Integrated Critical Thinking Questions encourage students to remain actively involved with the material.

CRITICAL THINKING QUESTION

How do women accomplish the kinkeeper role? What kinds of activities do women typically engage in that might serve to maintain ties among the network of family members?

Concept Reviews with Bulleted Summaries of Major Points at the end of main sections clarify and reinforce content, reiterating key aspects from the chapter.

Concept Review 10.1

- Less is known about the middle years of parenthood than either the transitional or later stages.
- Maternal and paternal roles are changing, largely as a result of changing patterns of work and family roles.
- The transition to parenthood causes many changes in lifestyle and family life and is often experienced as stressful.
- Parenthood may result in a decline in marital satisfaction.
- The middle years of parenthood represent the period when children come of age.
- Parents' assessments of their children's success may affect their own well-being and sense of self.

Understanding Development-in-Context is emphasized throughout the text to help students grasp and appreciate the nature and sources of diversity in development.

UNDERSTANDING THE DEVELOPMENTAL CONTEXT

Emerging Adulthood: The Age of Possibilities

Arnett (2000) describes ages 18 through 25 as a new life stage in industrialized societies, a transitional period between adolescence and young adulthood when one has great freedom and independence with relatively few long-term adult commitments and the role responsibilities and social expectations associated with them. It is a period full of opportunities and many possible futures and offers the freedom to explore options in love, work, and ideology even more intently than in adolescence. Arnett calls it **emerging adulthood.**

Development in Adulthood

FOURTH EDITION

Barbara Hansen Lemme

College of DuPage

PEARSON

Boston   New York   San Francisco
Mexico City   Montreal   Toronto   London   Madrid   Munich   Paris
Hong Kong   Singapore   Tokyo   Cape Town   Sydney

Dedicated to Stefan, Lily, and Parker,
who are teaching us about development all over again

Executive Editor: *Karon Bowers*
Editorial Assistant: *Lara Torksy*
Marketing Manager: *Mandee Eckersley*
Editorial-Production Service: *Trinity Publishers Services*
Composition Buyer: *Linda Cox*

Manufacturing Buyer: *JoAnne Sweeney*
Electronic Composition: *Omegatype Typography, Inc.*
Interior Design: *Ellen Pettengell*
Photo Researcher: *June Whitworth*
Cover Administrator: *Kristina Mose-Libon*

For related titles and support materials, visit our online catalog at www.ablongman.com.

Between the time Web site information is gathered and then published, it is not unusual for some sites to have closed. Also, the transcription of URLs can result in typographical errors. The publisher would appreciate notification where these errors occur so that they may be corrected in subsequent editions.

Photo Credits: p. 11, Dion Ogust/The Image Works; p. 15, Barbara Hansen Lemme; p. 31, courtesy of NBTY, Inc.; pp. 43, 78, John Coletti; p. 47, Ted Streshinsky/CORBIS; pp. 50, 243 left, Elizabeth Crews/The Image Works; p. 52, J. Gilbert Studio; pp. 63, 97 right, 156, 205, 423, 480, AP/Wide World Photos; pp. 70, 184, Tony Freeman/PhotoEdit; p. 76, Lyrl Ahern; p. 87, Laimute Druskis/Stock, Boston; p. 97 left, Yasuhiko Ishii/Photo Researchers; p. 105, Peter Simon/Stock, Boston; p. 112, Jim Harrison/Stock, Boston; p. 132, Ken Robert Buck/Index Stock Imagery; p. 144, courtesy of Kodansha America, Inc.; p. 147, Brian Smith; pp. 175, 278, Mary Ellen Lepionka; pp. 188, 226, PhotoDisc, Inc.; p. 230, Barbara Rios/Photo Researchers; p. 243 right, Robert Harbison; 255, Jon Riley/Stone/Getty Images; p. 270, Jeffry W. Myers/Stock, Boston; p. 279, Lionel J.M. Delevingne/Stock, Boston; p. 282, Mike Mazzaschi/Stock, Boston; p. 314, Peter Menzel/Stock, Boston; p. Library of Congress; p. 325, Andersen Ross/Photodisc Green/Getty Images; p. 350, courtesy of AETNA Retirement Services and Ammirati Puris Lintas, Inc., New York; p. 355, Greg Ceo/The Image Bank/Getty Images; p. 363, ESRF-CREATIS/Photo Researchers; p. 371, George W. Gardner/The Image Works; p. 375, Index Stock Imagery; p. 395, courtesy of Key Ovation, LLC; p. 401 left, Aaron Haupt/Photo Researchers; p. 401 right, Pierre Roussel/Newsmakers/ Getty Images; p. 409, Cheryl & Leo Meyer/Index Stock Imagery; p. 448, A. Pasieka/Photo Researchers; p. 452, Harvey Stein/Photo Researchers; p. 454, courtesy of *Scientific American*; p. 461, North Wind Picture Archives; p. 475, Corbis-Bettmann Archive; p. 483, Jim Mahoney/The Image Works.

Library of Congress Cataloging-in-Publication Data

Lemme, Barbara Hansen
    Development in adulthood / Barbara Hansen Lemme.—4th ed.
        p. cm.
    Includes bibliographical references and indexes.
    ISBN 0-205-43964-0
        1. Adulthood—Psychological aspects—Textbooks. 2. Aging—Psychological aspects—Textbooks. 3. Adulthood—Physiological aspects—Textbooks. 4. Aging—Physiological aspects—Textbooks. 5. Aging—Social aspects—Textbooks. I. Title.

BF724.5.L45 2006
155.6—dc22   2004060179

Printed in the United States of America

10 9 8 7 6 5 4 3   RRD-VA 09 08 07 06

Contents

Preface

I am decidedly, emphatically, and proudly in midcourse. And I am here to tell you that this is a great place to be. You'll read more about midcourse in Chapter 2, but if you'd like to jump ahead, go to page 65. In this I feel a bit of a pioneer, and I like the feeling. My grandmother once told me that every stage in life has its wonders and its challenges. As in so many other things, she was right. Each stage has its own quality; each is inherently valuable. I also got the impression that she thought you should be "in" the stage you're in. Maybe a worthy goal for each of us as we move through the various phases of our lives is to pay attention to where we are, where we've been, and where we're going—to live fully, learn what we can from our experiences, and look to the next phase with enthusiastic anticipation rather than regret. I have traveled quite a distance in my personal journey since I wrote the preface to the third edition. Many of the topics in this text take on different relevance for me as my own position in the life constellation changes. And while I am the same person who wrote the first edition, I am a different version of that person, and my own development over these years has enriched my understanding and appreciation of the material represented in this book. I am more convinced than ever of its value and importance in an academic curriculum and its relevance for each of our lives.

What does it mean to be an adult? What are the core issues of adult life? To what extent do we change over the years, and to what extent do we stay the same? Is the way we age inevitable, or do we get the old age we deserve? What does it mean to age successfully? These and other fascinating questions comprise the terrain we will travel together in this text.

Having developed and then taught a course in adult development for over 25 years, I am sure of one thing. There is a fundamental difference in teaching a course in adult development and aging as compared to other developmental psychology courses, such as child or adolescent development. That is, students in adult development courses will, for the most part, be studying life stages and experiences that they themselves have not lived through and about which they may have inaccurate and negative stereotypes and biases. An instructor must address the essential challenge of engaging students and helping them relate to the core issues. This is not as easy as it may sound. Students have a natural affinity for children and children's development and issues, and they have a lifetime of their own experiences that helps them connect with course material in child development classes. Not so with adult development. Concepts involve a level of abstraction that is sometimes difficult to grasp. And the pervasive ageism in our culture acts as a barrier between students and many of the issues of middle and late adulthood. And yet, we live most of our lives as adults. What could be more relevant to an individual than to learn about adult development before or as one goes through it? Or as loved ones go through it? And what could be more relevant to a society undergoing a demographic transformation of historic proportions in which life expectancy is now about 77, the median age is 35, and those over 85 are the fastest-growing segment of the population? Of course, the classroom instructor is essential in bridging the divide by providing examples, anecdotes, audiovisual materials, speakers, and other in-class activities to bring the material to life. An excellent text can be an invaluable asset in this regard as well. The need to convey the importance of the material and to connect with the personal reality and professional aspirations of the reader have been uppermost in my mind since the first draft of the first edition of this text.

Goals and Thematic Approach

Throughout my career, I have been privileged to teach undergraduate courses in psychology to a heterogenous group of students from diverse backgrounds with varying skill levels, goals, and needs. Some are in college for the first time—in fact, some are the first of their families ever to attend college. Others are returning to complete an interrupted undergraduate education. Still others have advanced degrees and are taking additional courses for personal interest or to upgrade skills or retrain for new careers. My goal has been to write a book for this audience—as well as for instructors—that offers substantive, scholarly, comprehensive, and up-to-date coverage of the core concepts and issues in the field of adult development and that at the same time is engaging, interesting, and relevant to their personal and vocational lives. I have integrated an appreciation of the historical evolution of concepts along with the most current thinking in the field. In addition, I have offered a somewhat different approach to the organization and presentation of content—one that reflects my own experience as a classroom teacher and that seems to work for students. And I have aimed at a smooth, clear, personal writing style—as if I were conversing with the reader in the classroom rather than on the written page.

Theoretical foundations include the life-span developmental perspective and the contextual model of development, as represented by Bronfenbrenners's Ecological Systems Theory. This book recognizes that individuals exist within complex, multilayered environments and that the nature and structure of forces operating within these environments exert significant influences on development. Thus, the focus is on development-in-context. While the text's primary emphasis is on psychological theories and concepts, the approach is broadly multidisciplinary. Sociocultural, historical, biological, genetic, economic, and political issues are treated as well. The developmental significance of age, cohort, gender, race/ethnicity, socioeconomic status, and culture is emphasized and integrated throughout. A balanced view of development is presented—neither overly optimistic nor pessimistic—that stresses the nature and origins of developmental diversity.

Features

Consistent with the goals and thematic approach described above, I'd like to highlight three major distinguishing features of this text. First is a commitment to pedagogy, including personal anecdotes in chapter openers, clear chapter organization, an accessible writing style, in-text definitions of terms, end-of-chapter review questions, integrated critical thinking questions, listings of key terms referenced to page numbers, interim summaries in each chapter called Concept Reviews, and in-text references to

Web sites that direct students and faculty to resources available on the Internet. These pedagogical supports are designed to clarify and reinforce content, enhance comprehension, and maximize retention. Critical thinking questions encourage the reader to remain actively involved with the material and may be used by the instructor to stimulate class discussion. Concept Reviews and end-of-chapter review questions may also be used by the instructor as bases of discussions, review sessions, or quiz or exam questions. The integration of Web site references in the text itself encourages the reader to pursue additional information on topics of interest.

Second, my continuing commitment to examining development-in-context and the nature and sources of diversity in human development is evident throughout each chapter of the text in the inclusion of research and theory on the impact of gender, race/ethnicity, cohort, socioeconomic status, and culture on development. This emphasis helps the student to grasp and appreciate the nature and sources of diversity in development and assists the instructor in presenting a broader perspective and overcoming biases in the research literature, as discussed in Chapter 1. Examples of topics reflecting this approach follow:

Chapter 1: Ageism and cultural, racial, socioeconomic, and gender bias; difficulties in identifying and defining American ethnic groups

Chapter 2: Bronfenbrenner's Ecological Systems Theory; impact of gender, social class, and ethnicity on the development of generativity

Chapter 3: Influence of culture, gender, ethnicity, and age on the development of the self (e.g., collectivism versus individualism); interaction of gender, generation, and history; interrelationship of aging, personality, and culture

Chapter 4: Individual and cohort (generational) differences in cognitive development

Chapter 5: Psychosocial explanations of diversity in cognitive aging

Chapter 6: Age, gender, and ethnic differences in social network formation; gender and age differences in friendship; sexual orientation; male-female differences in sexuality and sexual attitudes; sexuality among older adults

Chapter 7: Age and gender differences in marital satisfaction; same-sex and non-married romantic relationships; racial/ethnic variations in family life; effect of cohort (generation) on intergenerational ties; cultural and ethnic differences in grandparenthood; influence of race/ethnicity on the caregiver role

Chapter 8: Increasing diversity in the workplace; significant coverage of gender differences in career development; cohort, gender, and social class differences in retirement patterns; ethnicity, social class, gender, and the economics of retirement

Chapter 9: Sources of diversity in primary and secondary aging; variations in physical development and aging among males and females

Chapter 10: Racial/ethnic, age, and gender differences in health and mortality

Chapter 11: Age changes and gender differences in the dimensions of subjective well-being; effects of gender, social class, race, and age on locus of control; age, gender, and ethnic differences in rates and nature of mental disorders, coping, and help seeking; need for culturally sensitive treatment; age, sex, and racial/ethnic variations in suicide risk

Chapter 12: Historical changes and cultural differences in attitudes toward death and the experience of grief; gender, age, and cultural differences in death anxiety

The boxed feature entitled "Understanding the Developmental Context" (introduced in the second edition and expanded in the third to highlight the impact of cohort, ethnicity, culture, and age on individual lives) has been enhanced with two additions: in Chapter 2, a discussion of a transitional developmental stage called midcourse, the time between the career building of early adulthood and the frailties of old age; in Chapter 5, a review of research (called Better Thinking through Chemistry?) on so-called brain-enhancing chemicals. These boxed features are now found in 9 of the 12 chapters; they have been added sparingly and only when an issue of special interest does not fit neatly into the body of the chapter.

Third, relevance to students' personal and vocational lives is stressed. This text takes a fresh look at the field and strives for new ways of presenting content, including expanded coverage of high-interest and highly relevant material often overlooked or given short shrift in other texts. Application to real life is integrated throughout, rather than set aside in boxes or end-of-text chapters, and emphasis is placed on relevant social issues. Each chapter opens with a personal anecdote that ties some aspect of the chapter content to my personal experience. The focus on application engages student interest and provides a bridge between theory, research, and practice, enabling students to connect the material to their own personal lives as well as demonstrating its utility in their careers. Some examples are listed below.

Chapter 1: Critical thinking approach to research, providing tools to enable students either to "consume" research more effectively in their personal and academic lives or to use it more effectively in their work; discussion of advantages and disadvantages of each method and design and of limitations and biases in the research; effects of changing demographics on U.S. society; causes and consequences of ageism

Chapter 2: Ecological Systems Theory; extensive coverage of research on generativity, including Kotre's theory and studies of its correlates and antecedents; Costa and McCrae's trait model of personality; hypothesized transitional stage called midcourse

Chapter 3: Development of the self and related components (self-esteem, self-efficacy, identity); individualist versus collectivist cultures; social and evolutionary origins of gender differences

Chapter 4: Decrementalist view versus continued potential view of cognitive development in adulthood (using the metaphor of the shipwreck versus the butterfly); comparisons of learning in childhood and adulthood, adult intelligence versus school intelligence, and analytical versus practical intelligence; creativity, wisdom, and expertise; cognitive intervention studies

Chapter 5: Brain plasticity; importance of "engaged lifestyle," challenging work, and intellectually stimulating leisure-time activities; neuroimaging techniques; research on so-called brain-enhancing chemicals; human factors research and applications

Chapter 6: Nature and impact of social support; life-span attachment theory and the effect of early experience on adult relationships; adult friendship; sibling relationships; leaving home; transitional stage of emerging adulthood; mate selection; sexuality

Chapter 7: Family systems theory and family development theory; changing family structures; benefits of marriage; life-span developmental view of parenthood (early, middle, and late stages); the "sandwich generation"; grandparents as surrogate parents; the caregiver role; family violence

Chapter 8: Changing work world and workforce; multiple roles (combining work and family); economics of aging as linked with gender and race/ethnicity; feminization of poverty; social history of retirement and its continuing evolution; Social Security—history, nature, current status, and major misconceptions; meaning, character, and importance of leisure over the life span

Chapter 9: Physical development, illness, and health (purposefully placed later in the book to reflect the life-span perspective and avoid a tone of deterioration and loss early in the course); sensory changes with age; environmental modifications to accommodate sensory aging

Chapter 10: Health promotion and illness prevention; transgenerational design; polypharmacy, signs of drug toxicity and adverse drug reactions in the elderly

Chapter 11: Happiness and subjective well-being; religion and spirituality; coping with stress; nature and benefits of positive emotions such as hope; depression and ruminative coping; Alzheimer's disease—causes, risk factors, diagnosis, treatments

Chapter 12: Right-to-die movement; improving care of the dying (end-of-life care); grief and bereavement

New to This Edition

Each chapter of the fourth edition has been carefully reviewed, revised, and updated, both to achieve greater clarity and flow of the material as well as to integrate new research and topics. The overall chapter structure of the third edition has been retained. Special attention was given to Chapters 5 through 11, which were more thoroughly revised and rewritten to accommodate new thinking, research emphasis, and empirical findings in these topic areas.

New material includes coverage of current research and emerging "hot topics":

Chapter 1: Expanded coverage of the causes and consequences of ageism

Chapter 2: Addition of Erikson's "virtues" to the discussion of his stages of psychosocial development; discussion of a proposed new transitional stage of development—midcourse; expanded treatment of Costa and McCrae's Five Factor Model of personality

Chapter 3: Expanded critique of the identity status model; additional discussion of the trajectory of self-esteem across adulthood

Chapter 4: Updated section on the major findings of cognitive aging research; additional material on the relationship between intelligence, expertise, creativity, and wisdom; enhanced coverage of cognitive intervention studies

Chapter 5: Integrated new material on the cognitive benefits of intellectually stimulating leisure-time activities, results of a meta-analysis of studies of prospective memory, neuroimaging techniques, and changes in the neurochemistry of the aging brain; a new Understanding the Developmental Context boxed feature called "Better Thinking through Chemistry?" that reviews research on so-called brain-enhancing chemicals, especially antioxidants and ginkgo biloba; expanded section on research and applications in the field of human factors

Chapter 6: Discussion of research on the detrimental effects of negative social interaction; enhanced coverage of social support, including the importance of social support to buffer workplace stress; added review of research on sexuality among older adults

Chapter 7: Updating of all statistics on marriage, families, and so on, using 2000 Census data as well as other sources; new and revised figures and tables; new section on the benefits of marriage; reorganized section on marital satisfaction; enhanced coverage of racial/ethnic variations in family life

Chapter 8: Updated statistics, where available, throughout; added/revised figures and tables on labor market and workforce trends, as well as for other topics; enhanced coverage of research on multiple roles; emphasis on considering retirement from an ecological and life-course perspective; broadened coverage of 21st-century retirement trends; expanded coverage of leisure, with reference to related topics in other chapters (e.g., discussion in Chapter 5 of the benefits of participating in stimulating leisure activities for cognitive function).

Chapter 9: Enhanced coverage of osteoporosis and comparative photos of normal and osteoporotic bone; expanded section on benefits of sleep and sleep disturbances; updated section on menopause and HRT to include findings from the Women's Health Initiative study; added discussion in section on changes in sensory capacity with age of the importance of visual accessibility and Web site design, as Internet use by adults over 65 rises dramatically

Chapter 10: Additional coverage of the causes and warning signs of heart disease and emphasis on gender differences; new section on overweight and obesity, including prevalence, possible causes of the recent dramatic increase in rates, and health risks; expanded coverage of the biopsychosocial model of health and illness; enhanced coverage of the benefits of physical activity, integrating recent research on the effects on brain structure and function; updated discussion of medication use among older adults to clarify risks and prevent adverse drug reactions

Chapter 11: Expanded discussion of the determinants of happiness; extended coverage of research on the relationship between religiosity/spirituality and physical health, longevity, and psychological well-being; added research on the benefits of positive emotions in coping with stress; expanded treatment of research on the origins of gender differences in depression; updated coverage of suicide risk among older Americans, with comparison by sex and race/ethnicity; integration of new research on the causes and risk factors for Alzheimer's disease, including the vulnerability hypothesis and research on the ApoE4 protein; addition of the Mini Mental Status Examination, often used to evaluate cognitive function and screen for dementia; review of new approaches to treatment of AD and current clinical trials

Chapter 12: New section on resilience in the face of loss

Acknowledgments

I am pleased to acknowledge those individuals who have contributed to the fourth edition of *Development in Adulthood*. First is my editor at Allyn and Bacon, Karon Bowers. Ours has been a delightful and productive partnership from our first contact. I appreciate her positive energy, creative input, enthusiastic support, and commitment to making this the best and most effective edition of this text. I would also like to thank editorial assistant Lara Torsky for her help and support on this project. Donna Simons, senior production administrator at Allyn and Bacon, provided valued production expertise and guidance and was particularly adept at assisting me with the selection of photos. Special thanks go to John and Evelyn Ward of Trinity Publishers Services, who again served as shepherds of this text throughout the production process. It is difficult to overstate the value of being in such trusted and capable hands. Through all four editions, I have benefited greatly from their masterful production management; brilliant and careful copyediting; substantive queries and prods as to content; and consistent encouragement, humor, and support. Their dedication to ensuring the quality and longevity of this text is sincerely appreciated.

I would also like to acknowledge the important contribution of the many publisher's reviewers who have offered valuable suggestions and constructive criticism for the various editions of this text. Their thoughtful comments have helped to improve each successive edition and are sincerely appreciated. They are Jane H. Adkinson, Stephen F. Austin State University; Paul C. Amrhein, University of New Mexico; Harriet Amster, University of Texas, Arlington; Janet Belsky, Middle Tennessee State University; Luciane Berg, Southern Utah University; Barbara Biales, College of St. Catherine; Megan E. Bradley, Frostburg State University; Alicia B. Casas Celaya, Northeastern State University; Stephanie Clancy, Southern Illinois University; Mary Corrigan, Wichita State University; Gary Creasey, Illinois State University; Lisa B. Elliot, Monroe Community College; Bernard S. Gorman, Hofstra University and Nassau Community College; Dorothy Jackson, Ohio State University; Janey W. Johnson, University of Maryland; Phyllis M. Ladrigan, Nazareth College; Dale A. Lund, University of Utah; Kathleen Malley, Boston University; David B. Mitchell, Southern Methodist University; Penney Nichols-Whitehead, Shippensburg University; Romy Nocera, Bowling Green State University; Jenny Overeynder, State University of New York at Geneseo; Lisa Pavlik, Bergen Community College; David Payne, University of Kentucky; Nancy K. Rice, State University of New York at Geneseo; Dean Rodeheaver, University of Wisconsin, Green Bay; R. Kevin Rowell, University of Central Arkansas; Jane Rysberg, California State University at Chico; Sue V. Saxon, University of South Florida; Patricia Pratt Summers, South Carolina State University; Kim Wallace, The University of Montana; Tonya L. Watson, Northern Arizona University; Wayne Weiten, Santa Clara University; Susan Krauss Whitbourne, University of Massachusetts, Amherst; Joseph L. White, University of California, Irvine; and Lisa Wyatt, University of Hartford.

Most important, I want to acknowledge and thank each member of my family, not only for their unfailing love and support and their faith in me, but also for their inspirational example, great humor and optimism, and strength of character and for enriching my life in countless ways—particularly my mom, my sister Lynne, our sons and daughters-in-law Matt and Kim and Mike and Anne, our daughter Becca, and especially my husband, Ron, who strives to live life to the fullest and who represents adult development at its best. I am blessed indeed.

I hope you'll find this fourth edition of *Development in Adulthood* to be a valuable asset to you in your examination of adult life. I end this message to you as I began: with a glimpse into my own personal feelings about adult development. Perhaps this poem will have resonance for you as well.

> I am a part of all that I have met;
> Yet all experience is an arch
>   wherethro'
> Gleams that untravell'd world, whose
>   margin fades
> For ever and for ever when I move.
>
> —Alfred Lord Tennyson, *Ulysses*

1 The Study of Development in Adulthood

I REMEMBER LOOKING OUT THE WINDOW as the plane began to descend and seeing nothing but ocean. Finally, a speck of land began to appear—the island on which I would spend the next week. It was a coral atoll, six feet above sea level, the district center of one of the island groups of the Pacific. I spent the next three months like this, moving among the islands of American Samoa and Micronesia, studying the effects of rapid cultural change. My first experience as a field researcher was an extraordinary one. Having grown up in the Midwest, this was my initial exposure to another culture, let alone cultures as diverse as those represented among these islands. My light Norwegian coloring set me apart from the native populations in such a way that for the first time I felt as an outsider feels. The inherent difficulties of doing research were compounded by the personal difficulties of adjustments to climate, food, and social customs, as well as loneliness, boredom, and, on occasion, anxiety. I met many local people, Peace Corps workers, politicians, international jet-setters, and famous oceanographers. I explored islands where some of the major battles of World War II took place, where tanks still stood sentry in the waters offshore, and where unexploded shells and mines kept some areas cordoned off all these years later. I mistakenly wandered into the compound of a U.S. president and found myself surrounded by machine guns. I was faced with the suspicion by some that I was a CIA agent. I saw my country from the vantage point of others for the first time. Just on the brink of adulthood, at age 21, I had an experience of a lifetime. And I was never the same.

This is a book about adult life, that period that begins around the end of adolescence—somewhere between age 18 and the early 20s in most cases—and ends with death. In other words, this is a book about most of the human life span. Each chapter opens with something from my experience that is related to the chapter content—like the story you just read. This serves both as a way of introducing myself and, hopefully, also connects the chapter with real life.

The goals of this opening chapter are as follows: to provide an overview of adult development as a field of study; to establish a perspective or point of view that will direct the chapters to follow; to review the major research methods and designs used to study adulthood; and, finally, to take a critical look at the limitations of the available research. So . . . this is the "road map" for the chapter. Let's begin with a few definitions.

Psychology is the scientific study of behavior and mental processes. **Developmental psychology** is the subfield that examines the nature and direction of change in the individual over time. Though the term **development** has many meanings, it will be used here to refer to systematic changes in behavior over time that result from interaction between the individual and the internal and external environment. **Adult development** is the branch of developmental psychology concerned with change in the individual after adolescence. It is the newest division within developmental psychology. **Adulthood** does not begin at any particular age; it is a period characterized by relative independence, financial and otherwise, from parents and the acceptance of responsibility for one's actions. There are probably 16-year-olds who meet the definition and 29-year-olds who do not. In addition, the point at which a given individual becomes an adult is often ambiguous, since our society lacks formal markers of the end of childhood. However, given these cautions, a shift toward adult roles and responsibilities usually occurs somewhere between the late teens and early 20s.

Demography and a Changing View of Adulthood

Prior to the end of World War II, most research in developmental psychology focused on children and adolescents. This is evident in the major theories of development that emerged in the first half of the 20th century. Both Sigmund Freud's theory of personality development and Jean Piaget's theory of cognitive development assumed that developmental change stopped at adolescence. These theories reflect the then-common view that psychological development was accomplished by the end of childhood. Maturity was viewed as a static period or plateau, never maintained for long, followed by aging, decline, and death. For example, G. Stanley Hall, one of this country's early psychologists and author of the first text on aging, thought of development as a journey up a hill toward maturity, after which the individual went downhill on the other side toward old age (Birren & Birren, 1990).

As the century progressed, two major **demographic trends** (changes in the characteristics of the population) caused some developmental psychologists to shift their focus from childhood to adult life. The first was a swelling of the numbers of older adults due to increased life expectancy. The second was the influence of a group known as the baby boomers.

Increased Life Expectancy

Average life expectancy (generally referred to as life expectancy) refers to the number of years an individual born in a particular year can expect to live, given the conditions present at that time. The average life expectancy for an infant born in Massachusetts in

1785 was 28 years. In 1900, it was about 45. And now it is about 77, though it varies depending on race and gender. These 20th-century gains in life expectancy were equivalent to gains made in all of the preceding 5,000 years. They were largely the result of dramatic reductions in deaths due to infectious illnesses, as well as improved nutrition and hygiene (a clean water supply, sanitation systems) and reductions in maternal and infant deaths during childbirth. (Of course, some people lived to be 75 in 1785, but most lives were shortened by disease, birth injury, and so forth.) This trend toward increased life expectancy and the resulting increases in the numbers of older adults has occurred in most of the world, though it began earlier in industrialized countries (Coleman & Bond, 1990). Yet while the population of the world is aging (meaning that the proportion of elderly within the population is increasing), not all countries are aging at the same rate. Nor is the United States the "eldest." Of the eight industrialized countries shown in Figure 1.1, the United States is projected to have the lowest proportion of elderly in the year 2025—20 percent, or one in five. Still, the Census Bureau (1992e) estimates that by the year 2050, one in every 12 Americans will be over age 80, and that 1,170,000 people will be 100 years old or older. Those age 85 and over continue to be the fastest-growing segment of the population, by percentage, increasing by 274 percent from 1960 to 1994 (U.S. Bureau of the Census, 1992d).

Thus, the nature of adulthood and aging is changing. Not only are there more older adults today, they are healthier and more active than ever due to better medical care and improvements in diet, exercise, and other lifestyle factors. These changes prompted distinctions between **chronological age**—actual age in years—and **functional age** (Birren, 1969)—actual competence and performance—as people began to behave less and less in accordance with age stereotypes. For many, functional age became younger than chronological age. For example, people in their 60s and beyond began to behave more like what was thought to be typical of people in their 50s—healthy, active, youthful-looking. Neugarten (1974) proposed the terms *young-old* and *old-old* to reflect these

FIGURE 1.1   *Percentage of Population Age 65+ in Selected Countries: 1990 and 2025*

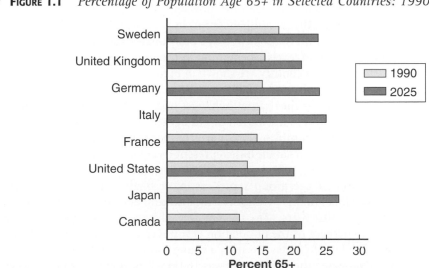

Source: U.S. Senate Special Committee on Aging et al., 1991.

changes. **Young-old** "refers not to a particular age but to health and social characteristics. A young-old person may be 55 or 85. The term represents the social reality that the line between middle age and old age is no longer clear" (Neugarten & Neugarten, 1987, p. 30). **Old-old** refers to the frail elderly, the minority of older people who often need special support and care. Baltes (1997) has proposed the term *fourth age* to refer to the period from age 80 on, which he sees as the major new frontier for developmental research and theory.

The view of maturity as a brief plateau followed by deterioration and loss thus has become increasingly obsolete, requiring a fundamental shift in our understanding of the nature of human development. The equating of development with childhood has given way to a conception of development as a lifelong process, beginning with conception and ending with death (Birren & Birren, 1990). One of the central issues in adult development pertains to explaining differences in developmental outcomes among individuals. While development was once viewed from a predominantly biological perspective, driven first by the forces of physical maturation and then physical aging, research has begun to show that psychological and sociological forces are equally potent influences on behavior throughout the life span. The differential effects of these multiple forces are now being described and studied.

Today we see greater scientific interest in adulthood and the ways in which adults continue to grow, adapt, and learn throughout their lives. The scientific study of aging (**gerontology**) was the initial focus of this new interest in adult development, with significantly less attention directed to the years between adolescence and late adulthood—the periods known as young and middle adulthood. However, the impact of the second major demographic phenomenon at work in our culture—the baby boom—led to an increased focus on these years as well.

The Baby Boom

The **baby boom** is composed of the 79 million individuals born after the end of World War II, between 1946 and 1964, now approximately one-third of the population of the United States, the largest generation in American history (U.S. Bureau of the Census, 1995). The boom was followed by a **baby bust**—a significant drop in the birth rate back to more normal levels—beginning in the mid-1960s. The fluctuating U.S. birth rates during the 20th century are shown in Figure 1.2. The 2002 birth rate is the lowest ever recorded (Martin et al., 2003).

Let's look at the dramatic changes occurring in the size and shape of the U.S. population, illustrated in Figure 1.3. The age structure in 1950 conforms to the **traditional population pyramid,** a Christmas tree–like form, with the largest age group being the youngest. The bars at the base represent recent births. The bars representing higher ages begin to narrow, reflecting mortality rates among these age groups. (The smaller bars in the 10–24 age group represent lower birth rates during the years of the Great Depression.) In this pyramid, births outnumber deaths, and the median age of the population is 30.2 years. (The *median age* is the age that divides the distribution in half, so that 50 percent of the population is younger, and 50 percent is older, than the median age. The United States was truly a young country both historically and demographically in 1790, when the median age was 16 [Hayflick, 1994].) Population size is 152 million.

The second graphic in Figure 1.3 represents a larger population in 1989; 249 million people. Notice how the structure is becoming increasingly rectangular. The baby

FIGURE 1.2 *U.S. Birth Rates: 1910–2002*

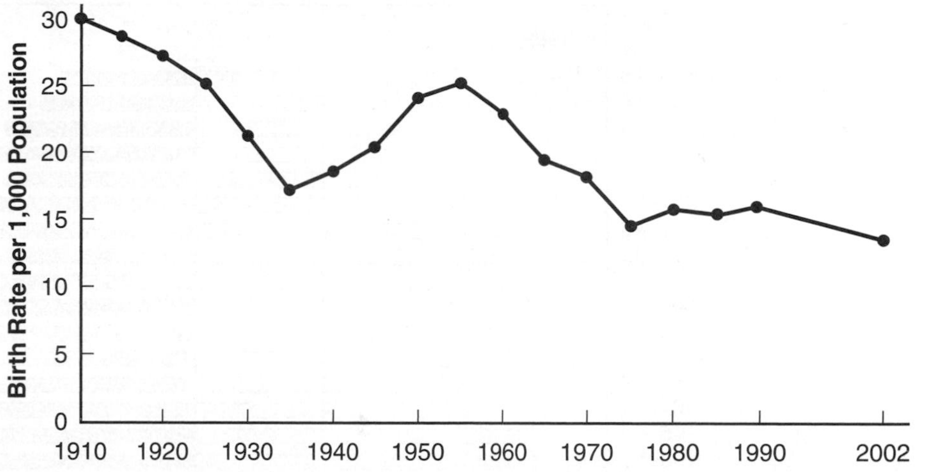

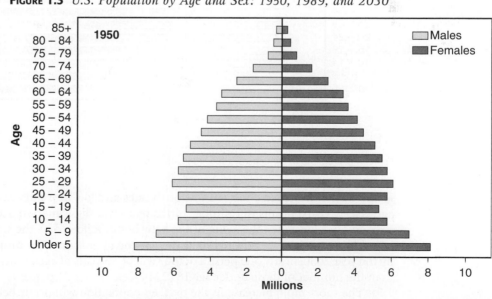

Sources: U.S. Bureau of the Census, 1983, 1990d; Martin et al., 2003.

boom, the front edge of which is now firmly into middle age, has produced a bulge in the population around the 25 to 44 age bars. The median age is now 32.6 years, and the ratio of births to deaths is 1.9 to 1. Note the growing disparity in numbers of males and females at the more advanced ages. The causes and ramifications of this trend will become apparent later in this text.

The third graphic in Figure 1.3 represents the projected shape of the population by 2030. Population size has increased to 301 million. The rectangular population structure

FIGURE 1.3 *U.S. Population by Age and Sex: 1950, 1989, and 2030*

(continued)

FIGURE 1.3 *Continued*

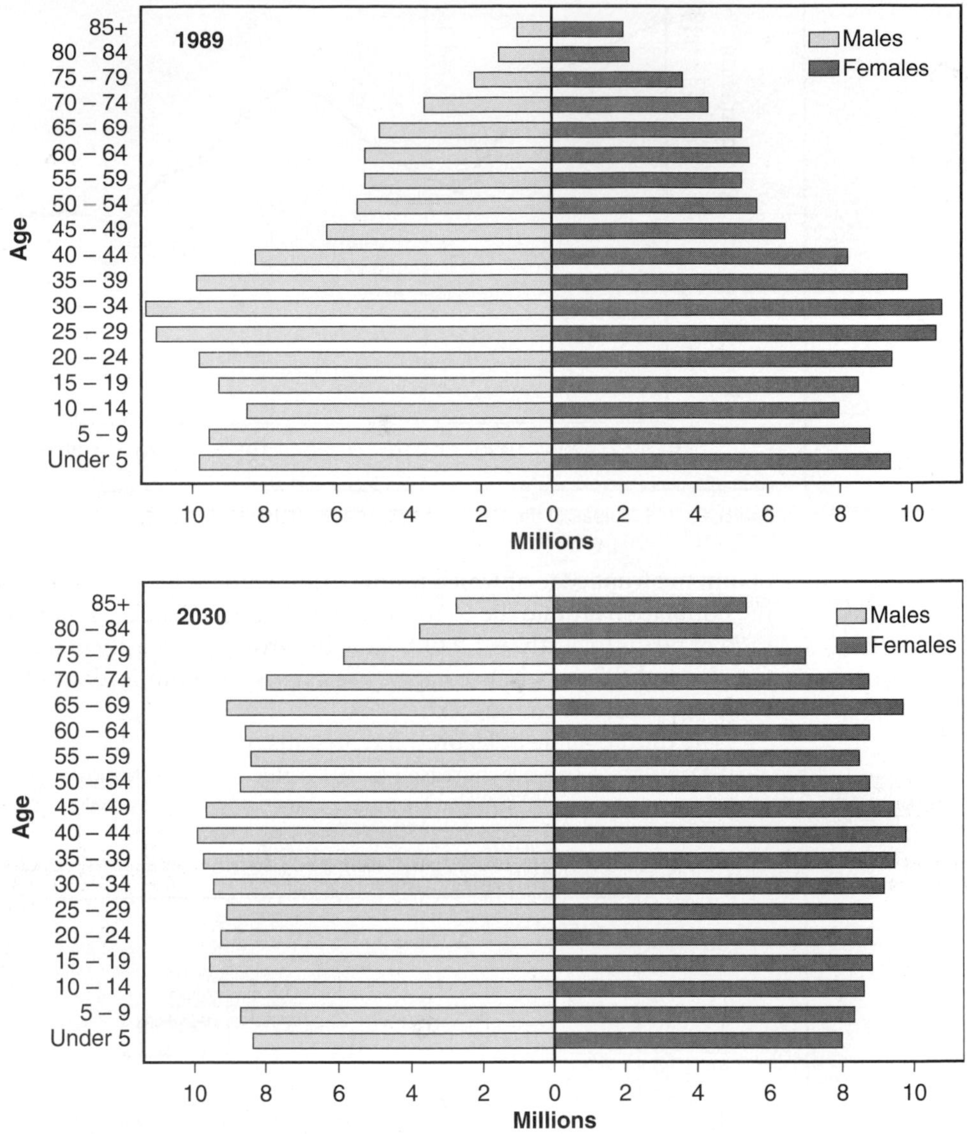

Source: U.S. Bureau of the Census, 1965, 1989, 1990d.

is due to the combined effects of low birth rates and low mortality rates. The median age is 41.8 years; deaths outnumber births by only a slight margin. Coupled with increased life expectancy, the aging of the baby boom followed by the smaller baby bust has led to what is often referred to as the *graying of America*. The projections are that by the year 2030, nearly one person in four will be 65 years of age or older, slightly more than the number of those under age 18 (22 percent versus 21 percent) (Figures 1.4 and 1.5). The most rapid increase in the over-65 population will occur between 2011 and 2039, when the baby boom turns 65.

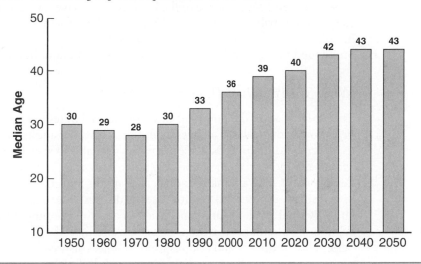

FIGURE 1.4 *Median Age of the Population: 1950–2050*

Source: U.S. Bureau of the Census, 1984, 1989.

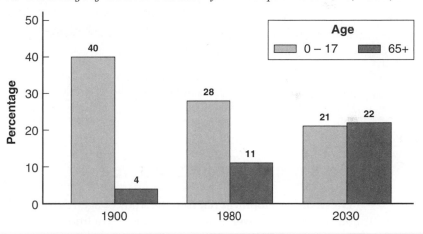

FIGURE 1.5 *Percentage of Children and Elderly in the Population: 1900, 1980, and 2030*

Sources: 1900 figures, which exclude Alaska, Hawaii, and Armed Forces overseas: U.S. Bureau of the Census, 1965. 1980 and 2030 figures: U.S. Bureau of the Census, 1989.

CRITICAL THINKING QUESTION

Can you identify the impact of the baby boom since the 1950s? More specifically, what influence has it had on our schools, advertising, housing market, employment patterns, styles in clothes, music, and so on? What changes are likely to occur in the future as a result of the aging of this huge group?

In sum, the demographic changes we have discussed—a significant increase in life expectancy and the presence of the baby boom—have transformed the structure of society and contributed, after World War II and especially since the 1960s, to a growing interest in adult life patterns. The initial interest in gerontology and late adulthood has broadened to include the early and middle years of adulthood as well.

Why Study Adult Development?

The study of adult development can be beneficial in several ways. First, given the growing number of adults of all ages, and especially older adults, we would be well advised to understand their needs and capabilities so that, as a society, we can provide for them as well as benefit from their contributions, even as they enter old age. Research in adult development may also help to dispel the myths and misconceptions of aging and the discrimination that often results. (See the discussion of ageism later in the chapter.) On an individual level, research and study in adult development may help each of us develop our potential and avoid experiences and lifestyles that undermine it. We may be better able to understand and respond to others, as well as to understand ourselves. In each of these ways, the potential for a more fulfilling life is enhanced.

Concept Review 1.1

- Two major demographic trends have contributed to increased interest in adult development: increased life expectancy and the baby boom.

- The age structure of the U.S. population—as well as that of other industrialized countries—is changing in significant ways.

- The study of adult development offers a number of benefits, including a better understanding of our own and others' needs and capabilities at all stages of adult life, including old age.

Life–Span Developmental Perspective

Life-span development refers to the study of age-related changes in behavior throughout life. In other words, in contrast to the traditional developmental perspective discussed earlier, life-span developmental psychologists are interested in studying constancy and change in behavior from conception to death. A number of theoretical perspectives associated with life-span developmental psychology are critical to our investigation of adult life. This collection of six beliefs, which constitutes not a theory of development but a way of thinking about development, is discussed below (Baltes, 1987). (See also Table 1.1.) As we discuss these six beliefs, notice how interrelated they are, one concept leading logically to the next to form "a family of perspectives" (p. 612).

Development Is a Lifelong Process

A **life-span developmental perspective** views human development as an ongoing process beginning at the moment of conception and continuing until the moment of death. No life stage is considered supreme in its regulation of development. At each

TABLE 1.1 *Six Key Perspectives on Life-Span Development*

DEVELOPMENT IS A LIFELONG PROCESS
Development continues throughout life; new possibilities may emerge at any age.

DEVELOPMENT INCLUDES BOTH GAINS AND LOSSES
At all points in the life span, development includes growth as well as decline.

DEVELOPMENT IS MULTIDIMENSIONAL, MULTIDIRECTIONAL, AND MULTICAUSAL
Throughout life, age-related change occurs in many different areas of development (cognitive, physical, and so on). This growth occurs at different rates and times, goes in different directions, and is caused by multiple factors.

DEVELOPMENT IS PLASTIC
Development can be modified or changed.

DEVELOPMENT IS EMBEDDED IN HISTORICAL, CULTURAL, AND SOCIAL CONTEXTS
Development is affected by the variables present in the various layers of the environment.

DEVELOPMENT IS A MULTIDISCIPLINARY FIELD
Development is best understood by knowledge integrated from psychology as well as related fields such as neuroscience and sociology.

Source: Based on Baltes, 1987.

FIGURE 1.6 *Life-Span Development: Gain-Loss Ratios in Adaptive Capacity*

One theoretical expectation concerning the average course of gain-loss ratios is a proportional shift across the life span.

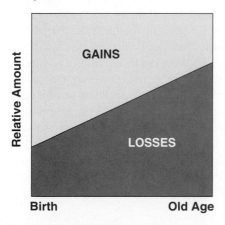

Source: P. B. Baltes, (1987). "Theoretical Propositions of Life-Span Developmental Psychology: On the Dynamics Between Growth and Decline." *Developmental Psychology, 23,* 611–626. Copyright 1987 by the American Psychological Association. Reprinted by permission.

stage, developmental processes and trends begun earlier may continue, while at the same time new possibilities may emerge.

Development Includes Both Gains and Losses

Remember that *development* traditionally has referred to growth during childhood and adolescence, while *aging* has referred to the processes of decline and loss associated with adulthood. The emerging view is to use development in an expanded sense to refer to age-related changes in either direction. Thus, "development at all points of the life course is a joint expression of features of growth (gain) and decline (loss)" (Baltes, 1987, p. 616). But these two forces do not exist in equal strength. Figure 1.6 shows a possible model of the relative strength of gains and losses over the life span. For Baltes (1997), the ultimate goal of human development is to achieve a positive balance of gains and losses for all ages of life. Examples of gains with age include improved emotional regulation and more satisfying personal relationships (Carstensen & Charles, 1998).

Development Is Multidimensional, Multidirectional, and Multicausal

Development has many dimensions and occurs on a number of different fronts—physical, social, emotional, cognitive, and so on. Each is related to the others, yet is also independent, following its own developmental pattern or trajectory and timetable

(Ferraro, 1990). They may also be of varying importance at different times during the life span, and change in any one area influences the others (Featherman & Petersen, 1986). In sum, age change throughout life occurs in many areas of development, proceeds in many different directions, and is caused by many different factors (Perlmutter, 1988). It is multidimensional, multidirectional, and multicausal.

Development Is Plastic

Individual development is characterized by **plasticity.** The idea is that, within limits, an individual's development is modifiable, based on life conditions and experiences. An individual's *actual* development therefore should be viewed as one of many originally *possible* outcomes (Lerner, 1984). The search is on to discover the degree to which individual development is modifiable, the conditions under which it occurs, and the constraints placed on it.

Development Is Embedded in Historical, Cultural, and Social Contexts

All aspects of development are affected by the environmental conditions present and the forces at work during an individual's lifetime. Paul Baltes (1979) has expanded the notion of environmental influence by describing three categories of events that influence developmental change over the life span: normative age-graded, normative history-graded, and nonnormative influences. All three "operate throughout the life course, their effects accumulate over time, and . . . they are responsible for how lives develop" (Baltes, 1987, p. 621).

Normative Age-Graded Influences

These are predictable, universally experienced events closely tied to an individual's age. For example, most individuals reach puberty around ages 12 to 14, and most women experience menopause in their late 40s and early 50s. Use of the term *normative* implies that development is highly similar across individuals and cultures; this is a developmental event that is normal. The forces underlying these events are often assumed to be biological—a reflection of a blueprint laid down in the genes. However, age-graded influences may also take the form of social customs. For example, in Japan strong pressure exists for women to marry by age 25. Thus, people of similar ages may show similarities in development because of age-graded influences. Normative age-graded influences are generally thought to be better explanations of development early in life. As people get older, they tend to become more different from each other as life experiences diverge. Thus, smaller differences would be expected between two one-month-olds than between two 80-year-olds. These increasing interindividual differences are the result of the next two categories of influence.

Normative History-Graded Influences

These sorts of events are the result of forces operating during a particular historical era. The idea here is that development is not just affected by internal, biological, and genetic influences, but also by forces unique to a period in history. This means that individuals raised in different historical circumstances may develop differently (Stewart &

Ostrove, 1998). Events such as epidemics, periods of famine, war, or economic growth; technological advances such as the automobile or television; or changing attitudes toward women are examples of history-graded influences. These forces make groups of people who experience them similar in some ways, and different from others who experience other history-graded events. A **cohort,** or group of people born at about the same time, experiences similar sociohistorical events at similar points in their lives. These events may have a significant effect in shaping lives within the group. The term **cohort effect**—the effect of year of birth—refers to essentially the same phenomenon as Baltes's normative history-graded influences. The idea is that if you want to understand someone—Freud, for example, or Lincoln, or Malcolm X, or your own parent— you must take the sociohistorical context into account.

Nonnormative Influences

All of us have experiences that are unique and that contribute to uniqueness in our development. Nonnormative events do not happen to everyone, or on any predictable timetable. Chance encounters with people or places may change the direction of our lives. My research experience in the Pacific, alluded to in the chapter opening, is an example. It not only transformed my worldview but also changed my perception of myself, and probably cemented my commitment to psychology as a career field as well—among other things. Other nonnormative events could be such things as serious illness or injury, a job transfer, or reading a life-changing book. These events contribute to the increasing diversity seen among adults as they age.

The life-span perspective is characterized by a recognition of the "reciprocal influences between the person and the environment" (Coleman & Bond, 1990, p. 28). For example, individuals to some extent create the environments that then influence them and to which they respond. The parent affects the child; the child then affects the parent. A corollary to the above point is that the individual is increasingly viewed as actively involved in development, rather than as a tabula rasa (blank slate), passively affected by factors within and without. One-way views of causality are being replaced

Normative history-graded influences include technological advances such as the automobile, television, and the computer, along with such things as periods of economic depression, famine, or war. These influences shape the development of those who experience them, making these individuals different than those who have not had the same experience.

by more systemic perspectives. "Biological and psychosocial aging occur interactively, and the changing organism is involved by a societal and cultural context that also changes, develops, and ages" (Featherman & Petersen, 1986, p. 343). For instance, loneliness or stress may undermine health and contribute to biological aging, just as ill health may undermine one's ability to respond effectively to life's challenges. The individual's stress level is also a function of what's happening in the larger environment—war, recession, natural disaster, or in contrast, peace, economic vigor, and so on. Each individual's behavior is a function of multiple forces. "This is a very important point as psychology has traditionally put its emphasis on measuring individual characteristics while tending to ignore the environment around" (Coleman & Bond, 1990, p. 28). This contextual view of development will be explored more fully in Chapter 2.

There is growing recognition of increasing diversity among people as they get older, in response to the complex and varied forces exerting a cumulative effect on development (Bengtson & Schaie, 1989). As Coleman and Bond (1990, pp. 27–28) point out, "The situations of older individuals will vary according to their histories. . . . Rather than growing more alike as we age, we therefore become more individual."

Development Is a Multidisciplinary Field

The perspectives described so far lead inevitably to the conclusion that development cannot be understood in psychological terms alone. Many observers (Baltes, 1987; Birren, 1989; Bourne, 1992; Flavell, 1992; Salthouse, 1991b; Schacter, 1992) cite the growing trend toward collaborative work across disciplines and the need to develop theories that can integrate knowledge generated in different fields. Contributions from fields such as sociology, anthropology, biology, and neuroscience are critical to an adequate understanding of the complexity of development over time.

In sum, then, these six theoretical positions constitute a metatheoretical view of individual development and serve as a framework within which we can examine the research findings in adult development. The goals of life-span research and theory are to gather information about the general principles that guide developmental change over time; to understand the variations across individuals as a result of genetic, biological, psychological, sociological, historical, and environmental factors; and to explore the plasticity in development (Baltes, 1987; Baltes, Staudinger, & Lindenberger, 1999). We turn now to an examination of the research enterprise itself.

Concept Review 1.2

- Life-span development focuses on the study of age-related changes in behavior from conception to death.

- The life-span developmental perspective is significantly different from the traditional view of development and is associated with six major theoretical positions.

Research Concepts, Methods, and Designs

Psychologists employ the scientific method in conducting research. We now turn our attention to one step of that process—the ways that psychological science gathers information. There are several reasons for doing so. First, and most practically, to understand research studies, we need a basic working knowledge of the language used by researchers in describing their work. So we will review terms central to the scientific study of behavior. Second, educated consumers of scientific information need to be able to evaluate the research being reported. Thus, we will review the components of good research as well as some common flaws and limitations. Third, some of you will have opportunities to conduct research of your own. A review of the various methods and designs, along with their advantages and disadvantages, will be useful. Our fourth and perhaps most important goal is to develop an appreciation of science as a way of generating new knowledge, and of finding answers to questions, resolutions to disputes, and solutions to problems (Miller, 1992). Understanding, evaluation, application, appreciation—these are our goals in the following pages.

Two Key Concepts in Research: Reliability and Validity

Two concepts that are critical to understanding and evaluating research are reliability and validity.

Reliability

Reliability basically means consistency or stability over time. In other words, will the results obtained be consistent if the study is done again, or are they influenced by some fluctuating factor, such that we cannot arrive at the same findings in all similar situations? Problems of reliability must be resolved for us to have confidence in the findings. Let's consider a couple of examples.

Test-Retest Reliability. If a research subject scored high on a measure of creativity one day and low on another day, these results would be inconsistent or unreliable. We could not be certain which (if either) is the real measure of the individual's creativity. In this case, the problem is with **test-retest reliability.**

Interobserver Reliability. If two observers rate the same adult's level of aggression differently, the ratings are not reliable. Which observer's judgment is most accurate? **Interobserver reliability** refers to consistency in the ratings or judgments made by independent observers.

Validity

Validity refers to whether the study examined what the investigator meant to study in the first place. Validity takes several different forms.

Construct Validity. **Construct validity** refers to the quality and appropriateness of the tool used for measuring a particular aspect of behavior. A measure is valid if it measures what it claims to measure. Questions of construct validity have been an issue for many years in regard to intelligence tests. Any studies using intelligence tests are potentially threatened by questions about what intelligence is in the first place and how it should be measured. This issue is discussed in more detail in Chapter 4.

Predictive Validity. **Predictive validity** refers to how well performance on a test predicts actual performance in real life. For instance, most college students have taken the

SAT or ACT. These tests are only useful to the extent that they can predict a student's future performance in college courses.

Internal Validity. **Internal validity** is an issue in experimental studies. It refers to the extent to which we can draw conclusions about the causal effect that one variable has on another (i.e., the effect of the independent variable on the dependent variable). If an investigator has been careful to design an experiment so that as many extraneous variables as possible are carefully controlled and the results are likely to be due to the independent variable, the study is said to have high internal validity. Let's say we wonder whether room color has any effect on concentration. We design an experiment in which subjects are randomly assigned to rooms of various colors and given some memory work. We are careful to control time of day, room size, furnishings, building location, and so on. What we do not know is that there is a flickering, buzzing fluorescent light in the green room. Comprehension is assessed after a fixed period of time passes, and results are tabulated. Subjects in the green room score significantly lower. We replicate the study the next day and get consistent results. Any conclusions based on this research would be threatened by low internal validity. In other words, the results may not be due to the independent variable—here, room color—but to another variable—distraction in the room. The study is not really measuring what we think it is measuring.

External Validity. **External validity** has to do with the generalizability of research results to the populations and/or settings that are of interest to the researcher. In other words, if the results of a study can be applied to other groups, situations, or times, they have external validity and are of greater general value. For example, do well-controlled laboratory studies tell us how people behave in real-life situations? Do studies of adults born in the early 20th century tell us about adulthood among those born in other historical periods? Or do studies of college students tell us about adults in general?

To sum up, reliability refers to the consistency or stability of results obtained, while validity refers to whether we have succeeded in studying what we set out to study. Various types of reliability and validity exist. Each contributes to the value of research results in understanding behavior.

Methods of Collecting Data

Research is undertaken because the investigator has an interest in a particular behavior, has developed a **hypothesis** or tentative explanation of the behavior, and wants to know if this best guess can be supported with factual data. For example, your hypothesis may be that alcohol interferes with REM sleep or that self-esteem increases with age. How would you collect data on these subjects? The method used will be determined by the nature of the question the researcher is asking. Three common methods are observation, self-reports, and case studies.

Naturalistic Observation/Field Method

Naturalistic observation involves describing the behavior of subjects in a real-life setting (the field), such as a factory, a church service, a PTA meeting, and so on. This is descriptive research—in other words, the researcher does not interfere with the situation in any way, but rather tries to create a record of what occurs. Naturalistic observation

Naturalistic observation, often used in cross-cultural research, offers an opportunity to describe behavior in its natural setting but at the price of lack of control.

is often used in the study of children, other cultures, and animals—for example, Dian Fossey's observations of the mountain gorilla in Kenya.

Advantages. The major advantage of the field method is its description of real-life behavior, as opposed to the more artificial behavior seen in a laboratory setting. It is the difference between observing chimpanzees in their natural habitat as compared to observing them in the zoo.

Disadvantages. This method has disadvantages as well. First, you have no control over the behavior you wish to observe. You may wait a long time to observe how the village chief interacts with other members of the tribe, for example. Second, natural settings are typically complex. You may find that there is so much activity you cannot take in all the important events at once. Your gaze may be distracted for a moment and you may miss a critical event taking place in another part of the setting. Third, there is the problem of observer fatigue and the need to look away occasionally, resulting in a noncontinuous observation. A fourth, more serious problem is the potential that bias or subjectivity on the part of the observer could color the observations—especially likely when the observer is from a different group or culture than the observed. Every effort must be made to obtain an objective record. Fifth, the possibility exists that the observer's presence may alter the behavior of the observed. Sixth, field studies are difficult to replicate, or duplicate, as the settings themselves are constantly changing. And finally, naturalistic observation provides a description, but not an explanation, of behavior. You may know what, but not why.

CRITICAL THINKING QUESTION
What techniques could be used to overcome some of the limitations described above?

Self-Reports: Interviews, Surveys, Questionnaires

Self-report methods rely on the research subjects' responses to a set of questions having to do with their attitudes, beliefs, behaviors, or experiences. The questions may be asked in person, over the phone, or in writing. For example, you may ask people of varying ages how old they feel, to get a sense of their subjective age. (My grandmother always said she thought of herself as 25 and confessed to some shock when she caught a glimpse of herself in the mirror or a shop window.) Or you may ask people to list the three most important aspects of their jobs, how they plan to vote in an upcoming election, and so forth. Sample selection is very important in survey research if it is to have high external validity.

Advantages. The major advantage of this method is that a lot of information can be collected rather easily from a large group of people.

Disadvantages. First, the quality of the questions will affect the validity of the data, so care must be taken to word them clearly, directly, and unambiguously. This is not as easy as it sounds—ask any teacher who has tried to write test questions that everyone will read the same way. Second, the quality of the data will be determined by the honesty of the subjects' responses to the questions. It is not that subjects are purposefully deceitful, although they can be, of course. Their responses are more likely to be distorted by faulty memory, the desire to present themselves in a favorable light to the researcher (known as the **social desirability bias**), or their interpretation of what is expected of them (the **demand characteristics** of the situation). Or subjects may not be able to provide accurate information because of the use of unconscious psychological defenses (such as denial).

Let's look at one example of questionable survey research. A government study of the incidence of rape in 1990 reported 130,000 attempted and completed rapes. In contrast, a study conducted by a psychologist found 683,000 women were raped in the same year—a rate over five times higher than that reported by the Bureau of Justice Statistics (Youngstrom, 1992c). Criticisms of the government study include the use of only one vague and indirect question, untrained interviewers whose race and gender were not matched to those of the subjects, and the presence of relatives during the interviews. Each of these conditions reduces the likelihood of full disclosure of any experience of rape.

The Case Study

The **case-study method** involves an in-depth investigation of one individual. Information is gathered through interviews, review of records, testing, observation, and so on. Case studies are often, but not always, conducted by clinicians to diagnose and treat a problem. They may also be used as a starting point in research. This method is most closely associated with Sigmund Freud, whose psychoanalytic theory was based on case studies of his patients.

Advantages. The major advantage is that a great deal of information is compiled that may be useful in this case; it may also generate hypotheses to be tested at a later time on others. Let's say, for example, that you study one highly creative individual and find something that you feel was critically important in the development of this individual's creative abilities. You could then expand your study to a larger sample to determine if the same factor was operative.

Disadvantages. Much of the information contained in a case history is *retrospective* (that is, it has to do with past events) and comes from interviews with the subject as well as relatives, friends, and others. All the cautions discussed for self-report data apply here as well. There is also a potential for bias in the researcher's interpretation or analysis of the data collected. Finally, because the study includes only one individual, the data collected may not be generalizable to anyone else. Additional research is needed to establish the external validity of any conclusions.

Now that we have reviewed some of the most common methods of collecting data, let's look at the difference between nondevelopmental and developmental research and how a research project is set up and organized—**research design.**

Nondevelopmental versus Developmental Research

Nondevelopmental research looks for relationships among variables that might be true of people regardless of age. We may want to know whether stress affects one's susceptibility to the flu, for example, or if there is a relationship between gender and language ability. **Developmental research** looks for relationships between chronological age (or the processes of growth and development) and another variable. For instance, we might want to know what happens to cognitive abilities or personality traits over the life span. We are essentially looking at whether and how people change over time. As we will see, developmental research must contend with some special challenges not present in nondevelopmental studies. Both types of research are valuable, and we will examine many instances of each in future chapters. However, different research designs may be used to study developmental versus nondevelopmental research questions.

General Research Designs

Two commonly used general research designs are correlational studies and experimental studies.

Correlational Studies

A **correlational study** seeks to determine if a relationship exists between two or more variables, and if so, to describe its nature and strength. For example, we may want to examine the relationship between exposure to the sun and skin cancer, class attendance and course grade, or length of marriage and marital satisfaction. These are variables that occur naturally among existing groups and that would be difficult or unethical to manipulate. Correlational studies merely describe, but do not create, these relationships.

There are two types of correlations. A **positive correlation** indicates that the two factors in question vary in the same direction—that is, as one increases (or decreases) in value, the other does also. So, for example, as the sun rises in the sky, the temperature goes up; as the sun descends, the temperature goes down. Or the more one studies, the higher one's test score is likely to be, and vice versa. **Negative correlations** reflect inverse relationships. As one variable increases, the other decreases. As stress increases, resistance to infection decreases, or as anxiety increases, test performance decreases.

Many correlational studies use the correlation coefficient. The variables studied are measured and the data are then plugged into a formula that calculates the degree of relationship, expressed as a **correlation coefficient.** Correlation coefficients vary between zero (no relationship) and ±1.0 (perfect relationship). The closer the correlation is to ±1.0, the stronger the relationship between the two variables measured and the more useful the correlation is in making predictions. Generally, correlations of ±.7 or higher are considered strong.

CRITICAL THINKING QUESTION

Which is the strongest correlation, a +.55 or a −.72? Why?

Advantages. Correlations are used in making predictions. For example, once the relationship between smoking and lung cancer was established, predictions could be made of risk from smoking. Car insurance companies often offer lower rates to drivers who do not smoke, because research has established that nonsmokers are less likely to have accidents.

Disadvantages. The major disadvantage of a correlational study is that it does not indicate whether a cause-and-effect relationship exists between the variables. Just because you wore yellow socks and got an A on the test does not mean that the socks caused the score, though lots of people have superstitions about these kinds of things. If we found that the sales of suntan lotion and the number of drownings that occurred were positively correlated, would that mean that buying suntan lotion causes you to drown, or that if you drown you buy suntan lotion? Of course not. The reason these two things vary together is that each is related to the weather. This is known as the *third-variable problem,* and it should always be kept in mind when interpreting correlational data. For example, a study on diet, lifestyle, and health found that a strong positive correlation existed between vitamin C intake and longevity (Cowley & Church, 1992). Those consuming the most vitamin C lived the longest. However, the researchers hastened to add that these two factors may vary together because of the effect of other variables; people who consume adequate vitamin C may have other characteristics, such as better overall diet, less smoking, greater exercise, or lower weight. So, the fact that two variables are related or occur together does not mean that one is causing the other. Correlations may, however, suggest hypotheses that can be tested through other means, such as an experiment. Researchers often combine research designs as a way of obtaining more powerful results.

Experimental Studies

Causal relationships can only be established through the use of an experimental design. An **experimental study** involves the creation of an artificial setting in which subjects are exposed to a certain treatment and their responses are recorded. The purpose is to determine if a causal relationship exists between the treatment (known as the **independent variable**) and the response (the **dependent variable**). You may wish to test a new drug in the treatment of AIDS, for example. Or you may want to know whether the type of music played in a grocery store influences buying. When I was in kindergarten, I became a "Polio Pioneer" by participating in the clinical trials of the Salk vaccine for polio. The study was designed to determine if the incidence of polio varied among those of us given the vaccine as opposed to a comparable group who were not. Let's look at the design of this experiment.

The hypothesis is that the vaccine lowers the risk of polio. To test the hypothesis, a sample is selected to represent the population we are interested in studying—in this case, children. I assume kindergarten-age students were recruited for two reasons: this is a high-risk age group, and, since they are often in school, they can be identified and recruited more easily than younger children. The school can also be used as the test site for administering the vaccine. Care must be taken to choose a representative sample. This increases external validity. Once a sample is chosen, the children are randomly assigned to one of two groups. What we want are two comparable groups, both containing boys and girls and having representatives of varying socioeconomic levels, geographic areas, races, and so on. The **experimental group** is exposed to the vaccine, which is the independent variable (the variable manipulated by the experimenter and the effect of which the experiment is all about). The other group serves as the **control group,** or comparison group, and is not given the vaccine, but rather a **placebo** (a pharmaceutically inactive substance). The study is run **double blind,** meaning that neither the children nor those interacting with the children—those giving the shots, parents, and so forth—know which child is in which group. This is to control for the psychological effects of being given a drug, and to guard against differential treatment based on group assignment.

In all other respects, the two groups are treated exactly the same way, exposed to the same site conditions, and so on, to control as many **extraneous variables** as possible—factors other than the independent variable that could influence the outcome of the experiment. In a well-designed experiment, there should be only one difference between the two groups—the independent variable. In such a study, internal validity is high. Otherwise, when the results for the two groups are compared, we will not be able to determine which variable or combination of variables produced the outcome. This is known as **confounding the variables**—actually, mixing their effects. (Remember the flickering light in the green room?) At the conclusion of the study, the dependent variable is measured. In this case, the dependent variable consists of the polio rates among the two groups. If a significant difference exists between the two, we can conclude that it is likely to be due to the vaccine. As you know, the vaccine was found to be effective, and I was delighted to have been in the experimental group. Some of my friends were not and had to go through the series of three painful injections all over again! This was well before the development of better needles and the oral vaccine.

This basic experimental design can be made more complex in a number of ways. For example, we could add a control group that receives no treatment at all, allowing an additional comparison to the effects of both the drug itself and the placebo. The simple one-condition experiment described above, however, illustrates the basic components of this design. (See Figure 1.7.)

CRITICAL THINKING QUESTION

Design an experiment to determine if taking an ACT preparation course affects performance on the ACT. Start by stating an hypothesis.

Advantages. Many psychologists favor the experimental method because of its ability to establish cause-and-effect relationships. Since the experimenter creates the situation, it also provides the greatest opportunity for control and precision; in other words, it has high internal validity. Experimental studies can also be replicated; others can attempt to duplicate the experiment and see if they get the same results. Consistent results give us more confidence in the findings. In contrast, my field research in the Pacific could never be adequately replicated because the field settings have changed so dramatically in the intervening years.

Disadvantages. In the early 20th century, as psychology was attempting to establish itself as a science and distance itself from its origins in philosophy, use of the experimental method was emphasized (Birren & Birren, 1990). Some critics feel that this

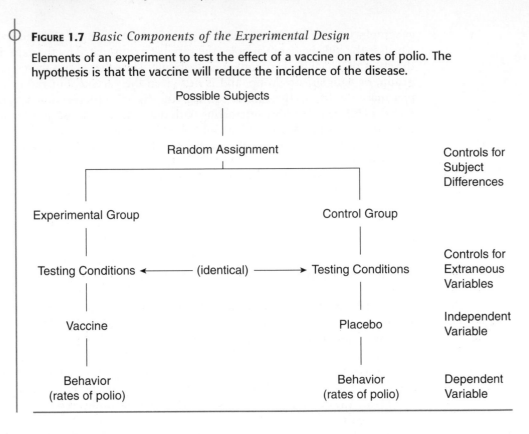

FIGURE 1.7 *Basic Components of the Experimental Design*

Elements of an experiment to test the effect of a vaccine on rates of polio. The hypothesis is that the vaccine will reduce the incidence of the disease.

trend has gone too far, resulting in studies that have low external validity and that fail to take into account the development of the individual over time and in an environmental context (Riegel, 1978). Subjects' behavior in the lab may not represent their behavior in real life. For example, carefully controlled laboratory studies of the effects of marijuana may not reflect the drug's effects when used in real life. Experiments conducted in the field reduce the artificiality of the setting, though they are still contrived and do not eliminate the effect of demand characteristics on the subjects. There are additional concerns over the ethics of some experimental treatments. And, of course, some experiments simply cannot be done—for example, purposely exposing individuals to hazardous chemicals to determine their effect. Studies of this sort could be done by identifying those to whom these experiences have naturally occurred. These **quasi-** or **natural experiments** respond to the ethical concerns, but they do so at the expense of experimental control.

Developmental Research Designs

Remember that developmental research is interested in change over time. The effects of age cannot be studied experimentally because age cannot be manipulated. I cannot decide that I want to see how my 20-year-old subjects will behave when they are 40 and make them 40. I either have to wait 20 years or try to study a comparable group of subjects who are already that age. A number of research designs are used in developmental studies to isolate the effect of age: the traditional cross-sectional, longitudinal, and time-lag designs, as well as the newer sequential designs.

Age, Cohort, and Time-of-Measurement Effects

Developmental research must consider the effects of three basic variables on the processes of change: age effects (represented by the chronological age of the subjects), cohort effects (due to the cohort or generation to which the subjects belong), and time-of-measurement effects (the environmental context, and therefore the influences at work, at the time the data were gathered) (Schaie, 1965).

Age effects represent differences in behavior due to inherent processes of change within the individual (for example, physiological development). Thus, differences we observe among individuals from age 20 to 50 may be explained by the normal patterns of change that occur in all of us as we get older. As discussed earlier, the idea of *cohort effects* is that people born during a particular period (say the 1970s) share certain sociohistorical experiences that make them different from those born in other periods. Cohort effects exert a lifelong influence. So it is possible that differences among age groups (for instance, 20- and 50-year-olds) are due to cohort, rather than age, effects— or both. **Time-of-measurement effects,** on the other hand, include those influences at work in the environment between and during the times behavior is measured (Botwinick, 1984). Examples might be the AIDS epidemic or a drastic change in the economy. These effects could also include events that affect the individual subject, such as loss of a loved one, illness, or marriage. Thus, the outcome of research may be influenced by the time when the study was done. Had it been conducted either earlier or later, the results may have been different.

In developmental research, these variables are often confounded, making it difficult to explain changes in behavior. That is, any or all of these effects, acting singly or in combination, may be responsible for the behavior of the subjects, differences among individuals and groups, and change over time. Let's say, for example, we begin to study a group of people at age 15. The year is 1962. The birth cohort is 1947. We follow them for 15 years, to 1977, and observe changes in their political attitudes. We find they become more liberal over time. How do we account for these changes? Are they the result of developmental processes related to age, such as identity formation? Are they a response to cohort experiences, such as coming of age during the Vietnam War and the social upheaval of the 1960s? Are they a reflection of events at the time of measurement, such as the state of the economy, or family or career issues? Or do changes in the subjects' political attitudes reflect all three?

To underscore the point, studies of 20-year-olds, part of the baby boom cohort, conducted in 1968 at the height of the Vietnam War may be influenced by the subjects' ages, their cohort, and conditions at the time of the study and might yield far different results than studies of 30-year-olds, part of the baby bust, conducted in 1995 (see Table 1.2). Depending on the type of dependent variable being measured, variations in the ages of the subjects, the cohorts to which they belong, and the sociohistorical influences at work at the time of the study can affect the outcome of the research. We might expect that the effects would be more significant in some types of studies than in others (for example, career development research as compared to studies of color perception). It will be important to keep these three variables in mind as

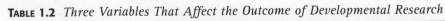

TABLE 1.2 *Three Variables That Affect the Outcome of Developmental Research*

	Age of Subjects	Subject Cohort	Sociohistorical Context at Time of Measurement
Study A	20	Baby boom: born 1948	1968: height of Vietnam War
Study B	30	Baby bust: born 1965	1995: peace and economic recovery

Note: Any differences observed between these two groups of subjects will be a function of their ages, cohort effects, and influences present in the environment at the time of the study.

we consider developmental research throughout this book. Though the newer sequential designs were developed to minimize the effects of cohort and time of measurement, some confounding of these variables is inevitable (Costa & McCrae, 1982), as we will see.

Cross-Sectional Studies

Cross-sectional studies have been the most commonly used of the developmental research designs. In a **cross-sectional study,** groups of subjects of different ages (and therefore different cohorts) are compared at one point in time. Time of measurement is thus held constant. These kinds of studies look for age-related differences. For example, we could compare the self-esteem scores of a group of 16-year-olds, 36-year-olds, and 56-year-olds to get a picture of what happens to self-esteem during adulthood.

Advantages. Cross-sectional studies are popular because they are relatively inexpensive, easier to manage, and less time consuming than other developmental designs. They also avoid the problems of subject attrition (subjects dropping out of the study) and practice effects (subjects being repeatedly tested) that plague longitudinal studies.

Disadvantages. Drawbacks include the confounding of age and cohort differences. In other words, differences among the groups may be due to their historical experience, not development or age. The results are thus contaminated by generational differences. For example, let's say we compare the intelligence test scores of a group of 18-year-olds and a group of 78-year-olds. We find that the younger group scores higher than the older group. Does this mean that intelligence declines with age?

CRITICAL THINKING QUESTION

What factors other than the age difference between the two groups might account for the differences in their scores?

The effect of such cohort differences was illustrated when the poorer performance of older as compared to younger adults on measures of memory, previously thought to be the result of the aging process, was later reexamined. It seems that when comparisons were made of college and noncollege subjects *of the same age,* similar differences in memory scores were obtained. This suggests that the discrepancies between the older and younger adults may not have been due to age, but rather to the greater experience of the younger adults, who were college students, with the types of memory tasks being tested (Ratner, 1987).

Because of the contaminating effects of cohort differences, cross-sectional data may lead to inaccurate conclusions regarding the age groups described. Cross-sectional studies can be thought of as describing, but not explaining, differences among age/cohort groups. They are perhaps best used when the range of ages across the groups is fairly small. A second disadvantage of cross-sectional studies is that they do not provide a picture of how individuals develop over time. In our first example, we have no idea how the 78-year-olds scored when they were 18. Nor do they focus on individual differences in development. Cross-sectional studies describe *age differences* among groups of people rather than describing or explaining *age changes* that occur in individuals over time.

Longitudinal Studies

In a **longitudinal study,** data are collected on one group of same-aged subjects (a birth cohort) over a long period of time. For instance, we might want to study the dietary habits of a group of people beginning when they are age 10 and ending when they are 60. When we conduct longitudinal studies, we are looking for age-related *changes* in individuals over time.

Advantages. Longitudinal studies provide a good picture of individual change over time and of developmental differences among individuals. One can look for the long-term effects of earlier events, make predictions and observe outcomes, and do retrospective analyses of developmental events to look for patterns of causation (Baltes & Nesselroade, 1979). For example, if some of the sample have exemplary health at age 40, the data may yield some information on possible determinants. For these reasons, the longitudinal study is preferred over the cross-sectional design. However, there are drawbacks as well.

Disadvantages. First, these studies are time consuming, and it is expensive to follow a group of people over a long period of time. Research grants are ordinarily given for three to five years, at which time significant progress must be demonstrated to maintain funding (Hayflick, 1994). This grant system thus tends to favor cross-sectional studies. Subject attrition is a significant problem, because if too many subjects drop out (due to disinterest, moving away, death, and so on), the sample becomes less and less representative. Sometimes, the group that remains is significantly different from the group with which the study began, and the generalizability of the results is threatened. In fact, it is usually the less able subjects who drop out, especially among older adults, leaving the more able ones to dominate the sample (Botwinick, 1984). For instance, if we wanted to study changes in the prevalence of chronic disability among older adults as they age, it would be important to maintain a low rate of subject dropout. Failure to respond to a survey is correlated with severe disability, institutionalization, and, of course, death. The loss of these subjects from the sample could thus lead to bias in the findings—here, an underestimation of the rate of disability. There are also concerns about practice effects as subjects are repeatedly interviewed, surveyed, tested, and so forth. Staff turnover, death, and delayed payoff for researchers (a great deal of time must pass before useful data are available) pose problems as well. In addition, the amount of data generated can be overwhelming. The Terman study of gifted children, which began with a sample of 1,528 kids in 1921, is still in touch with hundreds of subjects. Robert Sears, who took over the study on Terman's death in 1956 and who was one of the original subjects, estimated that they would eventually have about 4,000 pieces of data on each of those still in the sample (Goleman, 1980b). That is close to 4 million pieces of information! The final disadvantage has to do with the fact that the sample studied may not represent other generations. Age changes are confounded with cohort effects and time of measurement. For example, most of what we know about old age is based on a generation of people born around 1920. Do the patterns of change we observe in this group reflect the effects of age or the sociohistorical experiences of the group during the study as well as at the time of measurement? Does this knowledge tell us about the generations that preceded and that will follow this one? Or does their unique historical experience make them unlike those who went before and came after?

One of the most ambitious and best longitudinal studies on aging ever undertaken, the Baltimore Longitudinal Study of Aging (BLSA), began in 1958 under the direction of Nathan Shock, often cited as the father of gerontology in the United States. Since its beginning, the BLSA has included more than 1,500 male participants ranging in age from 17 to 96. In 1978, 700 women were recruited to participate. The purpose of the study is to examine the physical, emotional, and mental effects of aging among healthy people. Subjects return to the testing site at their own expense every two years to undergo several days of testing, involving over 100 procedures, some of which are boring, difficult, or uncomfortable. Yet there is a long waiting list to join the group. A very important finding is the tremendous diversity among individuals in how they age. For example, some 80-year-olds can perform at the level of the average 40-year-old (Hayflick, 1994). We will examine the findings of this study in greater detail in later chapters.

Time-Lag Studies

In **time-lag studies,** same-age groups are observed at different times. Age is held constant, while cohort and time of measurement vary. A time-lag design might be used to study changes in dating practices over time. For instance, the nature of dating among teenagers in 1960 could be compared with that in 1980 and 2000, or the nature of the father role could be examined in 1950, 1970, and 1990. Here, we are looking at cultural change.

Advantages. The time-lag study provides a picture of the effects of sociohistorical change at a particular point in development. We see how the same age group behaves in different historical periods and, thus, contexts.

Disadvantages. Cohort and time-of-measurement influences are confounded. So we could not be sure if any differences were the result of being born at a particular time in history, or the result of the general sociohistorical setting at the time the study was done. In addition, time-lag studies are expensive and time consuming. Finally, only one age is studied; thus, time-lag research focuses more on cultural change than personal development.

Sequential Designs

Sequential designs (Schaie, 1965, 1977) represent various combinations of the developmental designs we have just discussed: cross-sectional, longitudinal, and time lag. Cohort-sequential designs (two or more different cohorts are followed for a period of time) and cross-sequential designs (comparable cross-sectional studies are performed at different historical times) are among these alternatives. Gathering data on different cohorts of different ages at different times of measurement assists us in separating age-related changes typical among adults from effects that are unique to specific cohorts or historical eras. Table 1.3 provides an example of a sequential design.

Advantages. The sequential designs combine some strengths of both the cross-sectional and longitudinal approaches, while at the same time attempting to minimize the confounding of age, cohort, and time-of-measurement influences. Thus, they provide greater internal validity than either the traditional single-cohort longitudinal or the single-time-of-measurement cross-sectional designs. These designs represent an important contribution of adult development to research in developmental psychology.

Disadvantages. Though the sequential designs can partially overcome the limitations of the longitudinal, cross-sectional, and time-lag designs, their complexity has probably hindered their widespread use to date.

In sum, then, we have seen that each of the research designs has advantages and disadvantages and involves some confounding of age, cohort, and time-of-measurement influences. The particular choice of design will be dictated by the nature of the problem to be studied as well as by practical considerations of time and money. None of the methods and designs we have discussed is perfect. Designs can often be combined to achieve more sophisticated and informative results. If consistent results are obtained in different studies using different approaches at different times, our confidence in the findings is increased. As Botwinick (1984, p. 406) points out, "A single study should not constitute the basis for a fact."

TABLE 1.3 *An Example of a Sequential Design*

Birth Cohort	Time of Measurement[a]		
	1968	1970	1972
1929–1932	36–39	39–41	40–43
1925–1928	40–43	42–45	44–47
1921–1924	44–47	46–49	48–51
1917–1920	48–51	50–53	52–55
1913–1916	52–55	54–57	56–59
1909–1912	56–59	58–61	60–63
1903–1908	60–63	62–65	64–67

[a]Entries under time of measurement represent cohort ages.

Note: This design combines short-term longitudinal studies for a number of cohorts. Each row represents a birth cohort that was followed over a four-year period with measurements taken three times, at two-year intervals. Time-lag comparisons of two different cohorts at the same ages can be made at the 1968 and 1972 measurement points. For example, measurements taken in 1968 of the 1913–1916 cohort at ages 52–55 can be compared with measurements in 1972 of the 1917–1920 cohort at the same ages.

Source: Based on Lachman, 1985.

Concept Review 1.3

- Reliability and validity are key characteristics of good scientific research.

- Three common methods of data collection are naturalistic observation, self-report, and case study. Each has its advantages and disadvantages.

- Correlational studies seek to determine whether a relationship exists between two or more variables of interest and to describe its nature and strength.

- Experimental studies offer the most precise and controlled means by which to examine causal relationships.

- The outcomes of developmental studies may be affected by age, cohort, and time-of-measurement effects.

- Developmental studies, which aim to examine change over time, employ different research approaches, including cross-sectional, longitudinal, time-lag, and sequential designs.

Special Considerations and Limitations in the Research

Ethics

As in all psychological research, there are ethical constraints that guide the study of adulthood. These ethical standards have been established and published by the American Psychological Association. (View this document at www.apa.org.) Of paramount concern are respect for human dignity and autonomy, fairness, and protection from harm. Issues such as informed consent, humane treatment of subjects, the use of limited deception, and confidentiality must all be considered in designing and carrying out research projects. Kimmel and Moody (1990) identify additional ethical issues pertaining to the study of older individuals, particularly those who are frail, suffering from dementia, or in long-term-care facilities, among whom issues of informed consent pose special challenges. Deciding whether to go forward with research is often a result of risk-benefit analysis—that is, weighing the possible problems and dangers involved against the possible benefits derived.

Ageism

Ageism refers to stereotyping, prejudice, and discrimination based on age (Butler, 1969). When we stereotype, we treat all members of a group as if they were the same. When we are prejudiced, we prejudge people. We are biased against them because of the group to which they belong and our negative opinion of that group. (One can be prejudiced in favor of someone, though here the term is being used in a negative sense.) Discrimination refers to treating an individual or group unfairly. In his original formulation of the concept of ageism, Butler (1993) was concerned with older people's ageist attitudes toward the young, as well as vice versa. More typically, *ageism* means prejudice against the elderly. We often think of older people as one homogeneous group with certain negative characteristics, which then serve as the basis for unfair treatment.

CRITICAL THINKING QUESTION

While our focus here is on the problems that result for the object of stereotyping, prejudice, and discrimination, can you think of what functions they might perform for the person who holds these views?

A review of the literature on attitudes toward younger and older adults (Kite & Johnson, 1988) found age-related information to be very important in forming evaluations of people, especially in situations where personal knowledge of the individual is limited and comparisons are made between people of differing ages. Evaluations made in one-to-one situations are less affected by age and more affected by other personal characteristics. Research suggests that preschoolers have already begun to stereotype people based on age and that they hold more negative stereotypes of older people (Chitwood & Bigner, 1980). This is especially true if they have had little direct contact with older adults. There also seems to be a double standard of aging (Sontag, 1979); the consequences of aging are more negative for women than for men. In addition, men seem to be more aware of age in judging others and have a stronger youth bias (Kogan & Mills, 1992).

Ageism is perpetuated by the continued emphasis in our educational system on the early stages of growth and development. According to Hayflick (1994), 84 percent of secondary school biology texts do not mention aging, with the rest devoting only one to three pages to it. Texts at the college level are not much better. Fifty-one percent do not mention the biology of aging, and none contains more than a four-page discussion of the subject. The implicit message is that what occurs early in life is important, whereas changes after maturity is reached are not. The problem is compounded by the lack of teaching geriatricians, and in most medical schools, geriatric coursework comprises only a few hours of the four-year curriculum. Only 12 of 145 U.S. medical schools require a course in geriatrics (Blanchette & Flynn, 2001), and only three have a department of geriatrics, as compared to all medical schools in Great Britain and 19 of 88 in Japan (Scott, 2001).

CRITICAL THINKING QUESTION

What are the consequences of the lack of emphasis on geriatric training in U.S. medical schools?

Ironically, even the huge AARP (formerly known as the American Association of Retired Persons), with a current membership of over 35 million over the age of 50, possibly the largest membership organization in the world, feels the influence of negative stereotypes and attitudes toward aging and the aged. Established in 1955 by Ethel Percy Andrus, AARP downplays the word *retired* in its title to avoid scaring the youth-conscious baby boomers, who have begun to swell its ranks. The hope is that the acronym AARP will be accepted without people knowing exactly what it stands for (Rosenblatt, 1996).

Arluke and Levin (1984) illustrate the ageist view of older adults depicted in advertising. Ageism is also apparent in TV programming, where viewers over age 50, a fast-growing segment of the TV audience, find few of their cohorts in prime-time shows and those few usually relegated to supporting roles (Miller, 1995). TV programming reflects ageism in the advertising industry, which views those over 50 (the "mature" and "maturing" market) as a large group of poor people with little consumer potential (Lee, 1995), despite the fact that the discretionary spending power of Americans ages 50 and older is about 50 percent, that per capita spending peaks in the age 55–64 range, and that 65- to 74-year-olds outspend 35- to 44-year-olds. Lee attributes these ageist views to industry dominance by young adults in their 20s and 30s who know little about and do not want to be educated about older consumers. Thus, few positive models of maturity and aging are presented on TV.

Stereotyping causes us to treat all adults as if they were alike, and perhaps to see them as a group that represents a threat (Arluke & Levin, 1984; Ferraro, 1990). What we know, or think we know, about people dictates the social policies we develop and the decisions we make about how best to use scarce resources. Controversy about the Social Security system and other social programs that benefit the elderly is a case in point. The potential for generational conflict will be taken up again in Chapter 8.

A number of observers—for instance, Kimmel and Moody (1990)—point out that not all ageist attitudes are negative. While some people are gerophobes, others are gerophiles (Gutmann, 1988). Positive age bias may distort research and conclusions as well. For example, when observing that some older adults receive a better quality of care from their families than others do, one may conclude that some families are more neglectful. The truth may be that some older adults have a long history of abusive or in other ways dysfunctional relationships with family members that affect the quality of care they now receive from them. Bias in favor of the older adult may blind us to these realities.

Ageism leads to the same consequences as racism and sexism—it limits human opportunity and denies individuals the respect, freedom, and protection that everyone deserves. Rooted in our culture's "relentless hostility toward decay and dependency" (Cole, 1992, p. 17), ageism strips the last season of life of value and meaning. It may also create pessimistic attitudes about one's own future (Kremer, 1988). Ageism may even affect longevity. Individuals internalize age stereotypes early in life that affect perceptions of their own aging. A study of 660 men and women in Ohio, age 50 to 94, found that adults who developed positive attitudes about aging, as measured 23 years earlier, lived 7.5 years longer than those with negative attitudes (Levy, Slade, Kunkel, & Kasl, 2002). Self-perceptions of aging were more powerful than age, gender, socioeconomic status, loneliness, and functional health and had a greater effect on survival than lowered blood pressure or cholesterol, exercise, weight loss, or not smoking. As the authors point out, if an unidentified virus were found to reduce life expectancy by over seven years, research would focus on identification of the culprit and development of a cure. Here, denigrating stereotypes of the aged are the cause. A cure requires that they be delegitimized "by the same society that has been generating them" (p. 268).

Community programs that attempt to bridge the generations, such as those that recruit older volunteers to work with the public schools (for example, as living history speakers or tutors), offer one anitidote to ageism. Such programs create mutually beneficial interaction between young and old, promote positive images of aging, and present opportunities for those involved, including teachers, to learn more about the past as well as the aging process.

There is increasing awareness that growing old, like any experience in life, "cannot be understood apart from its subjective experience" (Cole, 1992, p. 17). A number of observers have called for greater emphasis on the actual experience of age as reported directly by the aged. In the absence of this kind of information, myths and misconceptions abound. Figure 1.8 illustrates the discrepancy between the stereotype and reality of old age. Note that younger people's assumptions about the problems of older adults are not supported by the reports of the elderly themselves and that elderly reports on quality of life have improved over the last 25 years. In fact, 44 percent of Americans over 65 describe the present as the best years of their lives, a 32 percent increase over 1974 (National Council on Aging, 2000).

Psychological research can contribute to a more accurate body of knowledge about human development, capability, and need throughout the life span. But just as it is endemic in our society, the problem of ageism infuses research, because it infuses the people who do the research (as well as the people who write textbooks—see Whitbourne & Hulicka, 1990). As Hayflick (1994) suggests, until recently those few researchers working in the field of aging risked ridicule from their fellow scientists for their efforts in an area often viewed as distasteful or unlikely to bear productive fruit. In addition to absorbing the stereotypes, researchers' objectivity may be threatened by their own, or others', aging. Growing recognition of the problem of ageism prompted the American Psychological Association to set up the Task Force to Develop Non-Ageist Guidelines

FIGURE 1.8 *Myths versus Realities of Late Adulthood*

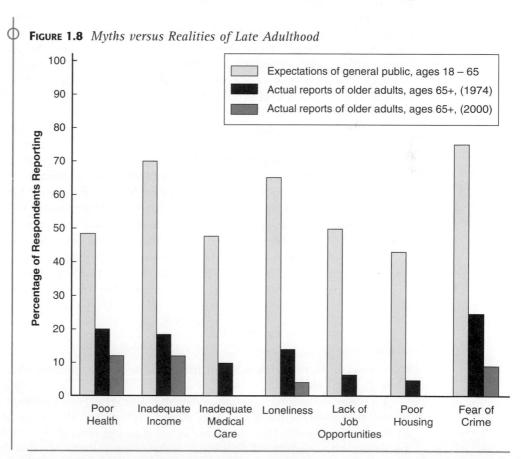

Source: National Council on Aging, 1981, 2000.

for Research. Many of the suggestions for avoiding ageist research practices are discussed by Kimmel and Moody (1990), who alert us to problems in sample selection, measurement, definition of terms, and data analysis and interpretation. Let's examine their concerns more closely.

There are special challenges in studying adults, who are more knowledgeable and sophisticated than children and adolescents and may be better able to figure out the researcher's hidden agenda. Neither are they captive audiences, easily found in preschool and school settings. (It has been said that much of what we know about psychology is based on studies of rats and college freshmen. In fact, when I was an undergraduate, in order to get credit for general psychology, each student had to participate in five research projects—a good way to make a pool of subjects available to the faculty and graduate students. But representative?) As Park and Cherry (1989) point out, finding representative samples of healthy adults can be difficult, leading to the use of *samples of convenience.* Thus, some developmental studies have failed to select samples representative of the diversity found among adults in relation to gender, race, class, immigration history, education, lifestyle, and so on. These demographic characteristics may be especially important in studies of some aspects of development, such as career development or health. In other research areas, such as basic perceptual processes, for example, these factors may be of less concern.

In addition, different types of tools commonly used to assess behavior may be required when applied to individuals of different ages and circumstances. For example, my father had a massive stroke when he was 75. In the weeks that followed, he was tested many times to assess the extent of the damage, design treatment, and develop a prognosis. One of these tests—the purpose of which was to determine the extent of perceptual loss—required Dad to put his right hand into a bowl of uncooked rice and feel around to see if he could identify by touch an object buried in the bowl. Dad refused. In talking with my father later, I discovered that the therapist had not explained the purpose of the task and that Dad felt foolish doing it. Rather than try to explain this to his therapist (although he understood and knew exactly what he wanted to say, getting it to come out was difficult and slow), he had just withdrawn and become uncooperative. Once the purpose was discussed with him, he readily agreed to give it a try. Patients are people first. Proud but wounded and humiliated, my father needed to be treated like the mature adult he was. A tool such as this might be used more easily with children, who generally like to play games and may be more comfortable with the task.

Other measurement tools contain obviously ageist items and must be changed. Consider the following word matrix item from a test published by the Educational Testing Service (Schaie, 1988, p. 179). The task is to fill in the missing word to complete the matrix.

youth	beauty	life
age	_____	death

The correct answer is *ugliness.* Surely items that do not promote ageist attitudes could be used in tests like these.

Problems in the interpretation of data may also arise. For example, it is well documented that people between the ages of 60 and 70 react more slowly than those between 20 and 30. But the difference amounts to less than one second. Studies are needed to determine when such small differences really matter. Slower reaction time may not make much difference for most daily tasks (such as home maintenance or balancing a checkbook), but may be very significant for tasks like driving; it may be irrelevant in many occupations (such as literary agent or museum curator), but critical in some, like air traffic controller. Additional research would help to clarify such issues. To borrow a phrase from Ferraro (1990, p. 14), we may be "majoring on the minors"; that is, making a big deal out of things with relatively little practical significance. These and other suggestions can help to minimize the problem of ageism in the study of adult behavior. But gender and ethnic bias raise additional concerns.

Cultural, Racial, Socioeconomic, and Gender Bias

Much of what is known about adult life is based on samples of White, middle-class American males studied mainly by White, middle-class American males. Despite growing awareness of the important impact of culture, race, socioeconomic status, and gender on behavior and development and on shaping individuals' experiences and life chances (Huyck, 1990), mainstream psychology has been accused of being "womanless" (Crawford & Marecek, 1989) as well as "raceless" (Graham, 1992). In a useful overview of these issues, Sampson (1993, p. 1219) summarizes critics' charges as follows: "Human nature has been addressed in terms of an implicit standard that turns out to be primarily White, primarily male, and primarily Western, especially United Statesian." He points out that, in general, psychology has not been accused of being intentionally biased and, to its credit, has attempted to respond to these challenges and seek remedies. While some of the charges may be overstated, legitimate questions continue to be raised about the potential influence of researcher bias in the design and interpretation of results as well as about the external validity—the generalizability—of these research findings (for example, see Basow, 1992; Gilligan, 1982). Let's examine these problems.

GET A KICK OUT OF LIFE. GET KNOX!

Knox NutraJoint PLUS Glucosamine Chondroitin & MSM MAXIMUM STRENGTH FORMULA with GELATINE

PROMOTES JOINT COMFORT 120 PLUS

KNOX NUTRAJOINT PROMOTES JOINT COMFORT.

There's no holding you back with Knox Nutrajoint. It has what it takes to support comfortable joint movement.* There's **Glucosamine** to lubricate cartilage*. **Chondroitin** to cushion joints*. MSM, an important contributor to cartilage health*... plus Knox's special ingredient, **Gelatine**, the building blocks for collagen, the chief structural protein in cartilage and bone* With Knox Nutrajoint, there's no stopping you now.

Available at Walgreens, CVS/pharmacy, Rite Aid, Eckerd, Shopko, Kroger, Albertsons, Safeway, A&P, Acme, City Markets, Dillons, Dominick's, Jewel, Genuardi's, Jewel-Osco, King Soopers, Cisco Drug, Pathmark, Price Chopper, Randalls, Sav-on, ShopRite, Stop & Shop, Tom Thumb, Vons, Waldbaums and wherever quality nutritional supplements are sold.
1-800-893-KNOX • www.nutrajoint.com

SAVE $3.00 on Knox NutraJoint Caplets

Media images influence the way we think about groups of people—males, females, Blacks, Asians, Whites, young, old, and so on. This ad plays off stereotypes of age.

Concerns about Researcher Bias

As Basow (1992, p. 22) points out, "Until our society is neutral with respect to gender, class, race, and sexual preference, it is impossible to assume that science will be. Therefore, it is incumbent upon all researchers to understand how the social context influences the research process." Since society may never achieve neutrality with regard to the factors Basow lists, we should consider the influence of bias in the research process.

Phares (1992) suggests that single-gender research is often conducted because of a faulty assumption that certain topics are relevant only to males or females. For years, parenting was seen as a female domain, and thus research on parent-infant relations focused almost exclusively on mothers. Aggression research, on the other hand, has focused primarily on males.

The dominance of research by White males may well have influenced the kinds of questions asked and the way the resulting research was designed, implemented, and evaluated. As Elkind (1996) points out, even the giants in the field are influenced by and can never entirely transcend the prevailing views of the social, historical, and cultural context in which they live and work, and which may affect assumptions regarding universality, gender, and so on. Burton, Dilworth-Anderson, and Bengtson (1991, p. 68) identify the central challenge as

> the social scientist's "ways of thinking." . . . Ways of thinking encompass the . . . value orientations, perceptions of the world, ideas about the group of people being studied, and theoretical allegiances. . . . Ways of thinking predetermine research questions, methodological procedures, the assessment of established "facts," the interpretation of facts, and the development of facts into general terms that serve as theoretical perspectives.

Some critics contend that the problem goes further (Foucault, 1981). "According to this view, versions of reality not only reflect but also legitimate particular forms of social organization and power asymmetries" (Riger, 1992, p. 730).

The race and gender of the investigator are, though seldom even reported, potentially important variables in research. As Bronfenbrenner (1979, p. 66) notes, the individual conducting the study is a part of the research setting, and therefore of the reciprocal relationships that exist within it. Graham (1992) points out that because of the lack of carefully controlled studies, we simply do not know what effect the experimenter might have on the results.

Concerns about External Validity

How relevant is the bulk of the extant research for women, African Americans, Hispanic Americans, Native Americans, the poor, and so on—groups whose life experience, values, aspirations, challenges, and needs may be vastly different from those on whom most of our research has been based (Blum, Harmon, Harris, Bergeisen, & Resnick, 1992; Youngstrom, 1992a; Stanford & Yee, 1991)?

Moghaddam (1987) suggests that there are "three worlds" of research and practice in psychology: one drawn solely from within the United States, one developed by researchers in other industrialized countries, and one being generated in developing countries. U.S. psychology, firmly based in American principles such as individualism, has been influential outside of its own sphere in both developed and developing countries, but American psychologists have remained largely unaware of the work of their colleagues in the rest of the world (Mays, Rubin, Sabourin, & Walker, 1996). As the United States becomes more internationalized through the influence of international trade, communication, and immigration, such insular behavior will make it increasingly difficult to understand and respond effectively to the problems affecting American society and its citizenry. "We continue to run the risk of developing theories, research paradigms, and service delivery models that are not sensitive to large portions of the populations that make up the United States" (Jackson, Antonucci, & Gibson, 1990, p. 118).

A number of investigators have pointed to the central problem of what constitutes the "norm" of human behavior and development. Many of the most influential theories in psychology have been based exclusively or primarily on studies of White males, though until recently this was not recognized as a problem, or even mentioned in discussions of theory in standard texts. For example, Kohlberg's (1969) theory of moral development and McClelland's (1953) theory of achievement motivation (McClelland, Atkinson, Clark, & Lowell, 1953) were based on male samples. Yoder and Kahn (1993) cite three consequences of adopting a White, privileged male norm: faulty overgeneralizations, exaggerations of difference, and evaluations of deficiency. When women and minorities are included, existing theories often need to be drastically revised (Stanford & Yee, 1991). Gilligan (1982) has offered intensive studies of the moral development of women, while Horner (1970) has contributed to the understanding of women's achievement.

"Psychology is sexist to the extent that its theorizing does not have equal relevance to individuals of both sexes, and greater attention is given to life experiences of one sex" (McHugh, Koeske, & Frieze, 1986). The difficulty comes in assuming that the behavior of this group is the norm, and that those who do not conform to this standard— women, Blacks, whoever—are, therefore, deviant (Gilligan, 1982; Basow, 1990).

Basow (1992, p. 20) also points to the problem of "shifting anchor points"—the idea that males and females may be held to different standards and that the same behavior may be interpreted differently, depending on the gender of the actor. Figure 1.9 provides a humorous look at this problem. This example also illustrates difficulties in defining what we mean by various terms—for example, *assertive* versus *aggressive*— when applied to males and females.

The concern over research bias has led to the formulation of guidelines for avoiding sexism in psychological research (Denmark, Russo, Frieze, & Sechzer, 1988). However, a review of the literature to assess change in selected indicators of gender bias suggests that room for improvement still exists (Gannon, Luchetta, Rhodes, Pardie, & Segrist, 1992). In addition, Denmark (1994) found little coverage of gender bias in research in current psychology textbooks, though she found overall improvement since an earlier study conducted in 1983 in regard to the inclusion of gender-related topics.

There is also growing recognition of and research interest in the diversity *within* groups of women and men (Yoder & Kahn, 1993). As Williams (1987, p. 21) says, "The intrasex differences in most psychologically relevant variables are so large, and overlap between the sexes is so extensive, that identification by sexual category offers little in the way of prediction of behavior." In other words, gender alone is not sufficient information

FIGURE 1.9 *How to Tell a Businessman from a Businesswoman*

A businessman is dynamic; a businesswoman is aggressive.
A businessman is good on details; she is picky.
He loses his temper; she's bitchy.
He's a go-getter; she's pushy.
When he's depressed, everyone tiptoes past his office; when
    she's moody, it must be her time of month.
He follows through; she doesn't know when to quit.
He's confident; she's stuck-up.
He stands firm; she's hard as nails.
He has the courage of his convictions; she's stubborn.
He is a man of the world; she's been around.
He can handle his liquor; she's a lush.
He isn't afraid to say what he thinks; she's mouthy.
He's human; she's emotional.
He exercises authority diligently; she is power hungry.
He is close-mouthed; she is secretive.
He can make quick decisions; she's impulsive.
He's a stern taskmaster; she's hard to work for.
He climbed the ladder of success; she slept her way to the top.

about an individual. We cannot assume that *all* males are a certain way or *all* females are another way. As a case in point, consider the fact that women have generally been found to be less assertive than men. However, this is not necessarily true for Black women and Black men. So, as Basow (1992, p. 19) asks: "Who then is meant by the terms *women* and *men?*" Denmark (1994, p. 331) found that psychology texts generally fail to make a distinction between gender and race such that "women's issues generally mean White women's issues." We are only beginning to identify and understand the other critical aspects of an individual's psychosocial identity, such as age, race, ethnicity, and social class. Gender cannot be viewed as separate from these other factors. In recognition of this reality, the American Psychological Association (1994) has recommended that samples be described by ethnic group. As Marecek (1995, p. 163) says, "If I were fitted out with skin of a different color, or transported into a different moment in history, I would no longer be the woman I am now." Of course, studies of race and ethnicity are challenged by the same level of within-group diversity as those of gender. (See the Box for a discussion of the difficulties of defining and studying ethnic groups.)

UNDERSTANDING THE DEVELOPMENTAL CONTEXT

Difficulties in Identifying and Defining American Ethnic Groups

The role of race and ethnicity has become an increasingly important concern among American psychologists (Rowe, Vazsonyi, & Flannery, 1994; Phinney, 1996). The goal of research in this area is to identify and understand the relationship between race, ethnicity, and psychological outcomes. The use of the term *race* is declining for a variety of reasons and is being replaced by *ethnicity,* referring to broad groupings of individuals based on culture of origin as well as observable physical characteristics such as skin color. The first difficulty comes in identifying, defining, and labeling meaningful ethnic groups. The U.S. Census Bureau currently uses five basic ethnic categories: Hispanic, non-Hispanic White, Black, Native American, and Asian/Pacific Islander. There are a number of problems with the use of these categories. First, the groups are internally heterogeneous. For example, the category Asian/Pacific Islander includes those with roots in cultures as diverse as India, Japan, the Philippines, and Korea. Similarly, Hispanics, who share a common linguistic heritage, and make up the largest and fastest-growing minority in the United States, may originally have immigrated from Mexico, Cuba, Puerto Rico, Central and South America, or else-

where. Among Native Americans, there are many culturally distinct tribes speaking some 200 different languages. Thus, any generalizations regarding these broad ethnic categories seem somewhat absurd. Second, there is enormous variability even within more narrowly defined subgroups, let alone within the major ethnic categories, in terms of such factors as recency of immigration, social class, geographic location, and education. Many of these variables interact and confound the effect of ethnicity, making it difficult to determine how ethnicity per se affects behavior and development. Third, ethnic groups do not remain structurally isolated but disperse and mix with other ethnic groups and the larger mainstream culture, further reducing the meaning of the ethnic label. Fourth, the assignment of individuals to ethnic categories is accomplished in a variety of ways—sometimes by self-report, appearance, school records, last name, and so on—undermining the legitimacy of the category labels themselves. Finally, there is a growing number of individuals of mixed ethnicity for whom the Census Bureau's categories may not be relevant. As Phinney (1996, p. 918) asks, "When we talk about American ethnic groups, what do we mean?"

According to Sue (1999), the relative scarcity of psychological research on ethnic minority populations is compounded by its low quality. He recommends that all studies address external validity issues and specifically identify the populations to which the findings can be applied. The magnitude of concern over research bias is increasing as the demographic composition of our society continues to change. The growing diversity of our population challenges our ability to apply existing research, policy, and programs to emerging groups (Burton et al., 1991, p. 67). According to Robin LaDue, in order for psychology to be relevant to society, it must be relevant to everyone (cited in Youngstrom, 1992a). Yet concerns continue to be voiced about the lack of progress in preparing psychologists to work with ethnic minorities (Youngstrom, 1992d) and women. The challenge will be the extent to which we can understand and appreciate the rich and increasing diversity of our society, while at the same time describing the experiences, problems, and challenges common to us all (Burton et al., 1991).

Efforts to overcome ageism, sexism, and racism in psychological research are of critical importance as scientific psychology attempts to understand human behavior and development and the economic, social, and political forces that influence it. These efforts may also benefit the application of psychological knowledge to societal problems. In Scarr's (1988, p. 56) terms, we are in desperate need of information that will "inform us of what we need to do to help underrepresented people to succeed in this society." As Sampson (1993, p. 1228) concludes, "Either psychology will listen and change, or it will lose its thrust as an important contributor to the tasks of our time." Awareness of the problem is the first step to that end.

Psychology is changing and responding to these concerns. Throughout this book, we will attempt to integrate the growing body of psychological research that identifies the different experiences of men as compared to women as well as the different ways the two genders experience the same events. (As an example, who do you think are generally more satisfied with marriage, men or women?) At the same time, we will examine the emerging research bearing on the role of ethnicity, age, and socioeconomic status in understanding individual behavior and development.

Concept Review 1.4

- Pervasive ageism in American society has the potential to affect the research enterprise in psychology in a number of ways.

- Greater awareness of various forms of bias in psychological research and theory has led to increasing consideration and appreciation of the role of gender, ethnicity, and socioeconomic class in human behavior and development.

REVIEW QUESTIONS

Demography and a Changing View of Adulthood

1. Discuss the two demographic changes that have contributed to a changing view of adulthood since the end of World War II.

2. What is meant by the "graying of America"? Describe the changes that are continuing to occur in the age structure of the U.S. population.

3. How can the study of adult development be beneficial?

Life-Span Developmental Perspective

1. Distinguish between normative age-graded, normative history-graded, and nonnormative influences.
2. Identify the key elements of the life-span developmental perspective.

Research Concepts, Methods, and Designs

1. Distinguish between reliability and validity as they apply to scientific research. Discuss the types of each.
2. Discuss the advantages and disadvantages of naturalistic observation, self-report, and case-study methods of collecting data.
3. Provide an example of a positive and a negative correlation.
4. Does relationship indicate causation? What is the "third-variable problem" in correlational studies?

5. Describe the basic elements of an experimental study. What is the greatest strength of this type of research? The greatest weakness?
6. Compare and contrast the cross-sectional, longitudinal, time-lag, and sequential designs.
7. In research, what is meant by the phrase "If it hasn't happened twice, it hasn't happened"? How is confidence in research findings increased?

Special Considerations and Limitations in the Research

1. Define ageism and discuss its potential impact on the research process.
2. Serious concerns have been raised about gender and ethnic bias in psychological research and theory. What is the basis of these concerns? Why is this a problem?

KEY TERMS

adult development, 2
adulthood, 2
age effects, 21
ageism, 26
average life expectancy, 2
baby boom, 4
baby bust, 4
case-study method, 16
chronological age, 3
cohort, 11
cohort effect, 11
confounding the variables, 19
construct validity, 13
control group, 19
correlation coefficient, 17
correlational study, 17
cross-sectional study, 22
demand characteristics, 16
demographic trends, 2
dependent variable, 18
development, 2

developmental psychology, 2
developmental research, 17
double-blind study, 19
experimental group, 19
experimental study, 18
external validity, 14
extraneous variables, 19
functional age, 3
gerontology, 4
hypothesis, 14
independent variable, 18
internal validity, 14
interobserver reliability, 13
life-span development, 8
life-span developmental
    perspective, 8
longitudinal study, 23
naturalistic observation, 14
negative correlations, 17
nondevelopmental research, 17
nonnormative influence, 11

normative age-graded influence, 10
normative history-graded
    influence, 10
old-old, 4
placebo, 19
plasticity, 10
positive correlation, 17
predictive validity, 13
psychology, 2
quasi- or natural experiments, 20
reliability, 13
research design, 16
self-report methods, 15
sequential designs, 25
social desirability bias, 16
test-retest reliability, 13
time-lag studies, 24
time-of-measurement effects, 21
traditional population pyramid, 4
validity, 13
young-old, 4

2 Theories of Psychosocial Development

HE WAS ONE OF THOSE GUYS who seemed to have it all—looks, brains, friends, charm, health, a wealthy and influential family in the city, a country club background—a real Big Man on Campus. He planned a career in medicine, following in the family tradition. The future looked bright. But then this was the late 1960s. The Vietnam War was at its height. Desperate young men were doing desperate things to stay out of the draft—marrying quickly, having children, going to Canada. Good grades would maintain your college deferment, a teaching job could protect you, a medical condition might get you out, and so on. Already struggling with the pressure of family expectations, his insurance was to enlist in the Marine Reserves. One weekend a month, two weeks in the summer, gladly exchanged for the risk of being drafted into the army, the infantry, the front lines. But when even this did not seem safe enough, he had himself committed to a mental institution, certain to put a blot on his record that the military would see—this BMOC, this frightened young adult. After that, things fell apart. Rumors circulated that he had fled to Thailand, maybe was involved in the drug trade—this son of wealth and privilege, this boy with the golden future. Two years passed. A phone call came at Christmastime—"Come back. You have to come back for New Year's. Everyone will be there. He'll be there. He's home." I wasn't prepared. The big, gorgeous athlete with the great smile, the one who always lit up a room, had become a small, frail, hollow-eyed, burned-out relic of himself—long, thin, straggly hair; beard; dirty, ragged bell-bottoms; muslin shirt; beads; sandals—you get the picture. Slow responses, slow speech. Ill. Completely stoned. Completely heartbreaking. The future seemed bleak.

> That was over twenty years ago. Today, he is an influential physician in the city. Married, four children. Handsome, dedicated, smart, well liked, and well respected. The realization of the promise we saw in him way back then, with a future that looks bright . . . indeed.

How do we explain development? How do we understand the path an individual life takes, such as the path just described? What are the most potent influences on adult life? Biology? Environment? Is there some predictable logic to the events of adulthood—stages comparable to the stages proposed to describe childhood? Are there some experiences we all share, or are our lives too diverse for such comparisons? This is a chapter about theories of psychosocial development—theories that attempt to answer these and other questions about adult life. (Cognitive and biological theories will be addressed in later chapters.) We will begin with a theoretical overview, taking a look at three perspectives on development—the organismic, mechanistic, and contextual models—as a framework for organizing some of the historical trends in developmental theory. We will see that the field is increasingly turning to a contextual view, reflected here in the section describing Urie Bronfenbrenner's Ecological Systems Theory. Next, we will review some of the most influential developmental stage theories, especially that of Erik Erikson, and consider the criticisms of the stage approach. The chapter includes a discussion of age norms and Bernice Neugarten's social age clock, which addresses the social meaning of chronological age. Finally, we will examine alternatives to the stage model, such as McCrae and Costa's Five-Factor Model of Personality.

Organismic, Mechanistic, and Contextual Models

One of the great debates in psychology is over the relative influence of nature (heredity) and nurture (environment) on behavior. Three basic positions—represented by the organismic, mechanistic, and contextual models of development—are possible. The various theories of development can be grouped according to the model of development to which they subscribe. These perspectives are not unimportant. As noted by Rosenberg, citing Kenneth Burke, "A theory is not only a way of seeing but also a way of not seeing" (1989, p. 43).

The **organismic model** stresses a natural unfolding of behavior according to a genetic blueprint. According to this view, as long as the environment provides basic necessities, like food and water, development will proceed according to its own timetable. The impetus for development resides within the individual, who is viewed as active. This inner-directed development unfolds according to a preset timetable into a series of fixed, universal stages. Arnold Gesell's (1949) explanation of early motor development relies heavily on this sort of nativist position; Piaget's cognitive-developmental theory does so to a lesser degree (Piaget & Inhelder, 1969). Early theories of development, beginning with that of G. Stanley Hall around 1900, tended to take this perspective. We will see this idea represented in the stage approach of the psychoanalytic theories.

The **mechanistic model,** on the other hand, views the individual as a passive recipient of environmental influence—a tabula rasa or blank slate to be written on by experience. All behavior is thought to be learned. There are no universals in development.

Rather, each of us is unique, because our life experience is unique. This view, heavily emphasizing nurture, is reflected in the strict learning theory positions of John Watson and B. F. Skinner and predominated in mid-20th-century American psychology. Beginning in the 1970s, however, seeds of change were found in social learning theorists such as Albert Bandura, who moved away from an extreme mechanistic view to acknowledge the influence of both inner and outer forces on development.

The **contextual model** views the development of the individual as the product of a complex interaction between the individual's biological/genetic nature and the various layers of the environment during a particular historical period. The contextual model thus recognizes the role of both nature and nurture in development and emphasizes the reciprocal nature of this interaction. It integrates elements of both the organismic and mechanistic views and has become increasingly influential.

The ecological model of Urie Bronfenbrenner (1979, 1989) places the emphasis squarely on the context of development. Birren and Birren (1990, p. 9) describe Bronfenbrenner's theory as "a potentially useful perspective for understanding adult behavior." Let's turn to a review of this approach to human development and its implications for the study of adult life.

Bronfenbrenner's Ecological Systems Theory

Bronfenbrenner presents a view of the individual as a "highly complex system in which biological, cognitive, emotional, and social elements are powerfully intertwined" (Bronfenbrenner et al., 1986 p. 1223). Developmental psychology, he claims, must move away from a fragmented study of variables to the study of the living organism as a system. The use of the term **ecology** (the science of relationships between organisms and their environments) acknowledges the contributions of the individual's biogenetic background, while at the same time emphasizing its interaction with an environmental context.

Rigor versus Relevance: Caught between a Rock and a Soft Place?

Bronfenbrenner's theory builds on and extends earlier work that began in the 1930s and 1940s with Kurt Lewin and the group of ecological psychologists at the University of Kansas, including Roger Barker (1968), Herb Wright, and Paul Gump. Central to the ecological model is the critical interaction between the person and the environment, expressed by Lewin (1935, p. 73) in the following formula: $B = f(PE)$. That is, behavior (B) is a function of the interaction of the person (P) and the environment (E). These early ecological psychologists were interested in the characteristics of natural settings and their effect on real-life behavior, in contrast to the highly structured, controlled laboratory experimentation of the behaviorists, who then dominated the field.

A rift developed between advocates of scientific rigor, who favored controlled laboratory research, and those who espoused naturalistic studies, which they felt were more relevant to real life. The discipline found itself "between a rock and a *soft* place. . . . The emphasis on rigor has led to experiments that are elegantly designed but often limited in scope" (Bronfenbrenner, 1979, p. 18), while the descriptive studies, though more relevant, were criticized for a lack of scientific objectivity and validity. Developmental psychology, dominated by those who stress rigor, became, for Bronfenbrenner (1979, p. 19), "the science of the strange behavior of children in strange situations with strange adults for the briefest possible periods of time." The experimentalists were probably not oblivious to the fact that behavior was the result of the interaction of many variables. But they felt that you could not study everything at once, so they began by isolating manageable units of behavior. They were also limited by the statistical techniques of the time, which could only handle single-variable effects.

CRITICAL THINKING QUESTION

Were those who emphasized laboratory experimentation more interested in high internal or external validity? How about the ecologists?

Bronfenbrenner's (1979, p. 21) work attempts to bridge the rigor-relevance gap by acknowledging the need for both, to be achieved through the **ecology of human development**:

> The ecology of human development involves the scientific study of the progressive, mutual accommodation between an active, growing human being and the changing properties of the immediate settings in which the developing person lives, as this process is affected by relations between these settings, and by the larger contexts in which the settings are embedded.

A Systems Approach: Reciprocal Interactions

One of Bronfenbrenner's major theoretical contributions is a broadened understanding of the environment, extending from the immediate settings in which the individual engages in face-to-face interaction with the values and attitudes—the ideology—that pervade the culture. The individual is seen as one element in a complex system of reciprocal relationships. Change in any one element of the system has ramifications for all other elements. So if we wish to understand behavior, we must understand the interactions between people and their present and past environments (Cole, in Bronfenbrenner, 1979, p. x). This is what is meant by the study of *development-in-context.*

Phenomenology: Through the Eyes of the Beholder

In addition to the contributions of the early ecologists, Ecological Systems Theory also incorporates a basic tenet of Jean Piaget in its stress on the individual as an active constructor of reality. Bronfenbrenner's view is phenomenological. **Phenomenology** stresses that reality *as perceived by the individual* is what is important. He captures this idea by citing the following dictum: "If men define situations as real, they are real in their consequences" (Thomas & Thomas, 1928, p. 572). Therefore, ecological research must approach the study of the environment through the eyes of the beholder—from the subject's point of view.

The Ecological View of the Environment

The environment extends far beyond the immediate settings in which the individual engages. It includes relationships among these arenas as well as influences emitted by larger settings in which the individual may not even directly participate. Bronfenbrenner conceptualizes the environment as a series of nested structures, each contained within the next and a part of the whole, with the individual in the center. Specifically, these are the microsystem, mesosystem, exosystem, and macrosystem (Figure 2.1).

The Microsystem

The **microsystem** is the innermost level of the environment. It includes immediate settings in which the developing person interacts directly with people and objects. The three main elements of the microsystem are the activities, roles, and relationships in which the person engages. Two-person relationships, or **dyads,** are the building blocks of the social structure and are reciprocal in nature. Positive, supportive dyadic relationships enhance the quality of interactions among others in the system. Remember that an important determinant of the effect of the microsystem is the way the individual perceives the system—its meaning in phenomenological terms.

The Mesosystem

The **mesosystem** is composed of relationships between settings in which the individual participates. So rather than constituting another layer of environment per se, it represents interactions between microsystems. For example, the ability of an individual to function effectively on the job is influenced by linkages between the job and home. Job and home are each microsystems; the relationship between them and the effects they have on each other are part of the mesosystem. Stress and conflict at home are likely to undermine job performance, while harmony and support at home may enhance it. Similarly, stress on the job may add stress to family life, and so on. Interconnections between other people in the setting are of equal importance. For example, a father is

FIGURE 2.1 *Topological Model of the Environment: A Schematic Diagram of the Levels of the Environment in Bronfenbrenner's (1979) Ecological Systems Theory*

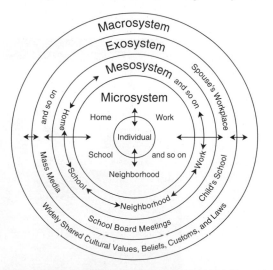

Note: Arrows across rings indicate reciprocal interactions at all levels.

affected by his relationships with his wife and daughter but is also influenced by the relationship *between* mother and daughter. Crouter and Bumpus (2001) describe a domino effect in which a father's stress from working long hours and feeling overloaded on the job may lead to general feelings of stress and burden, negatively affecting relationships with both spouse and children, thereby increasing his wife's feelings of role overload and level of conflict with their children, and the children's subsequent psychological adjustment. These outcomes alter the father's mesosystem in multiple ways, along with those of the mother and children.

Because the mesosystem is a system of microsystems, whenever the individual takes on a new role and enters the settings associated with it, the mesosystem is expanded. Similarly, termination of roles correspondingly reduces the mesosystem. These shifts in roles and associated contexts are known as *ecological transitions* (Bronfenbrenner, 1979, p. 6) and go on throughout the life span. For instance, when one marries or becomes a parent, other aspects of one's life are affected, just as when one starts or leaves school, changes jobs, or retires. These transitions have developmental significance and provide, "in effect, a ready-made experiment of nature with a built-in, before-after design in which each subject can serve as his own control" (p. 27). The systematic study of these transitions could be fruitful, though little of this type of research has been conducted. For example, with two married sons who have recently become parents, I am very interested in the transition to fatherhood.

Which settings have the most pervasive effect on adult life? Though research at the level of the mesosystem is limited, Bronfenbrenner identifies home and work as key arenas in adulthood (p. 236). The importance assigned to these two domains of adult life is reflected in later chapters of this text.

The Exosystem

The **exosystem** is made up of settings in which individuals do not actively participate, but that influence the microsystems in which they do act. For example, employees' work environments may be affected by events taking place at board meetings in which they

Bronfenbrenner's broad description of the environment includes the exosystem, made up of settings in which individuals do not actively participate but which can influence their more immediate environment, or microsystem. For example, decisions made at this corporate board meeting may affect individual employees in a number of direct ways.

are not involved, such as a decision to downsize a company. These events may have a ripple effect on the employees' home lives as well. Thus, a husband or wife may be strongly affected by his or her spouse's experience at work.

Similarly, decisions made at the local school board meeting may affect a working parent's ability to function effectively, both as a parent and as a professional. For example, the school calendar influences the kinds of child-care arrangements working parents must make to accommodate school holidays, teacher inservice days, and so on. Similarly, school systems that only schedule teacher conferences during the day discourage working parents' involvement in their children's education. On the other hand, school calendars and schedules that take into account the real-life situation of most parents could have more positive effects on other settings that the parents engage in and that directly or indirectly affect children.

The Macrosystem

The **macrosystem** represents the widely shared beliefs and values that determine how social groups—such as social classes, ethnic groups, or even entire societies—are organized. The macrosystem serves as a kind of blueprint, so that within a given social group or society, the micro-, meso-, and exosystems tend to be similar. For example, on the societal level, U.S. schools and offices share certain basic features because they derive from the same basic model. Schools or offices in other cultures would be different from ours but would share common elements among themselves. Within our society, the macrosystem varies somewhat by social class, and among different racial, ethnic, and religious groups.

A study of ethnic differences in adolescent school achievement conducted by Steinberg, Dornbusch, and Brown (1992) illustrates some of the ways in which the macrosystem influences behavior. The researchers were interested in studying the contrasting social ecologies of adolescents from differing ethnic backgrounds and their effect on academic performance. Specifically, they hoped to discover variables that would account for the higher achievement among White and Asian American as compared to Hispanic and African American teenagers. They found that White parents were more likely than Hispanic, African American, or Asian American parents to use an authoritative parenting style (characterized by warmth, firmness, and democracy). Children raised in authoritative homes have generally been found to be more competent on a variety of measures, including school achievement. Thus, the beliefs and values held by parents, and reflected in their approach to childrearing, may influence their children's development in important ways. However, the researchers found that the effect of parenting style among both White and minority students was moderated by ethnic differences in the values and norms of the peer group. So, for example, even the academic performance of African Americans raised by authoritative parents may be undermined by a peer group that does not value or support academic success. Conversely, Asian American children appear to benefit from a generally high level of support offered by their peer group, which serves to offset the disadvantages of being raised by more authoritarian parents (who employ a remote, rigid, and more power-oriented style). Thus, the multiple contexts in which individuals live (for example, home, peer group) interact and affect motivation, activities, goals, means of relating to others, and so on. Further, the nature of the context—here, its values and beliefs—varies among social groups.

Public policy also exists at the level of the macrosystem and reflects the beliefs and values of the society. Such policy has the potential to maintain or to change aspects of the environment that influence behavior. In other words, "Public policy has the power to affect the well-being and development of human beings by determining the conditions of their lives" (Bronfenbrenner, 1979, p. xiii). Examples include programs such as Head Start and Social Security, as well as policies affecting day care and family leave. Throughout this book, the impact of public policy will be woven into our discussions of adult life.

Ecology and Human Differences

One way to begin to understand cultural, racial, or religious differences among groups would be to systematically study the various layers of the environment in which these groups exist and their effect on behavior. Put simply, what are the qualities that characterize the environments in which people participate, and second, what are the effects of these qualities on their activities, roles, and relationships? How does individual behavior evolve in an environmental context?

The concept of social role is important to the understanding of individual differences in behavior. A **social role** is defined as a set of activities and relationships expected of a person who occupies a particular social position, and of others in relation to that person (Bronfenbrenner, 1979, p. 85). The second part of the definition is often overlooked, despite its significance. Not only does the role direct the individual's behavior, it dictates the behavior of others toward that individual as well. These role expectations are set at the level of the macrosystem, reflecting prevailing beliefs and values about how human relationships and enterprises should be organized. As a result, their influence pervades every level of the environment and every aspect of behavior. The importance of social role will be addressed a number of times throughout this book and will be especially helpful in understanding potential gender differences.

We should also remember that macrosystems and their component parts are affected by the larger sociohistorical context—in this sense, they are fluid, evolving. For example, compare the American macrosystem (as well as the other environmental systems) experienced by young adults in the 2000s to the one experienced by young adults in the 1940s. A number of differences are apparent, such as changed conceptions of male and female roles, opportunities for higher education, and economic conditions. Bronfenbrenner refers to this dimension of historical time as the *chronosystem* (the prefix *chrono* means time).

Sometimes, particularly during periods of rapid social and technological change, the macrosystem and its social institutions fail to keep pace with changes in individual lives—a situation referred to as **structural lag** (Riley, Kahn, & Foner, 1994). Individuals may be left with outdated (or missing) scripts by which to structure their lives. An example is the mismatch between the increasing health and longevity of older adults and the role opportunities available to them. A very good friend of mine is experiencing such a lag. Though he is just turning 50, he retired from the Air Force six years ago as a lieutenant colonel and is now working as a pilot instructor. His children have graduated from college and moved out on their own. He is struggling to find new meaning, fulfillment, and direction in his life now that his primary career and family goals—the focus of everything he's done up to this point in his life—have been achieved. Still healthy, vigorous, and capable, looking ahead to the next twenty, thirty, or more years of his life, the question he posed as we talked was a familiar one: "Now what? Is that all there is?" New roles for those in his position—and there are millions of them—have yet to be clearly defined.

One last comment about the macrosystem. Because of its pervasive influence over the other layers of the environmental system, changes in the macrosystem have the potential to change human behavior in significant ways. Consider, for example, the impact of a government's decision to go to war.

CRITICAL THINKING QUESTION

Check your grasp of these four levels of the environment by reading the following vignette and answering the questions based on Ecological Systems Theory.

> Martha lives in a modern capitalist society. She is an executive in a rapidly growing business firm and is married to Matt, an attorney in private practice. Their two children, ages 8 and 12, are doing well in school and have a wide circle of friends. Martha and Matt are very active in a number of community organizations. Martha's company has decided to expand and offers her the opportunity to move to Montana to open a new office.

1. *What do we know about the macrosystem in this case? How might it influence Matt and Martha—for example, their beliefs, values, social roles, and so on?*

2. *At what level of the environment was the decision made to expand the company and offer Martha a new job?*

3. *If Martha accepts this new job, which of her microsystems will be affected? How?*

4. *Identify possible implications for Martha's mesosystem.*

Bronfenbrenner's Ecological Systems Theory represents a contextual model of development, a perspective that, in acknowledging the interaction between the nature of the individual and the qualities of the environment, has become increasingly influential. Bronfenbrenner criticizes the bulk of developmental research for studying development-out-of-context: focusing on the characteristics of the person while forgetting the characteristics of the environment and, most important, the interaction between the two. The next section reviews another theoretical perspective in developmental psychology—stage theory.

Concept Review 2.1

- Theories of development can be categorized as organismic, mechanistic, or contextual, based on the degree to which they emphasize the relative influence of heredity and environment.

- Bronfenbrenner's Ecological Systems Theory represents the increasingly influential contextual perspective.

- A key tenet of ecological psychology is the reciprocal interaction between the individual and the environment.

- Bronfenbrenner describes the individual's environment as a system composed of nested layers: microsystem, mesosystem, exosystem, and macrosystem.

Ages and Stages: The Psychoanalytic Tradition

Stage Theory Defined

One of the strongest theoretical traditions in developmental psychology is that of **stage theory.** Proponents maintain that all of us, at about the same time in our lives, experience the same events, problems, or challenges—that there are universal sequences of change. Well-known examples of stage theories include those of Gesell, Piaget, Freud, Erikson, Havighurst, and Levinson. Stage theories tend to be organismic in nature, attributing change to an innate, genetic blueprint that governs development within individual members of the species in the same way (though they also, and to varying degrees, acknowledge the role of the environment). The stages are also viewed as sequential, so that successful completion of one stage is necessary for successful progression to the next, while failure to resolve issues or acquire skills at a more fundamental stage undermines success at later stages. Stage theory received an influential boost in the 1970s with the publication of a number of books describing variations on this theme (such as Levinson's *The Seasons of a Man's Life*). The 1980s brought increasing questions about the validity of the stage model, and criticisms have increased since. We will consider the criticisms as well as some alternative views later in this chapter.

Freud, Jung, and Erikson

The modern version of stage theory is traceable to Sigmund Freud's (1856–1939) theory of psychoanalysis. Freud described the psychosexual development of children as progressing through five fixed, universal stages, heavily biological in nature. His primary emphasis was on the first five or six years of life; he viewed adulthood as not much more than a reenactment of early experience, rather than a time of continued development.

Carl Jung (1875–1961) is often credited with extending the stage concept to adult development. Originally a devoted follower of Freud, Jung came to disagree with Freud's restricted emphasis on childhood and his neglect of the role of culture in development, among other things. An irreparable rift developed between the two in 1913, and Jung (1933) went on to develop his own view of human development. His conception of the life cycle focused especially on the second half of life, which he believed was dominated by a drive toward illumination of the self. He viewed age 40—the "noon of life" (p. 109)— as the beginning of the process of **individuation,** or becoming more fully oneself, a lifelong process of self-discovery and self-development marked by increasing introspection and a resolution of innate inner conflicts between polar opposites (masculine-feminine, creation-destruction, youth-age, and separation-attachment). Jung's emphasis on an important change beginning around age 40 is echoed in more recent conceptions of the midlife transition. Levinson (1978, p. 4) considers Jung to be "the father of the modern study of adult development."

Erik Erikson (1902–1994) can be viewed as the bridge between Freud and Jung— loyal to Freudian theory but extending the stage concept, bowing to Jung in his coverage of adult life and his emphasis on the critical role of culture. Erikson's (1950, 1968) theory is contextual in its emphasis on the interaction between the individual and society and is the first truly life-span stage theory. It has been so influential that we will devote the next major section of this chapter to a review of Erikson's contributions, with particular emphasis on the three adult stages and the ideas and theories generated by them. As Noam (1988, p. 3) says, "More than any other, his work has created the momentum towards a field of adult development. All present day theories of adult development are influenced by his vision, even when there is disagreement about model and method." McCrae and Costa (1990, p. 11) go as far as to say that "his theory of eight stages of life is probably the single most important theory of adult personality development."

Erikson's Eight Stages of Psychosocial Development

A loyal psychoanalyst who sees himself as building on the theory of Sigmund Freud, Erikson's focus is on the development of the ego, that part of the self that interacts in and with the real world through the use of such cognitive processes as perceiving, reasoning, and remembering. The ego progresses through a series of eight hierarchically arranged and universal stages, each characterized by a psychosocial crisis or turning point (Table 2.1). This process is governed by a preset plan, each successive stage precipitated by internal psychological developments as well as external social-role expectations. These stages essentially describe the development of different facets of the individual's identity in relation to the social world. The theory is based on the **epigenetic principle**—the idea that the parts give rise to the whole. "Out of this ground plan," Erikson (1968, p. 92) says, "the parts arise, each part having its time of special ascendancy, until all parts have arisen to form a functioning whole." Each stage adds to the others, eventually creating a new entity. Thus, the individual is viewed throughout the life span as a developing organism, with each stage influenced by and based on specific experiences at earlier stages.

Erik Erikson (1902–1994) contributed the first truly life-span theory of psychosocial development. His work has been extremely influential.

Erikson's studies of combat veterans, Native Americans, and others led him to conclude that development was not as universal as Freud conceived it to be. The sociocultural and historical context is therefore given more weight in Erikson's theory than in Freud's. Though the stages of development are preset genetically, the individual's unique experiences and the processing of those experiences give each life its unique quality and outcome. Thus, the person is seen as a biological/social/psychological organism; development is based in both biology and culture.

Each of Erikson's eight stages focuses on a **psychosocial crisis** in the life cycle. The use of the term *crisis* should be thought of in its Greek sense ("krisis") as a challenge or a turning point at which there are both danger and opportunity—"a turning point for better or worse" (Erikson, 1964, p. 139). Each stage is posited in terms of two alternative ways of dealing with the environmental challenge, one adaptive, one maladaptive. Successful resolution leads to the development of a basic psychological strength or virtue. Success or failure depends on experiences in earlier stages as well one's current life situation. For example, young adults who have developed a clearly articulated and integrated sense of self—an identity—should be capable of greater intimacy: closeness with and

TABLE 2.1 *Summary of Erikson's (1950) Eight Stages of Psychosocial Development*

Psychosocial Crisis/Approximate Age	Virtue
TRUST VERSUS MISTRUST (BIRTH TO AGE 1)	**HOPE**
The quality of parental care in meeting basic physical and psychological needs largely determines whether the child learns to view the world and people as safe and dependable.	
AUTONOMY VERSUS DOUBT (AGE 1 TO 3)	**WILL**
Parental responses to children's growing physical and mental abilities and their need to do things for themselves produce either a sense of self-government and self-sufficiency or self-doubt.	
INITIATIVE VERSUS GUILT (AGE 3 TO 6)	**PURPOSE**
Children given ample opportunity to initiate motor and intellectual activities learn to be self-starters, capable of planning and responsibility. Nonresponsive and derisive parents foster guilt.	
INDUSTRY VERSUS INFERIORITY (AGE 6 TO 11)	**COMPETENCE**
Children who are encouraged to make, build, and do things and who are rewarded for their efforts develop skills as well as pride in accomplishment and become productive and achievement oriented. Lack of opportunity and support, as well as criticism, leads to feelings of inferiority.	
IDENTITY VERSUS ROLE CONFUSION (ADOLESCENCE: THE TEENS)	**FIDELITY**
Adolescents must use newly developed cognitive abilities to develop a coherent sense of self that integrates past experiences with direction for future adult roles.	
INTIMACY VERSUS ISOLATION (YOUNG ADULTHOOD: 20S AND 30S)	**LOVE**
Young adults must develop the capacity to share with and care about others, without fear of losing their own identities. The alternative is to be alone.	
GENERATIVITY VERSUS SELF-ABSORPTION (MIDDLE ADULTHOOD: 40 TO 65)	**CARE**
Concern about future generations and the legacy one will leave behind is ushered in by a growing awareness of mortality at midlife. Those who fail at this task remain focused on their own needs and wants.	
INTEGRITY VERSUS DESPAIR (LATE ADULTHOOD TO DEATH)	**WISDOM**
Integrity refers to the ability to look back over one's life and see it as satisfying and meaningful. It also implies an acceptance of death. Those who despair see their lives as unsatisfying, have great regrets, feel that time precludes any attempts at change, and fear death.	

commitment to others. Those who have not successfully completed stage 5, on the other hand, may be threatened by intimacy, fearing a loss of self. Development is enhanced when resolution of the crisis is in favor of the positive alternative, though Erikson has often stated that some experience of the negative alternative may be beneficial as well. For example, while it is desirable for infants to acquire an overall sense of trust in others, some people should be mistrusted. In addition, even though an issue has its moment of ascendency in a particular stage of life, the issue is never resolved for good. Instead, it will reemerge in a different configuration at later stages. Though the formation of an identity is the primary issue of adolescence, for instance, this initial identity may be refined and reformulated many times throughout adult life. In order "to remain psychologically alive [the individual] must resolve these conflicts unceasingly" (Erikson, 1959, p. 51). Finally, positive as well as negative change can occur in regard to any of these issues at later stages.

In sum, beginning with its debut in 1950, and until fairly recently, Erikson's was one of the few theories to focus on adulthood. It is no wonder that his ideas are so often quoted. He has provided a broad outline of the development of the ego across the life span, acknowledging the multiple forces that contribute to individual development and interindividual variation—both internal and external, past and present. Development is described as an ongoing process, terminated only by death. The breadth of the theory has contributed to its appeal and its compatibility with other theories and disciplines. In addition, Erikson himself insisted on "historical relativism" and the need to revise theory in light of new circumstances (Weiland, 1993). Thus, he anticipated that his model would—and should—be adapted and reformulated. These are its strengths. Weaknesses include a lack of specificity about what behaviors to look for during the various stages (for example, how do we know the individual has achieved intimacy?) (Hamachek, 1990); questions about its applicability to development among women, other cultures, and so on; heavy reliance on clinical observations as opposed to empirical data; and more basic concerns about the stage model itself (which we will address in a later section).

It has been left to others to fill in gaps and to test, revise, and extend the theory. Whitbourne, Zuschlag, Elliot, and Waterman (1992) conducted a large-scale sequential study of three cohorts of men and women covering ages 20 to 42, using an Eriksonian-based quantitative measure of psychosocial development. They found quite a bit of support for Erikson's theory, while at the same time their data suggest that the developmental sequence and timetable he suggested for stages 1 through 8 may be much more variable across individuals, influenced by their life circumstances and social environment. Let's consider some additional expansions of Erikson's model.

Butler's Life Review

Erikson has described integrity as the acceptance of one's life as the one and only life possible, a coming to terms with the experiences and realities of a lifetime. Robert Butler (1963, 1968) has outlined one process that may be used by older adults to achieve this integration and acceptance. He calls it the **life review,** a period of purposeful reminiscence that involves a return to consciousness of past experiences and conflicts. Butler (1968, pp. 489–490) sees the life review as a normal and universal mental experience among older adults, prompted by approaching death:

> As the past marches in review, it is surveyed, observed, and reflected upon by the ego. Reconsideration of previous experiences and their meanings occurs, often with concomitant revised or expanded understanding. Such reorganization of past experience may provide a more valid picture, giving new and significant meanings to one's life; it may also prepare one for death, mitigating one's fears.

Support for the life review process may be one way others can assist older adults in integrating and accepting the life lived and adapting successfully to the last stage of development.

The nature of the life review is suggested in the following passage from Lillian Hellman's *Pentimento* (1974, p. 3):

> Old paint on canvas, as it ages, sometimes becomes transparent. When that happens it is possible, in some pictures, to see the original lines: a tree will show through a woman's dress, a child makes way for a dog, a large boat is no longer on an open sea. That is called

According to Robert Butler, reminiscence and the life review provide one way for older adults to
achieve integrity.

pentimento because the painter "repented," changed his mind. Perhaps it would be as well
to say that the old conception, replaced by a later choice, is a way of seeing and then seeing again. . . . The paint has aged now and I wanted to see what was there for me once,
what is there for me now.

Haight (1991) provides an integrated review of the literature from 1960 to 1990 on the
subject of life review and reminiscence. She found an increased interest over the 30-year
period, as well as evidence that life review and reminiscence are a promising therapeutic intervention. (See Chapter 11 for a discussion of the use of life review in the treatment of depression among older adults.) Additional research aimed at specifying the
exact nature and potential uses of the process and its relationship to adaptation is still
needed.

A Closer Look at Generativity

Stage 7—generativity versus self-absorption—is one of the least discussed and studied
stages in Erikson's model, though it is also one of the longest, extending from the end
of young adulthood to the end of the middle years. One observer has pointed out that
"for a motive so critical to our collective well-being . . . generativity has received only
incidental glances from psychology" (Kotre, 1984, p. 2). Let's examine some issues related to this stage, as well as some new ideas about the concept of generativity.

The awareness of one's own mortality—an awareness that seems to become more
"real" and therefore potent at midlife—raises the question of legacy, of what one will leave
behind of lasting significance. Erikson called this aspect of psychosocial development
generativity—a term that he apparently coined and that he defined as having an interest
in establishing and guiding the next generation. This suggests that the primary means by
which generativity is accomplished is through parenthood, but this is too limited an interpretation. According to Erikson (1950), having children does not in itself achieve generativity. Generativity is more broadly understood to mean a concern with future
generations and society as a whole, with the kind of world one will leave behind. Erikson

clarifies the term as follows: "It means to generate in the most inclusive sense. . . . I use the word 'generativity' because I mean everything that is generated from generation to generation: children, products, ideas, *and* works of art. In middle adulthood, one develops the capacity to care in a sense that includes 'to care to do' something, to 'care for' somebody or something, 'to take care of' that which needs protection and attention, and 'to take care not to' do something destructive" (Erikson, quoted in Evans, 1981, pp. 51–52).

Generative people are interested in making a contribution and leading a productive life (Hamachek, 1990). The opposite is for personality development to stagnate: the individual remains locked into personal needs and interests. While generative tendencies may appear earlier in the life course, Erikson states that it is in middle adulthood that they become the psychosocial focus of development. The "radius of care" expands beyond the self and the issue of identity prominent in adolescence, and intimate relationships with family and friends established in young adulthood, to the future of the community and society as a whole. Mature adults are able to "foster the development of others and contribute in some way to the culture in which they belong" (Peterson & Stewart, 1996, p. 21). McAdams and de St. Aubin (1992) conceptualize generativity as a multidimensional construct arising from the fusion of two deeply rooted desires: the agentic drive to be or to do something that transcends death and the communal need to be nurturant. In other words, "agency represents the self-asserting, self-protecting, self-expanding existence of the individual, while communion represents the participation of the individual in a mutual, interpersonal reality or in some larger organism" (Kotre, 1984, p. 16).

Kotre's Four Types of Generativity

Interest in generativity and its effects on personality in adulthood has increased in recent years, perhaps a reflection of the influence of the baby boom cohort, now in middle age and grappling with the "critical step from Me to Beyond Me" (Kotre, 1984, p. 24). Defining *generativity* as "a desire to invest one's substance in forms of life and work that will outlive the self," John Kotre (1984, p. 10) has extended Erikson's concept by delineating four major types, representing various ways the generative impulse may be expressed (Table 2.2).

TABLE 2.2 *Kotre's (1984) Four Types of Generativity*

Type	Description	Generative Object
Biological	Begetting, bearing, nursing offspring	Infant
Parental	Nurturing and disciplining offspring, initiating them into a family's traditions	Child
Technical	Teaching skills—the "body" of a culture—to successors, implicitly passing on the symbol system in which the skills are embedded	Apprentice, skill
Cultural	Creating, renovating, and conserving a symbol system—the "mind" of a culture—explicitly passing it on to successors	Disciple, culture

Source: John Kotre (1984). *Outliving the Self: Generativity and the Interpretation of Lives,* p. 12. Baltimore/London: Johns Hopkins Universit\y Press. Used by permission.

Generativity is an important aspect of adult psychosocial development and can be expressed in many different ways. Here, the ballet master perfects the student's pose.

Biological and **parental generativity** relate to the having and raising of children. These are the forms of generativity most people probably think of when first learning about this concept. **Technical generativity** "is accomplished by teachers at all stations of the journey through life, who pass on skills to those less advanced than themselves" (Kotre, 1984, p. 13). **Cultural generativity** moves beyond the teaching of how to do something, to the level of meaning: the fostering of the growth of others by passing on important values and ideologies through either tangible or intangible offerings to society. For example, an individual may work toward passage of a law, write a book or create a painting, restore a park, or serve as a mentor to a younger colleague, a concept we will explore more fully in Chapter 8 when we examine career development (Peterson & Klohnen, 1995). Unlike biological and parental forms, technical and cultural generativity can be expressed throughout adulthood. In fact, Kotre believes the most significant forms of cultural generativity occur after biological reproduction and promote the survival of future generations through the transmission of culture. Note that the distance between the actor and the object of generativity increases as one moves down the list of types, again illustrating Erikson's notion of an expanding radius of care.

Kotre emphasizes that the context in which generativity is expressed has changed significantly since the turn of the century. Extended life expectancy and the availability of birth control have provided new opportunities and outlets for generative behavior, as death is postponed and a span of child-free years opens up in the second half of life. Freedom from the demands and responsibilities of parenthood may provide other opportunities to express generative impulses, such as through community service.

Correlates and Antecedents of Generativity

Peterson and Klohnen (1995) and Peterson and Stewart (1996) constructed measures of generativity and applied them to the analysis of data drawn from samples of college-educated women during their 40s. The goal was to examine the correlates and antecedents of generativity at midlife. The researchers wanted to know what highly generative adults are like and how they got that way. In regard to the first issue, earlier research has suggested that generative individuals often assume leadership roles and are norm bearers who pass on cultural traditions to the next generation. Consistent with these studies, Peterson and Klohnen found that generative women are likely to display prosocial personal qualities such as empathy, self-control, and responsibility. Also in accord with earlier findings, these women were tolerant of differing viewpoints and tended to be psychologically healthy and fulfilled. Generative women who had careers found fulfillment in productivity and helping others; these subjects tended to be satisfied in their work and to be more motivated by a prosocial desire to help and care for others than by extrinsic factors such as money. Those not working in careers found fulfillment through parenting. Finally, generative women were invested in parenting but also expressed an expanded radius of care through their involvement in political activity. "These findings suggest that expressions of generativity are not limited to family or work life but are manifested as well in concerns for the wider national and international spheres" (Peterson & Klohnen, 1995, pp. 27–28). This may reflect Erikson's idea that generative individuals early in life develop a fundamental trust in the future of humanity (hope) and believe that constructive political activity can improve the human condition. This political involvement may facilitate Kotre's cultural generativity by allowing these women to pass on important values and ideas to others. As to the second question of antecedents, generativity at midlife was related to scores on personality measures obtained from these women as adolescents, supporting Erikson's contention that the psychological origins of generativity arise earlier in life. Highly generative participants also expressed gratitude to mentors in young adulthood (an influential teacher or boss), suggesting the importance of positive role models and an intergenerational link in generativity development and perhaps a desire to repay the debt by mentoring others. Findings such as these based on data drawn from longitudinal studies may be especially valuable, as they illuminate factors that contribute to generativity and could thus help facilitate the development of future cohorts of generative adults.

CRITICAL THINKING QUESTION

Can you identify findings from these two studies that illustrate the four types of generativity described by Kotre?

Both of these studies are based on primarily White, highly educated, affluent women. The authors stress that these women are in a good position to fulfill their generative impulses, while those who are less advantaged may face more frustrations and limited opportunities to do so. Peterson and Stewart (1996) suggest that immigrant and minority groups may face special challenges in regard to generativity as they grapple with which cultural values and traditions they should maintain and pass on to their children as they simultaneously attempt to integrate into the mainstream majority culture. Thus, future research must address the development and expression of generativity in men as well as in different social classes and ethnic groups.

Moments of Generativity, Not Stages

Many questions remain in regard to generativity, offering a rich research agenda. For example, how do you identify the generative person? How can generativity be measured? How do generative people get that way? What difference does generativity make in other aspects of the individual's life? Does generative behavior contribute to well-being? What is the relationship between generativity and gender? Social class? Culture?

On one point those currently researching this subject agree: the stage model of generativity as originally conceived by Erikson is outmoded. Kotre (1984) identifies the problems as follows. First, changes in the structure of the life cycle require changes in fixed-stage theories that are tied to age. Second, Erikson's theory contains a "scheduling dilemma." While childbearing is described as a prime component of generativity, Erikson places it in middle adulthood, when most childbearing and childrearing is over.

Third, the length of the stage suggests that it is the dominant issue for several decades of life, receding in importance in late adulthood as the issue of integrity takes center stage. Kotre finds no corroborating evidence in life histories. Rather, he describes a more intermittent pattern, with generativity arising, receding, and arising again at various points in adult life. In a study of age-cohort differences in a sample of 210 young, midlife, and older men and women, McAdams, de St. Aubin, and Logan (1993) found evidence of an increase in generativity from young adulthood to midlife, but no clear evidence of a decline in later life, as Erikson's model would suggest. Similarly, in a study of 333 women representing three cohorts, Zucker, Ostrove, and Stewart (2002) found that generativity increased from the 20s to the 40s and leveled off, but did not decline, into the 60s.

Instead of thinking of generativity as a stage, Kotre and others suggest it should be thought of as "an impulse released at various times between the late teens and old, old age. Different types of generativity, having their own schedules, will be released at different moments" (Kotre, 1984, p. 262). Stewart and Vandewater (1998) suggest there may be three different forms of generativity that follow different developmental paths. **Generative desires**—a longing to be productive and to make a contribution to society—peak in early adulthood, then decline. **Felt capacity for generativity** rises from early to middle adulthood and then declines a bit. It is at this point that individuals may have acquired the necessary resources, personal and otherwise, to feel capable and competent to carry out the generative contributions they envisioned earlier in life. Finally, **generative accomplishment,** a sense of having achieved a generative goal, may rise throughout adulthood, to peak in late life. In essence, the three forms are: I want to do it, I can do it, I've done it. Middle adulthood would be characterized by relatively high levels of all three forms, distinguished from other life periods by high levels of felt capacity for generativity. As currently conceptualized, then, generativity is not an internal, global personality trait, nor is it a fixed, universal stage of great duration. It is instead one aspect of the adult psychosocial agenda, perhaps most salient in the middle years of adulthood, which takes different forms and varies across roles, settings, and times.

In conclusion, a number of researchers are reformulating, expanding, and refining the concept of generativity. McAdams et al. (1993) describe it as one of the richest theoretical concepts in adult personality development, though it has only just begun to be explored empirically. They conceive generativity as constituting a psychosocial link between the developing person and the social world, a means by which an adult becomes integrated into social institutions and societal activities designed to maintain that which society has judged to be good and to better the world in the future. Adults express generativity in a number of different ways. It is a complex phenomenon, representing a "positive and proactive aspect of adult development and aging in modern Western life" (McAdams et al., 1993, p. 221), and deserving of continued research attention.

Levinson's Seasons of a Man's Life

During the 1970s, three books were published that contributed additional insights into adult development within the developmental stage model tradition (Vaillant, 1977; Gould, 1978; Levinson, 1978). Of these, the account by Daniel Levinson (1920–1994) of the life stories of 40 men, published in *The Seasons of a Man's Life,* has proven to be the most influential. A corollary volume on the seasons of a woman's life, the report of a study of 45 women begun in 1979, was published posthumously in 1996. While acknowledging a theoretical debt to Erikson and others, Levinson (1986, p. 10) clearly feels that adulthood cannot be understood by borrowing models from child development: "Adulthood has its own distinctive character and must be studied in its own right, not merely as an extrapolation from childhood." Let's examine his contribution to the stage model of development.

Purpose, Sample, and Method

The research that culminated in Levinson's book on male adult development began in 1966 and was motivated by both academic and personal interests: he was 46 and was grappling with personal issues that made him curious about midlife. His initial intention to study the midlife decade from 35 to 45 was later abandoned in favor of a broader study, extending from the late teens to the late 40s. His purpose was to search for preliminary answers to the following questions: "What does it mean to be an adult? What are the root issues of adult life . . . ? Is there an underlying order in the progression of our lives over the adult years, as in childhood and adolescence?" (Levinson, 1978, p. ix). He hoped that by constructing the stories of his subjects' lives, he could provide a developmental perspective on adulthood in men.

The sample consisted of 40 men, at that time aged 35 to 45, born between 1923 and 1934. The importance assigned to work as a basis of male identity was reflected in the choice of four occupational subgroups to comprise the sample: hourly workers in industry, business executives, university biologists, and novelists. All were American-born and had been married at least once. They differed in all other respects (education, race, marital status, religion, socioeconomic status, and so on). Levinson and his colleagues also used a secondary sample of historical and fictional figures.

His approach is social-psychological—that is, he attempts to describe how the individual engages with the external social world and the significance of that engagement for the adult self. The method used has come to be called a *Levinsonian study:* it consists of extensive biographical interviewing—in this case, totaling 10 to 20 hours per subject over a two- to three-month period, with a follow-up two years later. Though the primary sources of information were the men themselves, the team also interviewed wives, visited workplaces, and used various other sources of information. Levinson (1986) admits to methodological problems, including reliance on subjects' memory and reconstruction. The approach is also time consuming, expensive, and vulnerable to bias, both on the part of the subject and the interviewer. But it is, he feels, the only means of overcoming the fragmentation in so much adult development research and of examining the richness, meaning, and significance of an individual life.

Major Findings

The results provide a detailed structural view of development in adulthood, comprised of eras and periods that follow a universal, though not hierarchical, sequence. This is an important point. Like the seasons of the year, these periods follow one another and are interrelated, but one is not of greater value than another, nor does one period represent a more advanced level of development than the others. They are simply different. The segments of the life cycle are age-linked, generally varying only two years in either direction. This is one of the most controversial aspects of Levinson's model. Within this overall structure or design of adult life, however, there are infinite variations, as the individual engages with the social world in his own unique way, making his own choices, pursuing his own goals and values.

Eras, Transitions, and Periods. Levinson describes the life cycle as composed of a sequence of eras, as shown in Figure 2.2. Each **developmental era,** lasting about 25 years, has its own biopsychosocial nature—unique, though contributing to and integrated with the whole—like acts in a play, and represents a major change in the nature of our lives. There are lesser but crucially important changes within each era as well. The eras partially overlap, as one era comes to an end while the next is beginning. The change is accomplished during a long and complex **cross-era transition,** which normally lasts about five years and represents a fundamental turning point in the life cycle. Levinson (1996, p. 29) defines a transition as "a process of change that forms a bridge between X and Y. . . . To be 'in transit' is to be in the process of leaving X (without having fully left it) and, at the same time, of entering Y (without being fully a part of it)." The eras and

FIGURE 2.2 *Eras in the Male Life Cycle*

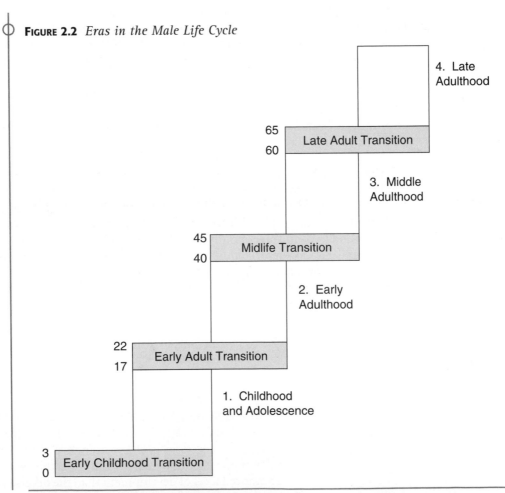

Source: Daniel J. Levinson et al. (1978). *The Seasons of a Man's Life.* New York: Ballantine Books. Copyright © 1978 by Daniel J. Levinson. Reprinted by permission of Alfred A. Knopf, Inc.

transitions are tied to well-defined average ages, with a range of ±2 years (Levinson, 1996). This, then, is the broad outline or macrostructure of the life cycle. The preadult era extends from conception to about age 22, ending as the individual becomes independent and begins to take his place in the world of adult responsibilities. Early adulthood lasts from 17 to 45. It is during this era that major life goals are pursued and crucial choices are made in regard to occupation, family, and lifestyle.

Of all the transitions, the **midlife transition** has received the most notice and has also been the subject of the greatest controversy. At its core is the experience of one's own mortality. Neugarten (1968) has described a changing time perspective that comes at midlife. Rather than thinking of one's life in terms of time since birth, we begin to think in terms of time left until death. As Karp (1988, p. 735) points out, "Once time is recognized as a diminishing resource, people have got to decide what they are going to do with that resource." (You may recall that this experience has also been cited as a stimulant to the expression of generative impulses.) Separating and at the same time connecting the early and middle adult eras, this transition represents significant change, especially in the direction of greater individuation, so that the self becomes more whole and integrated as it overcomes the polarities that exist within it (Levinson, 1986). Jung (1933) and later Neugarten (1977) and David Gutmann (1990) have spoken of the contrasexual transition that occurs as the demands of active parenting are reduced, usually at midlife. It is important to note that this change is brought about not by age, but rather by a structural change in the family and the parenting role. Postparental men allow nurturant and tender qualities to emerge and become more relationship oriented, while women adopt some of the achievement-oriented, competitive qualities typical of men, becoming more career oriented: "They do not at the same time lose their gender identities as men and women: instead, they revise their self-conception to include the new powers that accompany the midlife transformation. The result, for most men and women, is an expanded sense of self" (Gutmann, 1990, p. 172).

The middle adult era lasts from about age 40 to 65 and represents a period of culmination as one moves to more senior status in work and community. The late adulthood era, as well as Levinson's speculations about a late, late adulthood era beginning around age 80 (though not the major focus of his work), is described as well.

Within each era, we move from a novice phase to a culmination phase. Thus, during a transitional period, we have achieved the tasks of the previous era and feel a sense of mastery and competence, while at the same time we feel uncertain as to the tasks of the new era. We can be "both excited and terrified by the prospects of living in that era" (Levinson, 1986, p. 8).

Each major era is composed of more specific **developmental periods,** as shown in Figure 2.3. Notice the alternating stable and transitional substages. Stable periods, usually lasting five to seven years, 10 at the most, involve making key choices about the kind of life we want to live during that period, setting priorities, and pursuing goals compatible with them. But nothing lasts forever. In time, these choices become inadequate and come into question. This leads to the transitional period, during which we reassess the choices we have made, reaffirm some, explore options, and pursue new possibilities. These transitional periods normally last about five years and are characterized both by a sense of separation and loss as an old period ends and by the excitement of possibilities and potential as a new one begins. Levinson gives equal weight to both the structure-building (stable) periods and the structure-changing (transitional) periods, finding each to have great significance for the life course.

FIGURE 2.3 *Developmental Periods and Transitions in the Early and Middle Adulthood Eras*

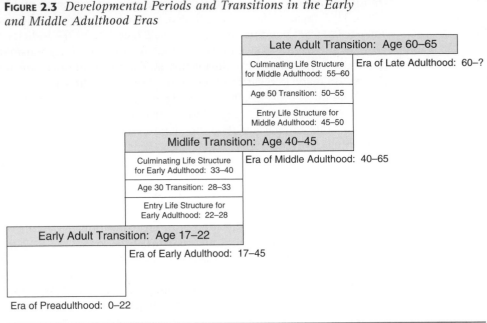

Source: Daniel J. Levinson et al. (1978). *The Season of a Man's Life.* New York: Ballantine Books. Copyright © 1978 by Daniel J. Levinson. Reprinted by permission of Alfred A. Knopf, Inc.

Life Structure. Levinson (1986) cites the **life structure** as the key concept to emerge from his research. It represents the underlying pattern or design of a person's life at a given time—the theme of the individual's life. The life structure is composed of major areas of choice and commitment (and the social roles and activities that go with them), which represent the way the individual has opted to relate to society. These central components have great significance for the self, receive the lion's share of the individual's time and energy, and influence other aspects of the person's life. Marriage/family and occupation are the most common central elements of the life structure, though the relative weight given to each varies from person to person. Other major choices might involve commitments to a religious ideology, ethnicity, a social movement, and so on. "These relationships are the stuff our lives are made of," Levinson (1986, p. 6) emphasizes, since "they are the vehicle by which we live out— or bury—various aspects of our selves and by which we participate, for better or worse, in the world around us."

The nature of the self and the context of the individual's life shape the evolution of the life structure (Levinson, 1996). Thus, Levinson emphasizes the reciprocal interaction of person and environment and the importance of the social context in development. Because adult life is characterized by periodic change, life structure is not permanent; rather, it evolves and is modified throughout the life cycle during the developmental periods described above. A growing sense of individuation of the self offers a clearer sense of who we are, what we want, and how to use our inner resources, leading to a better integration of the self with the external world and a more satisfying life structure (Levinson, 1986).

Major Points of Controversy

Though Levinson's model has been influential, at least three major aspects of it have been highly controversial. These are the method used by the team in conducting the research, the pattern of age-linked periods contained in the model, and the exclusive focus on male development. Let's consider each briefly.

Method. As indicated earlier, the biographical interview is vulnerable to criticism on a number of grounds, including its potential bias and the difficulty of replicating the findings. Levinson's rejoinder is that this is the only possible way of gaining a sense of the complexity of a life course. This remains an unresolved issue.

Age Linkages. This is probably the most troublesome aspect of Levinson's model. He himself professes surprise at his finding of such explicitly age-related periods, stating that he did not go into the research looking for these relationships. Rather, they found him. He further argues (1986, 1996) that the age linkages apply only to the basic framework of the life cycle, not to the timing of specific life events or the development of specific personality traits, which may occur at widely varying times. In fact, he readily acknowledges the great diversity seen in the concrete aspects of individual lives. As to the overall hypothesis of age-linked periods in the development of the life structure, Levinson (1986, p. 12) says, "I know of no systematic evidence disconfirming the hypothesis."

A lot of the energy in this debate has centered around the midlife transition, a concept that has caught the public's imagination and is one of the most often cited and controversial elements in Levinson's model. Though not the only one to postulate the existence of a major change point around age 40 (remember that Jung had described such an event, for example), Levinson's is the most visible of the recent descriptions. The real question to be addressed here is whether other researchers have been able to verify the existence of a major turning point around age 40. The evidence is mixed. While some researchers have found evidence of personality change at midlife (Helson & Wink, 1992; Stewart & Ostrove, 1998), others have not (McCrae & Costa, 1984). Perhaps the contradictory findings reflect variations in method (Levinson argues that brief interviews and questionnaires cannot uncover such things) as well as theoretical perspective. At the least, the notion of a universal *crisislike* transition has not found strong support in the research conducted to date.

Gender Parochialism. Levinson (1978, p. 9) himself describes his initial "strong desire to include women," deciding against it on methodological grounds. However, he promised a comparable study of women, a promise finally fulfilled by the publication of *The Seasons of a Woman's Life* in 1996. As Levinson (1978, p. 8) acknowledges, "It is essential to study the adult development of both genders if we are to understand either." A number of studies have used Levinson's approach to examine female development. Roberts and Newton (1987) reviewed the findings of four such doctoral dissertations. In general, these studies found that women passed through the same developmental periods at about the same ages. However, there were significant differences in the way developmental tasks were handled as well as in the outcomes of the periods. Specific differences will be discussed in later chapters, but basically, women's lives were found to be more complex and problematic. A study of 80 women by Mercer, Nichols, and

Doyle (1989) found that the subjects tended to experience developmental periods at later ages, to follow a more irregular pattern, and to focus on different aspects of the life structure than Levinson's men.

The Seasons of a Woman's Life summarizes Levinson's in-depth exploration of the lives of 45 women aged 35 to 45; three samples of 15 each represented homemakers and women with either corporate-financial or academic careers. Within each group the women chosen reflected a cross-section in regard to social class, education, religion, ethnicity, and marital and family history. He hoped to address two basic questions. First, is it possible to construct a gender-free model of adult development, an overall framework that describes what is common to both males and females? Second, within this overall model, is it possible to identify a gender-specific model? (Levinson, 1996, p. x). His findings indicate that women go through the same sequence of eras and periods at the same ages as men. "There is, in short, a single human life cycle through which all our lives evolve, with myriad variations related to gender, class, race, culture, historical epoch, specific circumstances, and genetics" (p. 5). Thus, though the framework is constant, specific life experiences within it vary. Women's development, as that of men's, is embedded in a particular sociohistorical context. As a result, women form different life structures within different opportunities and constraints. The important components of women's life structures, their specific nature, and the priority assigned to them may therefore differ from those of men. Two new concepts emerged from this study—"gender-splitting" and the "traditional marriage enterprise"—both of which will be addressed specifically in later chapters.

Many questions remain about the applicability of Levinson's model. In the meantime, we must be careful not to generalize findings beyond the samples studied.

Havighurst's Developmental Tasks

Robert Havighurst (1953) proposed an alternative stage model of life-span development based on the concept of developmental tasks. A **developmental task** is a major accomplishment required of an individual at a particular point in life; it is related to satisfaction and success in that and future periods (an example might be learning appropriate work-related habits and attitudes during adolescence). This concept has been incorporated by other theorists, such as Levinson. Havighurst's listing of developmental tasks of early, middle, and later adulthood is shown in Table 2.3. (He also listed developmental tasks for three earlier stages.)

CRITICAL THINKING QUESTION

Would you make any revisions, additions, or deletions to Havighurst's list, given the changing nature of adulthood that we have discussed so far in this book?

A Final Look at Stage Theory: Major Criticisms

As we have seen, Levinson's is one of the more recent in a long line of stage models of development that includes those offered by Erikson, Havighurst, and others. Personality psychologist Carol Ryff (1985, p. 99) believes that a major appeal of these approaches is the idea that individual development is characterized by "spiraling progressions of

TABLE 2.3 *Havighurst's (1953) Adult Developmental Tasks*

EARLY ADULTHOOD (18 TO 35 YEARS)
Selecting a mate
Learning to live with a marriage partner
Starting a family
Rearing children
Managing a home
Getting started in an occupation
Taking on civic responsibility
Finding a congenial social group

MIDDLE AGE (35 TO 60 YEARS)
Achieving adult, civic, and social responsibility
Establishing and maintaining an economic standard of living
Assisting teenage children in becoming responsible and happy adults
Developing adult leisure-time activities
Relating to one's spouse as a person
Learning to accept and adjust to the physiological changes of middle age
Adjusting to aging parents

LATER LIFE (60 ON)
Adjusting to decreasing physical strength
Adjusting to retirement and reduced income
Adjusting to the death of one's spouse
Establishing an explicit affiliation with one's age group
Meeting social and civic obligations
Establishing satisfactory living arrangements

improvement" throughout the life span. However, many developmental scholars continue to criticize this way of conceptualizing human development. The major criticisms of the stage theory approach are as follows.

First, an overemphasis on chronological age masks the variations that characterize individual lives. One appealing aspect of the stage model is, of course, that it imposes order and predictability on human life, but stage-structured models can appear rigid and deterministic (Weiland, 1992). The stage approach has a long tradition in child developmental theory. However, to reiterate, "there is far greater variability in the chronological age at which a given psychic crisis arises in later life, than is true of . . . youth . . . and the pattern of developmental tasks can vary more greatly, from one individual to another" (Peck, 1968, p. 92). Thus, critics maintain that stages described in adulthood must be less tied to chronological age.

A second problem is the lack of clear markers that define the beginning and ending of a stage. The usefulness of the stage model is undermined when demarcations between developmental periods are cloudy and ambiguous.

Others are concerned that the stage model offers a blueprint of idealized normality; consequently, deviations from the norm may be interpreted to signal maladjustment. In addition, the sequential nature of most stage models assumes that each stage is built on earlier ones: failure at one stage undermines success at the next. In these deterministic approaches, "history becomes destiny" (Falicov, 1984, p. 331). Divergent time schedules or sequencing of developmental tasks cannot be easily accommodated.

But perhaps the greatest criticism is that, to one degree or another, traditional stage models downplay the role of the sociohistorical context. Falicov (1984, pp. 332) cautions that "contextual modifiers are so powerful that it seems almost impossible to predict life cycle development without specifying development for whom, where, when, and under what circumstances."

To recapitulate, the stage theorists argue that personality change is normative, age-linked, and predictable, the result of the natural unfolding of a powerful inner plan across the various phases of life. People in their 20s tend to face different developmental tasks and be concerned with different psychosocial issues than people in their 30s, and so on. Others claim that life is not nearly so orderly and predictable, that change is based more on specific life events and role changes taking place within specific sociohistorical contexts. They stress diversity, not uniformity, in development across people. Chronological age is considered a poor predictor of psychological development. Let's examine Bernice Neugarten's concepts of the social age clock and the age-irrelevant society as examples of this latter point of view.

Multiple Meanings of Time and Age

Time and age are two concepts with multiple and complex meanings (Schroots & Birren, 1990). There is physical, objective time, measured by clock or calendar; biological time, described in circadian and metabolic terms; psychological time, as in the subjective experience of time duration; and social time, as in society's notion of when certain events or activities should occur in life. Similarly, there is chronological age, referring to the number of years that have passed since birth; biological age, meaning the amount of time remaining in an individual's life span; psychological age, in terms of the individual's adaptive capacities, such as memory, and also in terms of the individual's subjective feeling of age; and finally, social age, or one's roles or positions in social institutions, which are associated with chronological age, as indicated by such things as patterns of dress, language, and social deference (Schroots & Birren, 1990). As we discussed in Chapter 1, there is increasing desynchronization between the various types of time and age, so that chronological age is now an increasingly inadequate indicator, not only of biological or functional age, but also of psychological and social age. In other words, knowing an individual's age in years does not tell us much about what is going on in that individual's life. Changes in the rate and nature of biological and social aging have undermined the power of chronological age as an explanatory factor of psychological development (Schroots & Birren, 1990).

Rather than thinking of human life as governed by one clock—the passage of objective physical clock time—it is more accurate and useful to think of human experience in terms of a "clock shop" (Schroots & Birren, 1990, p. 47). These various clocks do not all tell the same time, though there are interrelationships among them. Biological and psychological clocks will be explored in more detail in later chapters. Our interest in this section is to examine the importance of the social clock and social age. What does time, or age, mean to the society, and therefore to the individual?

The Social Meaning(s) of Age

Our society places enormous emphasis on age as an organizing principle (Neugarten & Neugarten, 1987). Institutions such as schools are arranged around chronological age.

The sudden death of Olympic figure skating champion Sergei Grinkov at age 28 and the resulting widowhood of his wife and skating partner, Ekaterina Gordeeva, at age 24 illustrate off-time events.

Our behavior is greatly influenced by **age norms**—socially defined standards or expectations based on how old we are. Age is an important variable in how we relate to each other, not only in terms of forms of address, speech, and patterns of deference, but in whether we perceive others as having similar interests and friendship potential. We stereotype people on the basis of their perceived age. We also organize our personal lives around age, evaluating our behavior and progress toward life goals in reference to how we're doing "for our age."

Neugarten's Social Age Clock. Bernice Neugarten (1968) has suggested the term **social age clock** to refer to this internalized calendar, learned from society, which tells us about when in our lives we should be doing what. It is the same idea implicit in the phrase "act your age." For example, we have a sense of when we should finish our education, get our first full-time job, get married, have children, and so on. Socioeconomic status and the type of vocation one engages in affect this clock. Female Olympic gymnasts are considered old at 16, manual laborers reach middle age sooner than white-collar workers, professional athletes reach their peak in their 20s, whereas corporate executives, orchestra conductors, and Supreme Court justices may seem youthful in their 50s and 60s. **On-time events**—those that we expect to occur at about the time they do—seem to cause less stress than **off-time events**—those that occur either earlier or later than expected (Seltzer, 1976). Students often tell me, "I should be done with this by now," indicating that they feel behind in terms of their own social age clock. In the same way, early career success may pose problems as the individual wonders how to maintain this level of accomplishment throughout the remainder of the career cycle.

CRITICAL THINKING QUESTION

Would you expect the social age clock to be similar across cultures? Why or why not?

Resetting the Social Clock. By its very nature, the social age clock is influenced by the social environment. As the sociohistorical context changes, society's views of time and age change, and the social clock is reset. The demographic changes discussed in Chapter 1 have had profound effects on social age. For example, until this century, most parents died shortly after the last child left home. Today, most parents will experience a long post-parental period (Glick, 1977). The phenomenon of the so-called sandwich generation—middle-aged adults caught between the needs of children and parents—is also the result of changing demographics. In addition, more people marry later than they used to, have children later, retire earlier, live to become great-grandparents, and so on.

Fluid Life Cycle. All of this means that the life cycle is anything but neat and tidy. Neugarten and Neugarten (1987) cite the following outcomes. First, the boundaries between the major periods of life, which were once closely associated with chronological (and biological) age, have blurred. For instance, puberty, which used to be reached late in the teens, is now achieved at around age 12 to 14. But childhood does not end at puberty. Reproductive maturity is out of sync with psychological maturity. Second, new age groups have been identified, such as the young-old and the old-old, based more on functional ability than chronological age. By this definition, it is quite possible that people in their 70s would not be considered "old" in the traditional sense. Similarly, new life periods such as those mentioned above—the postparental period and the sandwich generation—have arisen. Moen (2003) describes an emerging stage called *midcourse* (see Box). Third, the timing of major life events has changed. Many people are in school for a much longer period of their lives than before, many women enter careers in midlife, and so on. Fourth, there is less consensus on how age-appropriate behavior is defined. Age norms have weakened. People now can have their first child in their 30s, start a new career at 50, retire at 55. Fifth, there is some evidence of a changed, more positive view of aging as health and vigor are maintained longer and longer. Overall, the life cycle has become more fluid, with traditional periods beginning to break down as age norms and age markers blur.

CRITICAL THINKING QUESTION

How do you define a "young woman"? A "young man"? When does middle adulthood end? What is the right time for people to marry?

Age-Irrelevant Society. Age norms have not disappeared altogether. Many people are well aware of how people their age are supposed to act (Karp, 1988). But the power of age norms over the way people conceptualize and live their lives is greatly reduced. Lives are more diverse than ever before, making chronological age less and less useful in helping us to understand what is going on in a person's life. When age norms more closely governed people's behaviors, when major life events occurred at more predictable times, it may have been more useful to think of the life cycle in terms of discrete stages. But different cohorts, with different expectations and experiences, exhibit different developmental patterns. They move through the life span differently. There are also cultural and ethnic differences in the way age is defined and the life schedule is described (Bane, 1991). There is no longer a single timetable. To echo a criticism we heard earlier, stage theories "decontextualize the meaning of behaviors" (Karp, 1988, p. 728). According to Neugarten and others, we are moving in the direction of an **age-irrelevant society** (Neugarten & Hagestad, 1976). Times surely have changed.

CRITICAL THINKING QUESTION

How might the loosening of age norms be beneficial to the individual and society? Are there ways these changes might pose difficulties?

Midcourse: Let's Retire the Term Retirement

What comes to mind when you imagine someone who is retired? My guess is that you are picturing the stereotype: a man in his 60s or 70s who is no longer working, has little to do, and contributes little to society. Is the stereotype accurate? What is the 21st-century reality? Phyllis Moen (2003) has offered the term **midcourse** to refer to the emergence of a new life stage "midway between the career building years of early adulthood and the frailties associated with later adulthood" (p. 87), spanning the years from about age 50 to 75. Forces such as the changing nature of work and workers (explored fully in Chapter 8) as well as demographic changes that have extended middle adulthood and delayed old age have produced a growing number of healthy, active, well-educated, skilled adults in their 50s, 60s, and 70s who are reformulating the 20th-century notion of retirement. Rather than a one-time one-way transition from full-time work to full-time leisure—a passage to old age and the loss of meaningful roles—retirement is increasingly likely to be a time of expanding options for productive activity—a beginning rather than an ending. It is also unscripted, as social norms, mores, stereotypes, expectations, as well as social institutions lag behind. Many of these "seasoned" adults may be transitioning out of their primary career jobs, but they are not moving to the sidelines of society. Midcourse adults remain socially integrated and engaged in productive activity in diverse ways: retiring from one job but working full time in another, starting second careers or businesses, working part-time or for part of the year, or being knee-deep in volunteer work. It is necessary to reassess notions of work, leisure, age, and retirement and invent new concepts, metaphors, roles, and opportunities to accommodate these new patterns. For example, perhaps the concept of retirement should not be so closely tied to age. After all, professional athletes retire in their 30s, military personnel retire after 20 years and start second careers, others retire two or more times during their working life, and some never retire. Society must provide midcourse adults with opportunities for meaningful and challenging activities, growth, and service. As a result, individuals will benefit from the boost to their health and well-being as society benefits from their talents and experience. I feel strongly that *retirement* isn't the right term for this life passage and sympathize with those who simply refuse to call themselves "retired." Now there is a term that fits.

CRITICAL THINKING QUESTION

How does Moen's (2003) notion of a new life stage called midcourse *relate to the concepts of cohort effect, structural lag, and the fluid life cycle?*

Concept
Review
2.2

- Stage theories of development, such as those of Freud and Erikson, take the position that all individuals progress through universal sequences of change at the direction of an innate, genetic blueprint.

- Erikson describes eight stages in the development of the ego, each characterized by a psychosocial crisis that can be resolved in either a positive or a negative direction.

(continued)

- Stage 7—Generativity versus Self-absorption—has received an increasing amount of research attention in recent years as investigators have attempted to refine the concept and describe its significance for adult development.

- Following in the stage theory tradition, Levinson offers a comparative description of the evolution of the life structure in adult men and women as they progress through a series of universal developmental eras and periods.

- Stage theory has been criticized on a number of grounds, the greatest criticism being that it downplays the role of the sociohistorical context.

- Neugarten has described the influence of the social age clock on individual development.

- Moen has proposed a new transitional stage called midcourse.

Trait Models: McCrae and Costa's Five-Factor Model of Personality

Robert McCrae and Paul Costa (1990) offer an alternative view of development in adulthood. Their five-factor model (FFM) of personality is based on five broad and enduring traits that they believe shape the process of aging as well as the individual's life course. These factors are neuroticism, extraversion, openness, agreeableness, and conscientiousness. It is on the basis of the "enduring core of the individual . . . [that] adaptation is made to an ever-changing life" (McCrae & Costa, 1990, p. 8). In other words, rather than focusing on the process of development (as in stage theory) or the impact of the environment (as in contextual theory), McCrae and Costa focus on the important qualities of the individual that direct the nature of interaction with the environment throughout adult life. They believe that somewhere between the ages of 20 and 30, "individuals attain a configuration of traits that will characterize them for years to come. From the perspective of the trait psychologist, adulthood begins at that point" (p. 10).

Defining a Trait

Trait psychology differs from other schools of personality theory in that it focuses on consistent differences, rather than similarities, between people. McCrae and Costa (1990, p. 23) define **psychological traits** as "dimensions of individual differences in tendencies to show consistent patterns of thoughts, feelings, and actions." Think of the five traits as summarizing individual differences in styles of thinking, feeling, and behaving. The use of the word *dimensions* indicates that people can be ranked based on the extent to which they possess one of the traits. Each trait is found in everyone to one degree or another, its distribution in the population being roughly equivalent to the normal curve. This means that most people possess the trait to a moderate degree, with few people showing extreme manifestations. The more of a trait a person has, the more likely the individual will be to show the behaviors associated with it, though behavior is of course modified by social-role expectations, the immediate context, mood, and acquired habits. Thus, the traits represent tendencies or predispositions to behave in a certain way, but they are not the sole determinants of behavior. Finally, they are assumed to be at least partially genetically based.

Defining the Five Factors

Neuroticism has to do with how likely an individual is to experience unpleasant, disturbing emotions (such as anxiety, hostility, insecurity, and guilt) and their corresponding thoughts and actions. **Extraversion** pertains to preferences for social interaction and activity, while **openness** refers to an individual's receptiveness to new ideas and experiences, as opposed to a preference for the familiar and practical. **Agreeableness** represents the degree to which a person is compassionate, good-natured, cooperative, and motivated to avoid conflict. Finally, **conscientiousness** has to do with self-discipline, organization, ambition, and achievement.

The five factors described by McCrae and Costa represent broad aspects of personality. Some of the specific qualities associated with each of them are shown in Table 2.4. The adjectives listed represent descriptions of low and high scorers on each factor. Culture may influence the manifestation of these common dimensions of personality (McCrae & Costa, 1997)—for example, the way fearfulness or responsibility is expressed, or the opportunities provided for social interaction or novel experience. The

TABLE 2.4 *McCrae and Costa's (1990) Five-Factor Model of Personality*

NEUROTICISM		AGREEABLENESS	
Calm	Worrying	Ruthless	Softhearted
Even-tempered	Temperamental	Suspicious	Trusting
Self-satisfied	Self-pitying	Stingy	Generous
Comfortable	Self-conscious	Antagonistic	Acquiescent
Unemotional	Emotional	Critical	Lenient
Hardy	Vulnerable	Irritable	Good-natured

EXTRAVERSION		CONSCIENTIOUSNESS	
Reserved	Affectionate	Negligent	Conscientious
Loner	Joiner	Lazy	Hardworking
Quiet	Talkative	Disorganized	Well-organized
Passive	Active	Late	Punctual
Sober	Fun-loving	Aimless	Ambitious
Unfeeling	Passionate	Quitting	Persevering

OPENNESS TO EXPERIENCE	
Down-to-earth	Imaginative
Uncreative	Creative
Conventional	Original
Prefer routine	Prefer variety
Uncurious	Curious
Conservative	Liberal

Note: The adjectives listed describe qualities associated with individuals who rank from relatively low (on the left) to relatively high in regard to each personality trait.

Source: R. McCrae and P. Costa (1990). *Personality in Adulthood,* p. 3. New York: Guilford Press. Reprinted by permission of Guilford Publications, Inc.

Revised NEO Personality Inventory (NEO-PI-R) has been developed to assess the five personality traits (Costa & McCrae, 1992).

McCrae and Costa's theory is relevant to what some consider the most important issue in personality theory—the question of personality stability versus change.

Do I Know You? Stability versus Change in the Adult Personality

The question to be addressed in this section has to do with whether the personality (or self) is stable over time and across situations or whether it changes. Described as "the central issue in the field" of personality theory (Kogan, 1990, p. 330), this controversy is reminiscent of the nature-nurture debate in that it is often viewed in terms of either-or—that is, people either change or they stay the same. The truth, of course, is not to be found in this sort of dichotomy.

A Historical View of the Issue: The Pendulum Swings

The stability of personality was an accepted tenet of psychological theory through most of the last century, clearly represented by William James (1892, p. 124) when he said, "For most of us, by the age of 30, the character has set like plaster, and will never soften again." This position was echoed in the Freudian view of personality as determined by experiences in the first five or six years of life, later behavior being viewed as an outgrowth of those early events.

By the 1970s, however, a number of books were published that espoused an alternate life-span view of personality as characterized by ongoing growth and change. These included the widely read *Passages* (Sheehy, 1976), as well as *The Seasons of a Man's Life* (Levinson, 1978), *Transformations* (Gould, 1978), and *Adaptation to Life* (Vaillant, 1977). Building on earlier work by Jung and Erikson, these portrayals of adult life described normal, universal stages of development and clearly turned the tide in favor of the view that personality is characterized more by change than constancy. Criticized for their reliance on self-report data and the subjective nature of conclusions drawn from lengthy interviews with research subjects, defenders claim that this is the only way of capturing the essence of human growth and change over time.

The plot thickened as longitudinal evidence of stability accumulated in the 1980s, most notably in the work of Robert McCrae and Paul Costa (1984, 1990) and the five-factor model of personality. Describing personality traits as enduring dispositions (aspects of the self that do not change), McCrae and Costa are strong advocates of the view that personality is stable over time. Support for this five-factor model has come from studies using different samples, methods, measuring instruments, and times of measurement, adding weight to the conclusions about personality stability (see, for example, Haan et al., 1986). Critics argue that trait theorists are by definition looking for characteristics that remain constant and can be used to define the individual over time. Their theory and method lead them to find that which they seek. As Helson and Moane (1987, p. 176) point out, personality inventories are designed to measure traits that endure, and the more reliable these instruments become, "the more insensitive [they] are to normative changes that occur with age."

What Changes and What Stays the Same?

Many observers have noted that the ongoing controversy in the personality and aging field has been healthy in that it has generated valuable research and stimulated a reformulation and refinement of the issues. At this point, the central question is perhaps better phrased not as whether the self (or personality) is stable or changes, but rather which aspects of the self change, how much, and under what conditions? Are there some aspects of the self that seem to be more stable than others? And what variables contribute to stability and change?

Personality Traits

McCrae and Costa offer compelling evidence that personality traits, as described in their five-factor model, remain stable from situation to situation and over the life span. That is, a person who is extraverted as a teenager is likely to be extraverted in middle age. This stability applies to everyone—male, female, Black, White, and so on—with few exceptions (such as those suffering from Alzheimer's disease). They note that "the same personality traits can be expressed in an infinite variety of ways, each suited to the situation" (1994, p. 175). Other researchers (Funder & Colvin, 1991; Roberts & Donahue, 1994) agree, concluding that although the specific situation may have a profound effect on what people do, individuals are still able to preserve their own distinctive styles *across* situations. Regardless of the specific context, extraverts are likely to be more sociable and talkative, neurotics more anxious and insecure. For McCrae and Costa, this stability originates in inherited biological predispositions. Thus, "personality forms one unchanging aspect of the self" (1990, p. 174). The proper perspective, according to their view, is this: "Ask not how life's experiences change personality; ask instead how personality shapes lives and gives order, continuity, and predictability to the life course, as well as creating or accommodating change" (McCrae & Costa, 1990, p. 177). For example, highly agreeable children (characterized by cooperation, compassion, and empathy) may develop behavior patterns that allow them to succeed academically and socially. Their early achievements and consistent agreeableness continue to benefit them into adulthood, leading to career and social success and greater psychological adjustment (Laursen, Pulkkinen, & Adams, 2002).

Recent research has examined age trends among the five factors to determine if they exhibit predictable developmental changes. Cross-sectional comparisons of adolescents and older adults in a dozen cultures have found consistent patterns of change with age across the five factors (Costa & McCrae, 1999; McCrae et al., 1999). College-age men and women score lower than older adults in agreeableness and conscientiousness, while scoring higher on neuroticism, extroversion, and openness. These findings suggest that neuroticism, extroversion, and openness decline, while agreeableness and conscientiousness increase as people mature. Costa and McCrae attribute these universal age trends to biologically based maturational changes. How do we reconcile these age trends with their assertion that personality factors remain stable over time? It may be that while one's relative position in regard to a trait does not change, the group as a whole is changing. So, the most conscientious person remains more conscientious than others the same age, but everyone in the group is more conscientious than they were when they were younger.

Accepting that traits remain stable does not necessitate a view that the self as a whole is constant, however: "Our finding of stability in this part of the self does not

What stays the same and what changes? These photos of the same individual at ages 5, 12, and 23 illustrate both similarity and difference over time. Evidence suggests that the self is also characterized by stability and change.

imply that other parts of the self do not change" (McCrae & Costa, 1990, p. 162). Less central aspects of the self, such as social behaviors, attitudes, and opinions, are more likely to be characterized by change. Similarly, identity, rooted as it is in social roles and relationships, may also change, though, as we will see in Chapter 3, the uncommitted identity statuses (diffusion and moratorium) might be thought of as fluctuating to a greater degree than the committed identity statuses (achievement and foreclosure) (Berzonsky, 1988).

Self-Concept and Self-Esteem

Are aspects of the self such as the self-concept and self-esteem characterized more by stability or change? In Chapter 3, the self-concept is described as a theory of the self constructed by the individual. Successful adaptation to the environment requires constant monitoring of information about the self and the effectiveness of various behaviors. Viewed in this way, the self-concept, like any theory, is continually tested, sometimes disconfirmed, and revised. In fact, if it is to serve the individual well, it would be "expected to undergo reformulation throughout the rest of the life cycle" (Marcia, 1988, p. 223).

We can think of the individual as continually attending to and processing information coming from direct experience as well as feedback from others to determine if it has relevance for the self. Gorrell (1990, p. 74) notes that "since individuals construct their own beliefs about themselves, they are the ultimate sources of self-concept change." Changes in the self-concept, then, are seen as originating within the individual, based on an assessment of self-relevant information.

Keep in mind, however, that research suggests that in general, we attend more closely to information consistent with existing beliefs, while we find ways to ignore or discount inconsistent information. In the same vein, Berzonsky (1988, p. 247) cites research in social cognition that portrays the normal individual as a "'cognitive miser' exerting minimal mental effort and utilizing a variety of self-serving confirmation biases to maintain existing beliefs."

Can these tendencies toward maintenance of the self-concept be overcome? And if so, how? Are some self-conceptions less resistant to change than others? As we will see in Chapter 3, the self-concept is hierarchically structured, with some self-conceptions more central and pervasive than others. More well-developed self-conceptions, the product of many experiences over a long period of time, are more resistant to change. Evidence also exists that more central, core self-conceptions are more stable as well (Gorrell, 1990; Snygg & Combs, 1949). Change in these deeper aspects of the self would be less likely. As Harter (1988, p. 55) points out, "One of the most basic needs of the individual is to maintain the unity and coherence of the conceptual system that defines the self." After all, if our self-concept were constantly buffeted by the various ups and downs of everyday life, any meaningful sense of self would be shattered. Our ability to plan for our future and predict our own behavior would be lost. This, then, is the press toward stability in the self theory. What are the presses toward change?

Historical and Social Context

Some models of the self account for change by looking at the social, cultural, and historical context. These approaches might consider the influence of historical events such as World War II, periods of relative social unrest such as the 1960s, the technological revolution of the 1990s and its effect on the world of work, the widespread effects of globalization and international terrorism in the early 21st century, and so on. The idea is that stability or change in the self may be influenced by stability or change in the sociocultural environment. Stable life circumstances and roles predict constancy in the self; changing life circumstances and roles predict change in the self. According to Helson and Moane (1987, p. 185), "If personality interacts with situations in any meaningful manner, it hardly makes sense to claim that personality does not change."

Role of Life Transitions

The self seems to be more volatile or fluid in certain periods in life. These are often transitional periods that offer the opportunity for "an organizational change, or a developmental spurt" (Noam, 1988, p. 11). New roles emerge, bringing with them new experiences and new relationships, all grist for the mill of change. One of the most significant transitions is from adolescence to adulthood—a transition viewed as a sort of natural disequilibrating event, or "crisis" in Erikson's terms, which the individual can use as a catalyst for exploration, new choices and commitments, and a reorganization of the self (Marcia, 1988). Other significant life transitions (such as marriage, parenthood, or retirement) might be expected to affect the self in comparable, though perhaps less dramatic, ways. The responsibilities associated with parenthood, for example, impel the self to adopt behaviors and attitudes consistent with the role, so that relevant developmental tasks can be accomplished.

Bloom (1964) theorizes that stability of the personality increases with age, a hypothesis supported by evidence from numerous studies (see, for example, Finn, 1986). Perhaps the greater stability seen with age is related to greater stability in the social context, as people settle into careers and relationships.

Is There a Change at Midlife?

Since the publication of books by Sheehy, Levinson, and others in the 1970s, there has been a lot of interest in the transition from young to middle adulthood—the so-called midlife crisis. While capturing the attention of the popular press and the public alike, as we have seen, research on the subject has been inconsistent. The stereotypical view of the 40-year-old man who walks out on his wife and children, gets an apartment in the city, buys a gold chain and a red sports car, while colorful, is inaccurate. Changes do occur in one's time perspective (from time since birth to time left until death and the accompanying feeling that time is running out) and the sense of one's position in the sequence of generations (particularly after the death of those in the older generation); these changed viewpoints often lead to a period of increased reflection and introspection as one contemplates the second half of life and one's goals and ambitions. These shifts may not, at least in the beginning, be particularly pleasant.

At a recent faculty meeting, a rather soft-spoken colleague, whom I did not know well, sat down next to me. I had a stack of books sitting in front of me having to do with adult development. He said, "So tell me about age 40." I said something about it being a great time in life because of the increasing freedom as children become more independent, along with the opportunity to get going on things one has always wanted to do, and so on, thinking I was being reassuring. He countered, "So how come I'm so depressed?" Coming from a man who is typically reticent, I thought his comment was striking and certainly illustrated the internal changes at work in many of us at about this time. As we talked more about this that day and subsequently, it was apparent that his "depression" was not of the clinical sort, but rather reflected the unease associated with important life changes.

At any rate, it is probably more accurate to think of these changes as manifestations of a *midlife transition* or a "midcourse correction" (Stewart & Ostrove, 1998) rather than a midlife crisis. After all, age 40 is the "noon of life," a time rightly devoted to "the illumination of the self" (Jung, 1933, p. 109). And as in all transitions, new role opportunities may present themselves and new experiences may lead to revision of some aspects of the sense of self. The second half of life may provide chances to explore aspects of the self ignored while trying to respond to the demands of young adulthood. As my friend Sally said at about this time in her life, "My house is like my life. I've done all of the basic construction—I just don't know how to accessorize."

Concluding Thoughts on Constancy and Change

In the final analysis, what can we say about the issue of change versus stability in the adult self? Surely the self must retain constancy so that we can predict our own behaviors and plan for the future with some degree of assurance that choices made today will be appropriate tomorrow. On the other hand, the human capacity for growth and change is one of the hallmarks of our existence. To assume that the future self could not rise above its present limitations contradicts what we know intuitively and empirically about ourselves. In truth, the self is characterized by both. "I'm different now, . . . but it's still me" (Rubin, 1981, p. 27). As Hamachek (1990, p. 679) points out, "It is precisely the feeling most people have now and then of *not* feeling so sure about their identity that enables them to sharpen, refine, and if necessary, redefine their self-concepts in light of changing life circumstances." Similarly, Bengtson et al. (1985) discuss the fact that perceived differences between the self-concept and the ideal self serve as motivation for change.

McCrae and Costa reconcile the apparent contradiction between stability and change as follows. While "adults' personality profile as a whole will change little over time . . . people undoubtedly do change across the life span. . . . The same traits can be seen in new guises: intellectual curiosity merely shifts from one field to another. . . . Many of these changes are best regarded as variations on the 'uniform tune' played by individuals' enduring dispositions" (1994, pp. 173–174).

In sum, the research suggests that some aspects of the self (notably, certain personality traits as well as core aspects of the self-concept) are relatively stable, while less central aspects of the self may change. Change is more likely during transitional periods and in response to changes in the sociocultural and historical context. In general, the self becomes more stable over time, perhaps as a result of cognitive processes and also as a function of a stabilizing of life circumstances. Evidence also exists that different patterns of stability and change are found among women than among men. Some discussion of this subject will be presented in the next chapter.

One can look for either stability or change and find it. Some metaphors may be helpful in crystallizing this issue. One can think of the life journey as a movement up a spiral staircase "in which we traverse, often again and again, albeit at different 'elevations,' many psychological territories we have traveled before" (Shneidman, 1989, p. 685). The new height allows the self to reorganize and, in Erikson's terms, "weave in" new information about the self in a new constellation. Like a symphony with its various movements, each stage of life has its own tempo, rhythm, and mood, tied to all the others by repeated themes, each theme reworked and modified at each step (Noam, 1988). One can focus on the new tunes or on the familiar melodies. This is the complexity of the human self.

Concept Review 2.3

- McCrae and Costa have described five influential personality traits: neuroticism, extraversion, openness, agreeableness, and conscientiousness.
- One of the major issues in the field of adult development is the extent to which individual personality changes or stays the same.
- Research suggests that some aspects of the self are relatively stable while others are more susceptible to change, and that change is more likely at some times in development than others.

REVIEW QUESTIONS

Organismic, Mechanistic, and Contextual Models

1. What is a contextual model of development? Contrast this with the organismic and mechanistic models.

Bronfenbrenner's Ecological Systems Theory

1. What are the major contributions of Bronfenbrenner's Ecological Systems Theory to our study of adult development?
2. Describe the components of the environment as conceptualized by Bronfenbrenner.

Ages and Stages: The Psychoanalytic Tradition

1. Identify the assumptions that stage theorists make about development.
2. What is meant by the term *individuation*? Who first introduced this concept?
3. Explain and illustrate Erikson's concept of a psychosocial crisis.
4. Discuss the eight stages of psychosocial development, according to Erikson.

5. Assess the nature of Erickson's influence on the study of adult development and the major criticisms of his theory.

6. Describe the nature and purpose of life review.

7. How is the concept of generativity being revised and reformulated by Kotre and others?

8. What characteristics seem to typify highly generative adults?

9. Identify factors that may contribute to the development of generativity.

10. Discuss the major findings of Levinson's study of adult men.

11. What is the nature of the midlife transition, according to Levinson? When and why does it occur? What are its purposes and outcomes?

12. What does Levinson mean by the life structure?

13. How do the results of Levinson's study of the life cycle in women compare with the findings from his study of men?

14. What are the major criticisms of Levinson's model?

15. Discuss the major criticisms of the stage model of development.

16. Define the social age clock and discuss its influence on the individual.

17. Give an example of an off-time event.

18. Illustrate how the social age clock has been reset.

19. What is the impact of the fluid life cycle and the age-irrelevant society?

20. How does the concept of midcourse alter traditional views on retirement as a life stage?

Trait Models: McCrae and Costa's Five-Factor Model of Personality

1. What is a trait theory of personality?

2. Compare and contrast contextual, stage, and trait models of development.

3. Explain and define McCrae and Costa's five factors. How do they influence adult life?

Do I Know You? Stability versus Change in the Adult Personality

1. There has been a lot of discussion about the issue of stability versus change in the adult personality. What are some of the factors that make it difficult to resolve this issue?

2. What is the position of stage theorists such as Levinson in regard to stability versus change? What is the position of personality theorists Costa and McCrae?

3. What aspects of the self are most likely to stay the same over time, and which are most likely to change?

4. What factors contribute to either stability or change in the self?

5. Do most people experience a "midlife crisis"? Discuss this concept and research findings related to it.

Key Terms

age-irrelevant society, 64
age norms, 63
agreeableness, 67
biological generativity, 52
conscientiousness, 67
contextual model, 39
cross-era transition, 56
cultural generativity, 52
developmental era, 56
developmental periods, 57
developmental task, 60
dyads, 41
ecology, 39
ecology of human development, 40
epigenetic principle, 47

exosystem, 42
extraversion, 67
felt capacity for generativity, 54
fluid life cycle, 64
generative accomplishment, 54
generative desires, 54
generativity, 50
individuation, 46
life review, 49
life structure, 58
macrosystem, 43
mechanistic model, 38
mesosystem, 41
microsystem, 41
midcourse, 65

midlife transition, 57
neuroticism, 67
off-time events, 63
on-time events, 63
openness, 67
organismic model, 38
parental generativity, 52
phenomenology, 40
psychological traits, 66
psychosocial crisis, 47
social age clock, 63
social role, 44
stage theory, 46
structural lag, 44
technical generativity, 52

3 The Self
Development and Issues of Culture, Gender, Ethnicity, and Age

LIKE MOST STUDENTS, I feel as if I have written hundreds of papers during my formal education, most of them long forgotten. But one from high school has remained in my memory. Not that I remember the content of what I wrote; it is the topic that has stayed with me. In fact, the topic was sort of famous around the school—it must have been *the* paper for our whole class, just as reading *Silas Marner* was *the* book for our sophomore year. It was the "Who Am I?" paper. As I think of it now, the assignment seems to have been an attempt to address the issue of identity formation among adolescents. I suspect my teacher was influenced by the then-emerging work of Erik Erikson (discussed in Chapter 2). Though I still have my cheerleading letter from junior high and a few crushed, dried corsages, among other mementos, I have not found this paper. I would like to see, from this vantage point, the person I was at that time, or at least the person I thought I was becoming. Would I recognize her? Would she be familiar to me? Wise? Naive? Interesting? Are you similar to the person you were years ago? Will you recognize yourself 20 years from now?

This chapter is devoted to an examination of the **self,** which consists of all the knowledge, feelings, and attitudes we have about our own being as unique, functioning individuals (Baron & Byrne, 1991). We will review the history of research on the self, its development and related components, such as self-concept, self-esteem, self-efficacy, and identity, and also examine the phenomenal self, our subjective experience of our own existence. We will then explore the effect of four variables on the self: culture, gender, race/ethnicity, and age. Throughout the pages that follow, we will attempt to integrate theory and research on what is the essence of human existence—an awareness of our own being in all its complexity and with all its ramifications. This is what we call a sense of self.

Defining the Self

Contributions of William James

Any review of the history of contemporary research on the self and related concepts must begin with William James, the great 19th-century American psychologist and author of the two-volume *Principles of Psychology* (1890). (By the way, if you are not familiar with James and his tremendous impact on psychology and philosophy, this might be a good time to find out more about him. He was born in 1842, died in 1910, and was the brother of novelist Henry James. His writing is described as lucid and readable.) The

longest chapter in James's book, totaling more than 100 pages, is titled "The Consciousness of Self." Here James (1890/1952, pp. 279–280) clearly identifies the self as central to understanding human behavior: "In its widest possible sense . . . a man's Self is the sum total of all he can call his. . . . If they wax and prosper, he feels triumphant; if they dwindle and die away, he feels cast down."

James (1892) distinguished between the **I-self**—the active observer of experience, the knower, and the **Me-self**—the observed, or what is known about the self. The assumption is that the I-self builds or constructs the Me-self through its processes of perceiving, interpreting, and evaluating information. The I-self, then, is the knower; the Me-self is the known. We will refer to these concepts later as the **phenomenal self** and the **self-concept,** respectively. Most research and theory on the self is actually directed toward the Me-self or self-concept. The I-self or phenomenal self, the subjective aspect of the self, has been largely ignored (Harter, 1988). This is due to difficulties in studying it scientifically.

William James (1842–1910) remains an influential figure in American psychology, though his most famous work, *Principles of Psychology,* was published in 1890.

CRITICAL THINKING QUESTION

Think about this sentence: "I see myself as an honest person." Can you distinguish between the I-self and the Me-self?

While James's influence on the developing field of psychology was noteworthy in many other respects, in the half century that followed the publication of his most famous work "virtually no research on the [self] was conducted. Indeed, the first systematic study . . . did not appear before a lapse of 60 years" (Rosenberg, 1989, p. 36). In reviewing this history, Morris Rosenberg argues that despite the relevance of the self for psychology as well as sociology and psychoanalysis, the dominant scientific models of the day in each of these fields stood as obstacles to research on the self and related subjects.* Let's look now at the evolution of thinking about the self, first in

*The synopsis of Rosenberg's views in this chapter is based on *Social Forces* (68 [1], 1989), "Self-Concept Research: A Historical Overview," by Morris Rosenberg. Copyright © The University of North Carolina Press. Used with permission.

psychology, and then in sociology and psychoanalysis, using Rosenberg's analysis as our framework.

Psychology

In psychology, a school of thought known as *behaviorism* became influential in the early 20th century and diverted interest from the self. Founded by John Watson in 1913, behaviorism emphasized controlled laboratory experimentation as the appropriate method and overt, observable behavior as the subject by which to establish psychology as a legitimate science. Thoughts and feelings, by definition subjective in nature, were regarded as unsuitable subjects of scientific inquiry. Thus, the study of the self conflicted with the goal of advancing scientific psychology. It was not until the 1940s that an alternative was proposed by Donald Snygg (1941; also see Snygg & Combs, 1949)—that of phenomenology.

Phenomenologists argue that it is not objective reality, but rather the individual's subjective perception of reality that is important. In other words, if you want to understand someone, you must try to see things through that individual's eyes. According to this model, the proper frame of reference from which to understand behavior is the internal mental and emotional experience of the person. The phenomenological perspective became integrated into humanistic theory, most obviously in the work of Carl Rogers (1951) and his Self Theory. It is also evident in Bronfenbrenner's Ecological Systems Theory, which emphasizes the individual's subjective perception of the environment, as we saw in Chapter 2.

Rosenberg (1989) claims that this alternative view gave legitimacy to a renewed scientific interest in the self among psychologists and led to a surge of research, which continues to this day. Lapsley and Power (1988), on the other hand, cite the "cognitive revolution" (the influence of Piaget and, later, information-processing theory) as bringing about an explosion of interest in such topics as self, ego, and identity. Whatever the cause, the concept of self is stimulating a great deal of research activity—testimony to its perceived relevance in understanding human development.

The work of contemporary psychologist Albert Bandura reflects a blend of each of the theoretical views just described. Bandura is a social learning theorist who has combined the best elements of Watson's behaviorism and the contributions of learning theorists such as B. F. Skinner with the more recent findings of cognitive psychology to study and describe attitudes toward the self and their impact on behavior. (See the discussion of self-efficacy later in this chapter.) Thus we see how the strands of many different theoretical traditions can be integrated into a more encompassing view of human functioning.

Sociology

Two major contributions to the study of the self emerged from the work of sociologists Charles Cooley and George Herbert Mead. In 1902, Cooley described the concept of the **looking glass self,** the idea that our sense of self is largely derived from our evaluation of social feedback from others. The people around us serve as social mirrors in which we see ourselves reflected. To Cooley, we are what we think other people think we are. (Here again, it is not the reality of others' evaluations that is important, but our phenomenal view of it.) Despite all the research and conflicting views of the self put forth

Our sense of self is to a great extent determined by how we evaluate feedback from others, a concept Cooley called the looking glass self.

in the intervening years, there seems to be general agreement on this point: our sense of self is primarily constructed from information received from others. It is, in other words, a social product. Our social relationships are influential not only in the formation of the self, but in its maintenance and change.

A second major contribution from sociology was the notion of the **generalized other.** Described by Mead (1934), this basically represented an extension of the role of social input in the formation of the self. Mead stressed that we actually begin to take the perspective of society (the generalized other) and its values and expectations in judging ourselves, thus incorporating societal standards into our sense of self. The influence of others and society in general on an individual's emerging sense of self becomes increasingly pronounced as cognitive maturity increases and perspective-taking skills develop (Selman & Byrne, 1974; Selman, 1980; Gurucharri & Selman, 1982). This is generally thought to occur during the stage of concrete operations, beginning about age 6. (Concrete operations represents the third of four stages of cognitive development in Jean Piaget's theory. At this level of thinking, individuals are capable of logic and also have the ability to consider more than one concept at a time, including the perspective of another person. They are no longer rooted in their own view of the world—or themselves.)

Psychoanalysis

The Freudians were indifferent to the concept of self, even though it would appear to lie at the heart of Freudian theory—as represented by the "ego," the conscious component of the personality that interacts with the real world. Rosenberg (1989) argues that the following factors contributed to the position of the self as a peripheral concept in the thinking of Freud and his followers. First, Freud used the term *ego* to refer to a set of cognitive processes such as attention, reasoning, and memory (his "secondary process thought"). Second, he focused on early childhood (a time when the concept of self is evolving but not yet formed). Third, he was more interested in the unconscious than the conscious, phenomenal world. The status of the self did not change significantly until the emergence of the neo-Freudians, including Karen Horney and especially Erik Erikson, in the 1940s and 1950s. Erikson (1968) proposed a theory of ego development and contributed a concept—*identity*—that brought the investigation of the self to center stage and continues to generate theory and research.

To sum up, despite a detour lasting about half a century, scientific interest in the concept of self and related components is currently abundant. The self is now viewed as central to our understanding of the individual's thoughts, feelings, and behaviors. While seen as an inherently social product, the self is also known to function as a social force, influencing behavior. Resting on the theoretical heritage of James, Cooley, Erikson, and others, the contributions of contemporary psychologists, sociologists, and psychoanalysts are enriching our grasp of this most essential aspect of human existence and experience.

Setting Things Straight: A Confusion of Monikers

Concepts related to the self "invoke some of the oldest, most enduring, and yet perplexing themes in social psychology" (Bengston, Reedy, & Gordon, 1985, p. 546). Originating in philosophy, especially phenomenology, the nature of the self and its components has been of interest, as we have seen, since the time of William James. However, during the intervening years, so many definitions of these components have been proposed and so many approaches to measurement and study have been used that some psychologists have suggested the terms be abandoned altogether (Allport, 1955). As a result, some clarification of terminology is necessary before we can proceed.

We have defined the "self" as consisting of all the knowledge, feelings, and attitudes we have about ourselves as unique, functioning individuals. Phenomenologically, the self reflects "one's sense of personal existence" (Hamachek, 1990, p. 677). This is what James referred to as the I-self. Though *self* is sometimes used synonymously with *personality,* an important distinction exists. *Self* refers to thoughts and feelings that the individual experiences, whereas *personality* and *personality traits* are judgments or inferences made by someone else about the individual. Put simply, the self is inside; personality is outside.

One of the first problems one notices in the literature related to the self is the inconsistent use of the following key terms: *self-concept, self-esteem,* and *identity.* To clarify and distinguish among them, they are defined here as they will be used in this chapter. Briefly, we will use the term *self-concept* to refer to our knowledge of ourselves, *self-esteem* to refer to our feelings about ourselves, and *identity* to refer to a sense of what we believe in and where we are headed in life. Let's delve into these three concepts.

Concept Review 3.1

- The "self" refers to all the knowledge, feelings, and attitudes we have about ourselves as unique, functioning individuals.

- William James makes a distinction between the I-Self and the Me-Self, also referred to as the phenomenal self and the self-concept.

- Sociologists such as Cooley and Mead have stressed the role of others (and society in general) in the formation of the individual self through their concepts of the looking glass self and the generalized other.

- There is currently a surge of interest in the study of the self and its development.

The Self-Concept: The Cognitive Theory of Self

Viewing the Self-Concept as a Self-Schema

The term *self-concept* refers to the information we have about ourselves, the way we perceive and describe ourselves, "a collection of beliefs about the kind of person we are" (Hamachek, 1990, p. 677). It is the equivalent of James's Me-self. Investigators commonly elicit this kind of information by asking subjects to respond to the question "Who am I?" For example, the "twenty statements test" (Kuhn & McPartland, 1954) involves giving subjects a single sheet of paper with 20 numbered blanks and asking them to write 20 answers to the question "Who am I?" Berk (1991, p. 434) describes the self-concept as a " 'personal theory' of what the self is like." The self-concept is, then, the result of a cognitive process, of "knowing"; it is a cognition, or mental concept—a self-cognition or self-theory.

Because this cognitive view of the self-concept relies heavily on the work of Jean Piaget, a brief review of his cognitive developmental theory may be helpful at this point. Piaget (1896–1980) identified three factors that contribute to mental development: (1) maturation (the genetically controlled growth of the brain and nervous system—the hardware necessary for cognitive processing), (2) experience in the world of nature and objects, and (3) interaction with others—particularly interactions that challenge the individual's existing understanding of things. But the mind does not just passively accept information. Piaget also described three intellectual tendencies that direct the way the human mind handles information. The first is the tendency to organize information into meaningful units called **schemas.** The second is to adapt to new information by either **assimilating** it (adding it) to existing schemas or **accommodating** it (changing existing schemas or creating new ones). The third tendency is to maintain a sense of cognitive harmony or balance, similar to the biological concept of homeostasis, which Piaget referred to as **equilibration.**

Information inconsistent with our existing worldview disrupts this equilibrium, placing us in an unpleasant cognitive state (conflict, dissonance, inconsistency) and requiring us to adapt in some way. Disequilibration is, in fact, the major impetus for cognitive development: as our current level of thinking becomes increasingly inadequate to deal with the information and experiences we are confronting, we become motivated to develop a more effective (and advanced) level of cognitive ability. Human beings are viewed, then, as active constructors of knowledge and understanding—of their reality.

Piaget's model includes four stages of cognitive development, culminating with formal thought in adolescence. As we will see in Chapter 4, a number of scholars have speculated about the existence of various types of postformal thought—additional modes of thinking that may evolve in adulthood, extending cognitive development beyond adolescence. Gisela Labouvie-Vief (1984, 1985) believes that there are three additional stages of thought, brought about by the clash between the logic of formal thought, which suggests that every question has one right answer, and an increasing awareness of the reality of life, with its complexities, ambiguities, and paradoxes. In the last of these adult stages, called *autonomous thought,* the individual is able to see how the self has influenced the construction of reality.

As applied to the development of the self, then, the ability to know the self is partly due to the biogenetic mental potential that emerges as the brain and nervous system mature, while the specific nature of self-knowledge comes from interaction with the world of nature and objects (learning from experience that you enjoy physical activity and sports, for example) and interaction with others. We tend to organize this accumulating information into a **self-schema** or self-concept (Markus, 1977; Markus & Nurius, 1986). More advanced levels of cognitive development allow a more complex understanding of the self to emerge (Labouvie-Vief, Chiodo, Goguen, Diehl, & Orwoll, 1995). Because information about the self is continually coming into the system as a result of experience and social interaction, the self-schema will be constantly evolving over the life span through the mechanisms of adaptation just described. However, research suggests that once formed, schemas strongly influence the future processing of information related to them. Let's look at the conclusions of this research more closely.

Cognitive Impact of the Self-Concept

While acknowledging that people develop in a social and historical context, "constructivists" point out that the self actively constructs and reconstructs that context (Ellis, 1991). In a real sense, "Individuals play a role in creating the reality to which they respond" (Berzonsky, 1989b, pp. 363–364). In this way, the self influences behavior, intentions, and aspirations in all the important aspects of a person's life (Gorrell, 1990). How can the schema of the self—the self-concept—exert this influence?

First, schemas seem to determine which items reaching the nervous system are selected for attention. After all, if we attempted to deal with every one of the stimuli coming in through the senses, we would be overwhelmed. This is extremely important, because stimuli not attended to are permanently lost to the information-processing system. You may be sitting in class when a particular concept is discussed, for example, but if you are not attending to the information, you will not have a clue what it means. For the same reason, you cannot learn anything by playing informational tapes while you are sound asleep. On the other hand, have you ever been at a party where there is sort of a buzz of noise from lots of simultaneous conversations, all blurred together, and then suddenly you distinctly hear *your* name above this buzz? The first step in processing information is paying attention to it. Schemas guide this attention.

Research confirms that information viewed as relevant to the self is processed more efficiently and retained more effectively than information thought to be irrelevant (for example, Higgins & Bargh, 1987). This is called the **self-reference effect** and explains why personal experiences are easier to remember than abstract examples (and why you heard your name in that crowded room). Good teachers make effective use of this phenomenon by using ample personal anecdotes to illustrate concepts, or by asking students to relate their own experiences to ideas being discussed in class. The self-reference effect may be the result of deeper processing at the semantic level (the level of meaning, as opposed to the more superficial processing of information based only on how it looks or sounds) and of greater elaboration or exploration of the information, both of which are known to enhance memory and retrieval. In other words, when we perceive information to be somehow related to ourselves, we take more interest in it, pay greater attention to it, explore it more thoroughly, and attempt to understand its meaning.

Further, there is evidence that once formed, the self-concept may be resistant to change. Stangor and Ruble (1989) suggest that early in the formation of a schema, we are more likely to attend to information *inconsistent* with it. This conflicting information may be easier to notice and remember. Once the schema is more fully developed, we are more likely to notice and remember information *consistent* with it, while ignoring conflicting data (and thereby maintaining equilibration). For example, we may discount criticism of ourselves because it conflicts with the way we see ourselves. In this way, the schema becomes stronger and challenges to it are more and more likely to fail. Thus, in the building stage of a schema the system is actively searching for varied information about the subject. Once the concept has formed, however, it may be self-perpetuating.

Kruglanski and Webster (1996) offer an alternative theory that may help explain the stability of the self-concept. They propose that individuals are motivated by a need for **cognitive closure,** defined as a desire for definite knowledge on an issue and an aversion to confusion and ambiguity. This need is assumed to represent a relatively stable dimension of individual differences—that is, among individuals the motivation toward closure varies along a continuum, with high need for closure at one end, and strong need to avoid closure at the other. The need for closure is also influenced by characteristics of the situation. Conditions such as time pressure, information that is difficult to process, an unpleasant or dull task, fatigue, pressure from valued others to reach a judgment, and so on could heighten the need for closure. The need for closure, in turn, produces two general tendencies: **cognitive urgency,** the inclination to reach closure as quickly as possible (to "seize" on a conclusion or an answer, to make a judgment), and **cognitive permanence,** the desire to maintain closure (to "freeze"). Those with a high need for closure, or those in situations that seem to require or heighten the desirability of achieving closure, are likely to reach a judgment quickly and then stick with it, despite future evidence that may contradict the judgment or decision reached. They may process less information before reaching a conclusion but paradoxically feel more sure of it under such conditions. These cognitive processes may affect the way individuals construct a self-concept. The perceived benefits of closure may lead individuals to seize prematurely on a sense of who they are and what they are like and then to freeze it, becoming less open to processing further information.

These processes may explain why some self-attitudes are maintained despite conflicting information. I am thinking, for example, of the anorectic adolescent, close to starvation, who looks in the mirror and sees herself as still overweight. On the positive side, the self-concept may be very resilient even in the face of negative and destructive social feedback. The same process that endangers the anorectic adolescent may save the older adult or the black teenager from the ravages of prejudice and discrimination.

CRITICAL THINKING QUESTION

How would the mechanisms described above explain the strength of attitudes such as racial prejudice? Why are attitudes so hard to change?

Finally, the way we define ourselves influences our social behavior. All statements made by a person that include the words *I, me, mine,* and *myself* reflect aspects of the self (Cooley, 1902). Thus, attitudes (for instance, "*I* like bananas"), intentions ("*I* plan to get *my* degree"), beliefs ("*I* believe education is the key to success"), norms ("In *my* group, people are punctual"), roles ("In *my* job, getting along well with many different kinds of people is necessary"), and values ("*I* think people should always try to do their best") represent various aspects of the self (Triandis, 1989). Our self-definition leads to behaviors consistent with that definition (Wicklund & Gollwitzer, 1982). For example, if people are given information leading them to think of themselves as "charitable," they give more money to charity (Kraut, 1973). People who think of themselves as "doers" of a particular activity are more likely to engage in that behavior (Greenwald, Carnot, Beach, & Young, 1987).

The self-schema (self-concept) begins to function like a "mental scaffold" on which we build and organize information related to the self, a vantage point from which we view ourselves and the social world in relation to ourselves. It directs our attention, affects what we remember and forget, and influences the activities in which we are interested or disinterested. Cognitive development and cognitive processes contribute to the way the self is structured, organized, and understood, and they are involved in its stability and/or revision. The content of the self—the knowledge that comprises it—comes from interaction with the environment and feedback from others as interpreted and evaluated by the cognitive processor. The I-self actively constructs the Me-self, which in turn influences future information processing and behavior.

How Many of You Are There?

Instead of thinking of the self as a unitary concept, it is more appropriate to think of *self-conceptions,* arranged in a hierarchical structure, with some more central, significant, and enduring, while others are more peripheral, trivial, and fleeting (Combs & Snygg, 1959; Coopersmith, 1967; Marsh & Shavelson, 1985; Rosenberg, 1979). At the top of the hierarchy is a general, abstract sense of self that remains consistent over time and across situations, while those that branch from it are increasingly concrete and tied to particular situations and contexts (Schell, Klein, & Babey, 1996). For example, you may have a concept of yourself as a male/female, son/daughter, sister/brother, student, and artist. In addition, you may have a concept of yourself as an occasional tennis player, a mower of lawns, and a good speller. Obviously, some of these self-conceptions are more central to the "real you" than others. Linda George (1980) has suggested the terms **hierarchy of importance** and **hierarchy of pervasiveness** to refer to the fact that some self-conceptions are more critical to the sense of self than others and will have greater impact on one's self-esteem and behavior. Hierarchical models allow individuals to define a broad, consistent sense of self, while at the same time acknowledging that we are different in different situations and at different times.

CRITICAL THINKING QUESTION

Which aspects of your self do you consider to be the most important and the most pervasive?

James (1890/1952) pointed out that the degree of similarity and level of organization among the different self-concepts would vary from person to person. For most, the selves are thought to be drawn together into a hierarchy that recognizes their differences as well as similarities and that places them at a level commensurate with their importance and pervasiveness. Changes in roles or developmental tasks may necessitate a reorganization of this hierarchy. Thus, we should also keep in mind that the current self-concept is in fact a "working self-concept" (Markus & Nurius, 1986), subject to modification and, in some unusual cases, dramatic change. There is also the notion of the "ideal self" or "possible self," the self we are working toward or can imagine ourselves becoming. These potential selves can serve as important motivating forces for the individual. In *The Seasons of a Man's Life* (1978), Dan Levinson incorporates this notion in his discussion of the "Dream," the sense of a future life and a future self that draws the individual into adulthood (see Chapter 8).

In sum, the self-concept (or self-conceptions) reflects our knowledge and beliefs about ourselves. It is the cognitive component of the self, a self-schema. It serves as a mental framework on which we organize information about ourselves and affects our perception and processing of information. The self-concept is hierarchical and complex and is believed to influence virtually every aspect of our functioning. It is not static, but rather dynamic, in that it is subject to revision and alteration.

Self-Esteem: The Assessment of One's Worth

The affective component of the self is **self-esteem.** It represents the individual's feelings toward and evaluation of the self, as well as an assessment of its worth along a positive-negative continuum. Put another way, self-esteem is the good-bad evaluation the I-self makes of the Me-self. An individual with high self-esteem has realistically appraised the self and accepts it, respects it, and finds it to have worth (Berk, 1991).

Importance of a Sense of Worth

According to Baron and Byrne (1991), of all the attitudes we hold, this central attitude about the self is likely the most important. The consensus of opinion is that self-esteem is a vital, fundamental human need (Greenberg et al., 1992). Coopersmith (1968, p. 218) views high self-esteem as "probably the most important requirement for effective behavior." To Greenwald (1988, p. 37), "The search for self-worth is one of the strongest motivating forces in adolescent and adult human behavior." Further, the ways in which different individuals build and attempt to maintain self-esteem are major contributors to differences in social behavior.

Numerous studies have found high self-esteem to be a valuable asset, with important implications for motivation and achievement, social relationships, health, and adjustment. For example, high self-esteem may motivate you to do things that benefit and protect you, because you believe you are worth it (Greenwald, 1988). This may at least partly explain why self-esteem is correlated with physical health (Antonucci & Jackson, 1983). Investigators have also found evidence that self-esteem has a major impact on affect, or mood. So, for instance, an individual high in self-worth will be relatively cheerful, while one low in self-worth will be relatively depressed (Harter, 1988). Research by Lund, Caserta, and Dimond (1993) found that self-esteem was among the best predictors of adjustment to the death of a spouse in later life. In general, high self-esteem is viewed as a central characteristic in mentally healthy individuals. (However, Heine, Lehman, Markus, & Kitayama [1999] found little evidence of a need for positive self-regard in Japanese culture, suggesting that this concept may be culturally based and characteristic of North American culture rather than a universal human need.)

Greenberg and his colleagues (1992) believe that the psychological function of self-esteem is to protect the individual from anxiety. They cite research indicating that people low in self-esteem tend to be anxious, that anxiety increases when self-esteem is threatened, and that strategies that defend self-esteem reduce anxiety. In one of their own studies, Greenberg and his associates found that subjects who received information raising their self-esteem experienced less anxiety than control subjects in response to a threatening film dealing with death. These results, coupled with findings from two additional studies, offer direct support for the hypothesis that self-esteem buffers anxiety in response to threat. Thus, the need for self-esteem may stem from a need for protection from basic fears. If so, future research may illuminate the processes by which self-esteem makes us feel safe and secure. Greenberg and his colleagues suggest that one way may be via a cultural belief that bad things do not happen to good people. Therefore, if individuals believe they are good and have worth, they are better able to maintain the illusion of safety.

Building Blocks of Self-Esteem

During early and middle childhood, children are developing a number of separate self-assessments—for example, in relation to their physical and academic selves. These are eventually integrated, probably beginning in middle childhood (ages 6 to 12), into a hierarchically organized system of self-assessments, headed by an overall or general self-esteem. This **global self-esteem** represents a synthesis of all the separate self-esteems in the hierarchy. So, we could think of our overall or global self-esteem as sitting at the top of a pyramid, a product of self-assessments in more specific areas of our lives such as social relationships, academic performance, work experience, and so on. Each of these could be further subdivided. For instance, our assessment of our social self might consist of assessments of our relationships with peers, romantic partners, and family members, while our academic self-esteem could be broken down into science, math, English, history, and so on. (See Figure 3.1.) As the individual progresses developmentally, new aspects of self-esteem emerge in relation to new roles and activities

FIGURE 3.1 *A Hierarchical Model of Self-Esteem*

This model suggests that global or overall self-esteem is based on self-evaluations in a number of life domains. The examples provided are not meant to exhaust the possibilities. Components of the hierarchy may be weighted differently at different ages and by different individuals and may be added in response to new roles and activities.

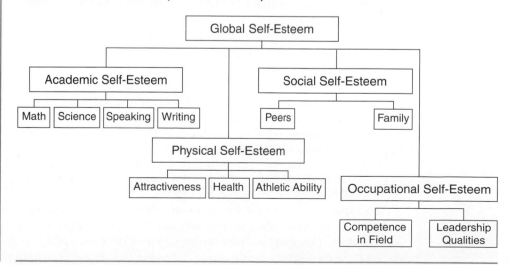

(competence in dating relationships in adolescence, for example, or worth as an employee or parent in young adulthood).

Cooley and Mead suggest that one of the major determinants of self-esteem is our perceptions of the value other people see in us. So, the higher the level of regard from others, the higher the level of regard for the self. Furthermore, feedback from some people is more significant than feedback from others and functions as a greater source of self-worth (Rosenberg, 1979). In childhood and adolescence, for example, parents are especially important sources of self-esteem.

Success experiences such as being chosen for a job promotion tend to have a positive effect on self-esteem, at least temporarily, while experiences such as failure, illness, or the loss of a loved one have been shown to have a negative effect. Major life transitions, such as that of retirement, could be expected to affect the components of self-esteem.

We also need to consider the importance individuals assign to the various "domains," or spheres of activity, in which they engage (for instance, school, athletics, home, work). Some of these domains will be considered more significant than others, based at least partly on the individual's assessment of the value placed on them by significant others and society in general. Thus, they may have a higher position in the self-esteem hierarchy described above. Success or failure in these domains will have much greater impact on overall self-esteem than success or failure in less important domains. These weightings would be expected to change with age: for example, with occupational self-esteem becoming more important in adulthood, while academic self-esteem recedes in significance.

Robert Atchley (1982) has offered an equation of sorts to clarify the relationship between self-esteem, self-concept, and the ideal self. Self-esteem is determined by the degree of concordance or similarity between the self-concept (the way we currently see ourselves) and the ideal self (the way we would like to be).

$$\text{Self-esteem} = \frac{\text{Self-concept}}{\text{Ideal self}}$$

A large discrepancy between the two would result in low self-esteem, while similarity between the two would result in high self-esteem. Low self-esteem could be raised in one of two ways, according to Atchley's model: either by lowering one's standards or enhancing one's view of oneself.

James concurs, suggesting that if one has no particular aspirations in a given field of activity, failure or incompetence in that activity will have little consequence for self-esteem. In fact, one way to raise self-esteem would be to simply lower one's expectations in those areas in which one is struggling. But what of domains considered so central to the individual's place in society that devaluation of the role is not feasible, and avoidance of activity in this domain is not possible? Wouldn't incompetence in these areas be especially damaging to self-esteem? (See Harter, 1988, for a discussion of these concepts as applied to children.)

CRITICAL THINKING QUESTION

What domains or roles do you think are so critical to adulthood that failure in behaviors associated with them could have particularly damaging effects on self-esteem? Could these domains be different for males and females?

Self-esteem thus represents the affective or evaluative component of the self: an assessment of the individual's self-worth. A sense of worth is considered to be a vital, fundamental need. As such, an individual's level of self-esteem has important consequences for many aspects of behavior. Like the self-concept, self-esteem is viewed as multidimensional, complex, and hierarchical in structure, rather than unitary and simple (Shavelson, Hubner, & Staton, 1976; Harter, 1990). Its primary determinants are one's subjective assessment of success in valued activities and evaluative feedback from significant others. Self-esteem is believed to go through an important period of organizational development in middle childhood, though it remains responsive to life experience. We turn our attention now to an exploration of a concept closely related to both self-concept and self-esteem: self-efficacy.

I Think I Can, I Think I Can: A Look at Self-Efficacy

Attitudes toward the self can and do motivate behavior, influencing our actions as well as our goals and ambitions. They are, in fact, the source of "will" and are self-fulfilling. One of the determinants of whether or not a person will attempt a task and persist at it is **self-efficacy** (Bandura, 1977a), or one's beliefs and expectations about whether one has the ability to successfully complete or accomplish a particular task. In other words, when considering whether to try to do something, we ask ourselves whether we have what it takes to pull it off. If we have high self-efficacy, we are more likely to attempt a task and more likely to succeed at it, which of course is the moral of the story in the classic children's book *The Little Engine That Could*. This reminds me of a quote attributed to Henry Ford: "Think you can or think you can't, either way you're likely to be right." Note that self-efficacy is defined in relationship to a particular task or goal,

Self-efficacy—a belief in one's ability to accomplish a task or reach a goal—contributes to achievement and coping/ adaptation.

rather than being described as a global attitude about the self. Also, as with self-esteem, it is evaluated along a positive-negative continuum.

Sources of Self-Efficacy

Bandura suggests four sources of self-efficacy beliefs: personal performance, emotional arousal, vicarious experiences with observed models, and encouragement and persuasion from others. So, if one has a history of personal success with a task, experiences positive affect such as pleasure rather than negative affect such as anxiety when engaged in this task, has seen others successfully accomplish it, and/or receives encouragement from significant others, one's perceived self-efficacy should go up and influence motivation positively. The reverse is also true. Thus, one's sense of self-efficacy is not static and fixed, but rather dynamic and subject to change (Berry & West, 1993). As self-efficacy fluctuates based on these four variables, motivation, effort, and persistence will vary accordingly.

Bandura (1991) states that personal empowerment through mastery experiences is the best contributor to strong and resilient self-efficacy and that overestimation of efficacy is okay, maybe even beneficial. What we need, according to Bandura, are resilient self-believers. Being more confident than you realistically should be is, according to Bandura, an asset because it makes you try harder. Additional effort enhances the likelihood of success, which in turn improves self-efficacy. (See Figure 3.2.) So, success breeds success. This reciprocal relationship between beliefs and behavior is evident throughout Bandura's discussion.

FIGURE 3.2 *Sources and Effects of Self-Efficacy*

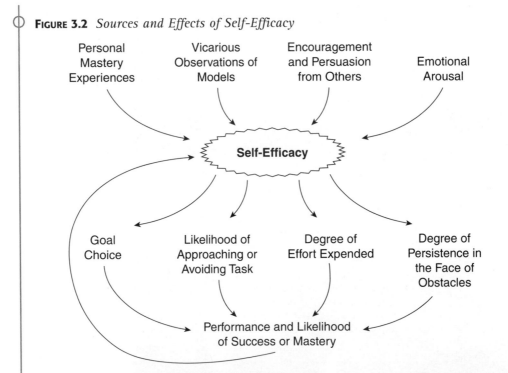

Correlates of Self-Efficacy

Perceived self-efficacy, then, affects one's motivation to attempt a particular task as well as the effort and persistence put forth in accomplishing it. In addition, those low in self-efficacy experience more negative emotions such as depression, helplessness, and low self-esteem (Devins et al., 1982) and have poorer coping skills (Mueller & Major, 1989). People high in self-efficacy perform better on a variety of tasks (Garland et al., 1988), have a higher tolerance for pain (Litt, 1988), and experience less stress (Bandura et al., 1988). See Table 3.1 for a description of traits associated with high and low self-efficacy.

Gender Differences in Self-Efficacy

Differences in the self-efficacy of males and females have been found to conform to the instrumental versus expressive roles that males and females in our society generally adopt. Consistent with the fact that society places greater value on the male gender role as well as its association with competence and achievement, Vollmer (1986) found that men tend to have higher self-efficacy than women. Not surprisingly, these gender differences affect career aspirations and decisions (Hackett, 1985). Gorrell (1990, p. 78) summarizes the findings of a number of studies by stating that "a person's sex-typed

TABLE 3.1 *Summary of Some Differences among People High and Low in Self-Efficacy*

High Self-Efficacy	Low Self-Efficacy
Set higher goals	Set lower goals
Exhibit greater commitment	Exhibit less commitment
Exert greater effort	Exert less effort
Exhibit greater persistence	Obstacles lead to giving up
Visualize success scenarios	Visualize failure scenarios
Are optimistic	Are pessimistic
Accept difficult tasks	Avoid difficult tasks
Are more adventurous	Are less adventurous
Are self-enhancing	Are self-limiting
View ability as a skill that can be developed	View ability as an inherent capacity
Attribute failure to lack of skill or effort	Attribute failure to lack of ability
Emphasize personal improvement and accomplishment of task	Emphasize comparison with others, evaluation of performance
Are resilient in face of difficulties	Feel cannot manage threats
Feel able to and do cope more successfully than others	Feel cannot and do not cope as successfully as others
Dwell on strengths	Dwell on deficiencies
Experience less emotional arousal, stress, depression, and anxiety	Are more prone to stress, anxiety, and depression
Have healthier autonomic nervous system functions	Experience damaging autonomic nervous system responses, such as repressed immune function

Source: Based on Bandura, 1977a, 1991. Used by permission.

beliefs form a significant portion of personal identity . . . , and a powerful element in those sex-typed beliefs is the sense of personal agency or control as evidenced by self-efficacy beliefs."

CRITICAL THINKING QUESTION

Based on self-efficacy theory and research, what types of careers would men and women gravitate toward or avoid? Why? Is this likely to change in the future? Has self-efficacy influenced your career plans?

Thus, it seems that a belief in one's abilities has a positive effect on a variety of aspects of performance. Self-efficacy demonstrates the interrelationship of cognitive, affective, and behavioral components of the self—what we think and feel about ourselves affects what we do.

Concept Review 2.2

- The self-concept can be described as a self-schema, or a personal theory we hold about what the self is like. It is complex and hierarchical in structure.

- The self-concept affects our attention to and processing of information and, once formed, is resistant to change.

- Self-esteem refers to an assessment of one's worth and has important implications for many aspects of behavior, including motivation, health, and adjustment.

- The major building blocks of self-esteem are success in valued activities and evaluative feedback from significant others.

- Self-efficacy reflects our beliefs and expectations about our ability to successfully complete a particular task; thus, it affects motivation and achievement.

- Albert Bandura has described differences among those high and low in self-efficacy.

Identity: Who Am I and Where Am I Going?

The development of the self takes on some important added dimensions during adolescence, that time beginning at about age 12 and ending somewhere between age 18 and the early 20s. This is a period marked by growing cognitive capacity as concrete thinkers become able to handle the abstractions of formal thought. It is a time of transition from childhood to adulthood, and from dependence to independence, when the individual is expected to make at least tentative decisions with regard to occupational choice and direction for the future. It is a time marked by increasing movement toward physical as well as psychological "leaving home." During adolescence, the first glimmers of a more truly adult self emerge, concerned with adult roles and responsibilities. These new aspects of self will have a pervasive influence over every aspect of adult life, guiding choices and directing action, while defining and providing purpose and meaning, or the lack of them. This transitional period is viewed, as are all transitional periods, as a time of both opportunity and danger, a time when development may proceed in either a positive or a negative direction, a time of exploration and experimentation, a time, in other words, of "crisis." (Remember that we are using the word *crisis* in its original Greek sense, to mean "a turning point.") Indeed, research by Haan, Millsap, and Hartka (1986) has found greater instability in personality during the late adolescence/ early adulthood transition than at any other time in the life span. This is truly an important and formative period in the development of the self.

Identity Defined: Erikson's Psychosocial Theory

The term most closely identified with the development of the self in adolescence is **identity.** Our definition of this concept is rooted in the theory of Erik Erikson (1968), summarized in Chapter 2. Erikson's work has stimulated a tremendous amount of research and has become the major model for understanding the development of the self in the critical transitional years of adolescence as well as during adulthood.

Stage 5 in Erikson's model of development is described as a crisis of **ego identity versus role confusion.** The task for the adolescent is to make commitments in the areas of occupation, religious and political ideology, and gender and sexual orientation and role. These commitments are an outgrowth of a period of active exploration of alternatives and, once made, lay the foundation for meeting the challenges of young adulthood, especially the task of forming and maintaining intimate relationships. The process of identity formation takes on special urgency in late adolescence, as both internal and external pressures toward commitment begin to coalesce. An inability to resolve the crisis and establish a tentative adult identity results in role confusion, characterized by a lack of clear direction and a vague sense of self.

In his *Identity: Youth and Crisis* (1968, p. 87), Erikson defines identity as follows:

> The wholeness to be achieved at this stage I have called a sense of inner identity. The young person, in order to experience wholeness, must feel a progressive continuity between that which he has come to be during the long years of childhood and that which he promises to become in the anticipated future; between that which he perceives himself to be and that which he perceives others to see in him and to expect of him. Individually speaking, identity includes, but is more than, the sum of all the successive identifications of those earlier years when the child wanted to be, and often was forced to become, like the people he depended on.

Notice that Erikson's model contains within it and/or implies significant concepts found in other theoretical models we have already discussed, such as phenomenology, cognitive theory, sociology, and social learning theory. Perhaps this explains the broad appeal as well as the theoretical utility of this model of the self. For example, Erikson describes the individual as *creating* an identity that includes, but yet is phenomenologically distinct from, the expectations and perceptions of others. This occurs in response to physical, cognitive, and psychosocial changes and the demands of entry into adulthood. In addition, the individual is attempting to integrate and synthesize all the existing *self-conceptions* developed up to this point, resulting in a new *schema* or *theory of self.* This new view of self provides a sense of continuity with past experience, but also incorporates the possibilities of new and future selves, preparing the individual to meet new challenges. The characteristics of unity and continuity of the self are key to understanding identity as Erikson defines it.

So, who am I? And what does it matter? In addressing the developmental importance of identity formation, Atkinson (1987) emphasizes the commitment to a sense of purpose in life and the choice of a life direction. No wonder the process is slow, gradual, and complex. Howard (1991) describes identity as a life story one constructs in late adolescence, which is influenced by the history and culture of one's time and has influence throughout the remainder of life. Some of these stories are better written and constructed than others, but whatever the quality, the story has ramifications: "Early in life we are free to choose what life story we will inhabit—and later we find that we are lived by that story. The eternal conflict of freedom versus destiny is revealed in the old Spanish proverb: Habits at first are silken threads—Then they become cables. The same could be said of stories" (p. 196).

Identity formation is viewed as a key developmental task of adolescence. Let's look at how this process takes place and at what variations exist in the way individuals handle this crisis.

Formation of Identity: Marcia's Identity Status Approach

Erikson's description of identity development was intended originally to be used for clinical purposes. As a result, it was vaguely defined. James Marcia (1966) operationalized Erikson's concept, extending its usefulness by providing a means by which it could be measured and tested. Marcia's model brought the research methods of social cognition to Erikson's psychoanalytic concept. This model has generated a large body of research in identity formation, while at the same time dominating much of the empirical literature on the subject.

Marcia describes four **identity statuses,** or outcomes of coping with and resolving the identity issue: identity diffusion, identity foreclosure, identity moratorium, and identity achievement. These identity statuses can be viewed as developmental progressions, with the first representing the least mature resolution and the last representing the most mature and desired outcome. As one moves through the transition to adulthood, the sense of identity should be strengthened as more and more alternatives are explored and either discarded as inappropriate or retained (Waterman, 1982).

Two criteria are used to assess an individual's identity status, evaluated by means of a semistructured interview lasting about 30 minutes. The first is crisis: the adolescent's active exploration of alternatives. This is normally a period marked by confusion, anxiety, inconsistency, and an active attempt to work through conflicts toward a unified definition of self. The second variable is commitment: the adolescent's degree of personal investment in choices made. Figure 3.3 depicts the four identity statuses in relation to these two criteria.

Identity Diffusion

Identity-diffused subjects are not currently in a state of crisis (although they may have been at one time) and have made no commitments. Further, they demonstrate no real concern over this status, or any compelling need to resolve the identity issue by adopting self-defining roles and values. This is essentially what Erikson meant by role confusion. For example, Jim could be described as irresponsible, spontaneous, and impulsive.

FIGURE 3.3 *Marcia's (1966) Identity Statuses*

	No Commitment	**Commitment**
No Crisis	Identity Diffusion	Identity Foreclosure
Crisis	Identity Moratorium	Identity Achievement

He has no specific career goals, no particular interests, and no set of values to guide his life choices. He seems to be "going nowhere" but is unconcerned about it.

Identity Foreclosure

The foreclosed identity status is characterized by commitment to vocational and ideological choices without having experienced a crisis. The choices these individuals adopt are not self-chosen through exploration and experimentation but are handed to them by or taken ready-made from parents or others. These people have become, in other words, what other people have suggested, prepared, or intended them to be. The use of the term *foreclosed* suggests that personality development has been taken over by or given up to forces outside the individual. Kathy, unsure of herself and unable to decide what she wants to do with her life, has succumbed to pressure to drop out of school, marry her childhood sweetheart, and "settle down." Doug, never having seriously considered any alternatives, has accepted his role in the family business and will commit himself to it full time on graduation from college.

Identity Moratorium

A "moratorium" refers to a time-out. In this case, the individual is in a state of crisis, is aware of the need to make choices, but is at present unable to do so. A moratorium signals a need for time. This is usually temporary; most people eventually move through a moratorium to identity achievement. Erikson also described a moratorium as a part of the identity formation process. Jerry, unable to fully commit himself to a career in law and confused about his values and the requirements of a legal career, decides to drop out of law school and go to Aspen, working as a bartender and earning enough to keep him in ski-lift tickets until he can "figure things out."

Identity Achievement

The most mature of the identity statuses, identity achievement refers to an individual who has successfully worked through a period of crisis and has made commitments that contribute to a definition of self. This is comparable to what Erikson described as ego identity. A person with this identity status is prepared to move on into adulthood equipped with a clearer sense of self, important beliefs, and life direction. Having considered a variety of careers and taken college courses in many different areas, Jane decided it was important to her to work with people and that her real love was psychology. She eventually completed a master's degree in counseling and now works with adolescents. She loves her work and feels that this is really what she was meant to do.

Variables Related to the Process of Identity Formation

Empirical studies have confirmed that while little attention is given to identity issues prior to high school, there is an increasing likelihood that alternatives will be considered and commitments made as the individual approaches late adolescence (Waterman, 1982). The process of identity formation is potentially affected by a number of variables, including parenting styles, the nature and quality of parent-child relationships, resolution of psychosocial issues at earlier stages, educational and work histories, exposure to a variety of models and alternatives, personality traits, level of cognitive development, and gender (Weinmann & Newcombe, 1990; Waterman, 1982).

For example, an authoritative parenting style (warm, fair, democratic) may contribute to identity achievement, whereas authoritarian parenting (power-oriented) may suppress experimentation and encourage premature commitments—foreclosure. Neglectful or permissive parenting may contribute to a lack of direction and increase the likelihood of a diffused status.

Achievement and moratorium subjects have been found to perform at a higher level on tasks of formal and moral reasoning and are more likely to be reflective than impulsive in making decisions. Additionally, these statuses show a more internal locus of control (see Chapter 11), higher self-esteem, greater need for achievement, and greater capacity for intimate relationships (see Bourne, 1978; Marcia, 1980). Some of these qualities (formal thought, for example) may be necessary, though not sufficient, for identity to be achieved.

Foreclosures, on the other hand, score high on measures of authoritarianism and need for social approval, report being very close to their parents, and score low on a scale of autonomy (reviewed in Bourne, 1978). Research on identity-diffused subjects is limited, though Marcia (1988, p. 217) describes this status as having the greatest degree of difficulty in life, "vulnerable to vicissitudes of external pressure, a sense of inner emptiness, and directionless." Like chameleons, they change from situation to situation (Berzonsky, 1988).

A Critique of the Identity Status Model

Problems with this model include questions about the validity and reliability of the instrument used to assess identity status, the need for replication of all findings, the need to expand samples beyond an overreliance on college students (do those who do not attend college go through the process in the same way?), and the need to include samples from other cultures. For a series of articles on these subjects, see the December 1999 issue of *Developmental Review* (volume 19, number 4).

Others have concerns about whether a "type model" of identity is realistic. Marcia himself (1976, as quoted in Bourne, 1978, p. 379) has said: "On reading a description of the identity statuses, as is the case with almost any typology, one begins to experience himself as a little bit of all of them. . . . No one is *just* a Foreclosure or Identity Achiever. Each person has elements of at least two, and often all four statuses." Similarly, it is possible that a person could have made commitments in some, though not all, areas relevant to identity and would therefore be difficult to accurately assign an identity status. Another issue pertains to the timing of identity development among recent cohorts, for whom the early 20s may be increasingly a time of extended moratorium as the requirement for longer periods of education have delayed the assumption of adult roles and responsibilities. The discussion of Arnett's (2000) concept of "emerging adulthood" in Chapter 6 (see the Box on p. 231) explores the idea that the achievement of adult identity may be taking longer than it did among previous cohorts.

Finally, some question exists about the stability of identity status in adulthood, prompting both Bourne (1978) and Waterman (1982) to call for increased research on age groups beyond the college years. As Bourne points out, " 'Identity' cannot properly be understood as a developmental end-point. . . . The maintenance of some flexibility of identity would seem at least as important as . . . a stable frame of reference from which one can actively participate in society" (p. 390). Rather, we should assume that the processes of identity formation extend into and perhaps throughout adulthood as the individual confronts the challenges of life, potentially leading to a stronger and clearer sense of ourselves (Zucker, Ostrove, & Stewart, 2002).

The Self in Cross-Cultural Perspective

The remainder of this chapter explores the effect of four variables on the self: culture, gender, race/ethnicity, and age. We begin with culture. The self is, after all, a social construct: "Humans do not have a basic, fundamental, pure human nature that is transhistorical and transcultural. Humans are incomplete and therefore unable to function adequately unless embedded in a specific cultural matrix" (Cushman, 1990, p. 601). The self is shaped by and expressed in the social context (from the micro to the macro level). Culture contains values, assumptions, and expectations that mold attitudes and guide choices. It imposes opportunities and limitations within which lives are lived. It also provides a worldview within which one interprets reality. As Kaufman (1986, p. 115) points out, "Culture provides an individual with a framework for making sense of and interpreting his or her own life and its larger contexts." Triandis (1996; Triandis & Suh, 2002) has said that culture is to society what memory is to individuals: it tells us what to attend to, what to expect, and how to interpret events; it includes what has worked for a society and thus what it deems worth passing on to future generations. Thus, to some extent, each culture may have its own psychology. Human beings are ethnocentric: we are so embedded in our own culture's way of thinking and behaving that we tend to believe other people see the world the same way we do. In fact, it is difficult to be aware of our own culture until we are confronted with another.

American psychology reflects the culture in which it developed. Thus, we should keep in mind the inherently ethnocentric nature of thinking about the self in Western psychology (Hermans, Kempen, & van Loon, 1992) and, until recently, the virtual exclusion of research and theory on groups other than the White male majority within Western culture itself. Failure to appreciate the importance of the social context may contribute to a distorted view of human nature and human behavior. The extent to which the body of research and theory related to the self applies to other cultures or historical periods is debatable. For example, Atkinson (1987) contends that the issue of forming an adult identity is probably much easier in technologically simple societies, where the options are fewer and the dictates of society stricter. According to Triandis (1989), the more complex a culture is, the more confused the individual's identity is likely to be. In our complex technological society, the sheer number of alternatives available to an adolescent is daunting, and the adult world to be entered is far more complex than in the past. Support for this position is provided by Katakis (1976, 1978, 1984), who asked 11- and 12-year-old children of farmers and fishermen in small Greek villages what they would be doing when they were older. They unhesitatingly said either farming or fishing. Greek children living in the more complex culture of large cities had no such clear sense of direction: their responses were often of the "I will find myself" type. In addition to raising concerns about the generalizability of findings to cultures significantly different from our own, researchers question the applicability of self-theory to ethnic minorities within the United States itself.

As Betancourt and Lopez (1993) point out, despite growing awareness of its importance in psychological development, the study of culture has achieved at best a secondary place in mainstream psychology. As a result, theories tend to assume that principles and findings can be universally applied. If the self is a social product, important differences in the sociocultural context of development would be expected to produce variations in the nature of the self. In turn, the sociocultural definition of the self would be expected to change social behavior (Triandis, 1989). To restate the point: different cultures may produce a different kind of self, which then causes people in different cultures to behave differently. We cannot separate the self from the culture that shapes it. If we hope to understand the way culture contributes to the development of the self, we need to determine which aspects of cultural variation might be important. The question is, then: What are the relevant qualities of the social environment and how do they affect development?

Collectivism versus Individualism

Triandis (1989, 1995, 1996; Triandis, Bontempo, Villareal, Asai, & Lucca, 1988; Triandis & Suh, 2002) suggests that one important dimension is the extent to which a culture is collectivist or individualist. He has described four major attributes that can be used to determine if a culture is *primarily* collectivist or individualist, along with about 60 other attributes that describe variations of these major types. Collectivism and individualism should not be viewed as polar opposites but rather as falling on a continuum. And in most societies they coexist to some extent. Triandis maintains that all people have predispositions to individualism and collectivism; the one predominantly expressed depends on the culture. He cautions against overgeneralization, pointing out that within any culture, variations exist by gender, economic class, minority or majority status, and so on. Thus, there is much variation *between* and *within* cultures. A summary of the major differences between collectivist and individualist cultures follows.

First, collectivists define the collective (family, village) as the basic unit of analysis. Thus, in **collectivist cultures,** individuals define themselves as part of a group(s). Concern with relationships is a defining characteristic. Markus and Kitayama (1991) have referred to this as the *interdependent self.* Second, collectivists place more emphasis on the welfare of the group and choose goals that are compatible with group goals. If there is a conflict between an individual and group goal, the priority is given to the group. Collectivists feel intense emotional attachment to the group and concern for its continued well-being. Third, their social behavior is governed more by social norms and other external social processes than by personal attitudes and feelings. Fourth, duties and obligations are very influential. Collectivists value such qualities as restraint and harmony, loyalty, humility, honoring parents and elders, belonging, obedience, reliability, and proper behavior. Vertical/hierarchical relationships (such as between a boss and an employee or between a parent and a child) are of greater significance and allow the collectivist to maintain a sense of belonging and interdependence that crosses generational and social boundaries and also to fulfill important obligations.

Individualists define the individual as the basic unit of analysis. Within **individualist cultures,** individuals define themselves as separate from the group, and the development of an autonomous, *independent self* is encouraged (Markus & Kitayama, 1991). Individualists place greater priority on personal goals over group goals and feel less attachment to and concern for the welfare of the group. The welfare of the individual and individual needs and feelings are emphasized. Social behavior is governed by internal processes such as personal attitudes and anticipated pleasurable outcomes. Having a good time and enjoying life are highly valued. If relationships become too costly, individualists are likely to drop them (see the discussion of equity theory in Chapter 6). Individualists value such qualities as self-expression, creativity, self-reliance, assertiveness, personal uniqueness, daring, individual freedom, equality, and inner-directedness. Horizontal relationships (with friends, coworkers, spouse) are of primary importance and allow the individualist to express individuality within ties with equals.

Examples of collectivist cultures include most of the Latin American, Asian, and African cultures, while most North American and Northern and Western European cultures would be classified as individualist. The picture is complex, however, since within the same culture, urban samples tend to be more individualist, while rural samples are more collectivist. There are also within-culture ethnic and social-class variations on this dimension. For example, within the United States, Hispanic samples are more collectivist than those of Northern and Western European heritage, as are working-class as compared to professional families. Individualism is more likely as cultures become more complex, affluent, and mobile. The collectivist-individualist dimension has a number of implications for the development of the self. While space does not permit a thorough review of this research, let's consider some examples.

First, childrearing patterns vary among collectivist and individualist cultures (Kohn, 1969, 1987; Triandis, 1989). Parents in collectivist cultures (and the American working class) emphasize obedience, reliability, and proper behavior. Children are socialized to

Collectivist cultures encourage individuals to develop strong attachment to the group and to place group goals above individual goals.

Individualistic cultures place great value on personal expression, competition, and individual achievement.

conform. In contrast, parents in individualist cultures (including those in the professional social classes) emphasize self-reliance and independence, allow children a good deal of autonomy, and place a high value on creativity and self-actualization. Thus, development of various aspects of the self is either encouraged or discouraged by the culture.

Second, the meaning of different aspects of the self also varies along this collectivist-individualist dimension (Triandis et al., 1988). In an individualist culture, self-reliance implies competition with others, along with freedom to do "one's own thing," while in a collectivist culture, it implies not being a burden to others. In an individualist culture, the individual achieves; in a collectivist culture, the group achieves.

Third, the mythology of a culture provides ideal types that become incorporated into the ideal self and form a standard on which self-esteem is based (Roland, 1984). Different cultures, with different value systems, hold up different heroes as a basis of self-evaluation. For example, American heroes are generally rugged, brave, and fiercely independent.

Fourth, identity is defined on the basis of different elements in collectivist versus individualist cultures (Triandis, 1989). In collectivist cultures, relationships are very important (for example, I am Becca's mother); in individualist cultures, possessions are a more important component of identity—the material things one owns as well as personal experiences and accomplishments.

Finally, the motives and behaviors of individuals in collectivist cultures are influenced to a greater extent by concerns about the welfare of the group, while those in individualist cultures are more concerned about personal welfare. A study of cultural differences in attitudes toward smoking offers an illustration (Marin, Marin, Otero-Sabogal, Sabogal, & Perez-Stable, 1987). The researchers found that a sample of U.S. Hispanics (collectivists) showed significantly more concern than a non-Hispanic sample (individualists) in regard to the following: the effect of smoking on the health of others; setting a bad example for children; harming children; and bothering others with the bad smell of smoking, bad breath, bad smell on clothes, and so on. The individualist sample of non-Hispanics was more concerned about their own experience of withdrawal if they quit smoking.

As these examples indicate, the collectivist-individualist dimension appears to be one important aspect of the cultural context, with important implications for the development of the self. See Oyserman, Coon, and Kemmelmeier (2002) for a comprehensive literature review and assessment of the individualism-collectivism model of culture and research issues. Our understanding of the self and its components will be enhanced by a broader appreciation of its cultural underpinnings.

CRITICAL THINKING QUESTION

If you had to label your family heritage and tradition as either collectivist or individualist, which would it tend to be and why do you say so? How has this orientation affected your values, relationships, goals, and priorities?

Most psychological findings come from studies of individualist cultures, such as in the United States, in which the individual is the unit of study. Major theories of psychological development, such as those of Erikson, Levinson, and Maslow, emphasize the development of an autonomous, independent individual. Our definition of psychological health includes self-sufficiency, self-actualization, self-efficacy, and so on (Enns, 1994). Yet most of the world's people live in collectivist cultures (for example, 70 percent live in non-Western cultures, with 35 percent of the population in China and India, while only 6 percent live in the United States) (Triandis, 1994). As Triandis (1996, p. 407) points out, "If psychology is to become a universal discipline it will need both theories and data from the majority of humans."

CRITICAL THINKING QUESTION

How might the Western world's definition of psychological health be viewed in collectivist cultures?

Concept Review 3.3

- Identity, as originally formulated by Erikson, represents the psychosocial crisis of adolescence and refers to a sense of who one is, what one believes in, and where one is headed in life.

- James Marcia has described four identity statuses: diffusion, foreclosure, moratorium, and achievement.

- The self is shaped by the cultural context in which it develops.

- Triandis stresses that one important dimension of cultural influence is the extent to which the culture is collectivist or individualist.

- Most psychological research, concepts, and theories have been based on individualist cultures.

Women, Men, and Identity Formation

An individual's position in the social structure—determined by such things as gender, race, socioeconomic status, and age—is associated with roles, statuses, experiences, and opportunities that influence and become integrated into the sense of self (Markus & Herzog, 1991). This is an important and relatively neglected area of research (George, 1990a). As we discussed earlier, the development of the self must be viewed in the context of an ongoing interaction between the individual and a particular historical time and a particular cultural place. An underlying assumption of this chapter is that though people experience many of the same life events—such as marriage, parenthood, loss of a loved one, illness, and so on—their responses to these events depend on the content and functioning of the self, which in turn is a product of the social, cultural, and historical context of development.

A word of caution is appropriate. Even when a group of people (for example, Whites, Blacks, males, females) share the same cultural experiences, certain aspects of those experiences will be more significant or meaningful to some individuals than to others. Thus, the relationship between an event and an individual self can only be understood in reference to that one individual life. The generalizations presented here must be understood in that light.

Traditional Gender Roles

Before proceeding, we need to clarify the use of the terms *sex* and *gender*. We will use **sex** to refer to the biological characteristics of males and females present at birth and **gender** to refer to the sociocultural aspects of being masculine or feminine, acquired as a result of socialization in a particular culture. Thus, gender is viewed here as being socially constructed. The **gender role** is society's description of characteristics associated with and behaviors appropriate for males and females. Gender roles are normative in the sense that these male-female differences are considered desirable.

Gender identity (thinking of oneself as either male or female) is generally thought to be set by age 3. After that, the individual attempts to think and behave in ways consistent with the appropriate gender role. (This is in accord with our discussion earlier that self-definition leads to behaviors consistent with that definition.) This sense of self as male or female turns out to be one of the most important determinants of behavior (McClelland, 1975). Gender roles act as perceptual filters through which we perceive and evaluate ourselves and others, and they also set up self-fulfilling prophecies (Basow, 1992). The expectations associated with these roles are deeply ingrained, communicated early in life, and function as stereotypes, or overgeneralized conceptions of the characteristics and abilities of males and females. Keep in mind, however, that meta-analyses of years of research on gender differences have concluded that actual behavioral differences between males and females are fewer in number and smaller in magnitude than gender stereotypes would suggest (see, for example, Linn & Hyde, 1989; Maccoby & Jacklin, 1974). The traditional gender roles have been described as expressive and instrumental (Parsons, 1949).

Nature and Impact of the Expressive and Instrumental Roles

The traditionally female **expressive role** is oriented toward establishing and maintaining relationships. The behaviors associated with it include nurturing, cooperation, sensitivity to the needs of others, dependency, and emotional responsiveness.

The male **instrumental role,** on the other hand, is goal and achievement oriented. The associated behaviors include dominance, assertiveness, achievement, independence, logical and rational thought, and competitiveness.

One of the consequences of these roles is that women often search for identity and find their worth in relationships: emphasis is placed on affiliation; connection; and empathizing with, caring for, and nurturing others. Men, on the other hand, focus on differentiation from others (separating and distinguishing themselves), autonomy, and personal success, searching for identity and finding their worth in work.

Society places much greater value on the instrumental role, equating it with competence and using it as a standard by which to judge the success and value of the individual. Males have a somewhat more positive self-concept, higher global self-esteem, higher self-efficacy, and generally overestimate their ability (Basow, 1992; Kling, Hyde, Showers, & Buswell, 1999; Vollmer, 1986). On the average, more males than females believe that they are good at a lot of things. In its emphasis on instrumental qualities, the male gender role contributes to a perception of ability and boosts confidence (Vollmer, 1986). Females have a somewhat more negative self-concept, lower self-esteem (especially beginning around age 12), lower self-efficacy, and generally underestimate their ability even when they have successfully performed a task (American Association of

University Women, 1991). Lower self-confidence may reduce motivation to attempt a task, especially if it is perceived as difficult.

Female accomplishments tend to be undervalued, even by females. In a longitudinal study of the high school graduating class of 1972, Adelman (1991) found that women outperformed men academically at every level from high school to graduate school and in all fields and courses, including calculus and statistics. Yet these women had lower academic and career aspirations, and their superior academic records were discounted and underrewarded in the job market (see Chapter 8). Basow (1992, p. 175) points out that "even when grades are the same for females and males in such fields as math and science, females think they are less competent than males think themselves to be." Gender roles have obvious implications, then, for the value placed on males and females in general, for society's judgments of their abilities, for their sense of self, and for their goals, aspirations, and eventual achievement.

Social versus Evolutionary Origins

Various explanations have been offered as to the origins of these gender differences. According to social role theory, while biological factors may contribute to male-female differences, their contribution is probably somewhat minor compared to that of environmental factors. The underlying assumption is that many behavioral differences between males and females are the result of social, not biological, forces. In other words, they are learned through socialization. Levinson (1996) uses the term *gender splitting* to refer to the pervasive and universal division of male and female, masculine and feminine, in human life. Gender splitting operates at all levels of society and causes men and women to live in different social worlds, develop different traits and identities, and engage in different types of activities. He views this splitting as both a product of and a contributor to a patriarchal society in which women are generally subordinate to men.

An alternative view is offered by evolutionary psychology, which suggests that the differences observed among men and women in their social behavior represent a successful adaptation to the differing sexual selection processes (or reproductive strategies) that operate in males and females (Archer, 1996). The basic assumption is that natural selection operated to select those social behaviors most likely to ensure that genes would be passed on to subsequent generations. Thus, the female, limited in the number of offspring she can produce, invests a great deal more in each one and is more discriminating in her selection of a mate, seeking a responsible, capable provider. The male, on the other hand, must maximize his attractiveness to the choosy female by appearing to be strong, powerful, and able to defend his interests. As a result, corresponding attributes—such as nurturing and attentiveness to emotional cues in the female, versus daring and ambition in the male—have been selected for survival. It is possible, as Archer suggests, that cultural processes such as gendered socialization have coevolved so as to reinforce existing evolutionary tendencies, enhancing traits that originally had great adaptive value in ensuring the transmission of genes to successive generations and enhancing the likelihood of the survival of offspring.

Levinson (1996) describes a gender revolution, a major step in social evolution, which began with the Industrial Revolution two hundred years ago and which is slowly transforming the meaning of gender, the relationships between men and women, and their place in society. Though the exact outcome of this revolution will not be clear for many years, the general direction is toward a reduction in gender splitting, leading to greater similarity in the lives and personalities of men and women. Pressures contributing to this change include increased life expectancy and a variety of economic changes that have altered the need for various types of work, including the domestic work of the traditional female. See the Box for an example of the powerful influence of social historical events on gender development.

Prominence of the Male Model of Development

When differences among males and females have been noted in developmental research, psychology has "tended to regard male behavior as the 'norm' and female behavior as some kind of deviation from that norm" (McClelland, 1975, p. 81). Many theories of development have been criticized on this basis, including those of Freud, Kohlberg, and Erikson. When women are found not to conform to the male model, they have been

---

UNDERSTANDING THE DEVELOPMENTAL CONTEXT

Does It Matter What Year You Were Born? The Intersection of Gender, Generation, and History

How does social history change life history? Stewart and Healy (1989) suggest that social historical events influence individual lives regardless of life stage, but the nature of the influence varies depending on the individual's stage of development. Thus, the same event can create *psychologically* different cohorts. Their view is that social historical events that occur in childhood shape the individual's basic views of life and the world; those that occur in adolescence shape the individual's sense of identity; and those that occur in adulthood influence the opportunities available to individuals, with a lesser effect on values and identity. A number of studies have focused on the impact of World War II on men's development (e.g., see Elder, 1986). Stewart and Ostrove (1998) have applied Stewart and Healy's model to the impact of women's involvement in the workforce during World War II on subsequent generations of women.

Many women entered the labor force during World War II, contributing to the war effort by taking jobs vacated by men serving in the military. The war provided an interesting opportunity for this cohort of adult women, whose traditional gender identities were forged primarily in the 1930s. For those in their identity-formative late teens or early 20s, the work experience may have been especially potent, contributing to the development of a vocational identity inconsistent with the postwar pressure to return to a conventional domestic life. For young girls, working women served as powerful role models, shaping their view of society and women's potential place in it. It is these girls who later became the leaders of the women's movement of the 1960s, opening social, educational, and occupational opportunities to the cohort just behind them, born in the baby boom years, 1946 to 1964. The women's movement promoted ideas about girls' participation in nontraditional arenas such as athletics, math, and science; equal pay for equal work; and egalitarian marriages. Stewart and Ostrove cite evidence that the baby boom cohort of women was profoundly affected by the social movements and events of the 1960s that occurred during their childhood and adolescent years. And it is, of course, some of these women, who later became psychologists, who have emphasized the importance of gender for individual development.

Does it matter what year you were born? The answer seems to be a resounding yes.

viewed as deficient or deviant. "Thus a problem in theory became cast as a problem in women's development" (Gilligan, 1982, p. 7).

The perception among some scholars that theory has failed to capture and explain the development of women has led to a growing body of literature challenging a purported male bias in the way psychological health and development have traditionally been defined (Westkott, 1989). This research studies women in their own right, rejecting "the model of the man as the only model of a seemingly full-fledged person" (Miller, 1986, p. xi). A closer look at this scholarship will help us to get the flavor of this point of view.

The developmental importance of such issues becomes apparent in adolescence, when, according to Erikson, the task of forming an independent identity takes center stage. How can she form an independent identity and fulfill the requirements of the female expressive role at the same time? A female could decide to "be more like a man," but in doing so she risks criticism from those who feel she is not doing her duty as society defines it. She is supposed to be giving, while men are supposed to be doing; she is to be the cheerleader, he is to be the star. Or, she can follow the prescription and find her self through her relationships with others, though in doing so she risks being described as "foreclosed," dependent, and "other-directed." In fact, as Miller suggests (1986), maybe the reason women have trouble knowing what they want is because their socialization is contrary to finding out. The focus is on others and what others want. Unable to enjoy growth in themselves, women are instead supposed to foster it in others. The key struggle as Gilligan (1982) sees it is in the contradiction between the way we have traditionally defined femininity and adulthood.

There is additional concern that women's strengths may be dysfunctional in society as presently organized. The expressive role is vulnerable, as evidenced by the high rate of depression among women as compared to men, much of which is attributed to women's position in society (see Chapter 11), as well as by the high incidence of violence against women (see Chapter 7). Because a woman is defined by connection to others, she has problems with separation and individuation—with establishing an independent identity. Of course, the male instrumental role is not without limitations. Males have problems as well. Because their gender identity is tied to separation and individuation, they may have trouble with relationships and intimacy (Freudenberger, 1987; Gilligan, 1982).

Identity Research and Women

What about the *process* of identity formation among females as compared to males? Research on this subject suggests that while the content of the choices males and females make may differ, the process used in making the choices seems to be far more similar than different (Levinson, 1996; Waterman, 1982). The gender differences that do exist are seen as arising primarily from the sociocultural environment, rather than from differing capacities within the individual. For example, while both the diffused and foreclosed statuses are viewed as maladaptive for males, who are expected to be independent and goal oriented, there is some question about the implications of foreclosure among women (Marcia, 1980; Bourne, 1978). Given the traditional expressive role, stressing as it does relationships with others and conformity to social norms, foreclosure may represent a form of identity achievement for females. So, instead of viewing foreclosure as an immature resolution of the identity crisis among females (in other words, a failure to achieve one of the major developmental tasks of adolescence), it may instead represent a successful accommodation to the female gender role.

Others have suggested that the timing of identity development may differ among women, depending on the choices made in regard to family and career. For example, O'Connell (1976) observed that women who pursued careers continuously without any break for childrearing tended to follow a male pattern, while women who were full-time homemakers or who resumed careers after an interruption for childbearing seemed to enter a moratorium phase in regard to identity that was not terminated until the children were of school age. The implication is that the female, wedded to husband and children, is unable to "achieve" an identity unless and until she can disentangle herself from these relationships. Again, an alternate view would be that women's identity is based on components other than the traditional male emphasis on career. Family-career issues and nontraditional role combinations are discussed in more depth in Chapter 8.

To sum up, the dominant view of identity formation has been that it is a process of separation and growing independence. This is problematic when this model is applied to women. In our culture, women tend to find their identity through attachment rather than separation from others. To the extent that traditional theories hold women to the same developmental standards as men, these theories deny women's uniqueness and the value of identity as women define it, and worse, may present them as somehow developmentally immature or flawed. Here again, our understanding of psychosocial development among males and females would be enhanced by acknowledging developmental realities. The challenge is made greater by the fact that gender roles in our society are in a state of transition, the outcome of which is uncertain. We must also keep in mind that what research there is primarily describes the experience of White middle-class America. Little is known about these issues as they affect other groups. For example, Binion (1990) points out that information about gender role development and attitudes among African Americans is virtually nonexistent.

Concept Review 3.4

- Gender, ethnicity, socioeconomic status, and age affect life opportunities and experiences that in turn influence the development of the self.
- Traditional gender roles are described as the instrumental male role and the expressive female role.
- Social role theory and evolutionary theory offer different explanations of the origins of gender differences.
- The same historical events affect individuals differently, depending on life stage.

Race/Ethnicity and the Development of the Self

The purpose of this section is to introduce the importance of race and culture in the development of the self. Following the suggestion of Phinney (1996), the term *ethnicity* will be used to refer to broad groupings of Americans identified by race and culture of origin, and *ethnic group* will refer to members of nondominant groups. Rather than focusing on all groups, we will attempt to review some of what is known about the development of the self among African Americans. Much of the material covered in this section could apply as well to other disadvantaged groups in our society, such as Native Americans. I have chosen to focus on African Americans for the following reasons: the visibility of this group within the culture as a whole, its experience of prejudice and discrimination, and its relative deprivation as a group within the larger culture. It is assumed that their visibility as people of color and their exclusion from many of the opportunities available to the White majority pose significant challenges to the formation of the self-concept, self-esteem, self-efficacy, and identity. In addition, more research on Blacks is available than on other racial/ethnic minorities. (Chapter 1, p. 34, provides a review of the problems posed by generalizations based on ethnic categories.)

Self-Esteem among Black Americans

To understand the development and experience of Black Americans, we have to overcome many of the same obstacles we faced in understanding the development and experience of American women. That is, we have to move beyond the application of the White male standard. Let's examine, as a case in point, the prevailing assumptions about self-esteem. You will recall that we defined self-esteem as the assessment of one's worth, primarily determined by one's subjective assessment of success in valued activities and evaluative feedback from others. Remember also that self-esteem is considered to have tremendous consequences for many other aspects of psychological functioning. Given the often negative stereotypes of Blacks, their experience of low social status and economic and social discrimination, along with their poor performance as compared to Whites on measures of academic and occupational achievement, one would expect to find that Blacks as a group have low self-esteem. In fact, "this prediction has been widely accepted by social psychologists, to the point that it has been assumed to be true" (Crocker & Major, 1989, p. 610). Yet research on global or overall self-esteem has consistently found that Blacks have self-esteem equal to or greater than that of Whites (Crocker & Major, 1989; Porter & Washington, 1979; Twenge & Crocker, 2002). These surprising results apply to other stigmatized groups, such as the physically handicapped, as well. Such findings may indicate that our understanding of the developmental foundations of self-esteem is not accurate, or at least may not be applicable to populations other than the White majority. An alternative explanation is offered by Crocker and Major (1989), who describe three protective mechanisms or strategies used by members of stigmatized groups.

The "Black Is Beautiful" movement of the 1960s was aimed at fostering strong identification among Blacks as a way of supporting self-esteem. Ethnicity has been found to be an important component of identity formation among Blacks.

Self-Protective Strategies

First, negative feedback received from others can be attributed to prejudice against the group and therefore be discounted as irrelevant for the self. This is consistent with research suggesting that attributing negative outcomes to external causes protects self-esteem. In this way, overt prejudice, easily detected, is less damaging than subtle, disguised prejudice, which may in fact be more prevalent today (Crocker & Major, 1989). This mechanism can be used even in situations where prejudice is not operative, however, and thus may lead to distorted views of the self and one's abilities as compared to others. Praise received from a prejudiced source, on the other hand, would be especially valued.

Second, members of stigmatized groups tend to selectively compare themselves with other members of their own group. This may be due to proximity, perceived similarity, or the desire to avoid painful comparisons with more advantaged groups. Whatever the reason, these in-group comparisons allow the individual to protect self-esteem. As Crocker and Major (1989) point out, the degree of contentment we feel is relative to the comparison standard we use.

CRITICAL THINKING QUESTION

How might segregation contribute to maintenance of high self-esteem among African Americans? What might you expect to happen initially after the experience of integration? What might be the effect of integration on the self-esteem of individuals from the more advantaged group?

The third strategy is "selective devaluing," placing less emphasis and value on those things the group does poorly and more emphasis and value on those things the group does well. This is consistent with research that found that we tend to place those domains in which we are less competent on the periphery of the self, reserving the central core for those domains in which we do well (Harter, 1988). Individuals might even devalue an activity with which they have no personal experience, relying instead on stereotypes about the group. For example, a girl may decide—before ever having taken a high school math class—that she will not do well in math because she has "learned" that math and science are male domains (Crocker & Major, 1989, p. 617). For the same reason, she may also see these courses as unimportant for her and avoid taking math classes as much as possible or take the least challenging ones. Through a process of selective devaluing, then, we may define ourselves less by our weaknesses than by our strengths. Remember also, however, that some domains are considered to be so important by society that it may be difficult to completely relegate them to an unimportant position in the self-structure, or to avoid them. Instead, it may be more a case of overvaluing the domains in which one's group is viewed as successful.

Once again, we should reiterate that not all members of stigmatized groups use these mechanisms, or use them effectively, and that some members do have low self-esteem. Research suggests, however, that those who identify strongly with the group, and view group membership as central to their sense of self, are likely to use these protective strategies and therefore effectively protect their global self-esteem. Thus, an individual who possesses a strong sense of identity as an African American should have high self-esteem.

There may be other means by which the self-esteem of Blacks and other stigmatized groups is supported, in addition to the three self-protective strategies described above. Not all Blacks (or women, or whoever) accept the negative stereotype held by the dominant culture (Coultas, 1989). Rejection of the stereotype also protects self-esteem. Further, studies find that African Americans rely heavily on reflected appraisals from friends, family, and community as a basis for personal self-esteem (Hughes & Demo, 1989), placing less emphasis on the attitudes of the larger society (the generalized other). Thus, self-evaluations at the level of the microsystem may be more significant for self-esteem than stereotypes held at the level of the macrosystem.

Negative Side Effects of These Strategies

While the processes described above may protect overall self-esteem, their use may also pose some problems for the individual. First, attributing all negative feedback to prejudice denies the informational value of that feedback if, in fact, it is accurate. Thus, the self may become increasingly distorted and unrealistic. Second, in-group comparisons may give a false sense of one's abilities as compared to the general population. As a result, individuals may see no need to improve and thus have little motivation to work hard to enhance their skills. This may, in turn, limit opportunities for achievement and advancement outside the in-group setting. Third, devaluation of activities highly valued by the larger society and overemphasis on activities viewed as less important by the larger society may, in the long run, render the individual increasingly disadvantaged in competition with those from other groups. If all you can do is X, and the society values Y above all else, success in the larger society is unlikely. Further, lack of skill to do Y may be misinterpreted as an indication of low ability, rather than low motivation.

Self-Efficacy among Black Americans

Black Americans score relatively low on measures of self-efficacy (Hughes & Demo, 1989). This is an anomaly, in that self-esteem and self-efficacy are normally positively correlated. Primarily based on experiences in which the individual has had the opportunity to master a task, this aspect of the self may be more affected by the larger society, more reflective of social class, education, occupation, and income. As Hughes and Demo (1989, p. 153) conclude, "It is a product of one's location in the social order. . . . Discrimination has largely relegated Blacks to subordinate positions and excluded them from positions of power, resources, and contexts of action that afford individuals the best opportunities to experience themselves as powerful and autonomous." Thus, while the self-esteem of Black Americans seems relatively unaffected by attitudes of the larger society, self-efficacy is viewed as being more directly influenced by inequality among the races. However, limited research on limited samples of Blacks in primarily cross-sectional studies impairs our understanding of these effects. Clearly, more research is needed.

Identity Formation among Blacks

Does Marcia's identity status model apply to the development of identity among Black adolescents? Aries and Moorehead (1989) report on a preliminary attempt to extend this concept to include ethnicity. The authors feel that, having been developed and used exclusively on White samples, the existing identity status interview may not adequately address areas—such as ethnicity—in which Black adolescents explore and question before making commitments. Thus, an additional section was added to the interview to assess these issues. Unlike the findings among samples of White adolescents, in which the ideological and sexual-interpersonal areas have been reported to be of central importance, ethnicity and occupation were found to be the most important determinants of identity among their Black sample. In fact, ethnicity "was most predictive of over-all identity status and . . . was singled out most frequently as most important to self-definition" (Aries & Moorehead, 1989, p. 80). If the identity status approach is to be used in the study of Black development, the centrality of ethnicity as expressed in this preliminary research would argue for an extension of Marcia's model to include this issue.

Thus, while Marcia's approach may be useful in understanding the development of Whites, it may be inappropriate when the subjects are Black—missing aspects of their experience crucial to understanding the process of identity formation in this group. "Black adolescents are caught between the cross-currents of two sets of values, Afro-American characterized by 'openness to self and others, tragedy and resilience, psychological connectedness and interdependence' . . . and Euro-American, characterized by 'individualism, competition and establishing power, dominance and control' " (Aries & Moorehead, 1989, p. 76). They are, in other words, caught between the more collectivist subculture and the more individualist larger culture. The Eriksonian model—on which the identity status concept is based, with its emphasis on separation and individuation—fails to reflect the importance placed in much of the Black community on interdependence, connectedness, and cooperation. Clearly, additional research is needed to illuminate racial and ethnic variations in the development of the self.

Race, Ethnicity, and Socioeconomic Status

Negative experiences that begin early in life and last a long time may have a cumulative negative impact on developmental outcomes. Thus, the social and economic circumstances common to so many Blacks in the United States may take their toll on biological, social, and psychological growth. In comparison to the population as a whole, Blacks have shorter life expectancy at birth and greater rates of disability and mortality at every point in the life span except after age 80 (Jackson et al., 1990). (Further discussion of this is offered in Chapter 10.) According to a report released by the United Nations in 1992, Black men in Harlem have a life expectancy of only 46 years, lower than the figure for some Third World countries (Longworth, 1992). Health problems include higher rates of hypertension, heart disease, asthma, and other stress-related problems (Heckler, 1985). Access to health care is also limited by geography, economics, and a reluctance to visit doctors, so that disease is more likely to be detected at a later, more advanced stage (Griffin, Thomas, & Curry, 1991b). These factors are complicated by poor nutrition and the stress of poverty. Rates of psychiatric disorders are also higher (Bulhan, 1985). In addition, many Black children grow up without fathers and are victimized by the high levels of violence and the prevalence of drugs in the surrounding community. In terms of education, Black children, especially males, are more likely to be identified as behavior problems, to be labeled as retarded, and to begin a pattern of underachievement that leads to high dropout rates (Griffin, Thomas, & Curry, 1991a). This pattern is thought to reflect socioeconomic factors such as those cited above, as well as the lower expectations of teachers and a misunderstanding of the Black child's behavior, culture, and learning style (Wiley, 1990). Failure to achieve in the educational arena limits occupational opportunities and perpetuates the cycle of poverty.

In this way, the realities of poverty and discrimination undermine the content of the self and therefore performance and achievement. Thus, socioeconomic status interacts with racial and ethnic factors, making it difficult to disentangle the effects of one from the other. Because much of the research on racial and ethnic minorities is in fact based on low-income samples, findings of racial and ethnic differences may be contaminated by the effects of socioeconomic status. Thus, caution must be exercised not to generalize findings based on research on low-income ethnic group samples.

Ethnic Groups and Core Characteristics: Hispanics, Asian Americans, and Native Americans

The implications of ethnicity for the development of the self will vary depending on a number of factors, including how closely one identifies with one's ethnic group (Phinney, 1996). For those with strong ties, the norms, values, attitudes, and behaviors that typify the group may contribute to the development of related psychological characteristics. A number of researchers have offered descriptions of the core characteristics generally associated with various ethnic groups. For example, Marin and Marin (1991) describe Hispanics as characterized by high levels of interdependence, a willingness to make sacrifices for the welfare of the group, conformity, a strong sense of attachment and loyalty to the extended family, a desire to avoid conflict, clearly defined gender roles, obedience to authority figures, and a relatively flexible attitude toward time. Asian Americans also place great value on familial obligations, give greater priority to group as opposed to individual goals, and value harmony in relationships (Uba, 1994). Similarly, Native Americans emphasize group welfare and value generosity, cooperation, family, and community (Attneave, 1982; Bennett, 1994). The descriptions of these groups are consistent with the broad differences between collectivist and individualist cultures described earlier. It is important to remember, however, that all such generalizations must be viewed with caution because of the tremendous heterogeneity within all ethnic groups, the reality of cultural blending, and ongoing cultural change.

Concept Review 3.5

- Race/ethnicity affect identity formation, self-esteem, and self-efficacy.

- Global self-esteem among Black Americans is equal to or greater than that of Whites, while self-efficacy is lower.

- Stigmatized groups may use a variety of protective strategies to maintain self-esteem.

- A number of factors complicate the study of the implications of ethnicity for the development of the self. These include the confounding of ethnicity with socioeconomic status as well as the tremendous diversity found within commonly used ethnic categories.

Effect of Age on the Self

Patterns of Age-Related Change in Adult Personality

McCrae and colleagues (1999) report the results of cross-sectional studies of adult personality development from five cultures (Germany, Italy, Portugal, Croatia, and South Korea), compared with data from samples in the United States. Personality was assessed using the Revised NEO Personality Inventory (a 240-item questionnaire designed to assess six specific facets of each of the five major personality traits: neuroticism, extraversion, openness to experience, conscientiousness, and agreeableness—see Chapter 2), administered to 7,363 subjects ranging in age from 18 to 83. Across cultures, older subjects showed small but consistent declines in neuroticism, extraversion, and openness, and modest increases in agreeableness and conscientiousness. The rate of change was highest from age 18 to 30, with lower rates of subsequent change (consistent with Costa and McCrae's [1999] view that personality stabilizes around age 30). In general, older adults differed from late adolescents and younger adults in the following ways: better at controlling impulses and less emotionally volatile, lower in thrill seeking and cheerfulness, more morally responsible and attuned to social demands, and generally less open to new experiences. No significant gender differences were found in these general patterns. (See also a comparison of 12 cultures by Costa & McCrae, 1999).

The similarity of findings among diverse cultures with very different recent histories argues against a cultural (nurture) explanation of these age-related changes. Instead, the investigators contend the changes in personality are the result of the unfolding of a genetic timetable (nature), representing universal maturational changes in adult personality. McCrae and his associates allow the possibility that these trends may be due to cohort differences, perhaps the result of worldwide events exposing younger subjects to better nutrition and health care or to mass media and its nontraditional values. Longitudinal studies will help to sort out these effects.

Why would age-related changes in personality be genetically programmed? Arguing from an evolutionary psychology perspective, different traits may offer advantages at different points in the life span and therefore may have evolved to support adult roles and responsibilities. For example, these investigators suggest that extraversion and openness might be advantageous among younger individuals who are seeking a mate, while conscientiousness would be beneficial to parents raising children. In fact, perhaps society accommodates these maturational changes in personality by "reserving heavy responsibilities for midlife adults, whose levels of emotional stability, dependability, and altruism are sufficiently developed to handle the task" (p. 475). In support of this view, a study of over 130,000 adults ages 21 to 60 found that the greatest increases in conscientiousness occur in the 20s, while increases in agreeableness peak in the 30s, supporting adult requirements for success in work and parental roles (Srivastava, John, Gosling, & Potter, 2003). Openness declines slightly as we get older, consistent with a reduced interest in seeking new relationships in favor of fostering fewer, more intimate and supportive social ties (see Chapter 6). McCrae and associates conclude that the accumulating evidence suggests a lawful pattern of adult personality development regardless of time or place.

Maintaining Continuity of the Self

Does aging per se affect the self? Does the self affect aging? Here again, the literature seems to present a paradox. On the one hand are those who contend that the stresses and losses of old age contribute to significant changes in the self, particularly in self-esteem. The lack of socialization for the role of the elder, the many role losses experienced by older individuals, and the devaluation of the roles still available cause a drop in self-worth and a resulting loss of self-esteem (see, for example, Rosow, 1973). This view depicts aging as an identity crisis. On the other hand is the growing body of research suggesting that age is, in fact, not a significant aspect of the self-concept and therefore not a significant determinant of self-esteem. This literature finds, instead, remarkable stability in self-esteem and self-concept with increasing age.

Researchers in adult development and aging have become increasingly interested in how older adults maintain a positive sense of self and of well-being despite the losses associated with old age (Heidrich & Ryff, 1993). Referred to as the "paradox of happiness" and "the invulnerable self" (Baltes & Baltes, 1990; Costa & McCrae, 1984), empirical studies document that older adults maintain high levels of subjective health, well-being, and life satisfaction despite changes in roles, relationships, and physical health. Indeed, even the oldest-old (age 85 and over) appear to retain a consistent sense of self over time, despite the massive internal and external changes that accompany old age (Troll & Skaff, 1997). The aging self seems to be remarkably resilient (Brandtstadter & Greve, 1994). Let's examine some of this research more closely.

Heidrich and Ryff (1993) addressed this question as it pertained to the physical health domain in a study of 262 community-dwelling women age 65 and over. These women were comparable to elderly women throughout the United States in terms of marital status, living arrangements, and employment status, as well as in number (mean = 3.6) and type of health problems reported. The most common of these were arthritis (65 percent), cardiovascular disease (52 percent), hypertension (37 percent), hearing loss (30 percent), cataracts (24 percent), and osteoporosis (19 percent). In addition, 21 percent scored above the cutoff for clinical depression. Self-report measures of physical and mental health status and aspects of the self-system were obtained. Findings supported the researchers' hypothesis that the self-system can mediate the effect of physical health on mental health. In particular, psychological well-being (both greater perceptions of life satisfaction and decreased psychological distress) was related to the extent to which these women maintained a sense of themselves as an integrated part of a social structure, with meaningful and valuable roles, positive identification with the elderly as a reference group, and positive perceptions of normal behaviors in old age. Thus, despite increasing physical health problems, these subjects were able to maintain good adjustment.

Let's consider this phenomenon from a cognitive perspective. Individuals are viewed as active constructors and interpreters of reality who organize self-relevant information into self-schemas. Strong beliefs are resistant to change. When we confront information that is inconsistent with our prior beliefs, we tend to disregard and doubt the information or discredit the source.

We would expect most self-schemas (such as a schema of good health) to be especially well developed and strongly held by older adults because of their years of accumulated experience and knowledge of themselves (Markus & Herzog, 1991). As a result, they may be resistant to revision through accommodation except when new information is very discrepant with the existing self-schema and encountered repeatedly (Whitbourne, 1985). Cognitive theories of the self would predict, then, that the more novel an experience and the more suddenly and repeatedly it is encountered, the more likely it is to significantly affect the self. Because most age-related change is gradual and is perhaps viewed as normal and expected and because many people retain continuity in roles and relationships, the self is not seriously threatened. This may offer a partial explanation of the paradox of happiness.

Social integration—having meaningful and satisfying social roles and relationships—is one factor in the paradox of happiness and the ageless self. These women are involved in an Elder Hostel/Habitat program.

Mac Rae (1990) reports on a study of 142 elderly women (the mean age was 76.8 years), conducted by personal interview and participant observation with the subjects.* The approach was phenomenological in that an understanding of the women's subjective experience of aging was the goal. Mac Rae found that 74 percent of the women did not think of themselves as old and that age was not a significant factor in their sense of themselves. In other words, age per se did not rank high in the hierarchies of importance or pervasiveness in regard to self-concept. Kaufman's (1986) findings are consistent: the elderly tend to emphasize continuity of self over time and to feel the same way they always have, in general not thinking of themselves in a context of aging. She refers to this as the **ageless self.** This does not mean that the self is frozen in some earlier configuration, but rather that there is a core of "real me" that continues despite physical and social change. She quotes Percy, at age 92, in response to being asked if he thinks of himself as 92 (Kaufman, 1986, p. 11): "No. I have the same attitude now, toward life and living, as I did 30 years ago. That's why this idea of not being able to walk along with other people—I'm more slowed down—it hurts my ego. Because inside, that's not really me."

In contrast to what she calls the "identity crisis literature which focuses on 'role loss' in old age," Mac Rae (1990, p. 250) focuses on "the roles and relationships that are retained." She concludes that the most meaningful determinants of self among these women are their social involvements and social network. To the extent that these are maintained, the individual is protected from damaging changes in self-concept and self-esteem.

In particular, the roles of homemaker and mother remained salient aspects of identity for these women, as did personal attributes such as interpersonal skills and a sense of humor. The ability to get along well with others was an especially prized attribute, and to the extent that they felt this was characteristic, their self-worth was enhanced. Thus, while "'women's work' may not be highly appraised by society as a whole, it is highly valued by this group of women" (Mac Rae, 1990, p. 257). Those behaviors typically associated with the female expressive role (nurturing, warm behaviors toward others) may in fact, in old age, have advantages over the male instrumental role. Unless the female becomes incapacitated, her role as a nurturer appears to be available for a lifetime. Though the roles may be redefined, they are never entirely lost: "Roles based on nurturant functions are durable and expandable. They can last as long as life and enlarge as needed, for there is always someone around who needs taking care of" (Meyerhoff, 1978, p. 263). Among this sample of older women, then, interpersonal re-

*The synopsis of Mac Rae's views presented in this chapter is based on *Canadian Journal on Aging* (9[3], 1990), "Older Women and Identity Maintenance in Later Life," by H. Mac Rae. Copyright © University of Guelph. Used with permission.

lationships comprise a central and pervasive component of self. "'Doing for others' appeared to be an important dimension of their interpretation of the meaning of life and the part they are to play in it. . . . Self can be found in 'doing for others'" (Mac Rae, 1990, p. 263). One would expect that loss of this capacity to be of service might have devastating effects on these women.

What about the viability of the traditional instrumental role in old age? Meyerhoff (1978, p. 262) observed that Jewish women were "better at being old" than were Jewish men, because the latter's "lifelong involvement with instrumental activities [was not] viable after retirement." If his sense of self is based primarily on one major role (here, that of work) and that role is terminated (as in retirement), the male may experience confusion about his identity and place in society. Unless meaningful substitute activities can be found for the work role, the male's sense of self and self-worth may be threatened. Indeed, research suggests that the consequences of retirement vary significantly depending on the individual's preretirement adjustment and current circumstances. Those for whom the work role is overdeveloped, as Meyerhoff suggests was the case with his sample, may have a more difficult time adjusting. Those with more diverse role involvement and who maintain meaningful activities, on the other hand, may experience no negative consequences of retirement. (See Chapter 8 for a more complete discussion of this issue.)

In sum, then, continuity of familiar settings, roles, and relationships contributes to stability in the sense of self as one ages. The elderly women in Mac Rae's (1990) sample built their identities on relationships with others, and in this way "were able to maintain continuity amidst discontinuity, a stability or sameness of self, while at the same time negotiating the inevitable changes in self that are part and parcel of life as a series of ever-changing experiences. . . . Lifelong self-meaning was sustained" (p. 265). Though society may define them as "old," they resist defining themselves (or constructing their self-schemas) in this way and are usually successful in doing so. This is perhaps a more impressive accomplishment if one considers what Grambs (1989, p. 7) describes as the "continuous and ubiquitous" age grading in our society. In other words, "age is akin to race and sex—it is a visible attribute others use to disregard the person and treat her categorically" (Eisenhandler, 1990, p. 4). (Of course we must remember that this sample represents a particular cohort of elderly women. The extent to which these findings will be applicable to future cohorts whose lives may follow more nontraditional paths remains to be seen.) Discontinuity of roles and unfamiliar settings would be expected to have the opposite effect. It is only when the context changes or major disruptions in lifestyle occur that the sense of self is greatly undermined.

You're Only as Old as You Feel: The Impact of Subjective Age

Definitions of age are legal, social (see Chapter 2 for a discussion of the social age clock and age norms), and subjective. Here, I wish to pursue the subjective experience of age. Surely one's felt age is influenced by legal and social definitions (the age at which one can vote or drive or the age at which it seems most appropriate to marry and have children). Yet as we have just seen, **subjective age** is sometimes independent of, or at least resistant to, these influences. The literature seems scant on the subject of "lived experience" (Keller, Leventhal, & Larson, 1989). In other words, we know little about what growing old means to the people actually experiencing it. Some authors have suggested that personal journals of later life offer a rich source of this information and ought to be studied (Berman, 1991). A personal journal is a genre of writing in which the inner life of the author is the prime subject matter, as opposed to a journal or diary of a military campaign or other specific experience. Berman describes some excellent published examples and points out that personal journals of older people ought to be of special interest to gerontologists "since they exemplify individuals' efforts to maintain a coherent life story despite the physical and social losses that accompany aging" (p. 35). A beautiful example of this perspective is found in the following excerpt from Elizabeth Vining's *Being Seventy* (1978, p. 5):

> Being seventy is not a matter of a single day. It takes a year; it is not finished until one is seventy-one. And so I think I shall pay special attention to this new year as it turns, keep a journal of its changes and insights, of the things I do or think for the first time because I am the age I am, and of those things I do for the last time or enjoy less keenly, of the compensations as well as the diminishments, and of the unexpected delights—for I am sure that there will be flowers in this landscape that do not grow elsewhere, and glimpses of unforeseen heights.

CRITICAL THINKING QUESTION

How could the personal journal be used by those who work with the elderly? What benefit might there be for the journal writer as well as for the reader? How does the genre of personal journal fit with Butler's concept of the life review (see Chapter 2)?

What do these experts teach us about their experience of aging? First, when does one develop a "sense of aging" (Sarason, 1977), of feeling old? As Grambs (1989, p. 9) notes, these "moments of changed awareness" occur at different points for different people. As we have seen, good health pushes the awareness of physical aging upward, whereas disabling illness can make even chronologically young people feel old, as well as making them appear old to others. Are you, then, only as old as you feel physically? Not exactly. Chronological age does contribute to felt or subjective age, but the relationship between the two is somewhat loose. Vining (1978a, p. 4), age 70, comments, "It isn't as if I feel old. I don't. Inside I feel often as gauche, as shy, as incapable of wise or effective action as I did at sixteen, or as surprised and delighted by unexpected beauty." On the other hand, I remember a faculty colleague, a dear friend with whom I had shared an office area for years, who one day realized he was the oldest person on the faculty. I remember being so surprised, saying it could not possibly be true, what about so and so, or so and so. Our joint review of the faculty directory eventually confirmed his original statement. At that moment, he became old in his own eyes. He retired the next spring, saying he guessed "it was time." Had he discovered others older than he, would he have felt this way? "Feeling" old is a product of many factors, including social comparison (as in this case), physical health status, role involvement, and age norms.

Patterns in Subjective Age

Montepare and Lachman (1989) describe patterns in subjective age among males and females from adolescence to old age. Figure 3.4 summarizes their findings. Note that adolescents generally hold older-age identities (that is, their subjective age is greater than their chronological age), those in early adulthood hold same-age identities, and the older one gets, the greater the discrepancy between chronological and subjective age.

FIGURE 3.4 *Age Identities for Men and Women across the Life Span*

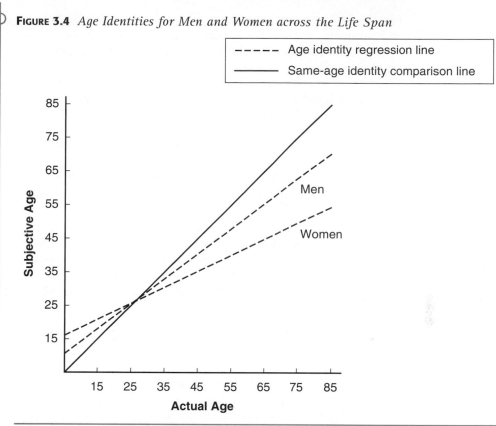

Note: The solid line represents the convergence of actual chronological age and subjective age (that is, for example, a 25-year-old feels 25 years old). The dotted lines represent Montepare and Lachman's findings in regard to the relationship between actual age and subjective age. Their research suggests that, except in the mid-20s, there is a discrepancy between an individual's chronological age and subjective age.

Source: J. Montepare and M. Lachman (1989). " 'You're Only as Old as You Feel': Self-Perceptions of Age, Fears of Aging, and Life Satisfaction from Adolescence to Old Age." *Psychology and Aging, 4,* p. 75. Copyright 1989 by the American Psychological Association. Reprinted by permission.

Beyond the early adult years, adults generally hold younger-age identities. (Barnes-Farrell and Piotrowski, 1989, found the mean discrepancy to be 5.6 years.) Further, note that the discrepancy is greater for women than for men. Ramifications for life satisfaction are not clear at this point, but what this and other similar studies tell us is that subjective age varies over the life span and appears to change in systematic ways. Once again, most older adults do not generally think of themselves as "old."

A number of studies suggests that individuals have "a fluctuating awareness of growing older" (Keller, Leventhal, & Larson, 1989, p. 81). In other words, age identity may not be stable, but episodic, varying with changing circumstances. When asked what kinds of things have made or might make them feel old, Mac Rae's respondents cited illness, disability, times of loneliness, death of a friend or loved one, or situations in which they were around young people. This concept is clearly exemplified in the following passages from May Sarton's (1988, p. 35) journal: "The stroke has made me take a leap into old age, instead of approaching it gradually." Her recovery changes felt age once again: "I am no longer the very old woman with a very old dog I was all spring and summer" (p. 188). These changes in age identity are partly the result of external events (here, a stroke), but also of the individual's cognitive evaluation of their meaning and significance. Threats to health signal aging in that they suggest social isolation, dependency, or a loss of roles. Once again, we see the I-self constructing the Me-self.

Sharon Kaufman has focused on the experience of illness in late life, especially the effect of chronic illness on the sense of self (see, for example, Kaufman, 1988). Through in-depth interviews of 64 stroke patients, she found that aging per se was not the most important aspect of the illness experience or the recovery process. Instead, problems centered on three issues (Kaufman, 1993): adjusting to changes in normal life patterns and routines that had been characteristic of the self prior to the stroke; a feeling of being different from one's former self as a result of the stroke; the failure to return to "normal" even in cases where there was no apparent remaining physical disability; and, most important, a need to redefine the self to incorporate the stroke experience. Completion of the last task signaled recovery for these subjects, while improvements in actual functional ability did not. Kaufman stresses that illness must be understood in terms of its meaning to the individual. This, again, is the phenomenological view. The self provides the framework for dealing with life events, including the aftermath of a serious illness.

Correlates of an Older-Age Identity

Aside from health, what are the other correlates of an older-age identity? The list includes being treated as old by others, negative comparisons with peers (perceiving oneself as worse off than others), loss of control, loss of a friend or loved one through death, retirement, and cognitive changes such as forgetfulness (Keller et al., 1989).

Eisenhandler (1990) presents a fascinating study of the possession of a driver's license as a disidentifier of old age. Older adults show great resistance to giving up their legal driving privileges—even though they will impose limits on themselves—to avoid the stigma of being "too old to drive." The driver's license is a symbol "widely understood as indicative of competency and adulthood in society" (p. 2). In addition, it represents independence and access to social roles and activities. In other words, it contributes to a sense of control over one's life. Even if it goes unused, the driver's license "protects the older adult from public or personal disruption of identity" (p. 4). The privilege of driving is eagerly awaited by teenagers in our society and reluctantly given up by older adults. As Eisenhandler points out, "The automobile is dear to older Americans because it is literally and figuratively a vehicle that transports the self" (p. 10).

CRITICAL THINKING QUESTION

What are the arguments pro and con for restricting driving privileges by age? What kinds of information would you need before you could make an informed decision on this issue?

Subjective Experience of Age: Positive or Negative

Finally, how do the majority of older people evaluate aging as a stage in life? Do their conceptions confirm or deny the generally negative stereotype of age? A number of studies have found that community-dwelling individuals have a generally positive outlook on this stage in their lives, accompanied by a realistic understanding of the problems and limitations that present themselves (Keller et al., 1989; Connidis, 1989). A negative outlook results from an accumulation of hardships, setbacks, losses, and disappointments. Specifically, the subjective experience of age is affected by a number of variables, including marital status (married people are happier, more satisfied, less lonely), level of expectations about being older (whether old age is better or worse than you thought it would be), financial status, number of children (the more children, the less worry about aging), and gender (women worry more about aging than men do, probably due to realistic concerns about loneliness and money) (Connidis, 1989). If most people do not think of themselves as old, this may be because, in their eyes, they do not fit the negative stereotype of being sick, dependent, and isolated. Also thought to be important, though not given much attention in the research literature, is a sense of purpose or meaning in life (see Chapter 11), and the extent to which the individual's life circumstances facilitate or undermine this (McCarthy, 1983; George & Clipp, 1991). In short, aging seems to be a generally positive experience for the majority of people, who apparently feel a sense of success and control over the changes associated with their chronological age.

It is important to remember one of the six key tenets of life-span theory: at all points in the life span, development includes both gains and losses. Are there benefits to the self in aging? Surely opportunities for continued growth exist. New roles may emerge—for example, grandparenthood. Carl Jung and Abraham Maslow, among others, portrayed the second half of life as providing the opportunity to work toward individuation and self-actualization, a deeper understanding of oneself and one's place in and relationship with the world and others. Perhaps accumulating knowledge and freedom from competing roles enable people to develop a kind of expertise in regard to the self. Stewart and Ostrove (1998) describe a clearer sense of identity and a greater sense of personal authority and efficacy, even exuberance, among samples of middle-aged women. Similarly, in a study of three cohorts of college-educated women currently in their 20s, 40s, and 60s, Zucker, Ostrove, and Stewart (2002) found increased identity certainty with age, along with higher levels of generativity and a sense of personal power, paired with lower levels of personal distress. The authors suggest that "rather than marking a period of decline, the 60s may be a time of considerable psychological well-being" (p. 242).

Personal journals of aging individuals contain numerous comments about increasing self-knowledge and self-acceptance, a lessening of concern with evaluation by others, of being better aware of one's qualities and strengths and better able to use them effectively—in general, of being more fully oneself. These capacities would certainly bring to the later years a sense of fulfillment and meaning, an opportunity to enjoy life intrinsically. As Vining (1978, p. 55) says, "At seventy I can afford to be an observer. I am out of the struggle. I no longer have to prove anything. I can enjoy the thing-in-itself, whatever it is, without regard to the prestige value or the effect that it may have on my career." Shneidman (1989, p. 684) describes the 70s as a potential Indian summer, "a period of relatively mild weather for both soma and psyche in the late autumn or the early winter of life, a decade of greater independence and increased opportunities for further self-development." It is important to understand the inaccuracy of the stereotype of aging for the majority of people and take into account the strengths and competencies, developed over a lifetime, that allow them to successfully confront the challenges of the later years. We should also recognize the circumstances that cause people to feel old and that undermine their sense of self and their ability to lead satisfying and productive lives. As discussed in Chapter 1, as we move toward a more age-irrelevant society, the meaning and significance of age for the self will change as well. As Kastenbaum (1995, p. 37) says, "It is becoming clear that at least some of us can do and be almost anything at any time in our lives."

Let's summarize the major points. First, aging can be a positive experience, a negative experience, or both, and the quality of the experience can and does fluctuate over time. As Neugarten (1977) pointed out long ago, age is an "empty variable." It is not time per se, but the events associated with the passage of time and the meanings individuals attach to them that are relevant. Thus, variables other than chronological age have greater impact on the self. Among these are health, finances, marital status, and role involvement. Second, the stereotype of old age is largely inaccurate. Most older people— estimates range as high as 80 to 90 percent (Butt & Beiser, 1987)—are well and independent and do not think of themselves as old. Aging happens so gradually that most people are not terribly aware of it until the late 70s. Because we tend to grow older in familiar surroundings and have learned to meet the demands they present, and because core aspects of the self have stabilized and we know ourselves well, we tend to see ourselves as we have always been—in a sense, "ageless." The research indicates that life stage or life events may tell us more about what is going on in a person's life than chronological age per se, and it may be more useful to group people for research purposes on these criteria in order to study their impact on attitudes toward the self (Bengtson et al., 1985). Finally, development throughout the life span includes gains as well as losses.

Impact of Age on Self-Esteem

At this point, there is no consensus in the research literature on the trajectory of self-esteem over the life span. Most studies of age differences in self-esteem have focused on childhood and adolescence, with few examining the pattern of development in adulthood and old age. Likely due to limitations in sample selection and data collection methods, the latter have produced inconsistent findings. While most show gradual increases in self-esteem throughout adulthood, others have found increases until old age, followed by either a leveling off or a decline in the later years of life. To address gaps in the research literature, Robins, Trzesniewski, Tracy, Gosling, and Potter (2002) examined age differences in self-esteem using cross-sectional data from a diverse group of 326,641 individuals age 9 to 90 collected over the Internet. The effects of gender, socioeconomic status, ethnicity, and nationality (U.S. versus non-U.S. citizens) were also considered. They found increasing levels of self-esteem throughout adulthood across essentially all demographic groups, peaking for most in the mid-60s, followed by a sharp decline around age 70. The results suggest "other than childhood, the mid-60s seem to represent the apex of self-esteem across the life course" (p. 430). The authors cite Erikson, Levinson, Jung, Neugarten, and social role theories as providing a theoretical explanation of these findings of high self-esteem in midlife. The essence of this perspective is captured by Gove, Ortega, and Style (1989, p. 1122):

> During the productive adult years, when persons are engaged in a full set of instrumental and social roles, their sense of self will reflect the fullness of this role repertoire . . . and there will be high levels of instrumentality, competitiveness and socioemotional support. Levels of life satisfaction and self-esteem will also be high.

How do we explain the drop in self-esteem found in late adulthood? After considering a number of possible explanations, such as role losses and changes in physical health, or limitations in the study such as cohort effects, the authors suggest an alternative perspective. They again turn to Erikson, Jung, Neugarten, Levinson, and others who suggest that older individuals, wiser and more accepting of their faults and limitations, have less need for self-promotion and self-aggrandizement. Thus, what appears as a drop in self-esteem may instead reflect a less inflated, more modest and balanced view of the self.

As indicated earlier, the majority of studies show either no age differences in global self-esteem among people living independently in the community or higher self-esteem among older cohorts (Bengtson et al., 1985). This is interpreted to mean that older cohorts started out with higher self-esteem than younger cohorts and/or that self-acceptance and self-worth are maintained or increase with age. A review of the formula for self-esteem given earlier may help us to understand how the latter might occur. Remember that there are two ways to raise self-esteem. The first is to improve the self-concept through doing more things better and placing greater value on the things one does well. People do become more skilled as they mature and more selective in their activities. This contributes to self-esteem. The second way is to decrease one's pretensions, to adjust one's goals, to become more realistic in one's aspirations (Brandtstadter & Greve, 1994; Rothermund & Brandtstadter, 2003b). This also results from maturity and accumulated experience.

Baltes and Baltes (1990) have offered a general model of adaptation, called **selective optimization with compensation** (SOC), which captures this idea and may help us understand how older people, faced with losses in many domains of their lives, nevertheless maintain a positive sense of self. According to the SOC model, "successful development is defined . . . as the maximization of gains (desirable goals or outcomes) and the minimization of losses (undesirable goals or outcomes)" (Baltes, Staudinger, & Lindenberger, 1999, p. 482). SOC suggests that when individuals encounter losses, such as those experienced with aging, they select the most important goals and focus their efforts on optimizing performance in these areas and finding ways to compensate for functional losses, while withdrawing from less important activities. Baltes (1997) points out that selection and compensation become increasingly important as we age in order to maintain acceptable levels of functioning and to progress in those activities most important to us. He describes an everyday example often used to illustrate this model. When the famous concert pianist Arthur Rubinstein was 80, he was asked how he was able to maintain his high level of piano playing. He answered that he played fewer pieces (selection), practiced them more often (optimization), and gave the audience the impression of playing speed by slowing down just before a fast segment of a piece (compensation).

We should remember the multidimensional nature of self-esteem. Age may affect one dimension or subdimension without affecting the others, though most research ignores this and focuses on global or overall self-esteem. Conceivably, then, one could suffer losses in some less important areas of self-esteem that would not significantly alter overall feelings of worth. On the other hand, losses in other critical domains might have disastrous effects.

Defenses Used to Protect the Self

As we have repeatedly seen, physical and mental well-being seem to depend on the extent to which an individual can find ways to maintain an overall positive view of the self (Markus & Herzog, 1991). Therefore, we should consider the strategies the I-self might use to defend the Me-self. Keep in mind that not everyone uses all of these and that some people may be more proficient in their use than others.

First, we control information about our pasts through repression and other mechanisms that allow us to remember what we want to remember (selective recall). Second, we tend to give more weight to what we think about ourselves and to discount conflicting feedback from others who do not know us as well. After all, who knows us better than we do? We may, in fact, attribute negative feedback to prejudice against older adults. Third, we may not apply negative stereotypes to ourselves, though we may have learned them and apply them to others. (I remember my 80-year-old father-in-law, one of the first drivers' ed teachers in our state, talking about "older" drivers disparagingly.) In other words, we engage in selective comparisons that assess ourselves favorably in relation to others (Heidrich & Ryff, 1993).

Fourth, we interact selectively in situations and with people who make us feel comfortable and support our self-theory, avoiding negative relationships and situations that threaten our competence. In other words, we pick our niches. (This may partially explain the appeal of a "retirement community.") Fifth, even if we no longer actively engage in a particular role, we may still identify closely with it. For example, the retired teacher may still think of herself as a teacher (Atchley, 1980). Sixth, we discount the importance of domains in which we are not competent (Harter, 1988) and may place more emphasis on our areas of expertise. (We discussed selective devaluing earlier in our discussion of self-protective mechanisms used by stigmatized groups.) Seventh, we tend to take more credit for our successes than our failures (Harter, 1988). Eighth, we tend to organize our self-concept in such a way that the central core elements of the self are positive attributes, while the more peripheral, least important elements are the negative attributes (Harter, 1988). Thus, we accentuate the positive. Harter also found that we tend to think of our positive qualities as personality traits, and therefore stable and enduring qualities of the real self, while our negative qualities are viewed as more ephemeral, fleeting behaviors not truly characteristic of the real self. Through these and perhaps other mechanisms, the individual may be able to retain a positive sense of self over time.

Causes of Low Self-Esteem in Late Adulthood

Up to this point, we have been talking about people who have had relatively high self-esteem throughout their lives, and the effect of the aging process on their sense of self. But some people have suffered from low self-esteem all their lives. If this is the case, they are unlikely to develop more positive self-images in late adulthood. This is partly due to the nature of forces maintaining the self as it is, and partly due to ageism and the real losses that occur during this period.

Others, however, experience a drop in self-esteem in their later years. This is most likely to be a result of significant losses, such as the loss of physical capacity (especially if it is sudden and disrupts favored activities) and loss of control. As we saw in the studies of stroke patients, time may permit these individuals to adjust, to cope effectively, and to employ self-protective strategies so that the loss of self-esteem may be moderated.

CRITICAL THINKING QUESTION

How might placement in a nursing home affect people's ability to defend their sense of self, particularly in regard to selective interaction and control?

Concept
Review
3.6

- There appear to be lawful and universal patterns of adult personality develop-ment in regard to the five major personality traits.

- Older adults, including the oldest-old, normally retain a consistent and pri-marily positive sense of self despite the realities of aging.

- Subjective age is influenced less by chronological age than by health, age norms, and role involvement.

- Contrary to the stereotype, the majority of studies find either no differences in self-esteem among older and younger adults or higher self-esteem among the older groups.

- Older individuals may defend their sense of self in a variety of ways, including selective optimization with compensation.

REVIEW QUESTIONS

Defining the Self

1. What does James mean by the I-self and the Me-self?
2. What explanation has been offered for the half-century delay in research related to the self following the publication of William James's *Principles of Psychology?*
3. The self has been defined as a social product. How do the contributions of Charles Cooley and George Herbert Mead help us to under-stand the role of others in the formation of the individual's sense of self?

The Self-Concept: The Cognitive Theory of Self

1. How does the self-schema influence our pro-cessing of self-relevant information?
2. If individuals rely heavily on accommodation when faced with new self-relevant informa-tion, will their self-concept be more likely to remain stable or to change?
3. Discuss the hierarchy of pervasiveness and the hierarchy of importance as they relate to the organization of the self-concept.
4. How might a high need for cognitive closure affect the formation of the self?

Self-Esteem: The Assessment of One's Worth

1. What are the primary determinants of self-esteem?

2. Based on Atchley's formula, describe two ways to raise self-esteem.
3. According to Greenberg et al., what is the psychological function of self-esteem?

I Think I Can; I Think I Can: A Look at Self-Efficacy

1. Bandura has identified four sources of self-efficacy beliefs. Which does he feel is most important?
2. What are the differences between those high and low in self-efficacy?

Identity: Who Am I and Where Am I Going?

1. What are the three key components of iden-tity, according to Erikson?
2. According to Marcia's model, on what basis is an individual assigned an identity status?
3. Compare and contrast Marcia's four identity statuses.
4. What are some of the concerns about the identity status model?

The Self in Cross-Cultural Perspective

1. Identify some of the ways the collectivist-individualist dimension of culture might affect the nature and development of the self.

Women, Men, and Identity Formation

1. Discuss the nature of the expressive and instrumental gender roles. Which of the two has higher status in our culture?
2. What difficulties do men and women face as a result of these gender roles?
3. Why is the male model of development considered to be inappropriate in describing female psychological development?

Race/Ethnicity and the Development of the Self

1. How does the self-esteem of African Americans compare with that of White Americans? How do researchers explain this?
2. What protective strategies do stigmatized groups use? What problems can arise from these strategies?
3. What are the possible ramifications of the lower self-efficacy found among Black as compared to White Americans?
4. Why must we be cautious about conclusions based on studies of low-income minority samples?

5. Summarize the core characteristics associated with Hispanics, Asian Americans, and Native Americans.

Effect of Age on the Self

1. How does adult personality change in relation to the five major personality traits?
2. Discuss research findings relative to the concept of the "ageless self."
3. What kinds of experiences make people feel old?
4. How do most older people feel about their aging?
5. Define *subjective age*. What pattern has been found in the relationship between subjective age and chronological age?
6. What happens to self-esteem with age, and how is this explained?
7. What defenses are used to protect the self?
8. What kinds of experiences are likely to lead to low self-esteem in late life?

Key Terms

accommodating, 80
ageless self, 112
assimilating, 80
cognitive closure, 82
cognitive permanence, 82
cognitive urgency, 82
collectivist cultures, 96
ego identity versus role
    confusion, 91
equilibration, 80
expressive role, 100
gender, 100
gender identity, 100
gender role, 100

generalized other, 78
global self-esteem, 85
hierarchy of importance, 83
hierarchy of pervasiveness, 83
identity, 91
identity achievement, 93
identity diffusion, 92
identity foreclosure, 93
identity moratorium, 93
identity statuses, 92
individualist cultures, 97
instrumental role, 100
I-self, 76
looking glass self, 77

Me-self, 76
phenomenal self, 76
schemas, 80
selective optimization with
    compensation, 119
self, 75
self-concept, 76
self-efficacy, 87
self-esteem, 84
self-reference effect, 81
self-schema, 81
sex, 100
subjective age, 113

4 Cognitive Processes in Adulthood, Part 1
Dimensions and Directions

IT WAS THE END OF THE SECOND SEMESTER of my freshman year. I had taken a particularly heavy course load that term and, like most freshmen, had begun to find my way around campus life, becoming involved in a lot of activities. I had a part-time job and a busy social life, and I played bridge in every spare moment. I was not sleeping much, pulling a lot of all-nighters, living on caffeine and nicotine. Burning the candle at both ends. From what I can piece together, it was early on the morning of my last final—a four-hour exam for a five-credit class in world history. I had been doing very well in the class and had studied hard for this exam. My best friend's mom was going to pick us up later that day for the 10-hour drive home, so in addition to taking finals, I had been busy getting packed up for the summer, closing up that year of my life to go back home. In retrospect, I know I was completely exhausted.

Suddenly, it was like someone pulled the plug on the computer. Everything went blank. I completely lost my memory for all the material I had been preparing for days. It was a surreal experience—like the academic computer files I had been working with went down temporarily and could not be accessed. And it was weird, because I knew who I was, and where I was, and what was happening around me, but I could not concentrate or focus, and I had this sense that if I took that exam, I would be capable of nothing but a blank piece of paper. Friends on my floor in the dorm came to the rescue, calling my professor and making arrangements for me to take the exam later that day. I remember someone insisting that I drink a glass of orange juice. To this day, I am not sure what happened, but I learned an important life lesson about limits. I was so badly frightened that I have never forgotten it. So although I still push myself hard and have a complex life, I am careful not to exceed them. And . . . I have an incredible curiosity about the workings of the human mind.

Well, you know what they say: "Live and learn." "Experience is the best teacher." I learned a lot from the experience described above—valuable lessons about myself, about friendship, and about priorities. The capacity to learn and remember is essential if individuals are to function effectively and continue to grow and develop. Imagine what it would be like if at some point in the life span human beings lost these abilities. What if they could no longer benefit from the lessons of their own experience, acquire new skills, or improve others? What if they couldn't learn the name of a new neighbor, remember the birthday of a grandchild, plan a trip to Europe, learn to use a new computer, improve their tennis game? Knowledge would be frozen. Formal and informal education would cease. The ability to adapt to changes in the environment would be lost. The same mistakes would be repeated. Fortunately, learning is not restricted to any age. Even elderly adults remain very active learners (Kausler, 1994).

What if these mental abilities weren't lost altogether, but rather changed with age? What would these changes be, and what might cause them? Might some abilities decline? Might others improve? Might new mental capacities emerge in adulthood? At what ages would these changes be likely to occur? And how would they affect individual behavior and development?

These and related questions have great importance for psychologists, as well as for each of us individually and collectively, given the rate of technological change and the demographic realities of an aging society. How will adults function in the world of the future? How can society make best use of their abilities and talents? What are the implications for the workforce, the economy, family life, individual fulfillment? How can we maintain and perhaps even enhance learning, memory, and problem-solving skills over the life span? These are the issues we begin to address in the following pages.

A Life-Span View of Cognitive Development

This chapter deals with the convergence of two major perspectives in psychology—cognitive psychology and life-span development. In doing so, it addresses the first of two fundamental questions: What happens to the mental abilities of normal individuals as they move through adult life? Chapter 5 will then examine theoretical perspectives on the second of these questions: What factors influence the course of adult cognition and in what ways? The research literature on aging and cognitive functioning is voluminous and increasing rapidly (Salthouse, 1991b). This chapter will highlight some of the significant findings and identify new theories on cognitive aging. We begin with an introduction to cognitive psychology.

Evolution of Cognitive Psychology

The Cognitive Revolution

The modern scientific study of cognitive issues—the *cognitive revolution*—can be traced to the mid- to late 1950s. During this period, a number of influences converged to shift psychology's research focus from overt behavior to a reemphasis on the importance of mental activity (Ashcraft, 1989; Bourne, 1992). These included dissatisfaction with behaviorism, the invention of the computer, and important discoveries by Miller (1956) and others in memory research. The outcome was **cognitive psychology,** the branch of psychology concerned with the scientific study of mental processes and activities, which today constitutes one of the key research areas in the field.

Broadly defined, **cognition** refers to the mental processes and activities we use in perceiving, remembering, and thinking and to the act of using those processes (Ashcraft, 1989). Cognitive psychology can be thought of as part of a larger network of scientific endeavor, sometimes referred to collectively as *cognitive science.* It is contributing to as well as benefiting from progress made in related fields, particularly neuroscience (which studies the structure and function of the nervous system) and neuropsychology (which attempts to understand the relationship between the nervous system and behavior). The ramifications of these research activities for our understanding of the mind—the mental processes and activities that are the province of cognitive psychology—are potentially immense.

Four Approaches within Cognitive Psychology

Cognitive psychologists approach the study of mental processes from different points of view. Some subscribe to an organismic perspective, others hold a more mechanistic view, while still others see development contextually. We touched on these three major theoretical models in Chapter 2. Let's apply them now to the study of cognitive development, and also review a fourth approach to this aspect of development—that of psychometrics.

Organismic Model. Piaget is the best-known cognitive representative of the organismic perspective (Piaget & Inhelder, 1969). In the organismic model, cognitive development is understood to proceed through a series of sequential, universal stages, tied to age and dictated by a genetic timetable, with each stage representing a qualitative change in cognitive ability. The source of development is thus primarily internal, within the organism, who is viewed as actively involved in constructing knowledge and adapting to the environment.

Mechanistic Model. Mechanists, on the other hand, view individual cognitive development as environmentally determined. The mind is written on by experience as if it were a blank sheet of paper. The individual is passive in this process, like a machine responding to external direction. And, because each of us experiences the environment differently, no universals in development exist. Cognitive change is viewed as age-irrelevant and quantitative in nature. Mechanistic views rely heavily on behaviorism and the work of Pavlov, Watson, and Skinner. More recent work by Bandura (1977b) and others has led to a modified mechanistic stance, which acknowledges some active cognitive involvement on the part of the individual.

Contextual Model. This approach, represented by the work of Baltes, Dittmann-Kohli, and Dixon (1984) as well as the Soviet scholar Vygotsky (1978), conceives of cognitive development as the result of a complex, reciprocal interaction between the individual's genetic nature and the various layers of the social, cultural, and historical environment. The complexity of this interaction results in great variability among individuals in all aspects of development. As a result, individuals will differ from each other in regard to the nature, direction, and timing of cognitive development.

While the organismic stage approach to cognitive development is no longer as preeminent as it once was (see Chapter 2 for an evaluation of stage theory in general), its notion of the individual as an active processor of information is central to current thinking in cognitive psychology (Ashcraft, 1989). Individuals are not blank slates that passively and uncritically accept whatever the environment presents to them. Instead, they are thinking, learning creatures by nature, intrinsically motivated to adapt to the environment. Their cognitive structures dictate both what they notice and how it is interpreted (Flavell, 1996). And despite the fact that cognitive psychology therefore explicitly rejects the behaviorists' mechanistic view of people as passive, reactive machines, it nonetheless recognizes the critical importance of environmental determinants of behavior. In acknowledging the role of both nature and nurture, the contextual model integrates important elements of the two earlier models, while extending our appreciation of the complex interaction among these influences. The contextual approach is becoming increasingly influential and is the model this book adopts.

Psychometric Approach. **Psychometrics** refers to the use of tests to measure psychological characteristics. The psychometric approach to the study of cognition differs from the others in that it is not really a theoretical approach (it makes no assumptions about the nature and origin of cognition, for example), but rather a method of describing cognitive performance through standardized measurement tools (Perlmutter, 1988). Traceable to their late-19th-century origins in Galton's unsuccessful attempts, intelligence tests have a long, complex, and controversial history. Among researchers in the psychometric tradition, Cattell (1963) and Horn (1982) have contributed the concepts of fluid and crystallized intelligence, discussed in a later section. Psychometric studies have generated a tremendous amount of valuable descriptive data about the cognitive performance of individuals across the life span.

Defining Adult Intelligence

Though it is one of the most widely used terms in psychology—as well as everyday life—the meaning of *intelligence* is controversial. Long-standing arguments exist over whether intelligence consists of a general ability (which, if you have a lot of it, would be of benefit in almost all cognitive tasks) or independent abilities (suggesting that you may be strong in some cognitive areas, weak in others, and so on). For example, Howard Gardner (1983, 1998, 1999) has described eight different intelligences (see Table 4.1) and suggested two others (spiritual and existential). The extent to which heredity and environment contribute to intelligence, and in what ways, is also disputed.

CRITICAL THINKING QUESTION

Assume that you are a superintendent of a public school system. Your district is reviewing its testing and assessment procedures to more accurately identify student strengths and weaknesses. Based on Gardner's view of intelligence presented in Table 4.1, how would you approach the assessment of intelligence? Would you continue to use standardized intelligence tests? Why or why not? Are there other measures you would want to implement?

TABLE 4.1 *Gardner's (1983, 1999) Frames of Mind*

Howard Gardner opposes the view that intelligence consists of a general ability that can be assessed on the basis of traditional intelligence tests. Instead, he has proposed that there are eight different intelligences, based in different parts of the brain and following different developmental trajectories. As a species, we have evolved so that we can analyze a number of different kinds of information. Each of us possesses all of these ways of thinking, though to varying degrees. So, an individual is likely to be stronger in some areas than in others, and areas of strength and weakness will differ from person to person. Standard IQ tests rely heavily on the first two intelligences described below: logical-mathematical and linguistic. These will probably sound familiar to you. The other six may surprise you. Gardner believes that we have erred by conceptualizing intelligence too narrowly, failing to recognize and develop other valuable forms of thought. His eight frames of mind are briefly described below, along with some careers that might utilize each strength. Of course, most tasks rely on combinations of these forms of intelligence.

Logical-mathematical intelligence: Often labeled as "scientific thinking," logical-mathematical intelligence refers to the type of thought used to solve math and science problems. It is linear and analytic. Scientists, mathematicians, physicians.

Linguistic intelligence: The ability to use language fluently. A poet is one example of a person who can use words to convey thoughts and feelings exceptionally well. Writers, translators, attorneys.

Visual/spatial intelligence: The ability to accurately perceive and remember visual stimuli, to find one's way around in space, to understand how space is organized, and to mentally transform three-dimensional objects. Artists, engineers, city planners, sculptors, navigators.

Musical intelligence: The ability to understand and produce music. Musicians, composers, conductors.

Bodily/kinesthetic intelligence: The ability to understand and use the body effectively. Athletes, dancers, surgeons, craftspeople.

Naturalistic intelligence: The ability to understand patterns in the natural world. Biologists, geologists, oceanographers.

Interpersonal intelligence: Refers to the ability to understand others, to know what motivates them, to read their cues, intentions, and desires. Politicians, teachers, therapists, salespeople.

Intrapersonal intelligence: Knowledge of one's own inner workings, having access to one's own feelings. This is a most private form of intelligence and is only apparent through language, music, or some other form of expression. Actors, spiritual leaders.

Within the field of psychology, intelligence has, for all practical purposes, come to be defined by the tests that measure it. In other words, intelligence has become equated with a score on an intelligence test. These tests, beginning with the Binet-Simon in 1905, were primarily intended to measure children's academic ability. Intelligence defined in this way refers to the degree to which one has the kind of academic skills children need to succeed in school, such as verbal and mathematical ability—but ignores such abilities as creativity. A very narrow definition indeed.

This use of the term *intelligence* becomes even more problematic when applied to adults. Academic intelligence is widely thought to be a poor reflection of the breadth of mental skills necessary to be successful in daily adult life (Baltes, Dittmann-Kohli, & Dixon, 1984). Cognitive competence in school might tap different cognitive abilities than cognitive competence in a sales situation or a military combat situation. A more appropriate, broader definition of the term for our purposes would reflect contextual views of development, which hold that "intelligence consists of the mental activity involved in successfully adapting to one's environment" (Berg & Sternberg, 1992, p. 221)—what has been called *successful intelligence* (Sternberg, 2004), or *practical intelligence* or *competence* (Birren, 1985).

Robert Sternberg's (1985a) triarchic theory distinguishes between analytic, practical, and creative intelligence. Analytic (or academic) intelligence is the type typically measured on intelligence tests. A comparison of the characteristics of analytic and practical problems follows (Neisser et al., 1996):

Analytic problems tend to	*Practical problems tend to*
be formulated by other people	require problem recognition and formulation
be clearly defined	be poorly defined
come with all the information needed to solve them	require additional information
have a single correct answer that can be reached in only one way	have alternative solutions
be presented out of context with ordinary experience	be closely tied to and require previous everyday experience
have little intrinsic interest	require personal interest and involvement

Further, it is assumed that different environments would necessitate different responses. The nature of intelligence would change with age if the environments to which people are exposed typically change with age as well. So the mental abilities required to be intelligent in one's teens might be different from those required later in life. The questions then become: What are the critical mental activities that facilitate adaptation? How can they be measured? Do they change systematically with age? Attempts to answer these questions are currently under way, as investigators grapple with identifying the components of practical intelligence and its assessment (Baltes, 1987; Schaie, 1990). The important thing to keep in mind is that **intelligence** is increasingly being described in contextual terms as the mental activity involved in successful adaptation to the environment.

Key Perspectives of Life-Span Cognitive Development

You may recall our discussion of the key beliefs associated with life-span development in Chapter 1. The next section reviews the components of the life-span perspective as a framework for considering the nature and fate of cognitive abilities in adult life. Such an application is particularly important because, as Baltes (1987, p. 613) points out, "The area of intellectual functioning is perhaps the best studied domain of life-span developmental psychology."

Development Is a Lifelong Process

Development, and in particular cognitive development, does not end at any particular age, and at each stage new possibilities may emerge. We will examine evidence of this adult cognitive potential—postformal thought, expertise, wisdom, and so on—in a later section.

Development Includes Both Gains and Losses

At all points in the life span, development includes growth as well as decline. We will consider research findings relative to cognitive growth, stability, and decline later.

Development Is Multidimensional, Multidirectional, and Multicausal

There are many different components of cognitive ability, with different patterns of change over time. Some aspects of mental functioning may be stable, while others may be in a period of growth or decline. Age change proceeds in many different directions and is caused by many different factors. As we will see, the concepts of fluid and crystallized intelligence illustrate this diversity. We will consider many other examples in this and the following chapter.

Development Is Plastic

Within limits, an individual's development is modifiable, based on life conditions and experiences. We will consider the issue of plasticity more fully in Chapter 5.

Development Is Embedded in Historical, Cultural, and Social Contexts

Cognitive development, like all aspects of development, is affected by the conditions present and the forces at work during an individual's lifetime. These can include prevailing attitudes as well as technological advances, economic factors, and so on. Thus, depending on the historical context, the level and course of intellectual development can vary dramatically. We will see that intelligence not only changes with age, it also changes with cohort (Baltes, 1987). The influence of cohort effects, in fact, confounded much of the early research into the question of what happens to intelligence with age.

Interindividual differences in development arise from the varying effects of the particular environments in which individuals live. The contextual view of intelligence described above, in which intelligence is seen as an adaptation to the environmental demands placed on the individual (Berg & Sternberg, 1992; Sternberg, 1985a)—a more "everyday" rather than "academic" intelligence—reflects this perspective.

Development Is a Multidisciplinary Field

Development cannot be understood in psychological terms alone. Contributions from other fields such as neuroscience will enhance our understanding of cognitive development in adulthood.

In sum, then, these six theoretical positions serve as a framework within which we can examine the research findings on cognitive processes in adulthood. We turn now to an examination of this evidence, beginning with research on the direction of cognitive change over time.

Growth, Stability, or Decline?

The remainder of this chapter addresses the fundamental issue of what happens to cognitive abilities with age. In particular, does growth, stability, or decline take place? Further, are the age trends consistent across various cognitive abilities? Across individuals? Cohorts?

The Shipwreck versus the Butterfly: Contrasting Metaphors of Adult Cognition

"Old age is a shipwreck." This statement, attributed to the French military and political leader Charles de Gaulle, represents the older decrementalist view of inevitable and universal deterioration with age. It contrasts sharply with a more recent use of the butterfly as a metaphor for "continued potential" (Perlmutter, 1988) in adult cognitive development, a conception reflected in the famous line from Robert Browning that the best is yet to be.

Which is it—the shipwreck or the butterfly? Let's consider the research tools, designs, and major findings.

Measurement Tools

In general, adult intelligence is assessed through the use of one of two types of psychometric tools (collectively referred to as CATs, for *cognitive ability tests*). The most widely used assessment device is probably the Wechsler Adult Intelligence Scale–Third Edition (WAIS-III), which measures 11 different abilities grouped into verbal and performance subscales. Verbal items include those that measure vocabulary, information, and comprehension; performance items include those requiring block design, picture arrangement, and picture completion. The verbal subscale relies heavily on language and taps stored information; the performance subscale does not require language fluency and asks the subject to manipulate information to solve a problem. The performance items are thought to be less dependent on educational and cultural background than the verbal items. Other researchers have used various subtests of the Thurstones' Primary Mental Abilities Test (Thurstone & Thurstone, 1949): verbal comprehension, word fluency, spatial ability, numerical ability, memory, perceptual speed, and inductive reasoning. To give you an idea of the types of questions found on these tests, examples of items from the subtests of the WAIS-III are included in Table 4.2.

CRITICAL THINKING QUESTION

On which subscales of the WAIS-III would you expect recent immigrants to the United States to perform better? What is the danger of using standardized intelligence tests with nonnative speakers?

Any test is a measure of performance on a particular day at a particular time and under particular circumstances. Salthouse (1991b) and others make a distinction between competence and performance. **Competence** is what one is capable of achieving under optimal evaluation conditions, while **performance** is what one actually does in a given assessment situation. The two are not necessarily identical, since the expression

TABLE 4.2 *Types of Items Found on the Wechsler Adult Intelligence Scale*

VERBAL SCALE

1. **Information:** Includes 29 questions that cover a wide range of general information, chosen to avoid specialized or academic knowledge. Example: What is a funnel? How much does it cost to mail a first-class letter?
2. **Comprehension:** Includes 14 items that assess understanding of common practices and ability to use practical judgment. Example: Why do people have insurance? Why do we use screens on windows?
3. **Arithmetic:** Includes 14 problems that are presented orally and are to be solved without paper and pencil. Tests numerical reasoning. Example: If an item costs $3, how many items can you buy with $36?
4. **Similarities:** Includes 13 items that ask in what way two things are alike. Measures abstract reasoning. Example: How are an ambulance and a fire truck alike?
5. **Digit span:** A series of between 3 and 9 digits are presented orally and must be repeated either forward or backward. Tests attention and rote memory. Example: Repeat the following numbers: 1 2 4 5 7 8 3 6 9.
6. **Vocabulary:** The subject is asked to define 40 words of increasing difficulty. Tests verbal comprehension. Example: What does *reliable* mean? What does *proliferate* mean?

PERFORMANCE SCALE

1. **Digit symbol:** A nonlanguage, timed code-substitution test. The subject is presented with a key containing 9 symbols paired with 9 digits. The subject is then presented with a series of numbers on the answer sheet and has 1½ minutes to fill in as many symbols as possible. Tests speed of learning. Example: 1!, 2@, 3#, 4*
   Fill in: 2_____, 4_____, 1_____.
2. **Picture completion:** Includes 21 cards, each containing a picture of an object from which some part is missing. Assesses visual memory and alertness. Example: What is missing from this picture?
3. **Block design:** The subject is shown a drawing of a block design and is asked to reproduce it using a set of one-inch blocks that are painted red, white, and red and white. Tests ability to analyze patterns. Example: Assemble the blocks to match this design.
4. **Picture arrangement:** The examinee must assemble a series of cards containing pictures in the right sequence to tell a story. Assesses understanding of social situations. Example: Put these pictures in order.
5. **Object assembly:** Includes four items, each of which contains cutouts that must be assembled to form a flat object. Tests understanding of part-whole relationships. Example: Put the pieces together to form a complete object.

Object assembly is one of the performance subtests on the WAIS-III.

of competence may be limited by factors other than ability. One must be careful, then, not to make assumptions about an individual's ability based on a limited assessment of performance. Are tests more accurate predictors of ability for some ages than others? Despite charges that they discriminate against older subjects, Salthouse concludes that there is no greater competency-performance discrepancy for one age group than another. In other words, psychometric tests are equally good (or equally bad) at measuring the cognitive competence of adults of all ages.

CRITICAL THINKING QUESTION

What are some of the variables that might affect an individual's performance on a test, regardless of age?

Other concerns have been raised about the use of these tests to assess cognitive development. First, serious questions exist about the validity of such measures when used to assess the cognitive ability of groups other than those against whom the tests have been standardized. The greatest objections have been raised over their use with racial and ethnic minorities (Helms, 1992). These groups generally do not fare well when their scores are compared to the White majority. The argument is that the language and concepts used bias the tests against minority individuals who may have had less exposure to this material, while at the same time failing to assess their unique cognitive style and strengths. We will have more to say about the effect of culture on cognitive style in Chapter 5. Thus, what these test scores actually represent is uncertain—cognitive ability or sociocultural background. Attempts to develop more culture-fair tests have met with mixed success. (For example, it has been difficult to identify items not influenced by culture and, therefore, fair to everyone.)

A similar concern has been expressed about the fairness and appropriateness of CATs when used in studies of older adults, given that the tests were originally developed for use with children. The fact that CATs are timed may discriminate against older adults, who may be slower to respond because of a greater desire to be cautious and answer correctly, or because of slower processing time in general. Thus, speed tests may obscure actual mental ability. (But some feel speed is an integral part of intelligence and so should be assessed.) In addition, younger cohorts may be more familiar with standardized testing in general and thus may be more test-wise, and perhaps less anxious, than older samples, for whom this experience is less familiar. Some observers also question whether the abilities measured have much relevance for intelligent functioning in everyday adult life. That is, the tests may lack ecological validity (Schaie, 1978). Potentially important aspects of cognition such as wisdom, creativity, social understanding, insight, long-range planning—abilities that might be especially important for effective adaptation in adult life—are not assessed adequately by current intelligence tests (Salthouse, 1991b).

Before we decide to "throw the bums out," we should consider Salthouse's (1991b) argument that these tests also have certain advantages. First, because CATs have been around since before the 1920s, a substantial body of comparative data is available that may provide insight into the nature of at least some aspects of cognitive aging within individuals and across age cohorts. For example, we might trace fluctuations in verbal ability within individuals and between groups of those tested over the last 70 years. Also, combining several different test batteries allows us to assess a fairly wide range of abilities, offsetting the criticism that the tests are too narrow (Salthouse, 1991b). On a more practical level, until better measures are devised, these tools may be superior to subjective assessments. Concerns over the methods used to assess adult cognition will be considered in greater detail in Chapter 5.

To sum up, psychometric intelligence tests measure only some aspects of cognition, and there are legitimate questions about what scores on these tests actually represent (Salthouse, 1991b). On the other hand, the tests have proven useful in research and also in clinical settings to diagnose the extent of cognitive impairment. They may not, however, be adequate predictors of everyday competence (Botwinick, 1984). They are best viewed as flawed but useful measures of some aspects of intellectual functioning.

Research Design

You may remember from Chapter 1 that two major research designs have traditionally been used to study development over time: the more common cross-sectional and the more favored longitudinal designs. Briefly, cross-sectional studies are criticized because they confound the variables of age and cohort. If differences are found between groups of older and younger subjects, we cannot be sure whether they are due to age or some aspect of historical experience. In general, cross-sectional studies of cognitive development have yielded somewhat more pessimistic findings of age-related change than longitudinal studies—that is, they suggest greater cognitive decline with age (Schaie, 1989, 1996). Longitudinal studies, on the other hand, while yielding a more accurate picture of individual development over time, are threatened by selective attrition and practice effects. Subjects drop out, leaving a more select group who may perform at a higher average level than the intact sample would have. Repeated testing may also give an advantage to the older sample. In addition, the effect of age may be confounded by the effects of nonnormative events (death of spouse, major illness) that are increasingly likely as participants get older. Finally, a longitudinal study is limited by its focus on only one cohort, which may not be representative of cohorts born either before or since. The best design combines elements of each of these traditional approaches.

Seattle Longitudinal Study

Data from a number of longitudinal studies covering wide age ranges are now available. A study that has examined cognitive aging extensively is K. Warner Schaie's (1996) Seattle Longitudinal Study (SLS). The database for this study consists of cognitive and other data on more than 5,000 subjects, studied at seven-year intervals, beginning in 1956. The SLS was designed to chart the course of five primary mental abilities from young adulthood through old age. Throughout, the focus has been on five major questions (Schaie, 1994):

- Does intelligence change uniformly through adulthood, or are there different patterns of change for different cognitive abilities?
- At what age do decrements in ability occur, and how great is the loss?
- Are there cohort (generational) differences in intellectual performance, and if so, what is the magnitude of the difference?
- What causes the large differences in age-related change among individuals?
- Can intellectual decline with age be reversed?

We will rely somewhat heavily on findings from this study for several reasons. First, unlike the earlier longitudinal studies that tended to include well-educated, more privileged subjects, the SLS sample was large and selected to be more representative of the population. Second, the sample includes a wide range of ages, consisting of individuals representing cohorts born between 1889 and 1939. Third, it is one of the few studies to use the same cognitive measures to assess adults from various age cohorts in both cross-sectional and longitudinal comparisons (Salthouse, 1991a). And fourth, several decades of data are now available.

Concept Review 4.1

- The modern scientific study of cognition can be traced to the cognitive revolution of the 1950s.

- Theoretical perspectives include the organismic, mechanistic, contextual, and psychometric models.

- Existing definitions of intelligence are controversial, ranging from the view of intelligence as a general ability to theories of multiple intelligence and from the traditional psychometric view to a more contextual approach emphasizing successful adaptation to the environment—so-called practical intelligence.

- The six key beliefs that constitute the life-span perspective can be applied to the study of cognitive development.

- Concerns have been expressed about the use of the two most popular measures of adult intelligence: the Wechsler Adult Intelligence Scale and the Thurstones' Primary Mental Abilities Test.

- Schaie's Seattle Longitudinal Study supplies several decades' worth of data on a number of major questions concerning adult cognitive development.

Evidence of Cognitive Decline: The Decrementalist View

As mentioned earlier, the traditional **decrementalist view** of cognitive development in adulthood is one of universal, inevitable, and pervasive decline. This view originates partly in the old dichotomy between development and aging—that is, the notion that development (meaning positive growth) is associated with childhood, and aging (meaning deterioration and decline) occurs in adulthood. The assumption is that aging is driven by a nonmodifiable genetic program that undermines all behavioral functions, including cognition. So according to this view, cognition is a victim of inevitable biological aging, and increasing cognitive decline is expected with increasing age. Investigators who adopt this position hope to describe what typically happens to our mental faculties as we age.

As we have seen, this position has been challenged in recent years by the view that development is a lifelong process characterized by both gains and losses, and that it is plastic—that is, modifiable. In addition, others have emphasized that even if age is found to be correlated with decline, we cannot assume that age is the cause of the decline (Perlmutter, 1988). It is not really age, but processes and variables associated with age that are responsible for the observed age trends: "Age is merely a surrogate, or a carrier, for the cumulative and aggregate effect of many different variables" (Salthouse, 1991b, p. 29). These investigators are searching for the specific factors that influence the direction, rate, and timing of age-related cognitive change.

Nonetheless, because of the dominance of the decrementalist view among researchers in the past, the bulk of empirical research in the field of cognitive aging has focused on the phenomenon of decline. And as a result, the negative relationship between age and cognition is now well established (Salthouse, 1991b). Though these findings have become increasingly unpopular because of their unrealistically negative portrayal of adult cognitive performance, Salthouse (1991b) argues that research on age-related declines may have tremendous practical benefits if, as a result, we learn to understand and perhaps intervene in this process. In fact, he feels the research emphasis on cognitive decline is of potentially greater value than research focusing on cognitive stability or growth.

Major Findings

Large Individual Differences

The picture that emerged from early cross-sectional studies of psychometric intelligence in adulthood basically looked like this: most abilities peak at midlife, followed by a plateau until the late 50s or early 60s, after which comes accelerating decline with age, the magnitude of which is typically small until the 70s (Schaie, 1989, 1990). More recent longitudinal studies have basically confirmed this pattern, though age changes are less pronounced and occur later. There is ongoing controversy about specific ages and rates of change. "For most people and most abilities, reliably detectable decline does not begin until the . . . late 60s and 70s" (Baltes, in Schaie, 1996, p. xxiv).

However, while the picture described above accurately reflects *group* data that have emerged from a variety of studies, it does not capture the immense variation among *individuals* in age-related cognitive development (Schaie & Willis, 1993). Research results are summarized by the use of averages, which often leaves the impression that all

50-year-olds or all 70-year-olds are functioning at the same level. In fact, a wide range of performance exists within each age group, with some 70-year-olds outperforming some 30-year-olds, and so on. A number of studies have found significant diversity among individuals in patterns of cognitive development, including those over 75, with many subjects remaining stable or improving, while some declined slowly, and others rapidly (see, e.g., Backman, Small, Whalin, & Larsson, 2000; Christensen et al., 1999; and Wilson, Beckett, et al., 2002). Wilson and colleagues conclude: "The observed heterogeneity in rates of change is not easily reconciled with the idea that cognitive ability declines inevitably or uniformly in old age as part of some developmental process. . . . Overall, the results suggest that change in cognitive function in old age is highly specific to the individual" (p. 190).

This section examines these interindividual variations in level and rate of change, based on Schaie's (1989, 1990, 1996) analysis of results from the SLS.

Because of its cohort-sequential design (which includes aspects of both longitudinal and cross-sectional designs; see Chapter 1), the sample included in the SLS represents a wide range of ages as well as birth cohorts. Data are now available from six measurement points over a 35-year period and allow comparisons of both individuals and cohort groups on the basis of five measures of primary mental ability (Schaie, 1990, 1994). They include verbal meaning—the ability to recognize and comprehend words; spatial orientation—the ability to mentally rotate objects in two-dimensional space; inductive reasoning—the ability to identify regularities and principles of rules, as in a number-series completion test; number—the ability to perform arithmetic computations quickly and accurately; and word fluency—the ability to recall words based on rules, such as words representing animals or starting with the letter s. Schaie (1989) considers these cognitive abilities to be essential to communicating with others, moving around in the environment, and solving the problems of everyday work and life.

Figure 4.1 shows the proportion of individuals who maintain stable levels of performance over a seven-year period, by age and ability. Note that between 60 and 85 percent of all subjects (depending on the age group) remain stable or improve on the five cognitive measures (Schaie, 1990). Even by age 81, significant decrement is observed in only 30 to 40 percent of the sample. Rather, about two-thirds of participants showed little or no decline (Schaie, 1989). Schaie (1990) points out that even by the 80s, none of the subjects showed universal decline on all of the cognitive abilities assessed. He concludes that old age may be characterized by an individualized pattern of selective maintenance of some abilities.

Additional analysis shows large variations not only in rate, but also pattern, of individual change, with some subjects remaining stable throughout, others showing continuous decline, and still others showing early decline followed by partial recovery or plateau or only late-life decline (Schaie, 1989).

Multidimensionality and Multidirectionality

Different components of cognitive functioning show different patterns of change over time. Cattell (1963) and Horn (1982) have developed a psychometric theory of intelligence that illustrates this point. According to this model, intelligence consists of two major clusters of abilities—fluid and crystallized intelligence. Baltes (1987; Baltes, Dittmann-Kohli, & Dixon, 1984; Baltes, Staudinger, & Lindenberger, 1999) has expanded this concept into a two-component model of intellectual development: the

FIGURE 4.1 *Proportion of Individuals Who Maintain Stable Levels of Performance over Seven Years on Five Primary Abilities*

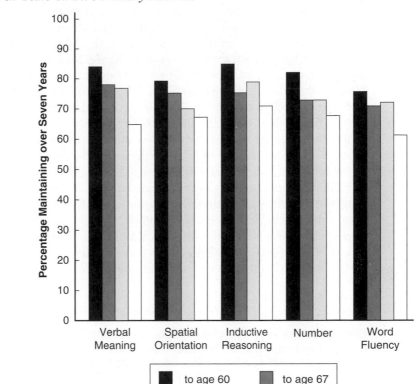

Source: K. W. Schaie (1990). "Intellectual Development in Adulthood." J. E. Birren and K. W. Schaie (Eds.), *Handbook of the Psychology of Aging* (3rd ed., pp. 291–309). San Diego, CA: Academic Press. Reprinted by permission of Academic Press, Inc.

mechanics and pragmatics of intelligence. Because these two models are very closely related, they will be presented jointly here. **Fluid intelligence** (the mechanics) refers to the inherited ability to think and reason. It is considered the more basic of the two, reflecting underlying information-processing and problem-solving capabilities—the brain's "hardware." Though influenced by experience, it is more heavily dependent on the state of the brain (Botwinick, 1984). These mechanical aspects of intelligence unfold as the brain and nervous system mature during the individual's development. Processing speed—the speed with which one can analyze information—is an example of fluid intelligence. The Digit Symbol Substitution subtest of the WAIS-III is a typical measure of cognitive processing speed. Other examples include attention, memory capacity, and reasoning ability. **Crystallized intelligence** (the pragmatics), on the other hand, refers to accumulated knowledge—information acquired and stored over a lifetime of experience—and the application of skills and knowledge to problem solving. Crystallized intelligence can be thought of as the mind's culture-based "software" (Baltes, 1997). The vocabulary subtest of the WAIS-III is a typical measure of knowledge. While primarily the product of education and acculturation, it is of course influenced by conditions in the brain and nervous system as well. Examples include proficiency in language and numbers and basic knowledge of the world, such as knowing how to conduct yourself during a job interview.

Extensive research on these two components of intelligence has generally yielded distinctly different patterns of age-related change. Measures that tap fluid intelligence show evidence of continuous decline beginning in the late 20s or early 30s (Salthouse, 1991a), while those tapping crystallized intelligence show evidence of growth with age and start to decline only in very old age, perhaps not until about age 90 (Baltes, 1987; Singer, Verhaeghen, Ghisletta, Lindenburger, & Baltes, 2003). Figure 4.2 depicts these findings. Some longitudinal analyses have raised questions about this picture, however, suggesting instead stability of fluid intelligence and all other abilities until the mid-50s to the early 70s, followed by a shift toward decline (Hertzog & Schaie, 1988).

The divergence of the developmental patterns of fluid/mechanic and crystallized/pragmatic intelligence illustrated in Figure 4.2 is referred to as *differentiation*. Some investigators report *dedifferentiation* (homogenization) very late in life; that is, the patterns of the two components—biological and cultural—begin to converge (Ghisletta & Lindenburger, 2003). They believe this is the result of accumulated biological impairments in the brain that become significant enough to undermine the previously well-

FIGURE 4.2 *Developmental Change in Fluid and Crystallized Intelligence*

One of the best-known psychometric structural theories of intelligence is that of Raymond B. Cattell and John L. Horn. The two main clusters of that theory—fluid and crystallized intelligence—are believed to follow different life-span developmental trajectories.

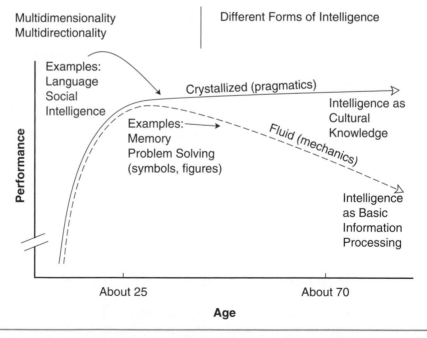

Source: P. B. Baltes (1987). "Theoretical Propositions of Life-Span Developmental Psychology: On the Dynamics Between Growth and Decline." *Developmental Psychology, 23,* 611–626. Copyright 1987 by the American Psychological Association. Reprinted by permission.

preserved crystallized intelligence. If and when it occurs, the decline in pragmatic abilities may be a signal of impending death.

Interestingly, and as would be expected according to Cattell, Horn, and Baltes, the verbal measures of the WAIS-III show an age pattern more similar to that of crystallized (pragmatic) intelligence, while scores on the performance subtests correspond more closely to those found in studies of fluid (mechanical) intelligence (Botwinick, 1984).

Other evidence of multidimensionality and multidirectionality comes from Schaie and Willis (1993), who report cross-sectional data measuring six primary mental abilities among samples whose average ages ranged from 29 to 88. Ability domains included inductive reasoning, verbal ability, verbal memory, numeric ability, spatial orientation, and perceptual speed. The peak ages for these abilities vary, as does the amount of change that occurs with age. They found verbal memory to be the best maintained and perceptual speed to be the most reduced with age. In short, "age differences are not uniform across abilities" (Schaie & Willis, 1993, p. 52).

Cohort Effect

What role does the cohort effect play in cognitive development? Do various birth cohorts show the same or different patterns as they age? Figure 4.3 shows age changes for the entire sample over a 28-year period on three measures of cognitive ability. The ages

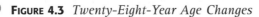

FIGURE 4.3 *Twenty-Eight-Year Age Changes*

Age changes over 28 years for the total sample for the abilities of verbal meaning, spatial orientation, and inductive reasoning.

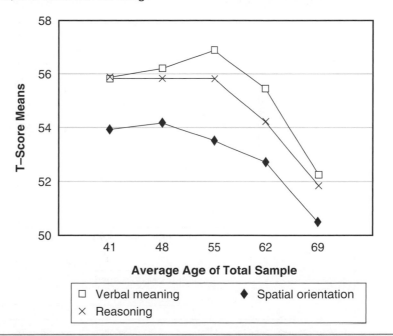

Source: K. W. Schaie (1989). "Individual Differences in Rate of Cognitive Change in Adulthood." In V. L. Bengston & K. W. Schaie (Eds.), *The Course of Later Life: Research and Reflections* (pp. 65–85). Copyright 1989, Springer Publishing Company, Inc., New York, NY 10012. Used by permission.

indicated on the graph represent the *average* age of the *total sample* at each of the five measurement intervals. The resulting pattern reflects the typical picture of change derived from group data that was described above—that is, a peak at midlife, followed by increasing decline with age. Notice also that the rate and pattern of decline vary across abilities, with spatial orientation the least well preserved of these three—again, multidimensionality and multidirectionality.

However, when the findings are broken down by birth cohort, different patterns emerge, as shown in Figures 4.4 to 4.6. The sample is shown separated into three subgroups, based on age at last time of measurement: middle age (average age, 57); young-old (average age, 71); and old-old (average age, 85). Thus, we see how the group that is currently middle-aged, young-old, or old-old performed at earlier ages. All three figures illustrate significant **positive cohort trends** (see especially Figure 4.5). In other words, later-born individuals perform at higher levels than did earlier-born individuals at the same ages on measures of verbal meaning, spatial orientation, and inductive reasoning. Schaie (1994) attributes these cohort differences largely to increased levels of formal education. All three figures also illustrate different patterns of change across cohorts and across cognitive abilities. There is also evidence not reflected in these figures that more recently born cohorts are at a disadvantage in comparison to earlier generations in number skill and word fluency (Schaie, 1996), illustrating negative cohort trends. The presence of significant generational shifts in cognitive performance (as great as 1.5 SD in the SLS data) illustrates the error of assuming that differences seen among adults of different ages are an inevitable developmental pattern.

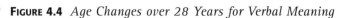

FIGURE 4.4 *Age Changes over 28 Years for Verbal Meaning*

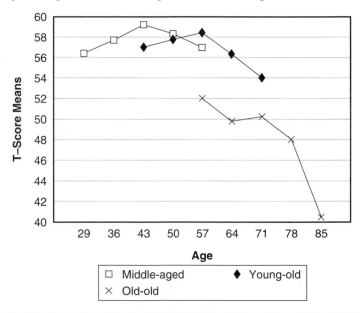

Note: Average ages for middle-aged = 57; young-old = 71; old-old = 85.

Source: K. W. Schaie (1989). "Individual Differences in Rate of Cognitive Change in Adulthood." In V. L. Bengston & K. W. Schaie (Eds.), *The Course of Later Life Research and Reflections* (pp. 65–85). Copyright 1989, Springer Publishing Company, Inc., New York, NY 10012. Used by permission.

FIGURE 4.5 *Age Changes over 28 Years for Spatial Orientation*

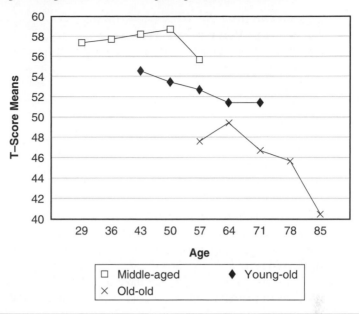

Note: Comparisons of all three cohorts at age 57 show clear evidence of a positive cohort trend.
Source: K. W. Schaie (1989). "Individual Differences in Rate of Cognitive Change in Adulthood." In V. L. Bengston & K. W. Schaie (Eds.), *The Course of Later Life: Research and Reflections* (pp. 65–85). Copyright 1989, Springer Publishing Company, Inc., New York, NY 10012. Used by permission.

FIGURE 4.6 *Age Changes over 28 Years for Inductive Reasoning*

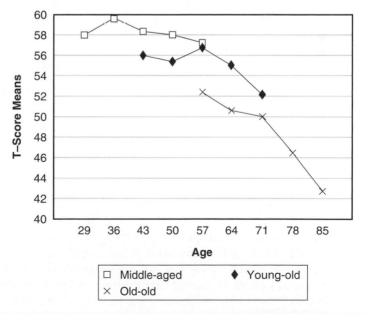

Source: K. W. Schaie (1989). "Individual Differences in Rate of Cognitive Change in Adulthood." In V. L. Bengston & K. W. Schaie (Eds.), *The Course of Later Life: Research and Reflections* (pp. 65–85). Copyright 1989, Springer Publishing Company, Inc., New York, NY 10012. Used by permission.

CRITICAL THINKING QUESTION

Can you think of other factors that might account for the positive cohort trends depicted in Figures 4.4 to 4.6? For the decline in number skill and word fluency?

Given what we know about our population demography, what can we expect about the future of these trends? Schaie (1990) predicts a reduction in the large discrepancies observed among younger and older cohorts, both because of improving conditions among successive generations of older adults and because maximal benefits for younger adults from better education and lifestyle have been achieved. In contrast to the positive cohort trends just discussed, Singer and colleagues (2003) propose a trend with effects in the opposite direction. As life expectancy in industrialized countries increases, a less select group of people will live to be very old, thus favoring earlier-born cohorts of the oldest old.

In sum, data from the SLS have conclusively shown substantial generational differences in primary mental abilities. The magnitude and direction of these trends vary by ability.

Magnitude of Change

We should keep in mind that even when decline is found, it tends to be of small magnitude at least until the 70s are reached, in the absence of pathology such as organic brain disease (Schaie, 1989). The vast majority of older adults function well within the normal range exhibited by younger adults and do not fall below the middle range of performance for young adults until their 80s (Salthouse, 1991a; Schaie, 1996). While decline certainly occurs in some areas of ability, we can expect competent behavior by many people even at advanced ages, especially in familiar settings. More deficiencies may be observed in these older adults in highly challenging, complex, or stressful situations (Schaie, 1990).

Conclusions

What meaningful conclusions can be drawn from the data on cognitive decline? First, large individual differences exist in the degree, rate, and pattern of cognitive change with age. These differences are masked in studies that report only group data. Second, a large body of evidence indicates that different aspects or dimensions of cognition follow different patterns of change over time, with some of these better preserved than others. Accumulated knowledge (crystallized or pragmatic intelligence) continues relatively unaffected by age, while processing ability (fluid or mechanical intelligence) declines, though the timing and degree are debatable. Thus, within individuals, the rate and pattern of change vary from one cognitive ability to another. Third, cohort trends illustrate the influence of the sociohistorical context on cognitive development. And finally, among healthy individuals, cognitive decline is normally of small magnitude, at least until very late adulthood. Performance is especially good in familiar settings.

Concept Review 4.2

- The traditional decrementalist view of cognitive development predicts inevitable and universal deterioration in mental abilities as individuals get older.

- Cattell and Horn distinguish between fluid and crystallized intelligence; Baltes proposes a similar model of the mechanics and pragmatics of intelligence.

- The data on cognitive decline reveal large individual differences; different patterns of age-related change across specific mental abilities; cohort effects; and, among healthy subjects, small magnitude of decline.

Evidence of Cognitive Growth: The Continued Potential View

As we have seen, the decrementalist view is that cognitive development in adulthood follows a pattern of universal, inevitable decline. We have reviewed the research literature on this subject and found that, while there is evidence of decline, it is limited to certain abilities and follows a highly variable pattern across and within individuals in rate, age of onset, and magnitude. Some individuals seem to be largely spared the kinds of decline that would be predicted by this traditional view. In fact, there does not seem to be much that is inevitable or universal.

Instead, accumulating evidence supports the **continued potential view** of cognitive development in adulthood—that some lifelong cognitive skills may continue to improve with age, and some new cognitive abilities may emerge in adulthood (Perlmutter, 1988). This model acknowledges the multidimensional, multidirectional, and multicausal nature of cognitive development throughout the life span. Perlmutter (1988), one of the most vocal advocates of this position, cites numerous lines of evidence in opposition to the inevitable decline model: the many individuals who have made important contributions late in life, studies of creativity in adulthood, studies of job performance among older workers, evidence of cohort effects, results of intervention and training studies, and surveys of older individuals themselves. All support a more optimistic view of adult cognitive potential. Newer studies indicate that many subjects show preservation of cognitive skills into the later decades of life and that mental decline is more the exception than the rule, assuming good health. For adherents of the continued potential view, the butterfly is a more appropriate metaphor than the shipwreck.

Because much of the research in adult development and aging has originated from what has been called the "misery perspective" on aging (Tornstam, 1992), the focus has been on the problems of aging. Though the intent was commendable—to identify the problems and develop policies to address them—the result is that older adults have been depicted as more needy, feeble, unhappy, and incompetent than they really are (Sherman, 1993). A number of authors have cited a growing imbalance in published reports of cognitive aging research, with data showing minimal or no age loss being selectively underreported (Cerella, Rybash, Hoyer, & Commons, 1993). A shift in focus away from a decline view to one of maintenance and improvement—a focus on what is going well, not on what is going wrong—could have a number of positive ramifications (Perlmutter, 1988). First, by dispelling the stereotype of older adults as feeble-minded and unproductive, it leads to more positive expectations of their abilities. The result could be an improved quality of life and a better utilization of adults' resources and contributions. This in turn might ultimately lead to a beneficial change in the age structuring of society. Second, adopting the continued potential view could direct research attention toward those biological, psychological, and social factors that facilitate and maximize cognitive development throughout the life span—those things that allow human beings to thrive rather than merely survive (Butler, Lewis, & Sunderland, 1991).

The biography of William Carlos Williams illustrates the richness of human potential (Mariani, 1982). Williams was a physician as well as one of the great poets of the 20th century. He suffered a stroke at age 67 and was hospitalized with severe depression at age 69. Though forced to give up the practice of medicine, he went on to write some of his greatest poetry. The point is that we should focus on a more comprehensive assessment of adult ability, including strengths and potentials, not just weaknesses and problems (Cohen, 1993).

Proponents of a continued potential view acknowledge evidence of cognitive decline but point out that when it occurs, it tends to be limited to those biologically based fluid or mechanical aspects of cognition. The more experientially based crystallized or pragmatic aspects of intelligence seem to remain stable or improve with age. The previous section focused on the former, examining the nature of cognitive losses. Our focus in this section will be on the latter—the gains possible even into old age.

As a beginning, let's examine Baltes's (1987) definition of pragmatic (crystallized) intelligence more closely. He includes the following components: (1) general factual and procedural (skill) knowledge, things like knowledge of historical events as well as skills such as riding a bike or solving an algebra problem; (2) specialized factual and procedural knowledge, such as that related to expertise in an occupation (for exam-

At ages 102 and 104, the Delany sisters published a book entitled *Having Our Say: The Delany Sisters' First Hundred Years.* These women are vivid examples of the cognitive potential that exists even late in life. Their autobiography provides a fascinating glimpse into personal and social history through the eyes of two black centenarians.

Having Our Say by Sarah and A. Elizabeth Delany with Amy Hill Hearth. Published by Kodansha America, Inc. © by Amy Hill Hearth, Sarah Louise Delany, and Annie Elizabeth Delany. Used with permission.

ple, accounting, automotive repair); and (3) knowledge about how to maximize the performance of cognitive skills, such as the use of repetition and review to enhance memory. Pragmatic intelligence tends to increase over time and is geared toward the application of knowledge to solve problems and adapt to different environments. The implication is that at different points in the life span, the contexts to which individuals are exposed and to which they must adapt—and therefore the nature of pragmatic intelligence—will change. Compare, for example, the kind of pragmatic intelligence required of a student in an introductory biochemistry class with the type demanded of a physician in a hospital emergency room. The specific knowledge and skills acquired—and therefore the nature and direction of cognitive development—will vary depending on the individual's life experience and as a function of gender, race, class, and culture. Intelligent behavior, then, is defined contextually in terms of the demands of the environment.

Adult Life-Span Learning

Learning is required throughout the life span for individuals to adapt to changes in their environments and life circumstances. This is even more true today, given the rapid pace of change and the difficulty of predicting the type of future world we will face. Little is known about adult learning because the emphasis has been on studying learning and cognitive development in early life, and because the kinds of learning that take place in adulthood differ from the types of learning usually studied. Research suggests that most learning abilities increase from the 20s to the 70s, and even the very old (85+) are capable of learning new things (Baltes & Warner, 1999). However, learning in adulthood is different from that in childhood because the needs of adult learners and the contexts in which adult learning takes place are significantly different (Sinnott, 1994a, b). Much of the learning that occurs among adults is motivated by the events and transitions adults experience, especially in the areas of work and family life; adult learning is closely tied to the context of the individual's life (Merriam, 1994). This learning may be formal (such as taking classes) or informal. Adults may find it necessary to learn new information or acquire new skills to find or advance in a job, take on new roles (such as parenthood), adjust to change (such as a move to a new community or a divorce), learn new leisure activities (such as golf), or engage in personal development activities (such as learning a second language). The learning demands placed on adults, the choices and opportunities they face, and the resources available to them will be colored by their social, cultural, and historical environment as well as by gender, class, and ethnicity. Thus, the pragmatic nature of adult learning is both stimulated and structured by adult life experience.

Older adults may use different cognitive strategies or approaches than younger individuals when faced with a cognitive task. While these differences were traditionally viewed as deficiencies, the emerging view is that the strategies used by older adults may in fact be adaptive to the changing experiences and demands present in adult life (Berg, Klaczynski, Calderone, & Strough, 1994). For example, Sinnott (1994b) characterizes learning among the young as focusing on the accumulation of facts (analytic, bottom-up processing), while learning among mature adults involves using higher organization to make sense of facts and to build a better theory (synthetic, top-down processing). Mature adults will need to be able to use both types of thought to deal with the issues of the future.

Quantitative versus Qualitative Gains in Adult Cognition

There is ongoing debate about whether cognitive development in adulthood involves essentially quantitative or qualitative gains. **Quantitative change** refers to variation in the amount of an attribute, whereas **qualitative change** refers to a difference in overall form or structure (Salthouse, 1991b). The increase in height from childhood to adulthood would be an example of quantitative change, while the transformation of a tadpole into a frog or a caterpillar into a butterfly would be an example of qualitative change. Applied to cognitive development, the debate is essentially whether we simply know more of the same sorts of things and know them in the same ways as we age, or whether we know different kinds of things and know them in different ways than we did earlier in life. Is adult cognitive development characterized by continuation down the same paths or new directions? For Baltes (1987), this remains an open question.

Quantitative Change: Does Cognitive Development End with Formal Thought?

According to Piaget (1972), cognitive development culminates in adolescence with the emergence of formal operations. Piaget describes cognitive development as proceeding through a series of four fixed, sequential, universal stages, each of which represents a qualitatively different and more advanced mode of thought: the sensorimotor stage (birth to age 2), the preoperational stage (ages 3 to 5), concrete operations (6 to 11), and formal operations (12 and up). **Formal operations**—the final, adult stage—includes the ability to think abstractly, to approach problems in an organized and systematic way, and to consider various hypotheses before reaching a solution. Though not all individuals have fully achieved formal thought by the end of adolescence (and some never do), no additional stages in the structure of intelligence emerge beyond this point. Once achieved, however, the capacities of formal thought may be applied in new contexts during adulthood. This is essentially a quantitative view of adult cognitive development, as opposed to the qualitative changes described in childhood. Further advances once formal thought is reached take the form of additions to *what* we know, not *how* we know it.

Qualitative Change: Postformal Thought

Some investigators take issue with Piaget's stance, proposing extensions to the theory in the form of various versions of **postformal thought** (for example, Commons, Richards, & Armon, 1984; Riegel, 1973; Sinnott, 1994a, 1998). They suggest that adults not only acquire more knowledge, they also develop new, qualitatively different ways of thinking. Riegel (1973), whose work has been credited with sparking this line of research (Baltes, 1987), even suggests that poor performance by older people on tests of formal thinking should be interpreted not as evidence of cognitive decline, but rather as evidence that this form of thinking has been replaced by a more advanced form of intelligence. Taken together, the work of this group attests to increases in cognitive power in adulthood—to developmental potential beyond formal operations—in opposition to the view of cognitive decline or even stability (Commons, Richards, & Armon, 1984; Richards, Armon, & Commons, 1984).

Some specific examples of these formulations include the following: Arlin's (1984) proposition that problem-solving operations are replaced with those geared toward

Formal thought allows the systematic testing of alternative hypotheses in solving a problem.

problem finding; Basseches's (1984) description of dialectical thought in adult cognition, which seeks out and tolerates, rather than attempting to remove, inconsistency; Commons and Richards's (1984) structural analytic thought, which can understand relationships between (in addition to within) systems or theories; Sinnott's (1998) emphasis on the examination of a vaguely defined problem from multiple perspectives in order to find the solution that best fits the particular context of the problem, a significant departure from traditional Piagetian theory, and which formal thinkers can be taught to do; and Labouvie-Vief's (1984) portrayal of postformal thought as autonomous, more complex and flexible, less constrained by the limitations of "strong" logic and the need to find one answer to a question or solution to a problem.

A common thread running through many of these descriptions of postformal thought is an increasing relativism, the realization that real-life problems do not always have absolute answers, that contradiction and uncertainty are realities of life, and that knowledge and reality are only true temporarily (Stevens-Long, 1990). There are also repeated descriptions of a move away from pure logic to renewed integration of logic and emotion (Rybash, Hoyer, & Roodin, 1986). Whether these various formulations will eventually prove to be descriptions of different facets of the same entity remains to be seen. Research on postformal thought has been described as being in a "state of imaginative, muddled suspense" (Arlin, 1984, p. 271).

Rather than expanding, extending, or otherwise revising the original conception of cognitive development put forth by Piaget, Broughton (1984) offers a compelling denunciation of the entire model. An advocate of the need for a "radical paradigm change," he contends that there is something fundamentally wrong with Piaget's conception of cognitive development as a normative model of adolescent and adult thought. He cites 15 major problems with the formal-operational model that, taken together, in his view require us to reject it. Among his objections are Piaget's emphasis on scientific logic as the epitome of human cognitive endeavor. Instead of looking beyond formal operations to describe postformal thought, Broughton argues that we should look beyond Piaget.

A long-standing controversy has also existed over the whole notion of universal stages in development. As Flavell (1992, p. 1000) points out, developmentalists essentially agree that cognitive development "is not as general stagelike . . . as Piaget and most of the rest of the field once thought." Instead, the mind is seen as developing in a more domain-specific, fractionated manner, though there is no consensus on the degree to which development is either general or specific (Flavell, 1992; Schaie & Willis, 1993).

Others argue that any conception of intelligence is culturally relative (Dasen, 1984) and rooted in a sociohistorical context (Bronfenbrenner, 1979). The nature of cognitive activity fluctuates as a function of historical change and cultural priorities—factors at the level of the macrosystem. Consider the types of cognitive activity necessary in hunter-gatherer societies as compared to rural, agrarian, or urban, industrialized cultures. Changes in the context introduce not only new content (new ideas, knowledge), but also new forms of cognitive activity. So, even if Piaget's description of cognitive development applies to our culture, it may not be an adequate description of other cultures or historical eras.

To reiterate, our understanding of adult cognitive development may have been limited by the view that advances in thinking culminate in adolescence with formal logic. Continued potential may exist for the development of other advanced forms of thought. Their nature and the factors that either encourage or discourage their emergence are not yet well delineated.

Expertise, Wisdom, and Creativity

Some investigators are less concerned with structures and stages of cognitive development and more concerned with the function of intelligence in adulthood. The focus of researchers in this group is on changes in crystallized intelligence, the pragmatic factual knowledge and skills that evolve in—and may be unique to—adulthood. Here, we consider research on expertise, wisdom, and creativity in adult life.

Expertise

Expertise refers to the development of advanced skills and knowledge in a particularly well-practiced activity—perhaps an occupation or a hobby. The assumption is that if one's involvement in this activity is maintained, the associated skills and knowledge may also be maintained or further developed (Baltes, 1987; Masunaga & Horn, 2001). Studies of expertise typically compare the knowledge base and performance of experts and novices in a particular domain or activity. A review of some of the findings follows.

First, not too surprisingly, a large, well-organized body of knowledge in a particular field is a prerequisite for expertise in that field (Bedard & Chi, 1992). Experts know more about their area of expertise and are especially familiar with the most critical information (Chi, Glaser, & Rees, 1982). This knowledge is also better organized and more accessible to them. It, in turn, influences the perception and processing of relevant information. For example, evidence suggests that experts can store more information relative to their area of expertise in long-term memory (Van Lehn, 1989). This was first demonstrated in studies of chess players: chess experts were better able to remember the position of pieces on a chessboard after a brief exposure than were chess novices (Chase & Simon, 1973). Chess masters are estimated to have about 50,000 chess patterns in memory, compared to about 1,000 for a good player and very few for a poor player (Chase & Simon, 1973). This vast storehouse of board patterns enables the chess expert to quickly recognize the positions of chess pieces on the board and to retrieve from memory information about possible moves and strategies (Gobet & Simon, 1996). Other studies have replicated these findings in other areas, such as memory of schematic drawings of electronic circuitboards, computer programming, engineering, architectural design, and medical problem solving (Bedard & Chi, 1992).

CRITICAL THINKING QUESTION

Which of Gardner's intelligences (see Table 4.1) is illustrated by chess masters' memory for board patterns?

Experts grasp more relevant and deeper aspects of a problem, focusing more on meaning, and utilize more effective, strategic problem-solving approaches as well (Anderson, 1993). They look ahead, considering implications and consequences of various courses of action (Gobet & Simon, 1996). A novice's approach to a problem is more superficial and less effective.

In addition, expert knowledge is more cross-referenced, better indexed. For instance, expert diagnosticians make connections between diseases that are related or that have similar symptoms, while a novice's knowledge is less integrated, focused more on the classic features of a disease, with fewer links across diagnostic categories (Bordage & Zacks, 1984). Thus, experts are better able to quickly understand the type of problem they are dealing with and the best approach to solving it. As an example, expert salespeople may be better at recognizing the type of customer they are working with and adopting the most effective sales strategy.

An expert's performance is faster, more efficient, more automatic, and more accurate (Bourne, 1992; Hoyer, 1987). Novices, on the other hand, not only know less but perform in a slower, more deliberate, step-by-step way. In other words, their behavior is more effortful. It is also less accurate.

Expertise is task specific and does not transfer from one domain to another. For instance, expert diagnosticians in one medical specialty, such as psychiatry, do not show the same level of proficiency in solving diagnostic problems in another specialty, such as cardiology.

CRITICAL THINKING QUESTION

What would be the primary reason expertise would not transfer from one subfield to another?

Finally, the high level of performance experts achieve comes only after extensive learning experiences and deliberate, intense practice. It requires a massive investment of time, typically beginning in childhood—usually a minimum of 10 years in most professional fields, and ideally under the supervision of a coach or teacher (Ericsson & Charness, 1994; Ericsson, Krampe, & Tesch-Romer, 1993; Hayes, 1985). Expertise is not innate. Thus, characteristics that motivate and sustain high levels of practice for many years (temperament, activity level, supportive environment, availability of resources such as coaches) are necessary for expertise to develop.

Masunaga and Horn (2001) theorize that the extended intense practice that leads to expertise stimulates the development of a type of memory they refer to as expertise working memory (EWM), which in turn supports reasoning in the area of expertise. EWM is separate from short-term working memory and "enables the expert to impose organization on information and thus make sense of it even when it is seen for only a brief moment" (p. 309). Research suggests that the ability to organize information significantly enhances the amount and duration of information in memory (Biederman, 1995). Thus, EWM would enhance the efficiency, accuracy, and speed of performance on expertise tasks.

Let's tie all this together with an example. Think of the difference between the expert and the novice skier. The expert has had many and varied experiences with different locations, conditions, types of equipment, and so forth, which can be applied to facilitate performance in the future. The expert grasps the situation quickly, knowing what to look for, what is important, and how to adjust to it. The expert's performance is not only better directed, but intuitive, faster, and more skillful. The novice, with limited experience, on the other hand, tends to approach the situation more tentatively, unsure what details to consider before acting. There are likely to be hesitations, false starts, mistakes, and failures.

Critical Thinking Question

Over the course of our lifetimes, through work and leisure activities, each of us probably develops several areas of expertise. Do you feel that you have acquired expertise in any particular activity? Why do you think so?

In some situations, expertise may actually limit performance. For example, because experts tend to interpret problems and process task-related information at a deeper level (the semantic level, based on meaning), they may overlook superficial details relevant to the problem. So, for example, novice computer programmers may be better than experts at answering detailed questions about how a program works (Adelson, 1984). In summarizing research on this subject, Ericsson and Charness (1994) point out that medical students have been found to match or even surpass medical experts when told to memorize medical information presented to them. However, the experts were better able to identify and remember the important facts needed to make decisions about a particular case, even though they may have forgotten detailed information about the patient. (These findings may shed some light on some of the more frustrating aspects of doctor-patient, or expert-client, relationships.)

To sum up, experts know more than novices. Their knowledge is better organized and their approach to problems is more effective and more efficient. As a result, experts perform better on tasks in their field of expertise. An expert's skill is domain specific, and little transfer occurs across domains. Expertise is the product of years of deliberate and intense practice. And finally, experts may not outperform novices in situations requiring knowledge of more superficial details.

What is the relationship between expertise and aging? Research by Hasher and Zacks (1979) suggests that automatic responses are less affected by age than more effortful ones. This may mean that the highly developed skills that constitute expertise represent one area of cognitive development that is largely spared as one ages. A study of expert pilots found that aviation expertise reduced age differences in performance on aviation tasks; the older experts performed at higher levels than both younger pilots and nonpilots (Morrow, Leirer, Altieri, & Fitzsimmons, 1994). Further, a study of baseball players found that elite performers not only played better throughout their careers, but were able to maintain their peak performance for a longer period of time, and their performance declined more gradually than their less expert counterparts (Schulz, Musa, Staszewski, & Siegler, 1994). Similarly, a study of players of GO, a very difficult and complex competitive game widely played in Japan, found that the amount of age-related loss in expert reasoning and memory decreased to no decline as level of expertise increased (Masunaga & Horn, 2001). In general, experts maintain a very high level of performance in their domain of expertise during a time when less accomplished individuals show clear effects of aging (Ericsson & Charness, 1994).

Wisdom

Traditionally the province of the humanities and religion, the scientific study of wisdom in psychology is in its infancy. This is in part due to the fact that wisdom is difficult to define and measure (Birren, 1985). Despite the association of age with wisdom that goes back to ancient times (Clayton & Birren, 1980), there are continuing questions about the origins and developmental course of wisdom over the life span. It is speculated that wisdom as a knowledge system may originate in adulthood. There are obvious overlaps between wisdom and such concepts as postformal thought, practical intelligence, expertise, and creativity. In fact, these may actually be aspects of wisdom.

There are two major branches of psychological investigations of wisdom (Baltes & Staudinger, 2000; Simonton, 1990). The first attempts to develop implicit or commonsense theories of wisdom: that is, how do people use the term and how do they know wisdom when they see it in everyday life (Clayton & Birren, 1980; Sternberg, 1985b). These studies conclude that wisdom is understood to be a rare and exceptional quality and to represent an ideal of human development. A consensus has emerged from these commonsense studies regarding the personal attributes of wise individuals (Baltes & Staudinger, 2000; Birren, 1985; Simonton, 1990). These attributes include a wealth of experience, high personal and interpersonal competence, the ability to listen and give advice, reflectiveness, mastery of emotional responses, creativity, and transcendence (the ability to overcome personal and environmental limitations).

The second, though less common, type of research on wisdom attempts to go beyond these implicit, everyday approaches to develop more explicit, empirically based theories. These investigations focus on the antecedents, correlates, and consequences of wisdom as well as the development of a means of measuring it. Much of this work has been done by Paul Baltes and his colleagues at the Max Planck Institute for Human Development in Berlin, Germany, and is referred to as the Berlin Wisdom Paradigm. Because of its current influence in the field, we will explore this model of wisdom more fully.

Baltes and his group of researchers define **wisdom** as "expertise in the conduct and meaning of life" (Baltes & Staudinger, 2000, p. 124). Embodying the best beliefs and principles that individuals and a culture can offer, it represents "the pinnacle of insight into the human condition and about the means and ends of a good life" (p. 122). Based on cultural-historical and philosophical analyses of the concept, the Berlin Wisdom

Paradigm lists general criteria describing the nature of wisdom (Baltes & Staudinger, 2000). The characteristics of wisdom are that it

- addresses important and difficult questions and strategies about the conduct and meaning of life
- includes knowledge about the limits of knowledge and the uncertainties of the world
- represents a truly superior level of knowledge, judgment, and advice
- constitutes knowledge with extraordinary scope, depth, measure, and balance
- involves a perfect synergy of mind and character—that is, an orchestration of knowledge and virtues
- represents knowledge used for the good or well-being of oneself and that of others
- is easily recognized when manifested, although difficult to achieve and to specify

These researchers have also identified a number of general conditions that contribute to the development of wisdom. First, as with any form of expertise, wisdom results from a period of intense learning, practice, and strong motivation to pursue excellence. Second, because of its complexity, wisdom is a product of the coalescence of many contributing factors. Third, wisdom results from the interaction of cognitive, motivational, social, interpersonal, and spiritual characteristics. Fourth, as with any form of expertise, guidance by some sort of mentor(s) and the mastery of certain types of critical life experiences are probably necessary.

Participants in their studies respond to hypothetical dilemmas these researchers feel capture the core essence of wisdom. For example, a fictitious 60-year-old widow who has recently completed a college degree and opened a business learns that her son has been left alone with two small children to care for. Subjects are asked to formulate a plan describing what the woman should do and consider in the next three to five years (Baltes, Staudinger, Maercker, & Smith, 1995). In another case individuals are asked what they would consider if they received a call from a good friend who had decided to commit suicide. There are no correct answers. Responses are judged on the basis of five wisdom-related criteria using a 7-point scale, with 7 being the highest. A response is considered "wise" if it is rated 5 or higher on each of the following five dimensions:

- Rich factual knowledge about fundamental matters of life (general knowledge about life matters, such as human nature, interpersonal relations, social norms, critical life events, a grasp of the issues involved in the dilemma, and understanding of emotions)
- Rich procedural knowledge about strategies useful in managing these life events (such as awareness of decision-making processes; ways of giving advice, prioritizing goals, and resolving conflict; and possible resolutions of the dilemma and the associated costs and benefits)
- Life-span contextualism (a view of people and events that considers their multiple contexts—e.g., family, school, work, and the public good)
- An explicit concern with universal values such as virtue and the common good that is balanced by relativism of values and life goals (recognition of differences among individuals and cultures and a realization that people's lives take different paths and that individuals have different values and priorities)
- Recognition of the essential uncertainty of life (a realization that there may be no perfect solution and that no one has all the answers) and the means to deal with uncertainty (Baltes & Staudinger, 2000; Staudinger, Smith, & Baltes, 1992)

The first two criteria are necessary but not sufficient to define wisdom-related knowledge, while the last three are considered to be more specific and unique to wisdom as the authors define it.

Baltes and Staudinger (2000, p. 136) offer the following illustration of a dilemma and two extreme responses.

> A 15-year-old girl wants to get married right away. What should one/she consider and do?
>
> Low wisdom-related score: A 15-year-old girl wants to get married? No—no way; marrying at age 15 would be utterly wrong. One has to tell the girl that marriage is not possible. (After further probing) It would be irresponsible to support such an idea. No, this is just a crazy idea.
>
> High wisdom-related score: Well, on the surface, this seems like an easy problem. On average, marriage for 15-year-old girls is not a good thing. But there are situations where the average case does not fit. Perhaps in this instance, special life circumstances are involved, such that the girl has a terminal illness. Or the girl has just lost her parents. And also, this girl may live in another culture or historical period. Perhaps she was raised with a value system different from ours. In addition, one has to think about adequate ways of talking with the girl and to consider her emotional state.

CRITICAL THINKING QUESTION

Can you formulate what you consider to be a "wise" and an "unwise" response to the other hypothetical dilemmas described above?

Baltes and Staudinger (2000, p. 133) note, "The perennial power of wisdom is its role as a reminder, a source, and a benchmark in the quest for excellence." As empirical research on this concept continues, we should achieve a greater appreciation of the nature, origins, and development of wisdom. While age is no guarantee of wisdom, the working assumption is that wisdom is more likely to be found among older people. How do we become wise as we journey through life? Can it happen formally, through professional training in fields such as clinical psychology or the ministry (Baltes, Staudinger, Maercker, & Smith, 1995)? Does it happen less formally, through workshops, seminars, psychotherapy, reading? Is it a product of personal life experience, such as the loss of a loved one? Are there certain cognitive prerequisites, such as postformal thought, that may underlie wisdom (Sinnott, 1993)? Do certain personality traits facilitate or inhibit its development? Questions remain about the role of gender in the development of wisdom (Orwoll & Achenbaum, 1993). Do men and women experience different challenges and opportunities that potentially alter the way in which wisdom is acquired and expressed? How do ethnicity, class, culture, and history affect these processes? These questions present a rich research agenda for the future.

Creativity

Other investigators are interested in the nature and development of creativity. Though the literature on this subject is much more extensive than that on wisdom, creativity remains, like wisdom, a difficult concept to define and measure. According to Botwinick (1984), **creativity** is identified through extraordinary products and achievements that are novel, original, and unique, but also relevant—either to a social or an esthetic need.

Historically, the study of creativity has focused primarily on the most eminent creators, those whose creative accomplishments represented the most rare and unambiguous examples of creative genius and whose creative ideas or products had a major impact on others (Sternberg & Lubart, 1996). This focus limited the empirical study of creativity because these individuals were by definition scarce and their creativity was difficult to study in the laboratory. A shift to the study of more everyday creativity—the type that enhances day-to-day functioning and is used to solve problems and adapt to change—occurred in the last half of the 20th century, though there are still those who feel that "Big C" creativity is not the same thing as everyday "little c" creativity.

Creative individuals have typically been identified either through psychometric measures or biographical and historical studies of actual creative achievements (Simonton, 1990). Standard intelligence tests do not measure creativity. Instead, they tap **convergent thought,** which is directed at finding the one and only true answer to a question. It is the kind of logical, analytic thought that Piaget focused on and that is stressed in school. Creativity, on the other hand, is often assessed by measures of **divergent thought,** which seeks alternative solutions or possibilities. The accompanying drawings illustrate the difference between these two types of thought. In the first example—convergent thought—the individual collects relevant information to arrive at the one correct answer. In the second example—divergent thought—the individual takes a question or problem as a starting point and generates multiple possible answers or approaches.

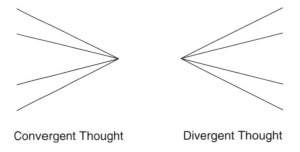

Convergent Thought   Divergent Thought

A convergent-thinking task might ask the individual to determine the velocity of an object when it hits the ground if it is dropped from a height of 200 feet. A divergent-thinking test might ask an individual to generate as many answers as possible to a question such as, "How many uses can you think of for a brick?"

Many tasks require the use of both types of thought. For example, one of our sons, a design major at a university, told me about a group project his industrial design class had been working on. Representatives from a large glass company had presented the class with a problem. They needed a new concept for a container to be used in laboratories to store liquids. After receiving detailed information about the way this container would be used, the class was sent off to "free associate" or brainstorm ideas. They considered various materials, shapes that would fit well in the hand, shapes that would be good for the storage of liquids, and so on. Then they began to systematically eliminate options in order to "converge" (his word) on the best design. According to Mike, they are encouraged to use this process of first employing divergent thought and then convergent thought in their design projects.

In addition to being recognized by their scores on divergent-thinking tests, creative individuals have been identified by the judgments of qualified experts, or by the frequency with which they have been cited in the literature (Botwinick, 1984). Each of these means of assessment, however, has problems with validity (Botwinick, 1984; Simonton, 1990) and begs the basic question: What is creativity and who decides what is creative and what is not?

Aside from questions of definition and measurement, our interest in this concept lies in how creativity changes as a function of age. History abounds with examples of creative brilliance late in life. Sophocles was in his late 80s when he finished the Oedipus plays, Cervantes completed *Don Quixote* at age 69, Claude Monet didn't begin his water lilies series until his 70s, Michelangelo was designing and painting until his death at 89, Verdi composed *Otello* at 73, Oliver Wendell Holmes was a Supreme Court justice until 91. Systematic studies of creativity over the life span have a long history, going back to Quetelet in 1835. Lehman's classic work, *Age and Achievement* (1953), represents a 20-year investigation of age-related changes in creativity in a variety of different fields of endeavor. There has been a burst of research activity in this area in recent years. Simonton (1991) summarizes the key findings.

One of the most solid empirical findings is that creative productivity tends to rise fairly rapidly to a peak, usually somewhere in the late 30s to early 40s, and then gradually declines (Lehman, 1953; McCrae, Arenberg, & Costa, 1987; Simonton, 1988). (See Figure 4.7.) This statement requires a number of qualifications, however, because it represents an average of many individuals. The age curve for a given individual may not conform to the group data for a number of reasons. First, the age curve is determined by "career age," not chronological age (Simonton, 1991). In other words, individuals who begin their creative activities in their mid-20s may reach their peak in their late 30s, though those who enter their career later may still be prolific much later in life. Probably the best-known example of this kind of late bloomer is Grandma Moses, who completed her first serious painting in her 70s.

Second, the age curve—specifically, the age at which the peak occurs and the magnitude of the postpeak decline—will vary according to the field of endeavor. Fields in which individuals reach an early peak (late 20s to early 30s) followed by a rather steep decline include lyric poetry, pure mathematics, and theoretical physics (Dennis, 1966;

FIGURE 4.7 *Creativity and Age*

This is a typical age curve showing the relationship between creative output and career age. Productivity rises rapidly to a peak, followed by a gradual decline until output reaches about half the peak rate (Simonton, 1988).

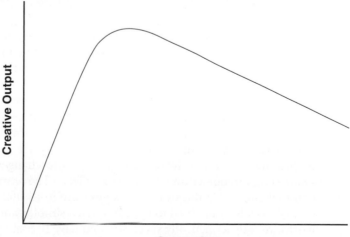

The creativity age curve is determined by the age at which one begins a career. Grandma Moses (seen here at age 88) is an example of a late bloomer who reached her peak late in life.

Lehman, 1953; Simonton, 1975). Disciplines in which individuals seem to peak around age 40, followed by a moderate decline, include psychology and sociology (Horner, Rushton, & Vernon, 1986). However, those engaged in novel writing, philosophy, history, and general scholarship peak later (late 40s or 50s), followed by minimal if any decline (Dennis, 1966; Lehman, 1953; Simonton, 1975).

CRITICAL THINKING QUESTION

What are the potential implications of the age curve in math and science for the preeminence of American scientific activity as the age structure of our society shifts?

These findings have been replicated in other cultures and historical periods (Simonton, 1975), lending credence to the notion that the forces behind the age curves are intrinsic to the particular creative endeavor (Simonton, 1991). For example, it may be that some creative activities require an abundance of enthusiasm, which peaks early in life, while others require the accumulation of experience (Beard, 1874)—crystallized knowledge and skills, perhaps even wisdom. Simonton's (1989) work on the swan-song phenomenon among classical composers may illustrate this point. Simonton studied 1,919 late-life works of 172 classical composers. He found that as these composers neared the end of their lives, their compositions changed—an effect he has called the **swan-song phenomenon** or last-works effect. (The term *swan song* comes from a legend that states that the swan only sings once in its life, shortly before death.) Works composed late in life tend to be rather brief, simpler, and more restrained than earlier works, yet are aesthetically successful and have become popular pieces in the classical repertoire. The musical creator seems to have reduced things to their essence in a last artistic testament, an accomplishment only possible later in one's career.

In addition to illustrating a possible integration of creativity and wisdom late in life, the existence of such swan songs argues against the loss of creative powers with age. In fact, Simonton (1988) suggests there may be a second (though lesser) creative peak later in life, a resurgence in creative output. In any case, the magnitude of the initial postpeak decline generally is such that in the decade of the 70s, creative output is about one-half what it was at its optimal period, a rate that generally exceeds the creative productivity of these individuals when they were in their 20s (Simonton, 1988). The bottom line: "The final phase of life can be, and often is, a period of phenomenal creativity" (Simonton, 1991, p. 16).

There is also the question of whether creative individuals are born or made. Most of the recent work on creativity hypothesizes that a number of factors must converge for creativity to develop, reflecting the contributions of both nature and nurture (Amabile, 1996; Simonton, 2000). These include personality variables (flexibility, openness to new experiences, risk taking, independence of judgment), motivational variables (an intrinsic interest in and love of the task, freedom from external constraints and pressures, and a willingness to engage in the same sort of systematic training and practice necessary for expertise), experiences that challenge and strengthen perseverance in the face of obstacles, and environmental variables (a sociocultural environment that values and supports creativity—for example, through the provision of mentors and role models early in life, forums for presenting creative works, and opportunities to associate with other creative individuals). Historical and political environments can affect the creative expression of an entire population. Citing historical examples, Simonton suggests that cultural diversity resulting from alien influence, open immigration, extensive travel, or study under foreign teachers may stimulate creativity in a civilization by enriching the cultural environment. An example is the Italian Renaissance. On the other hand, sociocultural forces are powerful enough to extinguish creativity, producing a lengthy "dark age."

Can creativity be taught, and can it be taught late in life? As part of a federally funded project to increase the independence of elderly individuals and integrate them into the community, the Quality of Life Program at the University of Georgia attempted to teach creative thinking skills (Goff & Torrance, 1991). These skills (representing "little c" creativity) were deemed to be important assets in adjusting to new challenges and problems. Preliminary findings are that those who participated in the training program showed evidence of significantly increased creativity in comparison to control subjects, whose scores declined over time. The apparent success of this program offers hope that creative powers may not only be maintained across adulthood, at least in some fields of endeavor, but that they may be enhanced and contribute to an improved quality of life among older adults.

Despite large advances in research on creativity, Simonton (2000) suggests that particular attention needs to be given to four areas. First, since most studies have focused on majority-culture White males, creativity among women and minorities is not well understood. Second, longitudinal studies are needed to increase understanding of the developmental course of creativity through the life span. Third, although we have an understanding of creative output in the arts, much less is known about scientific creativity. And finally, an understanding of creativity should lead to applications that stimulate the development of individual creativity.

What is the relationship among intelligence, expertise, creativity, and wisdom? A sufficient level of intelligence and expertise is necessary, though not sufficient, for a person to be either highly creative or wise. For example, an intelligent person may produce something that is functional and of high quality, but it may not be novel. Creativity requires both quality and originality and thus seems to go beyond intelligence. Yet combined creativity, intelligence, and expertise do not constitute wisdom. Leaders may be bright, innovative, and skilled, but they may lead people in a destructive direction. Robert Sternberg (2001) suggests that wisdom includes a synthesis of intelligence and creativity: creativity generates ideas, intelligence analyzes them to determine their quality, and wisdom ensures that they lead to a common good.

Successful Cognitive Aging

As we have seen, the decrementalist view of cognitive aging has fallen into disfavor, replaced by a more balanced view in which cognitive development in adulthood is characterized by both growth and decline—gains and losses. Though fluid abilities, such as speed of processing, may decline, crystallized knowledge and skills, like expertise, may expand. If so, what would constitute successful or optimal cognitive aging? Are there ways individuals can offset potential cognitive decline in later life?

Baltes et al. (1984; also see Baltes, 1987) have described successful adaptation to cognitive aging as *selective optimization with compensation,* a process whereby the individual maximizes cognitive strengths while developing compensatory skills to shore up weaknesses. The idea is that older individuals increasingly channel their cognitive abilities into areas of high priority and expertise. At the same time, a reserve capacity or energy is available to adults that gives the cognitive system a degree of plasticity. Though this reserve declines with age, even elderly adults generally have enough extra cognitive energy available to them to adapt to (compensate for) changing conditions. An example of this concept is provided by Salthouse (1984), who found that experienced older typists compensated for a reduction in speed by scanning further ahead in the material, thus maintaining a comparable level of performance to younger experienced typists.

Salthouse (1991a) has offered a second and essentially similar model of successful cognitive aging. He has described three strategies that can be used to cope with declines in cognitive ability: accommodation, compensation, and remediation. **Accommodation** refers to the tendency of older individuals to gradually disengage from those activities that stress their cognitive limits and to pour their energies instead into other activities where their accumulated experience is of great value. Just as the older athlete may turn to coaching, the older executive may turn to consulting. **Compensation** occurs when the same level of performance is maintained by changing the way a task is performed. The typists described above provide one example. Similarly, older tennis players may offset losses in speed and power by the use of superior strategy, enabling them to beat a younger opponent (Perlmutter, 1988). Or memory difficulties might be minimized by the use of written lists or reminders. Many older adults cope with the difficulty of monitoring medications through such memory aids. **Remediation** refers to cognitive intervention to restore cognitive abilities to a previous level, much as physical intervention is aimed at restoring a stroke patient to a previous level of functioning. Intervention studies provide practice or training on specific cognitive skills, and the performance outcome is measured.

Research on cognitive intervention and cognitive training since the early 1970s has demonstrated sizable and sustained, though not unlimited, plasticity even into old age on measures of both fluid and crystallized abilities (Baltes, 1987; Baltes, Dittmann-Kohli, & Kliegl, 1986; Baltes, Staudinger, & Lindenberger, 1999; Schaie, 1996; Verhaeghen, Marcoen, & Goossens, 1992). In other words, a portion of the cognitive decline that often accompanies age can be reversed through cognitive stimulation (Schaie, 1990). For example, practice or training can improve speed and reduce the effort involved in complex behaviors (Park, 1992). Based on cognitive intervention studies associated with the SLS, Schaie (1996) concludes that cognitive decline in old age may be the result of disuse rather than physiological deterioration in the brain, and these losses can be reversed through targeted cognitive intervention programs. For example, two-thirds of subjects age 64 and over who participated in a five-hour training program targeting spatial orientation and inductive reasoning improved. Forty percent of those who had experienced significant decline returned to the functional level they had exhibited 14 years earlier. Seven years later, participants maintained a substantial advantage over control subjects, a difference enhanced by booster training sessions. These types of interventions may be effective in helping older adults continue to live independently. The focus now is on establishing the limits or boundaries of this reserve capacity, a plasticity-within-constraints approach. It is important to point out, however, that adults of all ages benefit from these interventions. Thus, no intervention is likely to eliminate age-related differences.

The prototypes of successful cognitive aging that both Baltes and his associates and Salthouse offer suggest that high levels of cognitive performance can be maintained even late in life through various techniques that maximize strengths and minimize weaknesses. As people get older, some of their cognitive abilities become less efficient or impaired, but they are not broken. We are learning more about how to mend these abilities through remediation and environmental modification and design (Schooler, 1990). Certainly a stimulating, rich, socially supportive environment can assist this effort. As Salthouse (1991a, p. 38) concludes, "For most people there seem to be relatively few cognitive limits on what can be accomplished at any stage of life."

What factors might influence the nature, direction, and timing of age-related cognitive development? This is the question we turn to in the next chapter.

Concept Review 4.3

- The continued potential view maintains that some lifelong cognitive skills may continue to improve as we age and that new cognitive abilities may also emerge.

- Adult learning may be motivated by different factors and employ different strategies than learning early in life.

- Some believe that cognitive growth in adulthood consists primarily of an increase in the quantity of what is known, while others argue that the quality of thought also changes. The concept of postformal thought reflects the latter view.

- Expertise refers to the development of highly advanced knowledge and skills in a specific activity. Researchers are interested in its nature and developmental pattern.

- Wisdom may represent a type of expertise in the issues of life. Baltes and colleagues list five criteria in their operational definition of this concept. Research issues include the nature, origins, and development of wisdom.

(continued)

- Researchers studying creativity have traditionally focused on exceptional creative geniuses, though more recently interest in "little c" creativity has increased.

- Creativity is associated with divergent, as compared to convergent, thought.

- Researchers have identified a creativity age curve, though its specific nature varies among fields of endeavor.

- The development of creative potential results from the interaction of many factors.

- Successful cognitive aging involves adaptation through selective optimization with compensation.

- Cognitive intervention studies aimed at remediation of cognitive losses have demonstrated considerable plasticity and resilience among older adults.

REVIEW QUESTIONS

A Life–Span View of Cognitive Development

1. What is meant by the cognitive revolution? When and why did it occur?
2. Compare and contrast the four approaches to the study of mental processes. Which of these is becoming increasingly influential and why?
3. Contrast the psychometric and contextual definitions of intelligence.
4. How does Sternberg distinguish between analytic and practical problems?
5. Distinguish between competence and performance as these concepts relate to the assessment of cognitive ability.
6. Explain the concerns raised about the use of psychometric tests of cognitive ability. Are these tests so flawed that we should discontinue their use?

Evidence of Cognitive Decline: The Decrementalist View

1. Explain the decrementalist view of cognitive development in adulthood.
2. Distinguish between fluid and crystallized intelligence. What age trends have been observed in each?
3. What is the significance of a positive cohort trend?

4. Discuss the major generalizations that can be drawn from the findings on age-related cognitive decline.

Evidence of Cognitive Growth: The Continued Potential View

1. Explain the continued potential view of adult cognitive development.
2. Discuss the pros and cons of adopting either the decrementalist or the continued potential view.
3. Distinguish between quantitative and qualitative change as they apply to cognitive development.
4. What is postformal thought?
5. Define expertise in terms of the differences in the performance of experts and novices.
6. What are thought to be some of the major components of wisdom?
7. Illustrate the difference between convergent and divergent thought.
8. Describe the typical creativity age curve and the factors that contribute to individual differences in this curve.
9. What types of variables contribute to the development of individual creativity?
10. Discuss the patterns of successful cognitive aging that Baltes and Salthouse describe.
11. What conclusions can be drawn from cognitive intervention studies?

KEY TERMS

5 Cognitive Processes in Adulthood, Part II
Influences and Explanations

As we saw in the last chapter, the nature of cognitive development in adulthood is complex. Different dimensions of mental ability change in different ways, and there are large differences among individuals. Further, the extent of variation from one individual to another in cognitive functioning increases with age. Given the rapidly growing population of older adults, it is important that we understand the factors that contribute to these individual differences, particularly those that may lead to more optimal cognitive aging. Explaining these patterns of cognitive change requires the consideration of multiple causes. Making sense of the scientific literature in this area is difficult, because the research is complex, controversial, conflicting, and incomplete.

Research and Measurement Issues

Some critics charge that the evidence of cognitive decline is at least partly due to artifacts in the research—that is, characteristics of the research methods and designs used to study adult cognitive development. For example, some have asked whether the bulk of cognitive research has **ecological validity** (Botwinick, 1984; Hultsch & Dixon, 1990; Neisser, 1976). The question is whether the reliance on artificial laboratory techniques and psychometric methods and the focus on simple elements of cognition provide an accurate picture of how people really think and act. If older adults do not always perform at the same level as younger individuals on these sorts of artificial tasks, does this mean that their performance in their daily lives is impaired?

For example, the context in which a reasoning task is presented may be important. Ceci (1993) reports a study in which Brazilian construction foremen with less than a third-grade education were asked to solve a series of arithmetic problems involving proportional reasoning. Some of the problems were couched in a construction work context, some were couched in an unfamiliar context, while others were presented with no context at all but merely as numerical problems. The following problem is an example of the construction context (Ceci, 1993, p. 426):

> Suppose that a floor is 84 square meters in area, and I want to put under it a 5 cm base, comprised of 7 parts sand and 1 part cement. How many cubic meters of sand will be required to prepare such a base?

In comparison, the no-context problem was presented as described below:

> Suppose that the area of a rectangular box is 74 square meters, with a 5 cm altitude. For every 9 of A, there is 1 of B. How many cubic meters of A is needed to fill [the box] with a 5 cm mixture of A and B?

Results of studies such as these have found that problems presented in a real-life context were solved much more easily than the same problems presented with no such context. Thus, psychometric measures used to assess cognitive function may not give us an accurate picture of the everyday performance of individuals. This concern has led to an increasing interest in studying more everyday problem-solving situations—for example, memory for meaningful material, such as names.

Others are concerned about the characteristics of the subjects who generally participate in studies of cognition and aging. These concerns must be taken seriously because, as in all research, if the sample does not adequately represent the population, generalizations based on research findings will be in error. In particular, Poon, Krauss, and Bowles (1984) have pointed to the risks of both overestimating and underestimating the true effects of age on cognition when important characteristics of the samples studied are not considered. Most studies of cognitive aging have included White, middle-class samples (Schooler, 1990), with little research on intellectual aging within minority populations in the United States (Schaie, 1990) or in other cultures.

One of the most difficult problems in the study of aging is separating the "normal" effects of age from the effects of disease. In order to study normal age changes, participants who are sick must be excluded. Because cognition, like all psychological behaviors, rests on a physiological foundation, failure to do so could lead to a confounding of disease with age. In other words, if older subjects are found to perform at a lower level than younger subjects on a cognitive measure, we would not be certain whether this was the result of disease or normal aging. Evidence collected in the Seattle Longitudinal Study indicated that cardiovascular illness was associated with declines in mental abilities (Schaie, 1990). Concerns have also been raised about the inclusion of subjects who are in the early preclinical phase of dementia, particularly Alzheimer's disease. During this period, which may last as long as ten years, individuals have experienced cognitive impairment, but the symptoms are not yet sufficient to meet the clinical diagnosis. Thus, they are routinely included in cognitive aging research, leading to an exaggerated picture of age-related decline (Sliwinski, Lipton, Buschke, & Stewart, 1996; Sliwinski, Hofer, Hall, Buschke, and Lipton, 2003). The impact of **terminal drop** must also be considered—the finding that a marked decline in performance on cognitive measures occurs in the period preceding death (Siegler, 1975; Small, Fratiglioni, von Strauss, & Backman, 2003). If terminally ill patients (whether diagnosed or not) are included in the sample, their poor performance would artificially depress the average, inflating the appearance of cognitive decline (Baltes & Labouvie, 1973).

CRITICAL THINKING QUESTION
What factors might account for the phenomenon of terminal drop?

Concerns over sample selection led Christensen, Moye, Armson, and Kern (1992) to survey 197 cognitive aging studies published between 1984 and 1990 in four important journals. They found that random recruitment and the exclusion of subjects with relevant health conditions were rare. As a result, we must view conclusions of cognitive aging research with caution (Hayflick, 1994). Failure to eliminate subjects whose health has impaired their mental abilities leads to an underestimation of the abilities of healthy older individuals (Sliwinski, Hofer, Hall, Buschke, & Lipton, 2003). More attention to health screening in sample selection and the use of techniques such as the new brain-imaging technologies, which allow earlier detection of some relevant health conditions, may help to resolve these issues.

Additional concerns persist over the types of psychometric measures that are traditionally used to assess cognitive changes as individuals grow older. According to the **disuse hypothesis,** abilities that are not regularly used are lost. The basic idea is that people of different ages use different cognitive abilities. Tests may tap abilities that are not as widely used among older adults, so that their performance on these measures suffers. Ratner, Schell, Crimmins, Mittelman, and Baldinelli (1987) published an interesting study in which comparisons were made of the memory performance of college students, noncollege peers, and older adults. The college students not only outperformed the older subjects but also their peers who were not in college. The students studied longer and harder and used more effective organizational strategies to enhance their recall. The two out-of-school groups performed comparably. The authors speculate that being in school provides more opportunities and incentives to memorize material, thus enhancing some cognitive abilities.

CRITICAL THINKING QUESTION

Ratner et al. (1987) acknowledge that the college and noncollege samples may not be comparable. Can you think of differences between these two groups that may confound the findings?

Older subjects are not only further removed from their formal educational experience, but they generally have had less of it as well. Thus, differences found between older and younger subjects on cognitive tests may at least partially reflect differences in practice on cognitive tasks, rather than pure differences due to age. The heavy reliance on college samples as representatives of young adults makes this issue particularly relevant. If the performance of older subjects on CATs is diminished due to disuse or lack of practice of the tested skills, interventions to provide older adults with training or practice should improve their performance relative to younger adults, and, as we discussed in Chapter 4, the evidence suggests that this is indeed the case (Baron & Cerella, 1993; Schaie, 1996). Thus, disuse may contribute to the finding of cognitive aging.

Finally, in a review of studies of cautiousness among older adults, Botwinick (1984) identified two important findings. First, while older adults are not necessarily more cautious in all situations, they do tend to value accuracy over speed. That is, they are more concerned with coming up with the right answer than with a quick answer. The resulting slower performance of older adults on timed tests may lead to failure to complete all of the items and a lower score. Second, older adults may omit an answer if they are not confident it is correct, despite encouragement to guess. This is called the **omission error** and also leads to lower test scores. Taken as a whole, studies of cautiousness in later life suggest that older adults may know more than they show.

Continued attention to these research and measurement issues is essential if we are to untangle the relationship between age, cognition, and a host of other potentially influential factors. At least some of the decline found in cognitive aging studies may be the result of weaknesses in the research itself.

We turn now to the major explanations of cognitive development in adulthood, which have been organized into three categories: psychosocial influences, changes in the information-processing system, and physiological changes in the brain itself.

Concept Review 5.1

- Concerns have been raised about the ecological validity of much of the cognitive aging research.
- Other research issues have to do with sample selection and the potential effect of confounding variables on test performance.

Psychosocial Explanations

The contextual perspective views development as resulting from a series of reciprocal interactions between the individual and the environment throughout life. So as people age, we see the effects of both the biological changes that take place over the life span and the environmental contexts in which those changes occur (Arbuckle, Gold, Andres, Schwartzman, & Chaikelson, 1992). Chronological age, while a significant predictor, accounts for only about 25 percent of the total variation in cognitive ability from person to person (Moscovitch & Winocur, 1992; Salthouse, 1991b). Thus, a substantial 75 percent of individual differences is due to nondevelopmental factors and is not systematically related to age. This section explores some of the psychological, social, and cultural variables that contribute to the wide individual differences observed in cognitive development. As we will see, many of these factors are interrelated and vary as a function of an individual's position in the social structure.

Exposure to a Stimulating Environment

A number of studies have pointed to the positive effects of factors grouped here under the heading of exposure to stimulation. These factors include environmental complexity (Schooler, 1990); occupational type (Avolio & Waldman, 1990); occupational complexity (Kohn & Schooler, 1983; Schooler, Mulatu, & Oates, 1999); an active and involved lifestyle, exposure to cultural and educational resources, marriage (Gribbin, Schaie, & Parham, 1980); lengthy marriage to an intelligent spouse (Gruber & Schaie, 1986); and community versus institutional dwelling (Winocur & Moscovitch, 1990).

The basic hypothesis in all this research is that complex environments have a beneficial effect on cognitive functioning and that simple environments have a negative effect. The complexity of an individual's environment is defined by the type of stimuli it offers as well as the demands it makes (Schooler, 1990; Schooler, Mulatu, & Oates, 1999). Complex environments present more diverse stimuli and more complicated and ill-defined problems and thus require more decisions. When environments encourage, demand, and reward the use of advanced cognitive skills, individuals are motivated to develop and use their cognitive abilities. Simpler environments not only lack stimulation, but may not provide enough demand and reward for high cognitive effort and achievement, leading to a lower level of development and/or decline in intellectual function.

Schaie (1983) stresses the importance of an "engaged adult lifestyle" thought to result from the beneficial combination of high individual ability and favorable experiences, such as educational opportunities early in life. These early advantages promote high occupational achievement and a more complex and intellectually stimulating social environment in adulthood, which further challenges, promotes, and reinforces both the development and the maintenance of high levels of intellectual ability later in life. Supporting this view, Arbuckle, Maag, Pushkar, and Chaikelson (1998) found that an engaged lifestyle was the most consistent moderating factor in the degree of intellectual development and maintenance observed over a 45-year span in a group of World War II veterans. Further, they suggest that the importance of such a lifestyle may increase in later life.

What components of an engaged lifestyle are most influential? One variable that has received a great deal of attention is occupational complexity. Schooler, Mulatu, and Oates (1999) evaluated data from a 30-year longitudinal study begun in the early 1960s on the psychological effects of occupational conditions. Their central finding was that complexity of work and intellectual functioning continue to *reciprocally* affect each other throughout a person's working life. While substantively complex work has a significant positive effect on the level of intellectual functioning in workers of all ages, the effect is greatest among older workers. So, paid work that is intellectually challenging raises the individual's level of intellectual functioning, while paid work that is not intellectually challenging decreases it. The causal connections between the nature of one's work and intellectual development have been replicated in studies of women and other cultures. Subsequent research among men and women aged 41 to 88 confirmed that engaging in intellectually demanding leisure-time activities was associated with the same positive outcomes (Schooler & Mulatu, 2001). Further, Schooler and Mulatu speculate that doing complex paid work may increase the likelihood of pursuing cognitively stimulating leisure-time activities, thus compounding the intellectual benefit. The authors stress the practical applications of this finding: if society wishes to maximize the intellectual functioning of older adults, they should be encouraged to engage in activities that are cognitively complex. Heise (1987) hypothesizes that some of the intellectual decline seen among older individuals in Western cultures may result from their being forced into meaningless roles that present few challenging cognitive tasks.

While these studies suggest some of the factors that might influence cognitive performance in adulthood, they have not clearly identified the mechanisms through which this would happen. In short, they provide a hint of *why* without explaining *how* (Salthouse, 1991b). Is an active lifestyle preferable because it keeps people interested and motivated, because it has a bearing on degree of physical exercise, because of direct effects on neurons in the brain, or what? In addition, the direction of effect is not clear (Avolio & Waldman, 1990; Hultsch, Hertzog, Small, & Dixon, 1999). For example, if certain occupations are found to be associated with positive cognitive outcomes over time, is it because the job has a beneficial effect or because individuals with certain cognitive profiles tend to end up in these kinds of jobs or both? Or are other variables responsible for the observed relationship? Citing inconsistencies in research findings, problems in defining and measuring cognitive stimulation, as well as questions about the direction of influence just discussed, Salthouse, Berish, and Miles (2002) caution that definitive conclusions on the validity of the use-it-or-lose-it perspective may be premature. For the time being, however, they suggest that we act as if a positive relationship between cognitive stimulation and cognitive functioning exists; there is no harm in doing so, and future research may well confirm its value.

Psychological Factors

Researchers have become increasingly interested in studying relationships between various psychological characteristics and cognitive aging. Two personality variables that have gotten attention are self-efficacy and mental flexibility versus rigidity.

Self-Efficacy

A modest positive relationship seems to exist between self-efficacy (our belief in our ability to accomplish a task—see Chapter 3) and intellectual functioning, though the nature of the relationship remains unclear at present (Albert et al., 1995; Schaie, 1990). For example, do people's beliefs in themselves enhance their performance, perhaps through increased effort and persistence, or does good performance increase self-confidence, or both?

Mental Flexibility

Substantial evidence exists that mental flexibility (as opposed to rigidity) is associated with more positive cognitive outcomes later in life (Schaie, 1990). Schooler (1990) defines **mental flexibility** as the capacity to use a variety of approaches and perspectives, resulting in alternative solutions to cognitive problems. This characteristic probably interacts with a number of the lifestyle variables mentioned above to produce its effect. So, for example, environmental complexity may require and therefore enhance mental flexibility (Schooler, 1990). Job conditions that are challenging and offer opportunities for self-directed, complex work increase mental flexibility, while those that lack these qualities decrease intellectual flexibility (Schooler, Mulatu, & Oates, 1999).

CRITICAL THINKING QUESTION

Is there any similarity between mental flexibility and McCrae and Costa's description of the trait openness to experience (see Chapter 2)?

Emotional States

The effects of depression and stress have also been examined. Depression and cognitive abilities are negatively correlated. In severe cases, the effects of depression can be so profound as to be confused with dementia (Arbuckle et al., 1992). Stress has also been linked to cognitive decline (Amster & Krass, 1974). Research suggests that both depression and stress may burden and interfere with the individual's information-processing resources (Arbuckle et al., 1992; Hartlage, Alloy, Vazquez, & Dykman, 1993; Rabbitt, Donlan, Watson, McInnes, & Bent, 1995).

One intriguing hypothesis is that low self-efficacy may contribute to higher levels of stress and the resulting secretion of higher levels of glucocorticoids (see Chapter 9 for a more complete discussion of the physiological aspects of stress). These elevated glucocorticoid levels increase the risk of damage to cells in the hippocampus, a brain structure critical to learning and memory. Thus, high levels of stress may lead to physiological changes in the brain, which contribute to memory deficits (Seeman, McAvay, Merrill, Albert, & Rodin, 1996).

The links between psychological factors and cognitive abilities are ambiguous. The direction of causal relationships is unclear. For example, is depression causing the cognitive impairment, or is cognitive impairment causing the depression? There may be other factors causing both unhappiness and cognitive decline. Additional research may identify the critical variables, the nature of the relationships between them, and possible interventions to maximize cognitive performance later in life.

Demographic Variables

Socioeconomic Status

Level of education, occupational status, and income—all indicators of socioeconomic status (SES)—have been negatively correlated with rate of cognitive decline. That is, lower rates of decline are found among those with higher status.

Educational history has been the most consistent predictor of cognitive change (Albert et al., 1995). Again, these findings can be interpreted in a number of ways. For example, a positive correlation between level of education and level of cognitive functioning may not demonstrate that education is causing the cognitive ability. It may indicate that those with better cognitive abilities pursue more advanced levels of education. There is evidence that verbal ability is an important predictor of cognitive performance among older adults (Meyer & Rice, 1989). In addition, low levels of linguistic ability are a risk factor for dementia in late life (Kemper, Greiner, Marquis, Prenovost, & Mitzner, 2001). Perhaps education has beneficial effects through the develop of advanced verbal skills, so that highly educated samples may also be highly verbal. Or perhaps highly verbal people do better and advance further in school and also retain their cognitive abilities later in life.

One hypothesis is the concept of **neuronal reserve capacity,** developed by Albert and her colleagues at Harvard Medical School (Albert et al., 1995). They suggest that education early in life may directly increase the number and strength of synapses in the brain, thus protecting individuals from the effects of neuronal loss associated with aging by providing a reserve supply of connections. In addition, early educational achievement may also instill lifelong patterns of behavior that lead individuals to be exposed to and seek out rich, mentally stimulating environments (an engaged lifestyle), which contribute to compensatory dendritic sprouting (see the discussion later in this chapter) and thus maintain or enhance cognitive ability. Finally, the effect of education may interact with levels of self-efficacy, stress, and depression.

Similar complexity exists in the relationships between occupation, income, and cognitive development. In general, and for whatever reason, more privileged members of society show less cognitive decline. SES may be an indicator of the type of life opportunities and resources a person enjoys. Opportunities for education may be one of the most important contributors to successful or optimal aging.

Gender

The impact of gender has also been investigated, although there is relatively little research on gender differences in cognitive aging. Though some studies have shown older men to perform at higher levels than women on tests of intellectual ability (Rudinger, 1976), these differences have disappeared when the groups were matched for educational and occupational experiences (Berger & Gold, 1979). A number of studies have found that women who survive into very old age (85+) score higher than men on measures of memory and word fluency (see, e.g., Singer et al., 2003). According to Huyck (1990), there is no evidence that women and men differ in any systematic way in regard to overall intelligence or the degree to which intelligence declines with age. Gender differences are not found on most cognitive measures (West, Crook, & Barron, 1992). When they are, they tend to be rather small and with a lot of overlap between the sexes. In other words, if there is a difference between the average male and the average female on a certain measure, variation within the group is so wide that many members of each sex will exceed or fall below the average of the opposite sex. The well-publicized differences between school-age males and females in spatial, verbal, and mathematical skills (males have traditionally scored higher on math and spatial items, females on verbal items) appear to be narrowing as the experiences of boys and girls become more comparable. Even if cognitive skills are based in brain differences, they may be modifiable by experience. Thus, the evidence is scarce for an inevitable gender gap in most cognitive abilities. Rather, any findings of male-female differences among the current generations of adults may be partially the result of cohort effects—that is, historical differences in such things as gender roles and education.

Culture

Ceci (1993) argues that until recently, theories of cognitive development have tended to emphasize the psychological and biological processes and mechanisms of thought, while ignoring the context in which it occurs. The Russian psychologist Lev Vygotsky (1978, p. 126) states that cognition is "socially formed and culturally transmitted." Because cognitive processing is mediated by the culture in which an individual develops, variations from culture to culture in the direction and extent of cognitive development are expected (Ceci, 1993; Cole, 1990; Sternberg, 2004). For example, faced with cross-cultural research indicating that people in many cultures failed to reach the stage of formal thought without extensive schooling, Piaget revised his original view of stage four as universal to say that it was culturally variable (Rogoff & Chavajay, 1995). Identification of these cultural differences is relevant to our understanding and assessment of adult cognitive development. A number of cross-cultural studies suggest the impact of culture on thought. Though this growing body of literature can only be hinted at here, let's consider a few examples.

According to Schooler (1990, p. 352), "The nature of culturally available concepts places strong limits on the way people can think." What could this mean? Well, for example, performance on many kinds of tests is related to individuals' extent of formal schooling. Cross-cultural studies commonly find that, while adults in Western countries classify test items into taxonomic categories (for example, putting food items in one category, flowers in another, and modes of transportation in another), adults in many other nations sort by functional groups (for example, putting a hoe with a potato because the hoe is used to dig up the potato) (Rogoff & Chavajay, 1995). Classifying information by category seems to be a product of formal schooling, as does the use of a hierarchical organization system. Schooling and literacy also seem to affect the kind of evidence one is willing to accept as truth and therefore influence performance on tests of logical thinking. Logical thinking is typically assessed by use of a logical syllogism. In the 1930s, Luria (1976) used such a task with nonliterate Central Asian peasants: "In the Far North, where there is snow, all bears are white. Novaya Zemla is in the Far North and there is always snow there. What color are the bears there?" (p. 108). The peasants replied that they could only speak of what they themselves had seen, and since they hadn't been there, they could not say. The experimenter repeated the syllogism, asking what it implied. The peasants responded that if they had been there, or if they knew someone they respected who had been there, they could say. But otherwise, "those who didn't see can't say anything!" In contrast, Luria's literate research participants were able to solve the problem based on the logic of the syllogism alone, accepting the premise as true, while the nonschooled participants insisted that one should rely only on firsthand knowledge. Culture may affect test performance in still other ways. While Western societies associate speed of solving problems with intelligence, among Ugandan villagers intelligence is associated with being slow and careful (Goodnow, 1976). Culture appears to influence causal reasoning as well (Norenzayan & Nisbett, 2000). East Asians tend to explain behavior in terms of interactions between the individual and the context, while Americans tend to explain behavior primarily in terms of characteristics of the person.

The evidence also suggests that modes of thought or thinking styles vary among cultural groups. For example, while White Americans may be socialized to value linear problem solving, in which the "correct" answer to a question relies on using rational thinking, Black Americans may be socialized to value a more expressive, original processing style. Helms (1992) offers an example that illustrates the difference between the way Whites and Blacks might respond to the same question. She cites a sample Graduate Record Exam question, presented by Walsh and Betz (1985, p. 174), as follows:

> Old Mother Hubbard went to the cupboard
> To get her poor dog a bone
> But when she got there her cupboard was bare
> And so the poor dog got none.
>
> If the above is an accurate report of an event, which of the following headline versions gives an account that does not add to the given facts?
>
> A. Mother H Refuses Bone to Hungry Dog
> B. Mealtime Brings Only Bare Cupboard for Mrs. Hubbard and Dog
> C. Mother Hubbard Seeks Bone for Dog, Finds Empty Cupboard
> D. Dog Lover Unable to Continue Support of Pet
> E. Bone Missing from Hubbard Cupboard—Mystery Unsolved

The correct answer is supposed to be C, though Helms argues that one could also make a case for E. If we assume that Mother Hubbard was expecting to find a bone in the cupboard—why else would she have gone looking there?—the whereabouts of the bone does constitute a mystery. She further argues that, because Blacks are socialized from childhood on to develop creative, spontaneous, expansive thinking skills, they may be more likely to choose the more creative, less obvious alternative—that is, E. To date, however, no standardized CAT has incorporated this thinking style, despite the fact that it may be more common in the real world than the more rational style, which assumes there can only be one right answer to a problem. In sum, in order to understand an individual's thinking, an appreciation of the social, cultural, and historical context in which it developed and is used is essential.

The research cited in this section suggests that cognitive development and age-related cognitive decline are significantly affected by various psychological, social, and cultural factors acting alone or in combination. While not denying the role of biological factors and the aging process in intellectual decline in later life, some experts feel that individual differences in cognitive ability more strongly reflect differing psychological characteristics and social experiences (Schaie & Geiwitz, 1982). Not only *what* people think, but *how* they think can be affected by these variables. More privileged groups in society seem more likely to be exposed to environmental conditions that maximize intellectual development (Schooler, 1990). As Singer et al. (2003) point out, these greater cognitive resources "may have significant consequences . . . permit[ting] better everyday functioning . . . and protect[ing] individuals for a longer time from falling below critical levels or 'thresholds' of dysfunctionality" (p. 327). The pattern of intellectual development is not fixed in the genes at birth. Nor is decline inevitable. Rather, both individual and environmental characteristics affect growth, maintenance, and decline. Once again, we see the importance of the context of development and the person-environment interaction.

However, the relationships between variables such as those mentioned here and cognitive development are complex and, at present, not well understood. More explicit research is needed on what kinds of experiences in what patterns affect what aspects of cognition and in what ways (Salthouse, 1991b). At the very least, the simplistic view that there is a general pattern of inevitable and universal decline appears unwarranted.

Concept Review 5.2

- Continued exposure to a stimulating environment seems to benefit cognitive development throughout life, though the specific means by which this effect occurs is unclear. Much research has focused on the concept of an engaged lifestyle and occupational complexity.

- Investigators are studying a number of psychological variables, including self-efficacy, mental flexibility, stress, and depression to determine their relationship to cognitive aging.

- Individuals with higher levels of education, occupational status, and income show lower rates of cognitive decline.

- Gender differences in cognitive abilities appear to result more from cohort effects and differing experiences and opportunities than from inevitable, genetic/biological differences between males and females.

- Increasing attention is being paid to the effect of the cultural and historical context on the nature of thought as well as on the direction and extent of cognitive development.

Information-Processing Explanations

Perhaps the most popular approach to explaining age-related changes in cognitive functioning currently relies on the information-processing perspective. In essence, **information-processing theory** refers to a collection of concepts that attempt to explain the "black box" of the mind, that portion of experience between the stimulus input and the response output that the behaviorists ignored. It is not so much a theory of cognition as a perspective on how the mind operates, based heavily on an analogy with the computer as a symbol-manipulating system. The focus is on what the mind does with information once it enters the system: how it is transformed into terms the brain can handle (**encoding**), how it is maintained over time (**storage**), and how it can be found and reactivated when needed (**retrieval**). This section discusses attempts to identify components of the information-processing system that may be most responsible for age-related cognitive decline. These are *fluid* abilities. The assumption is that deficits in these components increasingly undermine cognitive performance with age.

An important body of evidence sheds light on what has come to be known as the **age-complexity effect** (Salthouse, 1991b, 1996). This term refers to the well-established finding that the magnitude of cognitive age differences increases as the task becomes increasingly complex. On the other hand, tasks that rely on well-practiced skills or areas of expertise or on familiar material are likely to show age-equivalent performance. Some attribute the age-complexity effect to deficiencies in the general purpose information-processing resources available to older individuals, such as attention, speed of processing, and memory capacity. Salthouse (1991b, 1996) describes these resources in terms of the metaphors of energy, time, and space.

Attention

Attention is considered a key component of the information-processing system and is the subject of great research interest. It has been defined as the mechanisms we use to prepare to process stimuli, focus on what to process, and determine how far to process it (Heilman, Watson, Valenstein, & Goldberg, 1987). Attention is vital because it determines what gets into the information-processing system to begin with. Others emphasize that attention is a limited mental resource that determines how many separate mental processes can be carried out simultaneously, noting that it is under the control of some central executive system that directs its use (Ashcraft, 1989). Individuals can only pay attention to a finite amount of information at any given time. The focus in cognitive aging research is on describing what happens to attention over the course of adult life.

Selective Attention

Some investigators hypothesize that the poorer performance of older adults on some cognitive measures is the result of a decline in the attentional resources available for processing information. (See McDowd & Shaw, 2000, and Rogers, 2000, for overviews.) For example, research suggests that an age-related decline occurs in selective attention—the ability to screen out and ignore (inhibit responses to) irrelevant stimuli and focus on information most important to the task at hand. This is especially apparent with demanding tasks (Hasher & Zacks, 1988; McDowd & Birren, 1990). Put another way, older adults may be more distractible, and this deficiency may be especially apparent in situations requiring a lot of information processing. An inability to inhibit responses to irrelevant stimuli would mean that some of the individual's limited attentional resources would be misdirected, undermining both speed and accuracy of cognitive performance (McDowd & Filion, 1992).

Automatic versus Effortful Processing

Hasher and Zacks (1979) have studied age differences in automatic and effortful processing. **Automatic operations** require little or no attention or conscious awareness and may be inherent or result from extensive practice. The encoding of spatial location information seems innate, so that we tend to remember where things happened, even without consciously trying to store that information. Have you ever driven home and, once there, wondered how you got there? The act of driving, which, when you were first learning, was accomplished only with great effort, has become sort of unconscious and undemanding of your conscious attention. So, under normal driving conditions, you can think of other things, talk to passengers, and so on, without disrupting your driving performance. **Effortful operations** do require attention because they involve deeper and more elaborate processing. And they do divert the attention available for other tasks. So you may not be able to solve complex mathematical problems while simultaneously listening to a conversation going on in the room. The underlying assumption here is that attention is a limited resource. Hasher and Zacks argue that age-related declines are limited to effortful processing, while tasks that have become automatic (and therefore require little attention) are largely spared these adverse effects. This may explain why expert skills show little evidence of decline with age. The jury is still out on this issue (Schacter, 1989; Botwinick, 1984).

Others counter that the cognitive deficits observed among older adults can be accounted for in another way—by a general slowing of information processing as a whole (Cerella, 1990; Verhaegen, Steitz, Sliwinski, & Cerella, 2003). In other words, the differences seen with increasing age are quantitative rather than qualitative. We consider this view next.

Speed of Processing

A second important information-processing resource is speed. Starting around age 25, the rate of information processing slows. Older adults are generally slower than younger adults on a wide range of tasks, and these age differences seem to increase with the complexity of the task (Birren, Riegel, & Morrison, 1962). Age-related slowing is one of the "least disputed . . . most pervasive . . . most clearly established . . . most reliable" findings in the psychology-of-aging literature (Salthouse, 1985). And it is of more than simply empirical interest, given its potential implications for occupational and everyday functioning. Yet, while this slowing-with-age phenomenon has been studied extensively, there is still a great deal of controversy over how to explain it and what it means (Salthouse, 1985; Myerson, Hale, Poon, Wagstaff, & Smith, 1990; Schulz, 1994).

One of the earliest studies of intelligence, response speed, and aging was published in 1936 by Irving Lorge. He tested adults of different ages using three intelligence tests, which differed in the degree to which they required a rapid response: one was short and highly speeded; the second was moderately speeded; and the third had liberal time limits. The greatest age differences were found on the highly speeded test, while the smallest differences were found on the least speeded test. Lorge concluded that speeded tests underestimate the cognitive power of older subjects, because the tests confound ability with speed. According to Lorge (1936, p. 110), "The reported deterioration is more apparent than genuine. . . . The inference of mental decline is an unfortunate libel upon adults." We have discussed the criticism that timed CATs discriminate against older adults. The assumption behind these criticisms is that the mental competence of older adults is not diminished; it simply takes longer for them to perform the necessary information-processing steps. Controversy still surrounds this issue, though substantial age-related differences persist in many measures even when time limits are removed (Salthouse, 1991b).

Generalized Slowing Hypothesis

There is an alternative view, referred to as the *Birren hypothesis* (Cunningham, 1989) or the **generalized slowing hypothesis** (Cerella, 1990). According to this perspective, which James Birren began to formulate in the 1940s, the slowing of information processing is not just a peripheral performance issue, but rather an integral determinant of cognitive ability. Put simply, according to this speed hypothesis, age differences in intelligence are the result of age differences in speed. Birren had observed, as had Galton and many others before him, that older people seemed on average to be slower at a wide range of tasks. However, Birren viewed this slowing not as a consequence but rather as a cause of many of the cognitive deficits observed among older adults. He suggested that a global slowing occurred in the central nervous system with age, the result of a primary process of aging in the nervous system (Birren, 1964). Thus, all behavior mediated by the central nervous system tends to slow down as the organism ages. A slowing of response is the direct result of normal aging, not the product of disease, brain trauma, or other similar factors. Further, a general reduction in the speed of all information-processing activities impairs not only rate of response, but also quality of response.

Salthouse (1994, 1996) concludes that slower processing impairs the quality of decisions because less information is available simultaneously (relevant information processed earlier has been displaced or has decayed and is no longer available by the time later information is processed). He offers the problems a slow juggler would have as a metaphor for this effect. Botwinick (1984) suggests that a kind of central power source exists that, when functioning optimally, makes for fast as well as good behavior of all sorts. According to Birren, this power source suffers with age, the equivalent of a pervasive electrical brownout that affects all cognitive processes in the same way. Birren's approach has the virtue of being economical. We do not need to look for age-related changes at each step of the information-processing system; the generalized slowing hypothesis would explain age-related deficits in all of them with one basic concept.

Processing speed is understood to play a vital role in cognitive aging (Myerson, Ferraro, Hale, & Lima, 1992). Lest we assume that it is the *only* factor, however, studies have attributed anywhere from 13 to 54 percent of the age-related differences among individuals on a variety of cognitive measures to speed factors, and up to 90 percent for some highly speeded measures (Salthouse, 1991b). So, the slowing of behavior accounts for some, but not all, of the age-related deficits observed among older as compared to younger adults (Botwinick, 1984). Further, some mental operations seem to show more evidence of slowing than others, suggesting that whatever mechanism is at work may not affect all cognitive processes equally. These results suggest a more local (as opposed to global) slowing in which some elements are slowed while others are not. Salthouse (1991b, p. 325) characterizes the hypotheses related to speed of processing as follows: "Slowing of all or some processes, by the same or varying amounts, due to one or several factors, affects a few or most cognitive tasks."

If we accept that generalized slowing occurs, what could be the cause? Let's look at three possible explanations: first, an increase in cycling time; second, loss of information; and third, defects in the neural network.

Increased Cycling Time. Salthouse (1985) suggests that a slowing of processing speed can be explained by analogy to a computer whose cycling time has increased. Thus, each processing step takes longer. While any one of these steps might not appreciably slow down the overall rate of response, when the slowing is aggregated over a number of steps, the slowing may become functionally important. Behaviors that have become "automatic," either because they are well practiced or simple, would be less affected. On the other hand, complex behaviors would be more affected because of the many processing steps they require. As a result, the total time difference in the performance of young and old adults would increase proportionately to degree of complexity.

Information-Loss Model. Myerson et al. (1990) have offered an alternative explanation, which they call the **information-loss model.** The authors provide the following analogy. Have you ever made a photocopy of something and then made a copy from the copy? The quality the second time around is not nearly as good as the first time, even though you may try to compensate by increasing the copying level and so on. Some information from the original is lost at the copy level. And each time you make a copy from a copy, the image is further degraded. The information-loss model is based on a similar phenomenon and makes the following assumptions. First, just as no machine is 100 percent efficient, no information-processing system is 100 percent efficient. Second, despite compensations, some small amount of information is lost at each step as information is processed in the nervous system. Though the system tries to compensate for this loss at each step (by holding onto the information longer so as to get more from

According to the information-loss model, the information-processing system loses some information at each step, just as a photocopy loses some detail each time a copy is made from a copy (as shown here). Information loss increases with age.

it, for example), there will be a residual loss. The next step will add more loss, and processing will become progressively slower. The loss and its effects accumulate with each step, just as the photocopy gets worse with each replication. Third, the rate of information loss increases with age. As a result, the whole system must function at a slower rate to compensate for the loss. Again, more complex tasks require more processing steps and are more affected by information loss along the way. Well-practiced, more automatic behaviors, on the other hand, would be less affected. This model maintains, then, that older adults differ from younger adults in the rate at which information is lost during processing and that this is a global change, affecting all cognitive tasks.

Disconnection Hypothesis. A third explanation is offered by Cerella (1990), who describes a change in the hardware of the nervous system in the form of breaks in the neural network. These breaks represent the death of individual neurons. This approach conceives of cognition as computation that occurs in a neural network composed of links and nodes. Processing consists of sending a message through the network in a fixed amount of time. The time is determined by the number of links in the network that the signal must traverse from beginning to end. Any breaks in the links would mean that the signal would have to make a detour, thus increasing processing time. Figure 5.1 illustrates a break in the neural network. The more breaks, the longer the time required to process the signal. Aging results in increasing numbers of breaks over time as neurons degenerate and die and alternate pathways must be used. Thus, differences in processing speed between younger and older adults would be accounted for by the accumulation of neural network breaks. The discrepancies would be more evident in more complex tasks, which rely on more complex neural networks.

FIGURE 5.1 *Schematic Neural Network Showing a Break in the Links and the Resultant Detour Traversed by the Nerve Impulse*

Accumulating breaks with age (representing the death of individual neurons) correspondingly increase processing time.

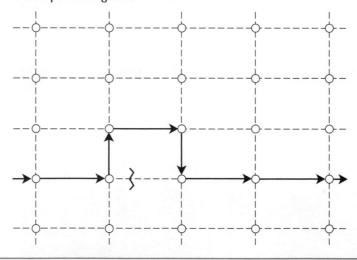

Source: J. Cerella (1990). "Aging and Information-Processing Rate." In J. E. Birren and K. W. Schaie (Eds.), *Handbook of the Psychology of Aging* (3rd ed., pp. 210–221). San Diego, CA: Academic Press. Used by permission of Academic Press, Inc.

All three models point to some mechanism in the central nervous system—the neural hardware—as the source of the increasing processing time required by older subjects. According to Cerella (1990), these biologically based models explain the observed phenomena without having to resort to explanations based on increased cautiousness, a greater emphasis on accuracy over speed, deficits in attention, and so on. This is not to say that these factors have no effect, but rather that their effect is no different in the young than in the old. Salthouse (1985), on the other hand, cautions that the data are not only sparse, but methodologically flawed as well.

Two final points bear mention. First, we have seen in earlier sections the danger of assuming that group data tell us about individual aging. The fact is that large numbers of individuals experience no cognitive deficits until advanced age or may even demonstrate improved performance over previous levels as a result of favorable life experiences or programmed interventions (Schaie, 1988). For this reason, we must be careful not to assume that the changes we are looking at are universal. Second, researchers may discover age-related changes that are both reliable and of significant magnitude but that are irrelevant to real-world functioning (Schaie, 1988). We have to be careful not to overintepret small changes as having practical significance. For example, most experimental studies find the absolute difference in reaction time between younger and older adults to be under one second (Cerella, Poon, & Williams, 1980). We should consider whether such a difference significantly impairs older adults in most circumstances, in what settings it is critical, and whether there may be compensations available to older, more experienced individuals that would make up for the slower reaction time. As Hunt (1993, p. 589) put it, "In most cases involving everyday activity, the young old contrast should not be thought of as a contrast between a fast and a slow computer, but as a contrast between a fast computer with a limited library of programs and a slow computer with a large library." In those situations where speed is more critical, interventions may be available that could improve processing speed. What we can say at this point is that there is consensus that information processing slows with age and that it is a pervasive phenomenon. Issues of cause and consequence remain to be resolved.

Several scholars have identified ways that slower processing speed may undermine memory processes, leading to qualitative, not just quantitative, differences in processing. Salthouse (1985) suggests that a slower rate of processing might lead to the use of different (less efficient?) strategies. He also notes that the system will be characterized by more partially processed information at any given moment and so be more susceptible to overload and distraction. Myerson et al. (1990) point out that slower processing due to information loss means that the amount of information available for storage and retrieval is reduced. Let's look at research specifically directed at age-related memory changes.

Memory

Calling it the binding and unifying force that holds our consciousness together, Hering (1920, p. 75) spoke to the critical importance of memory for our sense of self, our understanding of the world around us, and our ability to function within it: "We owe to memory almost everything that we either have or are." Given its central importance, it should not be surprising that many more experimental studies have been done on memory than on anything else in the psychology of aging, and that research activity remains strong. Most of these are controlled laboratory studies in which subjects are tested using verbal material. Concern over ecological validity has led to efforts to study memory for material considered to be more meaningful and relevant to everyday, practical cognitive tasks (Hultsch & Dixon, 1990). One of the most important changes in our thinking about memory is the recognition that it is not a unitary entity, but rather is composed of many diverse aspects, the relations among which are not yet well understood (Schacter, 1989).

Competing theories abound, none of which accommodates all the findings. Age-related declines in memory do occur and are of real concern to many older people. Yet one of the most striking aspects of the experimental literature is that age-related memory changes are extremely variable (Craik, 1994). It appears that some aspects of memory are well maintained as we age, while others are more vulnerable to the effects of aging. Much of the research on memory and aging is focused on determining which of the various aspects, forms, and varieties of memory are preserved and which decline with age in an effort to localize the source of age-related cognitive deficits (Hultsch & Dixon, 1990).

Short-Term and Long-Term Memory

One of the dominant conceptions of memory in the 1960s and 1970s was the "memory stores" model of Atkinson and Shiffrin (1968), who proposed that information passed through a series of storage bins of various sizes as it was processed. These stages of memory were called sensory, short-term, and long-term memory, with particular research attention being focused on the latter two. (See Figure 5.2.)

Short-term memory was considered to be a limited-capacity, temporary holding facility for information that had either just come in from the senses and needed to be processed, or had just been retrieved from permanent storage for temporary use. It was the midpoint between the senses and the permanent memory store, or **long-term memory.** Information was thought to move in and out of short-term memory in 30 seconds, unless the individual actively rehearsed it to keep it longer (as when you say a phone number over and over until you are able to complete the call). If you are familiar with using a personal computer, short-term memory would be roughly equivalent to the information you are currently working with on the screen, which either may just have been

FIGURE 5.2 *The "Stores" Model of Memory, Based on Atkinson and Shiffrin (1968)*

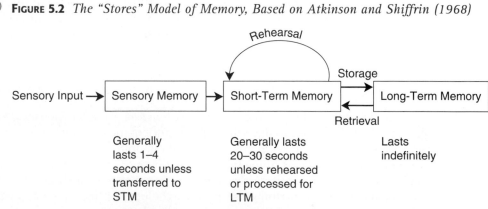

entered or may have been called up from a stored file. Once you have finished with this material, you can either let it leave the system, or you can place it in permanent storage—the equivalent of long-term memory. Long-term memory would be analogous to what is stored on the floppy disk or hard drive. Unlike your PC, however, your brain's long-term memory is thought to be a storehouse with an unlimited capacity.

Working Memory

By 1982, Crowder was chronicling the "demise" of the original concept of short-term memory. An alternative view—richer and more elaborate in its conceptualization—was presented by Baddeley and Hitch (1974; also see Baddeley, 1986, 2001) in the concept of working memory, which places less emphasis on the components of the memory system and more on the activities or functions of memory. Baddeley's group used a dual-task technique to study working memory. Subjects perform a primary task such as reading and comprehending a prose passage, while at the same time trying to remember a list of numbers. Or they might track a visual object, while at the same time performing a task that involves processing either verbal or visual images (Baddeley, 1986). They wanted to know whether the secondary task (hanging on to the set of numbers) would interfere with the primary task (reading comprehension). They found that subjects could handle the comprehension task as long as they had fewer than six digits to remember. Beyond that, comprehension began to suffer. Further, they found that visual, but not verbal, imagery tasks interfered with the visual tracking task. Their conclusion was that, unlike the traditional view of short-term memory as a unitary entity, working memory must consist of more than one component.

Baddeley and Hitch (1974) have partitioned working memory into three subsystems: the central executive and two support systems, called the phonological loop and the visuospatial sketchpad. **Working memory** can be thought of as the place where your current memory activity is being conducted, a "dynamic place where intermediate results of the memory processes are 'scribbled down' so they'll be available for later processing" (Ashcraft, 1989, pp. 54–55). Working memory represents the amount of cognitive resource that is available to process incoming information or previously stored information retrieved from long-term memory and to store new information (Park et al., 1996). In this model, working memory is limited by the amount of processing capacity (space) available—in other words, the number of tasks the system can handle simultaneously.

Consider, for example, a list of errands: the post office (mail a package, get a roll of stamps), the dry cleaner (pick up cleaning, drop off cleaning, and ask about fixing a zipper), the jeweler (order a new watchband, remember to take the watch with you, get a setting on a ring checked), the grocery store (a long list here), and so on. At what point do you feel your capacity to remember all this diminishing? When you feel your resource limit has been reached, you are experiencing the limits of working memory. The same occurs when you try to do complex mathematical computations in your head or understand a complicated set of instructions. There is a point at which you say the equivalent of "Wait a minute—I'm not getting this."

Working memory, then, is where conscious mental work goes on—the putting together of pieces of information to accomplish a task, some of it coming from the environment and some of it retrieved from existing storage in the memory system. And there are limits to how much you can do all at once. Your abilities are facilitated, however, by the three components of working memory mentioned earlier, which function to hold onto information while it is being processed.

The job of the **central executive** is to direct the use of mental resources such as attention and strategies such as organization—to control activity, direct the flow of work, and make decisions as an executive would. The central executive is assisted by the **phonological loop,** an auditory mechanism that temporarily holds acoustic and speech-based information, while the **visuospatial sketchpad,** a kind of chalkboard for pictorial representations ("the mind's eye"), performs the same function in regard to visual and spatial information. A couple of examples may help to clarify how these systems work. Let's say you are at the grocery store and your bill comes to $23.87. You have a $20, a $10, and two $1 bills. While you (actually your central executive) are deciding which bills to give to the checker and figuring out how much change you should get back, your phonological loop assists you by repeating (rehearsing) the amount you owe. Or, let's say you are walking across campus and you pass someone whose face you recognize, but you cannot place the person. As you pass, and the person is now out of sight, your visuospatial sketchpad will "sketch out" and hold onto an image of the person so you can remember the face while your central executive starts searching through memory files to figure out how you know her. Figure 5.3 illustrates these three components of working memory. The original multicomponent model proposed by Baddeley and Hitch has been revised over the years. Most recently, a fourth subsystem, the *episodic buffer,* has been proposed, providing interface between the other components and able to combine information from them with information from LTM (Baddeley, 2000, 2001).

To date, there has been quite a bit of empirical support for the working memory model (Schacter, 1989). However, we do not yet understand its neural bases—that is, how many different working memory systems there are, in which parts of the brain they are based, or how they interact (Smith, 2000). There is considerable research interest in executive processes such as those represented by the central executive, and their role in cognitive aging, though they are widely acknowledged to be very complex, difficult to assess, and not well understood (Salthouse, Atkinson, & Berish, 2003).

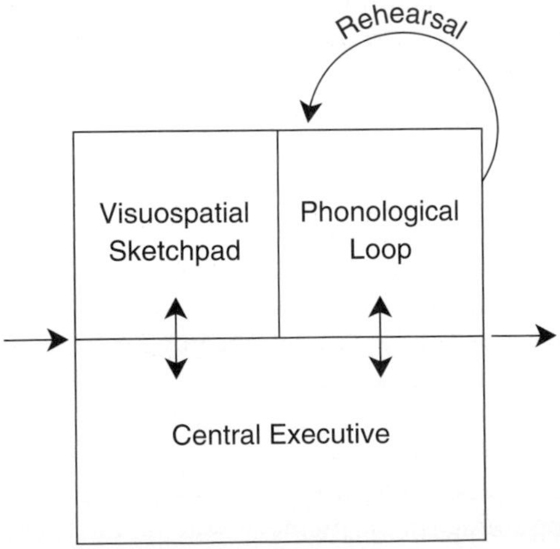

Cognitive aging research has demonstrated substantial deficiencies among older people on tasks that tap working memory (for example, Wingfield, Stine, Lahar, & Aberdeen, 1988). If we view working memory as a general mental resource, deficiencies in this aspect of memory would significantly undermine many cognitive activities (Hultsch & Dixon, 1990). Older adults may have a smaller "workspace" in which to keep in mind the problem while at the same time performing computations, storing intermediate solutions, and so on (Salthouse, 1985). If this is the case, the system would have to rely on techniques that take more time, such as swapping and transferring information back and forth to long-term memory. Speed of processing would be slowed, and the more complex the task, the greater the impairment. This is consistent with evidence we have cited earlier. For example, Kausler, Wiley, and Lieberwitz (1992) hypothesize that the problems older people have in recall of long-term memory are actually

FIGURE 5.3 *Three Components of Working Memory*

due to a problem in working memory—the difficulty of searching large storehouses of information to retrieve a particular item. The effort required to search a larger pool of knowledge overwhelms the elderly subjects' diminished working-memory capacity. Thus, they are at a retrieval-search disadvantage in comparison to younger subjects.

As discussed in the previous section, a number of researchers attribute age-related changes to a reduction in speed. A slower rate of information processing would affect the efficiency of working memory, especially for complex tasks, and in turn lead to reduced performance on tests of fluid intelligence (Fry & Hale, 1996). Thus, speed appears to be the more fundamental resource, and reduced speed is the primary cause of age differences in memory (Park et al., 1996).

Levels of Processing

The **levels-of-processing model** (Craik & Lockhart, 1972) focuses on the extent of processing that takes place during encoding; it predicts that information processed more elaborately and deeply will be more easily remembered than information processed more superficially. This model places less emphasis on the structure of memory and more on what the individual does with information. For example, the word *engram* could be processed based on the way it looks (the most shallow, structural level), the way it sounds (a deeper, acoustic level), or its meaning (the deepest, semantic level). (See Table 5.1.) Processing at the level of meaning would be expected to produce the most reliable memory. Modifications of this model suggest that different encoding processes may be more effective with certain kinds of material than with others, and that the usefulness of any encoding activity depends on and interacts with the conditions present at retrieval (Schacter, 1989). For example, semantic processing may not be as powerful as acoustic coding for a rhyming task. This is Tulving's (1983) **principle of encoding specificity:** the type of encoding should be appropriate to the task.

In general, however, older adults do not seem to process information as deeply or elaboratively as younger people (Craik & Simon, 1980). In other words, the quality of

TABLE 5.1 *Levels of Processing*

Level of Processing	Example
Visual	Remembering how something looks—for example, the length of a word, capitalization, and so on. Have you ever looked at a written word and said, "That doesn't look right"? Or have you ever said, "I'd know it if I saw it"?
Acoustic	Remembering how something sounds—for example, the number of syllables in a word, the letter it starts with, a word it rhymes with. Have you ever recognized someone by their footsteps? Or said, "I'd know it if I heard it"?
Semantic	Remembering the meaning—for example, the definition of a word. Can you come up with synonyms for the word *exhilaration?* Have you read a book or seen a movie and been able to tell someone the gist of it?

processing suffers with age. Some question exists about whether this is a performance problem (they could do better if shown how to) or a real processing deficiency (they are incapable of doing it) (Schacter, 1989). Craik (1986) feels that older people have a special problem with self-initiated retrieval—when the retrieval context does not provide much help or support in coming up with the to-be-remembered information and the individual must therefore exert more conscious effort. An example would be an essay question on a test. On the other hand, subjects who have a great deal of knowledge or experience in a particular area are likely to encode related information in a rich, elaborate way, enhancing later retrieval (Adelson, 1984). This potentially gives the edge to older, more experienced individuals (experts) relative to that domain. You may remember that experts tend to process information relevant to their area of expertise at a deeper, semantic or meaning level, while novices approach the information more superficially (how it looks, sounds, and so on). This gives the expert an advantage in most problem-solving tasks within the field of expertise, unless the problem requires detailed, superficial information, which the expert tends to overlook.

Again, Schacter (1989) concludes that it is difficult to draw any strong conclusions about the nature of age differences in level of processing. Empirical findings are inconsistent due largely to problems in the assessment of the processing strategies subjects are actually using.

Episodic, Semantic, and Procedural Memory

Tulving (1972, 1983) distinguished between **episodic memory** (knowledge of specific events experienced by the individual, stored along with information about time and place, much like a personal diary), **semantic memory** (consisting of highly overlearned general knowledge and vocabulary, the kind of information found in an encyclopedia or dictionary), and skill or **procedural memory** (the influence of previous experiences on present performance). (See Table 5.2.) Tulving suggested a hierarchical system in which procedural memory was the most primitive and first to develop, followed by semantic and finally episodic memory. The implication is that episodic memory is most vulnerable, and procedural memory least vulnerable, to the effects of aging (Craik & Jennings, 1992). Though it is not always easy to distinguish between them, the tentative assumption is that age differences in memory are more likely in episodic than semantic or procedural memory (Salthouse, 1991b).

TABLE 5.2 *Procedural, Semantic, and Episodic Memory*

Type of Memory	Analogy	Examples
Procedural	A "how-to" manual	Knowing how to tie a necktie or ride a bike Knowing how to prepare to write a paper
Semantic	Encyclopedia and dictionary	Knowledge of the Civil War Knowing what the word *over* means
Episodic	Personal diary	Memories aroused when a particular song is played Recollections of your first childhood friend

CRITICAL THINKING QUESTION
Are older adults more likely to remember how to roller-skate (assuming they once knew) or the name of their third-grade teacher? Why?

Implicit versus Explicit Memory

Much research interest has been directed at the distinction between implicit and explicit memory (Graf & Schacter, 1985), which evolved from observations of spared memory abilities among patients with amnesia (Greenwald, 1992). **Implicit memory** is "an unintentional, nonconscious form of retention," while **explicit memory** "involves conscious recollection of previous experiences" (Schacter, 1992, p. 559). Explicit memory can be seen in memory of facts that you have intentionally tried to remember (for example, trying hard to remember the name of your first date). Implicit memory can be seen in skill or procedural learning tasks (and is comparable to Tulving's procedural memory). For instance, you may be able to hop on a bike and ride like an expert without much conscious thought, even after years of no riding. Or you may be able to find your way to a particular location, though you are not consciously aware of how you will do it. A more dramatic example is provided by the following story (Adler, 1991). A young woman is found wandering aimlessly on the street. The police pick her up. She has no memory of who she is and is carrying no identification. The police ask her to start dialing phone numbers. One of the numbers she dials turns out to be her mother's.

Most laboratory memory studies tap explicit memory, which is normally assessed through recall or recognition tasks that require the subject to intentionally retrieve information learned during a prior study session. Implicit memory is often studied through priming tasks that do not require the subject to consciously recall a previous exposure to the material (Tulving & Schacter, 1990). For example, subjects are exposed to items such as words or pictures during a study session but are not asked to remember them. This is often done under the guise of some unrelated task. Then, at a later time, they are asked to identify degraded versions of the picture or to complete the stem or fragment of a word. If their test performance is better for items they have seen before than for those they have had no previous exposure to, priming is shown—in other words, evidence of implicit memory exists. For example, subjects asked to complete word fragments such as _ac_os_ _ or *tab*_ _ tend to provide words they were previously exposed to (*lacrosse, table*) (Schacter, 1989).

Different patterns of age-related deficits appear on explicit and implicit memory tasks, with implicit memory left largely unaffected, while explicit memory deteriorates with age (Light, 1988, 1991). The reasons for these differences are not understood. Much debate exists about whether the distinction between implicit and explicit memory is based in two neurologically distinct memory systems or different processing strategies or both (Schacter, 1992; Schacter, Cooper, & Valdiserri, 1992). The distinction between implicit and explicit memory may stem from the difference between automatic and effortful processing. Brain scan technology (such as positron emission tomography or PET), which allows researchers to get a picture of what is happening in the brain as an individual works on a task, should shed light on this question.

The use of memory aids, such as this medicine organizer, can effectively support prospective memory.

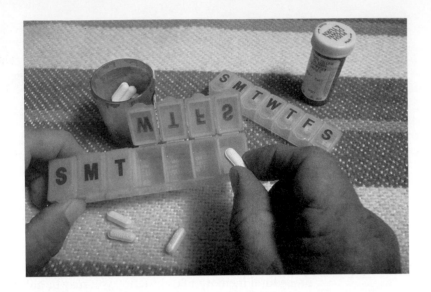

Prospective Memory

Prospective memory (PM)—remembering to do something in the future—has generally been thought to be highly susceptible to aging effects because of the greater demands these tasks place on self-initiated remembering. Older adults may be especially likely to forget when there is a delay between intention and execution (remembering to do something and being able to do it) (Einstein, McDaniel, Manzi, Cochran, & Baker, 2000). Many everyday prospective memory tasks are repetitive, such as taking medication. For these sorts of routine tasks, one needs to remember to do it and then that one has done it. Einstein, McDaniel, Smith, and Shaw (1998) found large increases in both omission errors (forgetting to do something) and repetition errors (forgetting that one has done something) among older adults, especially when faced with several concurrent tasks.

However, as in so many other areas of the cognitive aging literature, our understanding of PM is muddled by contradictions among studies examining various aspects of PM and using different methodologies. Henry, MacLeod, Phillips, and Crawford (2004) conducted a meta-analytic review of the studies on PM in order to address major issues relating to age effects and to resolve inconsistencies in the findings. They reached some surprising conclusions. First, contrary to prevailing opinion, PM is associated with less age-related decline than retrospective memory (memory for past events). In addition, while older adults perform more poorly than younger subjects in laboratory studies of PM, older subjects substantially outperform their younger counterparts in naturalistic studies. Whatever deficits are measured in the lab do not translate to everyday life, where older adults appear to benefit from experience and effective memory strategies, such as the use of memory aids, that compensate for any age-related decline in basic processing resources.

Memory for Meaningful Material

As the research just cited illustrates, we are becoming increasingly aware that any age-related memory change is a product of the interaction of characteristics of the individual, the context in which behavior occurs, and the task itself (Hultsch & Dixon, 1990). Along with concerns about the ecological validity of much cognitive aging research, this has led to increased efforts to study memory for more meaningful material, such as events, prose passages, names, faces, and so on. One well-documented problem is increased difficulty in word (and name) finding with age, and an increase in tip-of-the-tongue (TOT) experiences (Maylor & Valentine, 1992; Light, 1990). Maylor and Valentine point out that the difficulty in retrieving proper names may be especially frustrating because, unlike other words, substitutes for them cannot really be used. The problem may be that, due to cognitive slowing, retrieval takes longer among older adults. On the other hand, retrieval of names may be more difficult with age because the pool of names we know is greater (making the search more complex) and because the average amount of time that has passed since our last exposure to or recall of a given name becomes longer. These factors may explain the phenomenon better than aging itself.

Attitudes and Attributions

One of the issues that may bear on the cognitive performance of older individuals is what they and others expect their mental ability to be. Hertzog and Hultsch (2000) reviewed evidence indicating that while people perceive their memory to be declining as they grow older, their beliefs are not highly correlated with their actual performance on memory tasks. If older people believe that their memory and other cognitive abilities are deteriorating, this attitude may affect their confidence and motivation to try new things and learn new tasks. Thus, they may avoid these activities, setting up a self-fulfilling prophecy. Erber and her colleagues have conducted a number of studies on attitudes toward memory failure among younger and older individuals. Both young and old adults rated identical memory failures as more serious if the individual was old as opposed to young (Erber, Szuchman, & Rothberg, 1990). In addition, memory failure in an older subject was attributed to lack of ability, which is considered a stable trait, whereas the failure in a young subject was attributed to lack of effort and attention, which could presumably be remedied (Erber & Rothberg, 1991). Erber, Etheart, and Szuchman (1992) speculate as to whether this age-based double standard affects overall judgments of cognitive ability and the opportunities available to older individuals.

Summing Up Research on Memory and Aging

Each of the approaches to the study of memory discussed above is an attempt to localize age differences in specific aspects of memory. Despite active research efforts, none has been entirely successful in doing so. Many findings have not been replicated, possibly as a result of methodological problems, or perhaps because we have yet to identify the most important dimensions along which age differences exist (Salthouse, 1991b). Certainly memory is no longer seen as a unitary entity, but as an extremely complex phenomenon. Theoretical interpretations of the relationships among the varieties and forms of memory are "still very much up for grabs" (Schacter, 1989, p. 710).

Does memory decline with age? The answer seems to be yes . . . and no. No meaningful conclusions about age-related changes in memory can be reached without specifying what aspect of memory, or what type of memory task, is being discussed. Some aspects of memory seem to be spared any meaningful deterioration with age among healthy adults, while others show some evidence of decline. In general, those memory tasks that are complex, effortful, and require speed and the manipulation of a lot of new information simultaneously appear to become more difficult as we age. On the other hand, memory tasks that rely on accumulated experience and expertise—well-practiced, automatic processes—show less evidence of loss.

The research presented earlier in this chapter has a bearing on the way our memory ages. Those who are well-educated, healthy, optimistic, and flexible, and who live stimulating, cognitively challenging lives may be better able to avoid cognitive decline. Further, among those who show evidence of obvious deterioration, the negative effects of aging may be minimized by appropriate environmental support, compensation techniques (for example, providing cues and reminders, minimizing distractions), and cognitive interventions (such as instruction in effective processing strategies).

Status of Information-Processing Approaches

As we have seen, some investigators are attempting to localize the source of age-related cognitive deficits in a specific aspect of the information-processing system—for example, in one or another component of memory. Others believe the major culprit to be a reduction of some general processing resource—such as attention or speed—that underlies all cognitive activity. These various information-processing resources may be interrelated in various ways, or may reflect different facets of the same mechanism. Many cognitive processes seem to be age-sensitive. Research describing one or another of these aspects of cognitive functioning in adulthood (the "what") continues to accumulate, but conclusions as to the "why" and the "how" remain weak and general. We have talked in earlier chapters about the lack of integrated understanding of development in the field in general. This problem is no less evident here (Li, 2002). In fact, as Salthouse (1991b, p. 289) puts it, "One can obviously question whether progress is being made toward integrative understanding when the number of phenomena in need of explanation is apparently increasing rather than decreasing." Horn (1986, p. 43) laments the narrowness of much process-focused cognitive research: "There is a sense in which this work is not putting Humpty Dumpty back together again." Salthouse (1991b, p. 360) says simply, "Further research is needed."

The direction of future research is likely to change. As Hunt (1993) points out, the psychology of aging has been dominated by laboratory-based studies comparing the performance of elderly and young adults on tasks with questionable direct application to the cognitive activities of everyday life. He predicts a growing research focus on middle-aged adults, mainly because of interest in workforce capability. Researchers will also increasingly concentrate on meaningful tasks with application to everyday life. An understanding of the reasons for and prevention of the decline in fluid intelligence we have discussed will be critical in a world in which fluid intelligence will be in demand. The value of crystallized intelligence accumulated over a lifetime of experience may lessen in many fields as technology replaces the expertise previously provided by people. Greater value will be placed on the flexibility to frame new solutions to old problems, or to conceptualize new problems (or products or services) in the first place. A better understanding of how to encourage the maintenance of learning, problem-solving skills, and retrainability will be more and more essential as our aging society confronts the challenges of the 21st century.

Schacter (1989, 1992) is a vocal champion of a multidisciplinary approach to the study of age-related cognitive change—what he calls a cognitive neuroscience approach.

Rather than perpetuate the old dualism between mind and body through the segregation of research and theory into isolated disciplines, he feels it is helpful to combine cognitive research and theory with neuropsychological and neurobiological findings, thus contributing to a broader understanding of the phenomenon under study. Schacter's position is consistent with the interdisciplinary theme running throughout this book. We turn now to look at some of the relevant neurological issues, keeping in mind that the linkages between biological and psychological factors are not well understood (Craik & Salthouse, 2000; Ivy, MacLeod, Petit, & Markus, 1992). Attempts to relate the two remain to some degree "an adventure in correlating the mysterious with the unknown" (Owens, 1956, p. 157).

Concept Review 5.3

- Those who study cognitive aging from an information-processing perspective are interested in age-related changes in the way the mind encodes, stores, and retrieves information.

- The magnitude of variation in cognitive ability among people of different ages increases as the task becomes more complex—a finding known as the age-complexity effect.

- Research suggests that selective attention may decline with age, thus undermining effortful tasks, while those that have become automatic are largely unaffected.

- Birren has proposed the generalized slowing hypothesis to account for differences in the cognitive abilities of older versus younger individuals. This slowing may be due to increased cycling time, information loss, or loss of neural connections.

- The bulk of research has focused on the role of memory in cognitive aging and attempts to determine which aspects of memory are more likely to decline with age and which are best preserved and why.

Physiological Explanations

The changes that occur in the nervous system as we age may contribute to age-related changes in cognitive performance. This section examines some of the large-scale anatomical changes in the brain and changes at the level of the neuron. It also reviews evidence of plasticity in the aging nervous system.

Changes in the Brain with Age

Advances in neuroscience and neuropsychology are helping us to understand the relationship between brain and behavior more clearly. In this section, we review research in neuropsychology that attempts to understand age-associated changes in brain structure and function.

New brain imaging technologies may help to fill the gap in our knowledge of the aging brain. In particular, advances in magnetic resonance imaging (MRI) technology,

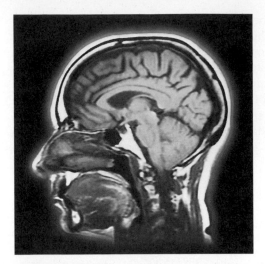

New techniques for producing images of brain structure and function, such as the magnetic resonance image shown here, hold great potential for increasing our understanding of cognitive changes that occur with age.

originally developed to provide information about brain structure, now allow us to see brain function through the use of **functional magnetic resonance imaging (fMRI).** fMRI detects changes in the magnetic state of blood as a result of oxygenation. Thus, it is possible to detect where brain activity occurs as people perform various cognitive tasks. fMRI has a number of advantages over existing brain-imaging technologies. First, this new technology will be more widely available than the positron emission tomography (PET) technology, which has been the best-known and most influential technique for getting images of human brain function up to now. Because PET facilities are very expensive to build and maintain, few of them exist, while clinical MRI scanners are already present in thousands of hospitals around the country. Second, unlike the PET scan, fMRI is noninvasive, so subjects can participate in MRI studies without the need for any injection. And third, the same machine can produce a structural MRI of an individual's brain just before or after an fMRI (Gabrieli et al., 1996). Thus, investigators can map brain functions onto brain structures. Finally, fMRI produces good technical resolution and has no known risks. Though fMRI is a new technology and there are some unresolved challenges in its use, it holds great potential for expanding our understanding of cognitive aging. In the future, scientists hope to develop less expensive and more portable techniques and to combine fMRI with other technologies (such as MEG—magnetoencephalography) to produce "brain movies." (See Buckner & Logan, 2001, and Raichle, 2001, for reviews of PET and fMRI methodology.)

Neuroimaging techniques can be applied to groups of adults of different ages to determine if there are differences in task-related activity in a given brain region (Grady, 2002). Various outcomes have been found, depending on the task and brain area studied. The groups may show similar brain activity, or the older group may show greater or lesser activity than those who are younger. It is not yet clear how to interpret these findings. For example, lower levels of brain activity could reflect either reduced functional ability or more efficient processing. Similarly, a higher level of activation in older adults could reflect either greater functional ability or greater efforts at compensation. Could differences between groups be due to performance differences rather than age per se, with one group being more or less skilled at the task than others? Similarly, when brain atrophy is found, what is its functional significance? While neuroimaging evidence alone cannot answer all the questions in the study of cognitive aging, it certainly contributes to our quest for understanding.

Advanced age is associated with a progressive loss of brain tissue, especially in the **cerebral cortex** (Ivy et al., 1992). This is the quarter-inch covering over the cerebrum where higher-order mental activities occur. By age 70, the loss of total brain mass is about 5 percent, by 80, 10 percent, and by 90, 20 percent (Minckler & Boyd, 1968; Wisniewski & Terry, 1976). Some brain areas are more vulnerable than others. The loss of neurons is especially marked in the **frontal lobe** of each hemisphere (Ivy et al., 1992; Parkin & Walter, 1992), the area identified by Baddeley (1986) as the location of the central executive function of working memory. The anterior portion of the frontal lobes, called the prefrontal cortex, comprises about 28 percent of the cortex and appears to be involved in monitoring and controlling our thoughts and actions (Shimamura, 1996). Other researchers have found damage to the **hippocampus,** a fingerlike structure in the limbic system known to be involved in memory (Moscovitch & Winocur, 1992). (See Figures 5.4 and 5.5.)

During normal aging, deterioration in the prefrontal cortex and the hippocampus may account for some of the memory and executive deficits seen in older adults (Mittenberg, Seidenberg, O'Leary, & DiGiulio, 1989) that show up as problems in finding the right word or remembering someone's name, absentmindedness (e.g., forgetting where one put one's keys), and difficulty remembering temporal order (e.g., forgetting when some recent event took place). However, most studies have failed to identify extensive neuronal loss in the cortex and hippocampus (Smith, Roberts, Gage, & Tuszynski, 1999). And these patterns of neuronal loss and their associated cognitive problems vary greatly in degree among older adults; indeed, some individuals in their 60s to 90s show no appreciable neuronal loss. This suggests the influence of a number of factors, such as degree of mental activity and aerobic exercise, as we will see. There is also evidence that various alleles of the Apolipoprotein E (APOE) gene on chromosome 19 have either a detrimental or protective effect on memory function in normal cognitive aging (Deary et al., 2004). The dire picture we used to paint of major cell losses in normal aging has clearly been contradicted by recent research. For the most part, in a healthy older adult, these changes are rather subtle and, while annoying to the individual, do not result in major cognitive impairment.

Are there other structural explanations for the types of cognitive deficits seen in older individuals? Smith, Roberts, Gage, & Tuszynski (1999) studied adult rhesus monkeys, which provide the best animal model of human aging. They found significant age-related cell atrophy (but not cell death) in the subcortical basal forebrain, the lower brain centers that support the more advanced brain structures involved in higher-order cognitive functions. The cause of this cell degeneration is unknown. Most significantly, the researchers were able to almost completely reverse these changes through human

FIGURE 5.4 *The Lobes of the Cerebral Cortex*

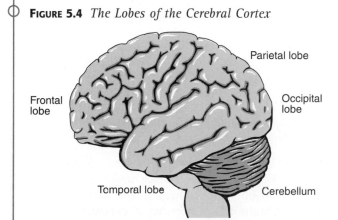

FIGURE 5.5 *The Hippocampus*

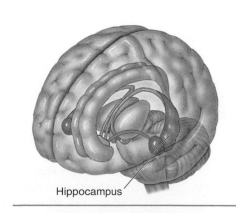

nerve growth factor gene therapy, suggesting that though these neurons have begun to degenerate, they have not died and can be returned to normal. These findings have potential implications for the prevention of normal cognitive aging as well as for the treatment of Alzheimer's disease.

Male and female brains may age differently. Gur et al. (1991) found evidence of sex differences in the way the brain changes with age. The researchers used magnetic resonance imaging (MRI) to study the brains of 34 men and 35 women age 18 to 80. Brain atrophy (reduced brain volume and increased cerebrospinal fluid volume) was more pronounced in men and was especially apparent in the left cerebral hemisphere. Not only was there less evidence of brain deterioration in the women, but the age effects were symmetrically distributed. The data also indicate that mental functions controlled by the left hemisphere, such as verbal abilities, are likely to be more greatly affected in older males than older females. Accumulating research indicates that the female sex hormone estrogen enhances cognitive function via properties that affect the structure and function of neurons in areas of the brain critical to learning and memory and that it may protect against age-related decline and Alzheimer's disease (Foy, Henderson, Berger, & Thompson, 2000). Concerns about the loss of estrogen among women at menopause (e.g., twice as many women as men develop Alzheimer's disease) have led to interest in the efficacy of hormone replacement therapy. These issues remain unresolved.

Though these neurological changes may be the primary cause of cognitive decline, Moscovitch & Winocur (1992) are careful to point out that they do not occur in isolation, but can be influenced (precipitated, enhanced, retarded, even reversed) by psychological, social, and environmental factors. Let's consider an example. We know that the system of blood vessels that feeds the brain deteriorates with age (Ivy et al., 1992). As the levels of oxygen, nutrients, and other vital substances normally supplied to brain cells by the blood are reduced, brain cells begin to die. The question is, what sets this process in motion? Ivy et al. (1992) suggest that reduced neural activity in the brain of an elderly person may result from changing work and/or social patterns. As neurons become less active, blood flow to those areas of the brain is reduced—sort of the law of demand and supply. As the blood supply decreases, brain cells begin to die. In other words, the chain of events could begin in a number of different ways, perhaps precipitated by psychosocial events. Moscovitch and Winocur (1992) advocate a more global approach to the study of cognitive decline in late adulthood, which would take account of the complex interaction of psychosocial, environmental, and biological aspects of aging.

CRITICAL THINKING QUESTION

Earlier in this chapter, we discussed the influence of a stimulating environment on age-related cognitive change. On the basis of research just cited, how might environmental richness and complexity affect the state of the brain?

Before we leave this section, it should be noted that changes in the circulatory system of the brain also lead to erosion of the **blood-brain barrier,** which protects the brain from many potentially harmful blood-borne substances. As this barrier deteriorates and becomes more permeable, the brain is at greater risk of exposure to a variety of factors. Whether this is in part responsible for the presence of one such substance in the brain, amyloid, which has been implicated in the development of Alzheimer's disease, is unknown. Chapter 11 includes a more in-depth look at this form of dementia.

Changes in and between Neurons, and Plasticity

Black, Greenough, Anderson, and Isaacs (1987) take issue with the view that the aging brain is in a state of inevitable decline, shriveling up and dying. They attribute this perception largely to studies of laboratory rats, who are normally housed throughout their lives in cages with little stimulation and no company and who are therefore not normal. "All too often these otherwise excellent studies can only tell us about bored old rats reared with too much food and not enough exercise" (Black et al., 1987, p. 126). They do not necessarily tell us much about normal rat—let alone human—aging. Recent work in neuroscience presents a much more hopeful picture of the brain's capacity to maintain, repair, and adapt itself. This work focuses on brain **plasticity**—the idea that the brain can modify its structure and function in a positive sense and that this capacity is maintained throughout adulthood and old age. This is a fairly new concept, contrary to the traditional view that brain tissue is static and unmodifiable, as well as unable to respond to damage (Cohen, 1990). The implication is that aging does not inevitably lead to a loss of function (Cotman, 1990).

Let's consider the structure of the **neuron** or nerve cell, the basic building block of the nervous system. Two parts of the neuron especially relevant to our discussion are the dendrites and axon (Figure 5.6). **Dendrites** arc short branching fibers that extend from the cell body and receive information from elsewhere in the nervous system. Dendrites comprise about 95 percent of the surface of nerve cells. The more luxuriant the dendritic tree, the more surface area and the greater the neuron's ability to receive information. While we used to think that dendrites atrophied with age, evidence now exists of normal dendritic growth between middle and old age (Coleman & Flood, 1986). The **axon** is a long fiber projecting away from the cell body and ending in a number of terminal branches that transmit information (in the form of nerve impulses) to

FIGURE 5.6 *The Neuron*

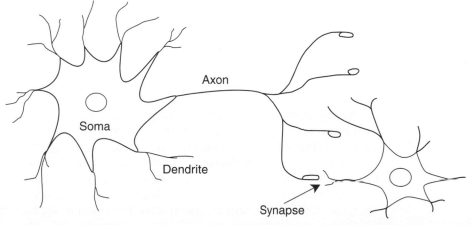

other parts of the system (another neuron, muscle, gland, and so on). Again, the more projections from the axon, the more it can reach out and the greater the communication capacity of the cell. The small fluid-filled space through which this transfer of information occurs is called a **synapse.**

Communication between neurons occurs at the synapse through the release of chemical neurotransmitters. A number of neurotransmitters have been identified, produced, and used in different parts of the brain, regulating different neural activities. One of these is dopamine. Among other things, **dopamine** acts in the frontal cortex, affecting functions such as attention, processing speed, and working memory (Li, 2002). Throughout adulthood, the amount of dopamine and the number of receptors responding to it decline at a rate of 5 to 15 percent per decade. Li theorizes that some of the cognitive deficits that occur with age may be the result of changes in the chemical systems that support communication among neurons. To date, the causes of these age-related changes in brain chemistry and their effects on brain function and therefore on information-processing abilities are not well understood.

Generally, the number of synapses is a structural representation of the functional complexity of the nervous system. In other words, the more synapses, the greater the informational capacity—the more information can be received and sent. And the number of synapses is determined by the dendritic and axonal branches available to communicate with each other. As an analogy, imagine that you live in a remote village in the early 20th century. Being a progressive sort, you have a telephone, but it is the only one in town. Who can you call? As more people get phones, more and more lines are added to the network, and the capacity of communication within the network increases accordingly. You can "reach out and touch" more people. It is the same with synapses. The more dendrites and axons (phones), the more synapses (phone lines), and the more impulses (calls) can be sent throughout the system.

As we have seen, some nerve cell loss occurs with age, though debate surrounds the actual degree of loss (Cotman, 1990). Cell death is due to a combination of factors both intrinsic and extrinsic to the individual; it seems to be especially likely among the larger neurons (Ivy et al., 1992). Their loss is mitigated, however, by the **redundancy** built into the system. Many networks of neurons carry on similar activities, so that, if one neuron or set of neurons is damaged or dies, its function can normally be taken over by other neurons. For example, brain-imaging studies have found important differences in the number of brain areas older adults use to perform a verbal working memory task as compared to younger subjects, illustrating recruitment to compensate for age-related declines (Azar, 2001). Basically, it is as important to know *how much* damage has occurred in the brain as to know where the damage is located. While the brain can compensate for minor losses, extensive losses will probably translate into some loss of function.

The focus of research interest seems to be increasingly on the synapse. The selective loss of larger cortical neurons is significant, because they tend to make connections with more distant parts of the brain. In other words, they have many more synapses. As a result, as they die off, the amount of information coming into and leaving the cortex will be correspondingly decreased, impairing communication between these higher brain centers and the rest of the nervous system (Ivy et al., 1992).

But this is only part of the picture because, while degeneration and loss do occur, compensatory mechanisms are also at work. For example, axonal and dendritic **sprout-**

ing can take place in response to neuronal loss. As nerve cells die, surrounding cells develop (sprout) new dendritic and axonic fibers to fill the void (Cotman, 1990). In this way, lost synapses are replaced. An analogy may be made to the trees in a forest. When one tree dies, the opening left in the forest canopy does not remain for long, as existing trees surrounding the void grow new branches to fill the space.

Compensatory sprouting is believed to go on throughout life, though perhaps not as readily in advanced age. Black et al. (1987) speculate that this may be because of the aging body's reduced ability to provide the physiological support—glucose, oxygen, and so on—needed to maintain increasing numbers of synapses. In an intriguing study, Hall, Gonder-Fredericks, Vogt, and Gold (1986) found that 50- to 70-year-old adults performed significantly better on a memorization task if they drank a high-sugar drink (not an artificially sweetened one) just beforehand.

Some evidence exists that the sprouting of nerve fibers (and the maintenance or restoration of function that results) is regulated by a group of chemicals including **nerve growth factor,** collectively referred to as **neurotrophins** (Cotman, 1990; Woodruff-Pak, 1993). If this is confirmed, it might some day be possible to improve brain function in older adults by administering this or other substances therapeutically. This is impossible at the moment, however, because, while growth factors are produced and act in the brain, they are made up of large molecules that are prevented from entering by the blood-brain barrier. Thus, they cannot be given orally or by injection.

The same sprouting phenomenon has been observed in some parts of the brain in response to environmental enrichment (Turner & Greenough, 1985) and is thought to represent learning and memory in the brain (Greenough, 1984, 1988). In one study, Greenough, Larson, and Withers (1985) taught adult rats to reach for food with their nonpreferred paw. After the rats had had 16 days of training, motor neurons controlling the newly trained paw had developed dendritic branches as elaborate as those controlling the preferred paw. In another series of experiments, Black et al. (1987) found that the brains of old rats moved to toy-filled social environments developed a thicker cortex and more extensive dendritic branching than those left in standard lab cages. The body of research in this area indicates that the most effective enrichment is offered by environments that provide novel objects and that are social, involving two or more animals (Woodruff-Pak, 1993). The basic idea is simple: environmental stimulation may translate into more neural connections by enlarging the dendritic tree. We should also stress that decreased stimulation will diminish a neuron's dendrites, reducing the functional capacity of the system (Diamond, 1993).

Research also attests to the value of aerobic fitness in maintaining the health of the brain, improving executive control functions, and enhancing reaction time and the rate of information processing (Kramer & Willis, 2002; Woodruff-Pak, 1993). Older men and women who have maintained their physical fitness through jogging have shown reaction times similar to those of college sophomores. The cognitive benefits of moderate exercise also appear to extend to those who begin their fitness program in later life. While neither the mechanism involved nor the extent to which physical activity affects cognitive function is clear, regular exercise may postpone, arrest, or even reverse age-related changes in information processing (Bashore & Goddard, 1993).

Other lines of research suggest the importance of diet to brain health. See the Box for a discussion of the effect of dietary supplements on cognitive aging. The role of exercise, diet, and sleep will be examined further in Chapters 9, 10, and 11.

CRITICAL THINKING QUESTION

Based on the research cited in this chapter, identify specific *activities that may help individuals to retain good brain health and function with age.*

UNDERSTANDING THE DEVELOPMENTAL CONTEXT

Better Thinking through Chemistry?

In recent years, wild claims about the benefits of one or another brain-enhancing chemical have led a lot of people to conclude that they should run to their local farmers' market, pharmacy, or health food store to load up on so-called cognitive enhancers or brain nutrients. (For a thorough discussion of these substances, see Gold, Cahill, & Wenk, 2002; and McDaniel, Maier, & Einstein, 2002.) What's it all about? Is there in fact an herb to treat every ailment? Can diet prevent, forestall, or reverse cognitive decline? Though many substances have been cited, antioxidants and ginkgo biloba are among the most often touted as good for maintaining brain function, especially memory, and staving off age-related losses.

A number of studies suggest that a diet rich in antioxidants, such as deeply colored fruits and vegetables (e.g., blueberries, carrots), may be beneficial. Antioxidants control inflammation and neutralize damaging free radicals produced as the brain metabolizes the large amounts of oxygen it needs to function. (See Chapter 9 for additional discussion of free radicals.) Oxidative stress impairs brain function, can lead to cell death, and is implicated in the development of Alzheimer's disease. These effects may be more apparent in older organisms, as normal repair mechanisms become less effective. Antioxidants are believed to retard or reverse free radical damage to neurons. They may also improve cardiovascular function, which may in turn benefit the brain through improved blood flow and prevention of cardiac disease. Evidence from animal studies is more supportive of the beneficial role of antioxidants in enhancing cognitive function than is research currently available on humans, largely because there is a lack of placebo-controlled studies on humans.

Ginkgo biloba is an herb derived from the leaves of the gingko tree, indigenous to Korea, China, and Japan. Its use to treat biological and psychological conditions has a long history in Chinese medicine. Today, it is perhaps the most widely used herbal supplement to enhance cognitive function. As with almost all herbal supplements, its use (purity, safety, and efficacy) is poorly regulated by the government, as it is not officially classified as a drug and therefore falls outside existing law. Like many other plants, ginkgo biloba does have antioxidant properties and may also have positive effects on the cardiovascular system. As a whole, the research literature on its cognitive effects is limited, weak, and inconclusive.

The authors of both reviews reach the same conclusion: "All in all . . . the current data do not allow strong scientifically based recommendations for any of these memory nutrients. However, the data also do not allow us to conclude that these nutrients are ineffective in boosting memory. Like Gold et al., we believe that there are enough positive results with at least some of these nutrients to suggest that this is an important area for further research" (McDaniel, Maier, & Einstein, 2002, p. 35). These authors cite the need for the following: additional research on healthy middle-aged as well as older adults; research directed at clarifying which nutrients benefit which kinds of cognitive processes; and studies that recognize that combinations of nutrients, rather than any one acting singly, may more effectively address the complex changes that occur in the brain as we age.

Oh . . . and by the way, the brain also benefits from ample sleep. That means, for most of us, at least eight hours of sleep per night. (Read more about the benefits of sleep for learning and memory and overall health on pp. 366–367 in Chapter 9.)

Until very recently, our understanding of brain development was based on the assumption that all of the neurons we will ever have are produced through mitosis during prenatal development. This means that in adulthood lost cells cannot be replenished. This view was altered by the publication of results from a team of researchers at Princeton University in the fall of 1999 (Gould, Reeves, Graziano, & Gross, 1999). Their study of adult macaques (primates) found that new neurons are continually added to several regions of the cortex involved in learning and memory. Earlier studies by Gould and her associates (e.g., Gould, Tanapat, McEwen, Flugge, & Fuchs, 1998) had found evidence of neurogenesis in the hippocampus of several types of monkeys. These studies indicate that though most neocortical neurons are produced prenatally, neurogenesis does occur in the adult primate brain, specifically in areas that play a vital role in behavioral plasticity. These researchers suggest that immature neurons may be capable of rapid structural changes and that this process may serve as the basis for adult capacity for learning. Just as environmental stimulation in early development seems necessary to prevent the "pruning back" of young neurons, so might these new neurons die without stimulation from complex experiences. Finally, the production of neurons throughout adulthood results in "a continuum of neurons of different ages that may form a basis for marking the temporal dimension of memory" (Gould, Reeves, Graziano, & Gross, 1999, p. 551). Future studies will hopefully provide an explanation of the factors involved in the generation and survival of neurons that should enhance our understanding of both normal and abnormal brain development and help to explain the profound impact of environment and life experience on adult brain function. If these findings hold true for other primates and humans, we will have to revise our view of brain development and the way the adult brain responds to experience.

This emerging view is of a dynamic (rather than static) nervous system in which neuronal connections remain somewhat plastic (as opposed to being totally hard-wired early in life). Neurons retain the capacity to respond both to environmental stimulation and to the neuronal loss associated with age. Again, development is characterized by both gains and losses, their relative dominance being affected by many factors, including the individual's behavior and environment. A point seems to occur, however, at which cell loss becomes so extensive, and the compensatory mechanisms sufficiently impaired, that a net loss of functional capacity results. This probably does not happen until very old age in most cases and may be forestalled through environmental interventions. For those without disease, the brain is able to age remarkably well.

Applications and Implications of Cognitive Aging Research

Much of the basic, theoretical work we have been discussing has practical significance and can be used to improve the quality of life as well as the productivity of adults of all ages (Fisk & Rogers, 2002; Park, 1992). For instance, research in the field of **applied cognitive aging** attempts to solve real-life problems of older adults by utilizing what is known about their cognitive abilities. The ability declines observed in many community-dwelling older adults are largely reversible through appropriate educational intervention programs, such as those discussed at the end of Chapter 4 (Schaie, 1996).

Research in the field of **human factors** makes use of what is known about the cognitive, perceptual, and motor behaviors of the individual to design safer and more efficient tools, technologies, and environments. Are existing products and systems easy for most of us to use? The answer is no (Fisk and Rogers, 2002). People of all ages report similar types of problems, though these are exacerbated in older adults: for example, difficulty understanding (or even being able to read) printed material or an inability to physically manipulate the product. Such problems may be merely annoying, or in some cases dangerous, as when using home health care systems. And products touted as simple to use are often quite the contrary, as in the case of a blood glucose monitor designed for home use by diabetics that in fact requires more than 50 steps. By "knowing the user," those working in this field hope to achieve the goal of optimizing an individual's performance (e.g., reducing pilot error or surgical error by redesign of instrumentation) (Charness, 1992). Environmental modifications to accommodate the decreased visual and auditory capabilities of older adults are an example of these applications (see Chapter 9 for a more extensive discussion of this issue). Another approach may be to change the way information is presented so that it is more easily understood and remembered. Investigators might determine how best to structure prescription labels and directions so as to encourage medication adherence, for example (Park, 1992). This field has also focused on issues of safety and productivity in the workplace, an emphasis likely to be of increasing concern with the graying of the labor force (Charness, 1992).

Wendy Rogers and Dan Fisk are codirectors of the Human Factors and Aging Laboratory at the Georgia Institute of Technology. They are the psychologists on an interdisciplinary research team focused on developing psychological and computer support systems to enable older individuals to remain independent and in their own homes (Rogers & Fisk, 2004). Called the Aware Home Research Initiative, its goal is to identify the sensory, motor, and cognitive impairments that often undermine day-to-day functioning and then match existing technologies or develop new ones to address those needs. Such technologies might include reminder systems, automated virtual coaches that guide the use of complex technologies, and object finders. Visit the Web site at www.cc.gatech.edu/fce/ahri/. As Fisk and Rogers (2002) and Park (1992) point out, the aging of American society provides a potent demographic imperative for the use of basic research findings in these ways.

Final Comments on Cognitive Development

Research in adult cognitive development is flourishing, though a continuing need exists for theory that can integrate the accumulating findings and offer a coherent sense of what it all means. It is not entirely clear what effect age changes in the brain have on actual performance on cognitive tasks (Craik & Salthouse, 2000). Denise Park assesses our understanding of the aging brain to be equivalent to our understanding of cardiovascular disease and smoking 30 years ago. "The aging mind is a new frontier" (Park, quoted in Azar, 2001, p. 26).

Certainly there has been a move away from the decrementalist model of inevitable decline toward a more moderate view that acknowledges both compensation for loss and continued potential for cognitive growth. In addition, models of cognitive development are increasingly contextual and multidisciplinary, recognizing the multiple variables—psychosocial, environmental, and biological—that influence cognitive development and behavior. A wide range of unique influences contributes to the greater degree of interindividual variability observed in cognitive performance during the adult years. Those who maintain a high level of functioning tend to be healthy and mentally flexible, with high self-efficacy; have high socioeconomic status and a rich, stimulating, and supportive environment; maintain a high level of intellectual and physical activity; and have a larger working-memory capacity and use more efficient processing strategies. In addition, cognitive development in adulthood is to a large extent directed toward developing mastery and competence in particular domains important to the individual. These areas of expertise seem to be largely spared the negative effects of aging. Thus, we see evidence of intraindividual variation as well: an individual may function effectively in some cognitive domains but not in others. Interest in cognitive development continues at a high level. We can be optimistic that the future will bring better understanding of this most precious human capacity.

Concept Review 5.4

- New brain-imaging technology, such as the fMRI, may help us to better understand what happens in the aging brain.

- While there is a progressive loss of brain tissue with advanced age, especially in the frontal lobes of the cerebral cortex and the hippocampus, the degree of loss varies greatly among individuals and, among healthy subjects, seems to be relatively minor.

- The brain retains plasticity throughout adulthood and old age.

- The number of synapses in the nervous system is correlated with its informational capacity.

- Axonal and dendritic sprouting occurs in response to cell loss as well as environmental enrichment.

- Recent studies indicate that neurogenesis occurs in the adult primate brain.

- Cognitive aging research has practical applications that can help improve productivity and quality of life for adults of all ages.

REVIEW QUESTIONS

Research and Measurement Issues

1. A number of critics have expressed concern that the research in adult cognitive development is flawed. Discuss the major problems cited in reference to ecological validity, sample selection, and psychometric tools used to measure cognitive ability.

Psychosocial Explanations

1. Identify the major psychosocial variables known to be related to cognitive development in adulthood.

2. Explain the neuronal reserve capacity hypothesis.

Information-Processing Explanations

1. What is the information-processing perspective?

2. Identify the three information-processing resources that have been the subject of extensive research in cognitive aging.

3. Distinguish between automatic and effortful processing. Which is most affected by increasing age?

4. Discuss the three explanations offered to account for the generalized slowing observed among older adults.
5. Distinguish between short-term and long-term memory according to the Atkinson and Shiffrin "stores" model.
6. Explain the function and components of working memory as proposed by Baddeley and Hitch.
7. Discuss and illustrate the three levels of processing described by Craik and Lockhart. What is their relationship to memory?
8. Explain the differences between procedural, semantic, and episodic memory, as described by Tulving. Which seems most affected by age?
9. How do Graf and Schacter distinguish between explicit and implicit memory? Which of these appears to be largely spared in older adults?
10. What are the findings on changes in prospective memory as we age?

Physiological Explanations

1. Why does Schacter advocate a cognitive neuroscience approach to the study of age-related cognitive change?

2. What is an fMRI, and how may it help us to better understand cognitive aging?
3. Which parts of the brain are most affected by cell loss with age? Are these changes purely biological in origin?
4. Describe the major components of the neuron.
5. How does the number of synapses determine the functional complexity of the nervous system?
6. What is the significance of brain redundancy and plasticity?
7. Discuss the research evidence relative to sprouting, in response to both cell loss and environmental stimulation.
8. What conclusions can currently be drawn about the effects of antioxidants and ginkgo biloba on cognitive function?
9. Does neurogenesis occur in the adult brain? Discuss the research findings and their implications.

Applications and Implications of Cognitive Aging Research

1. Discuss the applications of research in the the fields of applied cognitive aging and human factors.

KEY TERMS

age-complexity effect, 172
applied cognitive aging, 195
attention, 172
automatic operations, 173
axon, 191
blood-brain barrier, 190
central executive, 180
cerebral cortex, 188
dendrites, 191
disuse hypothesis, 164
dopamine, 192
ecological validity, 162
effortful operations, 173
encoding, 172
episodic memory, 182
explicit memory, 183
frontal lobe, 188

functional magnetic resonance
   imaging (fMRI), 188
generalized slowing hypothesis, 174
hippocampus, 189
human factors, 195
implicit memory, 183
information-loss model, 175
information-processing theory, 172
levels-of-processing model, 181
long-term memory, 178
mental flexibility, 167
nerve growth factor, 193
neuron, 191
neuronal reserve capacity, 168
neurotrophins, 193
omission error, 164

phonological loop, 180
plasticity, 191
principle of encoding
   specificity, 181
procedural memory, 182
prospective memory, 184
redundancy, 192
retrieval, 172
semantic memory, 182
short-term memory, 178
sprouting, 192
storage, 172
synapse, 192
terminal drop, 163
visuospatial sketchpad, 180
working memory, 179

6 Social Development, Friendship, and Mate Selection

SHE HAD A WAY OF LOOKING AT YOU that spoke volumes. The family called it "the glare." The glare could be directed at you for what she thought was some serious transgression—like being disrespectful to a parent or failing to help with some task without being asked. And it had great motivational power. She was the matriarch of our family, the only grandparent I ever knew. She was bright, strong-willed, loving, blessed with a great and infectious sense of humor, and guided by strongly held and clearly articulated principles. And I was then, and am now, under her spell. Her life reflected the norms of her generation, yet at the same time anticipating the changes that characterize the lives of women generations later. Many of my attitudes about the second half of life were formed by her example. She is without question the template of my life, the model against which I compare myself. Who is yours?

Sigmund Freud was reportedly once asked what the goals of adult behavior should be—what a normal adult should be able to do. His reply was, "Lieben und arbeiten." Love and work. This chapter addresses one of the most important aspects of our lives—our close relationships to family and friends over the course of adult life. Beginning with an overview of social relationships, we will then examine the impact of early attachment experience on adult relationships. Research on the nature and function of friendship is reviewed. And finally, we'll consider the transition of leaving home, the process of mate selection, and examine some of the research on sexuality and sexual relationships. Throughout our discussion, two major questions will be addressed: What are the nature and function of our close relationships and how are they related to our well-being? How do relationships and patterns of social interaction change over time?

Overview of Social Relationships

Nature of Relationships

Need for Affiliation

Human beings are social animals. From the earliest interactions between infant and mother and throughout the life span, the individual's development is dependent on and shaped by the social world. Most human behavior occurs in the context of relationships with others. "Interpersonal relationships are the foundation and theme of human life" (Reis, Collins, & Berscheid, 2000, p. 844). Our ties to others originate in an innate need to establish relationships (deWaal, 1989; Wright, 1984), known as the **need for affiliation.** Throughout human evolution, forming and maintaining at least a minimum number of close interpersonal relationships were essential for reproduction and survival in hostile environments (Baumeister & Leary, 1995). Species characteristics—such as cooperativeness, group loyalty, adherence to social norms, fear of social exclusion, protest at separation, and distress at the end of a relationship—reflect the drive to belong to a social group (Baumeister & Leary, 1995; Brewer & Caporael, 1990). The strength of this need varies from person to person and may be influenced by biochemical factors such as the production of oxytocin, a hormone that appears to be associated with social bonding. Costa and McCrae (1984) have found substantial variability in the degree to which individuals are sociable or extraverted. These differences seem to be stable throughout the life span (see Chapter 2).

The need to affiliate also varies in relation to aspects of the situation (Hill, 1987). For example, anxiety tends to increase an individual's desire to be with others, especially those facing a similar threat (Schachter, 1959). A group of researchers studied the effect of preoperative roommate assignments on 84 men aged 41 to 70 who were about to undergo first-time, nonemergency coronary bypass surgery (Kulik, Mahler, & Moore, 1996). Patients were assigned to a room alone or to a semiprivate room with a roommate who was either cardiac or noncardiac and either preoperative or postoperative. Patients with roommates who were recovering from a similar condition (cardiac and postoperative) had the best health outcomes: they were less anxious before surgery, were ambulatory sooner after surgery, and were discharged sooner. Those with no roommates generally had the slowest recoveries. The researchers suggest that there are many reasons for the desire to affiliate under threat, including the need for information about the threat itself (cognitive clarity), the need to determine if one's emotional responses are appropriate (emotional comparison), and the need for emotional support and reassurance.

CRITICAL THINKING QUESTION

Why would postoperative cardiac patients seem to provide the best roommate match for the patients in the study described above?

Some researchers believe the tendency to seek social support in stressful situations is stronger in females than in males, due to natural selection (Taylor, 2002; see also Chapter 11). The idea is that throughout evolution, females relied on forming social alliances and eliciting social support in order to ensure their own and their infants' survival. Thus, women experiencing stress are more likely to engage in "befriending" behaviors, such as calling someone to talk when they're upset, or asking for directions when lost.

As we'll see, social isolation and loneliness have a powerful negative effect on physical and psychological well-being. The value and importance of social ties are well recognized. Indeed, throughout history, societies have used social rejection in the form of ostracism, banishment, and solitary confinement as a severe form of punishment for crimes against the community.

Reciprocity and Interdependence

The basic unit of the social system is the dyad, or two-person relationship. A dyad is reciprocal in nature, a two-way street—that is, each person in the relationship pays attention to and responds to the behavior of the other. These close relationships are also characterized by interdependence (Kelley et al., 1983): the individuals in the relationship rely on and influence each other and participate together in many kinds of activities over an extended period. Dyads with a high degree of reciprocity, interdependence, and mutually positive feelings are especially potent forces in development. Each member of such a dyad both contributes to and benefits from the relationship.

As discussed in Chapter 2, dyadic relationships are the building blocks of the microsystem, out of which larger and more complex interpersonal networks are formed (Bronfenbrenner, 1979). For example, the husband-wife dyad becomes a triad with the birth of a baby. Adding a third person to a situation makes for a much more complex social structure. Each parent now has a dyadic relationship with the baby, which is influenced by and also influences the relationship each has with the other. Thus, the family is really a system of reciprocal, interdependent relationships (Figure 6.1). Bossard (1945, p. 292) developed the following formula to calculate the number of interpersonal

FIGURE 6.1 *A Systems View of Relationships*

Dyadic relationships are reciprocal and act as the building blocks of larger social networks. Each dyad in the network influences and is influenced by other dyads in the system.

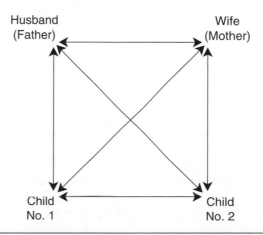

relationships within the family (*x* represents the number of interpersonal relationships, and *y* is the number of people).

$$x = \frac{y^2 - y}{2}$$

CRITICAL THINKING QUESTION

If a family consists of four living grandparents, two parents, and three children, how many total possible interpersonal relationships are there? If the three children eventually marry, what would the total be (excluding in-laws)?

Relationships are dynamic, rather than static; that is, they change as individuals change (Reis, Collins, & Berscheid, 2000). Because of the reciprocal nature of a dyad, developmental change on the part of one person in the relationship is likely to lead to developmental change in the other (Bronfenbrenner, 1979; Hagestad & Neugarten, 1985). Klein, Jorgenson, and Miller (1979) refer to these effects as **developmental reciprocities.** As a child grows and matures, the parental role itself changes, and with it, the behavior of the parent and the nature of the parent-child relationship. Pruchno, Blow, and Smyer (1984) have written similarly of "life event webs," suggesting that when one person undergoes change, role partners whose lives are interlinked will also experience change. Troll and Stapely (1986) found that illness in a grandparent was associated with a lowering of that individual's happiness as well as with increased distress among daughters in the middle generation. Similarly, Hagestad (1982) describes the **family ripple effects** of divorce. A divorce affects not only the divorcing couple, but also those with whom they have relationships: children, parents, siblings, and so on. Relationships within the family system are altered and in some cases terminated. For example, grandparents may lose touch with grandchildren, if their child is the noncustodial parent.

CRITICAL THINKING QUESTION

What would be some of the developmental reciprocities or ripple effects when one family member marries? Becomes a parent?

The Environmental Context

Relationships do not exist in isolation. Rather, they are embedded in and influenced by the various layers of the environment we discussed in Chapter 2—the microsystem, mesosystem, exosystem, and macrosystem (Bronfenbrenner, 1979). Thus, each dyad must be viewed as a relationship-in-context, embedded in a particular family, neighborhood, school, social class, society, and culture, influenced by gender, ethnicity, and so on.

Furthermore, these environments are not static. Just as each individual develops over time, elements of the social context, such as the family or even the society, are also developing (Antonucci, 1989). Relationships are dynamic and evolving.

Finally, social development takes place in a particular historical time and is subject to forces at work during that period. One of the clearest examples of the influence of historical context is the change in the nature of marriage and parenthood since the end of World War II. Family size has declined as parents have fewer children. The majority of married women now work outside the home. And the divorce rate has risen dramatically.

In sum, our focus is on close personal relationships that are characterized by reciprocity and interdependence and that influence development. Social relationships must be understood within a broad and evolving social and historical context. Elements of this context both influence and are influenced by the developing individual. As discussed in Chapter 2, $B = f(PE)$.

Benefits of Relating

What benefits do individuals derive from their relationships with others? Social interaction has many and diverse functions. We get information and assistance from others, learn about our culture and history, and identify and select mates through social interaction (Carstensen, 1992). We receive reassurance and help with coping during times of stress. In addition, interaction with others contributes to the development and maintenance of our sense of self (see Chapter 3). Relationships may provide companionship or someone we can confide in (Connidis & Davies, 1990). They may be a source of interest and fun. The priority we place on these functions may change at different points in the life cycle. Social interaction costs us as well—for example, in terms of energy and emotional risk. In fact, Carstensen (1992) suggests that one of the reasons we drop certain relationships while maintaining others is that they begin to cost more than we gain from them.

Links to Well-Being

Increasingly, research is focusing on how relationships contribute to individual well-being (Keith & Schafer, 1991). A number of investigators have found evidence of a link between social relations, health, and mortality (Blazer, 1982; House, Landis, & Umberson, 1988). One study followed a broad-based sample of 1,234 patients, who had just experienced an initial myocardial infarction, to try to determine which factors might predict a subsequent major cardiac event (Case, Moss, Case, McDermott, & Eberly, 1992). Subjects were followed for a period of one to four years. The recurrent cardiac event rate was 15.8 percent for those living alone, compared to 8.8 percent for those not living alone. The researchers concluded that, when compared with all other known risk factors, living alone is an important risk factor in a patient's prognosis.

CRITICAL THINKING QUESTION
How might living alone increase one's risk?

Similarly, social isolation has been found to be one of the greatest risks to the psychological and physical health of the elderly (Arnetz, Theorell, Levi, Kallner, & Eneroth, 1983; La Rue, Dessonville, & Jarvik, 1985). And the relationship between social relations and health is likely to be bidirectional. That is, social isolation not only undermines health, but poor health impairs social relationships. For example, many subjects in Thompson and Heller's (1990) study of 271 community-dwelling elderly women reported that poor physical health undermined social interaction in two ways: through reduced energy due to feeling down and depressed, and by limiting opportunities to form and maintain relationships.

Of course, not all relationships are constructive or beneficial to the developing individual. A number of researchers have emphasized that the quantity of social interaction—number of relationships, frequency of contact, and so on—may be less important than the quality of relationships, at least as perceived by the individual (Antonucci & Akiyama, 1991; Fisher, Reid, & Melendez, 1989; Thompson & Heller, 1990). Negative social interaction has a detrimental effect on physical and psychological health. The adverse effects of negative social exchanges may be disproportionately stronger and longer lasting than the more immediate benefits of positive interactions (Newsom, Nishishiba, Morgan, & Rook, 2003). Negative exchanges may lower self-esteem, undermine coping behavior, increase physiological arousal, trigger more cognitive rumination, and/or be assigned greater importance than positive exchanges by the individual. Satisfaction with intimate relationships has a .74 correlation with overall life satisfaction (Troll, 1986). A minimum level of positive social interaction is apparently essential to a sense of well-being (Thompson & Heller, 1990).

What are the characteristics of a high-quality relationship? And how do social relationships exert their beneficial effects? The publication of two important research reviews in the 1970s (Cassel, 1976; Cobb, 1976) generated a great deal of interest in the concept of social support and its relationship to both psychological and physical well-being. Let's examine this concept more closely.

Social Support

Social support consists of interpersonal transactions that provide the following: positive affect (admiration, respect, liking, love), affirmation (agreement with or acknowledgment of the appropriateness of some action or statement; reassurance of worth), and aid (some form of assistance) (Kahn, Wethington, & Ingersoll-Dayton, 1987). In simple terms, a supportive relationship exists when we believe that the other person cares for and accepts us and would back us and provide help if needed. Not all relationships provide support: "Although one cannot have social support without having a network, one may conceivably have a network without support" (Pearlin, Mullan, Semple, & Skaff, 1990, p. 586).

Impact on Quality of Life

Social support contributes to a sense of well-being and life satisfaction. Many researchers suggest that social support reduces uncertainty and enhances the individual's perception of personal control and social competence (Albrecht & Adelman, 1987; Pearlin & Turner, 1987; Sarason, Sarason, & Pierce, 1990). Others stress that self-esteem is greater when close relationships are perceived to be supportive (Antonucci & Jackson, 1987; Cramer, 1990a). The consensus seems to be that social support encompasses emotional closeness and warmth, acceptance, comfort, and assistance and leads to a more positive self-concept, improved self-esteem, and greater self-efficacy in the recipient. An individual with sufficient support feels better able to cope with life events (Antonucci

Supportive relationships help one deal with stressful events, illustrated here as Nancy Reagan is comforted by her children during interment ceremonies for the former president.

& Akiyama, 1991). The adequacy of the social support available is thought to partially determine well-being, performance in major social roles, and success in managing life events (Kahn, 1979).

Lowered social support may partially explain the negative effect that physical impairment has on psychological well-being. In a national sample of 4,734 adults aged 65 and older, Newsom and Schulz (1996) found that poor health can severely disrupt an individual's social support system, reduce perceived and actual support, and lead to lowered life satisfaction as well as increased risk of depression. Poor health and physical impairment may reduce the individual's ability to remain in touch with others because of a diminished ability to use the phone, drive a car, or use public transportation. Thus, there are fewer contacts with family and friends. Further, individuals may lose control over the timing and location of social interaction. And they may be less able to provide support to others, reducing the reciprocal nature of the relationships. The belief that help would be available if needed was particularly important to older adults in their sample and was correlated with increased well-being and a lowered risk of depression. Thus, one of the functions of social support as we grow older may be to provide a sense of control over our environment—the reassurance that tangible assistance will be available if needed. For those with few social ties, programs that offer assistance with household chores or provide home-based meals may make an especially important contribution to quality of life.

There is probably a reciprocal relationship between social support and emotional state. While social support may enhance positive mood, those who are happier and more optimistic are also more likely to attract others to them, thus further enhancing their social support network (Salovey, Rothman, Detweiler, & Steward, 2000).

Impact on Mental Health

Social support has been found to be equally important for mental well-being. "Relationships are people's most frequent source of both happiness and distress" (Berscheid & Reis, 1998, p. 243). A wealth of research has found that social support protects people from the negative psychological effects of stressful life events, such as the responsibilities of parenthood, the adjustments of divorce, or the difficulty of providing care for a loved one who suffers from a chronic illness (Basic Behavioral Science Task Force of the National Advisory Mental Health Council, 1996). For example, those with adequate social support are less likely to become clinically depressed. Research also suggests that those who suffer from schizophrenia and alcoholism are better able to function in the community, maintain treatment gains, and have fewer relapses and less frequent hospitalizations if they have supportive relationships. In contrast, those who are socially isolated or whose relationships offer little social support are less likely to use active coping strategies when faced with a problem and, when depressed, are more likely to passively worry and obsess (ruminate) about their symptoms (Nolen-Hoeksema, Parker, & Larson, 1994). Relationships that offer little support may create conflict and tension while at the same time denying the individual affirmation of beliefs and decisions as well as the opportunity to express emotional distress and to get practical help (money, services) when needed.

As we will see, social support may also cost as well as benefit those who give and receive it. Relationships in which one member receives a disproportionate share of support may lead to dissatisfaction and stress. The demands of caregiving can also take a toll. In our culture, women seem to bear a heavier burden for providing social support. This may affect women's psychological well-being, including their risk for depression (see Chapter 11).

Impact on Physical Health

Uchino, Cacioppo, and Kiecolt-Glaser (1996) reviewed 81 studies on the relationship between social support and physiological processes. They found reliable evidence that social support was related to positive effects on the cardiovascular, endocrine, and immune systems. These effects were evident among adults of all ages and were found in a variety of cultures. A study of New York City traffic cops, under high levels of daily stress from being insulted, cursed at, and threatened by motorists, found that workplace support in the form of encouragement, constructive feedback, and compassion buffered the effects of stress and was correlated with lower blood pressure (Karlin, Brondolo, & Schwartz, 2003). Interestingly, men benefited more when the support came from those in similar positions, while women received more benefit from support by immediate supervisors. The findings suggest that the way we treat each other at work may have a direct effect on cardiovascular health. Coworker support is especially important as a buffer in periods of high stress. Uchino et al. further suggest that the net effect of the influence of social support may be to slow the biological aging process itself. In addition, social support is related to a more effective immune response. In one study, subjects with a more diverse social network showed greater resistance to the cold virus, suggesting the value of support from a variety of relationships (e.g., family, friends, coworkers) (Cohen, Doyle, Skoner, Rabin, & Gwaltney, 1997). In the studies cited, emotional support offered by close relationships, such as those with family members, was found to be significant. A corollary to these conclusions is that disruption of these close ties is likely to have important physiological consequences for both health and risk of mortality.

What are the mechanisms by which social support affects physiology? Further research is needed to clarify this issue, but there are probably multiple ways this is accomplished, including the possibility that supportive relationships buffer the effects of stress on the individual (perhaps by bolstering individuals' confidence in their ability to cope or through cooperative problem solving aimed at dealing with and recovering from stress, for example). In general, positive emotions (such as those generated by social support) are associated with healthier patterns of physiological function, while negative emotions have the opposite effect (Salovey, Rothman, Detweiler, & Steward, 2000). In addition, supportive relationships may enhance health-promoting behaviors (e.g., exercise), both through social pressure and positive example. (See Figure 6.2.)

The beneficial health effects of social support may be especially important for older adults, who experience health-impairing changes in the cardiovascular, endocrine, and

FIGURE 6.2 *The Effect of Social Support on Health Outcomes*

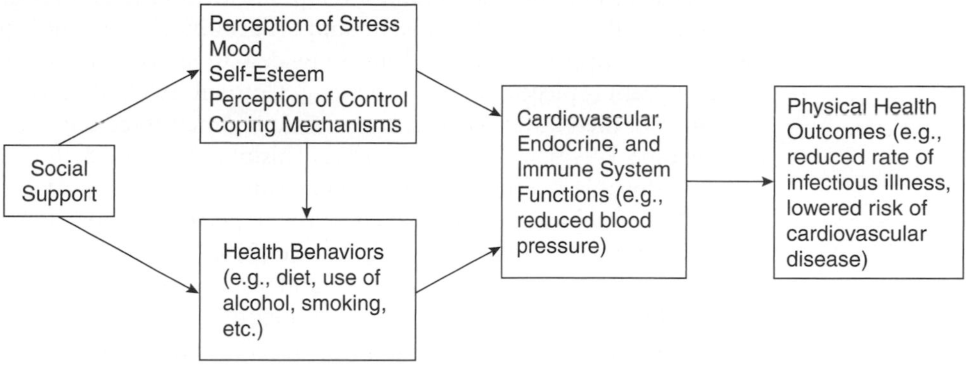

Source: Based on Cohen, Doyle, Skoner, Rabin, and Gwaltney, 1997; Salovey, Rothman, Detweiler, and Steward, 2000; and Uchino, Uno, and Holt-Lunstad, 1999.

immune systems (see Chapter 9). However, as House, Landis, and Umberson (1988, p. 544) point out:

> Changes in marital and childrearing patterns and in the age structure of our society will produce in the 21st century a steady increase of the number of older people who lack spouses or children—the people to whom older people often turn for relatedness and support. Thus, just as we discover the importance of social relationships for health, and see an increasing need for them, their prevalence and availability may be declining.

Clearly, supportive relationships seem to promote positive health outcomes. (See Table 6.1 for a summary of the possible benefits of social support.)

Interventions Based on Social Support

The accumulating research suggests that intervention strategies based on mobilizing supportive networks of relationships may have therapeutic benefits (Basic Behavioral

TABLE 6.1 *Benefits of Social Support*

Quality of Life	Enhances feelings of control and social competence
	Enhances self-concept, self-esteem, and self-efficacy
	Enhances ability to manage life events
	Contributes to life satisfaction, subjective well-being (happiness)
Mental Health	Acts as a buffer against stress
	Contributes to active coping behaviors
	Contributes to positive mood; reduces risk of depression
	Supports recovery (e.g., schizophrenia, alcoholism)
Physical Health	Produces positive effects on cardiovascular, endocrine, immune systems
	Reduces risk of illness; enhances treatment/recovery
	May slow biological aging

Science Task Force, 1996). One approach is to activate and bolster existing social ties. Another is to help the individual develop new ties, such as through mentoring programs, friendly visitor programs, or support groups. Breast cancer patients randomly assigned to a support group lived almost twice as long as a comparison group given routine treatment (Spiegel, Bloom, Kraemer, & Gottheil, 1989). Because of the strength and durability of their adverse effects, interventions aimed at reducing negative interactions may be especially beneficial (Newsom, Nishishiba, Morgan, & Rook, 2003).

Some people may be more adept at recruiting social support. What characteristics of the individual make it more likely that one person will help another and that support will be available when needed? Krause (2003) emphasizes the importance of social skills (the interpersonal abilities and traits needed to develop and maintain meaningful relationships) and states that their role in shaping supportive relationships is understudied. For example, how does one communicate pain and suffering to enlist needed help without appearing to be complaining and risking driving people away? Better understanding of these issues may lead to interventions based on bolstering or augmenting an individual's social skills.

Keep in mind that while social support is generally believed to have a positive effect on both physical and psychological well-being, individuals differ in the extent to which they require it. Those with a high need for affiliation need more support than those whose need to affiliate is low (Hill & Christensen, 1989). In addition, some situations generate a greater need for support than others (Baron & Byrne, 1991). For example, Keinan and Hobfoll (1989) found that the support provided by the husband in the delivery room had a positive effect on reducing anxiety and anger for first-time mothers only. The husband's presence or absence was less relevant in later deliveries. Finally, characteristics of the culture affect the availability of social support (Triandis et al., 1988).

Critical Thinking Question

In general, would you expect to find higher levels of social support in individualist or collectivist cultures? Why?

Is the source of support important, or will just anyone do (Connidis & Davies, 1990; Krause, 2003; Troll, 1986)? A study of widows (Bankoff, 1983a, b) suggests that some people are better sources of support than others in specific situations. In this case, the most effective sources of comfort were mothers and friends who themselves were widowed. Parental support available early in life may be especially critical for successful development throughout adulthood (Shaw, Krause, Chatters, Connell, & Ingersoll-Dayton, 2004). The key factor may be whether we are receiving the support we need and expect from a particular relationship. Jones, Hobbs, and Hockenbury (1982), for example, define loneliness as the experience that results from a discrepancy between the relationships we desire and the ones we have.

The need for support and the ability to be supportive would be expected to ebb and flow over the life course. The positive outcomes associated with social support may derive not only from receiving it, but also from giving it to others. Though much remains to be learned about the development and effects of social relations over the life span, we can conclude that social relationships have an important impact on physical and psychological well-being and that relationships offering social support seem particularly essential.

Convoy Model of Social Relationships

Troll (1986, p. 301) describes a **social network** as "a loose affiliation of people surrounding a designated central person," consisting of both kin (relatives) and nonkin (such as friends and neighbors). What happens to this network of social relationships over the life course?

Kahn and Antonucci (1980) have offered an interesting model of life-span social relations known as the **convoy model.** The idea is that an individual is enmeshed in a social network of emotionally close others that moves with the person through life, just as a convoy of trucks moves along the highway. They do so because of the mutual benefit derived from their association: the individual both gives social support to and receives social support from those in the convoy. In empirical studies based on this model, the convoy has been represented by a concentric three-circle diagram that maps an individual's network relationships (Antonucci, 1986). Networks can be identified by asking people to name important individuals in their lives and then to describe the quality and function of those relationships. The closest and most important people—those we consider so important that we cannot imagine life without them (for instance, spouse, best friend, parent)—are in the inner circle. Those considered to be less close but still important go in the middle and outer rings.

Developmental Patterns

Convoy building itself may follow a developmental course. Based on the findings of a number of studies, Carstensen (1992, 1995; Carstensen, Isaacowitz, & Charles, 1999; Lang & Carstensen, 1994) describes the following process. Late adolescence and early adulthood are a time for social exploration and the expansion of the range of social contacts as individuals investigate the world and gather information on how it works and how they fit into it. When information seeking is the primary goal, contacts and relationships with a wide range of people are valuable. During this period, individuals are actively involved in establishing independence from the family of origin and in friend and mate selection. By the early 30s, convoy members have been chosen. Relationships with those selected become increasingly close and satisfying as time goes by, while less satisfying and more casual, peripheral relationships, such as those with acquaintances, are dropped. As a result of this "proactive pruning process" (Carstensen & Charles, 1998), our networks become more selective as we move through life. The primary goal is now to maximize social and emotional gains and minimize social and emotional risks. This pattern forms the basis of Carstensen's (1991) **socioemotional selectivity theory (SST).**

Social interaction declines in old age (Carstensen, 1991). If human beings are social animals, why do we observe this reduction in social interaction among older adults? The two most prominent traditional theories of social aging—the disengagement and activity theories—explain it as follows. According to **disengagement theory** (Cumming & Henry, 1961), old age is characterized by a process of mutual withdrawal between the individual and society in symbolic preparation for death. The range and rate of social activity would be expected to decline as the individual voluntarily withdraws from social roles and becomes more distanced from others. The **activity theory,** on the other hand (Maddox, 1965), asserts that life satisfaction is increased to the extent that people remain actively involved in social roles and relationships and that when disengagement occurs, it is imposed, not chosen. In other words, barriers to social interaction emerge as people age, such as a lack of opportunity for social contact after retirement.

Socioemotional selectivity theory offers an alternative explanation of the reduced rates of social interaction observed among older adults. According to this view, the reduction in social interaction among older adults is a part of a developmental process that begins early in life and by which social relationships are progressively narrowed. Contacts with acquaintances begin to decline in early adulthood and continue to do so during middle age (Carstensen, 1991). At the same time, contacts with relatives and close friends increase. The individual is actively selecting among relationships but not withdrawing from relationships in general. Those selected are those that offer the most social support; less intimate relationships are progressively dropped. Older individuals continue to give, not merely take, in these social interactions. For example, in a study of adults aged 70 to 104 years, subjects reported that they continued to provide emotional support in their relationships, thus maintaining reciprocity and interdependence. Indeed, older people report great satisfaction with their social relationships and are less likely to feel lonely than young and middle-aged adults (Lang & Carstensen, 1994). Basically, then, as we get older, we become more involved with fewer people—those who comprise the convoy. Similarly, other research has shown that, beginning in early adolescence, relationships become more purposeful over the life course (Troll, 1986).

SST suggests that the goals of social interaction shift over the course of adulthood, partly as a function of the individual's perception of time and the future (Carstensen, 1995; Lang & Carstensen, 2002). For example, when time seems limitless and the knowledge base is small, as in childhood and early adulthood, long-term goals have greater priority. As a result, the acquisition of information is the most important goal of social behavior. So an ambitious graduate student is willing to put up with the behavior of an obnoxious professor because the long-term benefits of doing so outweigh the short-term discomfort. However, later in life, when time is perceived as limited, attention shifts to the present, and emotional needs and how one feels have greater importance. Relative to younger people, older adults are less likely to engage in unpleasant or unsatisfying relationships. They are highly selective, with a marked preference for those they know well.

Younger people faced with a limited future show a similar pattern of change in social preferences, suggesting that it is not age per se but the sense of time that motivates individuals to be increasingly selective. Endings other than the approach of death (graduations, retirements, geographical moves) may have a similar effect. A college senior who perceives her remaining time on campus as limited may be less interested in meeting new people, preferring to spend time with longtime friends (Carstensen, Isaacowitz, & Charles, 1999). Consistent with this theory, in a study of 156 long-term marriages in middle and early old age, Levenson, Carstensen, and Gottman (1993) found that older couples seem to strive for a kind of "emotional homeostasis," using strategies that maintain a positive climate and avoiding conflict to help preserve the relationship. Thus, these patterns of social interaction are seen as highly adaptive.

Lansford, Sherman, and Antonucci (1998) studied three nationally representative samples (participants ranging in age from 21 to 93 years) interviewed at three different historical times (spanning the years 1957 to 1980) and found consistent support for SST. No significant differences were found related to cohort, gender, race, or socioeconomic status, suggesting that this theory has broad applications.

One might suspect that older adults would be especially vulnerable to a loss of social support because their social networks are at greatest risk for changes in membership due to events such as retirement, health problems that impair socializing, death, and so on. Yet, consistent with both the convoy model and SST, Gurung, Taylor, and Seeman (2003) found that despite a decrease in the number of social ties reported, the amount of support available to older adults actually increases. Thus, older adults do not appear to lose social support as they age.

Carstensen views socioemotional selectivity as an example of selective optimization with compensation (Baltes, 1987). (This concept was introduced in Chapter 3 and discussed in relation to cognitive development in Chapter 4.) Individuals proactively manage the social and psychological resources that contribute to successful development (Lang & Carstensen, 2002). Social contact is not the same thing as social support. Individuals concentrate their social energies in the most satisfying relationships, compensating for a reduction in the quantity of social contacts by enhancing the quality of those that remain—developing deeper, more intimate relationships with those select few. Put another way, we put more eggs into fewer baskets. In sum, "reductions in social activity may reflect discriminating choices rather than disengagement or a lack of social opportunity" (Carstensen, 1992, p. 338).

CRITICAL THINKING QUESTION
How might selectivity theory explain the low rates of social interaction frequently observed among nursing home residents, despite the fact that potential social partners are plentiful?

Composition

Though there is great variation among studies in terms of the typical size of the personal social network, most are probably composed of about 5 to 10 significant relationships (Antonucci & Akiyama, 1995). At least half of these are usually kin relationships, and family members normally occupy the most prominent positions in the network.

Who is chosen for membership in the convoy, and why? A number of factors are known to be particularly important in determining the composition, function, and relative importance of members in the individual's social network. Among these are marital status, the presence or absence of children, and proximity to family. The networks of single individuals as well as married couples who are childless include a higher concentration of friends and siblings (Connidis & Davies, 1990). Among those who are married with children, spouse and children are more dominant and friends and siblings less dominant (Johnson & Catalano, 1981).

Finally, while the "inner circle" is typically filled by family members, those who do not have kin or whose families do not live close by develop networks in which friends play a larger part than those who have kin nearby (Lang & Carstensen, 1994; Stoller & Earl, 1983)—another example of compensation. In addition, Lang and Carstensen (1994) found evidence that very old subjects (aged 85 to 104 years), in comparison with old subjects (70 to 84), had a larger proportion of friends and neighbors described as "not close" in their networks. The researchers hypothesize that these more diversified networks may allow very old adults to meet their increasing needs for various types of assistance without overburdening very close friends and family.

Gender may also play a role in network composition. The evidence suggests that women's networks are larger and may include more family members (Antonucci &

Akiyama, 1991) as a result of their greater role in maintaining family ties (Rosenthal, 1985)—a role referred to as that of the **kinkeeper.** Men's smaller networks, on the other hand, rely more heavily on friends. Married men's social relationships are primarily activated through their spouses (Antonucci & Akiyama, 1995). A broad range of social ties may be especially beneficial to women. While men view their wives as their major source of emotional support, women report receiving less emotional support from their spouses and significantly greater levels of support from their children, friends, and other relatives (Gurung, Taylor, & Seeman, 2003).

CRITICAL THINKING QUESTION

How do women accomplish the kinkeeper role? What kinds of activities do women typically engage in that might serve to maintain ties among the network of family members?

Finally, culture affects the composition of the social network. For example, Triandis et al. (1988) point out that in collectivist cultures (see Chapter 3), the most important relationships are vertical—for example, parent-child—whereas in individualist cultures such as the United States, the most important relationships are horizontal, as in spouse-spouse or friend-friend.

Levitt, Weber, and Guacci (1993) examined a number of these issues. The researchers used the convoy model to explore generational and cultural similarities and differences in social network relationships. The sample included 159 women representing three generations from English- and Spanish-speaking family lines. Convoy size (mean = 14.9 people) and the amount of support the individuals received did not vary across the generations, though older respondents felt they gave less than did younger and middle-generation respondents. Close family members were the primary source of support for all generations in both cultures. However, age-related differences existed in the overall structure of the convoy, with more friends and fewer family members represented in the convoys of the younger generation of adults, and the balance of friends and family members shifting in favor of family among the convoys of those in the middle and older generations. The authors speculate that the more extensive networks of friends may help young adults achieve independence and establish intimate relationships. Then, once commitments to marriage and parenthood have been made, the social convoy becomes increasingly family focused. This does not mean that friends are unimportant later in life but suggests that fewer friends are considered close enough to be a part of the convoy. And life stage, not age, contributes to this change. Though this pattern was found in both the cultures studied, the networks of the Spanish-speaking respondents were more family focused. This is consistent with other studies that have found greater family involvement among Latin American populations (Bengtson, Rosenthal, & Burton, 1990). Additional research is needed to determine if the pattern described here applies to men and other cultural groups.

According to the **functional-specificity-of-relationships model,** relationships tend to become specialized in terms of the kinds of functions they serve in an individual's life. We may rely on some relationships for emotional support, others for companionship, and still others for advice and assistance. Since people have many needs that can only be met in relationship to others, they require a number of different relationships (Weiss, 1974). As Connidis and Davies (1990, p. S142) put it, "No one type of relationship can satisfy all . . . needs. Instead, diversity in social networks is essential."

Social networks are continually evolving as relationships are terminated through separation or death, new relationships are forged, or old ones renegotiated (Connidis & Davies, 1990). Those who are unmarried and childless, particularly if they are male, may be at greater risk of lacking the diverse social network required to meet their needs and maintain well-being (Connidis & Davies, 1990).

Equity Theory: A Theory of Social Interaction

Many models and theories attempt to explain the rules by which social relationships operate. One is **equity theory** (Adams, 1965; Greenberg & Cohen, 1982), which asserts that individuals attempt to maintain relationships that are fair and just. To elaborate, "A relationship is perceived as fair if the outcomes each participant receives are proportional to the contribution each makes" (Baron & Byrne, 1991, p. 261). We not only expect our favors to be returned, but we expect to return the favors of others, either in kind or with something equivalent. So, for example, if I drive this week, I expect that you will drive next week. Or, if I take care of your dog while you are on vacation, I would feel comfortable asking you to take in my mail and water my plants while I am gone.

According to this theory, equitable relationships are comfortable, whereas inequitable relationships are not. People want to feel that they are being treated and treating others fairly, that what they are getting out of a relationship is equivalent to what they are putting into it. If an imbalance is perceived, the relationship will be viewed as unfair or unjust, and satisfaction with the relationship will be correspondingly reduced: "When individuals find themselves participating in inequitable relationships, they become distressed. The more inequitable the relationship, the more distress the individuals feel" (Walster, Walster, & Berscheid, 1978, p. 6). Those who are overbenefited may feel guilt, while those who are underbenefited may feel anger and resentment (Walster, Walster, & Berscheid, 1978). Perceived equity not only affects degree of satisfaction or distress but also commitment to the relationship (Sabatelli & Cecil-Pigo, 1985; Utne, Hatfield, Traupmann, & Greenberger, 1984). The discomfort associated with the inequity may prompt an increase or decrease in partners' contributions in order to restore balance. Or it may lead to distortions of reality so that a perception of equity is achieved (Keith & Schafer, 1991). According to Antonucci and Jackson (1989), this kind of cognitive manipulation is common.

Despite early claims that intimate relationships might be somehow exempt from these kinds of exchange orientations, the principles of equity theory have been found to apply equally well to close personal relationships. Some evidence indicates that equity in intimate relationships is a predictor of psychological well-being. For example, the presence of inequity in a long-term intimate relationship has been associated with depressive symptoms (Keith & Schafer, 1991).

Research suggests that over time, long-term intimate relationships tend to be perceived as more equitable, becoming less dominated by concerns of repayment of favors. At some point, "the closest of friends (as well as most lovers and spouses) do not feel obligated to give or expect to receive a specific repayment for each service rendered; rather each feels the total amount of favors he gives and receives will average out over the course of the friendship" (Davis, 1973, p. 132). In the case of the marital relationship, spouses may begin to think of themselves less as individuals and more as partners:

"The maturing marriage relationship requires a shift from . . . thinking in terms of 'you' and 'me' to a sense of 'we-ness'" (Keith & Schafer, 1991). Whatever contribution the individual makes benefits the partnership—and therefore both individuals—directly.

To summarize, in a newly formed relationship, the perception of equity or inequity will affect the degree of satisfaction the participants derive from it as well as the commitment they make to its continuation. As the relationship matures, however, the contributions made to and benefits derived from it are likely to be seen as averaging out over time, so that less emphasis is placed on specific exchanges.

Relationship Orientation and Gender

Research suggests that males and females follow somewhat different patterns of social interaction. One of these differences may be in their general attitude toward the exchange of resources in close relationships, known as **relationship orientation** (Jones & Vaughan, 1990). A **communal orientation** focuses on the needs and well-being of the other person, while an **exchange orientation** focuses on making sure the benefits derived are comparable (Clark, Mills, & Powell, 1986). Women report that they provide more support for and receive more support from more different types of people than men do (Antonucci & Akiyama, 1991). But these close relationships do not come without cost to women, who report being less happy as the number of close and important relationships goes up (Antonucci & Akiyama, 1987). A number of early studies found that females tend to be more communal—more generous, less self-interested, and less exchange oriented—than males in their social relationships (Keith & Schafer, 1991). Males, on the other hand, are more exchange oriented (Jones, Bloys, & Wood, 1990). Thus, for example, wives may be less likely to perceive a relationship as inequitable than husbands (Keith & Schafer, 1991). However, changes in the marital structure, such as the birth of a baby or the retirement of the husband, may bring concerns about equity to the fore, with wives more likely to report feeling underbenefited at such transition points. Keith and Schafer (1991) speculate that changes in women's roles may lead to changed expectations in regard to equity.

CRITICAL THINKING QUESTION

What effect do you think the changing role of women in our society might have on their perceptions and expectations of equity?

In sum, "social relations occupy different roles in the lives of men and women. These consistent gender differences suggest that the developmental experiences of men and women may be fundamentally different" (Antonucci & Akiyama, 1991, pp. 40–41).

Ethnic Differences

Despite the fact that there is greater sensitivity to and research interest in the impact of ethnicity on social development in adulthood than there used to be, a number of methodological problems hamper investigations on this subject (Barresi, 1990). One of the most fundamental problems is that studies vary in the definition of ethnicity on which they are based (Barresi, 1990). Some adopt a broad definition, which overlooks significant variation within the group. For example, Hispanics might be compared with Whites, overlooking the tremendous heterogeneity within both groups. Others take too narrow an approach—as, for example, in the case of studies confined to low-income minorities. The problem with the latter, and with much of the research in this area, is that it confounds ethnicity with social class. This makes it difficult to determine whether group differences are due to the influence of ethnic or socioeconomic influences (Antonucci & Akiyama, 1991; Mitchell & Register, 1984; Mutran, 1985). As Barresi (1990) points out, little research has been done on ethnic groups from higher socioeconomic statuses.

Other methodological problems include the questionable validity of measurement tools when applied to groups other than those on whom they were standardized, discrepancies that can enter into questions when translated into other languages or used with those who are not native speakers, and sampling problems due to the limited accessibility of ethnic groups and the difficulty of identifying random samples (Barresi, 1990). Finally, there is a lack of longitudinal research that could examine the process of social development among these groups.

While it is probable that genuine differences exist among U.S. ethnic groups in the structure, function, and development of social relations, the research to date is limited and inconsistent (Antonucci & Akiyama, 1991). What there is has focused primarily on African Americans and Hispanics; there is also a need to study Native Americans, Asian/Pacific Islanders, and White ethnics (Barresi, 1990). Finally, cross-cultural research has only begun to scratch the surface of cultural variations in relationships (Reis, Collins, & Berscheid, 2000). We discussed some of this literature in Chapter 3, with regard to individualism and collectivism. The bulk of the extant research has examined Western cultures.

Concept Review 6.1

- The need to affiliate varies among individuals and in relation to characteristics of the situation.

- Close personal relationships are characterized by reciprocity and interdependence.

- Research has identified links between social relationships, psychological well-being, health, and mortality.

- Social support is an important component of high-quality relationships.

- The convoy model and socioemotional selectivity theory offer descriptions of the development of a social network of close relationships over the life span.

- Relationships perceived as equitable are more satisfying and longer lasting.

Impact of Early Experience on Adult Relationships

Erikson's Psychosocial Stages

Many theorists have stressed the continuing influence of early experience on later social behavior. Erikson's theory represents the traditional psychoanalytic view that early experience has long-term effects. You may recall that his model begins with a description of the crucial nature of mother-infant interaction and its consequences for the development of trust or mistrust. Erikson's (1963, p. 263) description of the psychosocial crisis of young adulthood—intimacy versus isolation—focuses on the importance of establishing intimate relationships with others:

> The young adult, emerging from the search for and insistence on identity, is eager and willing to fuse his identity with that of others. He is ready for intimacy, that is, the capacity to commit himself to concrete affiliations and partnerships and to develop the ethical strength to abide by such commitments, even though they may call for significant sacrifices and compromises.

Note that in Erikson's hierarchical stage approach (see Chapter 2 for a more thorough review), the capacity for intimacy relies on the successful resolution of crises at earlier stages of development—especially the formation of an identity in adolescence. Erikson (1968, p. 101) makes this explicit in the following passage: "It is only after a reasonable sense of identity has been established that real *intimacy* with the other sex (or, for that matter, with any other person or even oneself) is possible." Note also that intimacy refers to a quality of relationships with others in general, not just romantic ties. Failure to develop this capacity leads to self-absorption and isolation from others.

Erikson's description of this psychosocial stage is consistent with some of the ideas discussed earlier in this chapter. The capacity for intimacy is emerging at a time of expanding social interaction, when, according to convoy theory, people are establishing networks that will provide mutual support over time. Failure to form intimate connections with others could conceivably lead to problems in convoy formation and resulting deficiencies in social support, with significant consequences for physical and psychological health.

Attachment Theory

In their search for continuity of influence between early experiences and the quality of relationships across the life span, a number of investigators have turned to **attachment theory.** This approach offers a life-span perspective on the development of bonds of affection (Ainsworth, 1989; Shaver & Hazan, 1988). **Attachment** refers to an emotional bond between two people; it "is essentially being identified with, having love for, and desiring to be with the other person, and represents an internal state within the individual" (Cicirelli, 1991, p. 305).

Attachment theory is the product of the joint work of John Bowlby and Mary Salter Ainsworth (Bretherton, 1992). It is perhaps most closely associated with Bowlby (1969, 1973, 1980), whose three-volume work on the subject of attachment, separation, and loss explored the formation of an emotional bond between infant and primary caregiver and the consequences of separation from the attachment object. Ainsworth and her colleagues (Ainsworth, Blehar, Waters, & Wall, 1978) extended this work by describing the normal process of attachment in the first year of life and by examining individual differences in the quality of infant attachment.

This early attachment experience and the attachment style that results may exert a continuing influence on subsequent relationships (Ainsworth, 1989; Bretherton, 1992; Feeney & Noller, 1990; Shaver & Hazan, 1988; Vormbrock, 1993). Bowlby himself (1979, p. 129) stressed that "attachment behavior [characterizes] human beings from the cradle to the grave." To understand how this theory might illuminate the nature of adult relationships, we first need to review its key components.

Behavioral System

The concept of **behavioral system** comes from the field of ethology, which deals with the bioevolutionary bases of behavior. It refers to a genetically determined, biologically based constellation of behaviors and feelings selected through evolution because of their survival value. Bowlby viewed attachment as rooted in such a system, called the **attachment behavioral system,** which he believed was universal to the species. Others are the caregiving and reproductive behavioral systems. The purpose of the attachment system is to promote proximity between infant and mother, enhancing the likelihood of protection and survival. As a result, infants are believed to be innately driven to form a secure attachment (Shaver & Hazan, 1988). They are preprogrammed to behave in ways that arouse and draw the caregiver into a relationship. Signaling behaviors such as crying, cooing, and smiling are examples of these proximity-promoting behaviors. Though indiscriminate at first, these behaviors become increasingly directed at one special person as the attachment process proceeds. As Ainsworth and associates (1978) have demonstrated, the mother's sensitivity and responsiveness to the infant's signals will shape the quality of the attachment between them. An attachment is normally evident by about six months of age and is considered to be one of the social milestones of the first year of life.

Ainsworth (1989) describes the attachment relationship to the mother as one of a number of important ties formed with others over the life span. She refers to these ties collectively as **affectional bonds.** An affectional bond is "a relatively long-enduring tie in which the partner is important as a unique individual and is interchangeable with none other. [These relationships are characterized by] a need to maintain proximity, distress upon inexplicable separation, pleasure or joy upon reunion, and grief at loss" (p. 711). The mother-child and father-child bond, sexual pair bond, and ties to siblings and close friends are examples of affectional bonds. These relationships may be driven by additional behavioral systems, such as the reproductive, caregiving, and sociable systems (Ainsworth, 1989; Greenberg & Marvin, 1982).

Quality of Attachment

The attachment object fulfills two primary functions: providing a haven of safety to which the infant can run when distressed as well as a secure base for exploration. Attachment relationships vary in quality, depending on the extent to which they accomplish these goals. Ainsworth et al. (1978) have described three attachment styles: secure, anxious/ambivalent, and avoidant. The development of a **secure attachment** relationship with the caregiver is the norm in our society, characteristic of 62 percent of all infants (Campos, Barrett, Lamb, Goldsmith, & Stenberg, 1983). Securely attached infants have experienced available and responsive caregiving. They generally appear to be happy and secure and are comforted by the presence of the attachment object. **Anxious/ambivalent** infants (15 percent) have experienced inconsistent and inappropriate caregiving. They seem drawn to the caregiver but unable to trust her. The third style, **avoidant,** describes 23 percent of infants and is the result of unresponsive, sometimes even rejecting, caregiving. These infants appear to derive no comfort or security from the caregiver. Throughout life, secure attachments buffer the effects of stress by offering the individual a sense of reassurance and security in the face of a perceived threat, providing a haven of safety and a secure base. (Note that relationships characterized by social support also provide protection from stress, as discussed earlier.)

Working Models

The attachment behavioral system has an inner, cognitive component in addition to the overt behaviors that it directs. Infants develop mental representations of the attachment object and of themselves as a result of their experience during the attachment process. Bowlby (1982) refers to these as **working models.** They are comparable to what cognitive social psychologists might call schemas (see Chapter 3). For example, the infant may conceive of the caregiver as responsive or unavailable and of the self as worthy or unworthy of care, since "the model of the attachment figure and the model of the self are likely to develop so as to be complementary and mutually confirming" (Bowlby, 1973, p. 238). At what point these mental models actually form is not yet known (Ainsworth, 1989). Their presence and specific nature are thought to be the key to the long-term effect of the early infant-mother attachment relationship (Ainsworth, 1989; Hazan & Shaver, 1987), enabling us to carry the relationship and its significance over distances of time and space. As Mary Engelbrecht says, "Wherever you go, there you are." Experience shapes our beliefs and expectations about ourselves, others, and our relationships with them. These working models then affect our behavior and our relationships, which may further influence our beliefs and expectations (Wachtel, 1977).

Sperling and Berman (1994) state that adult attachments are regulated by the internal working models formed early in life. Thus, attachment styles developed over the course of childhood and adolescence tend to be stable over the life span, influencing all of the individual's close relationships (Main, Kaplan, & Cassidy, 1985). Let's examine some of this research.

Attachment Theory and Romantic Love

Romantic love has become an increasingly popular topic of empirical study, in part due to the emerging view that it is a universal, biologically based process (as opposed to the view that it is a historical-cultural invention of Western cultures, originating in 12th-century Europe) (Hazan & Shaver, 1987; Gelman & Kandell, 1993). The application of attachment theory to romantic love relationships has been most fully developed by Cindy Hazan and Phillip Shaver (1987; also see Shaver & Hazan, 1988), who maintain that attachment styles originating in infant-mother interaction influence these relationships in important ways. They view romantic love as a biological process that evolved to promote attachment between adult sexual partners who were likely to become parents of an infant who would need their care (Hazan & Shaver, 1987).

Evidence for continuity in attachment style comes from self-report studies in which subjects were asked about their relationships with their parents (attachment history), their experience in romantic relationships (relationship style), and their attitudes about romantic relationships (working models) (Hazan & Shaver, 1987). In line with their hypotheses, the authors' findings indicated the following similarities between attachment history and adult romantic ties: the relative prevalence of attachment style in adulthood was roughly equivalent to that found in infancy, attachment style predicted the actual differences in the way the subjects experienced romantic relationships, and attachment style was consistent with subjects' mental models and attachment history. No significant sex differences were found. Before we look at these results in more detail, we should note that Hazan and Shaver (1987) caution against an overemphasis on attachment as an explanation of relationship quality. Other factors unique to particular partners or circumstances will also influence the degree of security or anxiety in a relationship.

Secure Attachment Style

The majority of subjects classified their adult attachment style as secure, identifying most closely with the following statement: "I find it relatively easy to get close to others and am comfortable depending on them and having them depend on me. I don't often worry about being abandoned or about someone getting too close to me." These subjects described their important love experiences as happy, friendly, trusting, accepting, and supportive. Their relationships tended to last twice as long as those with other attachment styles. They viewed themselves as likeable and easy to get to know and viewed others as generally good-hearted and well intentioned. They described their parental relationships as warm and loving. This is not surprising, since "the best predictors of adult attachment type were respondents' perceptions of the quality of their relationship with each parent and the parents' relationship with each other" (Hazan & Shaver, 1987, p. 516). Not only do secure subjects seem to be more successful in relationships, they are also described by peers as more socially skilled, cheerful, and likeable than either the anxious/ambivalent or avoidant subjects (Kobak & Sceery, 1988).

Anxious/Ambivalent Attachment Style

Subjects classified as anxious/ambivalent felt the following statement best described their feelings: "I find that others are reluctant to get as close as I would like. I often worry that my partner doesn't really love me or won't want to stay with me. I want to merge completely with another person, and this desire sometimes scares people away." These respondents described their important love relationships as involving jealousy, emotional ups and downs, desire for reciprocation, and intense sexual desire. They viewed their parents as unpredictable and unfair. They lacked self-confidence and viewed others as unwilling to commit to a long-term relationship. They typically fall in love quickly and easily but find the relationship unsatisfying.

Avoidant Attachment Style

The avoidant style was characterized as follows: "I am somewhat uncomfortable being close to others; I find it difficult to trust them completely, difficult to allow myself to depend on them. I am nervous when anyone gets too close and often, love partners want me to be more intimate than I feel comfortable being." These subjects typically feared intimacy, and described their important love relationships in terms of jealousy and lack of acceptance. They viewed their parents as demanding and uncaring, and themselves as disliked by others and independent. They described romantic love as hard to find and rarely lasting.

A study by Feeney and Noller (1990) replicated the basic findings just described. They found that secure subjects were distinguished by their positive, self-assured interactions with others and their high levels of self-esteem. The most essential feature of the avoidant subjects was avoidance of intimacy, whereas the anxious/ambivalent subjects tended toward dependence, possessiveness, and a strong desire for commitment. Feeney and Noller (1990) conclude that attachment style is likely to influence the individual's interpersonal relationships because it represents the individual's beliefs about the rewards and dangers of involvement with others.

Of course, adult romantic love differs from the attachment seen in infant behavior in at least two important ways: the fact that it includes sexual attraction and behavior as well as reciprocal caregiving (Shaver & Hazen, 1988). These features reflect the activation of two additional behavioral systems in addition to the attachment system: the reproductive and caregiving systems. Though relationships vary in the weights assigned to each of these components, prototypical adult romantic love contains all three (Shaver & Hazan, 1988). Further, because the attachment behavioral system is the first to develop, Shaver and Hazan believe it serves as a foundation for and influences the course of the other two systems.

Reorganization of Mental Models

As we have seen, a number of empirical studies have demonstrated that an attachment history leading to an anxious/ambivalent or avoidant social style is associated with impaired adult relationships. In addition, there is evidence of continuity between attachment history and the relationships one develops with one's own children (Fonagy, Steele, & Steele, 1991; Main & Goldwyn, 1984). Studies indicate that a mother's working model of attachment may play a significant role in the quality of her parental behavior and the resulting attachment security and adjustment of her children (Eiden, Teti, & Corns, 1995; Van IJzendoorn, 1995). This continuity effect is thought to be mediated by mental representations of self, other, and the nature of relationships. Negative attachment experiences seem to teach people that they are bad and undeserving of love and that others cannot be trusted or depended on.

Yet some people are able to overcome their negative parent-child relationships. Attachment theorists maintain that the development of attachment is not fixed in the first year of life but occurs over a long period of childhood and adolescence and is modifiable in either direction during that time. "We would not expect a child to be permanently scarred by early experiences or permanently protected from environmental assaults. Early experience cannot be more important than later experience, and . . . a changing environment should alter the quality of a child's adaptation" (Sroufe, 1978, p. 50). According to Crandell (1992), this may occur through a process whereby working models of attachment are reorganized. We do not know when in the process of development these representational models first become consolidated. Nor do we know the degree to which these models are plastic—that is, modifiable (Reis, Collins, & Berscheid, 2000). Some suggest that gaining access to and resolving the emotional pain associated with childhood experiences are important in overcoming these patterns, while repression leads to their repetition (Fraiberg, Adelson, & Shapiro, 1975; Main & Goldwyn, 1984).

Crandell (1992) designed a pilot study to investigate whether insecure attachment with parents could be overcome by a secure relationship with some other adult, and whether such an experience must occur before a certain time in order to have its salutory effects. Her findings suggest that subjects who were able to reorganize their working models and establish secure, satisfying relationships as adults had had the experience of a secure relationship with some other adult in either childhood or early adolescence (Crandell, 1992). Even for these subjects, however, the transition to establishing more satisfying intimate relationships was turbulent. This difficulty in modifying mental models is consistent with our discussion in Chapter 3 about the self-perpetuating nature of cognitive schemas. On the other hand, subjects who had not undergone this reorganization were involved in relationships characterized by either great conflict or a lack of emotional connection.

Crowell, Treboux, and Waters (2002) examined the stability of adult attachment style among 157 couples during the transition to marriage, with measures taken three months before and 18 months after the weddings. They found that secure attachment styles were very stable, suggesting that this style is difficult to "unlearn, undermine, or distort" (p. 476) even if the partner is insecure. This is a good thing. On the other hand, a number of those classified as insecurely attached at the first measurement had become more secure a year and a half into their marriages. How did this occur? Those most likely to become secure were more highly educated, lived away from their parents, and/or lived with their spouses before marriage. The authors believe that the opportunity for new experiences (new ideas, people, and relationships) and the openness to them, along with physical and psychological separation from parents, facilitated a reorganization of working models formed early in life. They view marriage as "a powerful opportunity for change" even if, in contrast to conventional thinking, the partner is insecure. "The results suggest that a committed, devoted, but insecure partner can be as effective as a secure partner in fostering growth and change in the individual and may even be relatively tolerant and supportive of a partner's secure-base 'missteps' " (p. 476). The authors conclude that opportunities for change in adulthood clearly exist.

Interestingly, difficulty in establishing satisfying, trusting relationships with others may extend to the therapeutic relationship, making it difficult for these individuals to benefit from such interventions (Bowlby, 1988; Crandell, 1992). As Crandell (1992, p. 10) says, "It is quite possible that from a state of being nurtured emerges the capacity to be nurturing and in the absence of this core experience, individuals are impaired in their ability to relate to another human being, whether it is a lover, a friend, a therapist, or one's own child."

Concluding Thoughts

While the attachment theory approach discussed here is only one of a number of competing perspectives on adult relationships and romantic love, it offers several advantages. First, it provides a life-span perspective on the development of affectional bonds. Bonds among parents and children, close friends, and romantic partners are seen as sharing common elements. Second, attachment theory offers insight into the origins of various relational styles and the forces shaping the quality of adult relationships (Shaver & Hazan, 1988). Researchers examining different models of developmental influences on adult romantic relationships have reached conclusions consistent with attachment theory. For example, Conger, Cui, Bryant, & Elder (2001) found that the socialization practices of parents were the best predictors of the quality of children's early adult romantic relationships. The emphasis on the influence of working models is also consistent with the notion of scripts and schemas in cognitive psychology, discussed in Chapter 3. Thus, attachment theory allows us to integrate ideas from several other fields, notably ethology and cognitive psychology.

However, we must be careful not to lay everything at the feet of attachment history. While correlations between variables pertaining to parents and current attachment style were statistically significant, they were not strong (Hazan & Shaver, 1987), suggesting that other important variables require investigation. Certainly the environmental context as well as characteristics of the partner in the relationship can be powerful determinants of the quality and form the relationship assumes. As Hazan and Shaver (1987) point out, an avoidant partner might make the most secure partner anxious. In addition, the continuing opportunity to engage in other, potentially more satisfying relationships might lead to revision of mental models, thereby weakening continuity of attachment style.

Much of the research on which our discussion is based suffers from methodological limitations. Studies rely heavily on self-report data. Thus, we have a subjective view of the relationship, and it is gathered from only one partner in the dyad. Naturalistic and laboratory observations of relationship behavior as well as interviews with both partners could enhance our understanding of adult relationships (Ainsworth, 1989; Hazan & Shaver, 1987). Finally, while attachment theory assumes that its concepts are universal, others call for research directed at examining cultural variations in the attachment process, particularly among non-Western cultures (Rothbaum, Weisz, Pott, Miyake, & Morelli, 2000).

Concept Review 6.2

- Evidence suggests that early attachment experiences and the resulting attachment style influence the individual's relationships later in life.

- Working models represent cognitive schemas for such things as "self," "love," and "relationships" and may be the key to the long-term effects of the early attachment experience.

- More research is needed to determine whether, when, and how working models and attachment style may be modified.

Friendship

Friendship is one of two major social domains, the other being the family. As Ainsworth (1989) points out, the term *friendship* can connote many different kinds of associations, from casual acquaintanceships to more intimate and enduring bonds. Our interest here is primarily in the latter.

Research Problems

Though there is growing research interest in the nature and development of friendship, studies of the development of friendship in adulthood are rare (Tesch, 1983). Many of the studies that do exist are based on adolescent or college samples (Sapadin, 1988) and so may tell us little about friendship among young, middle-aged, or older adults. Definitions of key terms such as *friendship* and *intimacy* vary widely among studies, making it difficult to compare findings and leading to inconsistent conclusions (Caldwell & Peplau, 1982; Roberto & Kimboko, 1989; Sapadin, 1988). As in almost every other aspect of adult development research, few longitudinal studies exist that could illuminate cohort differences as well as patterns of friendship maintenance and change over time (Griffin & Sparks, 1990; Roberto & Kimboko, 1989; Tesch, 1983). Instead, we get a "snapshot picture" of these relationships (Roberto & Kimboko, 1989, p. 11). Finally, Caldwell and Peplau (1982) warn against overgeneralizing the results of friendship studies, given evidence that friendship patterns vary by sex, age, marital status, employment, and other variables.

Nature of Friendship

Why Do We Make Friends?

Many theorists speculate that a basic behavioral system has evolved in human beings—Marvin (1977) calls it the **sociable system**—which motivates them to seek and maintain relationships with peers because there is survival value in doing so (Ainsworth, 1989). Group membership offers protection as well as assistance with tasks that have traditionally required cooperation (such as hunting). The operation of this system may explain why infants seldom show any fear or wariness around unfamiliar age peers, though they may show distinct signs of fear of strange adults (Ainsworth, 1989). So, we may be driven to seek proximity with peers, and some of these relationships may become sufficiently close and satisfying to be called friendships. As in other significant social relationships, the partner in the friendship dyad is viewed as important, unique, and irreplaceable in the relationship (Wright, 1982).

Unique Qualities of Friendship

Friendship is a voluntary association between equals who are high in similarity and whose primary orientation in the relationship is toward enjoyment and personal satisfaction. Let's examine these relationships more closely.

Friendship is distinct from other social relationships in a number of ways. First, the role of friend is present from early childhood to old age, in contrast to many more structured social roles, which are limited to certain portions of the life span—such as those of spouse, parent, worker (Tesch, 1983).

Second, unlike family ties, friendships are voluntary and are less regulated by societal and legal rules (Sapadin, 1988; Wiseman, 1986). Friendships have "broad and ambiguous boundaries" (Wright, 1982, p. 3). This may also mean that individuals have highly subjective definitions of what friendship is and what it means to be a friend.

Third, friendship is based in similarity. Friends are usually chosen from those of the same age, sex, and background (Aizenberg & Treas, 1985; Botwinick, 1984). This contributes to commonality of needs, interests, experiences, and perspectives. Morgan's (1986) concept of a shared knowledge structure and Stephen's (1986) notion of a web of shared meaning stress the importance of friends "speaking the same language" and "seeing things through the same eyes." "Congeniality of interests and activities" is important, both in the initiation and in the maintenance of a friendship (Ainsworth, 1989, p. 714).

Fourth, friendships are primarily oriented toward enjoyment and personal satisfaction, as opposed to the accomplishment of a particular task or goal (Wiseman, 1986). In fact, negative affect is a predictor of termination of a friendship, especially in the early stages of its development, while mutually positive feelings are associated with its continuation (Hays, 1985). Hays (1989, p. 35) suggests that "fun, enjoyable interactions may be the requisite base upon which all friendships must be built."

Fifth, though trust is an important element of most close relationships, it may be especially so in friendship because of its voluntary nature (Jones, Bloys, & Wood, 1990).

Blau (1973, p. 67) offers an effective summary: "Friendship rests on mutual choice and mutual need and involves a voluntary exchange of sociability between equals." Friends are often defined in terms of intimacy, dependability, sharing, acceptance, caring, closeness, and enjoyment (Sapadin, 1988).

Casual versus Close Friends

Like other relationships, friendship is dynamic and evolving (Hays, 1989). A number of studies have examined differences between casual friendships and those that have developed into closer, more intimate associations. Here are a few key findings. First, in its early stages, a friendship may have a sort of amorphous, unstructured quality. However, as the relationship progresses, the partners may develop expectations about how the relationship should function (Wiseman, 1986).

Second, close friendships are also characterized by greater interdependence, contact, and support than casual friendships (Hays, 1989; Kelley, 1979). Subjects in a study by Roberto and Kimboko (1989) indicated that the difference between a friend and a close friend was mostly a matter of degree.

Third, while close friendships offer greater benefits, they also entail higher costs, such as conflict, dissatisfaction, inconvenience, and the expenditure of emotional and tangible resources. The cost-benefit ratio seems to be more closely monitored in the early stages of a friendship (Hays, 1989). As the relationship progresses, the relationship orientation may shift from an exchange to a communal type, in which the mutual well-being of both partners is of greater concern than "keeping score" (Jones & Vaughan, 1990; Kelley, 1979). Friendship, particularly close friendship, is a challenge, requiring the individual to balance "freedom with commitment, intimacy with distance" (Sapadin, 1988, p. 401).

Functions of Friendship

Friendship serves many purposes. These purposes may vary by life stage or particular circumstances. In addition, different friends may play different roles. Regardless of age, having friends is beneficial (Reis, Collins, & Berscheid, 2000). Because friendships involve voluntary, mutually satisfying relationships between people with many commonalities, friends contribute to self-esteem (Blau, 1973; Wright, 1982). They also serve as confidants, models of coping, and, by offering support during difficult times, serve as buffers against stressful life experiences (Aizenberg & Treas, 1985). Cramer (1990b, p. 290) found that one particularly potent form of emotional support provided by friends is acceptance: "being available, listening attentively, enabling you to say what you want and being understanding." Hightower (1990) found evidence that harmonious peer relationships in adolescence were correlated with positive mental health in middle adulthood. A number of studies have found friendship to have a significant positive effect on morale, happiness, and life satisfaction among older adults (Aizenberg & Treas, 1985; Fisher, Reid, & Melendez, 1989; Roberto & Kimboko, 1989). Some studies have found morale in the elderly to be more strongly related to interaction with friends than with adult children (Wood & Robertson, 1978). Friends may have stimulation value, adding interest and opportunities for socializing to life, expanding the individual's knowledge, ideas, or perspectives (Rook, 1987; Wright, 1982).

Friends are a major source of enjoyment, generating greater positive affect than inter-actions with family (Larson, Mannell, & Zuzanek, 1986). They may also have utility value, contributing assistance and resources to help the individual meet needs or reach goals (Wright, 1982). Hartup and Stevens (1999) describe friendship with socially well-adjusted individuals as being like money in the bank, "social capital" that can be drawn on when needed. On the other hand, poorly adjusted friends can drain resources, in-creasing one's own risks.

Friendship versus Kinship

Researchers disagree about whether friends supplement (and can substitute for) fam-ily relationships or are functionally different and independent of them (Aizenberg & Treas, 1985). According to the functional-specificity-of-relationships model, different types of relationships serve different purposes, so that they are not interchangeable components of the social network.

A number of researchers have compared the nature of friend versus family rela-tionships. Regardless of age, friends offer enjoyment, respect, trust, affection, accep-tance, and spontaneity. Friends are most often named as those with whom adults of all ages enjoy spending time and engaging in leisure activities and who have the most pos-itive impact on psychological well-being (Antonucci & Akiyama, 1995). Because friend-ship is voluntary, being chosen as a friend seems to contribute significantly to positive feelings about the self. As stated earlier, friends are typically highly similar to one an-other. This contributes to the positive qualities of these relationships.

Family members, on the other hand, are relied on to provide more significant and long-term assistance when necessary, offering reciprocal support within and across gen-erations. These relationships are not voluntary, but rather obligatory. Hochschild (1973) feels that family ties are so dominant that their strength and nature may, in fact, dictate friendship patterns. Aizenberg and Treas (1985) describe Cantor's hierarchical model of social support in which family members are preferred regardless of the task, with children preferred over more distant relatives, and friends and neighbors preferred over governmental agencies. Those with no or poor relationships with family have lower lev-els of well-being, perhaps because the absence of ties that should be present leads to shame or embarrassment. Unlike friends, family members are often very different in terms of personality, interests, age, and cohort; they may not have a lot in common ex-cept kinship. People of all ages report that family members "get on their nerves" more than friends do. Destructive family ties are also difficult to sever.

Others point out that friendship and kinship relations often overlap (doesn't everyone have an "aunt" or "uncle" who is not really a family member, for example?), and that friends and family members can and do substitute for one another (Adams, 1967; Ballweg, 1969). For example, a friend might step in to augment the social sup-port system in times of need. The answer may be that though relationships tend to spe-cialize, and family ties may be stronger and more dominant, some crossover and substitution are possible when needed, as in times of crisis and when kin either do not exist or are not available. Both types of relationships are important. The marital rela-tionship may be unique, representing a blending of family and friendship characteris-tics. This may explain its significant impact on life satisfaction and well-being (Antonucci & Akiyama, 1995).

Gender Differences

There is a lot of interest in determining whether and how friendship differs among men and women (Reis, Collins, & Berscheid, 2000). Gender role seems to have a pervasive effect on patterns of casual friendship, while studies of especially close and long-lasting friendships have found no significant differences among men and women (Aizenberg & Treas, 1985; Wright, 1982). Further, even when differences are found, they are not so substantial as to be able to predict the quality of any one friendship between males or females (Wright, 1982). In addition, like other relationships, a friendship exists in a larger social context. For example, marital status may influence friendship patterns in significant ways, and these may vary for men and women (Sapadin, 1988; Tschann, 1988). Failure to take such influences into account may have confounded some of the research on gender differences in friendship, leading to conflicting findings.

Are Male or Female Friendships Superior?

Attempts are often made to build a case that either men's or women's relationships are superior. Tiger (1969) proposed that men had a stronger tendency to form intense, enduring same-sex bonds as a survival of their evolutionary past and the hazards of hunting and warfare. Wright (1982) cites evidence that historical and literary sources seldom represent female friendship, at least not positively.

Sapadin (1988, p. 401) suggests the existence of a "friendship myth," an idealized image of what a friend is, which serves as a standard against which friendships are compared:

> For most of recorded history, this friendship myth has been modeled on the characteristics of men's friendships—bravery, loyalty, duty and heroism. Indeed, women were considered incapable of true friendship because it was thought that they did not possess these qualities. More recently, a new "friendship myth" has developed in our culture that emphasizes deep bonds of trust, caring, and intimacy, qualities more characteristic of women's relationships. Now it is questioned in some circles whether men can ever be intimate or nurturing enough to be "real" friends with each other.

The current consensus is that the male gender role mitigates against the development of close friendship in males (Levinson, 1978; Lewis, 1978), leading to emotional inexpressiveness (Dosser, Balswick, & Halverson, 1986). Studies on gender differences in friendship have yielded remarkably similar findings (Sapadin, 1988). Women's relationships are generally described as closer, deeper, and more intimate than men's. Taylor (2002) argues that women's more social nature evolved to enhance female survival and is thus biologically based and evident from birth.

Among the unique qualities of friendship is a primary orientation toward enjoyment and personal satisfaction. Male friendships in particular seem to focus on doing things together, whereas female friendships focus on emotional support.

Females report offering more support in their relationships (Hays, 1989) and also being more satisfied than males with their same-sex friendships (Wheeler, Reis, & Nezlek, 1983). Male friendship tends to be more group and activity oriented and more guarded, less self-disclosing, and less intimate (Caldwell & Peplau, 1982; Sapadin, 1988). Female friendship has a more communal, or helping, orientation, as compared to the exchange orientation more typical of male friendship (Jones, Bloys, & Wood, 1990). While women's friendships may provide greater nurturance and intimacy, more commitment and involvement in the relationship are also expected (Sapadin, 1990). Men may expect and get less and may be more tolerant of conflict in the relationship. Finally, Roberto and Kimboko (1989) found greater levels of continuity in close friendships over time among women. Throughout life, women have more close friends than men do and see them more often than men see theirs.

In a summary of research on gender differences in close relationships, Hinde (1984) concludes that male friendships are based on shared activities, while female friendships are based on emotional support. When asked what they would prefer to do with a friend, 84 percent of the male subjects in Caldwell and Peplau's (1982) study chose "doing some activity," while 57 percent of the females chose "just talking." When men do talk with friends, it is generally about some activity. This characterization is in keeping with the male instrumental and female expressive gender roles (see Chapter 3). Wright (1982) summarizes the research by describing male friendship as "side-by-side" and female friendship as "face-to-face." However, deep and long-lasting friendships of men and women are both side-by-side and face-to-face. He cautions that there are more similarities than differences in male and female friendship and that there is no basis for assuming the superiority of either. Despite all the reports of gender differences, both sexes experience benefits like trust, acceptance, sharing, and enjoyment in their friendships (Sapadin, 1988; Wright, 1982).

Friendship Development over the Life Span

Weiss and Lowenthal (1975) studied various aspects of friendship in four generations of subjects: seniors in high school, newlyweds, middle-aged adults, and preretirement adults. Rate of interaction declined after high school and rose again in the oldest group. Similarly, Hartup and Stevens (1999) found that middle-aged adults spend less than 10 percent of their time with friends; newlyweds have the largest friendship network. About 7 percent of adults report having no friends; this number increases to 12 percent for women and 24 percent for men among those over 65 (Dykstra, 1995).

Descriptions of the qualities of friends and friendships were essentially similar across the four age groups in the Weiss and Lowenthal study. Likewise, Candy, Troll, and Levy (1981) found that the functions of friendship remained constant in a group of women between the ages of 14 and 60. Regardless of age, people consistently cite mutuality and reciprocity (both offering and receiving support) as a key element of friendship (Hartup & Stevens, 1999). Several studies suggest that friendships may become less oriented toward the self and more oriented toward others in adulthood; friendships also become less focused on similarity, with a corresponding increase in the appreciation of the uniqueness of the friend (Candy, Troll, & Levy, 1981; Tesch, 1983; Weiss & Lowenthal, 1975). Unfortunately, all of these studies were cross-sectional.

CRITICAL THINKING QUESTION
Why would rate of interaction with friends decline after high school and remain relatively low until later in life?

Friendships are often durable, lasting over many years. In a study of 115 males and females age 60 and over, 68 percent reported having a close friend throughout their lives, 17 percent since they were teenagers (Roberto & Kimboko, 1989). Only 4 percent indicated that they did not have a close friend until later in life. Similarly, 72 percent of respondents in a study by Field and Minkler (1988) reported that most of their friends were people they had known for years. Interestingly, women's friendships were more likely to be continuous from childhood and adolescence, while males who maintained friends were more likely to have done so since midlife. Fifty-three percent of subjects in the same study indicated that friends had become more important to them as they got older. Women indicated that this was primarily because of an increase in available time; women (but not men) also attributed the growing importance of friends to greater need. Men most frequently said that friends had taken the place of family members. Among older adults, friends may fill the gap in support left by loss of a spouse. Dykstra (1995) describes the emotional support and assistance of friends as a major protection against loneliness for those without partners.

Older adults risk losing friends through death, illness, or geographic mobility. Given the importance of friendship for health and well-being, these losses could be significant (Hogg & Heller, 1990). Is it easy to make friends late in life? Roberto and Kimboko (1989) report that 68 percent of their sample had not made any new close friends within the last year, though 94 percent indicated that they currently had at least one close friend. All of Kaufman's (1986) subjects (age 70 to 97) mentioned that they had outlived many of their friends. The sadness caused by these losses was aggravated by their perception that they would not be able to make a close friend in old age. "In old age, most friends are old friends," according to Carstensen (1991, p. 198). As one woman said, "The friends I've made recently I consider very much on the surface. When you're older you don't go deep into friendship. . . . You have no place to grow together" (Kaufman, 1986, p. 110). In addition, as the columnist Russell Baker (1991) pointed out, the older you get, the fewer the people who share your culture, your experience of the world, and your history. As we lose those with whom we share knowledge and meanings, we experience a different kind of loneliness. Perhaps we feel more comfortable with people who have shared "memories of the same ball players, movie actors, automobiles, politicians, dances . . . slang . . . clothing styles" (Kalish, 1975, p. 87). Remember that similarity of experiences and perspectives is an important basis of friendship.

Bernice Neugarten (1995–1996, p. 1) speaks eloquently of the "costs of survivorship":

As I grow older, I am more than ever struck by the psychological costs of growing very old. As a young or middle-aged person, I stood in a landscape populated by friends and rivals, by seniors, peers, and juniors, by mentors, colleagues, and students. But as I have aged past the median life expectancy, my landscape has begun to thin out. As those who occupied my social environment die, the psychological environment is also impoverished. . . . In my observation, and for people of my generation, the experience of the thinned landscape is significant. Really old friends cannot be replaced.

She goes on to say that the experience is different for women, who have a more complex and extensive social network than men. The result is that women have "a less acute sense of being alone in the world."

Hogg and Heller (1990) suggest that social isolation among older adults may be due in part to deficiencies in social skills such as assertiveness, empathy, and role taking, which are necessary to initiate and maintain new friendships. The need to replenish components of the social network may require older adults to brush up on or learn relevant social skills.

The Future of Friendship

Several observers speculate that friendship may assume even greater importance to future generations of elderly. For example, baby boomers will have fewer children in their support network, and their daughters, who have traditionally been the primary kinkeepers and caregivers, will be employed and therefore less available (Fisher, Reid, & Melendez, 1989). Friends may be increasingly relied on to fill this gap.

Concept Review 6.3

- Friendships are voluntary relationships between equals who are highly similar and whose primary goal in the relationship is enjoyment and personal satisfaction.

- The nature and function of relationships with friends differ from those with kin.

- Research on gender differences in close relationships suggests that, despite many similarities, male friendships are often based on shared activities, while female friendships are based on emotional support.

- Though friendships may be very durable, rates of interaction with friends tend to decline after high school and remain relatively low until later in life, when friendship once again increases in importance.

- Because of the significance of shared experiences and meanings among friends, the loss of friends later in life may be especially difficult.

Leaving Home: Transition from the Family of Origin

A major developmental task of the transitional period from childhood to adulthood is that of **leaving home.** This is not meant in the physical sense, but rather in the psychological sense of finishing the developmental tasks of adolescence, establishing an initial adult identity, and beginning to make the choices and commitments expected of adults in our society. (See Chapter 3 for a review of identity formation.)

Hamburg and Takanishi (1989) argue that adolescence may be a more difficult transitional period—and that adolescents may be more vulnerable—than ever before. To support their case, they cite the lengthening of this period (starting earlier, lasting longer), the increased disjunction between biological and social maturity, the greater complexity of adult roles and the difficulty of preparing for them, the erosion of support systems, and greater access to risky, even life-threatening behaviors. This longer and more complex period undermines self-confidence and self-esteem. Adolescence is viewed as a critical transition because potentially self-damaging behavior can be chosen that will affect future development, perhaps even survival, and because choices made during this time can set limits on future opportunities.

Our culture has no formal means by which one moves from childhood to adulthood, nor is there a fixed timetable that establishes a norm for when one should leave home (Haley, 1980). Some adolescents leave home gradually, in stages—for example, when they go off to college. Others leave abruptly, perhaps even defiantly. Still others never leave.

The 1990s witnessed the growing phenomenon of young adult children—both female and, increasingly, male—who leave home and then return, while others delay leaving home at all well into their 20s. The terms *boomerang kids* and *incompletely launched young adults* have been offered to describe these trends. In 2000, 56 percent of males age 18 to 24 lived at home with one or both parents, while 43 percent of females did so (perhaps reflecting earlier marriage for women than men) (Fields & Casper, 2001). Various factors—such as financial and personal setbacks, inability to find work or to live independently on a starting income, as well as the comforts of parents' more affluent lifestyle—may be involved. For whatever reason, a rather large number of educated young adults may not completely leave home during the traditional 18- to 22-year-old period. Is this a temporary trend or the emergence of another shift in the phases of the life cycle? Time will tell. (See the Box for a description of emerging adulthood—a new conception of development in the years from ages 18 to 25.)

CRITICAL THINKING QUESTION
Do you think you can leave home psychologically without leaving home physically? Can you leave home physically without leaving home psychologically?

A major developmental task in the transition to young adulthood is that of psychologically leaving home. This separation from the family of origin has ripple effects for the family system.

Emerging Adulthood: The Age of Possibilities

Arnett (2000) describes ages 18 through 25 as a new life stage in industrialized societies, a transitional period between adolescence and young adulthood when one has great freedom and independence with relatively few long-term adult commitments and the role responsibilities and social expectations associated with them. It is a period full of opportunities and many possible futures and offers the freedom to explore options in love, work, and ideology even more intently than in adolescence. Arnett calls it **emerging adulthood.**

Acknowledging a theoretical debt to Erikson (identity moratorium—see Chapter 3), Levinson (the novice phase—see Chapter 8), and Keniston (1971; a transitional stage called "youth"), Arnett makes a strong case for this new life stage. Developing over the last half century, emerging adulthood is necessitated by the need for extended education beyond high school and the delayed marriage and parenthood that usually results. The percentage of Americans continuing their education beyond high school rose from 14 percent in 1940 to more than 60 percent by the mid-1990s. Also, the median age of first marriage has risen to an all-time high: age 25 for women and age 27 for men. Parenthood occurs later as well. Asked whether they feel they have reached adulthood, a majority of respondents in their late teens and early twenties answer "in some respects yes,

in some respects no," suggesting a subjective sense of being no longer an adolescent but not yet an adult. Emerging adulthood is marked by a great deal of change (for example, the highest rate of residential change of any age group). It is also a time when many types of risk behaviors peak, such as unprotected sex, reckless driving, and most types of substance abuse. Arnett explains this as the outcome of identity exploration coupled with freedom from parental monitoring and less role constraint.

The product of culture and history, emerging adulthood offers a new way of thinking about and understanding the period between the late teens and the late twenties. This stage does not characterize the developmental course of all individuals even in industrialized cultures; for example, it is expected to be less common among those of low socioeconomic status with fewer opportunities and limited occupational futures. However, Arnett predicts it will become more pervasive worldwide, as developing countries become more integrated into the global economy and generate more higher-paying jobs requiring advanced education and training.

Emerging adulthood represents an age of possibilities, a time when personal freedom and exploration are higher for most individuals than at any other point in development and when many future directions remain open to realization.

Because the family is a system of interdependent, reciprocal relationships, any change in its composition can be disruptive. And, as mentioned earlier, developmental change on the part of one member of the family is likely to have ripple effects for others: "The meaning of a child's leaving home must also be read in terms of its impact on the family as a whole—especially on the parents" (Goleman, 1980a, p. 61).

CRITICAL THINKING QUESTION

Leaving home illustrates the concept of developmental reciprocity. What is the developmental significance for the family—particularly the parents—when a child leaves home? How are functions, roles, and developmental tasks affected? What are the possible ramifications when a child does not leave when expected?

How do parents influence a child's leaving home? In examining the parental contribution to an adolescent's successful transition from the home, Hightower (1990, p. 272) notes that effective parents create "a safe structure from which to venture forth and to establish confident membership in the social world outside of the home." In other words, they offer a safe haven and a secure base for exploration. In their classic study of adolescence, Douvan and Adelson (1966) comment that an adolescent needs to abandon the family without being abandoned by it. I remember when I got my first apartment after leaving graduate school. I was living in a town not far from my parents. I still had a key to their house and felt free to walk in any time, check out the fridge, use the washing machine, and so on. But I resisted giving Mom a key to my place, despite her logical arguments that she should have one. I think now that this was symbolic of exactly Douvan and Adelson's point: I had left home, left my parents, but I always knew that they were there for me. Of course, not all families provide this type of support. Some may have abandoned the adolescent prematurely, while others may encourage continued dependency. Family relationship patterns may complicate leaving home in a number of ways. In addition, individual differences among adolescents affect the leaving-home process. Haley (1980) suggests that female children, only children, and youngest children may have more difficulty.

CRITICAL THINKING QUESTION

How might the leaving-home process be affected by a single-parent versus a two-parent family structure?

So, what is the function of separating from the family of origin? It signifies a transition to the tasks and commitments of adult life: "Leaving home is an apt metaphor for finishing the developmental tasks of adolescence; this act, more than any other, symbolizes childhood's end" (Goleman, 1980a, p. 61).

Mate Selection: Who Marries Whom and Why?

Making and maintaining a mateship is one of the most crucial aspects of adult development (Kelly & Conley, 1987). Establishing a long-term primary intimate relationship has enormous positive consequences for the individual, affecting the definition of the self as well as psychological well-being (Erikson, 1950; Keith & Schafer, 1991). One's mate becomes the primary component of the social support system (Newcomb, 1990), perhaps explaining why married men are repeatedly found to live longer and healthier lives than their nonmarried counterparts (Butler, Lewis, & Sunderland, 1991; W. Gove, 1972; Verbrugge, 1979).

Americans are committed to marriage. We continue to have one of the highest marriage (and remarriage) rates in the world. Increased life expectancy has made it possible for more of these marriages to be long lasting. Many first marriages now reach their 50th anniversary, while others last into the sixth and seventh decades (Dychtwald & Flower, 1989).

Although in some cultures marriages are still carefully arranged by parents and motivated by economic and political considerations, people in the West generally marry for love. We choose our mates primarily through dating, which often culminates in the 20s in a walk down the aisle. So, although dating begins long before young adulthood, by this time mate selection is likely to be if not the major purpose, at least one of them.

CRITICAL THINKING QUESTION

Aside from mate selection, what are the functions of dating?

Because it is one of the most important choices we make, the process by which we select a mate has been studied extensively. Is this a choice guided purely by passionate emotion, or is there some logic to the selection of a marriage partner? Let's examine the relevant theory and research.

Studies of mate selection typically involve administering questionnaires that ask respondents to rank the importance of various qualities in their choice of romantic partner (Feingold, 1992). As you may recall from our discussion of self-report data in Chapter 1, there are concerns about this heavy reliance on subjective reports. For example, subjects may not be consciously aware of the factors operative as they select romantic partners. Because mate selection studies usually work backward from established couples, subjects may not remember the process accurately; also, they may rank the qualities they believe conform to societal values more highly to make themselves look good (the social desirability bias) (Aron, Dutton, Aron, & Iverson, 1989; Feingold, 1992). As Aron et al. (1989, p. 254) point out in discussing their research on the phenomenology of falling in love, "These accounts represent as much construction as description."

Mate selection is a complex process affected by a number of variables (Aron et al., 1989; Feingold, 1992; Hartin, 1990). Factors that promote initial attraction may be different from those that determine whether the relationship progresses and ultimately survives—such as social approval from significant others and the availability of alternative partners. Feingold (1992) suggests that we select partners based on a principle of **successive hurdles.** In other words, various screens or filters are imposed that select some individuals for continued consideration, while eliminating others. Those who make the "first cut" are then evaluated based on of the next level of criteria. Some filters can be thought of as passive elements of the mate selection process: they operate without the individual's participation. Others are active elements: the individual's personal preferences are at work (Mascie-Taylor & Vandenberg, 1988). Let's consider what some of these hurdles or filters might be.

Propinquity: "The Girl (or Boy) Next Door"

Let's begin with the obvious. To be attracted to someone and establish a relationship, you first have to meet that person. This is the first and broadest of the hurdles that must be overcome and is an example of a largely passive element in the mate selection process. **Propinquity** means physical proximity or closeness. If you live in St. Louis, there may be a perfect mate for you in Phoenix, but you'll probably never meet. You *are* likely to meet people who live near you, work in the same office, or sit near you in class. These random contacts determine your circle of acquaintances. If the circumstances of your life bring you into repeated positive or at least neutral contact with another person, you will probably gradually come to know and like each other. This is known as the **repeated-exposure effect** (Zajonc, 1968). So, propinquity, which is often a matter of chance, brings us into contact with a pool of potential mates. One way to increase the pool, of course, is to increase your exposure to different environments. In addition, propinquity helps us to overcome the barrier against interaction with strangers (Baron & Byrne, 1991). Finally, propinquity helps explain why people in our society tend to choose partners from their own social class, because our place of residence, school, and work environment are correlated with socioeconomic status (Feingold, 1988). Thus, we tend to interact and become familiar with people from similar backgrounds.

Attractiveness: "I Know What I Like"

Some of the people we become familiar with are more attractive to us than others. At this point, more active elements of personal preference play a role. Each of us has our own notion of what "good looking" means. But we may not pursue the most attractive person around as a potential partner. According to the **matching hypothesis,** we are likely to select someone whose physical attractiveness is similar to our own (Kalick & Hamilton, 1986), perhaps to avoid the possibility of rejection (Bernstein, Stephenson, Snyder, & Wicklund, 1983) or the stress and tension that may result from a mismatched, inequitable relationship (Keith & Schafer, 1991). Berscheid, Walster, and Bohrnstedt (1973) found that dating and marriage partners were more satisfied with their relationship if they rated themselves as matched.

There is strong evidence that males assign greater weight than females to physical attractiveness as a factor in mate selection. According to the **evolutionary hypothesis,** we are genetically predisposed to select a mate who can reproduce, nurture, and ensure the survival of our offspring. Natural selection has resulted in the development of gender differences in the criteria for choosing a mate (Symons, 1979), based on differences in male and female reproductive capacity. Because females have a limited ability to reproduce, they invest more in each offspring and prefer males with the status and resources to promote their survival (Trivers, 1972, 1985). Women are consistently found to be more discriminating than men in their selection criteria in terms of a potential mate's character (Archer, 1996). Males search for females who have physical attributes that correlate with youth and health as indicators of their reproductive capacity. The findings of a meta-analysis of literature on mate selection are consistent with this view (Feingold, 1992). Women place a higher priority on SES, ambitiousness, character, and intelligence, while males focus on physical attractiveness. Similarly, in a study of 37 cultures, Buss (1989) found that males value physical attractiveness and youth more than females, while females value financial capacity, ambition, and industriousness more than males. Interestingly, preliminary evidence suggests that an increase in a woman's SES does not alter this fundamental gender difference—her standards simply go up correspondingly (Townsend, 1989). Women appear to be most attracted to men who show signs of both dominance and prosocial behavior, indicators, perhaps, that they have the ability to accumulate the resources needed to provide for an offspring and would be willing to share those resources with a mate and children (Buss, 1995; Jensen-Campbell, Graziano, & West, 1995).

Aside from explaining differences in mate selection criteria, the evolutionary model may also be used to explain the tendency for females to prefer same-age or older partners, while males prefer younger partners (Baron & Byrne, 1991)—progressively younger than themselves as men grow older (Kenrick & Keefe, 1992). Women's age preferences show less variation over the life span.

Males and females also tend to differ in their preferences for the way a relationship develops (Feingold, 1992; Hendrick, Hendrick, Foote, & Slapion-Foote, 1984). Males are more often "fast movers," meaning that they seek "chemistry" and physical involvement early in a relationship. Women, on the other hand, tend to be "slow movers" who often prefer romantic relationships to develop more gradually, with friendship and emotional intimacy preceding physical intimacy. This is consistent with the priority given to physical attractiveness by males, who tend to screen out potential partners more quickly than females do. Females, on the other hand, tend to get to know the person, including the person's other, less visible attributes—a much longer process.

Similarity (Homogamy): "Birds of a Feather"

Similarity (**homogamy**) generally results in liking (Griffin & Sparks, 1990; Klohnen & Luo, 2003). People tend to marry those similar to themselves in terms of age, physical attractiveness, personality traits, attitudes, cognitive abilities, education, and social-class background (Epstein & Guttman, 1984; Kelley et al., 1983; Vandenberg, 1972). This is believed to be a function of the filtering out of dissimilar individuals based on propinquity, as mentioned, but is also due to personal preference (Caspi & Herbener, 1990; Mascie-Taylor & Vandenberg, 1988). One explanation is **niche picking,** a model of gene-environment interaction in which people seek out and prefer environments, activities, and relationships compatible with their genetic dispositions (Scarr & McCartney, 1983). Caspi and Herbener (1990) view this as one of the reasons that personality stabilizes in adulthood—the pervasive effect of a highly similar marriage partner, who reinforces existing activities and dispositions. Rosenbaum (1986) has suggested that another process is at work in promoting partner similarity: dissimilarity leads to avoidance of social interaction. Known as the **repulsion hypothesis,** Rosenbaum's concept would account for the choice of a similar partner because all others would have been screened out. In any case, as Caspi and Herbener (1990) conclude, homogamy is the norm in marriage. And being birds of a feather appears to pay off. Spouses who are similar to each other experience greater satisfaction in their marital relationship (see, for example, Bentler & Newcomb, 1978).

Reciprocity: "You Scratch My Back and I'll Scratch Yours"

Once the other person is judged to be attractive and to have desirable characteristics, signs that the attraction is mutual are sought (Aron et al., 1989). Not only does reciprocity boost self-esteem, it also reduces the likelihood of rejection: "The most powerful determinant of your attraction to another person is any indication, in word or deed, that he or she likes you, evaluates you highly, and wants to be with you" (Baron & Byrne, 1991, p. 258).

Complementarity: "Completing the Self"

When a potential partner possesses desirable characteristics and shows evidence of reciprocal attraction, that individual may be perceived as an opportunity for self-expansion

(Aron & Aron, 1986). In other words, one way to enhance the self is to psychologically incorporate the resources of the other person through establishing a close relationship (Aron et al., 1989). So, we may fall in love with those who possess qualities we lack but value—people who complement us in some way.

According to Hartin (1990), a marital partner is often chosen to meet needs of which neither partner is aware: "A spouse is usually chosen as the best person available who will play a colluding role in allowing the individual to work on unfinished developmental tasks, master formerly unconquered anxieties, or represent to the individual the undeveloped aspects of himself/herself" (Hartin, 1990, p. 38).

Our discussion of attachment theory focused on the long-term influence of early parent-child relationships. The relationship *between* the parents is also influential, since the parental marriage serves as a model—to be imitated, avoided, or remediated in the child's later marriage. Wamboldt and Wolin (1989) describe a process by which intergenerational family influence occurs through the medium of the family myth, which arises from experiences in the family of origin. The **family myth** includes shared perceptions of the family's identity, the nature of the world, and the family's place in it. Our hopes, dreams, and aspirations for our marriage are reflected in the attitude we develop toward our family myth and the mate we select to fulfill them.

Wamboldt and Wolin (1989) examined the way this myth may be carried forward into the mate selection process. A pilot project using a semistructured interview was conducted to ascertain subjects' family myths and their attitudes toward them. Sixteen premarital couples were interviewed. Questions included the following: "What are the most important similarities and differences between the families you each came from?" "What aspect of your family's way of being would you most want to carry into your future?" "Given the family that you have come from, can you see any reason why your partner is a particularly good choice for you?" (p. 151).

Three different patterns emerged from these interviews: accept and continue, process and struggle, and disengage and repudiate. The first pattern reflects pride in the family and a deep, personal incorporation of the family myth. These families apparently functioned well and are a positive role model for mate selection and the creation of a marital family. The second pattern, process and struggle, represents unresolved issues left over from the family of origin. These individuals describe much about their family's functioning that they like, but they also are aware of some basic flaws that need work. They may attempt to choose a mate who will compensate in some way for these areas of inadequacy. The third pattern represents severe inadequacy and even failure in the family of origin. Because the family myth serves as a negative role model, the individual may choose a marital partner who represents the antithesis of the early family experience.

The researchers suggest that couples made up of individuals who are both accepting and continuing their family myths probably have the best chance of marital success. Because mate selection among these couples is based on similarity, they benefit not only from the support of each family, but from the positive role model the family myth provides. Couples processing and jointly struggling with unresolved family issues have more difficulty and must adjust to the complementary aspect of the partner's personality that originally seemed attractive. Finally, couples engaged in repudiating the past are likely to have the greatest difficulty, partly because they know what they do not want but may be unsure what they *do* want and how to get it.

The Right Person at the Right Time: "Timing Is Everything"

The final hurdle in mate selection may be whether the person who is able to make all the preceding cuts shows up at the right time. Temporal readiness refers to the fact that people often marry within a limited time frame. All things being equal, the person we happen to be dating at the "right time" in terms of our own developmental and social clocks is likely to be the person we marry.

CRITICAL THINKING QUESTION

Given that many American men and women will divorce and remarry, do you think the process of mate selection described above applies only to the selection of a first marriage partner? If so, how might it differ for subsequent marriages?

Sexuality

By age 30, most Americans are either married or living with someone. Thus, establishing a long-term, intimate relationship is a dominant issue of early adulthood. What is the role of sexuality in adult life? While we can only begin to delve into this issue, let's consider some major points.

Male-Female Differences in Sexual Attitudes

A number of studies have found significant differences in male and female sexual attitudes (Buss & Schmitt, 1993; Oliver & Hyde, 1993). Across cultures, men show a much greater interest in casual sexual encounters (sex without commitment, such as one-night stands, brief affairs) and a desire for many more sexual partners throughout the lifetime than do women (more than 18 for men; 4 or 5 for women). In a twice-replicated study, 75 percent of men (but 0 percent of women) approached by an attractive stranger consented to a request for sex (Clark & Hatfield, 1989). Of course, just because men desire many casual partners doesn't mean they act accordingly; there are costs to consider as well. Also, social constraints and lack of opportunity may obscure these differences to some extent (Archer, 1996).

CRITICAL THINKING QUESTION

How would you explain male-female sexual differences on the basis of evolutionary psychology and mate selection theory (discussed in Chapter 3 and earlier in this chapter)?

Sexuality among Young and Middle-Aged Adults

In 1994, following in the footsteps of ground-breaking research by Kinsey, Pomeroy, and Martin (1948, 1953) and Masters and Johnson (1966), a group of social scientists at the University of Chicago published a report on the sexual practices and beliefs of American adults (Michael, Gagnon, Laumann, & Kolata, 1994). Investigators spent seven months interviewing a carefully chosen sample of 3,432 respondents age 18 to 59 about all aspects of their sex lives, histories, and attitudes. Widely viewed as one of the most comprehensive and methodologically sound studies on this subject, the findings shattered many myths and misconceptions. The report describes such things as how often people have sex and with whom, the nature of actual sexual practices and preferences, and changes in sexual patterns and attitudes among the cohorts represented. As is the case with most research in this area, however, the team ignored the issue of sexuality among older adults. Some key findings:

- In contrast to adults in the 50- to 59-year age group, younger cohorts tend to become sexually active earlier, to have more partners, and to have their first sexual experience outside of marriage.
- Eighty-three percent of those surveyed had one or no sexual partner in the last year.
- In regard to frequency, though the rates vary somewhat by age and gender, about one-third of American adults have sex with a partner two or more times a week, one-third have sex a few times a month, and the remaining third a few times a year or less.
- Individuals who are married or living with someone have the most active sex lives.
- Approximately 85 percent of respondents indicated that they were satisfied with their sexual relationships.
- The majority of respondents report traditional sexual practices and preferences, with vaginal intercourse almost universally the most common sexual activity among heterosexual couples.

CRITICAL THINKING QUESTION

How do you account for the lack of research interest in sexuality among older adults?

Late-Life Sexuality

Many young people, especially men, fear the loss of sexuality with age. These fears are largely unwarranted. Though there is significantly less research on sex and sexual relationships among older adults, the basic message is that one is never too old. For many, sexuality continues until the end of life. Zeiss and Kasl-Godley (2001) reviewed the data on sexuality among older adults and offer several conclusions. First, though older adults experience physiological changes that affect sexual response (e.g., increased time needed to become sexually aroused and achieve orgasm), most compensate successfully. Second, older couples report a steady level of interest, activity, and satisfaction, regardless of individual variations in patterns of sexual activity. Factors that affect sexuality include health, sociocultural attitudes toward sexuality, psychological well-being, and satisfaction with the relationship. For both men and women, changes in sexuality and sexual relations may have more to do with sociology and psychology than biology. Among older women, for example, the biggest problem may be the lack of a sexual partner (Michael, Gagnon, Laumann, & Kolata, 1994). Finally, most research to date has focused on White, well-educated, healthy, heterosexual older adults; research on other groups is needed.

It may be helpful to remember that sexuality and sexual expression do not only refer to intercourse (Travis, 1987). Regardless of age, adults have sensual and emotional needs that may be met by close physical contact such as holding and touching. Sexuality is an often overlooked component of successful aging. The aging of America may lead to an increase in research in this area.

CRITICAL THINKING QUESTION

How might the functions of dating differ among older adults as compared to those in their teens and 20s?

Sexual Orientation

The research literature in regard to sexual orientation leaves a number of unresolved questions. One of the most important of these has to do with the origins of heterosexual, gay, lesbian, and bisexual identities. Is sexual orientation an inborn characteristic determined by genetic or biological factors, fixed either before birth or very early in life? Or is it best thought of as the product of social and psychological influences, remaining somewhat plastic over time (Patterson, 1995)? Though a number of possible factors have been identified, according to Baumrind (1995, p. 132), at this point it is "impossible to disentangle the biological and psychological contributions to the behavioral differences that constitute sexual orientation." Even the size of the gay and lesbian population remains a subject of debate. Studies of sexual orientation and development have tended to focus on small samples of White, middle-class, urban subjects and relied heavily on retrospective data and self-report instruments (Baumrind, 1995; Patterson, 1995). Thus, the role of social class, race, ethnicity, culture, and gender is not well understood, and the validity of the data is questionable. Because the vast majority of research on human development has focused either primarily or exclusively on heterosexual patterns of development, much remains to be known about non-heterosexual social and psychological development. Though the research literature is growing rapidly, at this point we are left with more questions than answers about the developmental origins of sexual orientation and its effect on individual development.

Concept Review 6.4

- Psychologically leaving home represents the completion of the developmental tasks of adolescence and the transition to an adult identity, roles, and responsibilities.

- Establishing a long-term primary intimate relationship is an important developmental task of young adulthood and has significant consequences for psychological development and well-being.

- Mate selection is a complex process by which the pool of potential mates is progressively narrowed. Among the important criteria are propinquity, attractiveness, homogamy, reciprocity, complementarity, and timing.

- Males and females hold significantly different sexual attitudes.

(continued)

- Though recent large-scale survey research has revealed valuable information about sexual attitudes and practices among young and middle-aged adults, studies of sexuality among older adults are lacking.

- Questions about the origins of sexual preference and its developmental consequences remain at this point unanswered.

REVIEW QUESTIONS

Overview of Social Relationships

1. What are the major characteristics of close personal relationships?
2. What is social support, and how is it related to individual well-being (physical health, mental health, and quality of life)?
3. Discuss the developmental patterns involved in convoy building.
4. What factors influence convoy composition?
5. How does the socioemotional selectivity theory explain the reduced rates of social interaction observed among older adults, as compared to the disengagement and activity theories?
6. According to equity theory, what is the effect of perceived inequity on a relationship?
7. Differentiate between a communal and an exchange relationship orientation and discuss gender differences in regard to them.
8. Identify research problems in studying ethnic differences in social behavior.

Impact of Early Experience on Adult Relationships

1. What is the purpose of the attachment behavioral system?
2. How does the concept of working models explain the relationship between early attachment experience and later social relationships?
3. Discuss Hazan and Shaver's findings on the relationship between attachment history and adult romantic love relationships.
4. Can working models be reorganized later in life?

Friendship

1. Define the sociable behavioral system. What survival value might such a system provide?
2. How are friendships different from other types of social relationships?
3. How do close friendships differ from more casual ones?
4. What are the functions of close friendships?
5. Discuss the research findings on gender differences in friendship patterns.
6. How do friendship patterns change over the course of adult life, including old age?

Leaving Home: Transition from the Family of Origin

1. What is meant by "leaving home," and what is its developmental significance?
2. Why do some observers feel that adolescence is a more difficult transitional period than ever before?
3. How can parents facilitate this transition?
4. Describe the nature of Arnett's stage of emerging adulthood.

Mate Selection: Who Marries Whom and Why?

1. How is mate selection research generally conducted, and what are the limitations of this approach?
2. Explain how a mate might be selected through a process of overcoming successive hurdles.
3. How does the process of mate selection differ among males and females?
4. What is the "family myth" and how might it influence mate selection?

Sexuality

1. Discuss some of the major findings of recent research on sexuality among young and middle-aged adults.

2. How does age affect sexuality?
3. What are some of the limitations of research on sexual preference?

KEY TERMS

activity theory, 209
affectional bonds, 217
anxious/ambivalent attachment, 217
attachment, 216
attachment behavioral system, 217
attachment theory, 216
avoidant attachment, 217
behavioral system, 217
communal orientation, 214
convoy model, 209
developmental reciprocities, 202
disengagement theory, 209
emerging adulthood, 231

equity theory, 213
evolutionary hypothesis, 234
exchange orientation, 214
family myth, 236
family ripple effects, 202
friendship, 223
functional-specificity-of-relationships model, 212
homogamy, 235
kinkeeper, 212
leaving home, 229
matching hypothesis, 234
need for affiliation, 200

niche picking, 235
propinquity, 233
relationship orientation, 214
repeated-exposure effect, 234
repulsion hypothesis, 235
secure attachment, 217
sociable system, 223
social network, 209
social support, 204
socioemotional selectivity theory (SST), 209
successive hurdles, 233
working models, 218

7 | Family Ties, Transitions, and Challenges

ONE WEEK FROM THIS SATURDAY, my family will pass through a major transition in its development. The oldest child of the youngest generation, my sister's daughter, the first of my parents' grandchildren, will be married. She and her husband-to-be will establish a family of their own. In the next few years, children may come along, making the rest of us great-grandparents, grandparents, great-aunts and great-uncles, and so on. This is just the beginning of a more pervasive change in the structure and function of my extended family, as it reaches out to encompass this new offshoot. The cycle of generations takes another turn.

This chapter examines some of the family issues that emerge over the course of adult life. The meanings of two terms related to family forms need clarification. The **nuclear family** is composed of mother, father, and young children and can encompass one's family of origin or marital family. The **extended family** includes those directly related to nuclear family members; these individuals are also known as kin and include grandparents, aunts, uncles, and cousins.

Family Development

The family constitutes the second major social domain (the other being friendship). Family relations are a vital aspect of life. One general orientation that can be used to examine family issues and their significance for adult development is to take the family itself as the unit of study. The **family development perspective** studies the family as a dynamic system of interdependent relationships and examines the way it changes from the time of its formation until its dissolution (Hill & Mattessich, 1979). Consistencies in development across families are sought, in order to describe a universal pattern in the developmental life of the family unit.

Family Life Cycle

According to the **family life cycle model,** families pass through predictable, universal stages in their development. These stages represent qualitative changes in the composition, structure, and function of the family during a particular period. Each stage is associated with a set of developmental tasks that must be accomplished for the family to function effectively and promote further growth. Families in similar stages are thought to be engaging in similar activities and grappling with similar issues, though of course individuals and individual families may experience these events differently. Thus, a particular life stage is thought to tell us something about the role structure of the family and the interrelationships of family members—their needs, expectations, benefits, and responsibilities (Aldous, 1978; Mattessich & Hill, 1987). Further, as with individuals, families do not wake up one morning and find that they have made an abrupt move to a new and different stage of family life. Instead, there are periods of overlap and transition from one phase to another. In fact, each stage has its origins in earlier stages and reaches fruition in those yet to come (Duvall, 1977). Transitional periods are thought to be stressful, as family members renegotiate their relationships, roles, and expectations (Lavee, McCubbin, & Olson, 1987). Issues of timing (for instance, early versus late marriage, parenthood) as well as the consequences of not going through a stage (for example, involuntary childlessness) are also of interest (Aldous, 1990). The family life cycle has been studied in relationship to the psychological well-being of family members using indicators such as marital satisfaction, general life satisfaction, role strain, self-concept, and mental health (Keith & Schafer, 1991; Mattessich & Hill, 1987).

The primary focus of the family life cycle perspective, then, is the internal organization of the family system, how it changes over time, and the ramifications of these changes for the family unit and the individuals in it. According to this view, the family can be thought of as growing up and maturing, just as individuals do (Duvall, 1977).

One especially influential model of family development is that of Duvall (1977), who depicts the family life cycle as consisting of eight stages, listed in Table 7.1. Note that one of the primary factors used by Duvall in determining the family's position in the life cycle is the age and school placement of the oldest child: "The oldest child is always taking his family with him or with her out into the growing edges of family experience" (Duvall, 1977, p. 145). The family essentially repeats these experiences with subsequent children, perhaps benefiting from past experiences. In any case, later-born

According to the family life cycle model, families in similar stages of family life engage in similar activities and grapple with similar developmental tasks.

TABLE 7.1 *Duvall's Eight-Stage Family Life Cycle*

Stage	Brief Description

1. Married couples (without children)
2. Childbearing families (oldest child, birth–30 months)
3. Families with preschool children (oldest child, 2½–6 years)
4. Families with schoolchildren (oldest child, 6–13 years)
5. Families with teenagers (oldest child, 13–20 years)
6. Families launching young adults (first child gone–last child gone)
7. Middle-aged parents (empty nest to retirement)
8. Aging family members (retirement to death of spouse)

Source: Evelyn Mills Duvall (1977). *Marriage and Family Development.* New York: Harper & Row. Copyright 1957, 1962, 1967, 1971, 1977 by Harper & Row Publishers, Inc. Reprinted by permission of Addison Wesley Educational Publishers, Inc.

children experience a family at a different point in its development than do firstborns. Because people marry and have children at different ages, chronological age alone is not necessarily a good indicator of a family's location in the cycle (Brubaker, 1985). One's position in the family life cycle has an effect on subjective age.

Census data have been used to plot the time each stage usually lasts (Figure 7.1). In the figure, look at the relative amount of time devoted to each stage. Though when we think of the family we almost automatically think in terms of parents raising children, note that, according to Duvall's model, the periods of active parenting constitute less than half of the family life cycle (Duvall, 1977). Later-life families—those that are beyond the active childrearing years and that have begun to launch their children—have increasingly become the focus of research attention (Brubaker, 1985).

Family Developmental Tasks

The concept of developmental task originated with Robert Havighurst (1953), who described six stages in the life span as well as the tasks that should be accomplished in each (see Chapter 2). The term *developmental task* refers to an ability or challenge that, if achieved or resolved at the appropriate point in development, leads to satisfaction in the present stage and lays the foundation for future success. The fact that each member of the family is at a different developmental level, dealing with different developmental issues, often creates tension and conflict within the family unit. Further, the degree to which an individual can accomplish his or her own developmental tasks is often heavily influenced by the developmental issues of other family members (Goleman, 1980a). This kind of friction is normal and expected.

Families can be thought of as grappling with developmental tasks as well. As a social support system (Shanas, 1979b), the family has a number of basic functions, such as protecting its members, socializing children, and caring for elderly relatives. Some of these are expectations are derived from the culture and others are self-imposed; some are ongoing, while others are specific to family life cycle stage. A **family developmental task** is "a growth responsibility that arises at a certain stage in the life of a family, the successful achievement of which leads to present satisfaction, approval, and success with later tasks—whereas failure leads to unhappiness in the family, disap-

FIGURE 7.1 *Family Life Cycle by Length of Time in Each of Eight Stages*

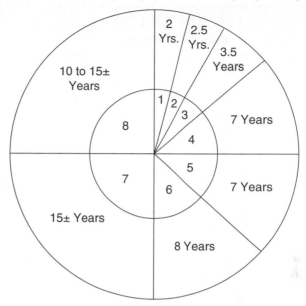

1. Married couples (without children).

2. Childbearing families
   (oldest child, birth–30 months).

3. Families with preschool children
   (oldest child, 30 months–6 years).

4. Families with schoolchildren
   (oldest child, 6–13 years).

5. Families with teenagers
   (oldest child, 13–20 years).

6. Families launching young adults (first
   child gone to last child leaving home).

7. Middle-aged parents
   (empty nest to retirement).

8. Aging family members
   (retirement to death of both spouses).

Source: Evelyn Mills Duvall (1977). *Marriage and Family Development.* New York: Harper & Row. Copyright 1957, 1962, 1967, 1971, 1977 by Harper & Row Publishers, Inc. Reprinted by permission of Addison Wesley Educational Publishers, Inc.

proval by society, and difficulty with later developmental tasks" (Duvall, 1977, p. 177). As the family moves through the life cycle, its responsibilities change. Table 7.2 describes the developmental tasks associated with each of the stages in Duvall's family life cycle model.

Cycle of Generations

The word *cycle* implies, according to the dictionary, a "recurring series." As Duvall (1977, p. 157) points out, the life cycle of a family has no beginning and no end; it is a part of a spiral of generations: "No matter where you start to study a family by means of its family life cycle, there are always relevant roots in the . . . past to be considered. Wherever you are at the moment, you have grown out of the stage just before and are

TABLE 7.2 *Stage-Critical Family Developmental Tasks through the Family Life Cycle*

Stage of the Family Life Cycle	Positions in the Family	Stage-Critical Family Developmental Tasks
1. Married couple	Wife Husband	Establishing a mutually satisfying marriage Adjusting to pregnancy and the promise of parenthood Fitting into the kin network
2. Childbearing	Wife-mother Husband-father Infant daughter or son or both	Having, adjusting to, and encouraging the development of infants Establishing a satisfying home for both parents and infant(s)
3. Preschool-age	Wife-mother Husband-father Daughter-sister Son-brother	Adapting to the critical needs and interests of preschool children in stimulating, growth-promoting ways Coping with energy depletion and lack of privacy as parents
4. School-age	Wife-mother Husband-father Daughter-sister Son-brother	Fitting into the community of school-age families in constructive ways Encouraging children's educational achievement
5. Teenage	Wife-mother Husband-father Daughter-sister Son-brother	Balancing freedom with responsibility as teenagers mature and emancipate themselves Establishing postparental interests and careers as growing parents
6. Launching center	Wife-mother-grandmother Husband-father-grandfather Daughter-sister-aunt Son-brother-uncle	Releasing young adults into work, military service, college, marriage, and so on, with appropriate rituals and assistance Maintaining a supportive home base
7. Middle-aged parents	Wife-mother-grandmother Husband-father-grandfather	Rebuilding the marriage relationship Maintaining kin ties with older and younger generations
8. Aging family members	Widow/widower Wife-mother-grandmother Husband-father-grandfather	Closing the family home or adapting it to aging Coping with bereavement and living alone Adjusting to retirement

Source: Evelyn Mills Duvall (1997). *Marriage and Family Development.* New York: Harper & Row. Copyright 1957, 1962, 1967, 1971, 1977 by Harper & Row Publishers, Inc. Reprinted by permission of Addison Wesley Educational Publishers, Inc.

heading into the stage ahead." Each of us, for example, is a part of the family life cycles of generations ahead of us (as child and grandchild), as well as those behind us (as parent and grandparent), and so on.

In our culture, individuals often witness concurrent family cycles spanning three and maybe even four generations. The oldest of these families may be in the final stage of family life, while the middle family unit is launching its children. Some of those same children may be initiating the development of a new family. Thus, a woman in her 40s may be dealing concurrently with the developmental issues of several family life cycles. She may be offering support to aging grandparents as well as to parents entering retirement, while at the same time being actively involved in launching her own children, perhaps even taking on the grandparent role herself. Tied by mutual interdependence, contributing as well as receiving various forms of support, a rich and diverse network of cross-generational relationships increasingly typifies family life. One of the advantages of the life cycle scheme is that it encourages us to take this long view of the family and its individual members, each of whom has relationships to others in the same and past and future generations.

Limitations of the Family Development Model

Family development and life cycle models have been criticized on a number of grounds. One of the obvious problems with any typology is that not every family fits. Those who never marry, childless couples, divorced or remarried couples, and so on do not follow the "normative" pattern laid out by any life cycle model. It is difficult to identify family life cycle stages that hold for all families, because families themselves are so varied (Duvall, 1977). And no model of family development can accommodate all individual variations in life patterns. For example, how does having a first child at 20 versus 40 influence the family life cycle? Is the empty-nest experience of 40-year-old parents comparable to that of 60-year-old parents? Researchers have also raised concerns about the effect of the historical context on family timetables (Aldous, 1990; Elder, 1984). Sociohistorical variables such as periods of war or economic depression, as well as changes in male and female roles, influence when we marry, when and how many children we have, and so on.

In addition, others have suggested that historical trends toward increased life expectancy, fewer numbers of children, and earlier retirement have led to new stages in family life; for example, the extended postparental stage may be subdivided into preretirement, early retirement, and late retirement phases (Swenson, Esker, & Kohlhepp, 1984). As Aldous (1990, p. 572) points out, models of family development have had to be modified over the last few decades, broadening their focus to include other than "first-marriage, two-parent, nuclear families" (for example, Hill, 1986; Mattessich & Hill, 1987), as well as the variations resulting from income, education, social class, and race (Norton, 1983). These modifications and extensions are ongoing and have responded to some, but not all, concerns with the family development perspective (Aldous, 1990).

Changing Families, Changing Times

As a social institution, the family reflects broad-scale changes that have transformed society as a whole. Demographic studies have documented the effects of macrosocietal changes in the population on the nature of American family life, changes that have been especially pronounced since the late 1960s (U.S. Bureau of the Census, 1992b). These include trends in the structure and composition of the family, the sequencing and timing of stages in the family life cycle, and the psychosocial environment and functioning of the family unit (Aizenberg & Treas, 1985; Glick, 1988).

Families are becoming increasingly diverse in both form and function, and definitions of what a family is vary among cultural and ethnic groups (Blieszner &

Bedford, 1995). Certainly, "the family has become a more complex institution than it once was" (U.S. Bureau of the Census, 1992b, p. 12). Though it is beyond the scope of this book to consider these changes and their implications in detail, some of them are highlighted below.

Increasing Numbers of Singles

The U.S. Census Bureau uses the term *household* to refer to the people who live in a housing unit and distinguishes between family households (composed of at least two people related by birth, marriage, or adoption) and nonfamily households (either a person living alone or a householder living with others who are not related). In the past, a large majority of households were made up of families, but that proportion is now significantly lower (dropping from 81 percent in 1970 to 69 percent in 2000). Most nonfamily households are one-person households. The total of all households consisting of an individual living alone—including young adults as well as the elderly—increased from 7 percent in 1940 to 26 percent in 2000 (Glick, 1988; Fields & Casper, 2001). A number of factors have contributed to these trends.

While the United States continues to have one of the highest marriage rates in the world, increasing numbers of young adults are choosing to live alone or at least to delay getting married. Delaying of marriage since 1970 has led to a substantial increase in the percentage of young, never-married adults. (See Table 7.3.)

The higher divorce rate has also contributed to the number of adults living alone. The number of one-parent families (which, by the way, used to be the result of widowhood but now generally stems from divorce or, secondarily, from never marrying to begin with) has shot up from 3.8 million in 1970 to 19.8 million in 2002 (Fields, 2003b). The overall number of children under age 18 living in one-parent households increased from 9 percent in 1960 to 28 percent in 2002: 69 percent lived with two parents, 23 percent with a single mother, 5 percent with a single father, and 4 percent with neither parent (Fields, 2003b; Glick, 1988). The incidence of one-parent families varies dramatically among racial/ethnic groups: 53 percent of Black children, 30 percent of Hispanics, 20 percent of Whites, and 15 percent of Asian/Pacific Islander children were living with a single parent in 2002 (Fields, 2003b).

Another factor is income from Social Security, which has helped many older adults to maintain their independence. The likelihood of living alone is greater among women, who comprised 58 percent of all adults living alone in 2000, and increases with age, especially among women, who typically outlive their husbands and are less likely to remarry. In 2000, 8 percent of women and 12 percent of men age 25 to 34 lived alone, whereas 49 percent of women and 21 percent of men over 75 lived alone (Fields &

TABLE 7.3 *Percentage of Never-Married Adults, by Age and Sex, 1970 and 2000*

	1970	2000
Women age 20 to 24	36%	73%
Men age 20 to 24	55	84
Women age 30–34	6	22
Men age 30 to 34	9	30

Source: Based on Fields and Casper, 2001.

Casper, 2001). The increase in individuals living alone is not limited to the United States but has also been observed in other developed countries.

Reduced Family Size

Like the average household size, the average family size is down, with most people having one or two children—compared to the three or four typical of 40 years ago. Figure 7.2 shows the overall trends. Fewer children and longer life expectancy have increased the empty-nest period from an average 1.6 years in the late 1800s to 13 years (Glick, 1977).

FIGURE 7.2 *Average Size of Households and Families, 1960–2000*

A household consists of all the persons who occupy a housing unit. These persons may be related, unrelated, or living alone. A family is a group of two or more persons related by birth, marriage, or adoption residing together. Because there are fewer children per family, more one-parent families, and a growing number of people living alone, the average sizes of households and families have declined. The trend toward smaller families and households began in the mid-1960s with the end of the postwar baby boom and has continued to the present, reaching a level of 2.62 persons per household, on average, in 2000 and 3.18 persons per family.

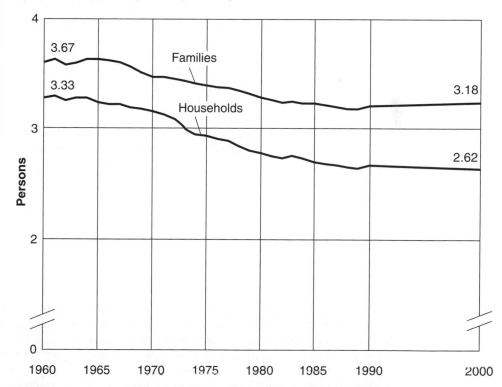

Sources: Fields and Casper, 2001; U.S. Bureau of the Census, 1999; U.S. Senate Special Committee on Aging et al., 1991, p. 14.

CRITICAL THINKING QUESTION
Why are people having fewer children today?

Family Composition Tilts toward Elders

Family membership is more heavily weighted toward older individuals as a result of increased longevity coupled with declining fertility rates. The average married couple has more living parents than children (Preston, 1984).

A More Vertical Family Structure

Family structure has become more vertical, with more generations alive at the same time and fewer members in each one—a "beanpole" family structure (Gatz, Bengtson, & Blum, 1990). Hagestad (1985) reports that of the women who died in one Pennsylvania county, 60 percent had great-grandchildren and 20 percent had great-great-grandchildren. Families spanning four generations are more common as a result of increased life expectancy and declining ages at marriage and childbearing in those cohorts. The result is **generational acceleration,** a shortening of the average number of years separating adjacent generations, down from about 30 years in 1900 to about 20 years today (Hagestad, 1981; Troll, Miller, & Atchley, 1979). Consequently, it is becoming more common for parents and children to find themselves growing old together (Aizenberg & Treas, 1985). In fact, by the 2020s, the baby boom may turn into a great-grandparent boom.

Intergenerational family roles have become more prominent and longer-lasting (Mutran & Reitzes, 1990). Young people today are more likely to have older relatives in their kinship network than at any earlier time in history (Aizenberg & Treas, 1985). These relationships, sharing as they do a long history, may be rich and deeply rooted, but may also cause stress and tension as the family system attempts to respond to the divergent developmental needs of its members (Aizenberg & Treas, 1985; Gatz et al., 1990).

Middle-Generation Squeeze

The **middle-generation squeeze** (Brody, 1981) (also referred to as the sandwich generation) has come to typify the experience of many in middle age, caught between the competing demands to care for parents and children and deal with their personal aspirations at the same time. The nest, which may have been empty or near empty, is being refilled, both psychologically and physically, by returning adult children or frail elderly relatives, only to reempty with the death of parents or the departure of children (Aizenberg & Treas, 1985; Clemens & Axelson, 1985). This situation is complicated by the increasing involvement of women—the traditional kinkeepers and caregivers—in the workforce (Gatz, Bengtson, & Blum, 1990). (See Chapter 8.) Those now in late adulthood have a large reservoir of kin on whom to rely for various kinds of support. The baby boom generation will, in contrast, have a relatively smaller pool of family resources available (Aizenberg & Treas, 1985). This is expected to change the nature of intergenerational support and exchange.

The Nuclear versus the Traditional Family Structure

Our discussion up to this point has taken as an assumption the characteristic family structure in industrialized society—the nuclear family unit composed of husband, wife, and children. Yet even within the United States, let alone in other cultures of the world, not all families conform to this model. Little attention has been given to cultural diversity in family structure, and much of that research has focused narrowly on disadvantaged and minority families, especially among Blacks and Hispanics (Johnson, 1995).

In most ethnic groups in the United States, immigrant families are characterized by traditionalism (Johnson, 1995). The **traditional family** is hierarchical in structure, with older members and males having higher status and power than younger members and females. The values of ethnic family life include respect, obligation, and interdependence. The family unit includes an extensive kinship system. Because of the emphasis on vertical intergenerational ties, networks of support and assistance are generally stronger in these families. The traditional family system is prominent among Asian and Hispanic immigrant groups, as well as among some European Catholic families. This family structure is somewhat difficult to maintain in American society, so change in the direction of the nuclear family model is evident among successive generations of immigrant families. In contrast to the traditional family, the nuclear family structure is more isolated from the kinship system. There is a more egalitarian relationship between husband and wife, and the function of the family unit specializes primarily in the raising of children. Older family members have a less advantageous position in the family unit.

As we have seen, the number of intact nuclear families has declined significantly since the 1960s, primarily as a result of divorce as well as the increase in single parents who have never married. Families are grappling with changes that are without historical precedent and whose implications are not completely clear. The family constellation is more complex and varied as a result of the broad changes sweeping over society. As demographer Paul Glick (1988) points out, when social change comes rapidly, as in recent decades, adjustment can be especially difficult and stressful. On the bright side, however, he predicts more moderate changes in family demographics in the decades ahead. Nonetheless, no single model of family development can accommodate the diverse patterns characterizing American family life today.

Concept Review 7.1

- The family development perspective studies the nature and life course of the family unit.
- The family life cycle model views the family as passing through a series of predictable, universal stages in its development. Each stage presents developmental tasks.
- Families are becoming increasingly diverse in both form and function.

Marriage: Establishing a Family of One's Own

Statistical Trends

Let's consider some of what we know about the state of marriage in our society. Here are some basic facts drawn from the Census Bureau as well as the National Center for

Health Statistics, a division of the Department of Health and Human Services that began keeping these sorts of statistics in 1964:

- Close to 90 percent of Americans eventually marry at least once. This remains the overwhelming pattern, though, as discussed, growing numbers of adults are living alone. (This includes those who have never married as well as those who are divorced and widowed.)
- In 2000, the median age of first marriage in the United States was 25.1 for women and 26.8 for men—the highest ever. For comparison, in the mid-1950s it reached a low of 20.1 for women and 22.5 for men (Figure 7.3). In 1996, the median age of marriage for women in Canada was 26.0; Germany, 26.2; Brazil, 22.6; India, 22.0; and Egypt, 21.9 (Noble, Cover, & Yanagishita, 1996).
- The nation's overall marriage, divorce, and remarriage rates stabilized in the 1990s (U.S. Bureau of the Census, 1992b, 1998). Marriage and remarriage rates are lower and divorce rates higher than those in the late 1960s. In the late 1990s, the divorce rate was three times what it was in 1960; there were 70 million people in the United States who had been divorced at least once (Amato & Booth, 1997).

FIGURE 7.3 *Median Age at First Marriage, by Sex, 1890–2000*

In recent years, men and women have had the highest median age at first marriage (26.8 and 25.1) since data were first collected on this subject in 1890. For both men and women, the median ages at first marriage were lowest in the mid-1950s and have been rising since, increasing more than four full years.

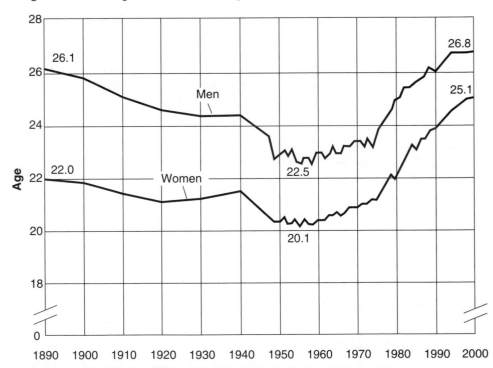

Sources: Fields & Casper, 2001; U.S. Bureau of the Census, 1991a, 1995, 1998.

- The average marriage lasts seven years. First marriages that end in divorce in a few years and produce no children are referred to as "starter marriages" (Amato & Booth, 1997).
- More than 40 percent of U.S. marriages involve a second or subsequent marriage for the bride, groom, or both (U.S. Bureau of the Census, 1992a, 1992b, 1995; U.S. National Center for Health Statistics, 1991).
- Rates of cohabitation, marriage, separation, divorce, and remarriage vary greatly by race/ethnicity, and these differences have increased over recent decades (Bramlett & Mosher, 2002).

CRITICAL THINKING QUESTION
What factors do you think are responsible for the fact that many young people are waiting longer to marry?

Components of Romantic Love

The scientific study of love goes back only about 30 years. A number of studies have attempted to identify the components of romantic love and their fate over time. These efforts share the view that love can survive over the years of a marriage, but that "it would be defined differently at different times" (Troll, 1986, p. 7).

For example, Ainsworth (1989) maintains that sexual pair bonds involve the operation of three basic behavioral systems: the attachment, reproductive, and caregiving systems. Thus, marriages are reciprocal relationships based on emotional, sexual, and familial interdependence. Over the course of the relationship, sexual attraction, which may have been the most important component in the beginning, begins to give way to the attachment and caregiving systems. Relationships that depend solely on sexual attraction tend to be short-lived, whereas those involving the caregiving and attachment components can be sustained over a long period. Caregiving is evident both in care provided to the partner and in the nurturing of children. The attachment component, though equally important, may be less evident. Hazan and Shaver (1987) point out that once established, a secure attachment, whether between child and parent or husband and wife, is often taken for granted. The strength of an attachment may be latent, observable only when the relationship is threatened or terminated (as in widowhood). These disruptions "'activate the attachment system,' to use Bowlby's phrase. . . . Loneliness and grieving are often signs of the depth of broken attachments" (Hazan & Shaver, 1987, p. 523).

A similar distinction has been made by Elaine (Walster) Hatfield and Ellen Berscheid (Berscheid, 1988; Berscheid & Walster, 1974; Hatfield, 1988), who distinguish between **passionate love**—intense emotion, sexual feelings, complete absorption in the other—and **companionate love**—warm, trusting affection. They suggest that passionate love burns brightly early in a relationship and then fades, while companionate love grows over time. Sternberg (1988) has expanded on this distinction, breaking companionate love down into two further components: **intimacy**—sharing, warmth, and closeness, which essentially amount to friendship—and **commitment**—the intent to maintain the relationship.

During the first year of marriage, while overall rates of companionship do not change, the nature of shared activity shifts from being primarily recreational to being more of a working partnership (McHale & Huston, 1985). In other words, being together is less the focus of marital activity and more incidental to the completion of tasks. Instead of going out to dinner and a movie, you do the laundry together.

Changes in the nature of the marital relationship can be trying to newly married couples, who may experience something different than what they expected in the relationship. In a study of 346 recently married couples (Arond, 1991), 41 percent of the sample reported that the adjustments were more difficult than they anticipated, 49 percent were having serious problems, and half were not certain the marriage would last. The authors portray marriage as a developmental process. In the transition from prenuptial bliss to reality, from the family of origin to the marital family, and from a passion-based to a companionate relationship, commitment to stick with the relationship may determine which marriages are likely to survive. In addition, having or being a spouse who has the qualities of a good friend—caring, integrity, sensitivity, warmth, acceptance—will be a tremendous asset. Patterns are set early on. Failure to resolve the issues of early marriage will have negative consequences later in the relationship.

So, marriages are dynamic relationships. Many of the changes that occur enrich the partners' life together. In describing the changing nature of her relationship with her husband, author Anna Quindlen (1988, p. 82) noted, "I still believe in magic, and it's still there. . . . But what I didn't know about marriage, the less magical parts of it, has become more important to me. Now we have history as well as chemistry."

Marital Roles

Particularly in this era of great change in gender roles, newly married couples may have a difficult time negotiating the role each partner will play relative to the relationship and the family itself. How will the work of the home and family be accomplished and by whom? How will decisions be made? Marriages can be categorized according to the way these questions are answered. For example, two major types of marriage have been identified in terms of the roles and statuses assigned to the marital partners: traditional and egalitarian. In a traditional marriage, the husband is the dominant, undisputed head of the household. The wife defers to him in all important matters. Household tasks are likely to be divided in stereotypical ways, with the wife taking care of the inside (including children), while the husband attends to the outside. In other words, there is "men's work" and "women's work."

In his description of a **traditional marriage enterprise,** Levinson (1996) emphasizes a clear split between the roles of female homemaker and male provisioner, with women centering their lives in the domestic world (composed of household and its surrounding familial and social world) and men centering their lives in the public sphere (composed of occupations and nonfamilial institutions). He points out that we are in the midst of a gender revolution that is changing the meaning of gender, the place of women and men in society, and the relationships between them in all aspects of life. At the heart of this change is a breakdown of the homemaker and provisioner roles and the associated dichotomy between the domestic and public spheres. The lives and personalities of men and women are becoming more similar, and new forms of marriage are emerging as more women both choose and are required to work outside the home and to commerce in a more equal way with the public sphere.

An **egalitarian marriage** (or *peer marriage*), in contrast to the traditional marriage, is a more democratic relationship of equals, in which power and authority are

In an egalitarian marriage, power, authority, and responsibility for household tasks are shared.

shared. Today, almost 60 percent of wives work, and a significant number of them earn more than their husbands. In these sorts of marriages, a premium is put on the partners' ability to communicate, negotiate, and resolve conflict. Traditional marriages are more likely when only the husband is employed.

A number of investigators (for example, Maret & Finlay, 1984; Scanzoni, 1978) maintain that the spouse with the greater earning power also has more bargaining power and a greater say in the domestic division of labor and other matters. According to this logic, as a woman's relative earning power increases, she is more likely to expect and demand greater equity in the relationship. Whether or not she gets it is another matter. Neither a wife's employment nor a husband's retirement affects the household division of labor as much as we might expect (Brubaker, 1985). For example, Walker (1970) found that employed mothers did about five times more housework than their husbands. Research by Berardo, Shehan, and Leslie (1987) confirms that even when they are employed, wives retain responsibility for the vast majority of the housework.

In any case, the degree to which the partners *agree* on marital gender roles seems more important to marital satisfaction and individual well-being than the nature of the marriage itself (Bowen & Orthner, 1983). Li and Caldwell (1987) found that the degree as well as the nature of incongruence affect marital adjustment. The worst scenario occurs when the wife is more nontraditional than the husband; the greater the discrepancy, the poorer the quality of the marriage.

Alternative Unions (Same-Sex and Nonmarried Romantic Relationships)

Some adults have marital-like partnerships, either heterosexual or homosexual, which are referred to here as alternative unions. Systematic research attention to same-sex romantic relationships emerged in the 1970s but is hampered by many of the same problems that characterize the early research on heterosexual couples: small samples of primarily White volunteers, with data from only one partner, based on anonymous self-reports (Huyck, 1995). In addition, research on these unions is complicated by problems in defining *homosexual* and determining the criteria for a relationship. Estimates of the prevalence of same-sex unions therefore vary, with some studies relying on self-definitions and others on census data. There are problems with both sources of information. Same-sex couples may face distinctive problems. For example, legal, social, and familial pressures that act to keep a heterosexual marriage intact may act to break up a homosexual relationship (Huyck, 1995). Difficulties also arise in later life in regard to inheritance, bereavement when a partner dies, and so on. The effects of gender and cohort also seem significant in these relationships—that is, the experiences of lesbian females versus gay men and older versus younger individuals may be quite different.

The number of unmarried couples living together has increased sevenfold since 1970. By age 30, about half of American women have cohabited. Among all racial/ ethnic groups, cohabitations are less stable than marriage. For a comprehensive review, see Bramlett and Mosher (2002). Some of these relationships eventually culminate in marriage. Most of the research on premarital cohabitation suggests that couples who live together before marriage have higher divorce rates. Studies also suggest that those who live together are less committed to the relationship, more independent, less religious, hold less traditional beliefs about marriage, and have more strained relationships with both sets of parents (for instance, see Newcomb, 1986). Additional research is needed to fully appreciate the effects of premarital cohabitation on the subsequent course of a marriage.

Benefits of Marriage

Regardless of age, sex, or cultural background, married people tend to be happier than those who are unmarried (Reis, Collins, & Berscheid, 2000). In comparison with those who are single, separated, divorced, or widowed, married adults, especially men, experience better overall well-being and lower rates of such indicators of psychological distress as depression and anxiety (Basic Behavioral Science Task Force, 1996). The most critical aspect of marriage for psychological well-being seems to be the emotional support it offers.

Married men and women also tend to have lower mortality, less risky behavior, more monitoring of health and compliance with medical regimens, more satisfaction with their sex lives, higher incomes, and more savings (Bramlett & Mosher, 2002). While some of these benefits may be due to a selection effect, with healthier, happier, more successful people more likely to get married to begin with (see, e.g., Johnson, McGue, Krueger, & Bouchard, 2004), research suggests that at least part of the benefits result from marriage itself.

CRITICAL THINKING QUESTION

How might marriage contribute to the positive outcomes described above?

Marital Satisfaction

For many of us, the marriage relationship is the most intimate and among the longest lasting of all close relationships. Socioemotional selectivity theory suggests that its importance increases across the years of adulthood, as we focus more and more of our interpersonal efforts on a more select group of relationships (see Chapter 6). As a result, the quality of the marital relationship is especially significant. A tremendous amount of research has been done on the causes and consequences of marital satisfaction as well as on its developmental pattern.

Qualities of High-Satisfaction Marriages

All marriages are not created equal. What distinguishes "good" marriages—those high in satisfaction—from less successful partnerships?

While there is no one formula for a happy marriage, researchers have identified a number of factors that have an important bearing on marital quality. Skolnik (1981) suggests the following key factors: affectionate and enjoyable personal relations, togetherness, good parental role models, acceptance of conflict as normal, and homogamous personalities. A number of studies find that satisfaction with the sexual relationship is strongly related to satisfaction with the relationship as a whole (Huyck, 1995).

The personality traits of the two spouses may also be critical to marital outcome. Kelly and Conley (1987) report findings from a longitudinal study of 300 couples over a period of 45 years (the Kelly Longitudinal Study of Marital Compatibility). They conclude that the personality characteristics of the marital partners determine whether the relationship is stable and mutually satisfying or not. The best indicators of marital distress are high neuroticism in both husband and wife and low impulse control in the husband. Personality is thought to have a formative influence on the cognitive and behavioral patterns established in the marriage. Neuroticism increases the likelihood of overreactions and conflict and disrupts patterns of communication: "Neuroticism acts to bring about distress, and the other traits of the husband help to determine whether the distress is brought to a head (in divorce) or suffered passively (in a stable but unsatisfactory marriage)" (Kelly & Conley, 1987, p. 34).

Similarly, Levenson et al. (1993) maintain that the most important determinant of marital satisfaction is the extent to which the couple is able to resolve conflict. Indicators of distressed marriages include reciprocal expression of negative feelings and behaviors (Basic Behavioral Task Force, 1996). A successful marriage requires more than love. Effective problem-solving skills and good communication seem to be necessary. The effects of incomplete resolution of important issues can accumulate over time and play a major role in eroding marital stability. Perhaps those most satisfied with their marriages have learned to adjust to transitions in their lives and in the life cycle of the family. Rather than altering the marital relationship, events such as retirement seem to highlight both the positive and negative aspects of a marriage (Brubaker, 1985). Because people carry their patterns of behavior with them throughout the life cycle, the quality of a marriage after such events is best predicted by the quality before. But bear in mind the eye of the beholder. Skolnik (1981) reports a correlation of only .31 between the satisfaction ratings of husbands and wives (with husbands more satisfied than wives).

Patterns of Marital Satisfaction

In general, the data have been contradictory. Most studies conducted before the 1960s found a gradual decline in marital satisfaction over time. For example, Pineo (1961) described an apparent "loss of fit" between the partners as the relationship went on. But more recent studies have not reported this pattern (Brubaker, 1985). Some have described a linear increase in marital satisfaction over time (Gilford, 1986). Others report essentially no change: those who were happy still are; those who were not still are not (in marriages that have remained intact) (Clark & Wallin, 1965). Still other studies—perhaps the majority—have found a curvilinear pattern, with satisfaction declining with the arrival of children, then increasing again after they leave home (for instance, see Rollins & Feldman, 1970). We'll have more to say about this finding in the section on parenthood. Clearly, the research has discovered a diversity of patterns: some marriages get better, some get worse, some remain about the same. Many variables are operating in any long-term intimate relationship, and the effects of these variables affect the course of the marital partnership over time.

Karney and Bradbury (1995) reviewed the major theoretical perspectives on marriage (social exchange theory, behavioral theory, attachment theory, and crisis theory) as well as the findings of 115 longitudinal studies (representing over 45,000 marriages) conducted since 1938 on change and development in marriage. Their goal was to integrate the findings and shed light on how marriages develop, succeed, and fail. They have proposed a model of marital development that integrates three categories of variables: the enduring vulnerabilities that couples bring to a marriage (including personal qualities such as neuroticism, as well as personal experiences such as an unhappy childhood); stressful events the couple encounters (including developmental transitions and other incidents and circumstances); and adaptive processes (the ways couples respond to events and circumstances). The model focuses on the interaction between vulnerability and stress and their effect on the way couples cope; this interplay accounts for changes in marital satisfaction as well as the timing of these changes. All married couples must adapt to a variety of stressful events over the course of their married life. Their ability to adapt depends on the amount of stress they encounter and the vulnerabilities the partners possess. Couples with good coping skills and few stresses and vulnerabilities will likely have stable and satisfying marriages. Couples with many vulnerabilities, high levels of stress, and poor coping skills will experience low marital satisfaction, separation, or divorce. Further, the quality of a previously satisfying marriage may decline when stress overwhelms coping resources.

Most long-term marriages of older adults are characterized by more affection and less expression of negative feelings (anger, contempt, sadness, and so on) than are marriages of middle-aged couples, regardless of severity of marital problems (Carstensen, Gottman, & Levenson, 1995). This finding suggests an age-related trend toward more positive affect. There may in fact be different developmental patterns for positive and negative marital feelings. In a study of three generations of married couples (Gilford & Bengston, 1979), young adults were found to be high on both positive and negative feelings, the middle generation reported lower levels of both positive and negative feelings, and the older group had more positive and fewer negative feelings. Troll (1986) suggests that negative feelings may decline steadily, while positive feelings may follow a curvilinear pattern. Longitudinal data from the Berkeley Older Generation Study indicate increased satisfaction and feelings of closeness from middle age to old age among couples who had been married 50 to 69 years (Field & Weishaus, 1992). Marital satisfaction and contact with children were positively correlated. Similarly, in a study of 156 long-term marriages, Levenson et al. (1993) found less conflict and more pleasure in older versus middle-aged marriages. Some marriages persist despite poor marital quality and low levels of satisfaction. Among long-term marriages, just as among young marriages, the least satisfying are characterized by the greatest expression of negative emotion (Carstensen, Gottman, & Levenson, 1995).

Gender Differences in Marital Satisfaction

In regard to gender, marriage appears to benefit men more than women. At all ages, men are more satisfied with their marriages than are women (Holahan, 1984; Levenson, Carstensen, & Gottman, 1993). According to Hess and Soldo (1985), women get physical and mental health benefits from good marriages, whereas men benefit regardless of the quality of the marriage. Levenson et al. (1993) hypothesize that the health toll of staying in an unhappy marriage falls heaviest on women because in our culture, the wife assumes the primary responsibility for trying to resolve an ailing marriage.

The marital behavior of men and women is consistent with their expressive and instrumental gender roles. Regardless of age and length of marriage, women express more positive and negative emotion than men and are more likely to confront a problem in the marriage, while men are more likely to withdraw from conflict and to "stonewall," or be nonexpressive, when experiencing strong negative emotion (Carstensen, Gottman, & Levenson, 1995). Husbands' defensive behaviors place further stress on their wives.

Cohort Effects

It is not clear to what extent the available data describe the pattern of development in marriage per se, as compared to the influence of cohort effects on those marriages previously studied (Huyck, 1995). Certainly, important changes have occurred in the age at first marriage, rates of cohabitation and divorce, and perhaps even in the expectations with which individuals enter marriage. Marriage among future cohorts may have a different meaning and follow different patterns than those described among earlier generations.

So what do we know about marriage after all this? We know that almost all of us will eventually marry and that marriage is associated with many benefits. The greater the similarity of the marital partners on such dimensions as personality, social background, marital role models, attachment history, and gender-role definitions, the fewer the sources of conflict and the greater the likelihood of marital compatibility and stability. Couples with good social and conflict resolution skills do a better job of navigating this intimate personal relationship. Those who make it through the apparently more difficult middle stages of the marriage, when the raising of children predominates, generally report high levels of satisfaction in their marriages, and correspondingly in their lives. We know that the spouse is an integral part of the social network, the major provider of social support. We know that men generally derive greater benefit from marriage than women. We know that the quality of our marriages will affect our children and their marriages. And we know that a lot of marriages do not make it and that this disruption of our support system can be devastating. We turn now to a consideration of divorce.

Divorce

Divorce, and the remarriages and stepfamilies that usually follow, has become so commonplace that it can now be thought of as normative, rather than an aberration (Carter & McGoldrick, 1988; Darden & Zimmerman, 1992). Remarriages have always occurred, though they used to be caused by the death of a spouse; now they are most often the result of divorce. The Census Bureau (1992a) estimates that approximately 50 percent of first marriages end in divorce, and the majority (some studies cite about 65 percent of women and 70 percent of men) remarry. A **remarried family** is a marriage in which either the husband or wife is in a second or subsequent marriage, while a **stepfamily** is a remarried family that includes children under the age of 18 in the home who were born to one of the partners prior to the remarriage (Glick, 1988).

There is some good news. The divorce rate, which had been steadily climbing since the 1950s, dropped in the 1990s, though modestly. Such a trend could be related to the increase in age at first marriage, known to be inversely related to likelihood of divorce (U.S. Census Bureau, 1992b). Others believe it is an artifact of demographics: the baby boom is now moving out of the prime divorce years, taking the divorce rate with it. But that does not mean younger cohorts will not show equally high rates of marital failure, especially given the example of their divorce-prone elders.

Amato and Booth (1997) reviewed data from a national sample of couples getting divorced and concluded that unrealistic expectations of marriage and widespread acceptance of divorce lead many couples to end marriages that could be salvaged. Rather than being precipitated by strong grounds, such as high levels of conflict, hatred, and discord, marriages are ending for a whole "kitchen sink" of reasons. The authors express concern about the negative consequences of these unnecessary family breakups on children.

An interesting relationship exists between income level and likelihood of divorce. The higher a man's income, the more likely his marriage will stay together, while as a woman's income increases, marital stability declines (Glick, 1984). Further, the Census Bureau reports (Reardon, 1993) that couples are nearly twice as likely to separate or divorce if they are living in poverty. The same report shows that the most stable families are those in which the husband works full time and the wife works part time.

CRITICAL THINKING QUESTION

Age, education, and income are negatively correlated with divorce. What factors might account for these correlations?

The probability of marital disruption also varies by race/ethnicity. Figure 7.4 shows the similarity of White and Hispanic women's probabilities of divorce, the higher likelihood of disruption among Black women, and the lower likelihood among Asian women.

Adjustment to Divorce

Studies of adjustment to divorce have typically focused on the wife's experience. This is because women are normally granted custody of the children, making the mother's adjustment more important in terms of the children's welfare and also providing an opportunity to study their adjustment at the same time (Bursik, 1991). Common emotional reactions include hostility and anger, depression, lowered self-esteem and self-concept, and feelings of social isolation and abandonment (Salts, 1985). One study found that ample social support, high scores on a masculinity scale, and low levels of acrimony toward the ex-spouse were strong predictors of good adjustment (Bursik, 1991). Disruption of the social network (including disapproval from extended family members and strained relationships with married friends) was especially difficult to deal with. Those who perceived social support to be available were better able to deal with the stress of the divorce.

Few noncustodial parents maintain consistent contact with their children. Nearly half of all children between the ages of 11 and 15 who are living with their custodial mother report that they have had no contact with their fathers in the past year (Basic Behavioral Science Task Force, 1996). The effect this has on the father's well-being, as well as his children's, needs further study.

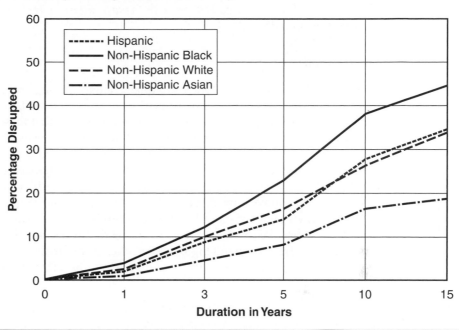

FIGURE 7.4 *Probability That the First Marriage Breaks Up,* *by Duration of Marriage and Race/Ethnicity*

Source: Based on Bramlett and Mosher, 2002.

Economic Consequences

Emotional and psychological adjustment may be complicated by socioeconomic changes following divorce. These are likely to be particularly disadvantageous to women. Estimates of the financial impact of divorce on women vary. According to Waldman (1992), the average woman's family income drops 23 percent following divorce. Peterson (1996) estimates that women typically experience a 27 percent drop in standard of living, while their ex-husbands experience a 10 percent increase. In 2001, 25 percent of all custodial mothers were living below the poverty line (U.S. Bureau of the Census, 2003). In 2002, 63 percent of custodial mothers and 39 percent of custodial fathers were awarded child support payments. (Those with no award at all either did not pursue an award or couldn't find the other parent.) Of those awarded support, 45 percent received the full payment, averaging $5,800 per year (U.S. Bureau of the Census, 2003). Payment of child support is more common among noncustodial parents who have regular visitation and/or joint custody of their children (U.S. Bureau of the Census, 1995).

According to these statistics, then, a significant percentage of noncustodial parents (who are primarily fathers) are not contributing at all to the financial support of their children. Unpaid child support is a major reason for needing public aid and a major factor in the feminization of poverty (see Chapter 8). The problem of so-called dead-beat dads is a complicated one and cuts across socioeconomic lines. Little relationship seems to exist between a man's income and the likelihood that he will pay court-ordered support (Hewlett, 1986; Waldman, 1992).

CRITICAL THINKING QUESTION

Since economic factors do not seem to explain nonsupport, what other explanations are there?

Remarriage

The majority of those who divorce eventually remarry, though remarriage rates among divorced women have declined from 65 percent in the 1950s to 50 percent today (Bramlett & Mosher, 2002). A number of studies indicate that these marriages are even more likely to fail than first marriages (U.S. Bureau of the Census, 1992b). Hartin (1990) points out that second marriages *should* be better than first marriages. After all, the partners are older, presumably more mature, and more experienced in intimate relationships. They may have learned from the experience of the first marriage and may be especially committed to making a success of the second one. However, second and subsequent marriages are plagued by complications that do not exist in a first marriage, a fact often overlooked by the partners as they enter the new relationship. One source of difficulty, of course, is resolving issues left over from the first marriage. According to Hartin (1990, p. 39), remarriage is more likely to be successful if the partners have achieved the following:

- Psychological closure on the first marriage (a sort of emotional divorce)
- Understanding of the reasons for entering the first marriage and for choosing the first spouse
- Understanding of each partner's contribution to the failure of the first marriage
- A clearer sense of what they want from a relationship and how to behave in it
- Reestablishment as independent individuals

Then the couple can face what may be the most difficult challenge of all—managing the complex configurations that result when the new family attempts to integrate the fragments of the two former families, which may of course include children. Recent research on mother-stepfather families suggests that while marriage may reduce some of the economic and other stresses that single mothers face, these families may also face difficulty integrating the stepparent into the ongoing parent-child relationship and forming a new family system (Basic Behavioral Science Task Force, 1996). These issues, more than anything else, may distinguish first and second marriages. Women with no children at the start of a second marriage are least likely to experience a second marital disruption (Bramlett & Mosher, 2002).

Widowhood

Widowhood—the loss of a spouse through death—is a major characteristic of family relationships later in life.

Because women tend to marry older men, and because men die earlier than women, widowhood is primarily a female phenomenon. In the United States, **widows** (women whose husbands have died) outnumber **widowers** (men whose wives have died) five to one (U.S. Bureau of the Census, 2003). As a result, most research has focused on widows, not widowers. Women live 15 years as widows on the average (Carstensen, 1991). In addition, men are over five times more likely to remarry than women following the death of their spouse (Aizenberg & Treas, 1990), since men have a larger pool of available partners. Among adults age 65 to 74, 78 percent of men but only 56 percent of women are married (Federal Interagency on Aging-Related Statistics, 2004).

According to the Holmes-Rahe Social Readjustment Rating Scale (Holmes & Rahe, 1967), the death of one's spouse is the most stressful life event. Adjustment to widowhood is partially a function of the circumstances of the spouse's death. For example, when the death occurs suddenly and unexpectedly, the surviving spouse is thrust into widowhood with little preparation. Life changes dramatically overnight. In other cases, the death may have followed a long battle with illness, around which the couple may have totally reorganized their lives. In addition, the surviving spouse may have been significantly involved in caregiving activities. Though the death is expected and some preparatory grief may have begun, adjustment to the loss is complicated by the dual need to adjust to the death as well as the end of the caregiver role, and the accompanying feelings of grief intermingling with relief.

The impact of widowhood is also a function of timing. Remember that events that occur at an expected stage in life—"on time"—are generally less stressful than those that occur "off time" (Seltzer, 1976). In the case of widowhood, the early death of a spouse may be more devastating. Stroebe and Stroebe (1987) found that younger widowed individuals were at greater risk of negative outcomes than those who were older. On the other hand, for some, the experience of widowhood later in life may be complicated by coexisting concerns about health, disability, and the ability to continue living independently without the care and support provided by the spouse. In such a case, the death of the spouse may symbolize for the survivor the difference between being old and not old (O'Bryant & Hansson, 1995). Those who have been recently widowed are over twice as likely to be placed in a nursing home as the nonwidowed (Wolinsky & Johnson, 1992).

Widowhood entails two major challenges: resolving the grief over the loss of a loved one and building a new life as a single person (Brubaker, 1985). Bankoff (1983b) has described three stages in this process. The first stage, called the *crisis-loss phase,* is a period of disorganization and chaos lasting days, weeks, and sometimes months. Anger, disbelief, and confusion about what the future will bring are characteristic of this stage. Symptoms of depression, such as apathy and withdrawal, are common correlates of grief. Widows and widowers cite difficulties with practical matters, such as finances and household tasks, as well as feelings of loneliness and loss, as they feel the void left in the social network by the death of the spouse (Lopata, 1979). In addition to dealing with their own feelings, spouses also recognize that others in the family, especially children, are suffering as well. The family itself will need time to reorganize. The second stage, called the *transition phase,* occurs as the individual's grief lessens in intensity and the possibility of a new life emerges. The development of a new identity as a single person and the rebuilding of a social system begin. The third stage, which might be referred to as the reorganization phase, involves the establishment of a new life (perhaps even a remarriage) and a return to normalcy as the individual adjusts to the loss. Each person grieves at a different rate, though several studies suggest that by six months the intensity of feelings has usually diminished significantly and the reorganization has begun. This is not to say that a person ever completely gets over the loss of a loved one. (See Chapter 12.)

As in any crisis, social support is important to the survivor's ability to cope. The social support network is usually activated immediately after a death occurs. However, this burst of assistance is usually short-lived and may not come at a time when it can most readily be accepted by the bereaved (normally when the initial shock has subsided): "Generally, the social network is on alert but not on active duty several weeks after the death" (Brubaker, 1985, p. 95). While children are often quite involved in providing support, the type of support they offer follows gender lines. Daughters provide more support than sons, especially emotional support; sons tend to provide more task-oriented assistance (Lopata, 1973, 1979). In the case of widows, especially valuable support in the initial stages of grief comes from their mothers (many of whom are probably also widowed) and from other widows (Bankoff, 1983a). Most widows prefer to live alone rather than with family members; when they do live with others it appears to be more out of economic necessity than preference (O'Bryant & Hansson, 1995).

Gender Differences

A number of investigators have looked at gender differences in widowhood. Because they are much less likely to remarry, widows might be expected to suffer greater loneliness than widowers. But several studies show that widows have more social contacts outside the home than married women, as if they divert attention that was focused on their husbands to other family members and friends (Anderson, 1984; Atchley, Pignatiello, & Shaw, 1975). Women have a more extensive social network than men do to begin with (Kohen, 1983), and this pays off later in life (Longino & Lipman, 1981). Remember, however, that the quality—not quantity—of relationships is critical to psychological well-being. As for widowers, a man's wife is often his best friend; he may have few others (Troll, 1982). In addition, the wife is typically the social manager and liaison for the family, and her death may cut him off from these ties. As a result of greater social isolation, his grief may be more intensely felt (Berardo, 1970). Greater difficulty living alone and the need for companionship may be reasons men remarry so frequently (Vinick, 1978). Women also benefit from the presence of other widows, who may serve as role models and significant sources of comfort in the early stages of grief. Males may suffer from a lack of such role models (Brubaker, 1985).

The biggest problem for women may well be poverty, because of the loss of the husband's income or, in many cases, retirement benefits, and also because of women's limited earning capacity (see Chapter 8) (Troll, 1986). The problem is magnified among minority women, whose husbands die earlier and whose financial status tends to be lower to begin with.

Of course, aside from these group differences, individuals will face the shift from the role of married to single person in their own ways, some more successfully than others. Those who have developed good coping skills, a rich and supportive social network, economic security, and diverse interests are better prepared to face this challenge.

Concept Review 7.2

- The median age of first marriage in 2000 was the highest on record.
- The nature of romantic love changes as the marital relationship evolves.
- Marriages are often categorized as traditional or egalitarian.
- The quality of the marital relationship is significant for each partner's psychological and physical well-being, especially so for the woman.

- A number of factors have been found to contribute to high-satisfaction marriages, including low levels of stress and partners who bring few vulnerabilities to the relationship and have effective coping skills (such as good communication and conflict-resolution skills).

- Much of the research on adjustment to divorce has focused on the custodial mother, for whom economic consequences are particularly significant.

- Remarriages are less successful than first marriages.

- The experience of widowhood is affected by a variety of factors, including timing and gender.

Parenthood

Though the number of children per family has declined and more parents are waiting longer than the traditional year before having a first child, most married couples eventually have children. In 1957, at the peak of the baby boom, the **fertility rate** (the number of births per female) in the United States hit a high of 3.8 births per woman, fell to a low of 1.7 in 1977, and has remained at about 2.0 over the last 20 years (Exeter, 1991; U.S. Census Bureau, 1998). The number of childless women aged 40 to 44 has almost doubled in the last 20 years, primarily as a result of greater career choices for women, though greater acceptance of childlessness and the delay of parenthood and resulting loss of fertility also play a role.

Fertility rate varies by race/ethnicity and place of birth. In the United States in 2002, Hispanic women had the highest fertility rate (Downs, 2003). Fertility of native-born women is lower than that of foreign-born women (U.S. Bureau of the Census, 1995; Downs, 2003). In 2002, 33 percent of all births were out of wedlock, up from 26 percent in 1994. Broken down by ethnic group, the rates were 25 percent of all births for White women, 36 percent for Hispanics, and 65 percent for Blacks. (See Figure 7.5.)

CRITICAL THINKING QUESTION
Why do people have children?

A Life-Span View of Parenthood

Traditional research has emphasized either the early, transitional years of parenthood, including the period just before and after the birth of a child and those years when the child and also the parental experience are young, or the later years, when parents are aged and children are in middle age. Hagestad (1987) has referred to these as the "alpha" and "omega" phases. Despite this emphasis, studies generally made little attempt to relate experiences in the alpha and omega phases. Left relatively unexamined are the middle years of parenthood, extending from the period when children are growing up

FIGURE 7.5 *Births Out of Wedlock, June 2002*

Percentage of babies born out of wedlock in the preceding 12 months to women in specified categories.

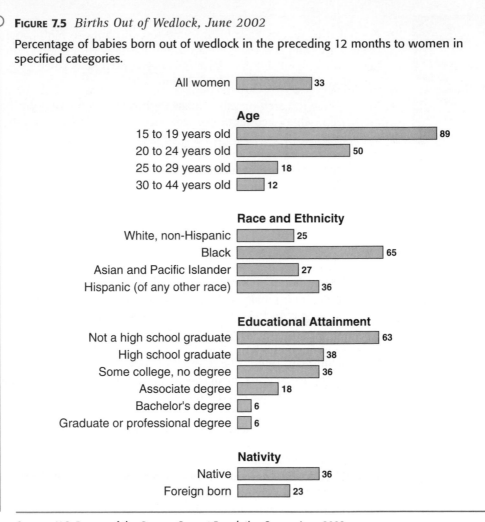

Age

All women	33
15 to 19 years old	89
20 to 24 years old	50
25 to 29 years old	18
30 to 44 years old	12

Race and Ethnicity

White, non-Hispanic	25
Black	65
Asian and Pacific Islander	27
Hispanic (of any other race)	36

Educational Attainment

Not a high school graduate	63
High school graduate	38
Some college, no degree	36
Associate degree	18
Bachelor's degree	6
Graduate or professional degree	6

Nativity

Native	36
Foreign born	23

Source: U.S. Bureau of the Census, *Current Population Survey,* June 2002.

through the leaving-home phase and early adulthood, when parents are in midlife (Seltzer & Ryff, 1994). Also, traditional research has focused on the effect of the parent on the child's development; few studies have examined the reciprocal nature of parent-child relations and the impact of parenthood on the parent. In contrast, a life-span view of parenthood recognizes that the parental role represents a lifelong commitment and that the parent-child relationship not only extends to the end of life, but also is affected by the developmental history of that relationship. Each phase of parenthood possesses its own character and is worthy of study. The life-span view also recognizes the reciprocal nature of the parent-child relationship, and that the parental role and a given parent's experience must be understood within the context of individual development, family development, culture, and cohort.

Parenthood is considered to be one of the most significant developmental tasks of adulthood (Dion, 1985), perhaps marking the end of immaturity better than any other role (Hoffman & Manis, 1979) and affecting definitions of self, relationships with others, and lifestyle. In addition to one's other roles, one is now also a parent. Parenthood is the means by which most adults develop generativity (Erikson, 1950). Gutmann (1990) has stressed the importance of parenthood in organizing male and female gender-role behavior. The birth of the first child represents a major transition in *family* life as well as individual development. Husband and wife are now also mother and father, altering the structure and function of the marriage as it shifts from a dyad to a triad. There are also developmental reciprocities—other members of the family become grandparents, aunts and uncles, cousins. One's position in the sequence of generations changes as well; no longer a member of the youngest generation in the family, there is now a new generation for which to be responsible. In the same way, older generations in the family shift up, to the status of grandparents or great-grandparents.

Changing Roles

The maternal and paternal roles are changing, primarily in response to shifts in the patterns of work and family roles. Full-time motherhood is no longer the norm. For the first time in history, more than 60 percent of women with children under the age of 18 are working outside the home (Matthews & Rodin, 1989). In 2002, 55 percent of mothers with infants were in the labor force, up from 31 percent in 1976 (the first year such data were collected) and down from the peak of 59 percent in 1998. (See Figure 7.6.) Evidence also exists that at least some fathers, who in the past often viewed parenthood as secondary to their role as chief breadwinner, are beginning to place more importance on their involvement with their children, trying to achieve more balance between their work and family roles. Evidence of subtle shifts in this direction include an increase in the

FIGURE 7.6 *Labor Force Participation among Mothers with Infants, 1976 to 2002*

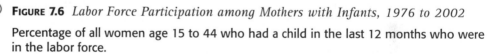

Percentage of all women age 15 to 44 who had a child in the last 12 months who were in the labor force.

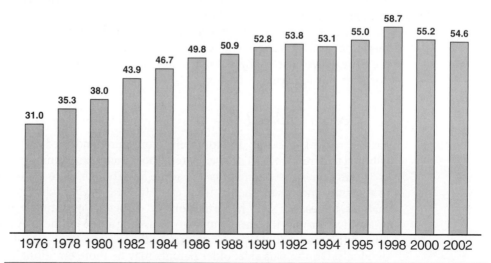

Sources: Downs, 2003; U.S. Bureau of the Census, *Current Population Survery,* selected years, June 1976 to June 2002.

number of single fathers as more men seek and get custody after divorce; an increase in the number of men who are present at the birth of their child and take time off following the birth; an increase in the number of men who report being involved in primary care of children; an increase in the number of men who drop children off and pick them up at day-care centers, take them to doctors' appointments, and so on; the increased visibility of men with babies in advertisements; and an increase in the number of men who turn down job transfers so as not to uproot their families (Coley, 2001; Lawson, 1990; Seligman, Rosenberg, Wingert, Hannah, & Annin, 1992).

I have witnessed a dramatic change between my father's generation of men and my own. Dad was very much a man of his age, completely uninvolved in any form of primary child care. He waited, smoking and pacing in the waiting room, as we were born. He never changed, bathed, dressed, or fed any of us when we were children. My husband, on the other hand, is one of the "new" fathers, present in the delivery room, and as involved as I am in the raising of our children. In fact, my daughter was a week old before I ever changed a diaper. Observers are quick to point out that this is a gradual change—not yet a revolution. While a minority of men are full partners with their wives in the responsibilities of parenthood (Deutsch, 2001; Hochschild, 1989), I (and our kids) happen to be among the lucky ones.

We will talk much more about the nature of work and family roles in Chapter 8. But before we leave this topic for now, consider how organized our society is around the notion of the traditional American family—for example, the placement of changing tables in public places, the scheduling of school activities and pediatricians' office hours, the content of men's and women's magazines. How easy do we make it for men (or working women, for that matter) to get information about and attend to the routines of active fatherhood? We "shower" the expectant mother with attention; we do little for the expectant father. In a thought-provoking article, Shapiro (1987) describes the double bind of men who are expected to be active participants in the birth of their child, yet simultaneously treated like outsiders. Their physical presence is expected, their emotional presence unwelcome. Shapiro identifies seven major fears and concerns common to expectant fathers that are normally not addressed, leaving them to deal with these feelings on their own and further isolating them. Among these are fear of the death of the spouse and/or child, doubts about their own ability to rise to the challenge of fatherhood, and fears about changes in the marital relationship and "being replaced" by the baby. If we expect fathers to be active parents, we need to provide the social supports for this to occur.

Delayed Parenthood

Factors related to career development, economics, and medical advances have contributed to a trend toward delayed parenthood. Increasing numbers of women and men are having their first babies after the age of 35. Though there are some increased risks to the fetus and the mother in these cases (greater likelihood of chromosome abnormalities, increased risk of hypertension and diabetes, for example), these can normally be avoided through increased monitoring, as long as the mother's overall health is good. One of the most difficult problems may be the increased rates of infertility in older individuals. On the plus side, older parents may be more emotionally mature and self-confident, better established in their careers, more financially stable, better with discipline and setting limits, and more involved with their kids (Furstenberg, Brooks-

Gunn, & Chase-Lansdale, 1989), though they may not have the energy of younger parents. Financial responsibilities of later-life pregnancies may postpone or eliminate parental retirement. Of greater concern to some observers are the social aspects of these "off-time" pregnancies and the ramifications for the family system (Gorman, 1991). For example, a very late pregnancy may deprive the child of relationships with grandparents or with same-age cousins. As with all family events, there are ripple effects. The same can be said, of course, about the consequences of pregnancy too early in life, which has the effect of lowering the teenager's educational and occupational achievements, increasing the risk of divorce, and creating problems for the parent (now grandparent) generation (Burton & Bengtson, 1985; McLaughlin & Micklin, 1983).

The Transition to Parenthood: Changes in Lifestyle and Family Life

Parenthood is a normative family transition: most adults become parents, at fairly predictable times. Parenthood is an expected role for which there is anticipatory socialization and social support; the assumption is that it is a positive experience. Despite this, the evidence suggests that it causes considerable stress. Surveys of large numbers of adults suggest that those with children at home experience more distress and less well-being than nonparents (McLanahan & Adams, 1987; Umberson & Gove, 1989). Seltzer and Ryff (1994) suggest that this may be due to inadequate preparation for this demanding role—that is, many adults may not have the skills or the values (such as self-denial) to be successful. So, the fact that most people expect to and do become parents does not guarantee success and satisfaction in the role. My own experience is that parenthood is one of the most satisfying and joyful aspects of adult life. But it is also one of the most challenging and demanding. The role requirements associated with parenthood are extensive, and the changes they produce are complex. Let's consider some of these.

First, there is a tremendous increase in workload, as the demands of caring for the child are added to existing responsibilities. I remember being amazed and absolutely overwhelmed by the sheer amount of work that one little baby could generate. My entire day revolved around changing, feeding, and holding the baby. I would just get her cleaned up, and she would throw up all over everything—or worse. I literally could not get anything else done. Fatigue and the frustration of seeing laundry and dust pile up and knowing that you have to get to the grocery store, prepare meals, and so on can really throw you, even if (as I did) you think of yourself as an organized, competent adult. It takes a while to reestablish a schedule and a sense of equilibrium. You gradually realize that you will "never" sleep late again, and that your leisure time is permanently diminished—and you get used to it. Parents' daily schedule is reorganized around the baby's needs, and physical living space is reorganized to accommodate the baby's "stuff"—and there's a lot of it (changing table, crib, diaper pail, and so on).

Second, there are changes in the family structure. By the very nature of a triad, each spouse must now compete for attention with the baby. Because the mother remains the primary caregiver, her increased workload means less time to spend with her husband, who may begin to feel left out. Even in previously egalitarian marriages, a tendency exists for the marriage to shift toward a more traditional division of labor after the first baby is born (Cowan & Cowan, 1992; Lamb, 1978; McHale & Huston, 1985).

Third, social life is also likely to change. For many parents, recreation is now found at home, doing things as a family unit, instead of going out and seeing friends as much.

Financial burden increases as well, partly due to increased costs, but also due to lost income if the wife stops working.

So, contrary to the myth that the birth of a child will save or even improve a marriage, children seem to put a significant strain on the husband-wife relationship. Of course, many other factors determine the way a family responds to the transition to parenthood. Problematic factors include a rocky marriage; lack of assistance and social support; little preparation or prior experience with children; financial concerns; emotional difficulties; an unwanted pregnancy; a difficult, sick, or disabled child; and work-role stress. All these circumstances can complicate the picture and undermine the new parents' ability to adjust successfully and fulfill the requirements of the parental role (Belsky, 1985b; Fleming, Ruble, Flett, & Shaul, 1988).

Where's Daddy?

"Historically, fathers have been a rather invisible group in the study of child development and family processes, with their influence rarely considered and their voices scarcely heard" (Coley, 2001, p. 743). Most of the research on the transition to parenthood focuses on changes in the woman's role from wife to mother. Little research examines the shift from the husband to the father role. However, we might expect the father's adjustment to be less extensive, since he is not expected to give up his career and does not assume primary caregiving responsibility.

A great deal of research has also been done on the mother-infant bond (see, for example, Klaus & Kennell, 1982). Ainsworth (1989) views this bond as an outgrowth of the caregiving behavioral system and thus as genetically based. Research into father-infant interaction is less extensive, though some studies show that fathers can effectively undertake the primary caregiver role, despite weaker biological underpinnings and lower social acceptance of the role for males (Ainsworth, 1989; Geiger, 1996). The fact is that they seldom do.

Phares (1992) cites a number of factors to explain the paucity of research on fathers, including the false belief that fathers are more difficult to recruit as subjects in research than mothers. Indeed, fathers are often studied indirectly, through mothers' reports of their behavior, raising questions about the validity of the data (Boyd, 1985; Coley, 2001). Phares concludes that the primary reason is probably the assumption that parenting is women's work, not men's. Citing Boyd (1985), she comments that "before the mid-1970s, fathers were not included in child development research because the cultural norm dictated that the father's role was to provide for the family financially, and it was considered unmasculine for men to be involved in taking care of their children" (Phares, 1992,

Even the most mature and well-organized parents find their lives turned upside down as they adjust to the new responsibilities of parenthood. Though there is relatively little research on fathers, their parental role is considered to be substantial and significant.

p. 659). Deutsch (2001) concurs that cultural images of motherhood reduce the position of fathers to "second-best substitutes." The father, considered unimportant to the child's social and emotional development, was simply left out of the theory and research on child development.

Research in the last 20 years has shown that early theories about the father's role are inadequate and based on outdated norms. Though fathers' involvement is not at the same level as that of mothers, it is considered to be substantial and significant, and similar in effect to that of mothers (Barnett & Baruch, 1987; Coley, 2001; Lamb, 1986). Studies of parenthood should no longer rest on the assumption that parenting is only a woman's role, but should include both parents.

Children and Marital Satisfaction

One aspect of the transition to parenthood that has been studied extensively is marital satisfaction. Most studies reveal moderate negative changes in marital quality after the birth of the first child—specifically, a decline in marital satisfaction, especially for women, and increased marital conflict (Cowan & Cowan, 1988). This pattern is not descriptive of all families, however. Belsky (1985b) points out that families change in different ways and that these changes are likely to be multiply determined. Decreased satisfaction with marriage may be the result of increased workload, especially for the wife, less time spent together, and increased financial difficulties (White, Booth, & Edwards, 1986). Rollins (1989) reanalyzed the data on declining marital satisfaction originally published in 1970 (Rollins & Feldman): "The result was that, with the amount of companionship held at a constant level, there were no differences in marital satisfaction of married men or women at different stages of the family career" (p. 191). He suggests that couples may avoid the consequences of role overload by paying special attention to communication and companionship with the spouse. Thus, the U-shaped pattern of marital satisfaction—initially high, decreasing with the arrival of children, and increasing after children leave—does not appear to be inevitable.

Though many women feel vulnerable, inadequate, and depressed in the first few postpartum months, and positive feelings toward their husbands decline, feelings about the baby become consistently more positive over time (Fleming, Ruble, Flett, & Van Wagner, 1990). Women report increasing feelings of closeness to the infant, as well as enjoyment of child-care activities, and a reduction in concerns about their new role. This is probably the result of both improved health and greater experience in mothering. Parenthood also brings many joys and satisfactions, possibly increasing the parents' sense of meaning in life (Umberson & Gove, 1989).

One variable that has received quite a bit of attention is the couple's expectations about parenthood. Belsky (1985), for example, designed a study to examine the effect of violated expectations. Specifically, he wanted to know if declines in marital satisfaction were the result of a discrepancy between the anticipated and real experiences of parenthood. He concluded that for both spouses, but especially for women, "the more events turned out to be less positive (or more negative) than anticipated, the more marital satisfaction declined—as did efforts to maintain the relationship" (p. 1041). These effects were most pronounced in the last three months of pregnancy and the first three months after the birth of the child. Because the responsibilities of parenting fall more heavily on women's shoulders, failure to accurately predict the nature of the role would lead to greater stress for them. Further, Ruble and her colleagues (1988) found that women generally expected the division of child-care and household tasks to be more equally shared than they actually were. The shift toward greater traditionality in the marriage may have caused a drop in marital satisfaction. In another investigation, Hackel and Ruble (1992) conducted a longitudinal study of 50 couples during the transition to first parenthood. Interestingly, they found that women's reaction to doing more household work and child care than they expected depended on whether they held traditional or nontraditional beliefs about gender roles.

One final note on this body of research. McHale and Huston (1985) conducted a longitudinal study of newlywed couples. They found that those who remained childless during the first year showed the same pattern of change in marital satisfaction as those who became parents. This suggests that the oft-reported declines might at least partly reflect the changing nature of the romantic relationship in the early stages of marriage and may not be entirely due to the birth of a baby.

The Middle Years of Parenthood

The middle years of parenthood, though woefully understudied, represent the longest phase and are among the most interesting, perhaps even the most meaningful. This is the period during which children come of age. How do adolescent children affect the development and well-being of their parents, who are often in midlife? What is the impact on the parents of a child's leaving home, not leaving home, or returning after having left? What is the effect of being a parent of an adult when one is in the prime of life oneself?

The Empty Nest

The postparental family, often referred to as the **empty nest,** is largely a recent phenomenon, the combined result of living longer and having fewer children. There used to be great concern about the well-being of the mother, in particular, as the kids began to leave home. After all, traditional women devoted themselves full time to motherhood. What would they do to fill the void? Again, though individuals react differently to these sorts of life events, studies increasingly show that most parents look forward to launching their children and that this is reflected in greater life satisfaction. The quality of the parent-child relationship as well as other conditions in the lives of both parents and their children affect the nature of this family transition and the ongoing intergenerational relationship.

CRITICAL THINKING QUESTION

Based on everything we have said so far, what are the satisfactions and rewards available to parents once their children have left home?

As we discussed in Chapter 6, recent cohorts of young adults are leaving later and are also more likely to return. Studies suggest that among parents age 45 to 54 who have adult children, 45 percent have an adult child who is living at home (Aquilino, 1990). In 2003, 22.8 percent of women and 30.6 percent of men age 18 to 34 lived with at least one of their parents (Fields, 2003a). Perhaps surprisingly, the majority of these parents had good relationships with these children and were satisfied with the living arrangement. Further study of this trend is warranted.

CRITICAL THINKING QUESTION

What factors contribute to an adult child living at home? What factors would contribute to the success of this living arrangement?

Culmination of the Active Parental Role: How Have the Kids Turned Out?

During the middle years of parenthood, parents have to renegotiate their relationship with their adult children, accept their life choices, relate to their spouses and children, and adjust to "how they have turned out." Tiger (1979, p. 960) has described parenthood as "a set of radically unselfish and often incomprehensibly inconvenient activities." Why do people do it? Perhaps because of the promise of the future, the hopes and dreams, that children represent (Ryff, Lee, Essex, & Schmutte, 1994). Ryff and her colleagues maintain that parents' assessments of how their children turn out in terms of their educational and occupational achievements, as well as their personal and social adjustment, represent "powerful statements about one's successes or failings as a parent" (p. 195). As a result, these assessments are expected to affect parents' well-being and evaluation of themselves. The team interviewed 215 midlife parents (mean age, 53.7). When asked what hopes and dreams they had for their children, both mothers and fathers mentioned happiness and educational success most frequently, followed by career success, a happy family, personal fulfillment, being a good moral person, and good health. As predicted, they found strong connections between parents' evaluations of their children's successes and failures and a number of measures of their own well-being, such as purpose in life and self-acceptance.

The Later Years of Parenthood

Few studies have attempted to connect experiences of parents and their adult children in the omega phase of parenthood with those in the alpha and middle phases. One of the issues that may dominate the omega period is the increasing need of aging parents for care and their dependency on their adult children. The research literature tends to focus on the nature of this experience for the caregiver (see the discussion later in this chapter), while little attention has been given to what it means to the parent to need and experience this caregiving. There is some evidence for the concept of a "support bank" (Antonucci & Jackson, 1990)—that is, contributions to a relationship earlier in life can be "withdrawn" legitimately later. Thus, parents who provided quality care to their children may feel less of a burden when they require assistance as they age (Beckman, 1981). It is also important to remember that at all stages of family life, relationships are reciprocal. We both give and get from our ties to others. Research is needed to address the parents' side of the parent-child relationship in old age and to examine the contributions that even aged parents make to their adult children. Though the years of active parenting have ended, parents of adult children may continue to enhance their children's development—for example, by serving as role models and sources of advice and support.

The Context of Parenthood

So far, we have been discussing the normative experience of parenthood. But for many, parenthood is nonnormative. This may be due to the timing of the role (unusually early or late), deviations from the traditional family structure (such as single parenthood or being an adoptive or stepparent), or characteristics of the child (for example, a child with Down's syndrome). We have seen that, in general, off-time events are more stressful than those that occur on time. We have also seen that variations in family structure are becoming more common, with the once-married two-parent family becoming less common. These alternate family structures may also contribute to changes in the experience of parenthood.

Traditional family research tended to treat all parents as if they were alike and to compare them as a group to nonparents. Increasingly, researchers are discarding this view of parents as a generic group and considering the impact of such variables as occupational status (working full versus part time or not working), socioeconomic status, ethnicity, and personality traits (Seltzer & Ryff, 1994). We must also be aware that cohort effects alter the nature and experience of parenting. What we know about parenthood may be peculiar to the cohorts studied and may not be generalizable to future generations of parents. More study is needed on the impact of such changes as the labor force participation of women, the changing roles of men and women, the effect of alternate family structures, the increasing use of day care, and the growing presence of adult children in the homes of their midlife parents.

Concept Review 7.3

- Less is known about the middle years of parenthood than either the transitional or later stages.
- Maternal and paternal roles are changing, largely as a result of changing patterns of work and family roles.
- The transition to parenthood causes many changes in lifestyle and family life and is often experienced as stressful.
- Parenthood may result in a decline in marital satisfaction.
- The middle years of parenthood represent the period when children come of age.
- Parents' assessments of their children's success may affect their own well-being and sense of self.
- Even as parents age and require more assistance from adult children, they continue to make important contributions to the parent-child relationship.
- Though parenthood is a normative experience, the nature of the parental experience is affected by the context in which it occurs.

Intergenerational Ties

Intergenerational relationships are those that cross generational lines. Here, we will examine the ties between parents and their adult children, and between grandparents and grandchildren.

Parent–Adult Child Relationships

The ongoing relationship between parents and their adult children is of growing interest as a result of longer life expectancy and the compression of generations. Parents and children are increasingly likely to grow old together (Aizenberg & Treas, 1985). As adults age, relationships with those in other generations increase in importance (Fingerman, 2001). The autonomy sought by a child in the stage of adolescence and leaving home does not signify a severing of the bonds of attachment to the parents (Ainsworth, 1989). Indeed, most adults continue to have meaningful, though altered, relationships with their parents. Fingerman (2001, p. 26) describes "the paradox of a distant intimacy": even though adults of different generations move apart and establish more distinct boundaries, their relationships grow closer. Cicirelli (1981) found that about 90 percent of adult children sampled felt "close" or "very close" to their parents. Maintaining or creating positive adult relationships with parents may benefit children's self-esteem and well-being (Welsh & Stewart, 1995). The remaining strength of their attachment is evident in the grief experienced when a parent dies. In addition, the working model of the parent and the parental relationship is retained cognitively and continues to be influential (Schmotkin, 1999).

Separate but Near

Older adults value their independence. They prefer to live close to, but not with, their adult children (Troll et al., 1979). And more older adults are able to live independently, due to improved health and economic status. Only 10 percent of parents over 65 (usually a mother) live with their children (most likely an unmarried daughter), and when they do, they are usually the head of the household (Troll, 1986). In cases where a parent lives with a child who is head of the household, the parent tends to be very old, poor, or sick. Although Hispanics, Blacks, and Asian Americans are more likely than Caucasian Americans to live in extended-family households, this is due more to economic need than choice (Carstensen, 1991). When socioeconomic status is controlled, family interaction patterns become highly similar. Given the choice, adults in both generations prefer to live independently.

Most parents (between 78 and 90 percent) live near at least one child and have regular weekly contact with their children, either visiting frequently or staying in touch by phone or letter (Shanas, 1979a; Cicirelli, 1983). Patterns of interaction established earlier in the life of the family tend to persist: those who have always visited frequently continue to do so; those who have not, do not (Leigh, 1982). A move to be near adult children when parents are older can have both positive and negative effects. On the positive side, parents may feel less tied to their own area of residence as they retire and their friends and neighbors retire and move away. This may free them to move closer to their family and to benefit from support and a sense of security as their vulnerability increases. This also allows parents to offer emotional and instrumental support, such as help with the care of grandchildren. Potential problems relate to integrating the lives of the various generations, negotiating boundaries so that each generation's privacy is respected, and dealing with any unresolved conflicts from earlier stages of the parent-child relationship.

Family systems vary markedly around the world, with different rules of marriage, inheritance, residence, and inclusion (Hashimoto, 1993). In the non-Western world, the most common living arrangement for older adults is coresidence with a married child.

For example, two-thirds of Japanese elderly currently live in multigenerational house-holds, usually with the eldest son, his wife, and children. Of the remaining one-third who have children, these older adults plan to move in with an adult child if necessary.

The Kinkeeper

In the Western world, families are believed to be held together by close ties between mothers and daughters (Troll et al., 1979). Women are, as noted earlier, the "kinkeep-ers." Studies indicate that, of the four possible parent-child dyads (father-son, father-daughter, mother-son, mother-daughter), the mother-daughter bond is the strongest throughout life, maintaining a consistent quality over time (Troll, 1986). Adult daugh-ters are more likely to live near and exchange help with their mothers than sons are (Cicirelli, 1983; Shanas, 1979a), and patterns of kin interaction normally follow the ma-ternal, rather than the paternal, side of the family. Family heirlooms and old photos are more likely to be from the mother's side of the family (Sweetser, 1963). Similarly, grand-mothers, especially the maternal grandmother, have more important relationships with their grandchildren (Cherlin & Furstenberg, 1985).

Interdependency and Mutual Assistance

The family continues in its role as a social support system, with parents and their adult children providing various types of assistance to one another. Parents may help with emotional support and advice or in more tangible ways, with money or babysitting, while adult children may reciprocate in providing emotional support, help with household tasks, or care during illness (Brody, 1985; Shanas, 1979a). This reciprocal assistance may shift in direction over the life of the family, focused more on children in the earlier stages and flowing more toward parents as they age. Over and over again, adult children have been found to be the chief source of support for elderly parents. One of the challenges of mutual dependence is for each generation to match the level of assistance to level of need. In other words, problems arise when too little, as well as too much, help is offered (Botwinick, 1984). Adult children tend to follow a "principle of least involvement in par-ents' lives" (Cicirelli, 1991, p. 302) in an attempt to preserve each generation's indepen-dence as long as possible. When ongoing surveillance of the situation suggests an increase in need, however, they become more involved in caregiving. Because of the likelihood that they will grow old together, adult children may at some point find their responsi-bilities to their parents increasingly burdensome because of their own aging processes. We will examine the dilemmas of caregiving in more detail in a later section.

A Comparison of Cohorts: The World War II, Baby Boom, and Baby Bust Generations

Parent-child relations are influenced by the social context in which they occur, so we must be cautious of making generalizations across cohorts. The World War II generation is characterized by the highest marriage rate of any cohort in the 20th century, high fer-tility rates and large numbers of surviving children, and increased life expectancy (Pillemer & Suitor, 1998). Their children, baby boomers, will share many years of adult life with their parents. Though they may anticipate a period of caregiving as their par-ents age, this burden will be lightened by the fact that their parents will more likely be married and that these responsiblilites will be shared with siblings. In contrast, baby boomers have lower rates of marriage, higher rates of living alone, higher rates of divorce, fewer children, higher rates of out-of-wedlock births, and live in a greater variety of family forms. With a greater likelihood of being single, with fewer children, and with parent-child relationships potentially impaired by disparate family forms and family dissolution, baby boomers may have fewer family resources available to them as they age. These boomer parents may also have fewer resources (financial and otherwise) to offer their own children, the baby busters, who will in turn have fewer siblings with whom to share family responsibilities for single aging parents. The effect that all this will have on intergenerational relationships remains to be seen. Will more flexible family forms in fact increase the types and extent of kinship bonds and the resources they offer? Or will friendship take on a more important role in filling the void left by fewer close family ties? The nature of parent-child relations as we know them today may be more a product of cohort and demography than of consistent characteristics of intergenerational ties. The current cohort of elderly has extensive resources of family support available. Future cohorts, many of whom will live alone, without the important support provided by a spouse and with fewer children, may not be so fortunate (Pillemer & Suitor, 1998).

Grandparenthood

The median age when people first become grandparents has been about 45 for the last 100 years (Hagestad, 1985). However, the aging of the population has increased the diversity of both grandparents, whose ages can range from 30 to well over 100, and grandchildren, who may range from newborns to retirees (Giarrusso, Silverstein, & Bengtson, 1996). According to Longino and Earle (1996), the children of the current generation will spend half of their lives as grandparents. Many will still be raising their own children and participating in the labor force at the same time. Interestingly, studies of grandparenthood tend to be studies of grandmothers; little is known about grandfatherhood (Brubaker, 1985). Other neglected topics are great-grandparenthood (the little research that exists suggests high similarity between the experiences of grandparents and great-grandparents), great-great-grandparenthood, and relationships between grandparents and their adult grandchildren (the majority of Americans age 65 and over have at least one adult grandchild) (Giarrusso, Silverstein, & Bengtson, 1996).

CRITICAL THINKING QUESTION

There are many reasons for the limited number of studies on grandfathers. How many can you think of?

Grandparental role expectations are not clearly defined (Brubaker, 1985). However, in a study of 125 grandmothers (Robertson, 1977, p. 171), 80 percent agreed that the following were characteristic of good grandparenting: "loves and enjoys grandchildren, sets good example (religion, honesty, right versus wrong), helps grandchildren when asked or needed, does not interfere too much in grandchildren's lives, is a good listener, doesn't interfere with parental upbringing or spoil grandchildren, and can use discipline with grandchildren if it is needed."

Grandparenthood means different things to different people (Kivnick, 1982a). For some, being a grandparent plays a central role in their lives; for others, it provides an

The majority of grandparents derive comfort, satisfaction, and pleasure from their role. Variation is found both in grandparenting style and in the different relationships established with different grandchildren.

opportunity to enjoy the benefits of being with young children without the responsibilities; for still others, it represents a means to immortality. Cherlin and Furstenberg (1985) found that grandparents not only differed from each other, they also had a different relationship with each of their grandchildren, partly as a function of the grandparent's age and sex, as well as the age and sex of the grandchild. Relationships with grandparents tend to be particularly close when grandchildren are young. Adolescents reflect their growing autonomy in these relationships (Kahana & Kahana, 1970). Satisfaction with the role varies as well, though the majority of grandparents in a study by Neugarten and Weinstein (1964, p. 200) "expressed only comfort, satisfaction, and pleasure." The grandparent-grandchild relationship is also a function of the relationship the grandparents have with their own children, which determines the degree of closeness and amount of contact that exists between the oldest and youngest generations (Matthews & Sprey, 1985).

The prevalence of divorce has meant loss of contact with grandchildren for many grandparents, particularly, of course, if they are the parents of the noncustodial spouse (Matthews & Sprey, 1984). The courts are increasingly being asked to untangle complicated questions of grandparents' rights. The strength of feeling these older adults have for the youngest members of their family is evidenced by their increasing tendency to seek legal remedies in such cases. Every state in the union has passed some form of grandparent visitation legislation since the late 1960s (Hartfield, 1996). Remarriage following divorce means that stepgrandparenthood is also increasingly common.

Troll (1983) refers to grandparents as "family watchdogs." Though they prefer to remain independent and somewhat detached from the lives of their children and grandchildren, they are ready to step in when needed, particularly by supporting the mother in her childrearing role (Hagestad, 1985). Just as parents turn first to children when they need help, children turn first to parents (Troll, 1986). Grandparents may help with the transition to parenthood, or in the adjustment to divorce (Aizenberg & Treas, 1985). In the latter case, grandparents, especially the parents of the mother (because of patterns of custody), may serve as agents of stability and comfort (Longino & Earle, 1996). The grandparent-child relationship can be mutually beneficial. For example, grandchildren may help fill the void a grandparent experiences in widowhood.

Another function of grandparenting is to bring "the past to the young," while grandchildren bring "the present to the old" (Troll, 1986, p. 307). Grandparents serve as symbols of family history and continuity as well (Johnson, 1985a). I never tired of hearing my grandmother's stories of "olden days" and family members who were only known to me through her verbal portraits. In traditional societies the elder holds a central position as cultural historian. Because all social roles exist within a larger ecological context, elders are affected by social and technological changes that transform the culture. We've seen evidence of the effects that social changes in the mainstream society—such as the higher divorce rate and extended life expectancy—are having on grandparents. We know much less about grandparenthood among ethnic minorities. See the Box for a discussion of the changing nature of grandparenthood among the Navajo of the American Southwest.

Grandparents as Surrogate Parents

Grandparents are increasingly stepping in as *surrogate parents* to take over the primary care of children when parents cannot—or will not—do so because of divorce, teenage pregnancy, single parenthood, drug and alcohol abuse, AIDS, incarceration, and/or unemployment. All of these factors are tied to poverty. By 2002, almost 4 million children

---

UNDERSTANDING THE DEVELOPMENTAL CONTEXT

Grandparenthood among the Navajo

One of the roles that grandparents may fulfill is that of family and cultural historian (Bengtson & Robertson, 1985; Kivnick, 1982b). Grandparents may serve as a bridge to the past, transmitting family and societal values as well as identity; as keepers of community (Barusch & Steen, 1996); or as cultural conservators (Weibel-Orlando, 1990). This role may be difficult to maintain when traditional societies experience rapid social and technological change. Grandparenting on the Navajo reservation in the four-corners area of the Southwest offers a

glimpse into the complex interplay between the cultural context and the maintenance of traditional roles (Barusch & Steen, 1996). Since the childhood of the current cohort of Navajo elders, two major technological changes have occurred on the reservation. The first is the rapid development of towns bordering Navajo lands. These border towns offer work, drawing the Navajo away from the reservation and its family-centered organization. The second is the availability of electricity and, with it, television, bringing to Navajo society the lifestyle, values, and attitudes of American society, which are in many ways alien to Navajo traditions. Both of these changes have undermined the central role of the elder as a source of cultural values, practical information, and identity—as representatives of what it means to be a Navajo. In addition, the past policy of only teaching the English language in schools has meant that the younger and elder generations are cut off from each other by a language barrier, the same phenomenon seen in immigrant families as younger generations become acculturated to the new culture. Less and less able to function as a bridge between generations, the grandparent's traditional role is weakened and devalued, and the elder is moved to the periphery of Navajo society. As Barusch and Steen point out, it is difficult to be a keeper of community in a changing world.

in the United States lived with their grandparents, a huge increase since 1980 and a serious indicator of the difficulties in which many American families find themselves (Fields, 2003b; Roe & Minkler, 1998–1999). In almost half the cases, the grandmother alone provides the care. About three-quarters of children are infants or preschoolers when they come to live with their grandparent, and 40 percent stay for five or more years (Fuller-Thomson, Minkler, & Driver, 1997). Surrogate parenting by grandparents offers both rewards and challenges, and most grandparents willingly accept the task of providing a safe haven for their grandchildren. Benefits include a renewed sense of purpose, an emotional bond with the grandchild, and the enjoyment children bring to one's life (Roe & Minkler, 1998–1999).

Sometimes the burden of helping out can be great, and under some circumstances the stress can be significant. For example, in one study, 86 percent of custodial grandparents raising children of drug-addicted parents felt anxious or depressed (Burton, 1992). Surrogate parents may experience health and economic problems, social isolation, and lack of institutional and government support (Minkler & Roe, 1996). Children living in their grandparent's household without a parent present are much more likely to be living in poverty and without health insurance (Fields, 2003b). These "custodial" grandparents have difficulty getting legal, permanent custody of the children and receive less than one-third the financial help offered to foster parents (Creighton, 1991). Insurance companies often refuse medical coverage for grandchildren who have not been legally adopted by the grandparent caregiver. Many school districts refuse to allow a child to register for school unless at least one natural parent lives within the boundaries established for that school. Reduced socialization with family and friends, shame, role conflict, and grief over the loss of their anticipated future pose other problems (Hayslip & Patrick, 2002). Legal and financial assistance are high priorities for these grandparents, as are support groups and referrals provided by AARP's Grandparent Information Center, opened in 1993 (www.aarp.org/confacts/health/grandsupport.html).

Surrogate parenting is especially likely in low-income inner-city areas, where grandparents are in some cases helping to prevent the collapse of the already overburdened foster-care system (Minkler & Roe, 1996). The problem is compounded among ethnic minority families by what Giarrusso, Silverstein, and Bengtson (1996) refer to as age-condensed family patterns. Teenage pregnancy among these groups can lead to grandparenthood in one's 20s or 30s, a pattern that may last over four or five generations. Higher fertility rates and the inclusion of nonbiological relatives in the family structure (referred to as "fictive kin") enlarge the social support network. This is a double-edged sword, however; one may receive support but may also have to *provide* support to many more people (Bengtson, Rosenthal, & Burton, 1995). African American grandchildren are about three times more likely than Whites to be living with a grandparent serving as a surrogate parent (U.S. Bureau of the Census, 1993). Rates are also higher among Latinos. These grandparents tend to have low income and multiple caregiving roles. Thus, their stress may be greater than that experienced by Whites.

Adult Sibling Relationships

Siblings are brothers and sisters—individuals who share the same biological parents. Social scientists have become increasingly interested in adult sibling relationships, which, though not yet well understood, may be an important component of an individual's social support system, particularly in old age (Cicirelli, 1991; Gold, 1987). Most of the current cohort of older adults have at least one living brother or sister with whom they stay in some kind of contact (Cicirelli, 1991). The importance of these bonds is expected to increase in the future as baby boomers, who have more siblings than preceding cohorts, but less stable marriages and fewer children on whom to rely for emotional and instrumental support, enter old age (Cicirelli, 1991; Gold, 1987). Thus, though the bulk of the research has focused on *inter*generational relationships, knowledge of *intra*generational ties may be increasingly valuable (Gold, 1987).

Sibling Relationships as Attachments

Cicirelli (1991) suggests that the origin and durability of the bond between siblings may be best explained by life-span attachment theory. Just as infants become attached to parents, children also become attached to siblings. These attachments persist into adulthood and are manifested by a desire to maintain contact (through such behaviors as calling and visiting) and to protect the relationship—for example, through helping and caregiving.

Unique Qualities

While sibling relationships share many common features with other emotional attachments, they are unique in at least four ways (Cicirelli, 1991). First, siblings share between 33 percent and 66 percent of their genes in common (Scarr & Gracek, 1982). The bond between siblings is not voluntary but ascribed by virtue of their biological linkage—they are born into the same family. As such, the relationship always exists, even though it may not be functional (Gold, 1987). Second, the sibling relationship is potentially the longest-lived of any family relationship, beginning as it does with the birth of the younger sib and ending with the death of one of them. Third, in addition to their shared genetic heritage, siblings share a long history of family experiences. This may produce similar perspectives and values, or at least an understanding of one another's point of view difficult to achieve in other relationships (Ainsworth, 1989; Gold, 1987). And fourth, the sibling connection is more egalitarian: siblings are likely to share relatively equal power in the relationship.

Pattern over Time

What is the normal course of sibling relationships over time? Bedford (1989) suggests that the level of involvement—extensive in childhood—decreases as the siblings enter adulthood and broadens again later in life.

In a qualitative study of sibling relationships in 60 individuals over 65, Gold (1987) found that 53 percent reported increased contact as well as a greater degree of emotional closeness in later years. Eighty percent enjoyed and sought increased contact with brothers and sisters. One of the most common reasons given for these changes was increased time available after the empty nest or retirement. Consistent with other research, 63 percent of the respondents indicated that sibling relationships played a secondary role during young and middle adulthood, when the developmental tasks associated with marriage, childrearing, and work took the spotlight. Other reasons cited for the changed relationship included a mellowing and desire to resolve old conflicts, increased worry about the health and well-being of the sibling, and greater need for support and assistance.

Functions of the Sibling Relationship

The special nature of the sibling connection may give it functions distinct from any others. Gold (1987) speculates that the desire to extend and enhance this connection in late adulthood may be an attempt to reconstruct the family of origin. Nearly all the subjects (88 percent) recognized the sibling relationship as the only remnant of the family of origin, and this shared survivorship enhanced its significance. In addition, an extensive shared history allowed the siblings to reminiscence together, a kind of collective life review that was mutually satisfying and was noted by 80 percent of the sample as the most frequent activity when siblings visited or corresponded. Siblings may also become primary convoy members later in life, filling voids left as other members of the social network drop out.

In fact, Cicirelli (1985) suggests that siblings may be the greatest untapped source of support for older adults. The potential availability of the sibling, even if never called on, may contribute to a sense of well-being. Though spouses and adult children are the preferred sources of assistance, siblings may serve as a sort of social insurance policy (Hochschild, 1973), ready to step in when alternative sources of support are unavailable. They appear to be especially important sources of psychological support—giving advice, boosting morale, and providing companionship (Cicirelli, 1991). These relationships may be more critical for the never-marrieds, who are more likely to turn to brothers and sisters for assistance (Johnson & Catalano, 1981). Finally, siblings provide support to aging parents as their level of need for caregiving increases (Cicirelli, 1991; Goetting, 1986). This may bring brothers and sisters closer together as they share caregiving tasks and responsibilities (Tonti, 1988).

Additional Questions

Cicirelli (1991) points to the need for greater understanding of ethnic and cultural differences in sibling relationships. There is some evidence that ties among siblings are

Connections among siblings may be an important component of an individual's support system, especially later in life.

stronger among lower socioeconomic groups, perhaps because there are fewer alternative sources of assistance available (Gold, Woodbury, & George, 1990). Studies examining half-siblings, stepsiblings, and adoptive siblings in adulthood are also needed. Do only children, those with nonfunctional sibling ties, or those with no living siblings develop "social sibling relationships" with age peers in adulthood as substitutes (Hochschild, 1973; Gold, 1987)? What is the impact of the death of a sibling on adult development (Brubaker, 1985)? What is the effect, if any, of gender on sibling relationships in adulthood?

Concept Review 7.4

- About 90 percent of adult children report being close or very close to their parents; this is evidence of the enduring importance of the parent-child bond.

- Older adults generally prefer to live close to, but not with, their adult children.

- Parent–adult child relationships continue to be characterized by reciprocity and various forms of mutual assistance.

- Relationships between parents and their adult children are influenced by culture, cohort, family history, and gender.

- Grandparenthood represents an opportunity for a fulfilling and satisfying role entry in middle to late adulthood.

- The nature of the grandparent role is somewhat unstructured and varies widely, though grandparents are a frequent source of support and assistance to their children and grandchildren in their several roles of parent, grandparent, and surrogate parent to grandchildren.

- Sibling relationships are unique and appear to become more important sources of support as individuals age.

Family Caregiving

Caregiving as a Normative Experience

One of the consequences of extended life expectancy is the increased risk of chronic illness leading to physical and cognitive impairment, and the likelihood that older individuals will need various types of assistance (Gatz et al., 1990). According to the U.S. Bureau of the Census (2003), about 20 percent of noninstitutionalized Americans age 5 and over have some type of chronic disability affecting everyday activities, and the likelihood increases with age, as does the need for assistance (Figure 7.7).

Help can be provided through either informal means (for instance, by family and friends) or formal mechanisms (institutions such as nursing homes). For every disabled elderly person residing in a nursing home, two or more equally impaired individuals live in the community through the efforts of family members, who provide assistance with medical and personal care and household chores (Federal Interagency Forum on Aging-Related Statistics, 2004). The family is also the source of emotional support, companionship, and caring, which is the form of family support that the elderly most want.

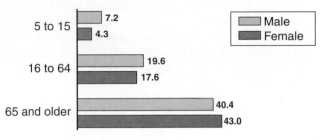

FIGURE 7.7 *Percentage of the Civilian Noninstitutionalized Population with Any Disability, by Age and Sex, 2000*

Note: Data based on self-report; includes sensory, physical, mental, and emotional conditions affecting physical, cognitive, self-care, and employment activities.
Source: U.S. Bureau of the Census, *Census 2000,* summary file 3.

Without the help provided by family members, as well as friends and neighbors, many more elderly would have to leave their homes and enter institutions.

The percentage of adults with living parents increased dramatically in the last century. For example, the number of middle-aged couples with two or more living parents rose from 10 percent in 1900 to 47 percent in 1976 (Uhlenberg, 1980). Brody (1985) has described long-term parent care as a normative experience, something that, as a result of changed demographics, adult children can now expect to do at some point in their lives. Because of the dramatic increase in the number of people needing care, and the implications for family members who provide this care, caregiving is a topic of great interest among gerontologists (George, 1990a).

Changed Nature of Caregiving

Not only do more people provide care for greater numbers of elderly than in the past, but the nature of caregiving has changed (Brody, 1985; Pearlin et al., 1990). First, medical advances have eliminated many of the acute causes of death, such as infectious illnesses, which predominated in the past. Today, as a result, people are most likely to die from chronic illnesses such as cancer. Medical science has also made it possible for people to survive longer after the onset of illness. This means that the caregiver role is extended over a longer period of time, during which the care recipient becomes progressively more dependent. Thus, caregivers "provide more care and more difficult care to more [family members] over much longer periods of time" (Brody, 1985, p. 20).

Who Is the Caregiver?

Most caregivers are older spouses and middle-aged adult children who provide care to an ill or disabled spouse or parent. When an older person needs assistance, there appears to be a hierarchy of preference in which individuals turn first to their spouse, then adult children, friends, neighbors, and eventually formal service providers (Cantor, 1980). Though the majority of studies have focused on primary caregivers, in most families, secondary caregivers exist as well. They may be involved in a variety of ways—for example, by providing respite for the primary caregiver or by handling finances (Malonebeach & Zarit, 1991). According to Stone, Cafferata, and Sangl (1987), about a third of caregivers are spouses, and 30 to 40 percent are adult children. Of these adult children, 80 percent are women, 50 percent are working (another 9 percent had quit to provide care), and 24 percent have a child under the age of 18. Eighty percent of these caregivers are involved in caregiving on a daily basis; 20 percent have been caregiving for five years or more.

The most likely person to provide care when an older person needs assistance is the spouse (Zarit, Birkel, & Malonebeach, 1989). These spouse caregivers are generally considered to be more vulnerable, since they are typically older, in poorer health, have lower incomes, and have been providing care for a longer period of time (Montgomery & Datwyler, 1990). In addition, as the spouse is often the primary source of social support, the loss of this resource as the patient's condition deteriorates may be especially difficult to bear. If the spouse is not available, the next most likely caregiver is an adult daughter. Because in the cohort now old, husbands are older than wives, wives live longer, and men are more likely to remarry, an older man who becomes ill is most likely to be cared for by his wife, who is also likely to be elderly and in poor health (Johnson, 1985b; Troll, 1986). For all the same reasons, when an older woman needs help, a daughter is most likely to provide it. Even when a spouse is the primary caregiver, adult children often serve as secondary caregivers and support systems for the caregiving spouse. Though the greatest proportion of daughters caring for a parent are in their 40s and 50s (remember the "middle-generation squeeze"), about a third are either under 40 or over 60 (Brody, 1985). As Brody (1985) has pointed out, a major new role has emerged for the young-old—that of caregiver for the old-old.

In families with more than one adult child, availability seems to determine which one assumes primary caregiving responsibilities (Gatz et al., 1990). Availability may be determined by geographic proximity, marital status, employment, or presence of young children. Families vary in how caregiving tasks are handled among siblings—for example, whether it is done cooperatively, by taking turns, and so on. According to Cicirelli (1991), siblings generally accept the unequal levels of responsibility as long as there are legitimate reasons for it. Abdication of responsibility without good reason is likely to generate resentment, however.

Why do women outnumber men in caregiver roles? A number of reasons have been cited, including the traditional gender roles of the female as kinkeeper and caregiver, which often cause women to live closer to parents and to have greater interaction with family members (Montgomery & Datwyler, 1990). However, we should emphasize that studies have found no difference in the sense of affection or obligation men and women feel for the elderly. The difference is in how they actualize that obligation (Montgomery & Kamo, 1989; Matthews & Rossner, 1988). So, though wives and daughters are shouldering the bulk of caregiving responsibilities, men's contributions should not be overlooked (Brody, 1985). The nature of their involvement often differs, tending to follow gender-role lines. Daughters are more likely to be involved in hands-on care (housekeeping, personal hygiene); sons are more likely to be involved with household repairs and finances (Cicirelli, 1981).

Caregiving Career

The more vertical family structure—in which more generations consisting of fewer members are alive at the same time—means that more than one older family member will probably need assistance, though fewer younger adults will be available to provide it (Gatz et al., 1990). Brody (1985) emphasizes that for many women, parent care is but one phase in a **caregiving career** that also includes child care, care for other elderly relatives, and, eventually for many, care for a dependent husband. Much of this caregiving may be concurrent and may extend well into later middle and early old age. In other words, caregiving is not a single, time-limited episode.

The caregiver role is a significant source of stress for these women, and, as unpaid labor, has no value for the future in terms of pension benefits or other financial resources. In fact, just when many women thought they could enter or reenter their careers, they are finding themselves involved in caring for their own or their husband's parents. As *Newsweek* (Beck, 1990) put it, they have moved from the mommy track to the daughter track.

Though some observers liken care of elderly family members to child care, others have pointed out critical distinctions (Brody, 1985; Schmich, 1991). For example, though young children live with their parents, aging parents often live far from their adult children, greatly complicating the provision of care. Second, the need to care for an elderly parent often occurs suddenly, after a heart attack, fall, or stroke, leaving no time for preparation. Third, formal care such as nursing home care is much more expensive than day care, averaging $55,000 a year, though it varies in different parts of the country (Hoffman, 2000). The developmental trajectory of the care provided to a child also differs from that provided to an ailing elder. Children become increasingly independent, so that the burden of primary care lightens over time. In the case of eldercare, the opposite is true: the care receiver progressively deteriorates, and the caregiver burden increases correspondingly. Emotional distinctions exist as well. Care of a failing parent forces one to anticipate the final separation from the elderly family member at the conclusion of the caregiving relationship. The caregiver experience may also prompt the caregiver to consider the possibility of eventual dependence on her own children (Brody, 1985). In addition, and especially for those caring for demented patients, grief and a sense of loss for the former person and relationship are typical (Gatz et al., 1990).

Caregiver Tasks

Gatz et al. (1990) list six types of help provided by caregivers:

- Emotional support and advice
- Instrumental help, such as cleaning, cooking, laundry, and so on
- Personal care—for example, bathing, dressing, toileting, assistance with walking, medications
- Managing finances
- Making decisions about care and arranging for formal service providers, such as nurses and other aides, to come into the home
- Direct financial assistance

The extent and duration of the care needed will, of course, vary tremendously across caregiving situations and will change over time, as the care recipient's condition changes.

Archbold (1983) distinguishes between **care providers,** who actually perform the care themselves, and **care managers,** who arrange for and coordinate services provided by others. Women tend to provide care, whereas men tend either to delegate caregiving responsibility to female family members or to purchase those services (Matthews & Rossner, 1988).

Many communities, religious and social organizations, social service agencies, and for-profit firms offer an increasing array of services to help those who need assistance as well as to relieve caregivers who live many miles from their ailing relatives. These include monitoring programs that regularly check in on older adults and programs that provide assistance with meals, transportation, home maintenance, and home health services.

Caregiver Stress

Caregiving is a stressful experience. Findings from a number of studies (see Schulz, Visintainer, & Williamson, 1990, for a review; also Bookwala, Yee, & Schulz, 2000) suggest that caregiver stress may have mental and physical health consequences for the caregiver. The rate of depression among caregivers is between 30 and 50 percent. In fact, family caregivers have been referred to as "hidden victims" (Crossman, London, & Barry, 1981; Zarit, Orr, & Zarit, 1985). Caregiver burnout can lead to institutionalization of the patient. Caregivers need support and respite. One doctor sometimes writes a prescription instructing the caregiver to take needed time away. Longitudinal data comparing caregivers with matched controls suggest that the higher rates of depression and anxiety disorders linked to the chronic stress experienced by caregivers persist for at least three years after the patient's death (Bodnar & Kiecolt-Glaser, 1994). In a study of 392 spouse caregivers and 427 noncaregivers aged 66 to 96 living with their spouses, spouse caregivers who reported strain were 63 percent more likely to die within four years than matched noncaregivers (Schulz & Beach, 1999). Their higher levels of depression and anxiety; lower perceived health; and reduced time to rest, recover from illness, or exercise are believed to contribute to the caregiver-mortality link. The authors emphasize the importance of focusing on the needs of *both* members of these older marital dyads. As Pearlin, Mullan, Semple, and Skaff (1990, p. 584) point out, "It is difficult to imagine many situations that equal—let alone surpass—the stressfulness of caregiving to relatives and friends with severe chronic impairments." The nature of this caregiving stress has become a prominent research topic (Pearlin et al., 1990). A complex web of interacting variables influences the degree of stress experienced by the caregiver. These include gender, age, race, education, socioeconomic status, work, family history, health, marital status, personality characteristics, and relationship with the care recipient (Brody, 1985; Dillehay & Sandys, 1990; Gallant & Connell, 2003; Haley et al., 1995; Hooker, Monahan, Shifren, & Hutchison, 1992; Majerovitz, 1995; Townsend & Franks, 1995; Yee & Schulz, 2000). Different caregivers respond differently to what might seem to be objectively similar caregiving circumstances, as a result of the operation of these multiple factors. Women have consistently been found to suffer greater burden and psychological distress than men (Bookwala & Schulz, 2000; Zarit, Todd, & Zarit, 1986). While the role of race/ethnicity is not well understood, there is some evidence that different groups experience the burden of caregiving in different ways. For example, Haley and colleagues (1995) found that Black family caregivers experienced more satisfaction and mastery and less depression in the caregiver role than White caregivers.

A number of stress and coping models have been offered to predict the consequences of caregiving for an individual caregiver. Though most emphasize the negative outcomes, positive outcomes such as increased competence, satisfaction, and closeness are also possible (Gatz et al., 1990). In general, those who feel their efforts to cope with the demands of the caregiver role are successful (coping efficacy) experience less distress (Gignac & Gottlieb, 1996).

Most Stressful Aspects of Caregiving

Investigators have attempted to determine which aspects of caregiving are the most burdensome. Whatever the specific aspects of the caregiving situation, Pearlin (1983) cites the transformation of a cherished relationship as itself a major source of stress. As the care receiver's condition deteriorates and need increases, caregiving may become the overriding component of the relationship. Problem behaviors (for example, incontinence, difficulty dressing, difficulty communicating) have a strong correlation with the degree of burden the caregiver experiences, as does the patient's emotional distress (Gatz et al., 1990). Degree of cognitive impairment has a greater impact on the caregiver's well-being than does functional impairment (Townsend & Franks, 1995). Those caring for individuals with dementia are in special need of support from their social network. Several investigators cite the emotional strain of dealing with increasing impairment in a person one is close to (Brody, 1985; Cantor, 1983). This emotional strain is related to restrictions on time and freedom, role overload, interference with lifestyle, and social isolation. Brody (1985) points out that despite extraordinary efforts to provide care for their ailing mothers, 60 percent of the sample studied felt guilty about somehow not doing enough.

Family Ripple Effects

Major life events produce effects that radiate throughout the family system, regardless of each individual's direct involvement in the event itself. The declining health of a family member and resulting need to provide care produce a host of such ripple effects. As Brody (1985) notes, we should remember that most adult children help their parents willingly and happily and derive satisfaction and personal growth from doing so. In addition, even though parents may be ailing, they continue to provide support and assistance to their adult children. But when parents begin to require more extensive help, the need to provide care affects not only the primary caregiver but the entire family system, altering its homeostasis and affecting relationships between family members (Brody, 1985; Gatz et al., 1990). Ripple effects include increased family tension, reduced time available to spend together, role overload, changes in lifestyle, and financial strain. Both primary caregivers and other family members report increased emotional distress. However, not all effects are negative. Some families report increased closeness and social support, along with increases in the amount of time spent together (Mellins, Blum, Boyd-Davis, & Gatz, 1993). Social support plays an important role in mediating the degree of stress experienced by the caregiver. The family provides much of this support. Family members can buffer as well as heighten the stress felt by the primary caregiver (Brody, 1989). Strengths as well as weaknesses in family relationships are highlighted, and unresolved issues may be resurrected by the caregiving role (Gatz et al., 1990).

Family–Workplace Stress Link

As we have seen, the nature of family caregiving is changing as the traditional mainstays of the family support system—wives and daughters—become employed outside the home in larger numbers. These "women in the middle" (Brody, 1981) are pulled by marital, parental, filial, and work responsibilities. Spillover between work and family roles can occur in both directions and be positive or negative, affecting caregivers' well-being (Stephens, Franks, & Atienza, 1997). Finley (1989) maintains that women's entrance into the labor force is unlikely to lead to parity with men in the caregiver role because gender differences in caregiving have become institutionalized. In other words, despite changes in gender roles, the traditional expectation that daughters will care for their parents is still widespread (Brody, 1985).

CRITICAL THINKING QUESTION

According to Bronfenbrenner's model (see Chapter 2), which level of the environment is illustrated by the interaction between work and family roles?

Given that the percentage of women in the labor force is projected to continue to increase, employers and employees alike will increasingly have to deal with linkages between family and work responsibilities (Fullerton & Toossi, 2001). Some women quit their jobs or reduce their work hours to care for an ailing spouse or parent (Stone, Cafferata, & Sangl, 1987). Others take time off without pay or rearrange their schedules so as to meet their varying obligations, giving up free time, socializing, and recreation rather than leave their jobs (Brody, 1985). Finch and Mason (1990) found evidence that, rather than make either-or choices between job and family, women are increasingly likely to seek out compromise solutions that allow them to meet family obligations without sacrificing career prospects.

Recognizing the pervasive need to provide care to elderly family members, some large corporations have begun to include eldercare in their employee benefit packages (Schmich, 1991). The U.S. Administration on Aging defines **corporate eldercare** as a service that a company provides to assist its employees with eldercare responsibilities. These companies recognize this as a way of recruiting and maintaining employees as well as reducing the work impact of eldercare on their workforce (through depression, time off from work, and so on). The benefits vary: some firms provide long-term care insurance for employees' parents or funds for respite care, while others offer flexible work schedules or extended unpaid leave, on-site eldercare facilities, counseling services, or educational workshops.

CRITICAL THINKING QUESTION

In what way(s) might the caregiver's job be a resource that could mediate caregiver stress?

What about the Care Recipient?

The care recipient's perspective has rarely been taken into account in the caregiving literature. Questions about what it is like to be a patient and to receive care are certainly relevant to our understanding of the caregiving relationship. (See Chapter 3 for a discussion of the effect of failing health on the sense of self.) The few studies that exist suggest that up to two-thirds of care recipients react negatively to help, experiencing depression and other signs of distress (Newsom, 1999). The sources and consequences of these negative reactions to being helped require further study.

To summarize, the evidence clearly indicates that families are the mainstay of the social support system of older family members. By all accounts, this informal support system seems to be working well, allowing impaired elderly to remain in their homes and avoid institutionalization. The elderly seem to be satisfied with their family relationships, feeling neither abandoned nor neglected by their children (Seelbach & Hansen, 1980). However, the increasing cost to these caregiving families in terms of emotional and physical energy, time, and money is extraordinary.

Concept Review 7.5

- The nature of care being provided to older adults today is more extensive and lasts longer than in the past.

- When an older person needs assistance, the most likely person to provide it is the spouse, followed by an adult daughter.

- Adult sons and daughters offer different types of assistance to their aging parents, consistent with their gender roles.

- The caregiver role is widely recognized as very stressful, though the nature and extent of the stress experienced by the caregiver is dependent on the interaction of a complex set of variables.

Family Violence

A Brief History of the Study of Domestic Violence

Though family relationships are the earliest and most enduring of our social relationships, they are not always positive. Indeed, for some, the family is the context for physical and emotional abuse, which has a profoundly destructive effect on development. **Domestic violence** is defined as a pattern of physical, sexual, and/or psychological maltreatment by one person in an intimate relationship to unfairly gain or maintain the misuse of power, control, and authority over another (American Psychological Association, 1996). Long considered a "domestic problem," a private matter, and therefore not the concern of the mental health or criminal justice systems, family violence is now viewed as a public concern, a serious social problem with the potential to significantly affect not only the victim but the entire family system and, ultimately, society as a whole. Violence signals a breakdown in one of the most basic purposes of family life—protection of its members. Assaulting or otherwise abusing a member of one's family should be no less a crime than doing the same to a stranger on the street. Yet, while our society disavows violence in general, it still subscribes to a belief system in which a man's home is his castle and what goes on there is no one else's business (Wodarski, 1987).

Interest in this subject can be traced to the 1960s and an influential article by Kempe and his colleagues (1962) on child abuse—the *battered child syndrome*. Since then, the focus has expanded to include wife abuse, husband abuse, parent abuse, sibling abuse, and elder abuse (first publicly recognized as a problem in the late 1980s). These various forms of family violence are not independent of one another; in fact, when one form of violence occurs in the family, other forms are more likely as well (Walker, 1999). Further, family violence is directly related to community violence.

As Straus (1990b) points out, the more violent parents are toward their children, the more violent these children are toward their siblings; the more violent husbands are toward their wives, the more violent the wives are toward their children. Perhaps surprisingly, "being a victim of violence is strongly related to engaging in violence oneself" (Straus, 1990b, p. 421). But we should emphasize that not all victims become abusers themselves, and some abusers grew up in nonviolent homes. The experience of violence is best thought of as a predisposing factor, influenced by interaction with other risk factors.

CRITICAL THINKING QUESTION
What might explain the tendency for abuse victims to become abusers themselves?

Family violence crosses racial, ethnic, class, and economic lines and exists at all stages of family life, though there is an as-yet-unexplained negative relationship between age and all forms of violence (Suitor, Pillemer, & Straus, 1990). However, it is not a gender-neutral problem. Estimates are that about 90 percent of abuse is committed by males (Stark & Flitcraft, 1988). Violence in families tends to flow along lines of power, making women and children the most likely victims (Killoran, 1984; Rennison & Welchans, 2000). The typical American woman is safer on the streets than in her own home, where the risk of assault is greatest (Straus & Gelles, 1990).

While an argument can be made that each form of family violence has distinguishing characteristics and its own set of contributing factors (U.S. Department of Health and Human Services, 1991), we will attempt here to provide an overview of the problem, touching on the central research issues and findings.

Incidence

Initial interest in the study of family violence sought to determine the extent of the problem. That question has not been clearly answered to date. In fact, strong disagreements continue to exist. First, empirical studies of domestic violence are hampered by inconsistent and evolving definitions of abuse (Emery, 1989; Straus, 1990a). For example, though distinctions used to be made between abuse and neglect (that is, between acts of commission and omission), current definitions now generally include neglect as a form of maltreatment. Debate also exists about whether violence should be defined in terms of actions or injuries (Stets & Straus, 1990). Further questions involve definitions of injurious acts—for instance, should only physical or also psychological attacks be included? Even more basically, what constitutes a physical act of violence? Estimates of child abuse vary from 1.5 million to 6.9 million acts annually, depending on whether hitting the child with an object is included in the list of abusive behaviors (Straus &

Gelles, 1990). Crime surveys are thought to underestimate domestic violence, because while most people think of being kicked by their spouse as wrong, they do not consider it a "crime" in the legal sense (Straus & Gelles, 1990). Thus, the National Family Violence Survey describes a rate 70 times greater than that based on the National Crime Survey, which is the only other national survey on the subject. A recent comment by one of my students illustrates the difficulty of agreeing on a definition of abusive behavior. She stated that the beatings she received from her father were not abuse, because she had done something wrong and deserved the punishment. Had her father beaten her for no reason, that, to her, would have been abuse. Some have argued that, for purposes of deciding which cases are in greatest need of intervention, we need to distinguish between *family maltreatment*, in which minimal physical or sexual harm occurs, and *family violence*, where there is serious and profound physical, psychological, or sexual trauma (Emery & Laumann-Billings, 1998).

Second, concerns have been raised about the accuracy of estimates derived from self-report data. Some forms of family violence (for example, husband abuse) may be especially unlikely to be reported. Others have criticized samples that typically exclude groups such as the very poor and homeless, among whom rates of violence would be expected to be high (Browne, 1993).

To summarize, the incidence of various forms of domestic violence is subject to debate, though a consensus exists that the prevalence is high and substantially underreported (U.S. Department of Health and Human Services, 1991). Emery (1989) predicts that debates regarding definitions are likely to continue and that, in fact, we will probably never reach a consensus on these definitions. He suggests that whether or not an act is "abusive" or "violent" is really a social judgment and is outside of the realm of social scientists, who are, however, bound to specify whatever operational definition they employ in their research.

With these cautions in mind, some often-cited statistics are listed below. Violence here refers to "physical assaults with the potential to cause physical harm, sexual aggression, forcible restraint, and threats to kill or harm" (Browne, 1993, p. 1077). These figures do not include all other forms of violence and neglect.

- A significant percentage—20 to 25 percent—of American families have experienced at least one episode of domestic violence (Sedlak, 1988; Stark & Flitcraft, 1988; Straus & Gelles, 1986).
- A minimum of 1.5 million women in the United States are physically abused or raped by male partners annually; a more accurate estimate may be as high as 4 million (Gazmarian et al., 2000; Straus & Gelles, 1990).
- Women are five times more likely to be victims of intimate partner violence than men; 33 percent of all women murdered are killed by an intimate partner (Rennison & Welchans, 2000).
- One-third of all American women will be physically assaulted (slapped, kicked, beaten, choked, or threatened or attacked with a weapon) at least once in the course of intimate relationships (Gazmarian et al., 2000).
- Abuse by a male partner is the "single major cause of injury for which women seek medical attention" (U.S. Department of Health and Human Services, 1991, p. 5).
- Spouse abuse is more common than automobile accidents, muggings, and cancer deaths combined (U.S. Senate Judiciary Committee, 1992).

- Rates of elder abuse vary widely, from 500,000 to over 5 million cases annually, depending on the definition and source of data used (e.g., crime reports, surveys) (Bonnie & Wallace, 2003; Chalk & King, 1998; National Center of Elder Abuse, www.elderabusecenter.org, 2004). Reports increase each year, and an estimated 16 percent of cases are referred for help, leaving 84 percent hidden.

The point here is that family violence is a real and prevalent condition of contemporary family life; its causes and consequences have important social implications. Though a thorough treatment of this issue is beyond the scope of this text, some of the most salient aspects of current research are summarized below.

Causal Factors

A central research concern is identifying the major causes of family violence. There seems to be universal agreement in the literature that the pattern of causation is extremely complex and that family violence cannot be explained by any one underlying cause or theoretical model (Emery, 1989; Emery & Laumann-Billings, 1998; U.S. Department of Health and Human Services, 1991). But family violence obviously has roots in a number of basic characteristics of the American family and American society (Straus, 1990a, b, and c). These include issues of male dominance, poverty, stress, and the experience of violence in childhood, as well as use of physical punishment by parents and social attitudes, such as public acceptance of violence and norms that devalue women (Cazenave & Straus, 1990; Emery, 1989; Geffner & Rosenbaum, 1990; Kantor & Straus, 1990; Murphy, 2003; Murphy & O'Farrell, 1996; Straus, 1990a, b, and c; U.S. Department of Health and Human Services, 1991; Walker, 1989).

Most research has focused on the abuser and attempts to develop a profile of characteristics that would aid not only in understanding but also in prediction and control. The early thinking was that abusers suffered from some sort of psychopathology. However, no "abusive personality" has been discovered, and the majority of abusers do not fit any particular model of pathology (Emery, 1989; Geffner & Rosenbaum, 1990). Instead, they are now believed to be responding to a constellation of influences ranging from individual developmental history to a host of situational and societal factors. A broad perspective is necessary: "The problem of violence against women cannot be fully understood, let alone solved, by focusing exclusively on individual psychology. Only by changing the social and cultural institutions that have given rise to the problem can a lasting solution be achieved" (Goodman, Koss, Fitzgerald, Russo, & Keita, 1993, p. 1055).

Some investigators have suggested that it may be useful to use Bronfenbrenner's ecological model as a way of conceptualizing and integrating the myriad variables implicated in the etiology of abusive behavior (Belsky, 1985a; Emery, 1989). (See Figure 2.1 for a review.) This model includes four levels: individual characteristics; the immediate social context (micro- and mesosystems); the broader exosystem; and the social and cultural context (macrosystem) (Emery & Laumann-Billings, 1998). The emphasis is on multiple risk factors and multiple pathways by which family violence may develop. Most models of abusive behavior are based on the underlying idea that aggression is a learned behavior, and that it is learned at home. As noted earlier, having experienced or witnessed family violence may predispose one to behave aggressively, but research has found that this is neither a sufficient nor a necessary cause.

CRITICAL THINKING QUESTION
Can you identify some macrosystem-level factors that may contribute to family violence?

Abuser and Victim Profiles

Attempts to develop a profile of the abuser as well as of the victim have been hampered by the many and interrelated variables involved in family violence. Tolman and Bennett (1990) warn of the pitfalls of these efforts, including the possibility of mistaking cause for effect (for example, low self-esteem) and of minimizing the real heterogeneity found among both victims and abusers. (See Holtzworth-Munroe & Stuart, 1994, for a description of three primary types of spouse batterers.) At the risk of overgeneralizing, profile sketches of the abuser and victim often include the following (for example, see Geffner & Rosenbaum, 1990; Overholser & Moll, 1990; Wodarski, 1987):

Abuser

- Male
- Traditional gender role
- Either experienced or witnessed abuse as a child
- Low self-esteem
- High need for dominance and control
- Dependence on victim to meet needs for dominance, and so on
- Great capacity for self-deception (denial)
- Attributes blame to external causes
- Socially isolated (lack of social support and social monitoring)
- Problem with alcohol
- History of head injury
- Under stress (poverty, unemployment)

Victim

- Female
- Traditional gender role
- History of experiencing or witnessing abuse
- Low self-esteem
- Passive, compliant
- Uses cognitive distortions to minimize the abuse
- Attributes blame to internal causes
- Socially isolated

CRITICAL THINKING QUESTION
What aspects of the traditional male and female gender roles would be relevant to the roles of abuser and victim?

Consequences of Family Violence

The consequences of being a victim of family violence vary depending on a number of factors, including the nature, frequency, and duration of the violent act; characteristics of the victim; the nature of the relationship between the abuser and victim; and the response of others to the abuse (Emery & Laumann-Billings, 1998). Victims of violence are obviously at risk for severe injury and death. They also suffer higher rates of stress-related illnesses, depression, and suicide attempts (Janoff-Bulman & Frieze, 1983; Murphy, 2003; Straus & Gelles, 1990). Studies of family violence have broadened to include the consequences of abuse not only for the immediate victim, but for the family system as a whole. For example, researchers have begun to study the children of battered women. They have also begun to look at the long-term consequences of experiencing violence in addition to examining the victim's current functioning. Interesting phenomena being pursued include the following:

- Nature and extent of the **intergenerational transmission of violence** (the idea that a cycle of violence is learned and passed down from one generation to another within the family)
- Discontinuities in the intergenerational transmission of violence—that is, protective factors correlated with the ability to overcome the experience of family violence
- Cognitive effects of victimization—for example, the effect on the sense of self, worldview, working models of relationships, and so forth
- Developmental effect on attachment and later relationships among children who have experienced abuse directly or whose mothers are abused
- Vulnerability to future abusive relationships
- Relevance of psychological concepts, such as learned helplessness and posttraumatic stress disorder, in explaining why women stay in abusive relationships
- Development of coping strategies by the victim that enhance survival but paradoxically undermine the ability to escape the abusive relationship (for example, denial, rationalization, repression) (Aber & Cicchetti, 1984; Cappell & Heiner, 1990; Emery, 1989; Follingstad, Neckerman, & Vormbrock, 1988; Sroufe & Fleeson, 1986; Walker, 1989; Widom, 1989; Wodarski, 1987)

Developmental Patterns in Adult Abusive Relationships

Expectations and behavior patterns established during dating and courtship are predictive of marital relationships. Studies suggest that violence during courtship may be widespread and may be a kind of training ground for later domestic violence (Roscoe & Benaske, 1985). One thing is certain—there is no recovery without intervention: "Violence between intimate partners always gets worse" (Walker, 1989, p. 697).

Walker (1979, 1984) has described a cycle of battering composed of three phases (Figure 7.8). The first stage is tension building, characterized by a number of minor incidents—pushing, shoving, verbal criticism—that gradually increase in severity. Eventually, the tension reaches a critical level and leads to an explosion—the second stage, involving the acute battering incident. This is usually the shortest of the three phases and results in the most harm to the victim. Because it leads to tension reduction for the abuser, abuse is reinforcing. The abuser rationalizes and minimizes the seriousness of the incident. Over time, this stage escalates; the battering becoming more frequent and more severe. During the third phase—loving contrition—the abuser expresses regret, is loving and attentive, and wants to redeem himself. This stage is reinforcing to the victim, often resulting in what has been called **traumatic bonding** or the Stockholm Syndrome, the development of an emotional attachment to the abuser (Dutton & Painter, 1981; Ochberg, 1980). The victim gains a false sense of hope that things will get better. As time passes, this stage gets shorter and may disappear altogether, replaced by a repetitive and escalating cycle of tension building and battering.

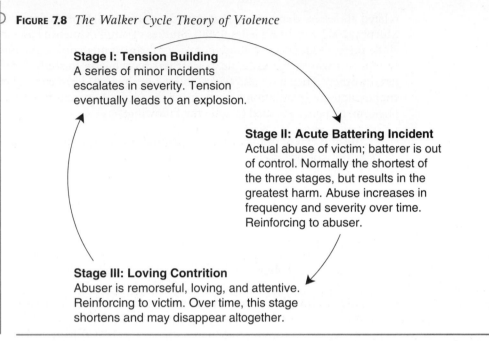

FIGURE 7.8 *The Walker Cycle Theory of Violence*

Stage I: Tension Building
A series of minor incidents escalates in severity. Tension eventually leads to an explosion.

Stage II: Acute Battering Incident
Actual abuse of victim; batterer is out of control. Normally the shortest of the three stages, but results in the greatest harm. Abuse increases in frequency and severity over time. Reinforcing to abuser.

Stage III: Loving Contrition
Abuser is remorseful, loving, and attentive. Reinforcing to victim. Over time, this stage shortens and may disappear altogether.

Source: Based on Walker, 1979.

Intervention

Research has also focused on the evaluation of various forms of prevention, intervention, and treatment. However, empirical studies of effectiveness have not kept pace with the development of new intervention strategies (Emery & Laumann-Billings, 1998). While increased efforts to assist the victims of abuse are necessary, there is also growing recognition of the need to help other family members and perpetrators as well (Emery, 1989).

Mutual frustrations occur as the legal and mental health systems attempt to confront the problem of family violence. Law enforcement is frustrated, for example, by the high rate of victim recantations. Victims call police, then later decide not to press charges. Mental health and social service workers are frustrated by law enforcement's limited ability to protect victims. But both systems must join in the effort to intervene and prevent future acts of abuse. For the cycle to be broken, the violence must stop, the abuser must accept responsibility for the abuse, the abuser and victim must be separated for a significant period of time to prevent the cycle from beginning again, and each must come to understand their role in the cycle.

The traditional police response to domestic assaults in the United States has consisted of police officers either providing some on-the-spot counseling or getting the abuser to leave the premises for a short while, neither of which is effective intervention. A field study by Sherman and Berk (1984) has been influential in demonstrating that the arrest of the offender is one of the most effective deterrents to future assaults, communicating to the offender that the behavior is a crime and will not be tolerated. Despite the fact that only 3 of the 136 arrested offenders in the study received fines or jail sentences, only 10 percent of them were arrested again for the same offense, as compared to 16 percent given counseling and 22 percent ordered off the premises. Similarly, a Bureau of Justice Statistics crime survey (Langer, 1986) found that only 15 percent of the women assaulted by husbands and boyfriends were assaulted again during the next six months if they reported the first offense to the police, compared with 41 percent who did not notify the police. While Lore and Schultz (1993) credit the Sherman and Berk study with the fact that over two-thirds of U.S. police departments now have a mandatory arrest policy in domestic violence cases, not all subsequent studies have replicated the reduced recidivism rates.

     Public education and early identification of families experiencing difficulty increase the likelihood that intervention will be successful. But, as Straus and Gelles (1990, p. 111) emphasize, "American society still has a long way to go before a typical citizen is as safe in his or her own home as on the streets or in a workplace."

Concept Review 7.6

- Rates of the incidence of domestic violence are not well established.

- Violence is the result of a complex pattern of factors interacting together.

- Family violence is believed to have far-reaching consequences for physical and psychological development and well-being.

- Intervention is necessary for the pattern of violence in family relationships to be broken.

REVIEW QUESTIONS

Family Development

1. Define the family development perspective.
2. How is family development viewed according to the family life cycle model?
3. Describe Duvall's eight-stage family life cycle.
4. Define and illustrate a family developmental task.
5. What are the limitations of the family development and family life cycle models?
6. Discuss some of the major demographic changes that have occurred in the American family in recent decades.

Marriage: Establishing a Family of One's Own

1. What are the methodological problems in the existing research on marriage?
2. Identify the demographic trends in American marriages, as indicated by data from the Census Bureau and the National Center on Health Statistics.

3. What are the components of romantic love and what is their developmental course, according to Ainsworth, Hatfield and Berscheid, and Sternberg?
4. Distinguish between a traditional and an egalitarian marriage. How are these roles related to marital satisfaction?
5. Identify some of the limitations in research on same-sex romantic relationships.
6. What are the benefits of marriage?
7. Identify the qualities of high-satisfaction marriages.
8. What effect do developmental events such as the empty nest and retirement have on marital quality?
9. Discuss the interaction of the three categories of variables in Karney and Bradbury's model of marital development?
10. Describe the pattern of marital satisfaction in long-term marriages.
11. Cite evidence indicating that men seem to benefit more from marriage than women do.

12. Give some possible explanations for the current trend in the divorce rate.
13. What is the relationship between income and likelihood of divorce? Ethnicity?
14. Discuss the factors that influence adjustment to divorce.
15. What are the economic consequences of divorce?
16. What additional complications distinguish subsequent from first marriages, and what conditions improve the likelihood of their success?
17. Why is more known about widows than widowers?
18. What are the two major challenges of widowhood?
19. According to Bankoff, what are the three stages of adjustment to widowhood?
20. How do males and females differ in their experience of widowhood?

Parenthood

1. Contrast the traditional versus the life-span view of parenthood and corresponding research.
2. How are parental roles changing?
3. What factors contribute to delayed parenthood? Is this considered a positive or negative trend?
4. What is the impact of parenthood on lifestyle and family life?
5. Why has so much research on parenthood focused on mothers and so little on fathers?
6. How does the birth of a child affect marital satisfaction?

Intergenerational Ties

1. What is meant by the phrase "separate but near"?
2. What is the significance of the "kinkeeper," and how is this role manifested in family life?
3. Discuss the nature and function of the relationship between parents and their adult children.
4. How clearly defined is the grandparent role?
5. What variables affect the relationship between grandparent and grandchild?

6. Describe the role of grandparents as "family watchdogs."
7. How does the divorce of adult children affect grandparents?
8. Describe the effect of the aging of the population on the experience of both grandparents and grandchildren.
9. Discuss the causes, prevalence, and consequences of surrogate parenting. What special problems are faced by grandparents who assume this role?

Adult Sibling Relationships

1. Why is interest in adult sibling relationships increasing?
2. How are sibling relationships unique?
3. Discuss the pattern of sibling relationships over the life span.
4. What are the functions of adult sibling relationships?

Family Caregiving

1. How and why has the nature of family caregiving changed in recent years?
2. What is the "caregiver career"?
3. Who is likely to be the caregiver?
4. What are the nature and origin of gender differences in caregiving?
5. What are considered the major sources of stress in the caregiver role?
6. What are the ramifications for the caregiver's family and work?
7. Discuss research limitations in family caregiving studies.

Family Violence

1. Why are estimates of domestic violence so difficult to establish?
2. Are abusers mentally ill?
3. What are considered to be the major causes of domestic violence?
4. Describe the general profile of the abuser and the victim.
5. What are some consequences of family violence?
6. Describe the three phases in Walker's cycle theory of battering. What happens to these phases over time?

Key Terms

8 Work and Retirement

MY GRANDFATHER WAS A TRAVELING SALESMAN. I emphasize *traveling.* His territory consisted of the United States east of the Mississippi and a good chunk of Canada. He covered his accounts by train, often being gone months at a time. With her husband gone so much, the responsibility of managing the household and its financial affairs fell almost totally on my grandmother. The Depression of the 1930s hit hard. To make ends meet, she moved her family into the downstairs of their home, renting out the upstairs bedrooms to boarders. She did piecework at home for a lingerie company, sewing rosettes onto ladies' undergarments for so much per thousand.

Finally, desperate to supplement the family's income, she got a job with an insurance company. This was an amazing feat for two reasons. First, few people hired women at that time—priority was given to men with families to support (the fact that women might be supporting families was rarely acknowledged). And second, her own husband had forbidden her to work, since it was considered unfeminine and a poor reflection on his status as breadwinner. But my grandmother was strong-willed and pragmatic, and she managed to keep the job and the household together for a long time before my grandfather found her out. (He came home unexpectedly and asked the kids where their mother was—they didn't come up with a convincing answer!) She eventually rose in the insurance business, becoming the first woman certified life underwriter in the city of Chicago. She worked until she was 85.

My mother, also a career woman, was tops in sales last fall—at age 75. And our daughter . . . well, at age 12 she doesn't know what she wants to be yet. Her generation of women faces an occupational future bright with expanded opportunities and at the same time overwhelming in the choices it presents. As my grandmother used to say, "There's a price for everything in life."

This chapter explores the place of work in adult life, the second of the major domains of adulthood identified in Freud's famous dictum, "Lieben und arbeiten"—to love and to work. We examine the impact of occupation on lifestyle, identity, and family relationships. We also review the tremendous changes in the nature of work and the labor force that have occurred in the past century, look at some projections for the future, and discuss their implications. We then turn to a discussion of the factors that influence the type of work we choose and review models of career development as well as research on gender differences. The chapter concludes with an examination of the social history of retirement, its recent emergence as a life stage, and its economic and developmental consequences for the individual and society as a whole.

Nature of Work

Significance of Work in Adult Life

Many of today's surnames—such as Cooper, Smith, Miller—reflect the occupations of our ancestors, a testimony to the importance of work throughout history. Our national origins in Puritan New England and our capitalist economy place heavy emphasis on productivity. As a result, both societies and individuals are described and evaluated—perhaps even defined—on the basis of what they "do" and how well they do it. Work is the central focus of some of the major theories of adult development (for example, Levinson, 1978; Vaillant, 1977). The choice of an occupation is one of the major developmental tasks of late adolescence and young adulthood—in fact, it is a choice that reverberates throughout our lives.

What are some of these reverberations? First, work is one of the main determinants of socioeconomic status and social class. Socioeconomic status is a composite measure that incorporates three interrelated but not completely overlapping variables: economic status, as measured by income; social status, as measured by education; and work status, as measured by occupation (Dutton & Levine, 1989). Occupation directly determines income and therefore influences things like lifestyle, type and location of residence, and perhaps geographic location. Where and how we live in turn affect how we spend leisure time, the kinds of schools our children attend, and so on. Because we spend so much time at work, our occupation also affects our social contacts and friendship formation. For most people, work is the primary determinant of status—or position in society—and is vital to the sense of self, contributing to both self-concept and self-esteem.

Our occupational role also defines society's expectations of us with respect to behavior, dress, and so forth. Figure 8.1 describes the explicit code of behavior for women teachers in the early 20th century. Today, few jobs entail such rigid prescriptions for behavior during and outside of working hours. Still, as Holland (1977, p. 5) put it: "Occupations represent a way of life, an environment rather than a set of isolated work functions or skills. To work as a carpenter means not only to use tools but also to have a certain status, community role, and a special pattern of living." In many ways, one is what one does, and choosing an occupation is equivalent to choosing a way of life.

Why Work?

Work means different things to different people, partly based on their own characteristics, but also based on the nature of the work itself. The question of what motivates

Figure 8.1 *Teacher Contract, 1923*

Though this particular contract is from Wisconsin, its basic elements were standard and used throughout the country.

This is an agreement between Miss _____, teacher, and the Board of Education of the _____ school, whereby Miss _____ agrees to teach for a period of eight months, beginning September 1, 1923. The Board of Education agrees to pay Miss _____ the sum of ($75) per month.

Miss _____ agrees:

1. Not to get married. This contract becomes null and void immediately if the teacher marries.
2. Not to keep company with men.
3. To be home between the hours of 8:00 p.m. and 6:00 a.m. unless in attendance at a school function.
4. Not to loiter downtown in ice cream stores.
5. Not to leave town at any time without the permission of the chairman of the Board of Trustees.
6. Not to smoke cigarettes. This contract becomes null and void immediately if the teacher is found smoking.
7. Not to drink beer, wine, or whiskey. This contract becomes null and void immediately if the teacher is found drinking beer, wine, or whiskey.
8. Not to ride in a carriage or automobile with any man except her brother or father.
9. Not to dress in bright colors.
10. Not to dye her hair.
11. To wear at least two petticoats.
12. Not to wear dresses more than two inches above the ankles.
13. To keep the schoolroom clean.
    a. To sweep the classroom floor at least once daily.
    b. To scrub the classroom floor at least once weekly with hot water and soap.
    c. To clean the blackboard at least once daily.
    d. To start the fire at 7:00 so the room will be warm at 8:00 a.m. when the children arrive.
14. Not to use face powder, mascara, or paint the lips.

people to work, then, is complex. Of course, most of us have to work for economic reasons, but is that the only motivator? In one study (Renwick & Lawler, 1978), male and female subjects were asked, "If you would continue to work even though you could live comfortably without doing so, what is the one most important reason?" The four most common responses were: "I enjoy what I do on my job" (29 percent of males, 28.6 percent of females), "I derive the major part of my identity from my job" (25.8 percent, 27.5 percent), followed by "Work keeps me from getting bored" (17.4 percent, 18.2 percent) and "My work is important and valuable to others" (13.9 percent, 10.8 percent).

The following list indicates some of the needs that work can fulfill. Individuals vary in the priority they place on these needs. Jobs vary in the extent to which they fulfill them.

- Material needs; financial security
- Self-esteem, self-respect
- Social acceptance
- Social status, respect from others
- Entree to the adult world

- Personal development and fulfillment (e.g., challenge, autonomy, satisfaction, enjoyment, meaning)
- Activity and structure in life, an antidote to boredom
- Social contact
- Generativity

CRITICAL THINKING QUESTION
Which of these factors is most important in regard to the place of work in your life?

The meaning of work apparently changes with age: older people place more value on the intangible aspects of a job, such as fulfillment, accomplishment, and friendship, and less emphasis on such aspects as finances (Birren, 1985). Men and women may differ in the values they assign to work as well, consistent with their expressive versus instrumental motivations (Gilligan, 1982). Aside from its role in the life of the individual, work also plays a major organizing role in society, structuring both time and activities (Sterns, Matheson, & Schwartz, 1990).

A Changing Work World: Work, Workers, Workplace

The world of work is changing dramatically, the combined result of economic and demographic trends along with technological innovations. Three major categories of change will influence the work experience of adults in the 21st century: changes in the labor market, changes in the workforce, and changes in the workplace itself.

Large-Scale Trends in the Labor Market

Major changes in the type of work that is and will be available are summarized briefly below.

- Decrease in goods-producing, manufacturing industries such as steel and textiles (the "postindustrial society")
- Decrease in agricultural occupations
- Decrease in low-skilled work
- Displacement of workers by technology
- Increase in service occupations
- Increase in high-tech occupations
- Increase in jobs requiring more education or training (Johnston, 1991; Johnston & Packer, 1987; U.S. Bureau of the Census, 1992e; U.S. Department of Labor, 2000, 2004a)

Job prospects will increase in fields like health, education, retail, trade, banking and insurance, government, management, sales, recreation/leisure, law, science, engineering, and computer-related occupations. These jobs will require workers to have much higher skill levels than in the past. In fact, for the first time in history, the majority of all *new* jobs will require some postsecondary education, though not necessarily a bachelor's degree. According to the U.S. Department of Labor (2004a), occupations requiring a college degree are growing twice as fast as others, and all but one of the 50 highest-paying occupations require at least a bachelor's degree. The Bureau of Labor Statistics (BLS) periodically projects the types of jobs that will be needed. Figure 8.2 summarizes the projections of occupations in the U.S. labor market to 2012. View the *Occupational Outlook*

FIGURE 8.2 *The Changing Occupational Structure, 1992–2012*

Major changes are occurring in the type of work that is and will be available in the United States.

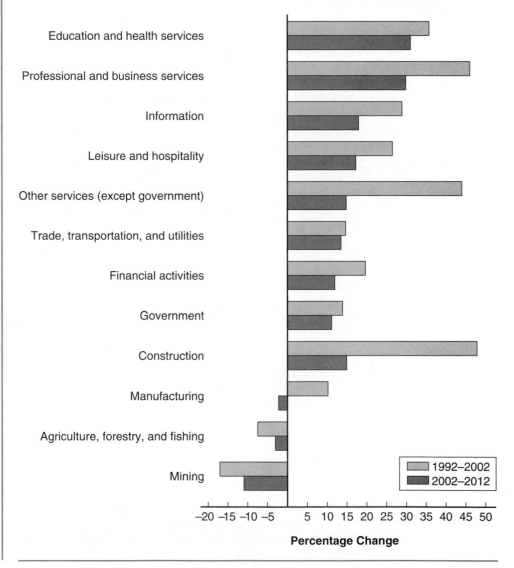

Percentage change in wage and salary employment in service-providing and goods-producing industry divisions, 1992–2002 and projected 2002–2012

Note: Education and health services is projected to grow faster (31.8 percent) and to add more jobs than any other industry sector (about 1 of every 4 new jobs).

Source: U.S. Department of Labor, Bureau of Labor Statistics, *Occupational Outlook Handbook,* 2004–2005.

Handbook of the U.S. Department of Labor for details about tomorrow's jobs at www.bls.gov/oco/home.htm.

Though the labor force will be expected to commit to more education and training, the investment in education generally pays off, as indicated in Figure 8.3.

Increasing Diversity in the Workforce

The workforce itself is changing in several significant ways: it is becoming older, more female, more ethnically diverse, and including more people with disabilities (thanks in part to assistive technology—e.g., large-screen monitors, voice recognition software) (U.S. Department of Labor, 2000, 2004–2005).

First, as the baby boom ages, the median age of the American worker, which was 38 in 1994, will rise to 40.6 by 2010 (Fullerton & Toossi, 2001). Those 55 and over are projected to increase from 14.3 percent of the labor force in 2002 to 19.1 percent in 2012. (Among countries in the European Union, it is estimated that by 2020, 40 percent of the workforce will be 45 to 65 years old.) At the same time, the impact of the baby bust will be felt: the pool of young workers between 16 and 24 will drop by about 8 percent. By 2012, this group is projected to comprise 15 percent of the labor force. See Figure 8.4.

Second, the workforce is becoming increasingly female. In 1960, about 36 of every 100 women participated in the labor force. By 1990, the figure was 57, increasing only slightly to 58 by 2000. The comparable figures for men were 80 of every 100 in 1960,

FIGURE 8.3 *Weekly Earnings, by Education*

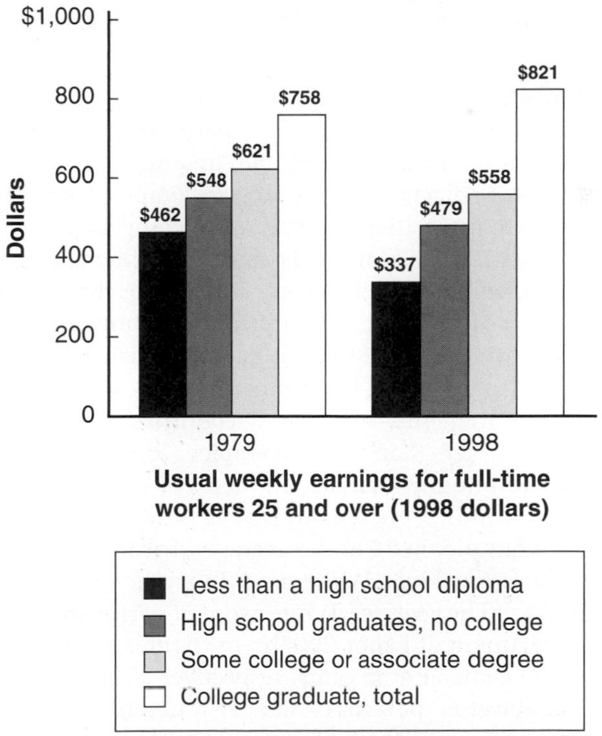
$1,000
800
600
400
200
0
Dollars
$462
$548
$621
$758
$337
$479
$558
$821
1979
1998
Usual weekly earnings for full-time workers 25 and over (1998 dollars)
Less than a high school diploma
High school graduates, no college
Some college or associate degree
College graduate, total

Source: U.S. Department of Labor, 2000.

FIGURE 8.4 *Percentage of Labor Force, by Age Group, 2002 and Projected 2012*

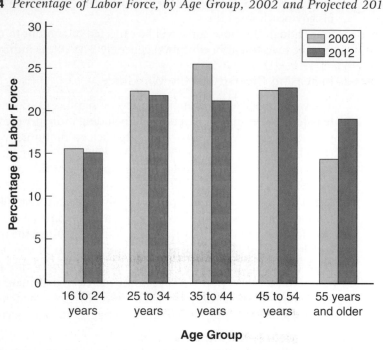

Source: U.S. Department of Labor, Bureau of Labor Statistics, *Occupational Outlook Handbook, 2004–2005.* Available online at http://bls.gov/oco/images/ocotjc03.gif.

down to 71 by 2000 (U.S. Bureau of the Census, August 2003). Women's share of the labor force will increase to 47.5 percent by 2012 (U.S. Department of Labor, 2004a).

Third, the racial and ethnic composition of the workforce is becoming increasingly diverse, a reflection of the changing composition of the U.S. population (see Figure 8.5). By 2010, minorities are expected to comprise 31 percent of the labor force (Fullerton & Toossi, 2001). Many will come from disadvantaged backgrounds. In addition, immigration will continue to contribute to the changing nature of the U.S. workforce. The number of Hispanics is projected to grow much faster than that of other groups (Bureau of Labor Statistics, 2004a). While industrialized countries such as the United States and Japan face looming labor shortages—the result of declining birth rates coupled with early retirements—developing countries such as Pakistan and Mexico are producing more workers than they can employ (Johnston, 1991).

Despite the increased numbers of women and minorities in the labor force, disparities in income remain sizable (a wage differential is referred to as a **wage gap**). For example, in 1940 the average African American man earned 40 cents for every dollar earned by a White man. Today, he earns 75 cents (U.S. Department of Labor, 2004a). The average White woman earns about 80 cents to a man's dollar (U.S. Department of Labor, 2004b); the figures for African American and Hispanic women are 65 cents and 55 cents, respectively. The Department of Labor (2000) concludes that about 60 percent of the pay differential is due to differences in skills, work experience, or the types of jobs held, leaving 40 percent to be attributed to discrimination. See Figure 8.6.

FIGURE 8.5 *The Changing Racial/Ethnic Structure of the U.S. Population*

By 2050, minorities are projected to rise from one in four Americans to almost one in every two.

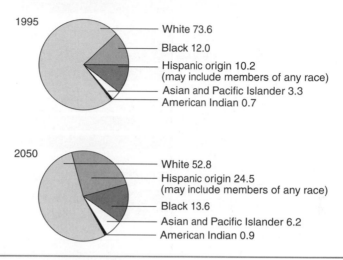

Percentage distribution of the population by race and Hispanic origin, 1995 and 2050

1995

White 73.6

Black 12.0

Hispanic origin 10.2
(may include members of any race)

Asian and Pacific Islander 3.3

American Indian 0.7

2050

White 52.8

Hispanic origin 24.5
(may include members of any race)

Black 13.6

Asian and Pacific Islander 6.2

American Indian 0.9

Source: U.S. Department of Labor, 2000.

Changes in the Workplace

In general, the kinds of jobs the U.S. economy is creating require much higher skill levels than in the past. Work is becoming increasingly cognitive and decreasingly physical. The U.S. Department of Labor has ranked all occupations on a scale of 1 to 6 (6 being the highest), based on the language, math, and reasoning skills required to perform them. The fastest-growing jobs have the highest skill ratings. In addition to these skills, globalization, new technologies, and the information revolution have also increased the demand for high-tech skills.

We hear a lot about the new high-tech jobs that are being created, yet technology is transforming not only the work we do, but also the way we do it. Most current jobs will continue to exist, though they will be performed differently, with job functions that utilize computers dramatically increasing. To illustrate, consider the change that has taken place in machine shops, from manually operated machine tools (e.g., lathes, drilling machines) to computer-programmed machine tools. Whereas manual operation required skills such as reading gauges and manual dexterity acquired through training and experience, computer-programmed tools require much less manual dexterity and much more computer literacy, perhaps including some programming familiarity (U.S. Department of Labor, 2000).

Level of education plays a critical role in occupational outcomes. Generally, the more education, the greater the likelihood of finding a job, earning a high income, and retiring with a pension. For example, in 1979 the average college graduate earned 38 percent more than the average high school graduate; today the figure is 71 percent. (See also Figure 8.3.) In 1970, fewer than 54 percent of all adults over 25 had completed high school and less

FIGURE 8.6 *Median Earnings, by Sex, Selected Occupational Groups, 2000*

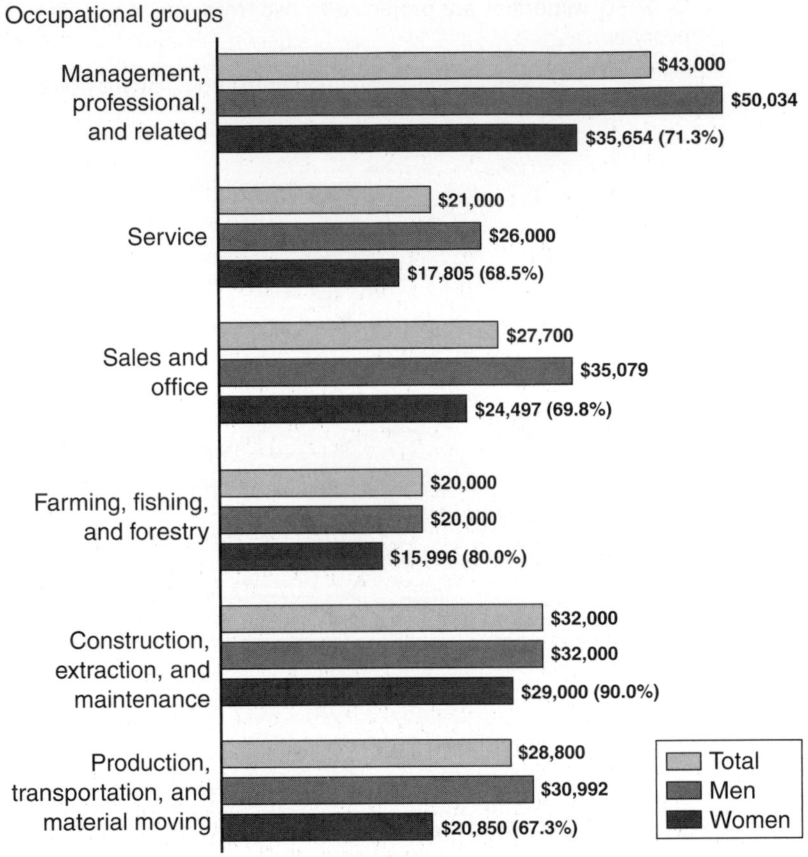

Occupational groups

Management, professional, and related
- $43,000
- $50,034
- $35,654 (71.3%)

Service
- $21,000
- $26,000
- $17,805 (68.5%)

Sales and office
- $27,700
- $35,079
- $24,497 (69.8%)

Farming, fishing, and forestry
- $20,000
- $20,000
- $15,996 (80.0%)

Construction, extraction, and maintenance
- $32,000
- $32,000
- $29,000 (90.0%)

Production, transportation, and material moving
- $28,800
- $30,992
- $20,850 (67.3%)

Legend: Total, Men, Women

Note: Percentage of men's earnings is shown in parentheses.
Source: U.S. Census Bureau, Census 2000, Sample Edited Detail File.

than 10 percent had finished college, compared with 83 percent and 24 percent today (U.S. Department of Labor, 2000). Though these figures are expected to continue to rise, they mask disparities across racial/ethnic lines. Of special concern are the far lower high school completion rates of Hispanics, whose proportion in the population is rising.

While high school and college completion rates are increasing, a significant number of job seekers lack the basic skills necessary to get and keep a job. Approximately 20 percent of the population reads at or below a fifth-grade level. In addition, the American Management Association surveyed midsized and larger businesses and found that the number of job applicants who lacked the math and reading skills necessary in the jobs for which they were applying jumped from 19 percent to almost 36 percent from 1996 to 1998 (U.S. Department of Labor, 2000). The AMA attributed the deficiencies not to a "dumbing down" of the workforce but to the higher level of skills required in the workplace. As the Department of Labor (2000) put it, the United States does not face a worker shortage, it faces a skills shortage. The fundamental challenge is to equip job seekers with the tools needed to succeed in the new economy.

The Labor Secretary's Commission on Achieving Necessary Skills (SCANS) issued a report in June 1991 titled *What Work Requires of Schools* (U.S. Department of Labor, 1991). Based on projections of future needs, this report defined five competencies as well as three categories of foundation skills that employees will need to be productive and successful (Table 8.1). Important competencies fall in the areas of use of resources, interpersonal skills, information, systems, and technology. The foundation skills are in basic areas such as reading and writing, thinking, and personal qualities. These are considered to be generic skills and competencies. The commission recognizes that specific jobs will differ in the degree to which these abilities are weighted, and that some additional job-specific skills will also be required.

Another way in which technology is transforming the workplace has to do with where and when work is done. The lines between work and home and work and leisure time are disappearing. In other words, the factory mind-set of the 1930s, with its five-day 40-hour work week in which a predominantly White male workforce arrived at and left the workplace at the same time, is breaking down. Technology (such as e-mail, voice mail, pagers, laptop computers, and mobile phones) allows workers to take their offices and work everywhere. Fifteen percent of workers report working at home during the week, either to finish or catch up on work or because it is the nature of the job (U.S. Department of Labor, 2002). Most of these workers are in managerial, professional, and sales occupations. Positive consequences include the flexibility to "go to work" without leaving home (home offices are becoming more commonplace) and to work nontraditional hours (wonderful for those with disabilities, family obligations, or remote residences). The downside is that work is becoming pervasive: one is always available, and the office never closes, leaving less time set aside for family or leisure.

One final change in the way work is structured deserves mention. The traditional work arrangement in which a full-time, year-round employee is given benefits, training, and/or a pension upon retirement is giving way to "just-in-time" employees—workers whom a business hires just when it needs them and for a delimited period of time. These

TABLE 8.1 *Worker Competencies and Skills*

FIVE ESSENTIAL COMPETENCIES
1. **Use of resources:** Allocating time, money, materials, space, and staff.
2. **Interpersonal skills:** Working on teams, teaching others, serving customers, leading, negotiating, and working well with people from culturally diverse backgrounds.
3. **Information:** Acquiring and evaluating data, organizing and maintaining files, interpreting and communicating, and using computers to process information.
4. **Systems:** Understanding social, organizational, and technological systems, monitoring and correcting performance, and designing or improving systems.
5. **Technology:** Selecting equipment and tools, applying technology to specific tasks, and maintaining and troubleshooting technologies.

THREE FOUNDATION SKILLS
1. **Basic skills:** Reading, writing, arithmetic and mathematics, speaking, and listening.
2. **Thinking skills:** Thinking creatively, making decisions, solving problems, seeing things in the mind's eye, knowing how to learn, and reasoning.
3. **Personal qualities:** Individual responsibility, self-esteem, sociability, self-management, integrity, and honesty.

Source: U.S. Department of Labor, 1991.

alternative work arrangements typify about 10 percent of workers (U.S. Department of Labor, 2001). Most are independent contractors; a growing number are agency temporary employees.

Implications of These Changes

The trends just described have societal implications in at least four major areas: education and training, the integration of women and minorities into the workforce, maintenance of productivity in an aging workforce, and balancing family and work issues.

Education and Training. Educational standards in the nation's schools need to be raised dramatically to produce the highly skilled workforce required in the future. In addition, we must continually reinvest in the workforce through ongoing education and training, so that it remains abreast of technological innovations and is adaptable in the face of job obsolescence. Lifelong learning will be the key to a competitive, productive workforce.

Education and training will be especially crucial for the growing number of minority workers, many of whom come from disadvantaged backgrounds and may be deficient in basic skills. The gap between the skill levels of those entering the workforce and the increasing skill levels expected of the workforce is a national problem.

Integration of Women and Minorities into the Workforce. Equal occupational opportunities must be available to women and minorities, on whom the economy will increasingly depend. This will require that existing disparities in income and advancement opportunities be addressed and eliminated and that pensions and other benefits be assigned equitably. The workforce itself will need to adjust to increasing cultural, racial, and gender diversity.

Maintenance of Productivity in an Aging Workforce. While an older workforce is more stable, experienced, and reliable, we must ensure that it also remains current, flexible, and adaptable. Here again, ongoing training will be key. In addition, until the large baby boom cohort begins to retire, those younger boomers and members of the baby bust are likely to experience slower career advancement. Some "cross-training" in related areas may keep them interested until opportunities to move up the career ladder emerge. The retirement of the baby boom members will present tremendous opportunities for talented and experienced workers to succeed, though the increase in retirement age may slow this process.

Balancing Family and Work Issues. Women's growing presence in the workforce means that the competing demands of work and family responsibilities must be addressed. To accommodate two-earner families, working mothers, and single parents, issues such as time away from work, flexible hours, part-time work, job sharing, stay-at-home work, day care, eldercare, and family leave will receive increased attention. In addition, support services for working families—including house cleaning, convenience products, and mail-order shopping—are likely to expand.

The world of work is changing in ways that significantly affect the work experience. These changes have important implications for occupational choice and preparation as well. We turn now from a societal view of the workplace and workforce to a more individual perspective on career development.

Concept Review 8.1

- The choice of an occupation is in many ways equivalent to choosing a way of life.

- Work means different things to different people and may fulfill a variety of needs.

- The world of work is undergoing dramatic change in three major areas: the labor market, the workforce, and the structure and skill requirements of the workplace.

Career Development

As we use the term today, **career** implies an occupation in which a person moves upward through a series of positions (a *career ladder*), each of which requires greater mastery and responsibility and offers increased financial return.

Career Cycle

Traditional views of career development attempted to identify a typical pattern of career progression. Research and theory focused primarily on men, and the career cycle that emerged essentially described a continuous process containing the following elements:

- A period of career exploration in adolescence, during which the individual experiments with a series of temporary jobs, learns appropriate work habits, attitudes, and behaviors (the "work ethic"), and begins to generate and consider career preferences and plans
- A crystallization of career direction during the college years, leading to the formulation of a Dream, commitment, and preparation
- Career entry, usually during the early 20s, when the individual achieves the first position in his chosen field and begins to learn the ropes
- A novice period, during which the individual begins to pay his or her dues, gain competence, and move up the career ladder
- At midlife, a period of assessment, both in terms of degree of progress in the career ("on time," "behind time"), the value of success or accommodation to failure, and reevaluation of the appropriateness of the career choice
- Career stability in middle age, in which gains are consolidated and maintained—a plateau of maximal achievement
- In the 50s, the beginnings of psychological separation, preparation for retirement, and increased interest in leisure and other activities outside of work
- And retirement, usually around the age of 65 (Erikson, 1968; Levinson, 1978; Super, 1957)

Challenges to the Traditional View: Increasing Diversity of Career Paths

This broad overview has been challenged on several fronts. The same general caution applies to these models as to all stage theories (see Chapter 2): they do not adequately describe the variety of patterns found among individuals as they progress through their working lives. A life-span approach acknowledges the potential for change at any point in the life cycle and recognizes the increasingly divergent career paths and timetables that typify contemporary adulthood (Sterns, Matheson, & Schwartz, 1990).

Perhaps more than anyone else, Donald Super (1957, 1985) prompted vocational psychologists to move beyond the subject of occupational choice to the study of how individuals develop careers and the relationship between career development and self-concept. His life-stage model of career development, which remains one of the most influential, describes four stages: exploration/implementation, establishment, mainte-nance, and deceleration. In the more recent formulations, Super (1984) has suggested that the order of the stages is not fixed and that individuals may progress through the sequence more than once, recycling through the stages at transition points. This dispels the myth that there is only one "right" career and that people stay in it all their lives. For reasons that originate in the individual as well as in the labor market, career stability no longer typifies the experience of established workers.

There is growing recognition that the work patterns and experiences of women and minorities (many of whom come from disadvantaged backgrounds) differ in signifi-cant ways from those of White men. For example, Gibson and Burns (1991) describe differences in preparation and training, occupational levels, opportunities for ad-vancement, availability of pensions, and so forth. Therefore, existing models are prob-ably better predictors of the careers of White males than of minorities and women.

Finally, we must remember that career development occurs in a socioeconomic context; thus, both occupational choice and the career cycle are influenced by condi-tions present in the macrosystem. And different cohorts, at different points in their ca-reer path at the time these events occur, are affected differently by them. For example, the corporate downsizing of the late 1980s and early 1990s effectively ended the careers of many white-collar executives who were nearing retirement age. For others not as far along in their careers, the effect may have been to invalidate long-standing assumptions about the value of company loyalty. Hiring freezes and the outsourcing of jobs have been common features of the early 21st-century labor market. What does this climate of uncertainty mean for career development? It may mean that employees feel greater pressure to work longer hours (the United States now leads even Japan in hours worked; Moen, 2003), to keep their résumés up to date, to be aware of other opportunities, and to be flexible and portable—able to change jobs more easily. As Moen (1998b) puts it, individuals need to "manage" their own careers and build career resilience.

Those younger employees who witnessed the fate of their older colleagues may have formed a different set of work-related attitudes, behaviors, and expectations. Today's new generation of workers (often referred to in the media as Generation X) brings ded-ication, independence, tolerance of diversity, and technological savvy to the workplace (Cohen, 2002). They value a sense of belonging and meaningfulness in work, involve-ment in decision making, and opportunities for professional development on the job and are perhaps less motivated by financial incentives than the baby boomers. Not wanting to be led down the same garden path as their predecessors, those in the post–baby boom generation—many of whom found it difficult to find work after grad-uation from college—may abandon the notion of a secure corporate career in favor of a more entrepreneurial approach. This trend may mesh well with the increase in free-lance work as companies contract out projects they would have given to full-time em-ployees in the past. These employees may gain freedom and flexibility as they sacrifice job security and benefits, and those who are able to market themselves and be adaptable will have a greater chance of success.

Those just entering their careers in the early years of the 21st century appear to face a different set of economic circumstances. The century began with a strong economy. Confidence and optimism were high, unemployment was down, corporate profits were up, and job prospects for college graduates were the best they had been in years. That changed rapidly. According to the U.S. Department of Labor (2004a), 2003 was the most difficult year for job seekers in 20 years. As the baby boom generation begins to retire, the competition for experienced employees among the smaller baby bust generation will heat up. Employers will likely take greater interest not only in recruiting new workers, but also in retaining them and upgrading the skills of existing employees. The nature of career development in this new environment remains to be seen.

What is clear is that the ground is shifting. Family considerations (e.g., child care, eldercare, the demands of a spouse's career) are no longer of concern only to women but increasingly intrude on the career paths of men as well (Moen, 1998a; U.S. Department of Labor, 2000). Moen (1998a, pp. 41, 44) sums up our discussion of the changes in the world of work and resulting structural lags in reference to career development:

> We are witnessing the restructuring of work as a consequence of the development of a more global economy, technological change, the shift to a service economy, and concerns over productivity and competitiveness. The rise in the contingent workforce, along with "downsizing" and the restructuring of job ladders, means that, for many workers, the traditional organizational career is rapidly becoming obsolete. The career paths of earlier generations are increasingly irrelevant as templates for contemporary workers. . . . Given the changes in the macroeconomy, work, longevity, retirement, families, gender roles, and the labor force, current assumptions and practices seem increasingly outmoded and inappropriate.

Why Do We Choose the Work We Do?

While we normally think of adolescence and early adulthood as the life stages during which occupational choices are first made, occupational development is best thought of as a lifelong developmental process. In fact, some observers have estimated that most individuals can expect to change careers at least twice during their working lives. So, while the initial occupational choice may not be a once-and-forever thing, it may set a direction and preclude other vocational options. Many variables interact to predispose people toward one type of work or another. Some of these are characteristics of the individual, while others are characteristic of the individual's environmental context. A number of the most important factors are described below.

Knowledge of Options

Occupational choice is complicated by the fact that there are estimated to be between 20,000 and 25,000 potential occupations, and most of us are unaware of many of them. However, it is not enough to know that an occupation exists. We also need to know the nature of the occupation, too. Careers may be considered or discounted based on stereotyped, inaccurate, or incomplete knowledge. Do you know what an intelligence analyst does? A food designer? A neonatologist? When we consider our future occupations, then, our knowledge limits our choices.

Market Conditions

As discussed above, career choice is influenced by economic and demographic forces that affect the availability of positions in fields of interest. In general, service occupations (including education, health services, business and professional services, and so on) are increasing, while manufacturing and agriculture-related jobs are decreasing (see Figure 8.2).

Family Attitudes, Traditions, and Expectations

As the major agents of socialization, families can directly and indirectly influence career choice by providing role models as well as exposure to experiences and options; by teaching value systems; through offering support and encouragement; by emphasizing family traditions, expectations, and pressures; and so on. For example, Adelman (1991) found that members of the high school class of 1972 perceived their parents to have lower educational aspirations for their daughters than their sons. These perceptions may partly explain the fact that as high school seniors, women in the sample had lower educational aspirations and career plans than men (though their eventual attainments exceeded their earlier goals).

Proximity Factors

There is no denying that being in the right place at the right time, or getting a tip or a reference from someone you know, can be influential. Even geography can determine occupational choice. Consider the lobster fishermen of Maine, or the coal miners of West Virginia.

Social Class

Socioeconomic status has an effect on occupational choice in a number of ways—for example, through determining available financial and social resources, educational opportunities, value systems, attitudes toward the self, and so on. In general, individuals of lower socioeconomic status tend toward jobs (in which upward mobility is limited

Family traditions and expectations influence career choice, as seen in this photo of the Panelli Brothers Italian Deli.

and movement is primarily horizontal), while those from higher socioeconomic backgrounds tend toward careers.

Gender Role

Both the individual's and society's views of appropriate male and female occupations may influence educational and career aspirations.

The Self

Holland's Personal Orientations. Some contemporary theories stress that occupational choice may reflect various aspects of the self. For example, Holland (1973, 1985, 1996) has developed an influential theory based on the idea that individuals attempt to choose work that matches their personality: "People search for environments that will let them exercise their skills and abilities, express their attitudes and values, and take on agreeable problems and roles" (1985, p. 4). The idea that people with certain personality traits may flourish in some occupations and wither in others is not new. However, Holland has contributed a typology that describes six personal orientations and their relationship to occupational choice (Table 8.2). Conducting a symphony orchestra might allow an individual to express both artistic and social aspects of the self. Owning and operating a family farm, on the other hand, would draw on realistic and conventional orientations.

Consistent gender differences have been found in both the personal orientations and associated occupations, with women generally overrepresented in the artistic, social, and conventional categories. Though personal orientation is only one of a number of factors affecting occupational choice, Holland suggests that this typology may be useful in understanding individuals' career pathways, work histories, vocational satisfaction, and levels of aspiration and achievement.

A good person-job fit leads to greater job satisfaction, career stability, and higher performance. Those with a clear sense of identity have a better understanding of their skills, interests, beliefs, and values. Thus, they are more likely to find work that is compatible and congruent with their personal characteristics. On the other hand, those with a diffuse sense of identity are more likely to make incompatible choices and to be dissatisfied with their work, leading to lowered performance and more frequent job changes.

Holland has continued to actively revise the typology in order to increase its ability to predict and explain career development. One area of recent research has been to link the six personal orientations to McCrae and Costa's five-factor personality trait theory (see Chapter 2). Holland (1996) has also speculated about how changes in the labor market and the skills and competencies that will be in high demand will affect some occupational groups more than others. Particularly hard hit will be realistic and conventional workers, who are in a shrinking labor market and whose preference for highly structured, predictable settings and traditional thinking and rule following will be less functional in a more chaotic occupational world requiring greater flexibility and adaptability.

CRITICAL THINKING QUESTION
Can you identify your personal orientation and two careers that would be compatible with it?

TABLE 8.2 *Holland's Personal Orientations and Their Relationship to Occupational Choice*

Realistic: Prefers activities that involve explicit, ordered, or systematic manipulation of objects, tools, machines, or animals. Has manual, mechanical, agricultural, electrical, and technical competencies. Perceives self as practical, conservative, having mechanical and athletic abilities, and lacking social skills. Values the concrete and tangible—for example, material rewards for accomplishments. Avoids interaction with people. Sample occupations include carpenter, truck operator.

Investigative: Prefers activities that involve the observational, symbolic, systematic, and creative investigation of physical, biological, and cultural phenomena. Has scientific and mathematical competencies. Sees self as scholarly, intellectual, skeptical, analytic, and lacking leadership skills. Values science—the development or acquisition of knowledge. Avoids persuasion or sales roles. Sample occupations include psychologist, microbiologist.

Artistic: Prefers ambiguous, free, unsystematic activities that involve the creation of art forms or products. Has artistic competencies in language, art, music, drama, or writing and lacks clerical or business system skills. Perceives self as original, expressive, nonconforming, introspective, and independent. Values creative expression. Avoids routines and conformity. Sample occupations include musician, designer.

Social: Prefers activities that involve helping, training, developing, treating, or enlightening others. Has human relations skills and is deficient in manual and technical skills. Perceives self as empathic, patient, helping and understanding others, having teaching ability, and lacking mechanical and scientific skills. Values ethical and social activities and social service. Avoids mechanical and technical activities. Sample occupations include teacher, clergy member.

Enterprising: Prefers activities that involve persuading, manipulating, or directing others. Has leadership, interpersonal, and persuasive skills and is deficient in scientific competencies. Sees self as popular, sociable, confident, and aggressive, with leadership and speaking skills, but lacking scientific ability. Values material achievement and social status. Avoids scientific or intellectual topics. Sample occupations include management, sales.

Conventional: Enjoys activities that involve establishing or maintaining order, routine, and standards, such as keeping records, organizing data, and operating business and data processing machines in a prescribed way. Has acquired clerical, computational, and business system skills and is deficient in artistic abilities. Sees self as conforming, orderly, and having clerical and numerical ability. Values economic and business achievement, power. Avoids ambiguous or unstructured activities. Sample occupations include bookkeeper, production editor.

Source: Based on Holland, 1985, 1996.

Career Self-Efficacy. Others stress individual **career self-efficacy,** the belief in one's ability to choose, prepare for, and be successful in a given occupation, as a determinant of occupational choice (Betz & Hackett, 1986; Lent & Hackett, 1987). (Bandura's concept of self-efficacy and its associated personal characteristics are reviewed in Chapter 3.) Consistent with Bandura's (1977a, 1991) conceptualization, those high in career self-efficacy envision a broader range of career options than those low in self-efficacy. Variations in self-efficacy may offer a partial explanation of the different patterns of occupational aspiration and choice observed among those from lower versus higher socioeconomic status and among women versus men.

Specifically, Hackett and Betz (1981) speculated that gender differences in self-efficacy may be a causal factor in the underutilization of women's career talents and their underrepresentation in many male-dominated, high-status, high-paying fields. In a study of college students, Betz and Hackett (1981) found that beliefs about one's abilities in a particular occupational area were a significant predictor of the occupations considered, while actual measured ability was not. Women's self-efficacy expectations were lower than men's in nontraditional occupations (such as engineering), but higher in traditional fields (such as nursing). The same pattern is likely among men. The investigators suggest that gender-role socialization results in the observed gender differences in self-efficacy, and influences the career choice and career-related behavior, such as academic preparation and choice of a college major, of young women and men.

CRITICAL THINKING QUESTION

Specifically, how might women's socialization into the expressive role and men's socialization into the instrumental role direct their courses of study, college major, and occupational choice?

To summarize, there is growing support for the application of self-efficacy theory to career choice and other aspects of the career development process. See Lent and Hackett (1987) for a review of the literature, a discussion of its limitations, suggestions for future research, and some interesting theoretical speculations.

We should also note that the relationship between personality and occupation is reciprocal—that is, not only does personality affect career choice, but the cumulative influence of work and the work environment may influence personal characteristics over time. For example, there is evidence that complex jobs that are cognitively challenging lead to increased mental flexibility, while repetitive, sedentary jobs may lead to mental rigidity (Avolio & Waldman, 1990; Kohn & Schooler, 1983; Schooler, 1990).

How Effectively Do We Choose?

Jarvis (1990) points out that career development may not be receiving the attention it deserves among young people, resulting in career indecisiveness and misdirection and tremendous human and financial cost to both employees and their employers. As evidence, he cites many statistics, a few of which are listed below.

- Sixty-two percent of all workers now in the labor force had no career plan when they started their first job.
- The majority of current college students do not have clearly defined career goals, as evidenced by widespread "major hopping."
- Most university graduates will not be working in jobs directly related to their majors five years after graduation.
- The median duration of first-job holding among young adults is less than one year.
- Young adults tend to stabilize in an occupation in their mid to late 20s, primarily because of financial or family obligations rather than because they have found an occupation they really like.
- Sixty-four percent of workers in one survey stated that if they could start over, they would choose another career. Over 50 percent said that they ended up in their jobs either through the advice of others or by chance.
- The majority of workers feel they could have been more satisfied and productive if they had known how to make better career decisions.

Macrosystem conditions discussed earlier may exacerbate this situation. It should be clear that the more people know about themselves and the labor market, the more likely they will be to make informed choices. A good fit (congruence) between the individual and the job is correlated with job satisfaction, stability, and achievement (Spokane, 1985). Of course, for one reason or another, many of us are not able to enter our first-choice career. It is perhaps comforting to note that everyone has the potential for success in a number of occupations, and that the first occupational choice is not necessarily the last.

Age and Job Satisfaction

Overall job satisfaction is significantly, though modestly, correlated with age (Warr, 1992). Older workers tend to have more positive feelings about their jobs than younger workers do. This may be due to job-related competence, seniority, and more opportunities to shape the job to fit personal needs and preferences.

Job absenteeism may be considered an indicator of job satisfaction. That is, absence from work may reflect a form of psychological withdrawal from an unsatisfying work situation. In a meta-analytic study of the research literature on age and both voluntary and involuntary (health-related) absenteeism, Martocchio (1989) found an inverse relationship between the age of the employee and the amount of time that employee was absent from work. Older workers were absent less often and for shorter periods of time than younger workers. Although the meta-analysis did not provide explanations for these findings, the results may suggest that older workers, in comparison to younger employees, have developed a better fit with their career niche and have a greater degree of job commitment and responsibility. The results of this study present a positive view of the reliability of older workers as a group, dispelling the myth that time lost from work increases with age.

Some aspects of occupational well-being seem to hit their lowest levels among middle-aged workers. One possible explanation of low satisfaction at midlife has to do with the worker's subjective sense of being on or off time in terms of progression up the career ladder (Lawrence, 1984). In other words, regardless of the individual's *actual* career position, a feeling of failed expectations could lead to reduced job satisfaction. And even those who are objectively and subjectively "successful" may not be spared. High achievers may experience success or encore anxiety, fearful that they may be unable to maintain the success they have achieved. Others have suggested that midlife issues of reassessment (see Chapter 3), and life cycle experiences such as children leaving home or the death of parents, may affect job motivation, performance, and satisfaction (Morgan, Patton, & Baker, 1985; O'Connor & Wolfe, 1987). In such cases, becoming a mentor or finding other new opportunities for growth may be helpful.

Growing Up and the Dream

Novice Phase

In his study of adult development in men, Levinson (1978) emphasizes work as the central feature of a man's adult identity, the primary basis of his life in society (see Chapter 2 for an overview of his theory). He describes a period called the **novice phase,** lasting from about age 17 to 33, during which the individual enters the adult world. Four developmental tasks are of primary importance during this time: the formation and cultivation of a Dream; the formation of an occupation; the formation of a mentor relationship; and the formation of intimate relationships, including marriage and family. Because of the central role of work, successful accomplishment of each of these tasks serves in one way or another to advance the individual's career.

The first of these tasks, the formation of the **Dream,** refers to developing a vision of the kind of life one wants to lead as an adult. Though not everyone has a Dream in this sense, Levinson considers it to be a distinct developmental advantage. The Dream facilitates separation from the family of origin and gives purpose, meaning, and direction to the early years of adult life, propelling the individual forward, guiding choices and commitments.

The second task of the novice phase is the formation of an occupation, a process that takes place over a long period and is not equivalent to merely choosing an occupational goal. Instead, it extends beyond the initial serious commitment to include career entry and movement up the career ladder.

One of the most interesting aspects of the novice phase as described by Levinson is the formation of an important relationship with a mentor. The **mentor** is an individual—usually a bit older and more senior in terms of career experience and status—who serves the multiple functions of friend, parent, spiritual guide, cheerleader, teacher, sponsor, and role model. The primary function of the mentor is to support the Dream and facilitate its realization. Finding an effective mentor is a distinct asset in the pursuit of career goals.

The final task involves the formation of intimate relationships. One of these is a relationship with a **special woman,** an important transitional figure who shares the young man's Dream, and through her faith in him, reinforces his belief and confidence in his career goals, and encourages him to move forward. Levinson maintains that his stage theory applies to individuals of all socioeconomic classes and in all occupations.

Levinsonian Studies of Women

Because Levinson's theory was originally based on a sample of men, some studies have attempted to determine whether women progress through the same developmental periods at roughly the same ages and in the same ways. In their review of four such Levinsonian studies of adult development in women, Roberts and Newton (1987) summarize findings on some key distinctions in the career development process.

First, women's Dreams differ from men's in many respects. Consistent with the views of Miller (1986) and Gilligan (1982), women's Dreams are more relational than individualistic, with occupation a central component in only a small percentage of those studied. Even among this group who placed career above relationships, concern with marriage and family became more central around age 30. Women's Dreams are typically more complex and diffuse, described as "split dreams" combining marriage, motherhood, and career. Their lesser clarity makes them correspondingly less motivating; family and career goals are often seen as mutually exclusive. As a result, women often sacrifice their own goals to those of their husbands. In general, women in these studies experienced lots of inner conflict and dissatisfaction, regardless of the choices made in terms of family and career commitments. Compared to the direction provided by a man's Dream, a woman's career direction may be more accurately characterized as "drift" (Williams, 1987, p. 370).

Gender differences were also found in regard to the other tasks of the novice period. Fewer women form mentor relationships, which poses a significant disadvantage in pursuing their goals and possibly denies them the opportunity to reach the highest levels of occupational achievement. In addition, the process of forming an occupation extends well into middle age. Compared to men their age, women may have a 10- to 20-year disadvantage. Finally, unlike men, whose intimate relationships often facilitate pursuit of the Dream, women are unlikely to find a "special man." In fact, husbands, who might be thought to fulfill that role, were described as the major obstacle to fulfillment of the individualistic aspects of women's Dreams.

These Levinsonian studies suggest that women's career development and occupational experience differ from those of men in a number of significant ways. These gender differences are explored more fully in the next section.

Concept Review 8.2

- Super and others studied the careers of large numbers of men and formulated a description of the typical career cycle.

- Career paths are becoming increasingly diverse, thus challenging the traditional view of the pattern of career development.

- Occupational choice should be thought of as a lifelong developmental process that is influenced by the interaction of many variables.

- There is a positive correlation between job satisfaction and age.

- Levinson has provided a detailed description of the novice phase of career development and the major developmental tasks of this period.

Gender and Work: Women's Career Paths and Special Career Issues

The career experience of women is not yet well understood (Ornstein & Isabella, 1990). Reflecting the traditional gender roles and males' greater career involvement, most of the career development research has focused on men, with the assumption that the theories, models, and concepts that emerged could be generalized to women. This assumption is being increasingly questioned as evidence accumulates that women's career paths, issues, and psychology differ significantly from those of men (Betz & Fitzgerald, 1987; Jenkins, 1989). For example, a study of men and women psychologists found different experiences throughout the career cycle (Cohen & Gutek, 1991).

Until recently, the vast majority of American women opted for the traditional roles of wife and mother. Other choices were frowned on, seen as second best, and thought to be necessary only when a woman lacked a man to provide adequately for her and her children. Today, however, because of social change, women have a much wider range of choices. The norm has shifted to a combination of domestic roles with either a job or a career, even among those who are married and have young children. Of course, different women have different priorities, and societal confusion about how working women are viewed persists.

Changing Nature of Women's Work and Working Women

Though women have always worked, the nature of their work changed dramatically in the 20th century. In the early 1900s, most working women were young and single. As the century unfolded, the major change was in the *type* of work women did, with fewer

women working in clerical jobs and more working in factories and agriculture (Keith & Schafer, 1991). This trend was accelerated by World War II, as women took over jobs vacated by servicemen—immortalized by "Rosie the Riveter." Their success changed the role of the American woman forever, despite the fact that most were forced to leave their positions once "the boys came home." (See also Box on p. 102.) Today, though women are moving into traditionally male occupations in greater numbers, progress in some areas has been slow. From 1983 to 2002, the proportion of young women employed as managers, administrators, or executives nearly doubled, though women are overrepresented in the lower-paying occupations within this category (U.S. Department of Labor, 2004b). (See Table 8.3.) There are also marked disparities favoring White over Black and Hispanic women. Many remain segregated in what are sometimes referred to as "pink-collar" jobs. These are generally low-paying positions, such as service-industry, office, and clerical work (for instance, receptionist, bank teller), in which there is little opportunity for advancement and in which being attractive, well groomed, self-effacing, and submissive are valued attributes.

This photo depicts women railroad workers in New Mexico in 1943. Women took over many traditionally male jobs as men entered the military during World War II. Women proved their competence and found the work and the income very satisfying. These experiences contributed to the changing nature of women's roles in American society.

In the second half of the 20th century, the labor-force participation rate of women doubled, with the majority of

TABLE 8.3 *Percentage of Females in Various Professions, 1972, 1984, 2002*

Profession	1972	1984	2002
Engineering	0.8	5.8	11.6
Law	3.8	15.8	29.2
Medicine	9.3	15.8	30.6
Business (executive and managerial)	17.6	32.4	50.5[a]
Writing, art, entertainment	31.7	42.7	49.8
Social work	55.1	64.3	74.0
Elementary and secondary education	70.0	70.9	75.7
Higher education	28.0	36.3	42.7
Library, museum curatorship	81.6	84.4	78.8
Nursing	92.6	95.8	92.9

[a]This percentage includes executives and managers at all levels. Women make up only 10 percent of senior management at major firms.

Sources: U.S. Bureau of the Census, 1998; U.S. Department of Labor, 2004a.

working women being married (Keith & Schafer, 1991; Spitze, 1988). (**Labor force participation rate** refers to the percentage of those eligible who are actually working or looking for work.) The labor force participation of men and women is converging (Fullerton & Toossi, 2001)(See Figure 8.7.) In addition, 72 percent of women with children under age 18 now work outside the home, as compared to the 47 percent who did so in 1975 (U.S. Department of Labor, 2004a). In 1955, 66 percent of American families consisted of a two-parent model, with husband as the breadwinner and wife as the homemaker; by 1985, that figure had dropped to less than 7 percent (Braverman, 1989). The predominant family form is now one in which both husband and wife work outside the home, constituting 59 percent of married-couple families in 2001 (U.S. Department of Labor, 2004a). This is variously referred to as the **dual-earner** or **dual-career family,** depending on the occupational level and commitment of the husband and wife. The nature of both work and family life have been fundamentally changed (see Figure 7.6, p. 267).

Women will constitute 47.5 percent of the American workforce by 2012. Their labor force participation, especially among midlife women, is increasing at the same time that middle-aged and older men's is decreasing (see Figure 8.11). Understanding the aspirations, abilities, and experiences of working women is therefore increasingly important. This section explores the nature of gender and work and includes three major

FIGURE 8.7 *Civilian Labor Force Participation Trends for Men and Women, 1980, 1990, 2000, and projected 2010.*

The labor force participation rate for women rose about 9 percentage points between 1980 and 2000 and is projected to rise further between 2000 and 2010. In contrast, the rate for men fell between 1980 and 2000 and is projected to fall again in the 2000–2010 period.

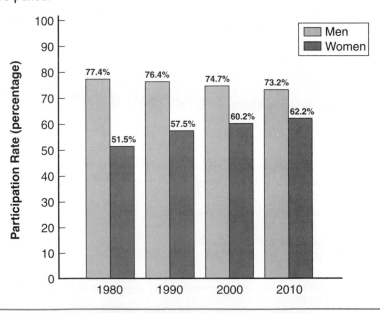

Source: U.S. Department of Labor, Bureau of Labor Statistics (2001, December 18).

topics: an overview of the major differences in the career patterns and experiences of women as compared to men, an examination of the economic consequences of the nature of women's labor force participation, and the costs and benefits of multiple roles.

Women's Career Patterns and Work Experiences

Why Do Women Work?

Women work for both extrinsic and intrinsic reasons. According to Williams (1987), women are motivated to work for three main reasons: economic need; in response to certain aspects of the domestic role that motivate them to seek an alternative to staying home (for example, tedium, isolation); and to meet psychological needs such as status and social contact, the realization of potential, and the desire to benefit society. Changing gender roles and increasing education also create greater opportunities for employment (Erdner & Guy, 1990), while changing norms may create social pressure to work.

Gender-Role Socialization

Many of the work-gender differences discussed below originate in the traditional gender roles toward which males and females are socialized. (See Chapter 3.) The male instrumental role, with its goal and achievement orientation, helps males succeed in work, while the female expressive role, with its emphasis on nurturing and dependency, may not. As a result, women may lack some of the skills, values, and attitudes toward the self that would lead them to the highest levels of occupational achievement. For example, girls may have less confidence in their ability, which can result in lower career aspirations. In fact, deviation from the female gender role may have interpersonal consequences such that a woman may be viewed as a less desirable romantic or friendship partner (Pfost & Fiore, 1990). In other words, women who pursue nontraditional occupations may pay a social price. The expectation of these negative social costs may affect women's career ambitions, steering them toward "safer" choices. Men seem to enjoy greater freedom in this regard.

Women's relationships may constrain career achievement in other ways as well. For example, in a study of psychologists, Cohen and Gutek (1991) found that women were less likely to move to advance their educational preparation or career development because of the potential effect on their partner's career or because the partner would not move with them. In many couples the wife's career is seen as secondary and the husband's as primary; thus her career goals may take a backseat to his.

The penalties for violating gender norms may also extend to the workplace and career progress directly. In three laboratory-based studies, researchers found that women who are seen as successful in a traditionally male-dominated field, such as finance or engineering, are viewed as "bitchy" in comparison to equivalently successful men; that is, they are considered more selfish, manipulative, untrustworthy, unsociable, and hard to work with (Heilman, Wallen, Fuchs, & Tamkins, 2004). Women who succeed in stereotypically female fields are not viewed in these terms. Such negative views can affect women's overall performance evaluations and career outcomes. The authors conclude that gender stereotypes may bias evaluations of women, penalizing them for success even when they have demonstrated their competence.

Discontinuity: The Interrupted Career Cycle

One of the unique features of women's career lives is the nature of the career pattern itself (Andersen, 1988; Ornstein & Isabella, 1990). Men's careers are essentially long and continuous, beginning after they complete their formal education and ending with retirement. There are traditionally few interruptions to this pattern, except perhaps for military service or illness. Women's careers are typically briefer and more **discontinuous,** interrupted by time out for childbearing and childrearing, as well as caregiving responsibilities to older family members (see Chapter 7 for a discussion of the caregiver role). Women may stop work altogether for a period of time, take extended leaves, or switch to part-time work to accommodate family responsibilities. The timing of career stages may also differ among men and women as a result (McHugh, Koeske, & Frieze, 1986).

A sporadic or discontinuous work history has important ramifications, in terms of both career progress and women's economic resources later in life (Hatch, 1990). Interruptions in the career cycle curtail advancement or limit one to part-time or low-paying work. Retirement income is directly related to work history and earnings. As women's work pattern is interrupted, earning potential declines proportionately. This pattern may also make them ineligible for full pension benefits (Hatch, 1990). As the family structure becomes more vertical (expanding in terms of the number of generations, contracting in terms of the number of family members in each generation; see Chapter 7) and the need to provide care for elderly family members increases, so does the likelihood that women's work histories will include more interruptions (O'Grady-LeShane, 1993). These work patterns have important long-term economic consequences for women: "The acceptance by women of caregiving responsibilities may endanger their future economic security and undoubtedly contributes to the high rates of poverty among elderly women" (Davis, Grant, & Rowland, 1990, p. 46).

Greater Diversity and Complexity

As a result of the kinds of issues raised above, women's career development is more complex than that of men (Betz & Fitzgerald, 1987). Women's work histories are also more heterogeneous, the diversity arising from different socialization experiences relative to work, both within and across generations of women (Lopata & Norr, 1980; Ornstein & Isabella, 1990). Some women assume the traditional role of full-time wife, mother, and homemaker and to some degree or other consider the work role to be undesirable or incompatible with their family life. Others defer their work goals until, for example, the kids are in school. Some career-oriented women defer family life until they are established in their careers. Still other women attempt to integrate work and family roles. Finally, there are those referred to as *career primary,* to whom marriage and parenthood are secondary to achievement in their chosen occupation. Of course, within these broad categories of women, tremendous diversity exists in terms of strength of commitment to various roles, timing, and so on.

The male instrumental role, on the other hand, clearly mandates work as a defining component of adulthood. Men are expected to assume the work role as soon as their formal educational preparation is complete, and to continue to work until retirement. This aspect of the male gender role has not undergone the fundamental changes seen in the female gender role in recent decades. Thus, the task of describing women's career development is increasingly challenging, as their work patterns become more complex and divergent.

Discrimination

Discrimination against women has been found in a number of areas, including advancement opportunities and earnings. In a longitudinal study of the high school class of 1972, Adelman (1991) discovered a paradox: women's credentials were not rewarded in the workplace despite the fact that they earned higher grades and attained a higher class rank than men in both high school and college, continued their education at a higher rate, and had more positive attitudes than men toward working conditions, relationships on the job, and the development of new skills. The study describes the educational and career experiences of women in the class of 1972 up to the age of 32. Women outperformed men academically at every level from high school to graduate school, and in all fields and courses, including statistics and calculus. However, Adelman asserts that their superior educational performance was discounted and underrewarded in the labor market. Women were more likely to experience unemployment, underemployment, and lower earnings than men. Some of these conditions persist.

Advancement Opportunities.   A firestorm of controversy was created in 1989 when Felice Schwartz suggested in a *Harvard Business Review* article that there be two career tracks for women: the **career primary track** and the career-and-family track—the **mommy track.** The idea was that women who opt to combine work and family roles should be viewed as less committed and motivated, and therefore less worthy of op-

portunities for advancement and positions of responsibility. These women would be relegated to a different level of career development within the organization. Critics pointed out that no such judgments were made of men who chose to have both careers and families. Despite the storms of protest, Schwartz may simply have been acknowledging reality. A de facto mommy track appears to exist, since surveys indicate that most women who rise to senior positions in their fields are either unmarried ("married to their jobs"?) or have no children. Ehrlich (1989) points out that 60 percent of top female executives are childless, while 95 percent of the men have children.

The **glass ceiling** refers to the existence of structural, though invisible, barriers that keep women out of top management positions. These barriers are based on biases and misconceptions of women's abilities and aspirations. Smith (1996) reports that out of the nation's top 1,936 corporate CEOs, nine are women. According to Meyerson and Fletcher (2000), 10 percent of senior managers of *Fortune* 500 companies are women. In 1980 two women were in charge of *Fortune* 500 companies; in 2005 there were seven (and 493 men). Most women remain in middle- and lower-level management positions. The presence of these barriers may have the effect of reducing women's motivation to reach the top (why try if you doubt you will make it?) and may be misinterpreted as a lack of ability or lack of interest. This may have the ironic effect of justifying the

Women who attempt to combine work and family roles may find themselves on the "mommy track" and consequently viewed as less committed and motivated, resulting in fewer advancement opportunities.

continued exclusion of women from these positions. The lack of mentors for women, mentioned earlier, also diminishes women's advancement. Many women don't encounter the glass ceiling until they are past 40, when they have established careers and are in line for a top executive spot. Not only are men more likely to be promoted and to be promoted earlier in their careers, they also receive the bulk of the types of positions that are the stepping-stones to the top (e.g., line positions with direct responsibility for profit and loss).

What will the future hold in regard to all this? There are some interesting trends. More than half of all college students are women, and, in some graduate and professional schools, women equal or exceed the number of men (National Center for Education Statistics, 2000). Women are also entering male-dominated professions in greater numbers. Thus, there are more women in the career pipeline. And many women (especially minority women) are circumventing the glass ceiling by becoming entrepreneurs, starting two-thirds of all new businesses. Many of these are Internet companies. In fact, e-commerce, where traditional power structures carry much less weight, may be an especially fertile ground for aspiring women. Women's skills in networking, fostering individual development, relationship building, and facilitating group processes may prove to be advantageous in the new workplace (Pfaff, 1999).

Earnings. A wage gap persists between male and female earnings and is wider for minority women (see the discussion earlier and Figure 8.6). Family responsibilities clearly play a role. The lower earnings of women with children are accounted for by their greater concentration in lower-paying fields (for example, teaching and nursing versus engineering and law) and by the fact that they represent a higher percentage of part-time workers.

Women's lower earnings not only limit current socioeconomic standing and lifestyle, as well as ability to save, but also negatively influence future and retirement earnings. In addition, lower salaries may make it difficult for women to pursue expensive advanced degrees, such as an MBA, thus further limiting advancement and earning potential (Kantrowitz, Rosenberg, Springen, & King, 1992).

Occupational Segregation

Women's work experiences are characterized by **occupational segregation**—that is, they are concentrated in occupations that are traditionally defined as feminine and in which few men are found, positions characterized by lower job security, lower pay, and fewer economic benefits (Hatch, 1990). This clustering begins in high school and college, where there is an unofficial men's curriculum and women's curriculum, with the former dominated by business and core science and engineering courses and the latter by human services and humanities courses (Adelman, 1991). This may reflect different value systems consistent with traditional gender roles, with women more oriented toward others and men more oriented toward individual success, autonomy, and achievement (Adelman, 1991; McCandless, Lueptow, & McClendon, 1989).

Mathematics, a curricular area that women are socialized to fear and avoid, has traditionally been an "occupational gatekeeper," regulating access to traditionally male-dominated fields (Adelman 1991; Sells, 1973). For example, among those in the class of 1972, 77 percent of economics majors were men, while 73 percent of education majors were women (Adelman, 1991). When women do enter the sciences, they tend to be found most often in the biological sciences and least often in mathematics and computer science. In 1998, women comprised the majority of those receiving doctorates in the social sciences (54.2 percent) and education (62.8 percent), while lagging far behind in such fields as the physical sciences (23.7 percent) and engineering (1.3 percent). Thus, women's occupational horizons are limited in part by their congregation in some curricular areas to the neglect of others—despite their fine academic performance even in traditionally male academic areas. Table 8.4 lists the 20 leading occupations of employed women in 2003.

Levinson (1996) points out that as women begin to enter a traditionally male occupation in larger numbers, and especially when they comprise over 50 percent of workers in that field, it is increasingly viewed as "women's work," with a corresponding reduction in status, pay, and attractiveness to men. The economic value placed on men's versus women's jobs (a reflection of the social value accorded to jobs primarily performed by women) is illustrated by a classified ad in our local paper some years ago: "Child-care worker, must be a high school graduate, $4.75–5.25/hour; janitor, no requirements, $5.50–6.00/hour."

Feminization of Poverty

The **feminization of poverty,** a term coined in the late 1970s, refers to the societal processes through which poverty has become concentrated among women and children (Minkler & Stone, 1985; Pearce, 1978). The federal poverty level for a family of four in

TABLE 8.4 *Twenty Leading Occupations of Employed Women, 2003*

Occupations	Percentage of Women
Secretaries and administrative assistants	96.3%
Elementary and middle school teachers	80.6
Registered nurses	90.2
Nursing, psychiatric, and home health aides	89.0
Cashiers	75.5
Customer service representatives	69.1
First-line supervisors/managers of office and administrative support	67.9
First-line supervisors/managers of retail sales workers	41.5
Bookkeeping, accounting, and auditing clerks	91.4
Receptionists and information clerks	93.2
Accountants and auditors	58.3
Retail salespersons	41.6
Maids and housekeeping cleaners	84.6
Secondary school teachers	53.5
Waiters and waitresses	68.1
Teacher assistants	90.9
Office clerks, general	83.8
Financial managers	51.6
Preschool and kindergarten teachers	98.3
Cooks	39.3

Source: U.S. Department of Labor, Bureau of Labor Statistics, Annual Averages, 2003.

2003 was an income of less than $18,979; for those 65 and over, it was $8,825 for individuals and $11,122 for couples. In addition to those officially below the poverty line, there are also many near poor who fall close to but do not meet the federal criteria. These guidelines simply identify those who are eligible for assistance and should not be taken as a definition of adequate income.

At special risk are women with young children and older, single, minority-group women. For example, while the overall poverty rate among families in 2003 was 10 percent, among families headed by a single female it was 28 percent (DeNavas-Walt, Proctor, & Mills, 2004). The poverty rate among Black women age 65 to 74 is 47 percent (American Psychological Association, 2004b). Cutler (1991, p. 18) refers to "the multiple jeopardies of age, ethnicity, and gender."

While the economic status of older Americans in general has improved dramatically in the last few decades (largely as a result of programs like Social Security and Medicare), these benefits have had less impact on women. Though Social Security is the most common source of income for older women, their work history and pattern of dependence on men leaves them with lower benefits in old age. According to the Social Security Administration (2004), at the end of 2003, women's average monthly Social Security retirement benefit was $798, compared to men's $1,039. Social Security comprises 54 percent of total income for unmarried women (including widows) age 65 and over, compared to 38 percent for men, and is the only source of income for 29 percent of unmarried elderly women. The problem is expected to worsen in the future for the following reasons. Though women are moving into the workforce in larger numbers than ever before, discontinuous work histories and occupational segregation combine to reduce present income and future Social Security and pension benefits. As Hatch (1990, p. 51) warns, "Largely as a result of their lifelong work experiences, women, along with many minorities, are at risk for poverty in older age—now and for the foreseeable future." Marital status is also important. Because more women in the future are expected to be single, poverty among older women is projected to increase (Keith, 1986). The high divorce rate, dismal performance of men in paying child support, lower remarriage rates of women as compared to men, and widowhood all contribute to the feminization of poverty. In fact, poverty among elderly couples and elderly men living alone is expected to virtually disappear by 2020, leaving poverty among the elderly to be exclusively a problem of poor elderly women living alone—widowed, divorced, or never married (Davis, Grant, & Rowland, 1990). Experts predict that 25 percent of today's young women will live in poverty in old age (Carstensen, 1991).

To reiterate, women's career patterns and work experiences differ significantly from those of men and are characterized by discontinuity, greater complexity and diversity, occupational segregation, and the experience of discrimination. While it is increasingly clear that the nature of career development varies significantly by gender, we do not yet have the rich, detailed, longitudinal data that would help us to understand women's career paths and issues (Ornstein & Isabella, 1990). It is clear, however, that women's work histories have important economic consequences, the effects of which will continue to be felt well into the future.

Multiple Roles: Combining Career and Family

All of us assume multiple roles throughout our lives. (Right now, for example, how many roles do you play in your life?) But some role combinations seem to generate more concern than others. In particular, as women increasingly seek to combine work and family roles, a great deal of research interest has been generated on the psychological and physical costs and benefits of doing so. Some historical perspective may be helpful in order to understand the strength and depth of the concern over women's occupational role.

As Barnett and Hyde state (2001, p.781): "One of the most dramatic markers of the late 20th and early 21st centuries is the astonishingly fast pace of change in the work and family roles of women and men in the United States." Until relatively recently, women were thought to lack the intellectual ability necessary to compete academically at the college level. When the actual performance of women belied these claims, some argued that even though they may have the cognitive potential, scholarly pursuits "would ruin their health or atrophy their reproductive organs," making them unfit to fulfill their domestic role (Furumoto & Scarborough, 1986, p. 37). Educated women, who had struggled to find institutions of higher learning that would admit them to begin with, were faced with a "cruel choice." For example, in the early years of this century, a woman who wished to teach at Wellesley College (a prestigious women's college and one of the few places where a college-educated woman could find an academic position) had to give up the idea of marrying and having a family. Wellesley, typical of colleges in its day, felt it was inappropriate to have married women faculty members. As Furumoto and Scarborough (1986, p. 40) sum up, "The accepted view in the late 19th and early 20th century was that, for a man, the potential for professional accomplishment was enhanced by marriage. For a woman, however, marriage and career were incompatible." Women's sphere was considered to be work inside the home, while men's was considered to be outside the home: women's work versus men's work. While the battle over educational opportunity has been waged and largely won, equal opportunity in the workplace is yet to be achieved.

The cultural pressure to stay home and be a full-time wife and mother and to forgo individual achievement has weakened in recent decades due to changing attitudes about the female gender role as well as economic necessity. The norm is currently some combination of work and family, with more and more women seeking advanced education and pursuing a career, and at the same time expecting to marry and have children.

Increased educational and occupational opportunities have led to greater numbers of U.S. families in which both husband and wife are employed full time. Many of these women, especially those employed in professional fields, view their work as a central component of their identity, not merely as temporary or as primarily motivated by economic necessity. Thus, they consider themselves to be involved in lifelong careers. Women today can expect to spend at least thirty years in the labor force (Barnett & Hyde, 2001). And their economic contribution is substantial; the average working wife with a full-time position contributes about 34 percent to the family's yearly income (U.S. Department of Labor, 2004a). In 2001, 24.1 percent of married women's earnings exceeded those of their working husbands (U. S. Department of Labor, 2004b, February).

Three Perspectives

We take as our starting point the fact that the majority of women now work outside the home alongside men—and that they will continue to do so. The issue we address in this section has to do with the experience of combining family and work roles (Williams, 1987; Crosby, 1987). While an extensive examination of this issue is unfortunately beyond the scope of this chapter, we will consider some of the benefits and costs of trying to "have it all." Three views exist.

Role Enhancement/Role Expansion Perspective. According to this view, multiple roles are advantageous to the individual (Barnett & Hyde, 2001; Marks, 1977; Sieber, 1974; Thoits, 1986; Verbrugge, 1983). Linville (1982, 1987) suggests that a complex self-structure (the result of defining oneself in relation to a large number of domains or in terms of a large number of attributes) enables the individual to cope more easily with a challenging or threatening event and offers protection from emotional turmoil. A variety of roles is viewed as increasing the individual's resources and potential rewards— material, psychological, and interpersonal (Barnett & Hyde, 2001; Barnett, Marshall, & Singer, 1992; Martire, Stephens, & Townsend, 2000; Moen, Dempster-McClain, & Williams, 1989; Repetti, Matthew, & Waldron, 1989). Despite the demands imposed by these varying roles, "alternative resources provided by multiple roles outweigh these stresses and help dampen their emotional effects" (Bolger, DeLongis, Kessler, & Wethington, 1990, p. 96). Thus, the more identities individuals have, the better their mental health is likely to be.

CRITICAL THINKING QUESTION

How might one role offset problems associated with another?

The research suggests that some of the potential benefits of occupying multiple roles may include:

- Stress buffering
- Improved physical health and greater longevity
- Improved mental health and reduced psychological distress
- Psychological benefits such as a greater sense of mastery, self-esteem, personal satisfaction, achievement, more potential sources of fulfillment, and higher levels of subjective well-being
- Greater social contact, integration, and sources of social support
- Greater independence
- Increased income and standard of living and greater ability to meet financial emergencies, with a corresponding decrease in financial stress

Baruch, Barnett, and Rivers (1983) studied 298 women age 35 to 55, with an average educational level two years beyond high school and an average annual family income ranging widely, from $4,500 to over $55,000. The women represented six population subgroups: employed women who never married, employed married women without children, employed married women with children, employed divorced women with children, full-time homemakers with children, and full-time homemakers without children. Using two criteria of well-being—mastery (feeling important and worthwhile) and pleasure (finding life enjoyable)—the researchers found the employed married women with children to have the highest well-being scores, while the full-time homemakers without children had the lowest scores. Paid work seems to be an especially potent source of mastery, while intimate relationships contribute a sense of pleasure to life. This study suggests that individuals can and do combine roles in ways that contribute to well-being. Studies find that men also enjoy benefits of their wives' multiple roles—better overall health, greater participation in parenting and increased emotional involvement with children, and reduced economic pressure (Gilbert, 1994).

In sum, then, the role enhancement/role expansion view sees multiple roles as advantageous to the individual in a variety of ways and portrays those with diverse roles as generally happier and healthier.

Role Strain Perspective. True to its historical origins, traditional research has focused on the problems women confront when attempting to combine work and family roles (Keith & Schafer, 1991). The basic idea is that occupying a variety of roles may lead to difficulty in fulfilling the various demands of each, resulting in stress—role strain or overload—and negatively affecting both physical and mental health. Research has also focused on the consequences for women's husbands, children, and marital and job satisfaction. Implicit in this view is the notion that work-family strain arises from role demands and expectations that render occupational and family roles incompatible, at least among women. According to Silverstein (1991, p. 1025), among others, many of these stresses are the result of the failure of both the workplace and the family to respond to changing realities (see also Chapter 7):

> The parameters of the workplace were originally designed for working men with wives at home to absorb the demands of raising a family and managing a household. To date, the world of work and particularly the career system has remained relatively inflexible to the needs of people (men and women) who both work and bear responsibility for raising a family. Similarly, the institution of marriage, like that of the workplace, has not been transformed to reflect the fact that both partners in a marriage now work.

CRITICAL THINKING QUESTION
What kinds of changes are necessary in both the workplace and the family to more successfully accommodate the reality that most men and women now work outside the home?

Research indicates that possible costs associated with multiple roles may include:

- Reduced discretionary time, both for leisure and for interaction with extended family and friends
- Greater marital stress
- Increased workload, especially for the wife, who retains primary responsibility for domestic chores and child care (see Chapter 7)
- Limitations on job mobility and career advancement
- Resentment and/or lack of support from others who hold a negative view of working mothers

While most of the research focus has been on role strain among women and on barriers that block women from equal access to occupational roles, many structural barriers also exist that limit men's involvement in family life. One way to reduce the strain on women would be to allow men greater access to family roles.

To sum up, the role strain view holds that work and family responsibilities are inherently conflicting and result in stress and strain, which can negatively affect both physical and psychological health and well-being.

Role Context Perspective. This view asserts that both the role enhancement/role expansion and role strain perspectives are overly simplistic, since they focus only on the number of roles an individual occupies and fail to consider the nature and circumstances of these roles (Moen, Dempster-McClain, & Williams, 1989). The role context perspective takes a more complex view, considering the *quality* of and interaction among the individual's roles, as well as the person's subjective assessment of them (Barnett & Hyde, 2001; Keith & Schafer, 1991).

Experiences in one role can either increase or buffer distress associated with another role (Stephens, Franks, & Townsend, 1994; Martire, Stephens, & Townsend, 2000). For example, the psychological meaning of work depends on the nature and level of work, its reciprocal interaction with the individual's other roles, and its importance to the individual (Keith & Schafer, 1991). So two people could occupy the same types and number of roles and yet experience different problems and rewards within them (Stephens & Townsend, 1997). A challenging and rewarding career coupled with marriage to a supportive husband is likely to have far different consequences for well-being than combining a low-status, low-paying job with marriage to a disapproving man. The point is that "women increasingly operate in two arenas; experiences in one arena are bound to be affected by experiences in the other" (Barnett, Marshall, & Singer, 1992, p. 42).

Thus, the role context approach takes a broader view of factors that influence the experience of occupying multiple roles. The bulk of the research literature indicates overall benefits for women's (and men's) health (Barnett & Hyde, 2001; Repetti, Matthews, & Waldron, 1989). However, Barnett and Hyde (2001) call for more research into the processes through which multiple roles are beneficial and the conditions that limit these beneficial effects. They also note that existing research has focused mainly on White, middle-class American samples in the 1980s and 1990s and thus may be relevant only to a certain group in a certain period of history. Future studies of more diverse cohorts are needed. As always, general statements may not apply to any one individual: outcomes vary according to a host of factors. It does appear, however, that "when quality roles are involved, quality rewards result" (Fowlkes, 1987, p. 9).

Finally, a number of factors contribute to successful role combination (Epstein, 1987; Gilbert, 1994). These include emotional support from significant others, shared values and beliefs about love and work, awareness of potential problems and resourcefulness in addressing them, confidence in one's goals and abilities, and societal and institutional support. Given the current reality of both work and family life, both men and women will have to learn to balance the requirements and responsibilities of multiple roles. (See Table 8.5 for a list of some facts affecting the future of work.)

CRITICAL THINKING QUESTION

There has been a lot of discussion about "family friendly" corporate policies. What kinds of policies might be included, and based on the foregoing discussion of multiple roles, how might they be in a company's self-interest?

TABLE 8.5 *Some Facts Affecting the Future of Work*

Baby boomers make up almost half (47%) of the workforce today.

Young women are enrolling in college at a higher rate (70%) than young men (64%).

Young people hold an average of nine jobs before age 32.

Employed mothers with children under age 13 miss an average of 6.4 workdays a year due to family-related issues.

From 1969 to 1996 families, on average, experienced a decrease of 22 hours a week (or 14 percent) of available parental time to spend with their children.

Small businesses employ about half of the nation's private sector workforce.

E-commerce revenue for 1998 was estimated at $300 billion—almost the size of the U.S. auto industry.

In five years, almost half of all workers will be employed in industries that produce or are intensive users of information technology.

American workers get only seven hours of sleep every night . . . 365 hours a year less than recommended. One in three adults say that their work has been affected by feeling drowsy on the job.

Source: U.S. Department of Labor, 2000.

Concept Review 8.3

- The nature of women's work and the types of women participating in the labor force changed dramatically in the 20th century.

- Though not yet well understood, the career patterns and experiences of women differ significantly from those of men.

- Women's career paths tend to be more diverse and discontinuous; in addition, women experience occupational segregation, limited advancement opportunities, and a significant wage gap.

- Poverty is concentrated among women and children.

- Research on multiple roles suggests that there are many potential benefits, depending on the quality of the roles and the particular circumstances of the individual.

Retirement and Leisure

Retirement constitutes a major developmental task of late adulthood and the final stage of the occupational cycle. It has become an issue of almost universal concern and one of the most researched topics in the field of gerontology (Palmore, Burchett, Fillenbaum, George, & Wallman, 1985). It is now as commonplace and expected an event of the second half of life as getting married and having children is of the first (Ekerdt, 1989). But it was not always so.

Retirement as a Life Stage: A Brief Social History

Retirement as we know it is a phenomenon of modern industrial society, a relatively new life stage that emerged only in the 20th century, gaining momentum following

World War II. In 1900, the labor force participation rate of males age 65 and over was 68.4 percent. By 1960, the rate had dropped to 30.5 percent, and by 1999, it was 16.5 percent (U.S. Bureau of the Census, 1999). What accounts for this dramatic shift in working patterns?

Prior to 1900, retirement was primarily for those with enough land or other resources to be able to stop working (Quadagno & McClellan, 1989). It was not a viable option for most Americans, who were self-employed and worked until they were physically or mentally disabled or died. Unemployment was feared and dreaded. The availability of retirement on a societal scale requires two prerequisites: an industrial economy productive enough to produce surplus, and the widespread availability of public and private pension systems to support individual workers after they leave the labor force (Palmore et al., 1985). These two criteria were not met until well into the 20th century.

The economic system that supports retirees began to be created in 1935 with the passage of the Social Security Act, which established a government program providing retirement and other benefits based on employment history. (The United States was way behind both Germany and Great Britain, which had enacted similar legislation in 1889 and 1909, respectively.) The Social Security Act was passed in response to widespread and growing unemployment among older individuals. These conditions, in turn, were the result of many factors, including abundant cheap labor because of open immigration, displacement due to technology, the effects of the Great Depression, and age discrimination. As family and community resources like poorhouses grew increasingly unable to care for the growing numbers of unemployed older workers, and with no government system of retirement support and no private pension plans, poverty among older adults skyrocketed. By 1940, when the first Social Security check was issued, 60 percent of the elderly were officially considered to be living in poverty. The dread that many felt of literally ending up in the poorhouse was a factor in the passage of the Social Security Act (Haber, 1993).

Age 65 was chosen as the age at which one became eligible to receive government benefits—an arbitrary choice, following the lead of Germany's Otto von Bismarck. In actuality, since life expectancy was considerably shorter at the time, few Americans were expected to live long enough to draw much in the way of retirement benefits. However, the first Social Security recipient, Ida Fuller of Ludlow, Vermont, paid $22 into the system before her retirement and, to the demographers' surprise, lived another 35 years, eventually receiving $20,940.85 in Social Security benefits by the time of her death in 1975 (Anderson, Borger, Hager, & Fineman, 1983). Not a bad investment!

Income supports developed rapidly following World War II. The growth of private pension plans picked up as large companies discovered such plans were a way of luring and keeping top employees, and unions began to fight for similar coverage in their labor negotiations. In addition, under the favorable economic conditions of the 1960s and 1970s, the Social Security system of benefits was greatly expanded (sowing the seeds, by the way, of its later distress). By the early 1960s, retirement emerged as a life stage, increasingly available to American workers and no longer viewed as dreaded unemployment or a sure trip to the poorhouse, but as earned leisure.

On a societal level, retirement helps to solve the problem of unemployment among younger workers (Quadagno & McClellan, 1989). Essentially, unemployment is shifted to those over 65—but it is called retirement—allowing younger people to move into the labor force. Though passage of the Age Discrimination in Employment Act (1986) now legally protects workers over 40 against being forced out of their jobs based on their age, it has not eliminated discrimination. In fact, many people have come to feel that older workers have a "duty" to get out of the way so that younger workers can take their place (Harris, 1981). On an individual level, this life period has been successfully "sold" as a positive life stage, characterized by autonomy, freedom, and the luxuries of time and an income sufficient to do some of the things one has always wanted to do but could not, because of family and work responsibilities. In 1974, Friedmann and Orbach noted, "There is good evidence that most Americans are coming to view retirement as a normally expected stage of life that follows a delimited period of work and one that has potentialities for its own intrinsic satisfactions" (p. 630). All in all, voluntary retirement has been viewed as a win-win situation: good for the economy as well as the individual.

CRITICAL THINKING QUESTION

How is retirement "sold" in the media? For example, how are retirees and their lifestyle depicted in advertising? Do you think you *will want to retire?*

Research Limitations

Before we begin our discussion of the developmental aspects of retirement, we should keep in mind that the research literature in this area suffers from the following weaknesses: inconsistencies in defining and measuring both retirement itself and adjustment to retirement, heavy reliance on cross-sectional studies, the use of primarily White male samples, and overreliance on data from previously retired cohorts (Erdner & Guy, 1990; Howard, Marshall, Rechnitzer, Cunningham, & Donner, 1982; Kim & Moen, 2001; Palmore et al., 1985).

Problems with definitions and measurement tools result in inconsistent findings and difficulty in comparing results across studies. Cross-sectional studies are subject to weaknesses such as the influence of cohort effects, while the lack of longitudinal data makes it difficult to study retirement as a long-term developmental process. The limited research on the retirement experiences of both women and minorities means that differences based on gender and ethnicity are not well understood.

Though retirement decisions are affected by ethnicity and gender, little is known about the factors that influence these decisions among African American and Hispanic men and women as compared to Whites (Honig, 1996). Research projects such as the Health and Retirement Study (HRS), a longitudinal study of health and retirement processes, have begun to address these issues more fully. HRS, which began in 1990, focuses on health, wealth, and retirement issues among 22,000 individuals over age 50. (For more information, visit the site at http://hrsonline.isr.umich.edu/.)

Finally, existing retirement research is based on the experience of previously and currently retired cohorts. The extent to which these findings can be generalized to future cohorts, who will be better educated, healthier, and more affluent, is not known (Easterlin, Macdonald, & Macunovich, 1990).

As we have seen in other chapters, these problems are not peculiar to retirement research, but progress in more fully understanding the retirement experience will depend on the extent to which they are successfully addressed.

A Life-Span View of Retirement

Throughout our discussion of the retirement experience, it may be useful to keep in mind the key life-span perspectives detailed in Chapter 1: that development is a life-long process that involves both gains and losses; that development is multidimensional, multidirectional, and multicausal; that development is plastic and is embedded in a historical, cultural, and social context; and that understanding development requires that we consider information from a variety of disciplines (Baltes, 1987). Think of retirement as a *process*, rather than an event, that spans a period of time (Kim & Moen, 2001). It is a complex phenomenon; each individual's experience of it and response to it depend on a multitude of variables.

Predictors of Retirement

The decision to retire is complex, based on a variety of factors. Palmore and colleagues (1985) summarize research findings in terms of five important predictors: health, socioeconomic status (education, occupation, income), demographic characteristics (age, marital status, number of dependents), job characteristics (self-employment versus employment by others, pension coverage), and attitudes toward work and retirement (job dissatisfaction, perceived pressure to retire). These variables have both direct and indirect effects and interact with one another. For example, number of dependents may influence perceived income sufficiency and therefore the timing of retirement. Self-employed individuals tend to continue to work full time. Most early retirement decisions seem to be influenced by subjective evaluations of health, work, and the attractiveness of retirement incentives and benefits.

Family considerations play a particular role in women's decision to retire (Vinick & Ekerdt, 1989). For example, women may retire earlier than men, timing their retirement to coincide with their husbands', or to care for a sick spouse or parent (Matthews & Brown, 1988; Shaw, 1984; Szinovacz, 1987). In addition, women's retirement decisions are better predicted by their husbands' pensions than their own (probably based on adequacy of benefits). Economic concerns are of special importance to widowed, divorced, and never-married women, who may want and need to work longer than they would if they were married. The economic consequences of women's work histories and their longer life expectancy contribute to their financial stress.

Retirement as a Developmental Process

Retirement (or perhaps more accurately retir*ing*) is currently viewed not as an isolated event but as an increasingly lengthy stage of adulthood. Adjustment to this life stage is a complex process that involves adaptation over a period of time and that must be considered within the broader context of the individual's life (Floyd et al., 1992; Howard et al., 1982).

Atchley (1976, 1988) has identified the following phases in the retirement process: preretirement, actual retirement (which may be followed by a honeymoon, immediate routine, or rest-and-relaxation phase), disenchantment, reorientation, routine, and termination. Preretirement includes preparation and the decision to retire. Expectations about what retirement will be like are formed. The honeymoon phase involves the initial enjoyment of the freedom from work and heightened activity—an attempt to do everything previously prevented by work. Not all retirees experience this euphoria; some settle quickly into a retirement routine, while others enter a period of rest and lowered activity. A disenchantment phase may follow as the novelty wears off and the problems of retirement appear, especially if retirement does not live up to earlier expectations. In the reorientation phase, the retiree adjusts, finding new interests and activities to take the place of work and eventually establishing a satisfying routine. The retirement period ends with a return to work, disability, or death.

Exit patterns from full-time employment vary. Some individuals retire gradually—for example, by cutting down on hours or workload. However, this is financially impractical for those entitled to a pension, as benefits are often based on income during the last three years of service, an incentive to maximize income during that period. A substantial minority move from a full-time career job (defined as one the employee has held for at least 10 years full time) to a **bridge job**—part-time employment in a new line of work and at lower pay or self-employment (Quinn & Kozy, 1996). Ruhm (1995) found that about a third of the men age 58 to 63 employed in 1989 were working in such jobs. These positions offer the advantages of flexibility of hours and different working conditions without threatening eligibility for pension plans. Labor force exit patterns are affected by gender and ethnicity; women are more likely to work in bridge jobs than men. Differences in exit patterns by race and ethnicity exist but do not fall into any obvious pattern (Quinn & Kozy, 1996). Many ethnic minorities may continue to work full time past the normal retirement age, even if they are in poor health, because of limited financial resources. Although the majority of workers do leave full-time employment and enter full-time leisure at the same time, the transition to bridge jobs is expected to increase in the future, the result of increased life expectancy and an aging population, combined with private sector incentives to retire (retirement incentive plans) and public sector (Social Security) incentives to continue working. Second careers are also a common phenomenon.

Impact of Retirement on Individual Well-Being

Much of the research on retirement has focused on its consequences for the individual's well-being. Because work is so central to male identity, and because the employment role influences so many other aspects of life, retirement has been thought of as a milestone event with enormous ramifications (Maxwell, 1985).

Theories of Retirement Adjustment

A number of frameworks have been suggested to explain how people adapt to retirement. Two of these are the crisis and continuity theories.

Crisis Theory. The traditional view was that retirement was bad for people—that it was hazardous to their physical and mental health. This "crisis" view held that the loss of the work role leads to lowered self-esteem and status, withdrawal, isolation, illness, and reduced life satisfaction. Stories were told of people who "retired and dropped dead." Part of the reason for these dire predictions was that early research failed to separate those who became ill and retired from those who retired and became ill. The kind of negative effects that used to be described as normal consequences of retirement actually were occurring among those who were unhealthy *before* retirement. Thirty years of research on the subject now indicates that retirement does not generally make people sick, depressed, lonely, or bored, and it does not cause death (Ekerdt, 1989). More recent research, which controls for preretirement characteristics, has largely discounted the crisis view.

Continuity Theory. The alternate view, referred to as continuity theory, holds that few individuals base their entire identity on work, that sufficient opportunities for satisfaction and maintenance of the sense of self remain, and that attitudes and activities undergo a minimum of change after retirement (Atchley, 1976). Thus, retirement is viewed not as a crisis but as an event having minimal long-term effects. In fact, research suggests that about 70 percent of retirees experience no serious adjustment problems.

Both views may be too simplistic, failing to account for the many and varied responses of individuals to the retirement experience and the fact that some adjust more successfully than others (Palmore et al., 1985). In addition, neither view acknowledges that the consequences of retirement may in fact be positive—for example, a reduction in work stress, opportunities for enjoyable leisure activities, increased companionship with one's spouse, and so on. The consequences of retiring are best understood from an ecological and life course perspective (Kim & Moen, 2001) within the context of the meaning of work for the individual, the individual's preretirement adjustment, and present circumstances (e.g., health, income). Responses to the retirement experience can be thought of as falling on a continuum, with very successful adaptation at one end, very unsuccessful adaptation at the other, and a wide range of possible responses in between (Howard et al., 1982). None of the existing models adequately accounts for the various responses of individuals to retirement.

Impact of Retirement on Marriage

As we saw in Chapter 7, traditional retirement has no real impact on marriage: "Virtually no study has demonstrated a strong negative impact of retirement on the quality of marriage" (Vinick & Ekerdt, 1989, p. 54). In a study of retired men and their wives, Vinick and Ekerdt (1989) found that overall level of satisfaction with retirement was high, with 60 percent of subjects describing their quality of life as somewhat or much better. About 50 percent reported increases in companionate activities with their spouse, one of the desirable aspects of retirement for married couples. Minor adjustment problems included impingement of the husband on the wife's territory and time as the couple readjusted their daily routine to accommodate the husband's retirement. Overall, the best predictor of marital satisfaction after retirement is marital satisfaction before retirement.

Higginbottom, Barling, and Kelloway (1993) studied 164 male retirees with a mean age of 69 years. They found that the quality of the retirement experience (and not retirement per se) influences marital satisfaction indirectly, through its effects on mental health. Unemployed men who were able to structure and fill their time meaningfully, who gained a sense of purpose from the activities they were involved in, and who maintained interpersonal contacts were more satisfied with retirement. This satisfaction spilled over into other domains of life and was associated with a sense of general well-being and life satisfaction and with reduced symptoms of depression, so that it indirectly contributed to satisfaction with marriage.

This picture of the impact of retirement on marriage describes the conventional situation in which both husband and wife are fully retired and is based on cohorts in which retirement was primarily an individual male passage. However, as the first generation of two-income families begins to retire, some unconventional situations arise that may be more problematic—for example, when a husband is retired but his wife is still actively involved in her career. In a longitudinal study of married workers and retirees age 50 to 74, Moen, Kim, and Hofmeister (2001) found that marital satisfaction was lowest among women who were still working but whose husbands were retired. Such situations will be increasingly common, given women's labor force participation rates and the typical age difference between spouses (Moen, 1998b). Unlike previous generations, when the typical wife was a homemaker, couples today increasingly have two retirements to think about. Among these "half-retired" couples (Winters, 1999), the first year or two may be very challenging as they renegotiate their relationship. Issues include restructuring schedules, how much time to spend together, how to divide the housework, how to help the retired spouse find a new life structure, and how to manage one spouse's increased leisure at the same time that the other has high career demands. Given that couples may live twenty or more years in this retirement relationship, its quality is significant.

General Conclusions about Retirement Adaptation

Our understanding of individuals' adjustment to retirement shares many elements with research on adjustment in general (see Chapter 11) and can be summarized by the following general statements:

- Individual responses to retirement vary widely.
- Retirement can be a source of stress or satisfaction.
- Ability to cope depends on previously acquired coping skills, along with the subjective appraisal of the experience as either challenging or threatening. Events that seem to be out of the individual's control are more likely to be viewed as threatening. Thus, individuals with previous success in coping with major life events and who retire voluntarily are more likely to adapt successfully than those with no previous coping success or who are forced to retire.
- Adaptation is easier when change is minimized and individuals retain ample sources of fulfillment and satisfaction. Those who have maintained a balance between work, leisure, family, and other roles experience less disruption than those for whom the work role was overdeveloped.
- Adaptation is easier when transitions occur gradually over time. Preretirement planning is associated with more successful adjustment. Similarly, gradual or phased retirement options that allow a reduction in work involvement over time may be more easily accommodated.
- Personal resources are of critical importance in adapting to retirement. The most important of these are sufficient income, good health, a social support system, and a high occupational level.
- Personal qualities such as flexibility and farsightedness and a positive attitude toward retirement are associated with successful adaptation.
- Circumstances in other domains of life have a bearing on the resources that can be brought to bear in retirement. Examples may include marital quality, relationships with adult children and aging parents.
- Retirement is increasingly a *couple* transition (Floyd et al., 1992; Howard et al., 1982; Kim & Moen, 2001; Moen, 1998b; Vinick & Ekerdt, 1989).

Most people adjust well to this new life stage. In general, the determinants of satisfaction for retirees are the same as those for nonretirees (for instance, health, income, supportive relationships, meaningful activities, and so forth). The widespread availability of preretirement planning programs is considered very beneficial in helping those contemplating retirement to avoid the pitfalls and take advantage of the opportunities (both financial and otherwise) that increase the likelihood of successful adjustment to retirement. As we will see, women and minorities face significant disadvantages in terms of their economic well-being, which has ramifications for life stress, health, and adjustment.

Economics of Retirement: Social Security and Pensions

Because of the significance of income to retirement satisfaction, the Social Security system and pension coverage have overwhelming importance for the nature and experience of retirement (Ekerdt, 1989). This section provides a basic overview of these systems, on which so many retirees depend.

First, **Social Security** is a government program of earned income that provides monthly benefits based on contributions during years of employment. Close to 95 percent of working Americans pay into the system, along with their employers, in the form of a payroll tax. One in six—46.5 million people—now receive benefits. The average monthly benefit for an individual retiree in 2002 was $895. (For information on your own future benefits, check www.ssa.gov.) Many people do not understand how the system operates. Let's consider six major misconceptions.

Major Misconceptions about Social Security

• *Misconception: Social Security is just a retirement program.* Social Security is not only a retirement program, but provides a package of protection that also includes disability and survivors' insurance benefits. Thirty-seven percent of those receiving benefits are nonretirees (including survivors, disabled workers, and dependent children). See Figure 8.8. Thus, it is best thought of as a universal pension and family insurance system.

• *Misconception: Social Security is a personal savings plan.* Social Security is a pay-as-you-go system, not a savings system. That is, contributions from current workers are immediately released to pay the benefits to current retirees and other recipients. This means that your benefits will depend on the contributions of future workers, so that the system represents an "intergenerational compact" (Brown, 1977) that successive generations are committed to uphold if it is to work. Ours is the only government that does not use general tax revenues to support its retirement income system.

• *Misconception: Social Security was intended to be an adequate source of retirement income.* Social Security was never intended to be the sole source of retirement income, but rather as a safety net. It was to be one of three pillars of retirement income, along with pensions and personal savings. The fact is, however, that the majority of Americans, especially ethnic minorities, rely on Social Security as their major—or sole—source of income. See Figure 8.9. Lack of attention paid to personal savings is of particular concern in regard to baby boomers, many of whom have done nothing to prepare financially for retirement. Generation Xers are not saving at sufficient levels ei-

FIGURE 8.8 *Persons Receiving Monthly Benefits, December 2002*

Forty-six million persons were receiving monthly Social Security benefits in December 2002. Of these, the majority were retired workers.

BENEFIT RECEIPT, BY TYPE OF BENEFICIARY

Type of Beneficiary	Total Number (in millions)	Total Percentage
Total with benefits in current payment status	46.5	100
Retired workers and dependents	32.4	70
Disabled workers and dependents	7.2	14
Survivors of deceased workers	6.9	16

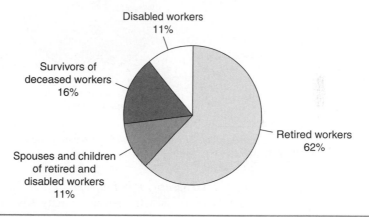

Percentage of Beneficiaries in Current Payment Status (by type)

Disabled workers 11%

Survivors of deceased workers 16%

Spouses and children of retired and disabled workers 11%

Retired workers 62%

Source: Statistical Abstract of the United States, 2003.

ther and are accumulating a huge level of debt that threatens their financial future (U.S. General Accounting Office, 2003).

• *Misconception: Retirees receive only what they have paid into the system during their years of work.* People will receive far more in benefits than they and their employers pay into the system. Many current retirees will draw out five times more than they paid in, recovering their entire contribution plus interest in 2.8 years (Anderson et al., 1983). This is a benefit to the employee, who receives good return on the investment. (Remember Ida Fuller?) This bonus is shrinking, though some critics feel it is still too generous. Men who retired in 1991 receive between 1.3 and 2.1 times, and women between 1.5 and 2.6 times, their contributions (U.S. House of Representatives, Committee on Ways and Means, 1991).

• *Misconception: Social Security payments are made only to those who need the benefits.* Social Security is a system of *earned* income based on contributions during years of employment and is not **means tested.** In other words, it pays regardless of need. This was done by design, so that there would be no stigma in receiving benefits: one is automatically eligible by virtue of being in the labor force: "Contributions, age, and physical well-being set or trigger benefit receipt, but level of current income does not" (Hudson & Kingson, 1991, p. 51).

FIGURE 8.9 *Percentage of Income from Social Security, 2001*

Social Security provides at least half of total income for a majority of beneficiaries. Social Security pays benefits to more than 91 percent of those age 65 or older. It is the major source of income (providing 50 percent or more of total income) for 65 percent of the beneficiaries. It contributes 90 percent or more of income for almost one-third of the beneficiaries and is the only source of income for 20 percent of them.

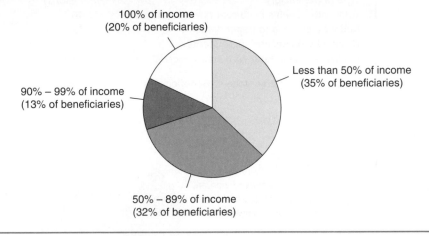

Source: U.S. Social Security Administration. Available online at www.ssa.gov/policy/docs/chartbooks/income_aged/2001/iac01.html#income.pdf.

• *Misconception: Social Security is in financial trouble and is in danger of going broke.* A 13-member federal commission, the Social Security Advisory Council, reviews the program every four years and recommends adjustments. Social Security is not going broke, though demographic changes require ongoing modifications to the system (Myers, 1998; Quinn, 2000). These might include reducing benefits, increasing payroll taxes, increasing the age of eligibility for full benefits (which, by 2022, will be 67), or (most controversial) changes in the way Social Security is funded. The biggest concern is over the large number of baby boomers who will begin retiring in the next decade. The basis of the concern is the **dependency ratio**—the number of workers paying into the system compared to the number drawing out. When Social Security was established in 1935, the dependency ratio was 35:1. It is currently about 3.3:1 and is projected to be 2:1 by 2050. (See Adamchak, 1993, for an extended discussion of the problems in accurately defining and calculating the dependency ratio and determining its consequences.) By 2050, there will not be enough workers to pay scheduled benefits at current tax rates. This problem can be remedied in a variety of ways, as suggested above. The baby boomers will begin to retire in about 2010. However, because the Social Security system is in a constant process of evaluation and adjustment, the retirement of the baby boomers has been anticipated. Social Security has been building a reserve to offset the extra demands on the system in the 21st century.

CRITICAL THINKING QUESTION
What would be the impact on the system if retirees received only the equivalent of their contribution to the Social Security system?

Private Pensions

Private pensions constitute a second pillar of retirement income. These plans combine contributions from both employer and employee during the employee's working years in a fund for the employee's retirement. In 2002, 53 percent of women and 54 percent of men employed full time were participants in a pension plan (Social Security Administration, 2004). Coverage is greater in large firms with over 1,000 employees than in small firms with fewer than 25 (coverage rates are 89 percent versus 23 percent), and among union members and those with higher incomes, and varies by industry. (See Figure 8.10 for sources of income among those 65 and over.) Pension coverage also varies by gender. Because of occupational segregation and discontinuous work histories, females are likely to receive lower pension benefits than men.

Employees must usually work in the job for 10 years to be **vested,** or entitled to draw some benefits on retirement even if they leave before the age of eligibility. Unlike Social Security benefits, most pension benefits are not **portable,** which means that if you leave your job before you are vested, you lose your benefits—you cannot take them with you. After vesting, you may be entitled to reduced benefits, but you lose the full long-term advantage of the plan. (Pension plans were originally developed to tie a worker to the job and reduce job mobility. You can see the effect here.) In addition, most pension benefits are not indexed to the cost of living, so that in periods of high

FIGURE 8.10 *Sources of Income, 2001, Age 65 and Over*

Social Security is a source of income for nearly all the aged. Nine out of 10 aged units receive Social Security benefits. Asset income is the next most common source of income, received by about 60 percent of the aged. Less than half (40 percent) receive pensions other than Social Security, and only 22 percent have earnings. Public assistance is received by 5 percent and veterans' benefits by only 4 percent.

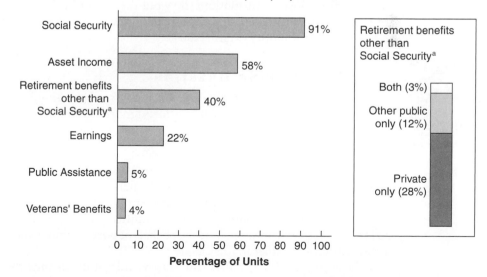

[a]Includes private pensions and annuities, government employee pensions, Railroad Retirement, and IRA, Keogh, and 401(k) payments.

Source: U.S. Social Security Administration. Available online at www.ssa.gov/policy/docs/chartbooks/income_aged/2001/iac01.html#income.

inflation, retirees on fixed incomes experience an erosion of their income. There is currently great concern over the underfunding of pension plans (Schwartz & Barrett, 1991), meaning that in many plans, a growing gap exists between what employees have been promised and the money that may be on hand to pay their benefits when they retire. In some cases, pension plans are eliminated when employers go bankrupt or due to buyouts and financial pressures.

In sum, economic well-being in the later years of life is significantly correlated with life satisfaction. Because the vast majority of Americans will continue to rely on Social Security and pension systems to support them in retirement, issues concerning these programs are of vital interest. Observers have expressed concern about discrimination against women and minorities in Social Security and pension policy (for example, see Choi, 1989; Rix, 1990). These groups are disadvantaged by their concentration in occupations with low pension coverage, their lower lifetime earnings levels, and their high job mobility, breaks in employment, and part-time work, which often make them ineligible for pension benefits.

Concerns also center on changes in pension coverage. Pension coverage is no longer growing and may in fact be in decline. Changes in the economy and the labor market do not bode well for the future of pensions as a source of retirement income. First, manufacturing jobs are decreasing, while service jobs, where pensions are less prevalent, are increasing. Second, there is an increase in both the subcontracting out of work and in part-time work; thus there are fewer full-time employees who would be eligible for a pension. Third, corporate downsizing has eliminated a large pool of middle management workers who would have drawn pensions. And finally, there is a shift from defined-benefit to defined-contribution pension plans. Defined-benefit programs are funded mainly by employer contributions. Defined-contribution plans are essentially employee savings accounts with tax advantages. The most common forms are 401(k) plans and individual retirement accounts (IRAs). Because they rely more heavily on employee contributions, they put the employee at greater risk. Unlike traditional pension plans that served as a social leveler, self-directed retirement plans tend to favor an elite minority (Walsh, 2004).

CRITICAL THINKING QUESTION

Are the changes in pension coverage just discussed an example of a normative age-graded influence, a normative history-graded influence, or a nonnormative influence?

Largely as a result of government programs such as Social Security, retirement is now a realistic economic option for many Americans. Poverty among the elderly has dropped from 60 percent in 1940 to 10 percent in 2002—a remarkable social achievement (U.S. House of Representatives, Committee on Ways and Means, 1991; Walsh, 2004). These figures, however, hide the pockets of poverty among older women and minorities discussed earlier in this chapter.

Those contemplating retirement must wonder if the income they thought would be sufficient to maintain a satisfying lifestyle will be eroded by family responsibilities or corporate and national economic crises. Their problems are ultimately our problems: "They are, after all, ourselves and our loved ones" (Nemschoff, 1992, p. 9).

Work and Retiring: The 21st Century

A Growing Retirement Period

Retirement as a social phenomenon continues to evolve. One major change is the growing length of the retirement period, the result of two factors: increased life expectancy and earlier retirement. **Early retirement** refers to retirement prior to age 65. The increasing popularity of early retirement is largely a response to the development of attractive **retirement incentive programs** (RIPs) associated with pension plans—offers of economic benefits available to those who opt to retire before the traditional age and within a specified time frame. RIPs are designed to encourage workers to leave the workforce as early as age 55 and thus to shave corporate payrolls or make way for younger, and cheaper, employees. Some experts charge that these so-called voluntary early retirement programs have actually evolved into "a systematic, institutionalized pressure . . . to encourage older workers to leave the labor force" (Schulz, 1992, p. 9). The popularity of early retirement means that the average worker now retires at about age 62 (Schulz, 1992) and can expect to live 15 to 20+ years after retirement (Morris & Bass, 1988; Palmore et al., 1985).

A Changing View of Retirement

As Ekerdt (1989) points out, we should think of retirement as an arrangement that suits our economic, political, and social needs and purposes. As these change, the institution of retirement will change accordingly. We are facing just such a prospect. Because of a number of factors—the fact that the vast majority of older Americans now retire, the growing length of the retirement period, the increasing health and affluence of retirees as a group, and national economic trends and concerns about the continued viability of the labor force—attitudes about retirement have begun to change.

Much of the attention has been on reassessing the trend toward early retirement (Rix, 1990; Schulz, 1992). An interesting paradox exists. First, the health and productive capacity of older Americans now make it feasible for work to extend much longer, into late adulthood. And second, since January 1987 (and full implementation of the Age Discrimination in Employment Act), mandatory retirement based on age is a relic of history. Older workers are, with few exceptions, legally entitled to work as long as they wish, assuming their performance remains acceptable. Despite this, they have been leaving the workforce. We have already documented the falling percentage of workers over age 65. The same trend is now evident among younger workers. In 1960, the labor force participation rate of men age 55 to 64 was 87.3 percent, dropping to 68.1 percent in 1998 (Fullerton, 1999). (The rate for women actually rose from 37.2 percent to 51.2 percent during the same period.) Projections are a 1.3 percent increase from 1998 to 2010 for men, to a rate of 69.4; and a 6.5 percent increase for women, to a rate of 57.7 by 2010 (Fullerton, 1999). Figure 8.11 illustrates these trends.

CRITICAL THINKING QUESTION

How do you explain the steadily rising labor force participation rates of women age 55 to 64, as shown in Figure 8.11?

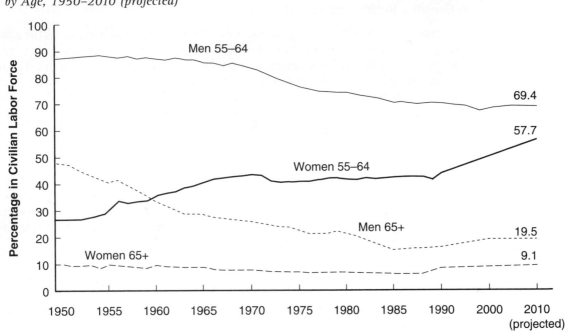

FIGURE 8.11 *Labor Force Participation (annual averages) of Older Men and Women, by Age, 1950–2010 (projected)*

Sources: U.S. Senate Special Committee on Aging et al., 1991, p. 95; Fullerton, 1999; Fullerton & Toossi, 2001.

So while most older adults are capable of working, and the right to work is guaranteed legally, the willingness to work seems now to be largely a function of Social Security and pension benefits (Rix, 1990). The fact is that many Americans can afford to retire and to do so earlier, and they are. The job market has also discouraged older workers who want to continue to work past the normal retirement age—for example, through economic disincentives that reduce income from pension benefits (Coberly, 1991). However, there are some interesting trends. Largely due to changes in Social Security and pension benefit plans, the labor force participation rate of men 65+ began to increase in 1985, reversing a long decline: growing from 16.3 percent in 1990, to 17.5 percent in 2000 and projected to be 19.5 percent by 2010 (Fullerton & Toossi, 2001).

As stated earlier, retirement has been successfully sold to the American public as a desirable life stage—maybe too successfully. There is mounting concern about the feasibility and desirability of a huge leisure class living as much as a third or more of its life in retirement at the same time that the pool of skilled labor is shrinking. Some argue that the emergence of new technologies and a service economy has reduced the importance of workers' muscle strength and quick responses. In such an economy, the knowledge, skills, and experience of older workers may be highly prized (Crystal, 1988; Myles, 1991). The prospect of labor shortages in the future has heightened concern over the loss of this talented labor pool.

Fears about the economic burden of the elderly on society—in terms of both retirement benefits and health care costs—have increased. Unfortunately, the elderly, who as a group have only recently risen out of poverty, have been unfairly targeted as the cause of poverty among other segments of society, leading to a new and dangerous form of ageism (Butler, 1993; McConnell & Beitler, 1991). In truth, older Americans represent 27 percent of the poor and near-poor. Eighty-three percent have incomes below $25,000 per year, and fewer than 3 percent have incomes above $50,000. As Hudson (1993, p. 79) warns, "Most troublesome of the anticipated trends has been widespread reinterpretation of policy successes in aging as policy excesses in which the aged find themselves transformed into an overindulged and singularly greedy population." Figure 8.12 illustrates the critical role Social Security continues to play in reducing poverty.

Older Americans should not be viewed as a homogeneous gray group. As we have seen, vast differences exist based on gender, race, class, cohort, and marital status (Hudson, 1993; Rank & Hirschl, 1999). This issue has significant age and gender implications, since

FIGURE 8.12 *Social Security's Role in Reducing Poverty, by Marital Status and Race, 1998*

Social Security plays a pivotal role in reducing poverty. Although there are aged beneficiaries with family income below the poverty line,[a] the poverty rate would be much higher if they did not have Social Security benefits. Nine percent of aged beneficiaries are poor, and 39 percent are kept out of poverty by their Social Security benefits, so that the total poverty rate without Social Security would be 48 percent. Although poverty rates vary considerably by marital status and race, the proportion kept out of poverty by their Social Security benefits is about 40 percent for all groups.

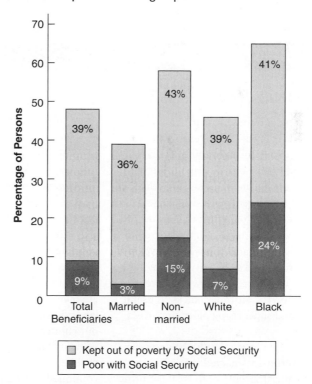

[a]Based on family income of aged persons to conform with official measures of poverty.
Source: U.S. Social Security Administration. Available online at www.ssa.gov/statistics/income_aged/1998/p.10.pdf.

it is the oldest-old, primarily female, who through no fault of their own are at greatest risk of both poverty and poor health. We should also remember that large numbers of elderly continue to make significant contributions to their families and communities, and to the economy as consumers. Thus, while we cannot ignore the real needs of some elderly adults, particularly the old-old, women, and minorities, we also cannot overlook the fact that rather than being a burden, the elderly are both economically and socially productive (Chawla, 1993). The challenge is to target benefits to those most in need—regardless of age—without undermining societal support for Social Security.

Many experts now predict that early retirement may soon be a thing of the past, hastened into extinction by the removal of barriers and the development of economic and other incentives to keep productive, experienced older employees on the job, or to lure them back from retirement. For example, the earnings limit for Social Security recipients has been eliminated (effective January 1, 2000), allowing older workers who have reached full retirement age to work and still receive their full benefits.

Some observers suggest that retirement and leisure will no longer be concentrated in the last stages of life, but instead that periods of intermittent "retirement" (for retraining, leisure, caregiving) may be sprinkled throughout adulthood. New work patterns and schedules, along with job redesign (such as job sharing, flextime, and phased retirement), are increasingly in evidence (Coberly, 1991; Rix, 1990). Unretirement programs and Retiree Job Banks are catching on at large companies such as The Travelers. Employers such as McDonald's have begun to specifically recruit older workers. (See Box.)

UNDERSTANDING THE DEVELOPMENTAL CONTEXT

Finding Niches for Golden Workers

Older workers bring a number of virtues to the workplace, including lower absenteeism, trustworthiness, maturity, experience, reliability, and a willingness to work part time or on temporary projects. They are also better educated and healthier than previous cohorts. Employers who wish to encourage older adults to stay in or return to the workforce must recognize that age is a dimension of diversity. While many organizations have developed educational programs and sensitivity training for a culturally diverse workforce, few have prepared managers to develop the attitudes and skills useful in working with and supervising older employees (Fyock, 1995).

Workplace adaptations may also be necessary. The Japanese government enacted legislation in 1998 offering financial incentives to Japanese firms that hire or retain workers over age 60. Grants are given for *kaizen,* or restructuring the workplace, to enable older workers to stay on the job (e.g., increasing illumination, redesigning tools to be ergonomically suited to older employees). Remember that Japan is aging rapidly and by 2020 will be the oldest nation in the world (see Chapter 1). Keeping workers healthy and on the job longer is thus a high priority.

Morris and Caro (1995) suggest that the involvement of adults age 55 to 75 in both paid and volunteer community service work is a major challenge of the 21st century, and they indicate there are many niches in which there are significant labor shortages and unmet community needs. In our culture, paid work and volunteer roles are important contributors to individuals' health and well-being. Policies and practices that encourage the continued active involvement of older adults in such roles can be in the best interest of both society and the individual.

Events in the lives of workers themselves may also slow the trend to earlier retirement. For many Americans who may have delayed marriage and parenthood in their 20s and 30s, early retirement may not be feasible, coming at the same time as college tuition or caregiving responsibilities for ailing older relatives. Spiraling health care costs along with the growing reluctance of employers to pay health care benefits may also keep workers on the job longer. The high divorce rate also may extend the working life of older women.

The field of financial gerontology offers a relevant concept. Financial gerontology is the study of the financial issues that relate to the process of aging and the social and economic trends affecting them. An important concept is the **human wealth span,** based on the assumption that how we live in later life is directly affected by what we do earlier in life. The human wealth span is divided into two phases: accumulation and expenditure/retirement. Earlier in the 20th century, individuals entered the workforce in their teens, retired about age 65 (if at all), and had a relatively short retirement period. As the century advanced, the trend was for people to enter the workforce later and leave it earlier, followed by an extended retirement period. This meant a much shorter accumulation phase and a much longer expenditure phase: retirement income had to be generated over a shorter time period, and the financial demands in retirement would be greater. Together with the decline in pension coverage discussed earlier, individuals often face a substantial financial burden.

CRITICAL THINKING QUESTION

Given the changes in the human wealth span described above, what do individuals need to do to prepare financially for retirement?

As a result of these factors, the 50-year trend for workers to withdraw from the labor force earlier and earlier seems to have been halted and possibly reversed (Fullerton, 1999). As Moen (1998b) points out, the notion of retirement as traditionally understood is blurring, as early retirement increases at the same time that retired workers return to work (either paid or volunteer, part time or full time) or begin second (or third or fourth) careers. Retirement is increasingly a transitional passage to new forms of work and productive activity, as opposed to a onetime, one-way passage from full-time employment to full-time leisure. (See the Box in Chapter 2, p. 65, on midcourse.) Indeed, surveys of baby boomers age 33 to 52 indicate that 80 percent of them intend to work at least part time after retiring (Lewis, 1999a). In a national survey of retirement attitudes, 61 percent of retirees and 70 percent of nonretirees said that retirement is a new beginning, an opportunity to be active and involved in their communities, start new activities, and set new goals (Lewis, 1999a). Similarly, Savishinsky (2001, p. 55) describes retirement as "marked by a rebirth of passion and purpose," with opportunities for diversification, enrichment, development of the self, and service to others. The coming wave of retirees wants far more than unlimited leisure; rather, they seem to want lives that are purposeful, useful, and productive. "Today's 50-, 60-, and 70-year-olds—and certainly tomorrow's—are unwilling to go quietly into their fathers' retirement lifestyle" (Moen, 2003, p. 91).

Clearly, the economy and its requirements are changing, along with the social needs of a demographically changing population (Morris & Bass, 1988). There is a structural lag as institutions, attitudes, and stereotypes fail to keep pace with the current realities and possibilities of an aging society. It is in the best interest of the individual and society to promote the productive involvement of those older workers who are redefining traditional ideas about career, retirement, age, and gender. A new sales job is under way.

Importance of Leisure over the Life Span

The meaning of leisure has evolved over the centuries. To the ancient Greeks, work was viewed as a means to valued leisure (defined as mental, physical, and social activities, especially music and contemplation), the goal of which was self-development and increased competency (Moen, 2003). With industrialization and the rise of the Puritan ethic, leisure became increasingly valued not as a goal in itself, but as R and R—a means to be better prepared for work. In the past, opportunities for leisure were severely limited. As we have seen, retirement as an exit from paid employment is a recent phenomenon. What is the meaning and importance of leisure in the 21st century?

RETIREMENT IS DEAD. IT'S BEEN REPLACED BY A NOVEL CONCEPT CALLED LIVING.

Who decided that at the age of 65 it was time to hit the brakes, start acting your age, and smile sweetly as the world spins by? Definitely not you. So we've packaged a unique set of tools, including annuities, 401(k)s, IRAs, mutual funds, and life insurance for you and your family. Everything you need to lay the groundwork for your next grand adventure. Whether that's finishing law school or turning your genius for the perfect omelet into a corner cafe. Because when you turn 65, the concept of retirement will be the only thing that's old and tired. For a free brochure, call 1-800-AETNA-60 or visit us at http://www.aetna.com.

Build for Retirement. Manage for Life.™

This ad reflects a number of important aspects of retirement at the turn of the 20th century, including changing conceptions of older adults and retirement itself, along with the importance of financial planning.
Courtesy of AETNA Retirement Services and Ammirati Puris Lintas, Inc., New York.

We often mistakenly think of retirement as the end of the productive period in life, to be followed by . . . we are not sure what. In a work-oriented society such as ours, this is a milestone event. During the 20th century, the time spent in working was cut by almost half, to an average of 14 percent of the hours that an average person lives (Dychtwald & Flower, 1989). During the same period, the average workweek dropped from 70 to 37 hours, weekends and evenings became private time off, vacations became common, and holidays grew like Topsy. All of this means that **leisure,** the time to do things one is not obligated to do and that are done for pleasure, which was once a rare commodity, has become commonplace.

Leisure does not have a very good reputation in American culture. Perhaps you have heard the phrase "Idle hands are the devil's playground"? An alternative view, harkening back to the Greeks, is that leisure should not be thought of merely as activity that is a frivolous waste of time—the dangerous polar opposite of work. Rather, leisure activity can be purposeful and goal oriented and make an important contribution to the quality of life. It can be a time for rest, surely, but also contemplation, scholarship, and self-realization. In fact, our words *scholar* and *school* derive from the Greek word for leisure, *skhole* (Dychtwald & Flower, 1989). So, leisure can be enjoyed for its intrinsic value, as "activity that is chosen for some anticipated experience, an action with meaning rather than simply a void of obligation" (Kelly, 1988, p. 109).

What do the first cohorts in our history to enjoy extended periods of earned leisure have to tell us about their experience? Typically, retired people report that they are busy and active (Kunkel, 1989, Savishinsky, 2000). Many enrich their lives and those of others through volunteer work. One place to go to find opportunities is the National Senior Service Corps (www.seniorcorps.org), which connects volunteers with programs. Remember that constructive use of time, purposeful activities, and interpersonal contact are the main determinants of retirement satisfaction (Higginbottom et al., 1993) and contribute to overall subjective well-being and physical and mental health (Chapter 6). Further, stimulating leisure activities benefit cognitive function (Chapter 5). Retirees also engage in the same kinds of nonwork activities that nonretired people do, simply reinvesting the "extra eight hours a day" in more of the same activities. They offer insights on the value of their newfound leisure: "The new freedom of my personal schedule is a delight. I can read, take a walk, sit in the garden, take a trip, as I wish. With fewer obligations, I have gained personal tranquility, I have time to enjoy my friends" (Miletti, 1984, p. 47). More generally, "Retirement is a very valuable time of life. There is time to know and grow in a different way" (p. 178). One of Savishinsky's (2000, p. 3) research subjects captured it eloquently: "Retirement is the gift of time, but its real burden is the rediscovery of choice, the responsibility for making up your own life."

As work patterns continue to change, we may see a new combination of work and leisure, sprinkled more evenly across life periods, as well as a new vision of leisure as a productive, fulfilling, expressive activity, and a source of well-being (Dychtwald & Flower, 1989). As we reinvent the meaning and the process of working and retiring in the 21st century, individuals have an opportunity to define retirement, rather than allowing retirement to define them (Savishinsky, 2000).

Concept Review 8.4

- Retirement as we know it today is a relatively new life stage that emerged in the 20th century and gained momentum after World War II. It is the product of economic and social trends and responds to the needs of both society and the individual.

- Most retirement research is based on cohorts of White males who are currently retired, though there are a number of studies currently under way to address other cohorts as well as females and ethnic minorities.

- The decision to retire is complex and based on a variety of factors that appear to vary by gender and ethnicity.

- Retirement should be viewed as a developmental process rather than an isolated event.

- Because financial status is a major predictor of retirement adjustment and satisfaction, the economics of retirement (Social Security, pension plans, and individual savings) are of considerable importance.

- Retirement as a social phenomenon continues to evolve in response to changes at both the macrosystem and microsystem levels.

REVIEW QUESTIONS

Nature of Work

1. How is choosing an occupation equivalent to choosing a way of life?
2. Discuss the various needs that work may fulfill.
3. Describe the major changes occurring in the labor market and the labor force.
4. Assess the impact of these changes for occupational choice and preparation as well as for the workplace and the nation.

Career Development

1. Describe the major elements of the career cycle.
2. Identify the causes of and the resulting changes in the traditional view of career development.
3. What are the major influences that shape occupational choice?
4. Identify the major idea behind Holland's personality orientation typology.
5. Discuss the four major developmental tasks of the novice period in Levinson's theory of men's adult development.
6. Assess the applicability of this model to women's development, based on the Levinsonian studies reviewed by Roberts and Newton.

Gender and Work: Women's Career Paths and Special Career Issues

1. Describe the changes that have taken place in women's work in the 20th and 21st centuries.

2. Compare and contrast men's and women's career paths and work experiences.
3. Differentiate among the three views of multiple roles: the role enhancement/role expansion, role strain, and role context perspectives.

Retirement and Leisure

1. Provide a brief overview of the history of retirement in the 20th and 21st centuries.
2. Identify the major research limitations in studies of retirement and their implications for our understanding of this issue.
3. What factors play a significant role in the decision to retire, and how are the predictors of women's retirement different from those of men?
4. Discuss the phases in Atchley's model of the retirement process.
5. Evaluate the crisis and continuity theories of retirement adjustment.
6. What factors affect adjustment to retirement?
7. Identify and refute the six major misconceptions of the Social Security system.
8. Are pensions likely to increase or decrease as a source of retirement income in the future?
9. Explain the trend toward early retirement and discuss its continued feasibility.
10. Evaluate the statement that leisure is simply a frivolous waste of time.

KEY TERMS

bridge job, 337
career, 311
career primary track, 325
career self-efficacy, 316
continuity theory of retirement adaptation, 338
crisis theory of retirement adaptation, 337
dependency ratio, 324
discontinuous work history, 342
Dream, 319
dual-earner/dual-career family, 322

early retirement, 345
feminization of poverty, 327
glass ceiling, 325
human wealth span, 349
labor force participation rate, 322
leisure, 350
means test, 341
mentor, 319
mommy track, 325
novice phase, 318
occupational segregation, 326

portable pension benefits, 343
retirement incentive program (RIP), 345
role context perspective, 332
role enhancement/role expansion perspective, 330
role strain perspective, 331
Social Security, 340
special woman, 319
vested pension benefits, 343
wage gap, 306

9 Physical Development and Aging

FOR A NUMBER OF YEARS, I have shared an office suite with my friend Ed. Known to be one of the most productive, reliable, and cooperative faculty members, Ed is also well liked by students and sought after for his expertise by community agencies. He is also, I might add, good-looking and quite a snappy dresser. I just heard that Ed would be retiring at the end of this academic year. I assumed he was taking advantage of the early retirement option available at our institution. And then I was told that my friend Ed is 74 years old! Later that day, I saw Paul Newman on a TV talk show. Still pretty darn gorgeous for a guy born in 1925. *Seventy-five.* What's your mental stereotype of age 75? Both of these men—oh, I could think of lots of women, too—some famous like Jane Fonda and some not, like my mom—epitomize one of the underlying themes of this chapter. People age differently, and successful aging is increasingly within our grasp. Well, Ed. I'll miss you. Here's to another 74.

We are benefactors of what Robert Butler (1988) has called the **longevity revolution**— the dramatic 27-year increase in average life expectancy that occurred in the 20th century (a gain nearly equal to that accomplished during the preceding 5,000 years) and its transforming social, economic, cultural, political, and personal implications. Has the greater quantity of life brought with it greater quality as well? Are our later years ones of health and vigor, or extended periods of disability and decline? Are we living better or merely living longer? This question constitutes the central focus of this and the following chapter, in which we address biological aspects of development in adulthood.

We begin by discussing the nature of aging itself. Then, following an overview of some physical changes that normally occur in adulthood, we turn to a review of the major theories of biological aging. In the course of the chapter, we will discover that for us, perhaps more than any other group in human history, the prospect of growing older holds brighter promise than ever before.

What Is This Thing Called Aging?

Though people have been aging since the beginning of time, scientific interest has only recently shifted from concern with early development and the acute infectious illnesses of childhood to an explosion of interest in adulthood, aging, and the chronic degenerative conditions that disable so many in later life. Fueled by the demographic changes whirling through Western societies, researchers have begun to illuminate the biological changes that characterize adulthood and the multiple forces that bring them about. They have discovered that much of what we thought we knew about aging is really myth, stereotype, and misconception.

Primary versus Secondary Aging

A first step in any scientific undertaking is to clearly define the object of study. Yet, despite the widespread use of the term by laypeople and experts alike, aging remains an elusive concept. There is at present no consensus on the nature of the fundamental biological process of aging, and thus no widely accepted formal definition exists (Achenbaum & Levin, 1989; Arking, 1991; Hayflick, 1994, 2003).

Efforts to clarify the nature of aging often make a distinction between primary and secondary aging (Busse, 1969). **Primary aging** refers to the normal and intrinsic processes of biological aging that are genetically programmed and that take place with the passage of time, despite good health and the absence of disease. These effects are considered to be primary in that they are fundamental and basic. A good example is menopause in women.

In contrast, **secondary aging** refers to age-related declines that are pathological and result from extrinsic factors, including disease, environmental influences, and behavior— for example, the effect of ultraviolet light exposure on cataract formation, noise pollution on hearing loss, or smoking on respiratory disease (Butler, 1988; Williams, 1992). Inadequate nutrition may be the direct cause of one-third to one-half of the health problems among the elderly (Hendricks & Hendricks, 1986). Thus, symptoms once attributed to aging may instead be the product of poor diet. These effects are referred to as secondary because, while they are often associated with age, people can theoretically age without experiencing them.

Let's examine primary aging in more detail.

Characteristics of Primary Aging

Conceptions of primary aging generally include the following common elements:

- A complex process of age-related structural and functional change over time
- Cumulative in its effects
- Consisting of changes that are deleterious (that is, they reduce function)
- Progressive (they take place gradually)
- Intrinsic (not due to an external cause)
- Inevitable (occurring under even optimal genetic and environmental circumstances)
- Universal (manifested in all members of a given gender of the species)
- Irreversible
- Begins after physical and reproductive maturity is reached
- Culminates in death (Arking, 1991; Kohn, 1985; Strehler, 1982; Williams, 1992)

Exposure to the sun contributes to the formation of cataracts and to wrinkling and cancer of the skin. These effects illustrate secondary aging.

Environmental factors can modify the primary aging process. For example, sun exposure appears to accelerate the aging of the skin. Similarly, primary aging can influence the secondary aging process, as when an older individual experiences a more severe reaction to infection. Though we cannot always distinguish between the two, primary aging is generally identifiable by its inevitability, universality, and irreversibility, while secondary aging appears among only a part of the population, is related to extrinsic factors such as behavior and socioeconomic status (though genetic traits may influence their effect), and may therefore be prevented or perhaps reversed. Secondary aging can be thought of as superimposed over the primary aging process (Schroots, 1988). Thus, "primary aging processes can be considered to represent the necessary or core aspects of aging, while secondary processes correspond to all the other factors often associated with increased age, and that frequently contribute to the observed levels of . . . performance, but which are not inevitable consequences of aging" (Salthouse, 1991b, p. 20). We will address these extrinsic factors in greater detail in Chapter 10.

CRITICAL THINKING QUESTION

Why would it be important to determine whether age-related changes occurring in an individual were the result of primary or secondary aging?

From Pessimism to Optimism

Our understanding of aging has evolved from a "litany of decrements" to the realization that, for years, "we allowed ourselves to attribute to age that which was due to disease, disability, and social adversity" (Butler, 1988, p. 145). In other words, we confused primary with secondary aging. For example, senile dementia (severe cognitive impairment among the old) was once considered a normal part of the aging process, something to be expected in advanced age. On the contrary, we now know that, far from being normal or inevitable, these cognitive impairments are the result of a specific organic brain injury or disease, most often Alzheimer's disease (see Chapter 11).

The fact that physiological or cognitive deficits are *correlated* with age does not necessarily indicate they they are *caused* by age—or by an underlying aging process. They may instead represent the effects of extrinsic agents working over a long period of time. For example, though the risk of lung cancer increases with age, it is not a normal outcome of growing older. Rather, in many cases it represents the end product of years of exposure to cigarette smoke. As Arking (1991) suggests, we have probably overemphasized the losses associated with increasing age, perhaps a result of the fact that much of the early research on aging took place in medical school geriatrics programs, where clinical samples were composed of the sick—not the "normal"—elderly. Though they lacked external validity, results of these studies were broadly generalized. The resulting myths, stereotypes, and distortions in our understanding of aging are slowly giving way to an appreciation of the distinction between normal aging and disease. The difficulty is in identifying what *normal* aging really is. The point here is that aging does not equal disease.

Current Conceptions of Aging

Beyond this basic distinction between primary and secondary aging, and as a result of the increased research attention focused on aging in recent years, a new and more accurate picture of normal, age-related biological change has emerged. Our understanding is enhanced by the growing availability of longitudinal data being generated by studies such as the Baltimore Longitudinal Study of Aging (BLSA), discussed in Chapter 1. These studies have debunked many of the myths of aging, which were based on earlier, flawed research. For example, cross-sectional observations of supposedly normal samples between 20 and 80 years of age led to the conclusion that kidney function declined with age. More recent analyses from the BLSA suggest no evidence of such decline (Williams, 1992). More than 2,500 volunteers ranging in age from 17 to 97 have participated in the BLSA since it began in 1958, traveling to Baltimore every two years for two and a half days of tests. These include a complete physical as well as tests of bone density, aerobic capacity, hearing, reaction time, glucose tolerance, lung function, and so on. There are 30 to 40 research projects under way at any one time. Attempts to recruit a more diverse sample of volunteers in recent years will increase the external validity of future findings. Research on normal aging will continue to benefit from this and other longitudinal studies currently under way. Some of the major elements of a newly emerging conception of aging are described below.

Development versus Aging: Is It All Downhill from Here?

The traditional distinction between development and aging can be summed up by the following analogy. Picture a series of stairs leading up the left side to a platform, and another series of stairs descending from the platform on the right. The platform symbolizes biological maturity. The steps leading upward represent the growth and development typical of childhood and adolescence, while those descending on the right signify the decline and deterioration traditionally thought to typify adulthood and aging. The structure also represents a timeline, beginning at the left, with the peak of development—the plateau—maintained for only a short time before decline begins.

This, in essence, is the decline or decrementalist view of age-related change in adulthood, heavily influenced by biological conceptions of the human life cycle (Schroots, 1988). In short, according to this view, after a brief period of maximal functioning, it is all downhill.

Baltes (1987) and others have argued against this dichotomy between development and aging, maintaining that each stage of development includes both gains and losses, though the proportion of each may shift with age (see Figure 1.6, p. 9), and suggesting that the term *development* be used to refer to age-related changes in either direction throughout the life span. (See Chapter 1 for an in-depth discussion of the elements of the life-span perspective.)

How might the application of this life-span perspective be beneficial as applied to the study of the biological changes that occur with age? First and foremost, a rejection of the decline view means a rejection of the notion that disease and disability are inevitable correlates of increasing age. This is not to deny the existence of some age-related decline, but rather to question the extent and the cause of such decline. Second, a life-span view motivates us to look beyond the genes for environmental and behavioral influences on development, and to identify factors that maximize development and health and prevent and forestall illness and decline.

While aging is increasingly conceptualized within the context of life-span development, the fact remains that much of the literature on biological development continues to use the term *aging*. So, while the life-span perspective constitutes the theoretical position adopted in this text, to be consistent with research and theory in this area we will follow convention and use the term *aging* to refer to age-related change that occurs after biological maturity is reached. The relationship between aging and development remains a point of controversy within the field (Achenbaum & Levin, 1989).

Ecology of Aging

The realization that aging is not a purely biological phenomenon has resulted in greater appreciation of the role of the environment in the aging process. People do not age in a vacuum. An ecological view of aging recognizes the complex and reciprocal interaction of the individual with the multiple layers of the environment (see Chapter 2). In other words, aging is the result of genetics and biology interacting with social, psychological, and historical influences. An integrated, multidisciplinary approach is required to understand it (Siegler, 1989). Biological reductionism—the tendency to attribute all change to biological aging—is to be avoided (Maddox, 1991), as is radical behaviorism, which attributes all change to environmental forces (Birren, 1988a). Either limits our understanding of the complex interplay between intrinsic and extrinsic forces acting on the individual.

Accumulating Effects over Time

Aging does not happen overnight. It is a complex process influenced by many factors, the effects of which accumulate over time. Birren (1988a) uses the analogy of repeatedly hitting a table with a hammer. Though the table eventually collapses, this is due not only to the final blow, but to the accumulating consequences of many small events interacting with qualities of the wood (for example, its hardness) and its environment (for instance, humidity). And so it is with human aging. What we see is the cumulative effect of years of experiences interacting with individuals' genetic qualities and current circumstances. A key research task has to do with identifying the antecedents of decline and disability in old age: "Explanations of aging must include not only biological factors, but also information about the social causes of differences in an environment, and the personal behavior which over a life time can have a great effect on health and mortality" (Birren, 1988a, p. 39).

Interindividual Variability

Attendance at a high school class reunion brings one point home clearly: people age at different rates and in different ways. In addition, differences between individuals increase over time, as the effects of both genetic and experiential variables accumulate (Schroots, 1988). The resulting heterogeneity is most evident at advanced ages. For example, one 75-year-old may be a much-respected Supreme Court justice, while another is confined to a long-term care institution, unable to remember his own name. So one indisputable conclusion has been reached: there is enormous diversity in how people age, and the range of individual variation increases as we get older (Hayflick, 1994). As we have said, chronological age is not a good indicator of functional age. Discovering the sources of this variability constitutes an important research issue.

Intraindividual Variability

When we attempt to describe the nature of age-related change in the body, we are immediately struck by the fact that the body does not age in a uniform, synchronized way. Instead, there are innate variations in the nature, rate, and timing of age-related decrements in functioning in different parts of the body. Different organs and systems reach their peaks at different times: about half of the body's internal organs reach their peak weight in the 30s, and the other half sometime between the 40s and the 70s. Thus, while some systems may be in a period of peak efficiency, others may be declining and others still developing. As we have repeatedly said, each stage is a mixture of growth and loss. There is no simple, overall pattern of growth that characterizes change across organs and systems (Arking, 1991). Instead, biological development involves an innate heterogeneity in growth patterns.

Decline with Age Is Not Universal

Some aspects of the body's functioning show no evidence of deterioration with age. For example, a study by Clarkson and Dedrick (1988) found that although there is an age-related decline in muscle strength over age 35, comparisons of women over 60 with college-age samples indicated no difference in the ability of muscle to repair and adapt to damage. So, while we tend to focus on areas of decline, we should remember that decay is not universal in every aspect of the body's functioning.

The Question of Functional Decline

When considering age-related change, it is critical to determine whether decrements in an organ system have any meaningful effect on the body's ability to function effectively. The body is "overbuilt": most of our organs and systems have a large reserve capacity, an extra capability not used under normal circumstances. It is a little bit like cars that have an extra gallon or two of gas in an auxiliary tank, which can be drawn on if the main tank runs out. Thus, age-related decrements may be hardly noticeable until they reach a certain threshold level, and that may be quite late in life, or only under conditions of maximal stress (Griffiths & Meechan, 1990). The question is, How much change is necessary to make a diffcrence?

Successful Aging

In a biological sense, **successful aging** (also referred to as healthy, optimal, or productive aging) refers to individuals who show minimal physiological losses across a number of functions compared to younger individuals (Arking, 1991). Like my friend Ed, mentioned in the chapter opener. What is the key to successful aging? Do you have to be lucky enough to inherit "good genes"? Rowe and Kahn (1987) make a distinction between "usual" and "successful" aging. Whereas in usual aging, external factors advance the primary aging process, in successful aging they have either a neutral or a positive effect. "The number of programmed inevitable and decremental aging changes that occur is probably much less than we have previously believed possible," Arking (1991, p. 166) notes. In fact, Rowe and Kahn (1998) state that genetic factors account for only 30 percent of the physical aspects of aging, leaving the rest to lifestyle and environment. So we have a lot more control over our aging and health than we used to think. Aging is no longer viewed as fixed or immutable, but rather as plastic, or modifiable through a variety of interventions—medical, behavioral, and environmental. Although we cannot stop the clock altogether, we can slow its rate and change its tone. And while the limits of this modifiability are unknown, the new view of aging brings with it the hope of a vigorous, healthy, productive period at the end of life. As the scientific maxim goes, "If you want to understand something, try to change it." Researchers in the field of aging are attempting to do just that.

Concept Review 9.1

- Scientists have only recently begun to study the biological changes that characterize adulthood and the interacting forces that bring them about.

- It is important to distinguish between primary and secondary aging.

- Conceptions of aging are changing dramatically, based on the growing availability of longitudinal data.

- Aging is to some extent modifiable. Thus, healthy, productive, successful aging may be an increasing reality.

Physical Development in Adulthood

The body reaches maturity sometime around age 25 to 30, considered to be the period of peak physical vitality and health. What exactly happens to the body after that, as we age? The exterior signs of aging—the graying and thinning of hair, the change in body proportions, and so on—are easily recognizable. But what about the more subtle changes, the ones going on inside the body and its various systems? Perhaps surprisingly, given our stereotypes of aging, with few exceptions our organ systems have the potential to maintain essentially the same biological function until very late in life—or at least as late in life as researchers have to date studied them (Williams, 1992).

This section provides a survey of some of the changes we can expect as we grow older. Though not by any means a comprehensive review, it should provide a feel for some of the normal changes in structure and function that typically occur as individuals move through the years of adulthood. The brain and nervous system were covered in Chapter 5. Here, we will discuss aging changes affecting the skin and connective tissue; the skeletal system; muscle tissue; the cardiovascular, respiratory, immune, endocrine, and reproductive systems; and the senses. A number of pathological conditions will also be covered.

Changes in the Skin and Connective Tissue

While it is probably true that nobody ever died of wrinkles, the aging of the skin has great emotional significance in our culture. Witness the astonishing growth in cosmetic surgery and the marketing of products that claim to restore that youthful glow. Women seem to be especially threatened by overt signs of aging because of the emphasis traditionally placed on women's appearance. While the aging of the skin has more psychological than medical significance, its impact on the sense of self should probably not be underestimated (Arking, 1991).

The skin is made up of several layers. The outer layer is the *epidermis,* the boundary between our bodies and the external world, where new skin cells are constantly being produced. The epidermis contains the pigment melanin, which gives the skin color. The *dermis* is a supportive layer of connective tissue (collagen and elastin) to which the epidermis adheres. It allows the skin to be flexible, stretch without tearing, and bounce back. The innermost layer is the *hypodermis,* a looser layer of connective tissue and varying amounts of fat cells, which acts as a shock absorber, storage depot, and insulation against heat loss.

As we age, the epidermis adheres less tightly to the dermis. The dermis thins, the weave of collagen fibers within it becomes looser, and the number of elastin fibers declines. In addition, some of the padding found in the fat cells of the hypodermis is lost. As a result, the skin becomes looser and more prone to wrinkles and sagging. The fact that men have a thicker dermis than women may partially explain why their skin is somewhat more resistant to the effects of age (Arking, 1991). Excessive exposure to the sun accelerates these changes.

Before we move on, we should expand a bit on the nature and role of **collagen.** Collagen is a protein composed of large, fibrous, elastic molecules. It is the basic structural component of connective tissue; as such, it is found in all body organs, bones, between cells, and so on. It occurs in pure form in tendons. Because of its elasticity, collagen acts as a rubber band, stretching and regaining its original shape. The loss of this elasticity with age has adverse effects not only on the skin, but also on bones, muscles, and organs. For example, muscles in the heart may become more rigid and unable to bounce back from strain, or bones may become more brittle. Despite the claims of cosmetic companies to the contrary, collagen cannot be absorbed through the skin.

Changes in the Skeletal System

The major age-related change in the skeletal system is the loss of bone. Contrary to what you might think, bone is not static but dynamic—that is, it is constantly being remodeled throughout life in a process by which old bone is reabsorbed and new bone is developed. Starting around age 30, the amount of bone reabsorbed begins to exceed that being synthesized, especially in the spongy interior layer of bone tissue that gives our skeletal system its strength. The remaining bone is left more porous, weaker, and more prone to fracture. The more bone mass one has as a young adult, the greater the likelihood of withstanding the normal process of bone loss later in life. In other words, sufficient reserves will be in place to maintain bone strength. Changes in collagen discussed above also contribute to increased brittleness. When a brittle bone is stressed, it is more likely to break cleanly, like a dry stick (Whitbourne, 1985). Such "clean" fractures are less likely to heal (Arking, 1991). Younger bone, on the other hand, bends and cracks like a green twig but is less likely to break cleanly.

Diet and exercise are two very important contributors to healthy bones. The body needs a constant supply of calcium. If insufficient quantities are taken in through the diet, the body will release stored calcium from the bones. Years of low calcium intake have a cumulative weakening effect and may be one of the most important contributors to the development of osteoporosis (see below). Foods rich in calcium include low-fat dairy products (such as milk, yogurt, cheese), seafood (for example, shrimp, sardines, salmon), and dark, leafy green vegetables (like kale, spinach, and broccoli), almonds, and foods fortified with calcium. Weight-bearing exercise (such as walking, jogging, cycling, or low-impact aerobics) is an excellent—perhaps the easiest—way to build bone mass and can improve the skeletal strength of individuals at any age. The maxim "use it or lose it" really applies here, as the bone responds to physical stress by forming new bone cells. Training for the Olympics is not necessary to get the benefits; even normal daily activity is helpful. Vitamin D is also important for strengthening bones, and the best source is exposure to ultraviolet light. Those who are disabled or living in institutional settings may benefit from regular excursions outdoors, even on gray days.

Osteoporosis

Osteoporosis (or porous bone) is a pathological condition that can be thought of as an exaggeration of the normal process of bone loss described above. It is a symptomless disease characterized by bone loss and deterioration of the skeleton leading to bone fragility and increased risk of fractures. Prevention is key, as osteoporosis can be treated but not cured. Treatment requires diagnosis, which can only be done through a bone mineral density (BMD) test, a painless, noninvasive procedure that uses x-ray technology to measure bone mass. Osteoporosis is defined as 25 percent bone loss compared to a healthy young adult, or 2.5 standard deviations below the mean on a BMD. The most recognizable sign is a curved or hunched back—osteoporosis can lead to vertebral fractures, resulting in pain, disfigurement, and loss of height. Fractures are also likely in the hip and wrist, though any bone in the body may be affected. The discomfort not only interferes with activities of daily living, such as walking, bending, cooking, and so on, but these activities (or even a simple sneeze or cough) can themselves cause fractures as the bones become more and more fragile (Licata, 1987). Bone fractures and their consequences increase vulnerability to other illnesses, such as pneumonia. Among those 50 and over, 24 percent die in the first year following a hip fracture (Brandt, 2001). Of those who survive, only one-quarter of those who break a hip after age 55 ever sufficiently heal to walk without assistance again (McAuliffe, 1988).

Women are at much greater risk of developing osteoporosis, especially after menopause. One of every two women and one in four men over 50 will develop an osteoporotic fracture. The sex difference is large, with the average male losing about 12 percent of his bone mass over a 30-year period, while a woman loses about 25 percent of hers in the same amount of time (Arking, 1991). Estrogen seems to protect bones in two ways: first, by suppressing the rate of reabsorption, and second, by increasing the body's ability to use dietary calcium. As estrogen levels fall following menopause, there is, then, a corresponding increase in bone reabsorption and a decrease in calcium utilization. Postmenopausal women have been estimated to lose 1.5 percent of their bone per year (Schlenker, 1984). Osteoporosis is a major cause of fractures in elderly women each year, one of the main reasons women enter nursing homes, and a leading cause of death among elderly women.

Risk factors associated with osteoporosis include genetic, nutritional, and lifestyle factors, as listed in Table 9.1. For example, the low bone density that leads to osteoporosis is under strong genetic control. An Australian research team (Morrison et al., 1994) has identified a single gene that accounts for a significant portion of an individual's overall risk. The gene influences how well the body utilizes vitamin D to build new bone. The beneficial allele (version of the gene) is recessive. Those who are homozygous recessive (genotype bb) have the densest bones, while those who are homozygous dominant (BB) have the least dense bones. Heterozygotes (Bb) fall in between. The BB combination could make an older woman four times more likely to experience a hip fracture. Variations in the presence of the different versions of this gene may contribute to variations in risk among different ethnic groups. The hope is that this genetic marker might be used to identify children prone to osteoporosis and prevent its development. Those at risk could be encouraged to consume adequate calcium, get regular physical exercise, and refrain from smoking, in order to build sufficient bone by early adulthood and retain it into old age. Other genes are suspected of involvement as well.

The progress of osteoporosis can be stopped and even reversed if it is diagnosed. Though the screening is widely available, many are unaware of it and most of those at risk aren't tested.

Exercise, estrogen therapy, and increased calcium intake may slow the rate of bone loss among postmenopausal women. Postmenopausal women who don't take estrogen, along with teenagers, pregnant women, and women who are breast-feeding, are advised to consume 1,500 milligrams of calcium a day. Adult women who are premenopausal require 1,000 milligrams a day. The problem is that the average adult diet includes under 600 milligrams. Vitamin D is also necessary, as it enables the body to process calcium.

TABLE 9.1 *Factors Associated with Increased Risk of Osteoporosis*

Genetic Factors	Nutritional Factors	Lifestyle Factors
Female	Low body weight	Smoking
Fair-skinned	Low dietary calcium intake	Lack of exercise
Small frame	High caffeine consumption	Some medications
Family history	High alcohol consumption	
	Chronic crash dieting	

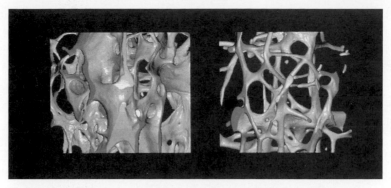

The low bone density associated with osteoporosis is evident by comparing these two images obtained by x-ray microtomography. The image on the left shows the bone structure of the vertebrae of a 50-year-old, while that on the right shows the change in bone structure and loss of bone mass in the vertebrae of a 70-year-old affected by osteoporosis. Osteoporosis is a major threat to the independence and survival of older women.

The best source of calcium is a varied diet, which contains vitamins and minerals that aid the body's use of calcium and help to build bone. The calcium content of a variety of foods is listed in Table 9.2. Drugs such as raloxifene, calcitonin, risedronate, and alendronate can help prevent or reverse osteoporosis. A number of other medications are in development.

The interaction of factors that lead to osteoporosis provides an excellent illustration of the relationship between primary and secondary aging. In this case, though the normal age-related loss of bone mass is not the same as osteoporosis, when combined with other factors such as poor nutrition and lack of exercise, osteoporosis may develop. Arking (1991, p. 211) states that "all aging changes represent a decrement in function." He goes on to suggest that these decrements serve as necessary, though not sufficient, preconditions for the possible development of pathology. An excellent source of information is the National Institutes of Health Osteoporosis and Related Bone Diseases National Resource Center (www.osteo.org).

Osteoarthritis

The most common form of arthritis, **osteoarthritis** is a degenerative joint disease that involves a breakdown of joint cartilage. Symptoms include pain, stiffness, and swelling.

TABLE 9.2 *Calcium Content of Selected Foods*

1 cup yogurt	345 mg	1 cup 2% cottage cheese	166 mg
1 cup skim milk	302 mg	¾ c. fortified oatmeal	163 mg
1 cup 2% milk	297 mg	1 cup cooked (fresh) broccoli	136 mg
½ cup tofu, firm	258 mg	1 cup cooked soybeans	131 mg
1 cup cooked turnip greens	252 mg	2 sardines	92 mg
1 oz. cheese	250 mg	¼ cup almonds	92 mg

Source: National Osteoporosis Foundation, 1991.

It is an extreme form of age-related changes that take place in the tendons, ligaments, cartilage, and fluid that lubricates the joints. It most often strikes in the knees, hips, and spine, and at its worst may leave the individual partially or totally disabled. Injuries, poor posture, or immobilization may be predisposing factors.

Changes in Skeletal Muscle

In humans, skeletal muscle is composed of postmitotic tissue. This means that muscle cells are established during fetal development and do not divide further after birth. So all of the muscle cells we will ever have are present when we are born, and once muscle cells die, they are not replaced. Exercise stimulates the growth of skeletal muscle by leading to an enlargement of existing muscle fibers. A number of factors can lead to muscle atrophy, or a decline in muscle mass, including lack of use, malnutrition, and denervation (changes in the nerves such that the muscle is not properly stimulated). The result is a decrease in either the size or the number of muscle fibers, or both (McCarter, 1978), and a corresponding loss of muscle strength and reactivity.

Because muscle tissue is so responsive to extrinsic influences, it is difficult to determine the nature and extent of intrinsic, primary aging processes and their effects (Arking, 1991). Some deterioration of muscle tissue probably takes place with age (McCarter, 1978), with muscle tissue eventually being replaced with fat. In addition to aging-related changes in the muscle tissue itself, concurrent changes in the circulatory and nervous systems as well as in the tendons and ligaments may also contribute to a decrease in muscle strength. However, there is reason to believe that changes in muscle strength are largely the result of factors extrinsic to the muscle and are not inevitable. For example, laboratory tests of muscle fiber from older individuals found no functional differences in comparison to fibers from younger samples, despite some structural deterioration (McCarter, 1978). Exercise is an especially potent factor in the age-related changes in muscle. Lifestyle changes such as decreased physical activity with age may be a major contributor to muscle atrophy in older individuals.

Changes in the Cardiovascular System

The cardiovascular system (composed of the heart and blood vessels) is responsible for delivering nutrients to and carrying waste from the tissues of the body. Fewer age-related structural changes occur in this system than one would expect, given the fact that about half of older adults have some degree of cardiovascular disease and that it is a leading cause of death among middle-aged and older adults (Arking, 1991). Here again, it is important to distinguish between normal changes that occur as a result of primary aging processes, and changes that are the result of disease. Williams (1992) concludes that, biologically, the heart can function just as well in later as in earlier years as long as it is free from disease.

Arteriosclerosis

Arteriosclerosis is a pathological condition in which plaque begins to accumulate on the interior walls of the arteries, reducing blood flow. It is age related in that risk increases with age, but it is thought to be the outcome of a variety of both intrinsic and extrinsic factors interacting over a long period of time. One of these is high blood cholesterol. The process is believed to be set in motion early in life, culminating in disease in the later years of adulthood. This condition may produce a heart attack, angina, or stroke (Hayflick, 1994). The causes and prevention of cardiovascular disease will be discussed more fully in Chapter 10.

Changes in the Respiratory System

Vital capacity refers to the total amount of air that can be forced into or out of the lungs. Normally, much of this volume is held in reserve: even during exercise we generally use little more than 50 percent of it (Griffiths & Meechan, 1990). However, a progressive loss of about 50 percent of vital capacity occurs between the ages of 30 and 80 (Kohn, 1978), due largely to decreasing elasticity and greater rigidity of lung tissue. Though in a normal adult the lungs may still be able to perform their function sufficiently well, at levels of maximal exertion they may no longer be able to meet the body's oxygen needs (Arking, 1991). As a result, the elderly are less able to respond effectively to stresses that increase respiration, and they are at greater risk from environmental pollutants, smoking, and respiratory diseases such as asthma and emphysema, which further reduce vital capacity.

Emphysema

Emphysema is a disease that develops in response to chronic irritation of the bronchial tubes by smoke, repeated infections, or other irritants. The response to chronic irritation is production of excessive mucus within the airways, which gradually accumulates, restricting airflow to the lungs. Additional stress is placed on the heart, which attempts to compensate by increasing blood flow. Individuals with emphysema suffer "oxygen hunger."

Changes in the Immune System

The **immune system** protects us from infection through various responses that attack and destroy microorganisms (viruses, bacteria) and other foreign materials that have invaded the body. The immune system is also a key defense against cancer, detecting and destroying cancer cells. The principal components of the immune system are the bone marrow and the **thymus,** an endocrine gland located above the heart. The spleen and lymph nodes are also involved. The immune system produces a number of types of cells—for example, B and T lymphocytes (B cells originate in the bone, T cells originate in the bone and mature in the thymus), subtypes of which are variously sensitive to the presence of certain molecules (antigens) that trigger an immune response.

The immune, endocrine, and nervous systems communicate with and influence each other through a complex series of feedback mechanisms. These connections are both neuronal and hormonal. That is, the brain may communicate with the thymus directly through the nerves, or indirectly through the secretion of chemical messengers. For example, **glucocorticoids** released by the adrenal cortex during stress suppress specific aspects of immune function. This **immunosuppressive** effect may make the body more susceptible to disease, especially under conditions of prolonged stress. The loss of regulatory neurons in the hippocampus with age may make it difficult to control glucocorticoid levels and may thus partly explain the higher levels of cancer seen in the elderly (Arking, 1991).

For its part, the thymus, through secretions of the hormone **thymosin,** may affect other components of these systems as well. Thymosin has a stimulating effect on immune function. For reasons that are unclear, the thymus begins to atrophy early in life, decreasing supplies of thymosin as well as reducing production of the full complement of lymphocytes. By age 50, most humans retain only 5 to 10 percent of the original mass of the thymus, and by age 60, the production of thymosin is undetectable (Hayflick, 1994). Some of these effects may be the result of changes in other systems with which the immune system interacts. The decline in immune system function may have important consequences for older adults. These consequences can include increased susceptibility to infectious diseases like pneumonia and the flu and increased likelihood of dying from them, increased cancer risk due to decreased surveillance, changes in blood vessel walls leading to arteriosclerosis, and an increase in autoimmune disorders such as rheumatoid arthritis or lupus (Schneider, 1992). Autoimmune disorders occur when the immune system begins to attack our own tissue. Studies suggest it may be possible to restore some of the immune system's lost function through treatment with thymosin.

Changes in the Endocrine System

The **endocrine system** is made up of the cells and tissues that produce chemical messengers called hormones. These are released into the blood and act on target cells. Like the immune system, the endocrine system affects every cell in the body, regulating such activities as growth, metabolism, reproduction, immune function, protein synthesis, and behavior. It is believed to play an important role in producing the changes associated with age. The levels of many hormones fall with age, including growth hormone (produced by the pituitary gland), testosterone, insulin, and thyroid hormone. Two age-related phenomena—menopause in women and enlargement of the prostate gland in men—are triggered by changes in the endocrine system. The reduced ability of older adults to recover from trauma or stress may be due to changes in the production or balance of certain key hormones or diminished ability of target tissue to respond to these chemicals (Hayflick, 1994). There is growing interest in hormone replacement therapy as a way of reversing the effects of aging, though its effectiveness and safety are not yet established.

Sleep Disturbances

Far from being a luxury, sufficient sleep is as important to health and well-being as diet and exercise. Though 100 years ago most adults slept about nine hours a night, today the median is six (Greer, 2004), leaving many adults moderately to severely sleep deprived. The fact that you don't feel tired is not an indicator of adequate sleep. Inadequate or lack of quality sleep can negatively affect all aspects of a person's life, including health, relationships, performance, productivity, and safety. Lack of sleep increases vulnerability to infection by suppression of immune function. Chronic sleep loss may increase the risk of a heart attack and hasten the onset and severity of diabetes, high blood pressure, and obesity. The benefits of sleep include improved health as well as increased attention span and memory, with benefits for learning, complex thought, and performance on a range of mental tasks. The brain appears to process and consolidate new information into long-term memory during periods of REM sleep, which predominate during the sixth and eighth hours of sleep. The brain also replenishes key neurotransmitters during REM cycles. Experimental studies have found that subjects' performance on memory tests improves without additional practice, providing they get enough sleep the night after the learning occurs. Sleep on subsequent nights cannot compensate. Depriving the brain of sufficient sleep thus interferes with memory formation and overall brain function.

Though all of us occasionally have trouble sleeping, disturbed sleep—for example, difficulty falling asleep or unwanted early morning wakefulness—becomes more prevalent with age (Morin, 1993). Occasional insomnia affects 30 to 40 percent of the general population (American Psychiatric Association, 1994) and rises to 50 to 60 percent among those age 60 and over; the rate of more serious and persistent sleep difficulties is between 10 and 35 percent among those over 65 (Libman, Creti, Amsel, Bender, & Fichten, 1997). Insomnia has been linked to a variety of factors, such as physical illness, pain, changes in central nervous system functioning, stress, and hormonal changes. In regard to the latter, one of the hormones thought to be involved in changing sleep-wake patterns is **melatonin,** a hormone produced by the pineal gland, in turn regulated by the hypothalamus (Haimov & Lavie, 1996). Melatonin is produced during the dark hours and reflects the light-dark cycle—high levels at night and low levels during the day. Melatonin production is abundant early in life and then declines. Changes in the secretion of melatonin with age may be associated with sleep disorders later in life. For example, Haimov and Lavie (1996) found significantly lower levels of melatonin as well as alterations in secretion patterns in elderly insomniacs as compared to matched controls. Because melatonin production is triggered by darkness, some researchers suspect that our artificially illuminated evenings and light pollution are suppressing its production, disrupting sleep and causing sleep pathology in some of us. The researchers caution that though exogenous melatonin may have some clinical use in the treatment of sleep disorders, we do not yet have reliable information about the long-term effects of its use. Other recommendations include practicing good sleep habits, such as avoiding the use of caffeine and alcohol after dinner and engaging in relaxation activities.

Changes in the Reproductive System

Though the reproductive systems of both males and females undergo some age-related changes, these decrements are much more extensive in the female. In the case of the human male, once puberty is reached and for the remainder of life, sperm are produced continuously and in large numbers. Levels of the sex hormone testosterone decline with age, though this does not seem to significantly impair male fertility. There does seem to be a general reduction in sexual interest, activity, and capacity, but great variability exists among men. Failure of potency (erectile dysfunction) is a common occurrence among older men and is often caused by vascular disease, though medications, thyroid disorders, and depression are among other causes (Morley, 1997). The efficacy of long-term testosterone replacement therapy is not yet known.

In the sexually mature female, one or the other of the two ovaries will release a mature egg cell into the Fallopian tubes each month. This egg cell or ovum may be available for fertilization by a sperm. Over the course of her lifetime, a woman may release about 500 ova, a fraction of the supply present in the ovaries at birth. Reproductive functions are ultimately under the control of the hypothalamus through secretion of hormones that stimulate the pituitary, which in turn releases hormones that influence the ovaries. The ovaries produce the female sex hormone **estrogen,** which not only regulates the menstrual cycle but influences as many as 300 other body functions, possibly through initiating gene activity that maintains normal function in those tissues. For example, it plays a role in the retention of calcium in the bones, causes thickening of the collagen that supports the skin, and influences the production of chemicals that affect mood.

Menopause

Menopause—the permanent cessation of menstruation and resulting loss of fertility—constitutes the major change that takes place in the female reproductive system. It normally occurs between the ages of 45 and 55, with the average at 50 or 51. Long considered a taboo topic and a stigma reflecting old age, menopause has emerged from the closet to become a prominent women's health issue. This is largely due to the huge number of baby boom women entering this period. While until the 20th century many women did not live long enough to reach menopause, or died shortly after their ovaries stopped functioning, today most women can expect to live about 30 years beyond age 50.

Menopause has both physiological and psychological significance, symbolizing for some the end of youth and femininity, while for others it brings freedom from fear of pregnancy and newfound vitality. Each woman's experience of menopause is different, the result of her own unique body chemistry, personality, and sociocultural background, which may influence the meaning she attaches to these reproductive changes. For most women, menopause is not a crisis; rather, most experience little difficulty (Gonyea, 1998). Increased scientific interest in this issue will ultimately benefit all women, removing the shroud of mystery and dispelling the misunderstandings and negative stereotypes that continue to surround this universal female experience (Mansfield, Jorgensen, & Yu, 1989).

The factors that initiate menopause are unclear; they may include age-related changes in the ovaries, the hypothalamus, or both. Because of their interconnections, any change in one could lead to a cascade of effects altering the activity of the other (Wise, 1986). Whatever initiates it, the most significant aspect of the process is a marked drop in estrogen levels, with widespread ramifications for tissues that rely on estrogen for their maintenance. The rate at which the estrogen supply diminishes is important to the woman's experience of menopause. For example, women who undergo surgical removal of the ovaries or chemotherapy experience a sudden loss of estrogen, with correspondingly greater severity of effect. In fact, much of what we thought we knew about menopause (and it was not pleasant) was the result of studies of these clinical samples. To this day, some confusion persists about what constitutes the "normal" experience of menopause (Mansfield, Jorgensen, & Yu, 1989).

CRITICAL THINKING QUESTION
Why would it be important to document the normal changes associated with menopause?

Women may experience symptoms of reproductive change up to a decade before menstruation actually stops. Generally, menstrual cycles become more irregular, further apart, and more variable in length from month to month. As with the male, the physiological changes associated with menopause need not interfere with sexuality. This is good news, since some evidence suggests that satisfying sexual relations are a positive indicator of longevity among women (Palmore, 1982). Other symptoms include hot flashes, drying and thinning of the skin (including vaginal dryness), redistribution of body weight, problems with short-term memory, and sleep disturbances.

Hot flashes, which occur to some degree in about 85 percent of menopausal women (Arking, 1991), seem to be especially troublesome. These bursts of heat and perspiration are the result of dilation of blood vessels in the skin. Though they vary widely in both frequency and severity (and some women do not experience them at all), they can occur up to 50 times a day, often disrupting sleep at night, and can last from a few seconds to an hour. They are unpleasant both for the experience of heat and excessive perspiration as well as for the chill that may follow. And they are embarrassing, striking unpredictably, whether a woman is at home preparing a meal or making an important presentation to a board of directors.

The consequences of menopause go well beyond symptoms of discomfort. Increased risk of both osteoporosis and heart attack are well documented. For decades the treatment of choice was **hormone replacement therapy (HRT),** particularly a combination of estrogen and progesterone (another female sex hormone), usually through daily pills or transdermal patches. HRT was touted not only for relief from the discomfort of symptoms such as hot flashes and disturbed sleep, but also as a protection from the more serious risks of heart disease and osteoporosis. All that changed in July 2002, when the National Institutes of Health prematurely halted one part of a landmark placebo-controlled longitudinal study of more than 16,000 women 50 to 79 years old that was designed to explore the long-term health effects of HRT. The study was part of the federally funded Women's Health Initiative (WHI), which will be discussed in more detail in Chapter 10. When the researchers analyzed the data they had collected five years into the study, they concluded that the risks to the experimental subjects, while small, outweighed the benefits and that the risks were great enough to discontinue the study. Specifically, the findings were a small but significant increase in risk of heart disease, breast cancer, stroke, and blood clots in the lungs. There were health benefits as well, including a lower risk of colon cancer and skeletal fractures (osteoporosis).

Questions remain about the effects of other types or dosages of hormone replacement, as well as nonhormonal prescription medications. There are also questions about the safety and effectiveness of over-the-counter products, the use of which has skyrocketed in recent years and which are not stringently regulated by the FDA.

Because each woman's medical history, family history, and lifestyle vary, she should consult her physician about the options available to her. For most women, the consensus is that HRT should not be used as a long-term treatment for disease prevention. Its main use is for short-term relief of the acute symptoms of menopause, when symptoms are severe and changes in lifestyle and nonhormonal strategies are ineffective. In those cases, the lowest possible dose should be prescribed for the shortest possible period of time.

Advances in medical treatment, changes in the opportunities available to middle-aged and older women, and a changing view of age and aging are likely to make the transition to menopause and beyond a more positive experience for women, now and into the future.

Changes in Sensory Capacity with Age

Sensory processes enable us to be aware of and interact with the external environment. And sensory abilities change with age. Diminished function of the sense organs reduces our capacity to stay in touch with what's going on around us and has important ramifications for our ability to live independently, to communicate, and for our social relationships, health, nutrition, and safety.

A loss of sensory information, particularly if it is severe, can also undermine higher-order mental abilities, which could explain some of the cognitive changes seen in older adults. A reduction in the sensory input reaching the brain—described by some as sensory impoverishment and sensory underload (Fozard, 1990; Sekuler & Blake, 1987)—reduces the brain's ability to respond to the environment as effectively, though this is probably not significant except in extreme cases. Age-related changes in the visual and auditory systems may undermine the functioning of working memory by impairing the efficiency of the visuospatial sketchpad and the phonological loop. Additionally, a generalized slowing of information processing with age could further aggravate the consequences of sensory losses, delaying response times to auditory and visual signals (Fozard, 1990). This might have implications for many behaviors, such as communication, driving, and so on. In more severe cases, the effects of sensory losses may be mistaken for signs of dementia (Sekuler & Blake, 1987).

Keep in mind that sensory aging normally occurs gradually, so that incremental changes may hardly be noticed until they reach the point where behavior is dramatically impaired. Some sensory changes may become apparent in middle age, though they become more pronounced—and harder to ignore—in late adulthood. Few people in their 70s are unaffected by at least some of them. But age of onset, rate, and magnitude of sensory change vary tremendously from person to person. Of all the senses, age changes in vision and hearing are by far the most studied and the best understood.

Vision

Because vision is the sense we rely on most, any change in visual ability has special significance. A number of age-related changes in the structure of the visual system affect seeing ability.

Older adults require more illumination to see well. Their vision will be most impaired in the dark, at dusk or twilight, or in dimly lit settings. This is due to various changes in the eye that limit the amount of light that reaches the retina, including lens clouding—or **cataracts**—and a smaller pupil—or **senile miosis.** Cataracts affect a majority of those over age 65 and, fortunately, are operable, resulting in over 2 million cataract surgeries annually in the United States alone (Goyal & Fine, 1993). Senile miosis refers to the smaller size and slower reactivity of the pupil with age. The pupil of a younger person rapidly changes size, letting in more or less light as the task and situation require. In the older eye, the pupil is not only more sluggish but no longer dilates as widely as before. The retina of an individual with senile miosis is estimated to receive only one-third as much light as the retina of a younger person (Sekuler & Blake, 1987). Because of needing greater illumination, older adults may find it difficult to do such things as find a seat in a dark theater or read a menu in a dimly lit restaurant. They may gradually find that they do not enjoy going out at night as much and begin to restrict their activities. The finer the detail of the task (e.g., reading, sewing, using small

Because of age-related changes in vision, older adults see more clearly when the visual image is larger, high contrast, and well illuminated. Road signs must be designed to enhance visibility, as illustrated here.

tools), the more light is needed. General household illumination should be updated to provide better safety and more comfort.

Older adults have problems with **visual acuity,** the ability to see detail clearly; they do not see as well as younger people. Their ability to see at a distance may be impaired, and they may have trouble picking out details. (Visual acuity is what is being tested with those "E" charts.) Acuity may begin to decline in the 40s, though the impairment is still modest up to about age 60, after which a more rapid decline sets in (Anderson & Palmore, 1974). Few older adults can see clearly without glasses. Loss of acuity is directly related to a reduction in the amount of light reaching the retina. This in turn is due to senile miosis as well as the yellowing of the lens (Ivy et al., 1992). One of the implications of these changes is that details (for example, in road signs) must be larger or sharper in order for the older eye to detect them.

A reduction in the amount of light reaching the retina also has the effect of lowering contrast sensitivity (Fozard, 1990). That is, it is more difficult for older adults to detect and differentiate between light and dark. They might miss a shadow that indicates a drop in the sidewalk, for example. Depth perception may be impaired, increasing the risk of falls. Modifications in the environment can help older adults overcome some of the resulting difficulty. Light switches could be painted a different color than the background so that they would be easier to see, or high-contrast color strips could be placed on stair treads to make them easier to distinguish (Sekuler & Blake, 1987).

You may have noticed that sometime around the age of 40, people begin to have difficulty focusing on things at close range. They hold things further away from their eyes in order to see them clearly. Of course, there comes a point where the arms are not long enough anymore! Activities like reading and threading a needle become more difficult. This is a condition known as **presbyopia**—or, more commonly, farsightedness. It is due to a stiffening of the lens of the eye and a loss of elasticity (a gradual process that begins, by the way, early in childhood). The lens no longer changes shape as easily as it did. Longitudinal data suggest that the greatest decline in close vision occurs between ages 40 and 55 (Bruckner, 1967). Presbyopia can be easily corrected with bifocal lenses.

Color vision is also affected. As the lens of the eye yellows, there is a loss of sensitivity to the shorter wavelengths of light. The outcome is a reduced ability to discriminate blues, greens, and violets. The ability to discriminate reds, oranges, and yellows is less affected. Any color coding, such as the color of various medications, should take this into account (Botwinick, 1984). Good color-rendering lamps (e.g., halogen) may enhance color discrimination.

In general, visual performance improves as the level of illumination increases, though no consensus exists at present on the most desirable level of illumination (Charness & Bosman, 1992). This is partly due to a complication caused by cataracts. In addition to clouding vision, cataracts scatter light and cause glare. So increasing the level of light available may respond to the greater need for illumination, but may aggravate the problem of glare. Increased sensitivity to glare affects night driving, making it more difficult and unpleasant. Older individuals can often adjust by restricting unnecessary night trips. Glare can also make highly polished floors treacherous. Glare is most acute when a bright object is seen against a dark background. One solution is to shield light sources so they provide good general illumination without causing glare. Another suggestion is to leave the level of illumination as much as possible in the hands of the individual (Botwinick, 1984). Sunglasses should be worn on bright days to reduce glare and to protect the eyes. There is growing suspicion that ultraviolet exposure may contribute to the development of cataracts.

Beyond the normal changes in vision that occur with age, the prevalence of low vision and its impact on functioning and quality of life among middle-aged and older adults has been underrecognized (Williams, 1995). Leading causes are the age-related diseases of cataract, glaucoma, diabetic retinopathy, and macular degeneration (Kupfer, 1995). More than two-thirds of those with low vision are over 65. Rates are higher among minorities and the poor. Diabetic retinopathy is the leading cause of blindness among those aged 25 to 65 in the United States. Prevention among insulin-dependent diabetics requires early detection and treatment. **Macular degeneration** is the leading cause of severe visual loss in those over 55, affecting an estimated 1.7 million Americans 65 and over. This age-related disease results in slow deterioration of the center of the retina, called the macula. The more common "dry" form of the disease is caused by a breakdown and thinning of macular tissue, resulting in a loss of central vision (blurriness or darkness) with maintenance of peripheral vision. The "wet" form involves the rapid growth of tiny blood vessels that break and leak blood and fluid into the area of the macula. Though there is no cure, early detection is important, as laser treatment (photodynamic therapy) of the "wet" form to seal the blood vessels and reduce the progression of the disease is more effective when performed early. Other treatment options are being investigated. The effect of vision loss on quality of life and the ability to carry on everyday functions can be devastating. The ability to read, see faces, drive, maintain a job, or live independently may be jeopardized. Older adults who are visually impaired are at greater risk of depressive disorders (Branch, Horowitz, & Carr, 1989).

Visual abilities unquestionably decline with age. Fortunately, most people can and do correct their vision with eyeglasses and are able to function very well. Behavioral adjustments on the part of the individual and design modifications in the environment can minimize the effects of many of the visual changes we have discussed. As our population ages, more attention will be given to the vision problems of older people.

One area of visual accessibility that has gained increased attention is the design of Web sites. Because of its inherently graphical nature, the World Wide Web poses challenges to users who are visually impaired. Internet use by adults over 65 is projected to increase dramatically (rising 358 percent from 2001 to 2005) (Stuen, 2002). Older adults are spending more time online, visiting more Web sites, and spending more money online than those who are younger; they constitute the fastest growing segment of Web users (Morrell, 2002). The Internet is a significant factor in the independence of all those with disabilities. Web design that increases visual accessibility by attending to typography, color, and contrast makes good market sense and has the additional benefit of increasing usability for everyone. See Figure 9.1 for practical suggestions on improving the legibility of printed material (books, instruction manuals, product descriptions, signs, Web sites, and so on).

For the first time, vision and hearing have been included in Healthy People 2010, a national disease prevention initiative sponsored by the U.S. Department of Health and Human Services, discussed in more depth in Chapter 10. The goal is to "improve the visual and hearing health of the nation through prevention, early detection, treatment and rehabilitation." For information on the vision objectives, visit http://healthyvision 2010.org.

The most important action people can take to preserve good eyesight is to get a comprehensive eye exam, which can detect eye diseases and conditions such as cataracts in their early stages and lead to effective treatment to maintain or restore good vision (Goyal & Fine, 1993).

Hearing

Hearing problems also increase with age, and hearing loss is one of the most common chronic conditions among older adults. A report on hearing impairment in the elderly

FIGURE 9.1 *Practical Tips for Improving Legibility of Printed Material*

Vision loss can make reading difficult by, for example, dimming as well as blurring the image. Listed below are several principles that can improve the readability of textual material.

High contrast: For many older or partially sighted readers, light letters on a dark background are more readable. The best contrast is achieved with white on black.

Large type, at least 16 to 18 points, is easiest to read.

Greater spacing between lines and letters assists readability.

Ordinary typeface, with uppercase and lowercase letters, is more readable than *italics,* s\anted, or ALL CAPS.

Standard typeface is more legible than decorative typeface.

Bold versions of any typeface are more readable because the letters are thicker.

A matte finish is preferred over a glossy finish, because it reduces glare.

from the U.S. Congress, Office of Technology Assessment (1986), found usually mild to moderate, but widespread, impairment.

One of the characteristics of older hearing is **presbycusis,** a decreased sensitivity to high-frequency sounds that becomes really apparent after age 50. The rule of thumb is that the higher the frequency and the older the person, the louder the sound needs to be to be heard (Botwinick, 1984). Consonants are higher-frequency sounds than vowels, so the older person will have more difficulty discriminating between words like *run* and *fun*. Because the voices of women are higher frequency than men's, and the voices of children and teenagers are higher frequency than adults', older people will have a harder time understanding their speech (Botwinick, 1984). This problem is magnified if the speech is rapid or if there is a lot of background noise (as in a crowd, or in traffic, or from a noisy fan). Thus, presbycusis is the primary cause of speech comprehension difficulties among older adults (Schneider, Daneman, Murphy, & See, 2000). Another implication of this progressive difficulty in hearing high-pitched sounds is that car horns, doorbells, and smoke and fire alarms are more difficult to hear, thus affecting personal safety. Any sound-based warning system should be designed to use low-frequency sounds and reverberation, which might attract the attention of hearing-impaired individuals (Charness & Bosman, 1992).

Accumulated exposure to "noise pollution" over time may be partly responsible for presbycusis. Presbycusis has been observed more often in industrialized than in traditional societies, where fewer noise hazards exist (Bergman, 1966), and develops earlier and is more severe among men than women (Sekuler & Blake, 1987). Loss of hearing sensitivity with age occurs more than twice as quickly among men as women (Hayflick, 1994). Men may be at greater risk because of exposure to high noise levels in their jobs, such as trucking, mining, and so on. If this is the case, one would also expect high incidence of hearing loss among musicians—which may partly explain their need for extremely high amplification! Preventive efforts are aimed at keeping the noise level low so that the environment does not produce hearing loss.

Another characteristic of elderly hearing is decreased ability to block out background noise. Identifying and locating sounds in noisy, crowded settings becomes progressively more difficult (U.S. Congress, Office of Technology Assessment, 1986). Again, older people may find such settings unpleasant and withdraw from interaction in them. This has become one of the main determinants of whether my mom enjoys a particular restaurant or not. There are several great ones close by that are "off her list" because they are too noisy, making it difficult for her to carry on a conversation. Since eating out is primarily a social experience, this is an important consideration.

Sekuler and Blake (1987) offer the following recommendations to help minimize the problem of background noise. First, the older person will be able to hear better when standing or sitting next to sound-absorbent materials, like drapes or upholstered furniture. Sitting in a high-backed chair will act as a shield. Hard surfaces such as large windows or bare walls should be avoided, since they aggravate the problem. Environments frequented by older adults should be designed to minimize echoes, reverberations, and noise (Charness & Bosman, 1992). This might include elimination of noisy air-conditioning systems or piped-in music, and the use of sound-absorbing materials on walls, floors, and so forth.

When hearing is impaired, so is communication. The typical complaint of someone suffering from classic presbycusis is that they can hear people talking but can't make out the words. The frustration and irritation that result may lead to more isolation than

Older adults may find crowded, congested settings unpleasant because of a reduced ability to screen out background noise and engage in conversation.

happens with visual loss (Butler, Lewis, & Sunderland, 1991). Older people may not only not hear as much, but they may begin to cover up their difficulty by, for example, smiling and nodding their heads at what appear to be appropriate times. In time, they may begin to avoid social situations out of embarrassment, and others may exclude them from conversations or social activities.

When we are talking to a hearing-impaired older person, Hull (1980) has recommended that we speak at a normal rate (unless your normal rate is fast—then slow down), with slightly greater intensity. It is helpful to minimize background noise and enhance the visibility of the speaker's face. This is so that the hearer can take advantage of visual cues such as lip movements and facial expressions to fill in the gaps.

While people usually think nothing of correcting vision with glasses, they are often reluctant to use hearing aids because of denial of the severity of the impairment, the associated social stigma of aging, and cost. In addition, the rather primitive technology available in the past often failed to deal effectively with the most common hearing problems and sometimes actually made them worse by boosting the level of all sound, including background noise, so that a "booming" effect resulted. Improvements in hearing aid technology, as well as advances in assistive listening devices, such as telephone amplifiers and alerting devices, can improve the functional ability and quality of life for those with significant hearing loss.

Finally, one in five adults over the age of 70 suffer from dual sensory impairment, the concurrent impairment of vision and hearing (Brennan, 2002). Minority individuals are at greater risk. This condition has been largely ignored in the research literature, though its effects are significant.

Taste and Smell

Reductions in taste and smell have implications for health and safety. These two senses overlap, making it somewhat difficult to isolate age-related changes in one or the other. Taste perception does not seem to be impaired in any significant way as we age, partly because taste buds are continually replaced throughout life (Ivy et al., 1992). However, smell does seem to be strongly affected, remaining relatively unchanged until about the mid-50s, when a decline begins (Ivy et al., 1992; Sekuler & Blake, 1987). Men lose the ability to identify odors earlier and more rapidly than women (Hayflick, 1994). According to the BLSA, a significant decline occurs around age 55 for men but not until 75 for women. Some studies have implicated smoking as a contributing factor to olfactory losses (Doty et al., 1984). By age 65, more than 50 percent of us show evidence of significant olfactory impairment (Doty et al., 1984). As a result, food may lose some of its appeal, seeming bland and boring, which increases the risk of loss of appetite and malnutrition. Older adults may compensate by eating spicier, more heavily seasoned foods. In addition, chewing food more carefully enhances flavor by increasing exposure to smell receptors. Foods with interesting textures, such as crunchy foods, may also help offset a reduction in the discrimination of flavor. Finally, because eating is such a social experience, the degree of social contact (or isolation) an individual experiences can either minimize or maximize the eating problems that result from changes in smell (Botwinick, 1984).

Insensitivity to smell places older adults at greater risk from other sources as well. They may be less likely to detect spoiled foods or smoke and natural gas leaks (Doty et al., 1984; Sekuler & Blake, 1987).

Touch

The sense of touch enables us to manually locate, identify, and manipulate objects (Ivy et al., 1992). Though age-related changes in touch have not been studied to the same degree as the other senses, we seem to experience a gradual loss in the sense of touch with age. The functional importance of these changes is not well understood, however. Findings on age changes in pain perception are unclear.

Overall, then, a gradual decline seems to occur in the capacity of the sense organs with age. However, these reductions are not normally debilitating and are often easily overcome. As Sekuler & Blake (1987) point out, our senses tend to hold up remarkably well, given the accumulated levels of exposure and use over a lifetime. They estimate, for example, that by the age of 60, your eyes have been exposed to more light energy than that unleashed by a nuclear blast.

Botwinick (1984) reminds us that the evidence on sensory changes with age is based on laboratory studies. As we have stressed before, the implications of these studies for functioning in everyday life are not clear. Even when sensory changes do have practical significance, the individual can often compensate, either with changes in habits, increased cautiousness, or the use of glasses or hearing aids. Fozard (1990) has suggested that older adults become experts at inferring what is going on around them as a way of compensating for less-than-complete information. We have also seen many examples in which the environment can be modified or redesigned to accommodate the needs of older adults. Limits imposed by society are sometimes worse than physical ones. Speaking to this issue, Hobman (1981) made the following observation: "The continued social well-being of older people, as with that of any other generation, largely depends on the degree to which they can continue to function as autonomous personalities able to control events rather than having to submit to external circumstances which restrict the lives of far too many people." Efforts should be made to ensure that older people's interaction with the world is not unnecessarily limited by age-related sensory changes.

In sum, it is clear that body tissues, organs, and systems undergo a variety of normal age-related decrements in both structure and function. The extent and timing of these changes vary tremendously, may in some cases have little functional significance, and are frequently amenable to intervention and perhaps even prevention. Some of these changes may serve as preconditions for disease, given the presence of other factors. As we learn more about normal biological aging, the recurrent message is that age and disease are not synonymous, and that both primary and secondary aging may be under greater control than we had previously thought.

Concept
Review
9.2

- In general, the normal biological changes in body tissues, organs, and systems that occur with age do not significantly impair the individual's function until very late in life.

- A number of pathological conditions are an exaggeration of normal age-related change (e.g., osteoporosis).

- Though sleep is important to health and well-being, many adults are moderately to severely sleep deprived.

- The nature of menopause, its consequences for women's health, and debate about HRT have become subjects of immense interest in recent years.

- Sensory aging becomes especially noticeable in late adulthood, though age, rate, and magnitude of sensory change vary significantly among individuals.

- Age changes in vision and hearing have been studied most extensively.

- While sensory aging has implications for many aspects of functioning (e.g., communication, safety), most normal age-related change can be easily accommodated by changes in individual behavior or environmental design.

Theories of Biological Aging

What causes the biological changes that occur as we age? While no clear answer to this question—no single comprehensive theory of biological aging—exists yet, there is certainly no shortage of contenders (Cristofalo, 1988). We used to think wear and tear was the primary cause of aging. Like a machine, the body just wore out over the course of a lifetime, succumbing in its weakened state to some external factor such as infection or stress. In recent years, evidence of a genetically based program of aging has accumulated, suggesting that aging and death are not random events but simply the final pieces of a developmental plan laid out in the blueprint that has governed age-related change from the moment of conception. Still more recently, scientists have begun to suspect that aging results when the damage caused by the internal processes of living accumulates and overwhelms the body's natural repair mechanisms.

Perhaps the truth is to be found in all these interpretations. As Schneider (1992) points out, the number of theories usually reflects the state of knowledge in a field. Thus, given the youth of biological aging research, we should not be surprised that dozens of theories have been offered. A comprehensive review is beyond the scope of this text; we will instead describe the major schools of thought and briefly discuss a few examples of each.

Theories of biological aging are usually grouped into two major categories: programmed (or developmental/genetic) and stochastic (or random) theories. **Programmed theories** take the position that aging is built into the system genetically, a sort of planned-obsolescence approach. Specific genes are thought to direct changes that ultimately lead to death. **Stochastic theories,** on the other hand, propose that aging is the result of living—the end result of accumulated damage caused by random events, both intrinsic and extrinsic, encountered in daily life. While convenient for discussion purposes, the organization suggested by this classification is more apparent than real. Theories overlap and are variously classified as programmed or stochastic by one or another reference. In addition, experts agree that these theories are not mutually exclusive (Gerhard & Cristofalo, 1992; Schneider, 1992). The process of biological aging is so complex that it is most likely the outcome of many processes interacting over time—both nature and nurture, planned and unplanned.

Aging by Design: Programmed Theories of Aging

Programmed theories of aging view it as an extension of the genetically controlled processes of development at work throughout the life span. Several lines of evidence point to the existence of such a genetic program (Finch & Tanzi, 1997). First, the maximum life span of an organism is a species characteristic. Humans live longer than dogs, which in turn live longer than fruit flies. Second, there is evidence of the operation of "clocks" that regulate biological events. Research by Hayflick (1965; also see Hayflick & Moorhead, 1961) and others has demonstrated that human cells taken from the body and allowed to divide in the lab have a limited life span of 50 plus or minus 10 divisions. Thus, it would seem that some sort of biological clock is operating at the cellular level. Biological clocks operate at the organism level as well—for example, the human female reproductive cycle is usually activated around age 12 and turned off around age 51. Third, longevity is known to be a familial trait. Studies of identical twins illustrate impressive similarity in length of life compared to pairs of siblings (Birren, 1988b). And fourth, age-related changes have a regularity that would be hard to explain as a result of random events.

It seems evident, then, that the genes play a significant role in the aging process. Some programmed theories focus on the coordinated effect of thousands of genes, while others examine the influence of one specific gene. Each, however, assumes the existence of an aging plan, activated some time after reproductive maturity, the nature and location of which are matters of debate. Finally, all such theories acknowledge the modifying effect of environmental variables.

Metabolic Theories

The common element in the **metabolic theories of aging** is the idea that human beings have a fixed lifetime supply of metabolic energy and that a positive correlation exists between metabolic rate and aging. This idea has been supported by experimental research on mice and rats indicating that if you cut their calorie intake by 40 percent, they live about 30 percent longer. In other words, if you reduce metabolism, you significantly extend life expectancy. However, the effect of metabolic rate is not simple. For example, a strict interpretation of this idea would suggest that the least active individuals (those burning the fewest calories) would be the longest lived. This is obviously not the case. Newer versions of this approach focus more specifically on damage to the **mitochondria,** components of the cell that produce about 95 percent of our metabolic energy, including that needed by the brain. This damage, a result of oxygen metabolism, accumulates with age and thus progressively impairs function in older cells. Whether calorie restriction has any useful application to humans is not yet clear.

Neuroendocrine Theories

The **neuroendocrine theories** (Finch & Landfield, 1985) focus on decreased function of the endocrine system and the neural centers that control it—particularly the hypothalamus and the pituitary gland. Because the neuroendocrine system regulates so many body functions, any progressive degeneration of this system would have widespread and deleterious effects on overall functioning, health, and survival. Scientists are studying various key hormones believed to play a role in biological aging, since the production of these hormones diminishes with age. For example, decreased estrogen is known to be involved in the aging of the female reproductive system. Researchers are also investigating the role of *dehydroepiandrosterone* (DHEA), secreted by the adrenal glands in diminishing amounts as we age. The effects of DHEA on aging are not well understood (Hayflick, 1994).

The pituitary gland produces an important substance known as *growth hormone* (GH). Though the pituitary never loses its capacity to produce this hormone, GH levels are very low in about one-third of the elderly. Rudman, Feller, and Nagra (1990) administered injections of GH each week for six months to a group of men over the age of 60 who had abnormally low GH levels. The results indicated a reversal of aging effects— for example, reductions in body fat and gains in skin thickness and spinal density. Additional research is needed to replicate these findings and determine their implications and generalizability.

Immunological Theory

Walford (1969) bases his **immune theory of aging** on two well-documented age-related changes in the immune system: a reduced ability to protect the body from infection and a striking increase in autoimmune disorders (those in which the body begins to attack its own tissue). He has focused on a cluster of regulatory genes called the *major histocompatibility complex* (MHC), which governs all major immune functions and which may trigger shrinkage of the thymus and other changes.

To sum up, programmed theories of aging attempt to account for the regularity and predictability in the aging process by identifying a genetic base for age-related change. They vary in the nature, identity, and location of the genetic control system they describe. Programmed theories stress the uniformity of age-related change but are less able to explain the tremendous heterogeneity in the nature and rate of aging across individuals. From this perspective, those who wish to intervene in the aging process would seek to control the aging program.

Aging by Accident: Stochastic Theories of Aging

The stochastic theories are essentially the descendants of the early wear-and-tear theory of aging, abandoned because of its oversimplification of the aging process (for example, even organisms in protected environments age) and its imprecision (how exactly are cells impaired?). These theories stress the damaging effects of random assaults such as disease, injury, exposure to toxins, and so on, as well as of the normal processes of life—like metabolism—over time. The damage accumulates either because of a failure in the body's repair mechanisms or because the damaged cells proliferate. Hayflick (2003, p. 65) takes the position that aging is "the random systemic loss of molecular fidelity that exceeds repair capacity after the age of reproductive maturation." In either case, the eventual outcome is organ failure and death (Arking, 1991).

Cross-Linkage Theory

Cross-linking (Bjorksten, 1968; Cerami, Vlassara, & Brownlee, 1987) refers to the chemical bonding of normally separate protein fibers, which impairs tissue function and causes aging changes. It occurs when glucose (blood sugar) irreparably attaches itself to proteins in the body, forming a gummy substance. This substance causes collagen and elastin to stiffen and lose elasticity and leads to clouding of the lens of the eye, clogging of arteries, and damage to the kidneys (Schneider, 1992). These effects are magnified in diabetes due to elevated blood sugar levels (Cerami, 1985).

Somatic Mutation, DNA-Damage, and Error Theories

Somatic mutation and **DNA-damage theories** (also referred to as *error theories*) hypothesize that random assaults on the DNA in the chromosomes of somatic (that is, non-sex) cells damage or alter the DNA and interfere with gene expression and therefore cell function. This damage could arise from exposure to radiation or from the action of free radicals produced in the body itself (see below). Each gene can be thought of as a code or recipe for the manufacture of a specific protein. (Proteins are essential to the structure and function of the body.) If this code is damaged or altered, the gene may not be able to produce its protein or may produce a faulty version of it. If the body's protein repair mechanisms fail, the result negatively affects the structure and function of cells, tissues, and organs. While there is little doubt that DNA damage may contribute to the aging process, Arking (1991) interprets the evidence to suggest that it may primarily be a consequence rather than a cause of aging. On the other hand, Hayflick (1994) contends some version of an error theory may eventually explain many age-related changes.

Free Radical Theory

One of the most compelling theories of aging, proposed by Denham Harman of the University of Nebraska in 1956, posits that damage done by free radicals is responsible for most aging changes. **Free radicals** are highly reactive molecules that carry an extra (unpaired) electron that allows them to bond readily with other chemicals. They are produced in the cell and may result from normal oxygen metabolism, as well as from radiation, ozone or other pollutants, or drugs.

Human beings require oxygen in order for metabolic processes that produce energy to take place. (These are called *aerobic activities*.) When an oxygen atom is broken down by the body to produce energy, the reaction strips away one of its electrons, creating an oxygen-free radical. The resulting molecule looks for another electron to complete its pair—the only way to do that is to steal one from somewhere else. This is the activity that causes the damage. Free radicals accumulate in the body, destroying fats and proteins critical to cell function and damaging DNA. (This may be one source of the somatic mutations described above. They may also damage the mitochondria; see the above section on metabolic theories.) Free radicals are believed to be responsible for functional and structural changes in the body characteristic of aging and are also thought to be involved in more than 60 disorders, including cataracts, arthritis, cancer, and heart disease (Arking, 1991; Levine & Stadtman, 1992). They may play a role in the development of Alzheimer's disease as well (see Chapter 11). **Free radical theory** suggests, then, that we may be victims of the necessary presence of oxygen in our cells.

The body produces an enzyme known as **superoxide dismutase** (an antioxidant) that neutralizes the free radicals produced by oxygen metabolism. However, this enzyme may not act quickly enough or thoroughly enough to completely prevent free radical damage. Even though as much as 99 percent of the damage is repaired, a little remains and accumulates. Eventually, enough "junk" builds up to impair the structure and function of the cells. Interestingly, the production of this enzyme is regulated by the major histocompatibility complex, also thought to play a role in the activities of the immune system (see above) (Cristofalo, 1988). Of course, any change in the availability of superoxide dismutase would have an impact on free radical damage. Finally, there has been some suggestion that foods rich in vitamins C and E may have antioxidant properties that could forestall aging by controlling free radical buildup.

To summarize, stochastic theories focus on the accumulated damage resulting from the processes of living. They offer a better explanation of the heterogeneity in aging across individuals than do the programmed theories. Any attempts at intervention derived from these theories would focus on avoiding this damage to begin with or boosting repair mechanisms to counter it. According to this view, "we are not programmed to die, merely insufficiently programmed to survive" (Kirkwood, 2000, p. 17).

In Search of an Integrated Theory

As Hayflick (1994, 2003) points out, we have made much more progress over the last 100 years in describing *what* happens as we get older than in explaining *why* it happens. He describes advances in understanding the fundamental aging process as moving at "glacial speed," largely because so little research is focused on the biology of aging, being instead directed at age-associated diseases. Put simply, we do not yet know why we age. Progress in uncovering the secrets of aging will be enhanced by discoveries in a variety of areas: technological advances in genetics and molecular biology; studies of human cells in vitro (in culture); research on cancer cells; comparative studies of other species; and studies of humans with diseases of premature aging such as Werner Syndrome, a rare disorder whose victims show signs of advanced aging in their 20s (Freeman, Whartenby, & Abraham, 1992; Gibbons, 1990; McCormick, 1992). Current theories of aging are by no means mutually exclusive, nor are they assumed to be the final word on the subject. Perhaps some of us have genes that grant us a slower systemwide internal clock that causes our cells to age more slowly, enabling them to better withstand the wear and tear of life. Or perhaps some of us inherit better internal repair mechanisms. And so on. It is likely that a variety of processes contribute to biological aging, and that accumulating evidence will cause us to discard some existing theories in favor of alternatives that reformulate, integrate, and add to the ideas reviewed here (Schneider, 1992). (See Table 9.3 for a summary of the aging theories discussed above.)

TABLE 9.3 *A Summary of Aging Theories*

Programmed Theories	Stochastic Theories
Metabolic theories: Focus on the relationship between metabolic rate and aging. Disproved in original form, newer versions focus on damage to the mitochondria and thus cellular energy production.	**Cross-linkage theory:** Cites a gummy substance produced when glucose bonds with protein as a cause of some aging changes.
Neuroendocrine theories: Focus on changes in the hypothalamus and pituitary gland that lead to decreased function of the endocrine system and widespread aging effects.	**Somatic mutation/DNA-damage/Error theories:** Maintain that damage to or mutations in the DNA of somatic cells impairs protein manufacture and therefore alters the structure and function of cells, tissues, and organs.
Immune theory: Points to programmed deterioration in the immune system as a cause of reduced resistance and increased incidence of autoimmune disorders.	**Free radical theory:** Argues that most age-related change is the result of damage wrought by free radicals—highly reactive by-products of metabolism.

The Goal of Aging Research: Adding Life to Years or Years to Life?

Average life expectancy (sometimes called *mean longevity*) refers to the number of years an individual born at a certain time can expect to live, given circumstances present during his or her lifetime. The average life expectancy for a baby born in 2001 is 77.2 years (National Center for Health Statistics, 2004). Life expectancy is closely related to sociocultural factors. **Active life expectancy** refers to the average number of years individuals of a certain cohort can expect to live in an independent state, free from significant disability (Olshansky, Carnes, & Cassel, 1990). **Life span** refers to the genetically based limit to life, the maximum number of years one could possibly live if free from all exogenous risk factors. Life span is a theoretical estimate, since it cannot actually be observed. This upper limit is thought to be about 120, although there are those who argue that the biological limit is closer to 85 for all practical purposes, and still others who claim there is no limit at all (see, for example, Barinag, 1991). The oldest verified age to which an individual has lived is 120 years (Olshansky et al., 1990).

Twentieth-century gains in life expectancy were largely the result of improvements in nutrition and sanitation, reductions in maternal and infant death during childbirth, control of infectious illnesses, and prevention and treatment of heart disease and stroke. The life span did not change—people still aged, but they were less likely to die prematurely from these causes (Hayflick, 2002). Even if the major causes of death (cancer and heart disease) are eliminated in the years to come, most experts feel that 85 is about the maximum average life expectancy achievable (Olshansky et al., 1990). However, unlocking the mysteries of biological aging raises two intriguing possibilities: first, of slowing the processes of degeneration and decline in order to improve health and vigor in the later years of life—in other words, forestalling aging within the existing life span; and second, of significantly extending the human life span itself. The latter possibility has raised a whole host of questions and ethical concerns (see, e.g., Cassel, 1992; Hackler, 2002; Hayflick, 2003).

CRITICAL THINKING QUESTION

Was Jonathan Swift correct when he said in Gulliver's Travels *that "long life is the universal desire and wish of mankind"? Is the extension of the human life span a good idea? What are the implications, and the pros and cons, for the individual as well as for society in general?*

Concept Review 9.3

- The causes of normal biological aging are not yet well understood.

- The many theories of aging can be grouped into two types: those that assume a genetic timetable is at work (the programmed theories) and those that view aging as a result of accumulating damage due to random events (the stochastic theories).

- Aging is a complex phenomenon that is likely to be caused by the interaction of many processes.

- Debate continues over the potential implications of extending the human life span.

REVIEW QUESTIONS

What Is This Thing Called Aging?

1. Differentiate between primary and secondary aging.
2. Compare the traditional view of aging with the emerging view.
3. What is meant by successful aging in the context of biological change?

Physical Development in Adulthood

1. Review changes in the skin that might lead to wrinkling and sagging.
2. Explain the role of collagen in the aging of the body.
3. Identify the major age-related changes in the skeletal system.
4. Define osteoporosis and identify those most at risk for developing this condition.
5. Discuss the role of exercise in age-related changes in muscle.
6. How can smoking lead to emphysema?
7. Assess the impact of age-related changes in the immune system.

8. Discuss the benefits of sleep and the risks of sleep deprivation.
9. How do changes in the reproductive system affect male and female sexuality?
10. Evaluate the significance of a drop in estrogen following menopause.
11. What are the major symptoms of menopause?
12. What are the current recommendations on hormone replacement therapy?
13. What kinds of visual problems typically develop in older adults?
14. How is hearing affected by aging?
15. Why do some observers feel that hearing loss may have a more significant impact than visual loss?
16. What are the potential implications of changes in taste, smell, and touch for older adults?
17. Discuss recommendations for individual and environmental adaptations to these sensory changes.

Theories of Biological Aging

1. Differentiate between programmed and stochastic theories of aging.

2. Briefly describe the three examples of each major class of aging theory.

3. How does life expectancy differ from life span?

KEY TERMS

active life expectancy, 382
arteriosclerosis, 364
average life expectancy, 382
cataract, 370
collagen, 360
cross-linkage theory of aging, 380
DNA-damage theories of aging, 380
emphysema, 365
endocrine system, 366
estrogen, 367
free radical theory of aging, 381
free radicals, 380
glucocorticoids, 365
hormone replacement therapy
     (HRT), 369

immune system, 365
immune theory of aging, 379
immunosuppression, 365
life span, 382
longevity revolution, 353
macular degeneration, 372
melatonin, 367
menopause, 368
metabolic theories of aging, 378
mitochondria, 379
neuroendocrine theories
     of aging, 379
osteoarthritis, 363
osteoporosis, 361
presbycusis, 374

presbyopia, 371
primary aging, 354
programmed theories of
     aging, 378
secondary aging, 354
senile miosis, 370
somatic mutation theories
     of aging, 380
stochastic theories of aging, 379
successful aging, 359
superoxide dismutase, 381
thymosin, 366
thymus, 365
visual acuity, 371

10 Health, Longevity, and Prevention

THE PHONE CALL CAME about 5:00 in the afternoon. It turned out to be one of those calls you hope you never get. I remember I almost didn't answer it because, as usual, I had about 10 different things going on—I had just gotten home from work, my three-year-old needed attention, I was about to start dinner—you know. Anyway, it was my parents' neighbor, a young woman who had befriended my father—he was retired and home most of the time, while my mom was still very active in her work and gone a lot. These two had become pals. She had just found my dad, sitting in the car in the driveway. She had called the paramedics—she thought he had had a stroke. Though my dad was 75 at the time, he had been healthy, active, vigorous—essentially the same dad I had always known. I had never really thought of him as old. He became old that day. And all our lives—Mom's, Dad's, their children's and grandchildren's—changed forever.

This chapter examines the relationships between aging, behavior, health, and illness—the intersection of our biological and psychological selves. We begin with an overview of the health status of adults, then address the leading causes of death and the effect of gender and race on health and longevity. Next, we review the concept of risk and discuss health promotion and intervention. The final section addresses concerns about the nature of medication use among older adults and discusses some issues surrounding long-term care.

Health, Disease, and Disability

Have you ever noticed that you take your health for granted until you get sick or suffer an injury? Only then do you appreciate how wonderful it is to feel well. Health is the variable most highly correlated with life satisfaction, subjective well-being, and morale (Larson, 1978). It is a topic of major interest in adulthood. **Developmental health psychology** is the study of the interaction of age, behavior, and health (Siegler, 1989). Investigators working in this area attempt to describe changes in health status over the course of adulthood, determine the nature and origins of age-related diseases, and describe the effect of health on behavior as well as the effect of behavior on health. Goals include the prevention of disease, the preservation of health, and an improved quality of life for those who suffer from disability and disease (Elias, Elias, & Elias, 1990). In order to accomplish these goals, health psychologists address basic questions such as: Who gets sick and why? Who is most likely to recover from illness and why? And how can we prevent illness and disability and promote recovery (Adler & Matthews, 1994)? We will address several of these issues in this section. Let's begin by looking at some of the difficulties that confront investigators doing research in developmental health psychology.

Defining and Measuring Health, Disease, and Illness

Let's say that we want to know the health status of samples of young, middle-aged, and older adults. One way to ascertain the state of the subjects' health would be to have them undergo a complete medical examination, including extensive diagnostic testing. However, in response to issues of cost, time, and ethics, studies often rely instead on individuals' self-assessments of their health. Subjects are typically given some sort of symptom checklist in an attempt to identify any existing diseases or conditions. These ratings might then be used to identify changes in health status over the adult life span, or they might serve as a means of sorting subjects into disease/healthy groups for further study and comparison.

The extent to which self-ratings provide an accurate gauge of health is the subject of debate (Elias et al., 1990; Siegler, 1989). The wording of the questions no doubt affects the quality of the information derived from these measures, as does the subjects' knowledge of their own health (Siegler, 1989). For example, some conditions—such as high blood pressure—are asymptomatic. Subjects would only be aware that they had these conditions if they had been medically diagnosed. Studies of "healthy" adults have probably been contaminated by the inclusion of subjects who are sick and do not know it.

CRITICAL THINKING QUESTION
To what extent might factors such as socioeconomic status and gender affect the amount of knowledge individuals have about their health?

So what does it mean to be "healthy"? At its simplest level, **health** is defined as the absence of disease. So, if an individual shows no signs of a diagnosable condition, the individual would be considered healthy. This is the definition of health implied in the measurement tools used in the majority of studies. However, in 1946 the World Health Organization defined health more broadly as "a state of complete physical, mental, and social well-being and not merely the absence of disease or infirmity" (cited in Birren & Zarit, 1985). This definition of health recognizes the complex interaction between physical, psychological, and social experiences and suggests a positive approach to the promotion of well-being rather than merely the elimination of disease.

Research has confirmed that subjective appraisals of health often conflict with more objective measures, yet are more important predictors of continued health and survival (Liang et al., 2003). Individuals often evaluate their health in reference to social, emotional, and spiritual well-being; comparisons with others; and functional status, in addition to their biomedical condition. Those who maintain positive assessments of their health, despite the actual state of health, fare better.

Antonovsky (1987) suggests that rather than thinking of them as either-or, health and illness should be conceptualized as falling on a continuum. Schroots (1988) makes an important distinction between disease and illness. **Disease** refers to the objective diagnosis of a particular disorder with a specific cause and characteristic symptoms. In contrast, **illness** refers not only to the existence of a specific disease, but also includes the individuals' subjective perception of and response to the disease and its effect on the psychosocial environment.

The point is that our picture of the health status of contemporary adults may be distorted in a number of ways by the manner in which we define and measure health, illness, disease, and disability.

A second group of difficulties occurs with studies that attempt to describe the effects of various diseases on behavior. These studies generally use the quasi-experimental design, in which existing groups of patients are compared with healthy controls. A major problem revolves around the fact that these patients are undergoing treatment—for example, they may be taking medication. Therefore, the effects of the illness are confounded with the effects of the treatment (Elias et al., 1990). Longitudinal studies are especially likely to be affected by confounding of variables. Not only does the subject age, but the illness advances, others may emerge, and numbers and types of medications may change over the course of the study. Under these conditions, it is difficult to untangle disease effects. Finally, the effect of the "patient" label must be considered in interpreting research results.

CRITICAL THINKING QUESTION
How might being labeled as a patient affect behavior?

Age and Health

What do we know about a person's health if we know the individual's age? How do the kinds of health-related problems that people experience change across the years of adulthood? As we have seen, age is not as clear an indicator of developmental status in adulthood as it is earlier in life. However, some general statements that describe the role of age in regard to health are listed below.

- Most adults are in good health and experience few limitations or disabilities. Between 2000 and 2002, 73 percent of adults over age 65 living in the community (that is, not in institutions) reported their health as excellent, very good, or good. (See Figure 10.1.)
- However, health and mobility decline with age, especially after age 80. Disease is more common among older adults.
- Most of the common diseases of later life have their origins years earlier, resulting in part from lifestyle and health practices. Social and behavioral factors are of critical importance in understanding health and aging. Both illness and health must be understood in a life-span perspective.
- Income is directly related to perception of health.
- The older the individual, the more difficult it is to recover from stress.

FIGURE 10.1 *Self-Rated Health Status: Percentage of Persons 65+ in Good to Excellent Health, by Age Group and Race/Hispanic Origin, 2000 to 2002*

Asking people to rate their own health as excellent, very good, good, fair, or poor provides a common indicator of health easily measured in surveys. It represents physical, emotional, and social aspects of health and well-being. Good to excellent self-reported health correlates with lower risk of mortality.

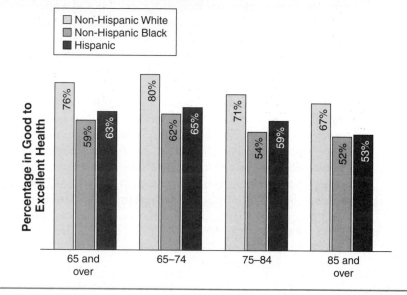

Note: Data are based on a three-year average from 2000 to 2002. People of Hispanic origin may be of any race. Data refer to the civilian noninstitutionalized population.

Source: Centers for Disease Control and Prevention, National Center for Health Statistics, 2004. Available online at www.agingstats.gov/chartbook2004/images/p_30.jpg.

- As individuals age, acute conditions decrease in frequency while chronic conditions increase in frequency. At least 80 percent of adults over 65 have at least one chronic condition, and 50 percent have at least two.
- Older adults typically have multiple disorders and sensory deficits that may interact. Treatments may also interact.
- In contrast to younger age groups, the elderly are likely to suffer from physical health problems that are multiple, chronic, and treatable but not curable. Acute illness may be superimposed on these conditions (Centers for Disease Control, 2004c; Estes & Binney, 1991; National Center for Health Statistics, 1990; Schroots, 1988; Siegler, 1989; www.agingstats.gov/chartbook2000/healthstatus.html).

Changes in Health across Adulthood

Verbrugge (1987) summarizes the health of young (age 17 to 44), middle-aged (45 to 64), and older (65+) adults as follows.

Young Adults. Young adults are in generally good health. They experience few trips to the doctor or hospitalizations. Respiratory ailments are the primary health problem: symptoms associated with colds are the most common complaint (nasal congestion, headache, tiredness, and so on). Few have chronic ailments—allergies are the most common problem—or limitations in daily activities. Fatal diseases are rare. Though death is relatively uncommon in this age group, the leading cause of death among young adult males is accidents; among young females, it is cancer. AIDS poses an increasing threat among this age group as well. About one-half of all new HIV infections occur among those under 25 (Centers for Disease Control, 2004d). HIV infection is the leading cause of death among African American males 25 to 44 years of age.

Middle-Aged Adults. A marked change in health status occurs from young to middle adulthood. The most common daily symptoms are musculoskeletal problems, especially among women (pain and stiffness in muscles and joints, sometimes in specific sites, sometimes all over), followed by respiratory ailments (headaches and cold symptoms are common). Disease becomes more commonplace in middle age. In contrast to young adults, who for the most part attribute their symptoms to acute infections, middle-aged adults point to diseases as the cause of their discomfort. Of the chronic conditions that emerge in middle age, five stand out: arthritis, hypertension, chronic sinusitis, heart conditions, and hearing impairments. These conditions may begin to cause limitations in daily activity. Fatal diseases also appear. In addition to heart diseases and hypertension, these include diabetes, arteriosclerosis, emphysema, and cancer. Office visits and hospital stays are more common. The leading causes of death are heart disease and cancer.

Older Adults. Musculoskeletal symptoms (primarily due to arthritis) are common among older adults: mostly pain symptoms, followed by stiffness. Acute problems diminish sharply. Four chronic conditions predominate—hypertension, hearing impairments, arthritis, and heart disease. These conditions are more severe than in middle age and limit work and leisure activities. The prevalence of chronic conditions varies by sex and race. Rates of hypertension and diabetes are increasing (Federal Interagency Forum on Aging-Related Statistics, 2004). Physician visits and hospital stays focus on life-threatening diseases. Heart disease is the principal cause of death, followed by cancer and stroke.

To sum up, people's overall evaluation of their physical health declines with age, though to a lesser degree than might be expected given the sharp rise in chronic health problems among the elderly. The types of daily symptoms reported change markedly across age categories, especially from young to middle adulthood. These constitute the essence of physical well-being for people, and their presence influences mental and emotional health as well. The rate of acute conditions drops with age, while the likelihood of suffering from chronic conditions increases sharply. Of the nonfatal diseases, rates of arthritis increase steadily, and sensory impairments appear, while life-threatening diseases also increase in frequency with age. Middle-aged and older adults are more likely to experience limitations due to their health status, too. Not surprisingly, adults have increasing contact with the medical establishment as they get older. And death rates rise rapidly across age groups.

Leading Causes of Death

Two-thirds of all Americans will die as a result of heart disease, cancer, stroke, chronic lower respiratory diseases, or an accident. While accidents fall in importance as people get older, 6 out of 10 elderly Americans die from heart disease, cancer, or stroke (Figure 10.2). Let's consider each of these briefly.

FIGURE 10.2 *Death Rates for Selected Leading Causes of Death among People Age 65+, 1981 to 2001*

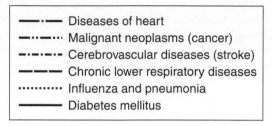

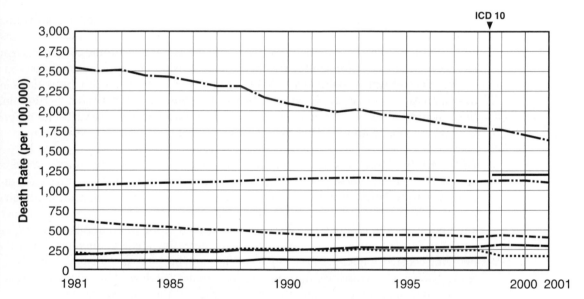

Source: Centers for Disease Control and Prevention, National Center for Health Statistics, National Vital Statistics System, 2004. Available online at www.agingstats.gov/chartbook2004/images/p_23.jpg.

Heart Disease. Since 1970, deaths from heart disease have dropped dramatically (down 40 percent). This has been accomplished through a combination of changes in lifestyle that have reduced major risk factors (smoking, cholesterol, hypertension) and promoted healthy behaviors (exercise, better diet), as well as through earlier detection and improved medical treatment. Still, cardiovascular disease is the leading cause of death among older adults in all industrialized countries.

While family history and genetic makeup increase the risk of heart disease, unhealthy behaviors also play a critical role. In fact, according to the American Heart Association, 82 percent of heart disease in women is due to unhealthy habits. The dramatic increase in obesity in recent years is of great concern, as unhealthy, high-fat diets are a major risk factor for heart disease. Obesity can also trigger diabetes; adults with diabetes are two to four times more likely to develop heart disease. Many Americans are diabetic and don't know it. The advice is simple: stop smoking, get at least 30 minutes of exercise on most days, eat a low-fat, high-fiber diet rich in fruits and vegetables, manage weight, and keep blood pressure and cholesterol low. An added benefit: protecting your heart may also protect your brain and reduce the risk of Alzheimer's disease (see Chapter 11).

Evidence is mounting that psychosocial factors—such as hostility, anger, stress, depression, and social isolation (low social support)—increase the risk of cardiovascular disease as well as affecting its development and outcome in those who already have heart disease (see, e.g., Rozanski, Blumenthal, & Kaplan, 1999; Krantz & McCeney, 2002; Krantz, Sheps, Carney, & Natelson, 2000). Attention is increasingly being given to interventions that address these factors.

Although heart disease strikes men earlier, once a woman reaches menopause and stops producing estrogen, her risk of heart attack goes up every year. Thus, longer life expectancy has brought higher rates of heart disease among women. Further, a woman who has a heart attack is twice as likely to have a second attack as a man and twice as likely to die. Treatment of women heart patients is complicated by the fact that they are likely to be significantly older (age 65 as compared to age 40) and may be suffering from other chronic conditions. The warning signs and internal manifestations of heart disease are often different in women than in men. Lack of knowledge about the nature of heart disease in women means that diagnoses are often missed (you are less likely to find it if you are not looking for it), and the effectiveness of available treatment strategies is unclear. As with men, however, prevention may be the key.

According to the American Heart Association (www.americanheart.org), some heart attacks are sudden and intense (the "movie heart attack"), but most start slowly, with mild pain or discomfort. The warning signs of heart attack vary among men and women and may include the following:

- Chest discomfort in the center of the chest that lasts more than a few minutes or that goes away and comes back (a feeling of uncomfortable pressure, squeezing, fullness, or pain)
- Pain or discomfort in other areas of the upper body, such as one or both arms, the back, neck, jaw, or stomach
- Shortness of breath, with or without chest discomfort
- Breaking out in a cold sweat, nausea, or lightheadedness

Cancer. Cancer refers to diseases in which abnormal cells divide without control. Cancer cells can invade adjacent tissue and can spread throughout the bloodstream and lymphatic system to other parts of the body. In the United States, one of every four deaths is from cancer. Since the risk of cancer increases with age, most cases affect adults beginning in middle age, with about 77 percent of all cancers diagnosed among those age 55 and older (American Cancer Society, 2004). Though a number of factors contribute to this phenomenon, time is perhaps the most important: cancer is a progressive disease and it simply takes time for it to develop (Ershler, 1992). The coexistence of other diseases, common in elderly patients, may affect the progress of the cancer and complicate its treatment.

Lung cancer is the most common cause of cancer death among both males and females in the United States. Cigarette smoking is the biggest risk factor, accounting for 87 percent of lung cancers (American Cancer Society, 2004). Individuals who stop smoking even after heavy long-term use reduce their cancer risk, although they remain at greater risk than those who never smoked. After ten years of not smoking, ex-smokers' risk of lung cancer decreases to 30 to 50 percent of the risk of those still smoking.

The occurrence of cancer varies by gender, as shown in Figure 10.3. Prostate cancer is the most commonly diagnosed form of cancer in males and the second leading cause of cancer deaths in males. African American men have the highest rate of prostate cancer in the world (American Cancer Society, 2004). Colorectal cancer (cancer of the colon or rectum) is the third leading cause of cancer-related deaths in males. Death rates among males have declined for all sites, with significant decreases for lung, prostate, brain, and other nervous system cancers.

FIGURE 10.3 *Leading Sites of New Cancer Cases and Deaths, 2003*

Estimated New Cases

Male		Female	
Prostate	220,900 (33%)	Breast	211,300 (32%)
Lung and bronchus	91,800 (14%)	Lung and bronchus	80,100 (12%)
Colon and rectum	72,800 (11%)	Colon and rectum	74,700 (11%)
Urinary bladder	42,200 (6%)	Uterine corpus	40,100 (6%)
Melanoma of the skin	29,900 (4%)	Ovary	25,400 (4%)
Non-Hodgkin lymphoma	28,300 (4%)	Non-Hodgkin Lymphoma	25,100 (4%)
Kidney	19,500 (3%)	Melanoma of the skin	24,300 (3%)
Oral cavity	18,200 (3%)	Thyroid	16,300 (3%)
Leukemia	17,900 (3%)	Pancreas	15,800 (2%)
Pancreas	14,900 (2%)	Urinary bladder	15,200 (2%)
All sites	**675,300 (100%)**	**All sites**	**658,800 (100%)**

Estimated Deaths

Male		Female	
Lung and bronchus	88,400 (31%)	Lung and bronchus	68,800 (25%)
Prostate	28,900 (10%)	Breast	39,800 (15%)
Colon and rectum	28,300 (10%)	Colon and rectum	28,800 (11%)
Pancreas	14,700 (5%)	Pancreas	15,300 (6%)
Non-Hodgkin Lymphoma	12,200 (4%)	Ovary	14,300 (5%)
Leukemia	12,100 (4%)	Non-Hodgkin Lymphoma	11,200 (4%)
Esophagus	9,900 (4%)	Leukemia	9,800 (4%)
Liver	9,200 (3%)	Uterine corpus	6,800 (3%)
Urinary bladder	8,600 (3%)	Brain	5,800 (2%)
Kidney	7,400 (3%)	Multiple myeloma	5,500 (2%)
All sites	**285,900 (100%)**	**All sites**	**270,600 (100%)**

Note: Excludes basal and squamous cell skin cancers and in situ carcinomas except urinary bladder. Percentages may not total 100% due to rounding.

Source: American Cancer Society *Surveillance Research*, 2004. Available online at www.cancer.org/downloads/STT/CAFF2003PWSecured.pdf.

Though breast cancer is the most common non-skin cancer diagnosed among women in the United States, death rates from breast cancer have declined significantly, which is attributed to better screening through mammography and improved treatment. However, female lung cancer deaths increased for several decades, leveling off in the late 1990s among White women, but not among Black women (American Cancer Society, 2004). Since 1987, more females have died from lung cancer than breast cancer. Women may develop lung cancer at a younger age and after fewer years of smoking than men. The greater risk of lung cancer among women is, in part, due to a smoking-induced genetic mutation in women's lung tissue, which is accelerated by estrogen. Women may also metabolize the carcinogens in smoke differently or have more trouble repairing damage to DNA. Colorectal cancer is the third leading cause of cancer deaths in females.

Cancer death rates also vary by race and ethnicity. Overall, cancer death rates among African Americans are about 30 percent higher than among Whites and more than two times higher than among Asian or Pacific Islanders, American Indians, or Hispanics (American Cancer Society, 2004). Rates for specific cancers vary among racial/ethnic groups as well. For example, in contrast to their White counterparts, deaths due to breast cancer in African American females continue to increase, in part because diagnosis is made at later stages of the disease.

Experts stress the importance of continued efforts at prevention, early detection, and treatment as well as research into the causes of the various cancers. It is estimated that 50 percent or more of cancer can be prevented through cessation of smoking and improved diet, such as reducing fat intake and increasing consumption of fruits and vegetables (U.S. Department of Health and Human Services, 2000). Physical activity and weight control (weight gain is a known risk factor for breast cancer among postmenopausal women) as well as limiting sun exposure and using sunscreen also help to prevent cancer. There is increased interest in the ability of vitamins E and C and beta-carotene to neutralize free radicals, thereby lowering cancer risk. As more is learned about the various forms of cancer, we may witness the prevention of the major human cancers through changes in lifestyle as well as medical interventions.

Stroke. A stroke is a type of cardiovascular disease. It occurs when the blood supply to part of the brain is cut off, either through a clot or a bursting of the blood vessel that normally feeds the tissue. Without a constant supply of oxygen delivered by the blood, brain cells begin to die. The nature and extent of the resulting damage depend on which part and how much of the brain is affected.

According to the American Heart Association (1997a, b; 2004), stroke is the third leading cause of death in the United States and the leading cause of severe disability, including paralysis, loss of speech, and memory impairments. Risk factors include obesity, smoking, high blood pressure, diabetes, heart disease, high cholesterol, drinking more than two alcoholic drinks a day, and a narrowing of the carotid arteries. One very important risk factor is a TIA (transient ischemic attack), a temporary interruption of blood flow that causes temporary strokelike symptoms. A person who has had a TIA is ten times more likely to suffer a stroke, 50 percent of the time within one year. African Americans experience higher rates of these risk factors and, as a result, have twice the risk of stroke.

Like a heart attack, a stroke is a medical emergency. New approaches to treatment must be administered quickly. But many people either deny or do not recognize the signs of stroke, and therefore patients may not receive the prompt medical attention they need. The five major warning signs are:

- Sudden weakness or numbness of the face, arm, or leg on one side of the body
- Sudden dimness or loss of vision, particularly in one eye
- Loss of speech or trouble talking or understanding speech
- Sudden, severe headache with no known cause
- Unexplained dizziness, unsteadiness, or sudden falls, especially in conjunction with other stroke symptoms

Stroke prevention is aimed at reducing the risk factors as well as screening for high blood pressure, cholesterol, and narrowed carotid arteries. The death rate from strokes has declined about 65 percent since 1960, primarily as a result of prevention efforts such as reduced smoking and better management of hypertension, along with better diagnosis and treatment.

Strokes are uncommon before age 50 but increase in frequency with age. Though older adults are at greatest risk for stroke, they are least likely to be aware of the warning signs and also most likely to have "silent" or symptomless strokes. These strokes occur in small vessels and, while initially harmless, can eventually disrupt brain function, causing memory problems or difficulty walking. Silent strokes are more frequent in women. To learn about stroke prevention, risk assessment, and warning signs, visit www.strokeassociation.org.

Health and Functional Status

One way to assess health status is by looking at the degree to which the individual can perform the functions necessary to live independently (in other words, degree of disability). These are referred to as **activities of daily living** (ADLs) and include such fundamental tasks as walking, bathing, dressing, getting to and using the toilet, eating, and transferring from a bed or a chair. A second class of activities, referred to as **instrumental activities of daily living** (IADLs), has more to do with carrying out the business of daily life and includes such tasks as getting around in the community, shopping, cooking, doing housework, and using the telephone. Older adults vary tremendously in the degree to which they are disabled by poor health—that is, in the number and severity of limitations in their activities. The presence of limitations in these areas is an important indicator of quality of life and has an impact on the need for various types of assistance, including long-term care. The design of products and environments to facilitate functional independence is also important. (See Box.) According to the U.S. Bureau of the Census (2003, March), rates of disability increase with age and are higher among the poor and among Native Americans and Blacks (as compared to Whites, Asians, and Hispanics). Also, because of their greater longevity, women comprise the majority of those over 65 with a severe disability.

Trends in Disability

Are rates of disability increasing or decreasing? As efforts to eliminate the fatal degenerative diseases that are the major causes of death succeed, and improved treatment delays death among those currently ill, there is growing concern that we are simply adding years of increasing disability—"trading off a longer life for a prolonged period of frailty and

*Transgenerational Design: Designing Products
and Environments for People of All Ages*

As people live longer, functional status becomes a critical concern. The concept of **transgenerational** (or universal) **design** is to make both products and environments compatible with the kinds of impairments and disabilities that can occur at any age but are more likely as we get older (Pirkl, 1995). Problems such as poor eyesight, failing finger strength, arthritis, and lower back problems can limit individuals' ability to function independently. Products designed to accommodate these disabilities can help us to remain active and independent and allow both young and old to accomplish the necessary activities of daily living (Clark, Czaja, & Weber, 1990). Design of transgenerational products has three aims: to bridge the demands of age changes, to respond to the widest range of ages and abilities, and to preserve the individual's sense of dignity and self-worth. Products, spaces, technologies, and services that accommodate the needs of a multiaged population not only increase individual independence, but also improve safety, comfort, convenience, and ease of operation—outcomes valued by all ages. Transgenerational design principles apply not only to the functional qualities of products and places, but also to their aesthetic aspects. Given the demographic realities, transgenerational design makes good economic sense. Beyond economics, matching products to the people who use them is important for consumers of all ages.

Transgenerational design can enhance the functional capacity of individuals of all ages by making products easier and more comfortable to use. The adjustable keyboard, low-stress mouse, and mousing platform shown here have been engineered to reduce repetitive stress injuries.

dependency" (Olshansky, Carnes, & Cassel, 1990, p. 639). In other words, concerns about the quality versus the quantity of life have emerged. In 1980, James Fries predicted that as a result of greater prevention as well as improved treatment, the portion of life spent in disease and disability would be compressed or delayed against a fixed life span, and therefore reduced. This optimistic view—the **compression-of-morbidity hypothesis**— suggests that poor health will, on average, occur later in life and be of shorter duration, thus giving people more healthy years. Though Fries's hypothesis has been controversial (Olshansky, Carnes, & Cassel, 1990) and we still lack sufficient data on the incidence of disease and disability among adults, evidence indicates that rates of disability among the elderly may be falling. Analysis of data from the National Long-Term Care Surveys (which regularly study about 20,000 people ages 65+) suggests that disability rates have declined since the early 1980s, when the surveys began (U.S. Bureau of the Census, 1995; see also Centers for Disease Control, 2004c). Rates of many chronic diseases are also falling (exceptions include hypertension and diabetes—likely related to increased rates of obesity). Some of this reduction may be due to surgical interventions such as cataract removal and joint replacement, as well as other treatments, though it also reflects the healthier behaviors and reduced risk that come with the overall higher educational levels and incomes of today's older adults. For example, disability was 42 to 67 percent lower for those with more than 16 years of education as compared to those with less than 11, and the disability rate among the nonpoor was 59 to 80 percent lower than among the poor (Manton et al., 1993). Efforts to better understand, treat, and prevent the nonfatal but highly disabling conditions of later life, such as arthritis, osteoporosis, sensory impairments, and Alzheimer's disease, will ensure that active life expectancy will increase, and longer life will also mean better health. We have reason to be optimistic.

Effects of Gender and Race on Health and Longevity

Health experience varies by race and gender, though our understanding of the health status of women and minorities is limited by the lack of available research on these populations.

Gender Differences

Despite the fact that women constitute the majority of the population, they have been routinely omitted from biomedical research (Denmark, 1994; Matthews et al., 1997). Typically, researchers study men and then generalize the results to women, even though there are known differences between male and female physiology. Research that does include women usually ignores older women, though they are often the ones most likely to suffer from the condition under investigation. For example, a famous study in the late 1980s found that taking an aspirin a day reduced the risk of heart attack by 50 percent. These results were quickly heralded as an effective preventive strategy. However, all of the 22,000 participants in the study were male physicians. Despite the fact that heart disease is the number-one killer of women over age 65, researchers neglected to determine if aspirin had the same salutary effect on women as on men.

Interest in studying women's health issues is growing, partly as a result of changes at the federal government level, including the creation of an Office of Women's Health within the National Institutes of Health (NIH), and the issuing of guidelines that require researchers who receive federal funds to include women participants. In 1991, NIH launched an enormous project called the Women's Health Initiative (WHI), a 15-year study of more than 161,000 postmenopausal women (age 50 to 79) from diverse ethnic groups and socioeconomic backgrounds. The study will explore the effects of diet, smoking, and other risk factors on the development of heart disease, stroke, osteoporosis, and breast and colon cancer among older women and minorities. These are the leading causes of death, disability, and frailty among older women. WHI will also evaluate the effects of hormone replacement therapy (see also Chapter 9), low-fat diet, and calcium—Vitamin D supplementation. (For a detailed review of WHI, see Matthews et al., 1997; visit the sites at www.nhlbi.nih.gov/whi and www.whi.org.)

A number of gender differences in health and longevity have been recognized. While men and women suffer from the same kinds of health problems, rates vary. In particular, men are more likely than women to develop and die from the most serious fatal diseases, while women are more likely than men to experience frequent, less serious acute conditions, as well as nonfatal chronic conditions that cause physical disabilities. For example, coronary heart disease is much more common among men, while arthritis and osteoporosis are much more common among women. However, it is a misconception to view heart disease as a man's problem, as it is the major cause of death among U.S. men *and* women.

Observed health differences between men and women may be attributable to biological and genetic factors but are also the product of socioeconomic experiences. For example, the data generally show that older women are at greater risk of functional impairment than older men. However, when economic and educational background are controlled, this gender difference disappears (Maddox, 1991). Further, the finding that American women generally enjoy longer life but worse health has not been replicated by research in the United Kingdom or Japan. For example, a longitudinal study of 2,200 older Japanese adults found that women not only had lower mortality rates but also had a lower risk of early onset of disability (Liang et al., 2003). The researchers suggest that rather than being universal, health trajectories over the course of adulthood may vary by context and be affected by a range of social, cultural, and psychological variables.

Female life expectancy in the United States exceeds that of males by about six years: for all races combined, 74.4 years for males; 79.8 years for females (National Center for Health Statistics, 2003). (See Table 10.1.) (The female advantage is 4.7 years in the United Kingdom, 4.8 in Sweden, and 6.8 in Japan.) In 2000, the sex ratio among those age 65 to 74 was 82 males to 100 females; the ratio among those 85+ was 41 males to 100 females (U.S. Bureau of the Census, 2001). The causes of this gender gap in mortality are complex and not well understood, though they are believed to include biogenetic as well as sociocultural and lifestyle factors operative throughout the life span: levels of stress, high-risk behaviors, exposure to hazardous environments, levels of physical activity, and so on (Herzog, 1989; Huyck, 1990). Nathanson (1977, pp. 145–146) has argued that women are more likely to engage in health-promoting behaviors and less likely to engage in risk-taking behaviors: "For all the causes of death where individual risk-taking behavior is clearly involved, rates for men are from two to four times higher than the comparable rates for women."

The implications of these gender differences are equally complex. For example, women's independence is at greater risk than men's in late adulthood, since their survival advantage may mean more years of chronic, debilitating illness. These conditions impair both ability and motivation to be physically active, leading to a downward spiral of physical limitations and frailty among elderly women—the less active you are, the weaker you get and the less active you *can* be. Lack of basic strength is blamed for the majority of falls experienced by over one-third of all adults over age 65 (Blake et al., 1988; Campbell, Borrie, & Spears, 1989).

TABLE 10.1 *Life Expectancy by Sex and Race, 1900–2001, United States (in years)*

	1900		2001	
	Male	Female	Male	Female
White	46.6	48.7	75.0	80.2
Black	32.5	33.5	68.6	75.5

Source: National Center for Health Statistics, 2003.

In addition, because of their employment history, women are less likely than men to have health insurance and the financial resources that give them access to the health care system. The fact that the majority of older women are widowed and living alone also means that they are less likely than men to experience the emotional support and caregiving provided by a spouse (see Chapter 7). Others claim that women, and in particular older and minority women, are the victims of bias and discrimination not only in health research but also in the health care system. For example, it is often considered "normal" for older women to be depressed and to have low self-esteem. Women may thus be denied treatment that could improve the quality of their lives.

Women over the age of 65 are a fast-growing segment of our population. Wisocki & Keuthen (1988) stress the importance of studying diseases of special concern to this group, such as osteoporosis, arthritis, and urinary incontinence. A major challenge for the future is to develop a health psychology that includes knowledge of women, their health status, and appropriate interventions.

Racial/Ethnic Differences

Minorities generally experience more health problems than Whites, and these problems tend to develop earlier in life, are more severe, and are more often fatal. However, health and longevity vary greatly both among and within racial/ethnic groups. Figures also vary by disease. For example, among adults 65 and over, rates of hypertension are 65 percent among Blacks, 49 percent among Hispanic Americans, and 47 percent among Whites (Centers for Disease Control, 2004c). Diabetes affects 25 percent of Hispanics, 23 percent of Blacks, and 14 percent of Whites. On the other hand, 22 percent of Whites have some form of cancer, compared with 10 percent of Hispanic Americans and Blacks.

The extent to which observed health differences are due to socioeconomic status (SES) and other factors besides race is unclear. SES is one of the strongest predictors of illness and health (Adler et al., 1994). Those higher in SES generally have better physical and psychological health than those lower in the hierarchy. SES differences in rates of illness and mortality have been found for almost all diseases and conditions.

Yet the nature of these relationships is unclear—that is, we are not certain how SES operates to influence the biological functions that determine health status. We know that SES is correlated with health-related behaviors, such as the quality of nutritional intake, a major factor in health and illness (Ryan, 1989). Adler et al. (1994) found that rates of smoking are inversely correlated with SES, while rates of physical activity and SES are positively correlated. In addition, psychological variables such as depression, hostility, and stress are all inversely related to SES. More research is needed to explore these and other potential explanations of the relationship between health and social class.

Attempts to improve the health status of disadvantaged groups must also confront the social, psychological, and physiological impact of poverty and living in what have been called toxic residential environments. These environments may lead to poor health through their effect on stress, smoking and use of other drugs, access to health care, and so on.

Relatively little is known about the health status and health-related behaviors of minority groups in general and some minorities in particular, such as American Indians (Blum et al., 1992). The majority of studies have focused on Blacks.

Health and Longevity among Blacks. The health status of African Americans is generally poorer than that of Whites, and they are more likely to rate their health as poor. In comparison to Whites, Blacks suffer higher rates of diabetes, hypertension, heart disease, arthritis, asthma, and other stress-related problems, as well as higher rates of death from cancer (Heckler, 1985; National Center for Health Statistics, 1990, 2000). In addition, access to health care is often limited by geography, economics, and a reluctance to visit doctors, so that disease is more likely to be detected at a later, more advanced stage. These factors are complicated by poor nutrition and the stress of poverty. Rates of psychiatric disorders are also higher (Bulhan, 1985).

In comparison to the population as a whole, Blacks have shorter life expectancy at birth and greater rates of disability and mortality at every point in the life span except after age 80 (Jackson et al., 1990). After that, Blacks can expect to outlive Whites, a phenomenon known as the **racial mortality crossover effect.** This may reflect a "selective survival" process by which those minority elders who live to advanced age are the most hardy (Markides & Mindel, 1987). As indicated in Table 10.1, average life expectancy for a Black male is 68.6 years, Black female 75.5 years, White male 75.0 years, and White female 80.2 years (National Center for Health Statistics, 2003).

Health and Longevity among Native Americans. The five leading causes of death among older American Indians and Alaskan natives are heart disease, cancer, unintentional injuries, diabetes, and cerebrovascular diseases (National Center for Health Statistics, 2004b). The leading health problem is alcohol abuse. There are important differences among tribes in terms of cultural beliefs and practices, diet, and so on; thus, care must be taken in generalizing about health issues for these groups.

Health and Longevity among Asians and Pacific Islanders. Asians and Pacific Islanders have lower rates of premature mortality and higher life expectancy than all other ethnic groups, though they do have higher rates of tuberculosis, hepatitis, anemia, and hypertension (Yee & Weaver, 1994). Again, generalizations are somewhat misleading, as some subgoups have poor health status. The overall relatively low mortality rate of Asians in comparison with other ethnic groups is thought to be related to socioeconomic status, culture, and lifestyle—for example, very few health problems are associated with smoking and alcohol.

Health and Longevity among Hispanics. Much of what we know about Hispanic populations is based on studies of Mexican Americans and may not be generalizable to other Hispanic groups (Yee & Weaver, 1994). Leading causes of poor health and death are heart disease, diabetes, cancer, and hypertension. Health problems are related to obesity, poor dietary habits, smoking, alcohol, and lack of exercise.

Summary. Preston and Taubman (1994) conclude that the poorer health and shorter life expectancy of Blacks in comparison with Whites is primarily due to racial inequality in education and income. Yee and Weaver (1994) agree that socioeconomic factors are a major (though not the only) contributor to the poor health of minorities, affecting such things as level of education, access to and utilization of health care services, and stress. They also suggest that for some of these groups, abandonment of traditional diets and lifestyles in favor of the mainstream American culture may have actualized existing genetic susceptibilities to certain health conditions. For example, the American diet may lead to higher rates of obesity and diabetes among these populations than among their White counterparts. Finally, perceived racism may activate physiological stress responses that affect health, as argued by Clark, Anderson, Clark, and Williams (1999).

Concept Review 10.1

- While the majority of older adults are in good health, rates of disease, chronic illness, and disability do increase with age.

- The most common chronic conditions among adults aged 65+ include arthritis, hypertension, and hearing and visual problems.

- The leading causes of death are heart disease, cancer, and stroke. Progress is being made in prevention and treatment.

- Rates of disability have been declining in recent years.

- Gender and race affect health status as well as longevity. More research is needed to clarify these effects and their causes.

Prevention of Illness and Promotion of Health

Hippocrates stressed that "the function of protecting and developing health must rank even above that of restoring it when it is impaired." In 2001, the American Psychological Association amended its bylaws to include "promoting health" as one of its major goals. Fries (1990, p. 2355) comments that managing old age better is best handled not by waiting around "for the cure" but by healthy lifestyles and environmental improvements that prevent disease and preserve fitness, vigor, and independence. Colten (1999, p.1) argues that health promotion among older adults is, in fact, "a responsibility of the pediatrician. The establishment of health-promoting behaviors in childhood is far easier than the breaking of disease-promoting habits in adults." Perhaps the point is best made in a classic essay by McKinlay (1981), who warns of the futility of using all one's resources to pull people out of a rushing stream without trying to find out who is upstream pushing them in.

Our health and the way we age are largely a matter of the way we live. Factors related to lifestyle can affect entire societies. For example, the social and economic difficulties experienced by the Russian population following the dissolution of the Soviet Union have led to a declining life expectancy. The average Russian male can expect to live 16 fewer years than his American counterpart—to age 59. The U.S. Public Health Service and a number of professional groups and organizations developed *Healthy People 2010,* a prevention agenda for the nation and a statement of national health objectives. This document has identified two major goals: to increase the quality and years of healthy life and to eliminate health disparities between different groups in the population. (Visit the site at www.health.gov/healthypeople/.)

Three Levels of Prevention

Prevention efforts can be thought of as falling into one of three levels. **Primary prevention** refers to efforts aimed at preventing or delaying the development of a disease

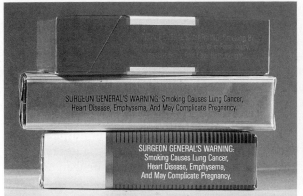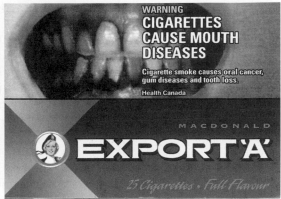

The health warnings on these cigarette packages are examples of primary prevention, aimed at preventing the development of smoking-related diseases and conditions in the population as a whole. Contrast the warning used in the United States on the left with one of a series used in Canada. Research has found that warnings with pictures are significantly more likely to persuade smokers to quit.

or condition. **Secondary prevention** refers to activities aimed at early diagnosis through screening when the condition is asymptomatic (before symptoms appear), and early treatment to cure or prevent the progression of a condition. **Tertiary prevention** comes after a diagnosis of a serious disease or disability and focuses on halting its progression and on rehabilitation, control of pain, and efforts to increase function. Table 10.2 lists examples of these three levels of prevention. German (1994) stresses that secondary and tertiary prevention efforts may be especially important in avoiding or limiting disability for older adults, including those in long-term care facilities, the majority of whom already suffer from an existing condition (or conditions).

Matching the Program to the Person

One of the challenges in prevention efforts is getting people to accept the message and actively participate in their own health care. The effectiveness of health promotion and prevention programs increases when they are matched to the target population (age, gender, and ethnic background). For example, women may be more receptive to prevention

TABLE 10.2 *Examples of Primary, Secondary, and Tertiary Prevention*

Primary Prevention	Secondary Prevention	Tertiary Prevention
Immunization	Screening for diabetes, cancer (e.g., prostate, breast)	Pain control for those with arthritis
Controlling risk factors through improved health habits (diet, exercise, not smoking)	Screening for depression	Very low-fat, vegetarian diet for those with heart disease
HIV-AIDS education	Controlling hypertension to avoid stroke	Rehabilitation following stroke

efforts (such as screening for cancer by Pap smears and mammography) if the provider is a female (Lurie et al., 1993).

Although the health of the U.S. population as a whole has improved since the 1980s, as we have seen, the health of minority groups has not. Rates of disease, disability, and mortality are, with few exceptions, higher than among Whites. Gornick et al. (1996) examined the effects of race and income on mortality and use of health services by those entitled to Medicare. The authors found that Black and low-income individuals received less preventive care (for example, fewer immunizations, fewer mammograms) and less adequate management of chronic conditions and had higher rates of hospitalization and mortality than White or more affluent Medicare beneficiaries. The authors suggest that these differences reflect a variety of variables, including educational and cultural differences that may affect use of services. To date, most health promotion and disease intervention programs have been geared to the dominant culture. According to Yee and Weaver (1994), in order to improve the health and longevity of ethnic minorities, these efforts must become "culturally competent"—that is, they must consider cultural differences in health beliefs and practices. For example, because many ethnic minorities come from collectivist cultures (see Chapter 3), programs that focus on the family may be more effective than those that focus on the individual. Further, individuals may be more receptive to health-related messages if they come from someone of similar background. Additional research is needed in order to effectively match the message, the program, and the provider to the culture of the target audience.

Risk Factors

Aging research has only recently begun to shift its emphasis from losses due to an inevitable biological aging process to sources of variability across individuals. We know that some people are at greater risk of disease and disability than others. A **risk factor** is a biological or behavioral characteristic that increases the likelihood that an individual will develop a disease (Siegler, 1989). (Stokols, 1992, would like us to consider environmental risk factors as well.) **Relative risk** describes the rate of a particular disease among those who have the risk factor(s) versus those who do not. Thus, the presence of risk factors does not indicate that an individual will inevitably develop a particular health problem but suggests that the probability increases as more risk factors are present.

As risk factors accumulate, the likelihood of sickness, disability, loss of productivity, and premature death increases, medical costs increase, and quality of life is impaired, especially as one gets older (Stamler, 2001; Mokdad, Marks, Stroup, & Gerberding, 2004). The best scenario is to enter young adulthood free of these factors and to stay that way. So it is important to recognize risk factors early and to adopt a lifestyle to address them.

Biological Risk Factors

The most important biological risk factors are age, sex, and family history (which is an indicator of genetic characteristics). Knowing your family's health history can be a tremendous advantage in preventing illness, disability, and death, though ironically, few people know for sure what their grandparents or parents died of and at what age. DNA testing can allow us to find out our genetic risk for various illnesses. One of the resulting challenges will be encouraging the positive utilization of genetic information.

Behavioral Risk Factors

Behavioral pathogens are toxic behaviors—personal attitudes, habits, and lifestyles that contribute to disease, disability, and death (Matarazzo, 1984). Among the major behavioral risk factors are smoking, use of alcohol, diet (especially in regard to cholesterol level), obesity, psychosocial stress, low internal control, and hostility (Siegler, 1989). Early claims of links between the Type A personality construct (hard-driving, competitive, time-urgent) and coronary heart disease have been modified to emphasize the importance of one Type A trait in particular—hostility (Wright, 1988).

A number of the behavioral risk factors are related to more than one disease. For example, smoking is linked to bone loss and osteoporosis; hypertension; stroke; coronary heart disease; cancer of the lung, mouth, larynx, bladder, kidney, pancreas, and stomach; and emphysema (Baum & Posluszny, 1999; Centers for Disease Control, 2004a; Siegler, 1989). According to the 2004 Surgeon General's Report (Centers for Disease Control, 2004a), smoking harms nearly every organ of the body, causing many diseases and reducing overall health.

A meta-analysis of the actual causes of death in the United States found that about half of all deaths in 2000 could be attributed to modifiable behavioral risk factors—that is, to preventable behaviors. Heading the list were smoking, poor diet and physical inactivity, and alcohol consumption (Mokdad et al., 2004). The researchers note that the most striking finding was the increase in the number of deaths due to poor diet and lack of exercise, which, if current trends of increasing overweight continue, may soon overtake tobacco as the leading cause of death. They estimate that, in 2005, the death toll from obesity will reach more than 500,000. They conclude: "Interventions to prevent and increase cessation of smoking, improve diet, and increase physical activity must become much higher priorities in the public health and health-care systems"(p. 1242).

A Closer Look at the Relationship between Mind and Body

While it is clear how factors like diet and smoking influence health, the link between attitudes and emotions and health may be less evident. The relation between the mind and the body—known as the mind-body problem—has been the subject of one of the classic debates in psychology. In the 17th century, the French philosopher and mathematician René Descartes described the mind and body as separate, noninteracting entities, a position known as **Cartesian dualism.** This position dominated medicine for 300 years. Though it persists in some quarters, it has been largely supplanted by the growing recognition that mind and body are reciprocally interconnected—that events occurring in one arena directly and indirectly affect events occurring in the other.

Some simple examples make the point. Have you ever been secretly embarrassed about something and felt your face get hot? Or been frightened and felt your heart start to race? I remember rushing to get to the psych building one day when I was in graduate school and brushing the edge of my foot with the heavy glass-and-steel door. It was a hot day, and I had on sandals. I raced to the elevator, got to my floor, opened my office, and happened to glance down at my foot. My little toe seemed to be dangling there at an odd angle. I remember actually saying to myself: "Ooh, I bet that hurts!" Suddenly, a rush of pain overwhelmed me and I felt faint, though I had been unaware of the injury until I actually saw my toe. All of these are examples of the reciprocal relationship between the mind and the body. But can the mind influence the body in such a way as to affect health? Can emotions and attitudes affect our susceptibility to infectious illness and the initiation and course of specific diseases? Though the mechanisms by which this may happen are not yet fully understood, the answer seems to be yes.

There has been growing interest in **psychoneuroimmunology** (PNI), a term referring to the study of the interaction of the mind, the nervous system, and the *immune system*. PNI examines how our beliefs, thoughts, and emotions influence our biological responses and therefore our susceptibility to illness. It reflects growing attention to the psychosocial components of health. In fact, psychosocial factors appear to be among the most powerful determinants of immune reactions (Cacioppo & Berntson, 1992) and thus may be important in the onset and progression of infectious disease and autoimmune diseases. This biopsychosocial model asserts that the "causes, development, and outcomes of an illness are determined by the interaction of psychological, social, and cultural factors with biochemistry and physiology" (Ray, 2004, p. 29). (See Cohen & Herbert, 1996, for a review of studies of PNI addressing the role of psychological factors in physical illness.) Testimony to the power of this view, in 1999 the National Institutes of Health awarded $2 million each to five mind-body centers to fund research by multidisciplinary teams (e.g., investigators from psychology, sociology, molecular biology, immunology) into links between emotions and health.

Psychosocial risk factors include loneliness, social isolation, lack of social support; lack of control, feelings of helplessness, pessimism; anger and hostility; feelings of loss or bereavement; and stress. Even commonplace stressful events can be threatening. For example, medical students (who are certainly familiar with test taking) show suppressed immune function during examination periods (Kiecolt-Glaser & Glaser, 1988). Those who experience a lot of stress may be more susceptible to a number of conditions, including cardiovascular disease and infectious disease (Adler & Matthews, 1994). In general, negative emotional states are associated with adverse health consequences (Kiecolt-Glaser, McGuire, Robles, & Glaser, 2002). Conversely, the holding of positive beliefs such as optimism, hope, and control are generally related to physical health and well-being (Salovey, Rothman, Detweiler, & Steward, 2000; Strickland, 1989).

How exactly do the negative health effects just mentioned occur? As Ray (2004) explains, there are four information-processing systems in each of us that continually communicate with and influence one another: the mind (representing the function of the brain), the nervous system, the endocrine system, and the immune system. It appears that the mind influences the body through direct links between brain centers and the immune system, as well as indirectly through the endocrine system, which controls body chemistry and therefore many body functions, including the activity of the immune system. Thus, for example, anger and hostility or grief may initiate a cascade of neurological and hormonal events, which, particularly if they become chronic (persist over a period of time), may negatively affect the body and therefore health.

Particular attention has been focused on the interactions among the hypothalamus, the pituitary, and the adrenal glands and the resulting effect of the brain on the immune system. One primary mechanism is through chemical alteration of the immune response. For example, psychosocial stress causes the secretion of substances that suppress immune system activity. As a result, the individual is more vulnerable to infectious illness and takes longer to heal after injury or surgery (Kiecolt-Glaser, Page, Marucha, MacCallum, & Glaser, 1998). In addition, excesses of stress hormones (for example, glucocorticoids) for long periods of time, as when individuals are under chronic stress, can accelerate aspects of aging, in particular degeneration of areas of the brain including the hippocampus (Sapolsky, 1992). The body's normal stress response is also associated with a number of maladies such as hypertension, some forms of ulcers, and colitis, among others (Cohen, Tyrrell, & Smith, 1993; Sapolsky, 1992). Further, the physiological stress response itself, as well as the health consequences of stress, changes with age, with the older individual being more vulnerable to negative stress-related outcomes (Kiecolt-Glaser & Glaser, 2001; Sapolsky, 1992).

In the context of health, the mind-body connection has thus been reformulated as the brain-immune system connection. Research in this area has been hampered by methodological and conceptual problems, including difficulty in defining and measuring such variables as stress, control, helplessness, and so on. Conclusions are best viewed as preliminary and tentative. But there is growing recognition that the cycle of disease may commence in many ways, including in the mind. The idea is that our attitudes and emotions may affect the functioning of the body, making us more or less vulnerable to disease. In addition to their biological effects, these psychosocial factors also influence health by either increasing or decreasing health-enhancing (e.g., exercise) and health-impairing (e.g., smoking) behaviors as well as health behaviors such as the decision to seek care if one believes one is ill (Baum & Posluszny, 1999).

Moderating or Protective Variables

Certain variables influence or moderate the effect of risk factors on health. For example, the health of individuals is also related to the quality of the social systems of which they are a part—marriage, friendship, and so forth (Siegler, 1989). Social support and social connectedness are consistently associated with lower rates of disease and longer life. After reviewing 81 studies, Uchino, Cacioppo, and Kiecolt-Glaser (1996) found that social support was consistently related to beneficial effects on the cardiovascular, endocrine, and immune systems. One mechanism that might explain these effects is the stress-buffering role of social support. (See Chapter 6 for a more thorough discussion of social support and health.)

CRITICAL THINKING QUESTION

Why is social support viewed as health protective? Through what mechanisms could it have an impact on individual health?

Positive beliefs constitute a second moderating variable. Personal control, along with a number of other positive and overlapping qualities including optimism, the ability to find meaning in one's life experiences, self-efficacy, and high self-esteem, positively affects mental and physical health, perhaps through its impact on perceived stress and coping responses (Adler & Matthews, 1994; Siegler, 1989; Taylor, Kemeny, Reed, Bower, & Gruenewald, 2000). These qualities also contribute to resiliency—the ability to bounce back after a setback or trauma—a quality known to predict successful aging. A feeling of hope and having some power over events is often beneficial in that it leads to active coping behaviors, including those that reduce risk and enhance health. For example, an individual at risk of developing osteoporosis may decide that she will take action to reduce the risk, such as maintaining a regular exercise program and eating calcium-rich foods. Actual and perceived control may decline with age, especially among those in poor health, and a feeling of low control might further undermine motivation to seek treatment or change health-damaging behaviors. Thus, beliefs and attitudes influence health and illness. (Personal control is discussed, along with related control concepts, in more depth in Chapter 11.) The outcome of our state of mind may be more direct. Our thoughts represent the functioning of the brain. Therefore, according to the biopsychosocial model, as we change our thoughts, we change our brain and therefore our physiology (Ray, 2004). Indeed, scientific evidence has begun to support the biblical axiom "a merry heart doeth good like a medicine."

A third moderating variable is the ability to cope with stress, including the stress of illness. Perceived stress, and in particular a feeling of being unable to cope with stress, negatively affects health through a complex series of physiological stress-related responses. Coping ability can either maximize or minimize the impact of stressors on health (Birren & Renner, 1983). (Stress and coping are discussed more thoroughly in Chapter 11.)

CRITICAL THINKING QUESTION

Observers have noticed that the moment very sick patients are diagnosed, their physical condition often deteriorates quickly. How might this phenomenon be explained? Why would it be important for doctors to present diagnoses as challenges, not verdicts?

One of the implications of the link between psychological factors and health is that patients (for example, those about to undergo surgery, those recovering from a heart attack, or those with cancer) may benefit from support groups and other psychological interventions that address psychosocial risk factors. These interventions can focus on feelings of stress, anxiety, and depression as well as boost the individual's social support and feelings of control. Outcomes may include better psychological adjustment and coping skills, faster healing and surgical recovery, reduced pain, greater compliance with treatment activities, healthier behavior patterns, and improved immune function. A number of research projects are under way to examine these possibilities.

The dominant health care model is shifting to one that focuses on building health rather than fighting sickness, recognizes the role of psychosocial factors in the development of disease, acknowledges the importance of the patient's belief system, and shifts the patient and physician roles to those of active participant and collaborator.

An Overview of Preventive Behaviors

An ounce of prevention is worth a pound of cure. Fortunately, risk can be lowered by changes in behavior. A high percentage of the disease and disability that afflicts Americans is the result of unwise choices in behavior and lifestyle: in other words, poor health is largely self-inflicted. Preventive behaviors include making dietary changes to reduce fat and increase consumption of fruits and vegetables, eliminating smoking and drug abuse, reducing alcohol intake, getting regular exercise, developing coping skills, and enhancing social support and internal control.

Many diseases and chronic conditions are appropriate targets for prevention, including coronary heart disease, cancer, stroke, arthritis, visual and hearing problems, hypertension, and osteoporosis (Rubenstein, 1997). These include the major causes of death as well as the most common chronic conditions among older adults. Examples of effective prevention strategies for each of these is provided in Table 10.3. A number

TABLE 10.3 *Prevention of Major Diseases and Chronic Conditions*

Disease/Condition	Example of Effective Prevention
Coronary heart disease	Regular physical exercise
Cancer	Eliminate smoking
Stroke	Control hypertension
Arthritis	Avoid stress on joints
Visual problems	Regular check-ups
Hearing problems	Avoid exposure to excess noise
Hypertension	Avoid salt
Osteoporosis	Adequate calcium intake

Note: Other prevention strategies in addition to those listed are also effective for many of these diseases and conditions.

Sources: Adapted from German, 1994; Rubenstein, 1997; Siegler, 1989.

of these strategies are effective for more than one condition. For example, avoidance of cigarette smoking offers primary prevention for stroke, cancer, and heart disease, as well as other conditions.

Changes in behavior can significantly reduce risk. Perhaps the best example of the effectiveness of intervention is in regard to cigarette smoking (McLeroy & Crump, 1994). Since the Surgeon General's report describing the health consequences of smoking was issued in the mid-1960s, there has been a growing societal effort to reduce the numbers of smokers in the United States and therefore to reduce mortality rates from heart disease, cancer, and stroke. Smoking rates among adults have dropped significantly since the 1970s. And as we have seen, death rates from heart disease and stroke have declined dramatically during the same time period. (See Figure 10.2.) A portion of these declines can be attributed to lower smoking rates. According to reports issued by the U.S. Surgeon General (1989, 1990), those who quit smoking reduce their risk of heart disease and stroke by more than half within one and two years of quitting, respectively. The American Cancer Society (2004) stresses that the younger you are when you quit smoking, the greater the benefits. Those who quit by age 35 avoid 90 percent of the health risks of smoking, though even those who quit after 50 substantially reduce their risk of premature death.

Dietary habits also play an important role in maintaining good health and preventing many of the diseases and chronic conditions associated with aging. In general, a healthy diet includes eating a variety of foods low in saturated fat, cholesterol, and salt, and high in fiber. Five to nine servings of fruits and vegetables should be consumed daily (a serving consists of ½ cup of cut-up fruit or vegetable).

As previously noted, the dramatic increase in rates of overweight and obesity is of great concern. Almost two-thirds of Americans are overweight (with a body-mass index of 25 to 29) or obese (with a body-mass index of 30 or more) (Centers for Disease Control, 2004b). Between 1991 and 2000, the prevalence of obesity increased 61 percent. The negative effects of excessive weight on health include increased risk of heart disease, stroke, diabetes, gout, gall bladder disease, several types of cancer, kidney dysfunction, liver damage, deterioration of the joints, endocrine system abnormalities, and resulting increased mortality (Pinel, Assanand, & Lehman, 2000). A variety of factors have been cited as contributing to the dramatic increase in overweight and obesity in the United States. These include food supply issues, such as increased consumption of prepared foods that are higher in fat and calories, dramatic increases in the number of meals eaten outside the home, and increased portion sizes; more urbanized environments that favor driving rather than walking; a more sedentary lifestyle, both at work and leisure, and thus low levels of physical activity; television viewing; and higher levels of stress (Centers for Disease Control, 2004b; DeAngelis, 2004; Stamler, 2001). These lifestyle and environmental factors may also interact with predisposing genetic factors in some individuals. From an evolutionary perspective, our human physiology, which evolved to be extremely sensitive to cues of finding food in an environment in which food was scarce, is now seriously out of sync in an environment in which food is plentiful, inexpensive, good tasting, often poor in nutritional quality, and served in super-sized portions. Primary prevention is the best approach to addressing this problem, as permanent weight loss has proven extremely difficult to achieve.

While we are increasingly aware of the importance of good nutrition throughout the life span, appropriate nutritional guidelines for older adults are not yet well understood and probably differ from the needs of younger adults. For example, while a low-fat, high-fiber, low-cholesterol diet is recommended for most of us, it may not be appropriate for many elderly patients. Andres and Hallfrisch (1989) report that up to 50 percent of nursing home patients, many of whom have trouble maintaining weight anyway, may be malnourished as a result of institutional adoption of these diets. As we get older, it is increasingly important to maintain adequate protein in our diets, as well as ample supplies of vitamins E, D, and B-12, folate (folic acid), and calcium. Unrecognized and untreated nutritional deficiencies—including dehydration, which can cause side effects that may be mistaken for dementia—may be extremely prevalent among older people, leading to unnecessary illness, the worsening of a coexisting health problem, hospitalization, and readmission after hospital discharge (Thompson, 1997). Relevant factors include poverty, social isolation, depression, medications, disability, and drug abuse. Increased attention to nutritional status during routine medical or other social service contacts would be of great benefit.

In many ways, older adults take better care of their health than younger adults, with people over 65 less likely to smoke, drink, be overweight, or report high levels of stress (U.S. Senate Special Committee on Aging et al., 1991). (Lower rates of smoking and drinking are due both to discontinuing these behaviors and to the deaths of smokers and drinkers.) However, the elderly are much less likely to exercise regularly. Let's examine the effects of exercise in more detail.

A Closer Look at the Benefits of Exercise

Regular physical activity provides a range of physical and psychological health benefits, enhancing the function of almost every organ and system in the body. Short- and long-term benefits include weight control, stress reduction, opportunities for social interaction, maintenance of strength and mobility, improved posture and balance, and increased longevity (Centers for Disease Control, 2004c; O'Brien & Vertinsky, 1991). Physical activity contributes to psychological well-being and is associated with lower rates of depression. Exercising regularly may also promote a more youthful self-concept, which in turn may encourage continued exercise.

Exercise helps to prevent and manage heart disease, high blood pressure, diabetes, osteoporosis, and osteoarthritis; helps to control cholesterol level; and is associated

Regular physical exercise produces a range of both physical and psychological benefits at every age.

with lower rates of colon and other cancers, stroke, and back injury (Centers for Disease Control, 2004c). A longitudinal study of women aged 40 to 65 who walked briskly (at 3 mph or one mile every 20 minutes—in other words, not casual strolling) at least three hours per week had a 30 to 40 percent lower risk of heart attack than sedentary women (Manson et al., 1999). This was essentially the same risk reduction as women who engaged in vigorous aerobic exercise such as jogging or bicycling. And the more they walked, the lower their risk. There is even speculation that some age-related changes in the immune system may in fact be the result of reduced muscle mass and the corresponding drop in an essential amino acid produced during muscle metabolism, especially among older, more sedentary individuals (Parry-Billings, Newsholme, & Young, 1992).

Aerobic exercise may also positively affect cognitive functions, especially among older adults, through increased blood flow as well as other mechanisms (Hawkins, Kramer, & Capaldi, 1992). In one recent study lasting six months, 124 men and women aged 60 to 75 who had not exercised before were randomly assigned to either a walking program or an anaerobic regimen of stretching and muscle toning (Kramer et al., 1999). Subjects were given a variety of tasks designed to measure executive activities controlled by the frontal lobes—the kinds of activities needed to live independently, such as the ability to plan, make and remember choices, and reevaluate decisions under changing circumstances. In one test, subjects were given task-switching exercises in which they were shown alternating letters and numbers and asked to quickly discriminate between vowels and consonants and odd and even numbers. The findings indicated that vigorous walking improves mental function: for example, the walkers' ability to switch tasks improved by 25 percent, while the nonwalkers showed little improvement. This is especially important because the participants had been relatively inactive all their lives: thus, it's never too late to get the benefits of exercise.

Subsequent research has found that aerobic fitness training substantially reduces age-related declines in tissue density in the frontal, parietal, and temporal cortices, thus enhancing the brain health of older adults (Colcombe et al., 2003). In addition, cardiovascular fitness improves the function of key brain areas that allow us to focus our attention and ignore irrelevant, distracting information (Colcombe et al., 2004). The researchers conclude that physical activity helps to build the brain and enhances brain health and plasticity, benefiting both brain structure and function. "Even moderate cardiovascular activity of the sort that is within reach of most healthy older adults results in improved neural functioning, and may help to extend or enhance independent living in older adult populations" (Colcombe et al., 2004, p. 3320).

Maintaining the health of the musculoskeletal system (the muscles and bones) is an important determinant of independence and functional well-being (Larson, 1991). Musculoskeletal conditions are the most common cause of disability in community residents (Manton, 1989). In fact, in regard to functional decline, about 50 percent of what we attribute to aging is actually the result of **hypokinesia,** the degeneration and functional loss of muscle and bone tissue from disuse (Drinkwater, 1988). Even small increases in activity can be beneficial, yet many adults report no leisure-time physical activity and only 10 percent engage in aerobic exercise three or more times a week. Because mobility is a survival need, older adults have a lot to gain from improving the amount of exercise they get.

Exercise may be an especially potent factor in maintaining older women's independence and avoiding institutionalization, given that women live longer than men, are likely to be living alone in the later years of adulthood, and suffer greater incidence of diseases such as osteoporosis and arthritis. Yet for most older women, exercise is an untapped resource, partly because of lifelong patterns of lower rates of physical activity than men (O'Brien & Vertinsky, 1991). In short, older women are less fit than they could be.

CRITICAL THINKING QUESTION
Would you expect this pattern to remain the same or change among future cohorts of older women?

Exercise can be beneficial even for the frail elderly. A study of frail, institutionalized residents between the ages of 86 and 96 showed dramatic average gains in muscle strength of 174 percent as well as improved mobility after an eight-week weight-training period (Fiatarone et al., 1990). Benefits included greater mobility (some subjects were no longer chairfast) and reduced risk of falls—and thus further disability and other health risks. In other words, functional capacity may be at least partly regainable through exercise, even among those whose mobility and strength is already diminished.

You Can Lead a Horse to Water . . .

People don't always change their behavior, even when there is ample evidence that they should. Witness the number of people who continue to smoke, despite a mountain of research on the negative health effects of doing so. How can we influence people to use health prevention information in a positive way? One way may be to make the benefits of doing so concrete. The problem is that the health benefits of exercise, diet, and so on lie in the future, where they are hard for people to grasp in real terms. So telling someone to exercise now to avoid a heart attack 10 years from now is often futile. In an innovative approach, Roizen (1999) and his team reviewed 25,000 scientific studies on the effects of various behaviors on mortality rates. They then identified and calculated the health effects of 125 major factors, including medical, genetic, psychological, lifestyle, and environmental risks, assessing how much each one raised or lowered one's biological age. The next step was to develop software that allows people to compute their biological age based on questions in 125 categories and to see how their good and bad habits affect their rate of aging in real terms, as well as the immediate benefit of making lifestyle changes. Compared to chronological age, one's RealAge is the biological age of the body based on how well it has been maintained. So two 40-year-olds may have very different biological ages, with one aging much faster (or slower) than the other. You can read more about this approach and take the RealAge test at www.re-alage.com. Roizen's hope is that putting health promotion and disease prevention information into a form people can understand will motivate them to behave in their own best interest and to live younger and healthier lives.

Context of Health and Illness: An Ecological View

Stokols (1992) proposes an ecological perspective on health promotion, recognizing that human health, well-being, and illness exist in a multilayered environmental context. He encourages us to think broadly and to focus not just on biogenetic, psychological, or behavioral factors in health, but also on the physical and social environment and the extent to which they promote or detract from health and well-being. For example, are physical environments comfortable, nontoxic, clean, controllable, aesthetically pleasing, and designed to minimize risk of injury? Is the social environment supportive, stable, responsive, low in conflict?

Risk is best understood by considering the interaction of genetic predispositions, factors in the environment, and behavioral differences among individuals (Adler & Matthews, 1994). Qualities of the environment interact with the biogenetic and psychological characteristics of individuals in important ways.

As McLeroy and Crump (1994) point out, the emphasis on health promotion and disease prevention represents an important change in our understanding of health and illness. We now recognize that disease originates from many causes, including psychological and behavioral factors, and we are developing a better understanding of the ways in which our emotions, attitudes, and behavior are linked to disease and the most effective ways to intervene. The important message is that many common diseases and conditions can be prevented, postponed, or controlled by variables under the individual's control. Society can also play an important role, not only by directly addressing the problems of poverty and discrimination, but also through educational programs, improving access to prevention and intervention services, and offering opportunities for individuals to remain physically active as well as vitally involved in their communities. Effective prevention and health promotion enhance the likelihood that each of us may experience healthy, successful, and productive aging. This is a worthy goal, well worth our ongoing efforts.

Medication Use among Older Adults: A Health Concern

Prevalence of Medication Use among Older Adults

Those over 65 are the largest consumers of prescription medications—about 50 percent of all medications are prescribed for this age group. The average older adult takes four and a half prescribed drugs, plus another two over-the-counter medications (OTCs), while those in nursing homes take an average of eight to ten prescription medications (Beers, 2001).

Older adults are also at highest risk of adverse drug reactions as a result of three major factors. First, physiological changes associated with age alter the action of drugs in the body. These effects are complicated by the chronic nature of illness among older cohorts, which means that drugs will be used over a long period of time. Second, many older people have multiple medical conditions, for which multiple drugs are prescribed. And third, older adults rely on OTCs with great frequency. **Polypharmacy** (the use of multiple medications) is a widespread and serious problem. Many drugs have **synergistic effects,** producing different outcomes when combined with other substances than they do when used alone.

Drug Impact on the Aging Body

Drugs affect the aging body differently than the younger body. According to Beers (2001), age effects in drug metabolism include the following: absorption, distribution, and clearance. For example, reduced liver and kidney function may mean that the drug is not broken down and eliminated from the body as quickly as in a younger person. Thus, higher concentrations of the drug may be present for longer periods of time. We also become more sensitive to most drugs as we get older, especially those that affect the central nervous system (Beers, 2001). Because of changes that occur in the blood-brain barrier with age, more drugs enter the brain at higher levels. Coupled with the older brain's increased sensitivity, this means "in the elderly, every drug can be psychoactive" (Avorn, quoted in Beers, 2001, p. 24). Many drugs can cause confusion or changes in the central nervous system in an older individual. Although tremendous individual variation in drug metabolism exists, and factors such as nutrition, smoking, and drug interaction must be taken into account as well, age effects may produce different drug reactions among older than among younger individuals.

Risks Due to Age Effects and Drug Interaction

Differential age-related responses to drugs and the likelihood of synergistic effects when drugs interact pose a number of risks to the elderly, including:

- Reduced therapeutic benefit from medication
- Unpleasant, unnecessary, and dangerous side effects
- Unnecessary disability and resulting loss of independence from confusion, depression, gait disturbances, falls (Feinberg, 2001)
- Adverse reactions have been associated with 32,000 hip fractures, 163,000 cases of mental impairment, and 61,000 cases of drug-induced Parkinson's disease each year (Feinberg, 2001)
- Inability to benefit from other forms of treatment (for instance, physical therapy) because of drug side effects
- Unnecessary hospitalizations—12 to 17 percent of acute hospital admissions may be due to adverse drug reactions ("Problems with Prescription Drugs Highest Among the Elderly," 1983)
- Significantly prolonged hospital stays and increased cost (Bates et al., 1997; Classen, Pestotnik, Evans, Lloyd, & Burke, 1997)
- Increased risk of death—adverse drug effects may cause more than 100,000 deaths in the United States annually and may be the fourth leading cause of death in those 65+ (Feinberg, 2001; U.S. Food and Drug Administration, 2004)
- Misdiagnoses (drug intoxication is often misdiagnosed as dementia)
- Time lost from work and other activities
- Drug-induced nutritional problems (many drugs affect nutrient intake and utilization—for example, laxatives, antacids, and so on)

Over-the-Counter Medications

Trends toward greater self-care and the increasing costs of medicine along with aggressive marketing have encouraged a boom in the sale of OTCs (Coons, Hendricks, & Sheahan, 1988). These drugs are more accessible and less expensive than prescription medications, and many of them are designed to treat some of the most common symptoms among older adults—pain, stiffness, and so on.

The use of these drugs further complicates the individual's medication regimen, increasing the risk of undesirable drug interactions and negative side effects. The reclassification of many powerful drugs that were once available only by prescription poses a hazard to many consumers, who wrongly assume that if a drug does not require physician involvement, it is relatively benign. Many do not even consider OTCs drugs (Ellor & Kurz, 1982). In reality, OTCs contain powerful substances—for example, Nyquil is 25 percent alcohol.

Thus, the risk of OTC-prescription or OTC-alcohol interaction is high, and these interactions have been shown to be a significant cause of hospitalizations (Caranasos, Stewart, & Cluff, 1974). In addition, OTCs often contain substances that are potentially harmful to those with heart disease, hypertension, and other diseases common among the elderly (Coons et al., 1988).

The increased use of herbs and botanicals also carries risk (e.g., allergic reactions, drug interactions, medical complications, side effects). For example, echinacea, an immune booster, can cause liver damage if taken for more than a few weeks at a time. Because the federal government categorizes them as dietary supplements, herbs and botanicals fall outside FDA regulations; thus, there are no assurances regarding purity, quality, or potency. And despite exaggerated marketing claims, there are few clinical studies of their safety and effectiveness.

Signs of Adverse Drug Reaction

The common signs of adverse drug reaction include confusion, depression, agitation, loss of appetite, weakness, lethargy, forgetfulness, tremor, constipation, diarrhea, and urinary retention. These effects are most likely at the highest dosages. Side effects may occur quickly or only after prolonged use of a medication(s), in which case they are less likely to be identified as drug induced. Because drug reactions can mimic other conditions such as Alzheimer's disease or depression, caregivers and health care workers should be knowledgeable about and alert to these symptoms and not automatically assume that they are due to illness. Experts caution that any symptom should be assumed to be a drug side effect until proven otherwise (Feinberg, 2001). Recovery from adverse reactions may be slower in older adults. Physicians are well advised to "start low and go slow" when prescribing medication, particularly among the elderly.

Avoiding Drug Toxicity and Overmedication

The role of the physician in medication use and misuse is significant. Because of their multiple health problems, older patients may see more than one physician. Under these circumstances, any one physician may be unaware of other drugs being prescribed, and the potential for adverse drug reactions is increased. Further, because geriatrics and geriatric pharmacology are relatively new disciplines, physicians often lack formal training in geriatric medication use and the special risks older adults face. Cameron and Richardson (2001) describe a "prescribing cascade" in which an adverse reaction to a drug is interpreted to be a new medical condition, leading to another prescription, which may then cause additional adverse effects, and so on.

Willcox, Himmelstein, and Woolhandler (1994) surveyed a national sample of 6,171 adults aged 65+ living in the community to examine the amount of inappropriate drug prescribing in this population (many earlier studies have focused on nursing homes). Of a list of 20 drugs generally considered inappropriate for those over 65, nearly a quarter of the sample had been prescribed at least one of the drugs (and 20 percent of this group received two or more), placing them at risk of adverse drug effects. A study of almost 800,000 subjects age 65 and over, using the outpatient prescription claims data base of a national pharmaceutical benefits manager, found that 21 percent filled a prescription for one or more drugs with the potential for severe adverse effects (Curtis et al., 2004). More than 15 percent received two drugs of concern, and 4 percent received three or more. Other studies have found that the likelihood of an inappropriate drug being prescribed was higher when multiple medications were prescribed and was double when the patient was a woman (Goulding, 2004). Lesar, Briceland, and Stein (1997) also found medication errors were common and were most often related to physicians' inadequate knowledge or use of knowledge regarding drug therapy, followed by lack of knowledge of patient factors (drug allergies, level of kidney function, and so on).

Physicians have also been criticized for failing to develop accurate medication histories (including OTCs, vitamins, hormones, and nutritional supplements), overprescribing, providing inadequate or ambiguous instructions, and failing to monitor drug regimens (Shimp & Ascione, 1988; Whittington, 1988). The excessive and inappropriate use of drugs such as antipsychotics and tranquilizers as chemical restraints in some nursing homes is of great concern. Overmedication or adverse reactions to drugs can lead to what is called the **excess-disabilities syndrome,** in which individuals function at a level lower than that of which they are capable.

The risk of adverse drug reactions increases with increasing numbers of drugs, as does the difficulty of managing the medications properly. For someone taking two medications daily, the risk of adverse effects is about 15 percent, while the risk rises to 50 to 60 percent for those taking five medications a day (Schwartz, 1997). **Nonadherence** (failure to take medication as prescribed) increases with complex medication regimens and among those with sensory or cognitive impairments who may have difficulty hearing, reading, understanding, or remembering instructions (Shimp & Ascione, 1988). A person may take a drug at the wrong time, in the wrong amount, or may not take it at all. Drugs must be taken at certain times of the day, perhaps several times during the day, some with food, some before or after a meal—this can be a nightmare for anyone, let alone someone who is ill, frail, depressed, or confused. A study by Park et al. (1992) found the highest rate of nonadherence among the old-old, primarily in the form of omission errors. Their findings suggest that external supports, such as the use of charts or containers organizing the medication that must be taken during the day, can significantly raise the adherence level of these older adults. There are many new products available to remind patients to take their medication, including watches that vibrate or chirp, e-mail reminders, medical pager services, and "smart" pill containers that track drug use (e.g., by recording how many times a bottle is opened during the day or the time elapsed since last opened).

Four basic rules of geriatric prescribing should be observed: start low; go slow; use as few drugs as possible; and watch for adverse effects (Monane, Gurwitz, & Avorn, 1993). Cameron and Richardson (2001) urge clinicians to ask themselves whether the use of medication can be avoided to begin with. If a drug is determined to be necessary, the goals of the treatment regimen should be clearly specified so that progress can be determined. Further, they recommend that the lowest possible dosage be used for the shortest period of time and that the patient be closely monitored for side effects, with special attention to age effects. They emphasize that adverse drug reactions are often misinterpreted as signs of aging or disease.

In addition, physicians and other health care workers must keep informed about new drugs and share information about medications and drug interactions with their patients. This is no easy task, since about 25 new drugs come on the market each year, and hundreds more are in development specifically for older adults. Better use of the expertise and patient contact function of pharmacists can also be helpful. Also, patients must take responsibility by becoming informed about the medications they are taking (knowing the names, why they have been prescribed, reading labels and inserts), taking medications as prescribed, informing physicians of their medication history and current status (including vitamins, OTCs, and so on), choosing a pharmacist carefully and using the same one, and reporting side effects.

In sum, the power of medications to either improve or undermine the health and functional status of the older adults who are their primary consumers and the special circumstances of their use among this population make the use of both prescription drugs and OTCs an important health care issue.

Long-Term Care

While space does not permit a thorough examination of all the issues surrounding long-term care, several points must be emphasized. First, because of the growing number of older Americans, the demand for long-term care will more than double by 2050 (Alecxih, 2001). However, much of this care can be provided in the home, as opposed to an institutional setting. The need for long-term care places a heavy burden on family caregivers and can quickly drain family financial resources. The availability of informal support may decline as a result of increased workforce participation of women, greater mobility among families, increased number of never-married and/or childless women in future cohorts, and divorce. Only about 5 percent of those over 65 currently live in institutional settings. Rates of nursing home residence declined over the past 20 years, reflecting lower rates of disability as well as the availability of other forms of residential care and services, such as assisted living and home health care (Federal Interagency Forum on Aging-Related Statistics, 2004). Despite this, the number of nursing home residents has been increasing because of the increased numbers of older adults.

Second, the nature and quality of long-term care facilities vary greatly, with most of the criticism leveled at those run for profit (as opposed to those run by religious or fraternal organizations or units of government). Detailed information on the past performance of nursing homes in the United States is available at www.medicare.gov (Nursing Home Compare) and www.aarp.org.

Third, as discussed in Chapter 1, few if any medical schools in the United States provide adequate geriatric training, thus limiting the practitioners available to treat the growing numbers of older adults as well as the academics to lead research programs and train future physicians (Blanchette & Flynn, 2001; Centers for Disease Control, 2004c). One result of lack of proper training is preventable nursing home admissions.

Fourth, a number of factors influence an individual's entrance into a long-term care facility, including health status (level of disability, cognitive impairment), marital status, availability of family caregivers, living arrangements, and income (U.S. Senate Special

Committee on Aging et al., 1991). The likelihood of living in a nursing home increases with age; 46 percent of the nursing home population is 85+ (Centers for Disease Control, 2004c). Women are twice as likely as men of comparable age to enter nursing homes. The typical nursing home resident is an 80-year-old white widow with several chronic conditions, who was previously a patient in a hospital or other health care facility (U.S. Senate Special Committee on Aging et al., 1991).

Fifth, due to a variety of factors, including the increasing diversity of our society, growing numbers of minority elders are entering nursing homes. This will require greater attention and sensitivity to cultural differences in the way care is provided—from food preferences to family decision-making patterns (Stanford & Schmidt, 1996).

Sixth, the cost of long-term care, which varies from $33,000 to $108,000 a year, is a major health care concern (Wollenberg, 2000). According to the AARP, the average cost of nursing home care is $55,848 annually (costs vary widely depending on geographic location). Though long-term care insurance is now available, many of those in the current cohort of elderly do not have it.

Seventh, the decision to enter a nursing home or to place a relative there is not made lightly. Rather, it is usually a decision of last resort, made only after the individual and the family can no longer maintain the individual at home. The experience of loss is a great threat to the adjustment of individuals entering institutional settings.

CRITICAL THINKING QUESTION

What are the losses an individual entering a nursing home may experience? How might these be addressed?

Criticisms of the quality of care provided in institutions, concerns over cost, the desire of most older adults to remain independent as long as possible, and growing evidence that most people are better off in their own homes have stimulated development of a large number of programs and services to support the elderly in the community. These include programs such as meals on wheels, adult day care, electronic monitoring, hospice services, and home health care agencies. Two important goals should be to avoid *inappropriate* nursing home placements and to maintain the autonomy of the individual as much and for as long as possible.

For those who have entered long-term care facilities, it is imperative to recognize the impact of both the physical and psychological qualities of this environment on the health and well-being of those who live—and work—there. Efforts to transform these environments to support and enhance the abilities, autonomy, and dignity of residents benefit all of us. (See, for example, Noell, 1996, for a discussion of alternative approaches in design of nursing homes.)

Successful Aging: A Multidimensional Effort

Much of the illness and disability previously attributed to an inevitable aging process is now known to be related to lifestyle and the behavioral choices we make. An understanding of how to change behaviors that threaten health and to develop and maintain those that promote it has been identified as a high research priority.

A life-span view of development maintains that the behavior of an individual is partly the result of the person's history. Thus, current health-related behavior is influenced by habits and attitudes acquired earlier in life. Efforts to intervene and modify these behaviors in order to eliminate behavior pathogens and enhance coping and health-promoting behaviors face difficult hurdles, since the development of healthy behaviors, attitudes, and lifestyles is perhaps best accomplished early in life.

Physicians who appreciate the role of psychosocial factors in health and illness can help to harness the benefits of the mind-body connection by enhancing feelings of control, reducing anxiety, and so on. This may mean something as simple as allowing the patient to take an active role in treatment decisions.

Similarly, such efforts as the education of individuals about their role in their own health outcomes, programs offered by employers to encourage wellness among their employees, and actions by citizens and policymakers to address environmental hazards can all have beneficial effects.

Finally, the reduction of medication-induced disability and programs that support the individual's efforts to maintain appropriate levels of independence and autonomy contribute significantly to the quality of life. If we choose to heed the messages inherent in the growing research literature, successful biological aging is increasingly within our reach.

Concept Review 10.2

- Our health and the way we age is largely a matter of how we live.

- Prevention can include primary, secondary, and tertiary efforts.

- Risk factors are biological, psychological, behavioral, or environmental characteristics that increase the likelihood that an individual will develop a disease or condition.

- Psychoneuroimmunology refers to the study of the interrelationships between the mind, nervous system, and immune system.

- Effective prevention exists for many serious diseases and conditions. Encouraging people to adopt healthy behaviors is an ongoing challenge.

- Polypharmacy is a serious and widespread problem, especially among older adults.

- The need for long-term care will continue to increase, and the population to be served will be increasingly diverse.

REVIEW QUESTIONS

Health, Disease, and Disability

1. What is developmental health psychology? What kinds of issues are of interest to researchers in this area?

2. Discuss two methodological challenges faced by those studying health, disease, and disability in adulthood.

3. How do health-related problems change across the years of adulthood?

4. Identify the three major causes of death, as well as the major nonfatal chronic debilitating conditions of old age. What are the trends in the incidence of these conditions?

5. Assess the nature and origins of gender and racial variations in health and longevity.

Prevention of Illness and Promotion of Health

1. Define the three levels of prevention and give an example of each.
2. Identify the major health-related biological and behavioral risk factors.
3. How can thoughts and feelings influence health?
4. Identify the major preventive behaviors.
5. What are the suspected causes and risks of dramatic increases in overweight and obesity?
6. Discuss the special dietary needs of older adults.

7. Assess the benefits of exercise in promoting health.
8. Explain the reasons for the high risk of adverse drug reactions among the elderly.
9. What are some of the common indicators of adverse drug reactions?
10. What steps can be taken to reduce the risk of medication problems?
11. Who is most likely to enter a long-term care facility, and why?
12. What are the trends in long-term care?
13. What special problems need to be addressed when an individual enters a long-term care facility?

KEY TERMS

activities of daily living (ADLs), 394
behavioral pathogen, 403
Cartesian dualism, 403
compression-of-morbidity hypothesis, 395
developmental health psychology, 385
disease, 387
excess-disabilities syndrome, 414

health, 386
hypokinesia, 409
illness, 387
instrumental activities of daily living (IADLs), 394
nonadherence, 414
polypharmacy, 411
primary prevention, 400
psychoneuroimmunology, 404

racial mortality crossover effect, 399
relative risk, 402
risk factor, 402
secondary prevention, 401
synergistic effects, 411
tertiary prevention, 401
transgenerational design, 395

11 Coping, Adaptation, and Mental Health

FOUR DAYS BEFORE CHRISTMAS Dad had another major stroke. It is now five weeks later, and the prognosis is not good. He is lethargic, unresponsive, weak. We struggle to determine how much of what we are seeing in his behavior is neurological (permanent damage done by the stroke itself), pharmacological (the result of the interaction of the many medications prescribed for him), or psychological (in other words, depression). As a family, we continue to press the doctors, nurses, and therapists to pursue all these possibilities. We are concerned about his physical as well as psychological treatment, the environmental settings around him, the attitudes of those with whom he has contact. Though my father's condition is certainly not a normal part of the adult experience, I am reminded once again that all behavior has multiple causes. Untangling their effects is tricky. I am also mindful of the intertwining of our lives as family members. As we work to help Dad deal with this latest challenge, the family unit and each of us as individuals must cope as well.

Experiences such as the one described above—dealing with the illness or injury of a loved one—are common elements of adult life. Any discussion of human development must address the issue of how we adapt to and overcome the challenges and hazards that confront us in daily life. While successful adjustment to life events, psychological health, subjective well-being, and life satisfaction are all topics of interest to developmental psychologists, until very recently the focus of research has been more on psychological dysfunction and emotional problems (Myers & Diener, 1995; Ryff, 1995). An important shift toward **positive psychology** has occurred, defined as "a science of positive subjective experience, positive individual traits, and positive institutions [that] promises to improve quality of life and prevent the pathologies that arise when life is barren and meaningless" (Seligman & Csikszentmihalyi, 2000, p. 5). The result? A model of the human being that includes the positive features that make life worth living and that allows individuals, communities, and societies to flourish. Reflecting this shift in focus, this chapter begins with a look at happiness, or what is often referred to as subjective well-being. We will then examine the nature and impact of psychological stress and individuals' responses to it—the so-called stress-and-coping approach. We know that failure to adapt can lead to both physical and mental illness. People respond differently to stress, and some of these responses are more effective than others. What accounts for these differences? One explanation has to do with the beliefs and attitudes people hold about their own behavior and experiences. Specifically, the extent to which individuals feel they have some control over their lives is thought to affect both their experience of stress and their style of coping. So the concept of personal control will be our focus in the next part of this chapter. The remainder of the chapter reviews the mental health status of adults, with particular attention to age and gender differences in rates and nature of psychopathology. The chapter concludes with a more detailed examination of two mental disorders: first, major depression; and second, the primary cause of dementia—Alzheimer's disease.

Happiness

Most People Are Happy

What does it mean to be happy? As used here, subjective well-being (SWB) or happiness refers to an individual's positive evaluation of his or her life (Diener, 2000). As Myers (2000) puts it, happiness is whatever people mean when they describe themselves as happy. The assumption is that if you *feel* happy, you *are* happy. In national surveys conducted in the United States between 1946 and the present, most people report being satisfied with their lives—both in general terms as well as in regard to specific domains such as finances, work, and family. In fact, throughout the world, most people report being at least moderately happy (Myers, 2000). As Diener and Diener (1996) argue, while it is important not to ignore the percentage who are unhappy and unfulfilled in their lives and who are less able to cope with life events, understanding who is happy and why may allow us to design better interventions to help those who are not.

Determinants of Happiness

Myers and Diener (1995) state that knowing a person's age, sex, race, or income (as long as it is enough to provide for the necessities) doesn't tell us much about happiness. No time of life is the happiest and most satisfying, and, negative stereotypes to the contrary, global or overall SWB does not decline as we get older (Pinquart & Sorensen, 2000). In fact, older adults experience less negative emotion but comparable levels of positive emotion as compared to younger adults (Carstensen & Charles, 1998). They also report greater control over their emotions and more stability of mood. Thus, emotional well-being (one component of SWB) seems to improve with age. In regard to gender, men and women are equally likely to describe themselves as happy and satisfied with their lives (Myers, 2000). Race and affluence do not predict happiness either. Clearly, we have to look further. So what are the origins of a person's happiness?

A number of studies have begun to identify factors that contribute to people's happiness. According to Lykken and Tellegen (1996), about half of the variance in adult happiness is due to genetic factors, with the other half determined by experience. Then is trying to be happier as futile as trying to be taller? Or was Abraham Lincoln correct when he said, "Most people are about as happy as they make up their minds to be" (Barton, 1976)? Lyubomirsky (2001) studied groups of people who rate themselves as either chronically happy or unhappy. She suggests that some people are happier than others because of a set of cognitive and motivational strategies they use in dealing with life experience. For example, in contrast to those who are unhappy, happy people are less sensitive to social comparison, less likely to dwell on themselves and their moods, and more likely to think about and evaluate events in more positive ways. In other words, happy people choose to see the world, themselves, and their circumstances in more positive and affirming ways that over time are associated with greater happiness and well-being. Questions remain as to whether these strategies can be taught and whether interventions designed to teach them can enhance individual happiness.

Ryff (1995) lists the following key dimensions of well-being: positive evaluation of the self and self-acceptance; positive relationships with others; autonomy or self-determination; environmental mastery (the ability to manage one's life and the environment effectively); a sense of purpose in life; and a feeling of growth and development as a person. In a number of cross-sectional studies designed to explore age differences, Ryff and her colleagues asked young, middle-aged, and older adults to rate themselves on each of these six dimensions. They consistently found that environmental mastery and autonomy increased with age, while purpose in life and personal growth declined. The other dimensions either remained stable or increased. While longitudinal data are needed to determine whether these are cohort or developmental effects, Ryff hypothesizes that the lower ratings of older adults on purpose and personal growth may reflect structural lag—that is, a lack of opportunity for continued growth and meaningful activity in the face of extended life expectancy. Gender differences were found on two dimensions: women consistently scored higher on positive relationships with others and personal growth. This is especially interesting in light of women's higher rates of depression (discussed later in this chapter).

CRITICAL THINKING QUESTION
Do you think the six dimensions of well-being described by Ryff would apply equally well to collectivist cultures?

According to Myers and Diener (1995) and DeNeve (1999), the following factors offer clues to the origins of SWB. (Note the overlap with those listed by Ryff, above.) First, happy people are characterized by self-esteem, optimism, a sense of personal control, and extraversion. (For an in-depth look at optimism, see Peterson, 2000.) Second, they have a supportive social network. In fact, their strong relationships are initiated and fostered by the positive social and emotional traits that characterize happy people. Thus, positive traits nurture strong ties that in turn support life satisfaction. Third, individuals who report being happy and satisfied with their lives are involved in meaningful, challenging activity (whether work or leisure). A fourth source of well-being comes from religious faith. Let's examine this issue a bit more fully.

Religious Involvement and Spirituality

Though a large part of many people's lives, religion and spirituality are long-neglected topics in scientific research. Miller and Thoresen (2003) believe this was largely due to assumptions that spirituality *could* not and *should* not be studied scientifically. This is changing, as evidenced by a burgeoning literature addressing research and theory in the psychology of religion. Space permits only a glimpse of some of the findings.

Research suggests that religiosity is generally positively related to physical health and longevity (at least partly because of healthier lifestyles, including lower rates of smoking and drinking); coping behavior; mental health (including lower rates of depression and suicide); and life satisfaction and psychological well-being—in other words, happiness (Kim, Nesselroade, & Featherman, 1996; Myers & Diener, 1995; Myers, 2000; Powell, Shahabi, & Thoresen, 2003; Seybold & Hill, 2001). Religious involvement may enhance well-being by providing social support as well as a belief system that offers hope and a sense of meaning and purpose in life. Further investigation of the mechanisms by which religious involvement produces its apparently beneficial effects on both mental and physical health is certainly warranted, since at this point these effects are not well understood (Miller & Thoresen, 2003). (See Seeman, Dubin, & Seeman, 2003, for a review of the evidence for biological processes that may link religiosity and spirituality to health.)

Investigators caution that existing studies suffer from a number of problems, including various vague definitions of religious and spiritual activity; lack of control of variables such as age, sex, education, and socioeconomic status; and biased samples. And even if these methodological problems can be overcome, correlation does not mean causation. That is, it is possible that other lifestyle factors, rather than religious involvement itself, are causing the positive health outcomes. Perhaps those most likely to be actively religious are also those least likely to be at high risk for poor physical and mental health.

High levels of religious involvement among many older adults suggest that this is a topic of particular relevance to studies of older cohorts and of aging in general. Contrary to the commonly held belief that people become increasingly religious as they age, longitudinal evidence indicates that religiosity is fairly stable over time, while spirituality seems to increase in prominence with age (Markides, Levin, & Ray, 1987; Wink & Dillon, 2003). Because the clergy is often the first place people turn in times of distress, alliances between the mental health and religious communities may be beneficial. Studies of religious involvement must also consider the diversity of religious traditions and their differential effects on health and well-being. Future research will help us to better understand these issues and the role of religion in health, well-being, and successful aging.

Concept Review 11.1

- Psychology has traditionally focused more research attention on unhappiness and dysfunction than on mental health and well-being. That focus has begun to shift with the emergence of positive psychology.

- In national and international surveys, most people report that they are happy.

- Studies have begun to identify a number of factors that seem to contribute to happiness and subjective well-being, including positive attitudes such as hope and optimism, social support, and meaningful activity.

Stress, Coping, and Locus of Control

Nature of Stress

Psychological stress encompasses the negative cognitive and emotional states that result when people feel that the demands placed on them exceed their ability to cope (Lazarus & Folkman, 1984). Stress occurs when a person perceives an event as threatening and feels overwhelmed, helpless, and unable to cope. The individual's assessment of the event is key—different people will be stressed by different things, depending on their subjective appraisal of the situation. So, for example, some people may find a test threatening, while others view it as a challenging opportunity to demonstrate what they know. Or one job seeker may consider an interview to be an exciting chance for advancement, while another interprets it as an opportunity for rejection. In general, situations are perceived as more stressful if they involve loss (or the threat of loss) of something highly valued by the individual (Hobfoll, 1989), and if they are perceived as unfamiliar, unpredictable, and out of our control.

Effects of Stress

Once we assess a situation as stressful, a chain reaction is set in motion with consequences for our emotions, thoughts, behavior, and physiology. There are many emotional responses to stress, such as anger, annoyance, or grief. Anxiety is an especially common and unpleasant emotional outcome and is potentially dangerous, especially if stress is severe and chronic. The general rule is that as stress increases, negative emotions increase. Stress can impair cognitive ability and task performance, disrupting attention, concentration, memory, and judgment. It can lead to interpersonal problems as the individual becomes self-absorbed, insecure, irritable, and so on. Stress is also implicated in a variety of psychological problems and disorders, ranging in seriousness from the relatively mild (such as insomnia) to the severe (for example, posttraumatic stress disorder).

Stress is very subjective. It is the individual's assessment of a situation, such as speaking before a large audience, that determines whether or not the experience is stressful for that individual.

In addition to these effects, stress is believed to have direct and indirect effects on physical health. Indirect effects might be changes in health-related behaviors, such as increased smoking or alcohol consumption. One of the direct mechanisms by which stress affects health is through alteration of immune system function. The physiological stress response includes the release of chemicals that suppress the activity of the thymus gland. This is the master gland of the immune system and orchestrates the activity of T cells, involved in fighting off viruses and bacteria. The result is that we are more vulnerable to a host of infectious agents. For example, Cohen et al. (1993; Cohen, 1996) demonstrated that psychological stress was associated with increased susceptibility to infection. They assessed the stress levels of 394 healthy subjects through the use of three stress questionnaires, then intentionally exposed the subjects to a common cold virus, quarantined them, and monitored them for the development of a clinical illness. Higher scores on the stress scales were positively correlated with risk of developing a cold. The effects of stress, then, are wide ranging and can be significant. Despite all the potential negative effects, stress may also have positive consequences. As Aldwin (1995) points out, coping successfully with highly stressful events may contribute to our development in adulthood, enhancing our repertoire of coping strategies, strengthening our sense of mastery, and leading to more effective adaptation in the future. But how do individuals manage and respond to stress?

Coping with Stress

Despite years of research and the importance of the topic, coping is not well understood (Somerfield & McCrae, 2000). We need to determine what works best, for whom, and under what circumstances. Since most stress and coping research has involved men, it is not clear whether there are consistent gender differences in male and female responses to stress. Taylor and her colleagues have recently offered a new paradigm to describe the coping behavior of women—the "tend-and-befriend" model (Taylor, 2002)—in contrast to the well-known fight-or-flight model they feel is more typical of the male stress response. In essence, they contend that women are more likely to protect themselves and their offspring through nurturing behavior and seeking support from others—behaviors based in the attachment and caregiving behavioral systems (see Chapter 6). Thus, women may be more likely to benefit from the stress-buffering effects of social support, with potential consequences for health and longevity.

It is clear that coping behavior is strongly influenced by an individual's personality traits. For example, those high in conscientiousness are more likely to follow doctors' orders; those low in neuroticism are more likely to attract and nurture social support. (See Chapter 2 for a discussion of McCrae and Costa's trait theory.) Though these traits tend to be stable and thus difficult to change, behavioral styles and attitudes also affect coping and are more likely to be amenable to change.

A number of studies have found that positive emotions are beneficial in coping with stress. They have a helpful effect by sustaining coping efforts, providing distraction or a "breather," and restoring resources. Fredrickson's (2000) "broaden and build model of positive emotions" is based on the finding that positive emotions build intellectual, social, and physical resources by broadening the scope of one's attention, thinking, and action. This may explain the benefits of interventions such as relaxation therapy. Positive emotions may also undo the harmful effects of negative emotions; this is called the "undoing hypothesis" (Fredrickson, 2001). Positive emotions also attract other people, thus bolstering social support. The benefits of positive emotions are immediate as well as long term, leading to psychological growth and enhanced well-being in the future.

Given their importance even during the most stressful times, how do people generate positive emotions? Folkman and Moskowitz (2000) discuss three types of coping associated with positive emotions during chronic stress: positive reappraisal, in which people focus on the good of what is happening or has happened; problem-focused coping, including thoughts and behaviors that manage or resolve the underlying causes of the stress; and the creation of positive events, in which people produce a psychological time-out by finding positive meaning in ordinary events (e.g., taking pleasure in an off-hand compliment or a beautiful day), having a good laugh, or deliberately planning positive occasions. Unanswered questions include the extent to which such coping mechanisms reflect underlying personality traits or can be taught.

Another approach, referred to as "hope theory," has been developed by Snyder and his colleagues (Snyder et al., 1991). Snyder contends that those who are hopeful and who act on that hope are healthier, happier, more successful, and live longer. Hope is often thought of as wishing for something. In contrast, Snyder defines hope as *working* for something with the expectation of its fulfillment. He believes that people can take control of their lives through personal effort, by setting clear goals and developing multiple routes to attain them. Further, he believes that this can be learned. Wonder how hopeful you are? See Table 11.1 for the Hope Scale, to date taken by more than 30,000 people and translated into about a dozen languages.

In sum, seeking social support, cultivating positive emotions, and acting on positive expectations (hope) enhance our ability to cope with stress. Ray (2004) emphasizes that it isn't the coping skills individuals actually have that are important; what matters

---

TABLE 11.1 *The Hope Scale*

For each of the eight statements below, select the number that best describes you:

1. Definitely false	5. Slightly true
2. Mostly false	6. Somewhat true
3. Somewhat false	7. Mostly true
4. Slightly false	8. Definitely true

_____ 1. I can think of many ways to get out of a jam.
_____ 2. I energetically pursue my goals.
_____ 3. There are lots of ways around any problem.
_____ 4. I can think of many ways to get the things in life that are most important to me.
_____ 5. Even when others get discouraged, I know I can find a way to solve the problem.
_____ 6. My past experiences have prepared me well for my future.
_____ 7. I've been pretty successful in life.
_____ 8. I meet the goals that I set for myself.

Add your answers for each of the eight items. The average score for college students is 48, which means a good, healthy level of hope. The standard deviation is 7, so a score of 55 or above reflects a high level of hope, while a score of 41 or below indicates that you may not be consistently hopeful. For more information, see Snyder et al., 1991; Snyder, 1994, 2000; McDermott and Snyder, 1999; or visit the hope web page: http://raven.cc.ukans.edu/~crsnyder.

Source: Snyder et al., 1991, and personal communication. Used by permission.

are the coping skills they *believe* they have. This leads us to examine the concept of personal control.

Beliefs about Personal Control

Many psychological theories of emotional well-being emphasize beliefs about the degree of control individuals feel over the events and circumstances of their lives. These beliefs in turn affect the amount of stress we experience and our responses to it. (For a broad historical and cultural overview of the concept of control and its status in psychology, see Shapiro, Schwartz, & Astin, 1996.)

Internal versus External Locus of Control

One of the best-known and most thoroughly researched theories of personal control beliefs is **locus of control,** first described by the social learning theorist Julian Rotter (1966). An **internal locus of control** refers to the belief that control over outcomes in one's life resides within oneself. Faced with a problem, individuals with a strong sense of internal control feel they can do something to cope with the situation. "Internalizers" are more likely to confront a problem directly in an attempt to deal with it because they expect their behavior to make a difference. They are also more likely to accept responsibility for what happens to them. **External locus of control** refers to the feeling that control of (and responsibility for) outcomes in one's life resides outside oneself, in fate, chance, luck, God, or other people. Faced with a problem, the "externalizer" thus feels powerless. Instead of using direct coping, this individual is more likely to respond to a problem defensively—for example, denying that the problem exists. Because stress means feeling overwhelmed and unable to cope, externalizers by definition experience more—and more intense—stress. Further, because they do not take effective action, the original problem may worsen.

Let's say that a group of individuals, some internalizers and some externalizers, are told by their physician that their blood cholesterol level is dangerously high. The internalizers are likely to modify their diet in an attempt to bring their cholesterol level down, while the externalizers may ignore advice about modifying their diet, feeling it does not matter what they do because their cholesterol level is out of their control.

Thus, locus of control may mediate the consequences of life events, including stress, through its influence on coping strategies. Those with a low sense of personal control may experience more stress, and stress may affect well-being by further eroding feelings of mastery or personal control.

CRITICAL THINKING QUESTION
Would you expect rates of depression to be higher among internalizers or externalizers?

Rotter believed locus of control to be a personality trait—a global, unidimensional characteristic of the person that is stable over time and across situations. According to Rotter's formulation, control can be thought of as lying on a continuum, with a highly developed internal locus of control at one end and a highly developed external locus at the other. He developed a measurement tool or scale consisting of a series of questions

TABLE 11.2 *Sample Items from a Locus-of-Control Scale*

The items listed below are examples from a locus-of-control scale developed by Rotter (1966). This scale, consisting of forced-choice items, assesses beliefs about whether control over events resides inside or outside oneself. "I" represents the internal option and "E" represents the external option.

"It is impossible for me to believe that chance or luck plays an important role in my life" (I) versus "Many times I feel that I have little influence over the things that happen to me" (E).

"I have often found that what is going to happen will happen" (E) versus "Trusting to fate has never turned out as well for me as making a decision to take a definite course of action" (I).

"It is not always wise to plan too far ahead because many things turn out to be a matter of good or bad fortune anyway" (E) versus "When I make plans, I am almost certain that I can make them work" (I).

Source: Adapted from Rotter, 1966.

that could be used to assess the degree to which individuals were internalizers or externalizers. (See Table 11.2 for some sample items.) So, according to Rotter, people tend to be one or the other, and, because the trait is stable over time and across situations, it will influence behavior in a variety of situations and contexts in the same way.

Consistent with his social learning perspective, Rotter believed that control expectancies were learned through the accumulation of experiences early in life. For example, when an infant's cries are responded to in a consistent way by a loving caregiver, the infant learns a sense of personal control: "When I need something and I cry, someone comes." In other words, I can influence what happens—an internal locus of control. Conversely, the infant whose cries go unheeded, and whose needs go unmet, learns a different message: "When I need something and I cry, nothing happens." As these experiences are repeated over time, this infant comes to believe that control over events resides outside the self—an external locus of control. These expectations about personal control persist and influence the way the individual responds to events and challenges later in life.

CRITICAL THINKING QUESTION
Do control beliefs function as self-fulfilling prophecies?

A number of studies have demonstrated the benefits of perceived control. For example, Langer, Janis, and Wolfer (1975) taught preoperative surgical patients that they could control their pain and distress by focusing their thoughts on the positive aspects of surgery. These patients requested fewer medications for pain and were rated as less anxious and distressed than control subjects not given this sense of cognitive control. Based on a longitudinal study of older adults, Krause and Shaw (2000) conclude that people may live longer if control over their most valued role is maintained. A sense of control has benefits for mental health as well as life satisfaction. Research concludes that an internal locus of control is correlated with subjective well-being among older adults (Kozma & Stones, 1978) as well as with a more positive view of aging itself—despite the presence of a significant number of negative changes in themselves and others in their lives (Keller et al., 1989). Nursing home residents given more control over their behavior and the decisions that affected them were better off physically and psychologically than those who did not receive this control (Langer & Rodin, 1976; Rodin & Langer, 1977). It is important to note, however, that some individuals do not want control. For these individuals, greater control may have negative rather than positive outcomes (Rodin, 1986). As O'Connor and Vallerand (1994, p. 190) suggest, "There are exceptions to the 'control-is-good' rule." The important thing for psychological adjustment is a good fit between the individual's need and desire for control and the environment.

CRITICAL THINKING QUESTION

Institutionalization may represent the ultimate loss of control. What kinds of things do people lose control over when they enter a setting such as a nursing home? How could the sense of personal control be enhanced in such situations?

General versus Domain-Specific Locus of Control

The concept of locus of control has received a lot of research attention over the years, and Rotter's original formulation has been challenged on several grounds. First, do you think people feel the same degree of control in all aspects of their lives? In other words, is locus of control a general attitude? Or does degree of perceived control vary from one area of life to another—is it domain specific? The internal-external locus-of-control construct is now thought of as being multidimensional and domain specific. That is, it varies across different aspects of a person's life. So, for example, you may feel you have a lot of control over your social life but little control over conditions at work. Loss of control in areas of life that a person values highly seems to have a correspondingly greater impact on well-being. For example, Krause and Baker (1992) studied the effect of financial strain on feelings of control in later life. They found that when people place a high priority on economic success, they are more likely to associate financial difficulty with reduced feelings of personal control. And, as older adults' feelings of control diminished, the subjects reported more somatic symptoms of distress (for example, headaches, tension, difficulty sleeping, and so on). Thus, threats to a sense of personal control in important domains of life may have a particularly pronounced impact on overall health and well-being.

Second, research suggests that control beliefs fluctuate over time in response to a variety of life events. Researchers are attempting to assess age-related changes across domains and to identify the situations and events that have a particularly significant impact on control beliefs. There are now 18 different locus-of-control scales that attempt to assess control beliefs in different domains as well as among different age groups, from preschool to elderly populations.

A Life-Span Look at Personal Control

Social psychologists have only recently begun to examine personal control beliefs from a life-span perspective. As a result, we know little about how the sense of control develops and changes over the life course, or of the nature and origins of individual differences in personal control (Rodin, 1987). There has been quite a bit of interest in how one's sense of control changes with age, because, while internality has been correlated with physical and mental health and an enhanced ability to deal with the developmental tasks of life, many events associated with aging could be viewed as leading to increasing externality.

Lachman and Weaver (1998) examined control beliefs in seven domains (e.g., health, work, finances) among a large sample of adults ranging in age from 25 to 75. In regard to feelings of control for their life overall, older adults reported greater control than young and middle-aged adults—despite their also reporting that they faced more constraints than younger individuals did. There were variations across domains, however, related to such factors as age, gender, education, and income as well as specific life experiences and their outcomes.

Maintaining a Sense of Control in Naturally Occurring Life Situations

Most of the research on the perception of control has been done in the laboratory. These studies typically expose subjects to some sort of short-term unpleasant stimulus (such as a noxious odor or a mild electric shock) under varying levels of control, and the effects are observed. The general finding, as we have noted previously, is that a perception of control is advantageous. Subjects who believe they have some control experience less stress and are more motivated to act.

Though valuable, such research may have limited ecological validity. Lab research cannot replicate the powerful, long-term situations that can threaten a sense of control in everyday life, such as a chronic illness, victimization by crime, or the loss of a job or a loved one. How do people in these low-control situations respond? How do they maintain a sense of personal control and the benefits of such beliefs? We know that loss of control can lead to increased stress and that individuals usually attempt to restore control. How can this occur in situations that provide few opportunities for control?

Baltes and Baltes (1986) have suggested a compensation model (referred to as *selective optimization with compensation, SOC*) whereby individuals who are faced with an uncontrollable situation compensate for their lack of control by concentrating on other areas where they *can* exercise control. For example, because many of the effects of aging are outside people's realm of control, older adults may concentrate on domains in which they have a greater degree of control, such as relationships with others. In this way, though control in some domains may be reduced, overall perceptions of control may be spared any negative effects The result? A sense of control over one's life in general remains high. (See Chapters 3 and 4 for a discussion of SOC as applied to the development of the self and cognitive aging.) Freund and Baltes (1998) administered a self-report measure listing behaviors that exemplified selection, optimization, and compensation paired with distractor items. Subjects were asked to choose the statement in each pair that was most similar to them. See Table 11.3 for examples. Subjects who reported using selective optimization with compensation as a way of managing life events scored higher on three measures of successful aging, including subjective well-being.

Similarly, when individuals cannot avoid or undo a stressful event, they may respond instead by employing a variety of techniques aimed at controlling the *consequences* of that event. Thompson, Sobolew-Shubin, Galbraith, Schwankovsky, and Cruzen (1993) studied the role of perceived control in a sample of 71 cancer patients

TABLE 11.3 *Sample Items from the SOC Questionnaire*

Subjects are asked to choose which of each paired statements best describes them. In the actual questionnaire, target and distractor items are randomly distributed in the two columns.

Target Behavior	Distractor
SELECTION	
When I think about what I want in life, I commit myself to one or two important goals.	Even when I really consider what I want in life, I wait and see what happens instead of committing myself to just one or two particular goals.
OPTIMIZATION	
When something matters to me, I devote myself fully and completely to it.	Even when something matters to me, I still have a hard time devoting myself fully and completely to it.
COMPENSATION	
When things don't go as well as they used to, I keep trying other ways of doing it until I can achieve the same result I used to.	When things don't go as well as they used to, I accept it.

Source: Adapted from Freund and Baltes, 1998.

between the ages of 29 and 80. They found that patients with higher perceptions of control were better adjusted and less depressed. Interestingly, these patients focused not on controlling the stressor itself—in this case, the cancer—but rather on their emotional reactions and daily physical symptoms, such as their level of pain—the consequences of the cancer. The investigators suggest that perhaps "psychological adjustment to a general life stressor gets played out at the level of the routine events of everyday life—as long as one has control at that level, one feels able to handle the larger event" (p. 301). Thus, compensation may be one strategy individuals use to maintain a sense of control in low-control situations. Even in very low control situations, people are likely to be able to find *some* aspect of the situation they can influence. For these cancer patients, control over the consequences of their diagnosis played a larger role in their adjustment than the belief that they could control the cancer itself.

Brandtstadter, Wentura, and Greve (1993; see also Brandtstadter & Greve, 1994; and Brandtstadter & Rothermund, 1994) propose that elderly people, while aware of age-related developmental losses, maintain a sense of control and a positive view of the self through the use of accommodative processes. That is, while optimizing their focus in some areas, they may disengage from certain activities, lower their level of aspiration, and adopt less demanding standards of performance. In this way, goals are adjusted and become more feasible. (See Chapter 3 for a more detailed discussion of the effect of aging on the self.) These accommodative processes allow the individual to cope successfully with the irreversible losses and uncontrollable events that typify later life and to buffer their impact. A sense of personal control and a positive sense of self are maintained, and feelings of helplessness and depression are minimized. Heckhausen and Schulz (1995; and Schulz & Heckhausen, 1996) offer a similar model of adaptation in which primary control (which refers to efforts to modify events in the external environment) increasingly gives way to secondary control (cognitive processes aimed at changing the self—e.g., attitudes, perceptions) as people get older and their personal resources are reduced. The goal is to optimize development by effectively selecting behaviors and compensating for failures.

Much remains to be learned about the nature, importance, developmental course, and consequences of control beliefs. One interesting topic for future investigation is the relationship between religion, spirituality, and beliefs about personal control. (See Zarit, Pearlin, & Schaie, 2003, for an integrative review of research on personal control.) Some general conclusions can be drawn from studies on this subject over the last 40 years. First, belief in personal control is generally beneficial to overall adjustment, performance, and health. People are better off if they are optimistic about their ability to influence events. Second, those with a low sense of personal control may experience more stress and may also respond to stress less effectively. Thus, a sense of control reduces the amount of stress experienced and also prompts the individual to attempt constructive action, which has at least the potential for success. Finally, feelings of personal control may be especially crucial in areas that people value highly and that may therefore have a significant effect on psychological well-being. Discovering strategies that individuals can use to maintain a sense of control when faced with the stresses of daily life as well as age-related change is a fertile area for research.

Concept Review 11.2

- Stress occurs when we feel threatened and unable to cope with the threat.

- Though not yet well understood, an individual's attempts to cope with stress reflect underlying personality traits as well as beliefs and attitudes, such as hope.

- The extent to which individuals feel they have some control over their circumstances influences the amount of stress they experience and their style of coping with it.

- Rotter developed the concept of locus of control (LOC), one of many related models of personal control beliefs.

- The LOC concept continues to generate a great deal of research as psychologists seek to understand its developmental history as well as the mechanisms by which a sense of control can be maintained.

An Overview of the Mental Health Status of Adults

Epidemiology is the study of the incidence, distribution, and control of disease. Epidemiological data thus provide evidence on the rates of various disorders. One source of valuable data about mental disorders is the Epidemiological Catchment Area (ECA) Survey (Regier et al., 1984). This study, sponsored by the National Institute of Mental Health, is one of the largest surveys ever undertaken to determine the prevalence of mental disorders in the United States. The sample included over 18,000 adults from five geographic locations in New Haven, Connecticut, Baltimore, St. Louis, rural North Carolina, and Los Angeles. A structured interview was used to collect information about symptoms on which diagnoses are based.

The results of the ECA survey contradicted two major misconceptions about mental illness in adulthood (George, 1990b). The first is that because of the losses and reduced resources associated with aging, older adults are at greater risk than younger adults. The second is that women are at greater risk than men. Both these statements are overly simplified and largely inaccurate. Let's look at the data bearing on issues of age and gender in rates of psychological disorders.

Age-Related Trends in Psychological Health

Jones and Meredith (2000) examined the developmental paths of psychological health for 236 male and female participants in a longitudinal study of human development. Using a measure of psychological health based on 73 different aspects of personality, subjects were examined at age 14, 18, 30, 40, 50, and 62. In general and on average, psychological health improved steadily with age. There were individual differences, however, with some individuals showing dramatic increases, while others showed smaller gains. And there was a strong positive correlation between psychological health in adolescence and adulthood: those with greater psychological health in their teens experienced greater increases in health later, though even those with low psychological health eventually showed improvement. No group or gender differences in the overall patterns were found. Because the sample consisted of intelligent, educated, successful people, studies of less advantaged individuals as well as those from other birth cohorts are needed in order to verify the generalizability of the findings. However, these results suggest that, despite the inevitable setbacks, losses, and challenges of life, it is possible to continue to gain in psychological health—as Vaillant (1977) suggested, using the irritating sand of life to create pearls.

Consistent with these findings, and despite the myths and stereotypes of old age, one general conclusion drawn from the data is that there is a lower prevalence of mental disorder among older adults than younger adults (Gatz & Smyer, 1992). For example, ECA data from four sites show the rates of mental disorder excluding dementia among adults age 18 to 64 to vary from 11.1 to 25.3 percent, while the rate among those age 65+ ranges from 5.8 to 13.9 percent. The prevalence of mood disorders, including depression, among older adults ranged from 1.5 to 2.9 percent, while rates for all other age groups varied from 2.5 to 7.6 percent. Dementia is the one disorder for which the rate does increase dramatically with age, especially after age 65. The majority of these cases are the result of Alzheimer's disease. Prevalence among those 65 and older is variously estimated at about 6 to 15 percent (Evans, 1989; Mortimer & Hutton, 1985; Ritchie & Kildea, 1995; Robins et al., 1984). Gatz and Smyer (2001) estimate the proportion of adults age 65+ with all mental disorders including dementia at about 22 percent. This includes those living in the community as well as those living in institutions (both psychiatric facilities and nursing homes). The most common disorders among the elderly are depression, anxiety, Alzheimer's disease, and substance abuse (alcoholism).

As Cohen (1990) points out, the coexistence of physical illness, which is quite likely among older adults, creates the potential for interaction between physical and mental disturbance. Thus, physical illness may cause mental distress, while mental distress may exacerbate physical illness. For example, Levitan and Kornfeld (1981) found that attention to the psychological status of cardiac surgery patients (for instance, through psychological intervention to address depressive symptoms) led to reduced length of stay in the hospital and improved treatment outcomes (such as lowered likelihood of institutionalization).

In sum, then, the general conclusion is that with the exception of the dementias, most mental disorders are most prevalent among young adults, with middle-aged adults experiencing intermediate rates. Though their status is complicated by the potential interaction with a coexisting physical illness, older adults are at lower risk for mental disorder than either young or middle-aged adults. Psychological health appears to improve with age.

Assessment, Diagnosis, and Treatment of Mental Disorders among Older Adults

Because a number of important risk factors for mental disorder are common among the current generation of older adults—for example, low levels of education and high rates of chronic illness—it is somewhat surprising to find lower rates of disorder in this group (George, 1990b). A number of investigators have suggested that existing data seriously underestimate the prevalence of mental disorders among older adults. For example, Jeste and colleagues (1999) believe the actual prevalence (excluding dementia) to be 16.3 percent, 25 percent higher than the 13 percent cited in the ECA data. If this is the case, older adults may not be diagnosed and therefore may not be receiving treatment that could help to alleviate their difficulties. Why might this be? Several factors make determining the rates of mental disorder among older adults especially difficult.

The first problem has to do with the commonly used diagnostic criteria. Unlike many physical illnesses, for which there are objective, easily measured markers, diagnosis of mental disorder is based on symptoms that are reported by the individual or observed by the clinician (George, 1993). These symptoms are then assessed in comparison to a set of standard criteria. Thus, the diagnosis of mental illness is often more difficult than the diagnosis of physical illness, regardless of age.

The most commonly used diagnostic classification system for psychological disorders is contained in the *Diagnostic and Statistical Manual of Mental Disorders (DSM)*, published by the American Psychiatric Association (1994). This manual has been revised a number of times since its debut in 1952; the current version is *DSM-IV*, published in 1994.

Some investigators have questioned whether the diagnostic criteria in *DSM* are "age-fair." In other words, criteria that are valid when used with younger individuals may be invalid when applied to older adults. Perhaps mental illness in older adults is manifested in a different way than it is in younger adults. For example, depression among the elderly may show itself in vague physical decline or multiple physical complaints (Cohen, 1990) rather than in the symptoms more typical among younger individuals (see Table 11.4). Existing criteria may therefore fail to identify disorders among older adults.

Second, symptoms of mental disorders such as depression and anxiety (for example, difficulty sleeping, changed eating patterns, or heart palpitations) mimic the symptoms of physical illnesses (Gatz & Smyer, 1992). Since the current cohort of older adults is much more likely to visit their physician than a mental health professional (George, Blazer, Winfield-Laird, Leaf, & Fishbach, 1988), it is likely that the symptoms would be attributed to a physical condition, leaving a mental disorder undetected.

Third, myths and stereotypes about aging may interfere with the identification as well as the treatment of psychological problems among older adults (Cohen, 1990).

Symptoms may be overlooked or dismissed as inevitable and "normal" aspects of aging. For example, we may assume that it is normal for older adults to be sad and depressed or that it is normal for older individuals to be confused and forgetful. In one study (Gallo, Ryan, & Ford, 1999), 75 percent of physicians viewed depression as "understandable" in older patients. As we have seen in earlier chapters, one of the critical challenges in developmental psychology is differentiating normal age-related change from disease. Our inability to do so impairs the likelihood that we will identify mental disorders.

Others have voiced concern over ageism in treatment, citing avoidance of older patients and negative outcome expectations among therapists (Butler, Lewis, & Sunderland, 1991; Dittman, 2003). For example, older patients may be viewed as more set in their ways and less able to change their behavior. In a study of 371 experienced practicing doctoral-level psychologists, James and Haley (1995) found evidence of age bias and even stronger evidence of health bias (negative attitudes toward and negative evaluations of those in poor health), regardless of age. Such bias may undermine the therapeutic relationship and set up a destructive self-fulfilling prophecy, adversely affecting treatment outcomes. These concerns may be especially relevant to older clients, who often suffer from coexisting physical health problems.

As we have noted before, few health care professionals are knowledgeable about and experienced in the treatment of older individuals. This includes practicing psychologists, few of whom have had any formal training (graduate coursework or supervised internships) in the psychology of aging (American Psychological Association, 2004a). Lack of preparation may increase reluctance to work with older adults. An awareness of cultural differences that may affect the manifestation, diagnosis, and treatment of mental disorders among the growing proportion of ethnic minorities will also be critical. To address these concerns, the APA has published *Guidelines for Psychological Practice with Older Adults* (American Psychological Association, 2004a).

Researchers estimate that up to 63 percent of adults age 65 and over with a mental disorder are not receiving treatment (U.S. Department of Health and Human Services, 1999). Failure in diagnosis and treatment may be especially likely among older individuals living in nursing homes. The National Institute of Mental Health estimates that 50 to 60 percent of nursing home residents have serious mental health problems (cited in Binney & Swan, 1991). Depression and dementia are especially common (Jakubiak & Callahan, 1996). Despite the fact that nursing homes are the largest single location providing care for those with mental illness, services are largely unavailable in these locations. One of the most common forms of care in these institutions is drug treatment, often with antipsychotic drugs. This is in spite of the fact that residents frequently have not been formally diagnosed with a mental disorder. Similarly, Rovner et al. (1990, 1991) found that nursing home physicians correctly diagnosed only half of the residents who were suffering from dementia and missed the majority of those suffering from depression. The latter is especially troubling because depression is associated with increased mortality and is often treatable. They conclude that mental disorders in nursing homes are often undiagnosed or misdiagnosed.

Cohort Effect

It is important to remember that existing data are based on current cohorts of adults. The extent to which differential prevalence rates are the result of developmental factors or cohort effects is not yet clear. In other words, the lower rates of mental disorder among today's older adults may be due to differences in the historical experience of the older and younger cohorts. If this is the case, rates of some mental disorders among future groups of elderly will be higher, as those now in young and middle adulthood move across the life span. Specifically, it is likely that rates of substance abuse, alcoholism, and depression will go up. On the other hand, rates of dementia caused by vascular problems may decline, reflecting improvements in nutrition and lifestyle.

Indeed, comparisons of survey data from 1957, 1976, and 1996 showed a significant increase in the number of Americans reporting an existing or impending mental health problem (from about 19 percent in 1957 to about 30 percent in 1996) (Swindle, Heller, Pescosolido, & Kikuzawa, 2000). Whether this is due to an actual increase in prevalence or greater willingness to discuss mental problems (or both) is unclear. Jeste and colleagues (1999) expect a greater increase in the rate of mental illness among the elderly in comparision to younger age groups—to 21.6 percent by 2030—as a result of the following: lower rates of death early in life from suicide or physical comorbidity among patients suffering from disorders such as depression, schizophrenia, and substance dependence due to better treatment and an overall higher standard of living; increased numbers of older adults and thus an increase in those who may develop late-onset disorders; and higher risk among younger generations. In any event, the sheer number of cases will increase even if rates remain constant, because of the large baby boom cohort.

Cohort not only influences experiences directly related to mental health outcomes, but also affects individuals' attitudes toward treatment. For example, future cohorts may be more likely to seek help from mental health professionals than those now old. This trend is evident in the results of a recent survey by the APA's Practice Directorate, showing that more Americans are seeking mental health treatment (American Psychological Association, 2004b). In addition, changes in family structure and dynamics—the high rate of divorce, smaller family size, and the entrance of increasing numbers of women into the workforce—may affect the care available to older persons (Gatz & Smyer, 1992). Thus, both the rate of mental disorder and the response to it may vary with birth cohort.

CRITICAL THINKING QUESTION

What sociohistorical experiences among cohorts of adults now in young and middle adulthood might explain the higher rates of mental disorders among these groups in comparison to older adults?

To sum up, there are legitimate concerns about the accuracy of prevalence rates of mental disorders among older adults. Evidence suggests there may be substantial error in diagnosis as well as extensive undertreatment of the elderly. These problems will increase as the numbers of mentally ill elderly go up. There is an urgent need for clinicians specifically trained in the identification and treatment of mental disorders in late life (clinical geropsychologists) and an equally great need to provide access to these services in the community as well as in the nursing home.

Gender Differences in Rates of Mental Disorders

Some confusion exists as to whether there are gender differences in the overall prevalence of mental disorders in adulthood (see, for example, George, 1990b; Gatz & Smyer, 1992; Smith & Baltes, 1998). There are known to be gender differences in the rates of *specific* disorders, however. Women are significantly more likely to suffer from mood disorders, especially depression, and anxiety disorders. Men, on the other hand, experience higher rates of substance use disorders (both alcohol and other) and antisocial personality. Though the reasons are unclear, these disparities in prevalence narrow and sometimes disappear altogether later in life, reflecting declining rates among the more at-risk group (Myers et al., 1984; Blazer et al., 1985).

Little research has been done on the differing experiences of older men and women and the effect of these experiences on psychological health. We do know that women experience significant risk factors such as poverty to a greater extent than men. (See our discussion of the feminization of poverty in Chapter 8.) Given the fact that women constitute the majority of older adults, and that their proportion increases with age, understanding gender differences in risk is important.

Some critics charge that the diagnostic criteria contained in *DSM-IV* are biased against women—that is, that they tend to lead to higher rates of diagnosis of mental disorder among women than among men. The argument is that the diagnostic criteria rate stereotypical masculine traits such as independence as healthier than traits traditionally considered to be feminine. Thus, held to a male standard, more women would be identified as suffering from a mental disorder than is actually the case. (See, for example, Kaplan, 1983.) Others argue that gender stereotypes associated with some diagnostic labels themselves, rather than the specific diagnostic criteria, may lead to biases in diagnosis. For instance, Ford and Widiger (1989) found evidence of bias in the diagnosis of antisocial personality disorder (males were more likely to be diagnosed) and histrionic personality disorder (females were more likely to be diagnosed). Issues of bias remain unresolved at this point.

Gender, Age, and Racial/Ethnic Differences in Help Seeking

In order for a mental disorder to be diagnosed and treated, the individual must come to the attention of the mental health system. Yet studies indicate that only 40 percent of those with a diagnosable disorder receive any formal care, and only 25 percent receive care from a mental health specialist (Kessler et al., 1994). Age, gender, and racial/ethnic differences exist in the help-seeking behavior of adults. At all ages, women are more likely to seek help with physical and mental problems than men (Addis & Mahalik, 2003; Kessler, Brown, & Borman, 1981). Older adults are just as likely to seek treatment for mental health problems as younger adults, though they have a stronger tendency to do so from their physician than a mental health professional (George et al., 1988). If, as some investigators suspect, primary care physicians are less likely to accurately diagnose and treat mental disorders, this may mean that older adults are receiving less adequate treatment for mental health problems than younger adults (George, 1990b). Treatment of the elderly individual is especially challenging and complex because of the high probability that physical and mental illness may coexist.

Identifying and treating the mental health needs of minority individuals is especially difficult. First, they are less likely to seek help than members of other groups (Abramson, Trejo, & Lai, 2002; Wyckle & Musil, 1993). Second, there is a need to develop diagnostic measures that are culturally valid and reliable (Sakuye, 1992). There has been progress, however. For the first time, *DSM-IV* addresses ethnic and cultural issues, including the role of culture in the expression and evaluation of symptoms, as well as the impact of culture on the therapeutic relationship.

Finally, a shortage of culturally competent and sensitive therapists exists. This is significant because there is evidence that the therapist-client match in language and ethnicity is related to the success of the treatment. The proportion of minority members of the American Psychological Association is far below that of the U.S. minority population (Fowler, 2002). The minority group population is growing, an indication that this problem will grow more serious with time. The number of minority students in the educational pipeline is not sufficient to keep pace with the need for mental health services among ethnic minority groups (Bernal & Castro, 1993). As a result, dominant-culture psychologists will continue to provide most of the treatment. They will require training to be more sensitive to relevant cultural issues. For example, those working with Native Americans must have an understanding of Indian culture and history and how such things as native belief systems may interact with treatment approaches. The knowledge base needed to train culturally sensitive mental health professionals needs expansion. For reasons already mentioned, much of this research will be done by those from the majority culture (Bernal & Castro, 1993).

To summarize, while progress has been made in describing the prevalence of mental disorders among adults and identifying differential patterns based on age and gender, clear explanations of these patterns are at this point unavailable. Men and women are believed to experience differences in risk for certain specific diagnoses. In addition, it appears that rates of mental disorder are lower among the current cohort of older adults. The evidence is primarily cross-sectional, however. The lack of longitudinal studies makes it difficult to determine whether this pattern is a reflection of age-related changes or differing degrees of risk among existing cohorts of adults. If the lower rate is the result of age-related change, suggesting that age somehow protects one from risk, we can be optimistic that future generations of adults might continue to show lower rates of mental disorder. Perhaps as we age, our accumulated experience provides us with the tools and resources to cope with life events more effectively. If, however, the differences are due to cohort effects, there is a need to determine what the social and environmental risk factors are and to focus on prevention. Does the higher risk of disorder among younger cohorts suggest that the environment (both physical and social) is more dangerous now than it was? If so, the prevalence of mental disorder will increase as the next generation enters old age (Gatz & Smyer, 1992). Finally, the increasing cultural diversity of our society requires that we develop a better appreciation of the impact of ethnic background on help seeking, diagnosis, and treatment, and that we train a cadre of mental health professionals sensitive to these issues.

Despite the fact that the majority of adults of all ages are in good mental health, there is a sizable minority whose quality of life, productivity, and physical health are profoundly affected by significant mental health problems. For these individuals, accurate diagnosis and effective treatment are a high priority. Efforts to reduce the incidence of mental disorders in the future, however, must focus on prevention.

Science of Prevention

Prevention efforts attempt to identify risk factors for the development of mental disorders as well as protective factors that are correlated with mental health. **Risk factors** are associated with a high likelihood of onset, greater severity, and longer duration of major mental disorders (Coie et al., 1993). **Protective factors,** on the other hand, are variables that increase individuals' resistance to risk factors and, therefore, disorders.

Prevention is logically aimed at counteracting the risk factors and strengthening the protective factors. (See NIMH Prevention Research Steering Committee, 1994, and Mrazek & Haggerty, 1994, for two major reports on the prevention of mental disorders.) The immense potential value of prevention is illustrated by the fact that delaying the onset of Alzheimer's disease by just five years could reduce the number of cases by 50 percent in one generation (Jeste et al., 1999).

Risk Factors

Current models of causation emphasize a complex interaction among genetic, biological, and psychosocial risk and protective factors. Any one psychological disorder is likely to be associated with many different risk factors, rather than just one. Thus, no simple cause-and-effect relationships exist. In addition, any given risk factor may be involved in the development of many different disorders. Further, a risk factor may have a different effect at different ages, so timing is important. Finally, the likelihood of developing a disorder increases as a function of the number of risk factors, their duration, and severity.

Wyckle and Musil (1993) identify the following social and cultural variables as having a particularly strong influence on mental health and well-being: gender, socioeconomic status, negative life events, physical health, race and ethnicity, and social support. For example, a depressed older adult is more likely to be a woman of lower socioeconomic status, who is unmarried or widowed, has experienced stressful life events, lacks a social support system, and has a coexisting physical illness (Blazer, Hughes, & George, 1987). Financial status may be a particularly powerful risk factor because of the potential stress resulting directly from insufficient financial resources as well as the impact of finances on such things as self-esteem, dependence on others, nutrition, access to health care, and so on. In addition, for elderly adults living on fixed incomes, financial strain may be especially likely to erode feelings of control (Krause & Baker, 1992). Moritz, Kasl, and Berkman (1989) studied the impact of living with a cognitively impaired spouse. They found that men who felt their financial resources were inadequate experienced more symptoms of depression than those who felt financially secure.

The correlation between economic strain and depressive symptoms may at least partially explain the association between gender, race/ethnicity, and mental health (Wyckle & Musil, 1993). As we have seen, women and ethnic and racial minorities are more likely to have lower socioeconomic status.

Protective Factors

The presence of protective factors can mitigate the effect of exposure to risk factors (see, for example, Rolf, Masten, Cicchetti, Neuchterlein, & Weintraub, 1990). Protective factors can be grouped into two general categories (Coie et al., 1993). The first group includes factors characteristic of the individual, such as temperament and coping skills. The second group includes characteristics of the individual's environment, such as the degree of social support available. As we discussed in Chapter 6, social support is a critical variable and is determined not by the number of relationships an individual has but by the quality of those relationships. A supportive social network may be especially important to the mental health of older adults (Wyckle & Musil, 1993). Help with such things as household maintenance as well as the companionship and acceptance provided by supportive relationships are associated with greater life satisfaction and lower rates of depressive symptoms.

A Life-Span View of Prevention

A life-span approach to mental disorders acknowledges and seeks to understand the great variability among individuals at risk of psychological difficulties. It recognizes the complex interplay of multiple causal factors—biological, social, psychological, and historical—on all aspects of development. Further, it views the prevention of mental health problems as a lifelong process. While some of the mental disorders that plague older adults represent a continuation of problems that originated earlier in life, others, called *late-onset disorders* (e.g., late-onset alcholism), emerge for the first time later in life. Some of these may reflect the failure of coping strategies that were sufficient at earlier stages.

Coie and his colleagues (1993) point out that longitudinal studies have the potential to significantly enhance our understanding of the onset and developmental course of psychopathology as well as the interaction of risk and protective factors over the life course. Current understanding is hindered by the scarcity of such studies.

They also emphasize the importance of the ecological, contextual, and systems theory views that human adaptation is best understood in terms of the interaction between the person and the environment ($B = f(PE)$—see Chapter 2). Such a perspective recognizes that individuals may respond to similar environments in different ways. It also emphasizes the role of the sociocultural context in the origin, course, and prevention of mental illness. Cultural norms, beliefs, and practices have a bearing on definitions of normal and abnormal behavior as well as on the operation of risk and protective factors. Behavior is the product of multiple and interacting forces, the influence of which may vary by age. Thus, for example, the impact of the death of a loved one on development would depend on such factors as the individual's temperament, the nature of the relationship, the availability of social support, the economic status of the family, the individual's gender, age, and so on. The success of any prevention program thus depends on recognizing the fit between the individual and the environment as well as the effect of the personal history, cultural context, and life stage of the person. In other words, programs must be matched to people (Stacey-Konnert, 1993).

Finally, one must remember that the goal of any prevention effort is the elimination of mental disorder, not the prevention of aging and old age itself. "While this . . . may sound foolishly simplistic, there is prevalent in this society a paradoxical view that to grow old well is to stay young. This view is a denial of normal development and should be rejected in favor of the goal of a fulfilled old age" (Stacey-Konnert, 1993, p. 78).

Concept Review 11.3

- Epidemiological data suggest that, with the exception of dementia, mental disorders are more prevalent among younger as compared to older adults. The extent to which this is the result of developmental or cohort effects is unclear.

- However, there is a great deal of concern about underdiagnosis and undertreatment of older adults.

(continued)

- Women are more likely to suffer from mood and anxiety disorders, while men are at greater risk of antisocial personality disorder and substance use disorders.

- There are age, gender, and racial/ethnic differences in help seeking.

- Demographic changes in our society necessitate greater understanding of and sensitivity to the effect of ethnic background and culture on the development and treatment of mental disorders.

- Increasing attention is being paid to an ecological view of the identification of risk factors in the development of mental disorders and protective factors that promote mental health.

A Look at Two Mental Disorders in Adulthood

Because it is beyond the scope of this chapter to review all of the specific mental disorders affecting adults, two disorders have been selected for closer review: major depression and Alzheimer's disease.

Major Depression

Called the common cold of mental illness, depression is the most common complaint among those who seek mental health care and the third most common reason why people visit physicians (Strickland, 1992). Each year, about 10 percent of American adults experience serious depression. Though *DSM-IV* identifies a variety of depressive disorders, the most common of these and the focus of our discussion is major depression. It differs from sadness or "the blues" both in intensity and duration. Major depression affects about 3 percent of the adult population and is occurring with increasing frequency in younger and younger populations worldwide. It is especially prevalent in more economically advanced countries. Though the reasons are unclear, greater social isolation, a feeling of powerlessness, and unrealistic goals established by media images have been suggested (Buss, 2000). Individuals are thus more likely to be faced with a sense of failure and insignificance and to lack the strong social ties that make one feel valued.

Depression is a phenomenon of the whole person. Thus, it affects and can severely disrupt all aspects of functioning—physical, emotional, social, cognitive. Occupational and interpersonal impairment often results. The emotional distress suffered by depressed individuals contributes to major health risks, such as smoking and drinking (McGinnis & Foege, 1993; Schoenborn & Horm, 1993). In general, depression increases the risk of illness, disability, and death (Meeks, Murrell, & Mehl, 2000). In addition, two-thirds of the 30,000 reported suicides in the United States each year may be related to major depression (Strickland, 1992). Without treatment, symptoms can last for weeks, months, or years. And while available treatment is estimated to be effective in over 80 percent of cases, few people recognize the signs of depression and seek help. Thus, only one in four depressed individuals receives treatment (Hollon, Thase, & Markowitz, 2002; Strickland, 1992). Abraham Lincoln is said to have battled severe bouts of it. Winston Churchill suffered from what he called "the black dog." So what is major depression exactly? How can it be identified?

Diagnostic Criteria

The essential feature of **major depression,** according to *DSM-IV,* is either a depressed mood or a loss of interest or pleasure in all, or almost all, activities. Major depression is identified by a combination of symptoms that interfere with normal activities such as eating, sleeping, working, and finding pleasure in life. These symptoms arc listed in Table 11.4. Five or more symptoms are required for a diagnosis. The symptoms must be psychological rather than physical in origin—for example, symptoms attributed to a physical illness or the use of medications or alcohol would be excluded. The symptoms must be relatively persistent—that is, present for most of the day, nearly every day for at least two weeks—and must occur together, forming a syndrome. Not all depressed individuals experience every symptom, and the severity of the symptoms varies from person to person. In general, depression makes you feel worthless, helpless, hopeless, and exhausted. It is important to remember that these negative thoughts and feelings are part of the depression and that they will begin to lift as the depression responds to treatment. ECA data suggest that 20 percent of those who develop major depression experience their first symptom by about age 19 (50 percent by age 26), though the disorder may not be diagnosed until years later (Mrazek & Haggerty, 1994).

Causes

Though major depression does run in families, it also occurs in individuals who have no family history of the disorder. It is associated with an imbalance of neurotransmitters in the brain—specifically, norepinephrine and serotonin; however, there is some debate about whether this chemical imbalance is a cause or a consequence of the depression. Whether or not one develops depression may depend on the interaction of a biological vulnerability, stress, and personal resources. This is a developmental diathesis-stress model. A **diathesis** is a predisposition to developing a disorder. The idea is that some people are more likely to develop a particular disorder or illness than others (e.g., perhaps due to genetic/biological factors, personality traits, or life experience) but that the

TABLE 11.4 *Symptoms of Depression*

Persistent sad, anxious, or "empty" mood
Feelings of hopelessness, pessimism
Feelings of guilt, worthlessness, helplessness
Loss of interest or pleasure in hobbies and activities that you once enjoyed, including sex
Insomnia, early-morning awakening, or oversleeping
Appetite and/or weight loss or overeating and weight gain
Decreased energy, fatigue, being "slowed down"
Thoughts of suicide or death, suicide attempts
Restlessness, irritability
Difficulty concentrating, remembering, making decisions
Persistent physical symptoms that do not respond to treatment, such as headaches, digestive disorders, and chronic pain

Note: A diagnosis of major depression is based on the presence of at least five symptoms of psychological origin occurring together and lasting at least two weeks.

disorder itself is triggered by stress. (Remember that being at high risk does not guarantee that the disorder will occur; it just increases the likelihood.)

The Institute of Medicine Report (Mrazek & Haggerty, 1994) identifies five risk factors: having a parent or other close biological relative with a mood disorder; experiencing a severe stressor; having low self-esteem, low self-efficacy, and a sense of helplessness and hopelessness (an external locus of control, pessimism); being female (see below); and living in poverty. There is a considerable amount of evidence linking lack of social support to depression (Smallegan, 1989). Social support—feeling loved, cared about, and accepted—may offer some protection from severe depression, perhaps through its stress-buffering effects. (The grief that results from the loss of a loved one is considered to be distinct from major depression. See Chapter 12 for a discussion of grief and bereavement.) The consensus is that depression is caused by a complex interaction of many risk factors.

Treatment

A meta-analysis of research on the effects of psychological treatments, summarizing 9,400 studies involving over a million subjects, found overwhelming evidence that these interventions work (Lipsey & Wilson, 1993). Cognitive-behavioral and interpersonal therapies are especially effective in treating depression. Psychotherapy may be aimed at changing irrational and negative thought patterns that magnify the stressful nature of life events and at developing more effective coping skills. The use of reminiscence and the life review process (discussed in Chapter 2) may hold special potential for application with older adults (see, e.g., Serrano, Latorre, Gatz, & Montanes, 2004). Butler (2000) notes how struck he has been by the need of individuals to synthesize and integrate the life they have lived. And while mini-reviews may be precipitated by events earlier in life, it is only at the end of life that it is possible to deal with one's life as a whole. The life review provides the opportunity to analyze past experiences, mentally resolve old conflicts and issues, reconcile with family and friends, and come to terms with one's life history and integrate it into the present, thereby enhancing feelings of self-worth and potentially achieving a sense of integrity. Not all of these reviews result in positive outcomes; there may be inner turmoil and a sense of failure, especially among those who conduct their life review alone. Those who allow another person to share in the process are much more likely to feel increased self-esteem and to avoid feelings of depression and isolation. As Butler (2000, p. 12) so eloquently puts it, to some extent we are reinventing ourselves "by altering reality and explaining misdeeds. Memoirs, autobiographies or life reviews do not necessarily represent the unvarnished truth, but they are the last possible edition of the volume each of us has spent a lifetime creating and amending. Written or spoken, life review is a last effort to integrate and reconcile one's public and private selves."

Antidepressant drugs may be effective when used in conjunction with psychological treatments. Used alone, the risk of relapse is as high as 60 percent. Antidepressants offer relief from specific symptoms by modifying the biochemistry of the brain. Though more effective drugs are available than ever before, some individuals do not respond to medication, and many individuals must put up with side effects, including nausea, weight gain, blurred vision, and insomnia, among others. Two-thirds of all prescriptions for antidepressant drugs are written for women (Strickland, 1992), yet few studies have examined the effects of these drugs on women as compared to men, their interaction with the reproductive hormones, or gender differences in effectiveness. For reasons discussed in Chapter 10, special care must be exercised before proceeding with the use of drug treatment in older depressed patients (see Ahmed & Takeshita, 1997, for a discussion of this issue).

A consensus statement formed by a panel of 20 eminent representatives from a variety of fields (Hirschfeld et al., 1997, p. 333) cautions that although increasingly safe, effective treatments are available, "the vast majority of patients with chronic major depression are misdiagnosed, receive inappropriate or inadequate treatment, or are given no treatment at all." The reasons are complex and include failure on the part of individuals to recognize symptoms and fear of stigma, lack of education on the part of physicians and mental health workers in the diagnosis and treatment of depression, and health care system factors such as inadequate insurance coverage. The costs of undertreatment to the individual and to society are substantial, including decreased quality of life, interpersonal impairment, economic losses due to occupational impairment, threats to health, and mortality.

Gender Differences in Depression

Studies of depression in the United States and other developed countries have consistently found that women are on average twice as likely to suffer from depression as men (Nolen-Hoeksema, 1990). Estimates are that about 12 percent of men and 25 percent of women will experience major depression at some point in their lives. The origin of this gender difference is not known but is thought to reflect a complex interaction of genetic, biological, cultural, and social factors. Evidence linking hormonal changes associated with reproduction to depression is limited and weak (Nolen-Hoeksema, 2001; Strickland, 1992). Recent research has focused on gender differences in biological responses to stress, with females generally showing heightened reactivity. Psychological, social, and cultural factors unique to women's experience, in combination with their biological reactivity to stress, are seen as potent explanations of the higher rate of depression among women. In particular, the following have been proposed as significant contributing factors: the experience of victimization (both physical and sexual abuse) (see Chapter 7); economic deprivation, poverty, and restricted occupational mobility (see Chapter 8); and gender-role expectancies that are restrictive, carry less power, respect, and status, lead to lowered self-efficacy and feelings of personal control, and that also demand emotional expressivity at the expense of self (for example, the caregiver role; see Chapter 7). Stress experiences and stress reactivity interact and feed one another: the greater the stress, the more heightened the response, with negative consequences for coping and health and an increased likelihood of additional stressful experiences (Nolen-Hoeksema, 2001).

More research is needed on the risk factors for depression as well as the coping strategies used by men and women in response to negative life events before the gender difference in depression can be adequately explained. Though depression is more likely among women, depressive illnesses affect men in large numbers. In 2003, the National Institute of Mental Health initiated a campaign to raise awareness of depression in men and to reduce the stigma of men seeking help.

Ruminative Coping

How do you behave once you are depressed? Just as some people have a higher risk of becoming depressed in the first place, Susan Nolen-Hoeksema (1987, 1990, 1991; Nolen-Hoeksema, Larson, & Grayson, 1999) has argued that the way people respond to being depressed can affect its severity and duration. In a series of both naturalistic and laboratory studies, she has found that those who engage in rumination experience more severe and longer-lasting depression, while those who engage in distraction experience relief. **Rumination** refers to repetitive thoughts and behaviors that focus your attention on your symptoms of distress (such as sitting at home thinking about how miserable you are) and the meanings and consequences of these symptoms (for example, worrying that you aren't going to be able to get your work done because you're depressed). Ruminative coping is a passive, not active, coping style. It is believed to worsen and lengthen depression in at least three ways. First, it enhances the effect of depressed mood on the individual's thinking so that there is a more negative bias—that is, people recall more negative memories and become more pessimistic about the present and future. Second, ruminative coping may interfere with attention and concentration and therefore undermine or lead to the neglect of everyday instrumental behaviors, which, in turn, may increase feelings of worthlessness and helplessness. Individuals who ruminate are less likely to do the things that need to be done and that might make them feel better, even though they know they should and that it might help them. And third, rumination interferes with good problem solving; individuals come up with fewer and less effective solutions. Ironically, those who ruminate have the sense that they are gaining insight into their problem, which is what keeps them ruminating, despite the fact that they are feeling worse and aren't coping effectively.

Distracting responses are thoughts and behaviors that take your mind off your depression and allow you to focus on pleasant or at least neutral things. They may relieve the depressed mood by offering positive reinforcement and pleasure as well as by preventing depression from interfering with concentration and judgment—thus enhancing problem solving.

CRITICAL THINKING QUESTION
What effective distracting responses have you engaged in to relieve feelings of depression?

Ruminative coping style seems to be a stable characteristic of the individual and is more common among women than men (in fact, it was originally proposed to help explain the higher risk of depression among women) (Nolen-Hoeksema, Morrow, & Fredrickson, 1993). Poor social support, additional stress, and an initially severe depressive reaction also contribute to a tendency to engage in ruminative coping (Nolen-Hoeksema, Parker, & Larson, 1994). Cognitive-behavioral therapy can be effective in helping those with a ruminative style get into a more active problem-solving cycle, focusing on specific actions to be taken as opposed to excessive, passive worrying.

Age Differences in Depression: A Paradox

While ECA data indicate the prevalence of major depression among community-dwelling adults 65+ to be between 0.5 percent to 0.95 percent (George et al., 1988), a population study reported by the Federal Interagency Forum on Aging-Related Statistics (2004) found significant symptoms of depression in 18 percent of women and 11 percent of men over 65. (Rates are much higher in institutional settings, such as nursing homes.) What accounts for the discrepancy? Studies have arrived at dramatically different conclusions about the relationship between age and depression, depending on how depression is defined and measured.

Those studies that rely on traditional clinical diagnosis find that rates go down with age. This is a somewhat paradoxical finding, since many of the most potent risk factors—severe stresses such as physical illness and financial difficulties (Williamson & Schulz, 1992)—are more prevalent in this group. Of course it is possible that the accumulated experiences and coping strategies acquired over a lifetime offer protection from depression in late life. But a number of other hypotheses have been offered. Because these studies are cross-sectional, the data may reflect cohort effects (either greater protection due to historical experiences among older generations or greater risk among younger groups, or both) rather than a developmental phenomenon. Or we may be seeing a selection effect: given that depression is correlated with mortality (Conwell, 1996), those most at risk for severe depression are more likely to have been eliminated from the population by late adulthood. It is also possible that because older adults are more likely to suffer from a physical illness, clinicians may be discounting depressive symptoms because they attribute them to the illness, thus excluding them on the basis of *DSM* criteria. Depressive symptoms such as sleep problems and reduced energy level are of special concern because they could easily be misattributed to a physical health problem (Berkman et al., 1986). The cognitive effects of depression may also lead to misdiagnosis as dementia. Coexisting dementia may also mask the symptoms of depression. Another explanation of the unexpectedly low rate of major depression among older adults is that major depression is primarily manifested through different symptoms among this group, such as physical complaints, again leading to misdiagnosis (Ahmed & Takeshita, 1997). Thus, the criteria may not be age-fair or appropriate for elderly individuals. Questions of fairness have also been raised about the applicability of *DSM-IV* criteria to racial and ethnic minorities, whose rates of depressive disorders mirror those of Whites, despite the presence of significant risk factors (Anthony & Aboraya, 1992). Finally, the criteria for major depression may ignore less severe but still significant cases of depression.

In contrast, studies that rely on self-report measures of symptoms—such as the widely used Center for Epidemiologic Studies Depression Scale (CES-D) or the Beck Depression Inventory—find that rates of depression go up with age. Many more adults at all ages report symptoms of depression than qualify for diagnosis (George, 1993). Yet while their symptoms may not be significant enough to meet the criteria for a clinical disorder, they may disrupt functioning in social relationships as well as on the job and reduce quality of life. This so-called **minor depression** (also known as mild or subclinical depression) is especially prevalent among older adults, suggesting they may be more prone to minor depression than younger adults. Gatz and Hurwicz (1990) suggest that older adults may experience a lack of positive feelings, rather than active negative feelings. There is also speculation that a different, yet unidentified depressive syndrome is present among the elderly. Older adults may be more likely to develop a **depletion syndrome** (Newmann, Engel, & Jensen, 1991; Newmann, Klein, Jensen, & Essex, 1996). The key features of this syndrome are self-worthlessness, loss of interest in things, strong feelings of loneliness, a general sense of hopelessness, and thoughts of death and dying. Other classic symptoms of major depression are absent. Thus, older adults may be at lower risk of major depression but at higher risk of depletion syndrome, which is not represented in the currently used diagnostic criteria.

Whatever the reason, many older adults (perhaps as many as 5 million individuals over the age of 65) are apparently struggling with some form of depression serious enough to impair their ability to function and to undermine quality of life. Because these symptoms do not meet the diagnostic criteria for major depression, their problems remain unrecognized and untreated (Schulz, Martire, Beach, & Scheier, 2000). Successful treatment offers many benefits, including improved quality of life, reduced physical illness and health care costs, and enhanced productivity and survival. Is minor depression a distinct disorder, different from currently recognized forms? Are there other unidentified forms of depression that are more likely with advanced age? If so, what is the nature and course of this disorder? What are the risk factors and treatments? These issues merit attention. It seems safe to conclude that there does not appear to be a general or dramatic increase in depression among older adults (Rothermund & Brandtstadter, 2003a). Despite the accumulated changes and losses of later life, most older adults exhibit resilience.

Suicide among the Elderly

Suicide is a more frequent cause of death among older adults than any other age category, though this is primarily a reflection of the especially high suicide rate among older White men, a rate three times the national average. According to the National Center for Health Statistics (2003), in 2001 the suicide rate for older White men was three times the rate for older Black men; almost twice the rate of elderly Hispanic and Asian males; eight times the rate for older White women; and nearly 22 times the rate for older Black women. (See Figure 11.1.) Firearms are the most common method of suicide among the elderly (Meehan, Saltzman, & Sattin, 1991).

Suicide rates among the elderly declined throughout much of the 20th century until 1980 (Conwell, 1993). The decline is attributed to such things as improved economic security resulting from Social Security and Medicare legislation, availability of antidepressant drugs, and other cohort effects. However, increasing suicide rates among younger individuals suggest that as these cohorts move into later life, rates among the elderly will rise. The 25 percent increase in suicides among those 65+ between 1980 and 1988 is thought to represent the beginning of this trend. Given the fact that the absolute number of elderly is increasing, even if rates do not increase the number of suicides is expected to double by the year 2030 (Haas & Hendin, 1983).

FIGURE 11.1 *Suicide Rates for People 65+, by Sex and Race/Ethnicity, 2001*

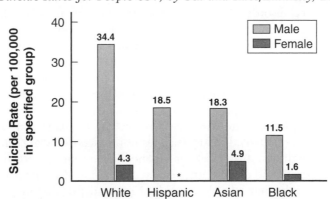

*Rate based on too few deaths to be reliable.
Source: National Center for Health Statistics, 2003.

Studies suggest that 90 percent of cases of suicide among the elderly, as in all age groups, are associated with a diagnosable mental disorder—two-thirds are attributable to major depression. Remember that members of this cohort are no less likely to seek help with their problems; however, they are inclined to seek it from their doctor. In fact, studies indicate that up to three-quarters of suicide victims visited their physician shortly before their death, but that the depression was either not diagnosed or not effectively treated (Clark, 1991).

In a study of elderly adults diagnosed with major depression, Zweig and Hinrichsen (1993) found the risk of attempted suicide was greater among those of higher socioeconomic status, those with a history of suicidal tendencies or attempts, and those experiencing interpersonal stressors, such as strain in their relationships with a spouse or adult child. This strain resulted either from maladjustment in the relative or the damaging effects of the patient's depression and the need for care.

Information about the state of mind of deceased suicide victims is collected through in-depth interviews with family and friends, a technique known as the psychological autopsy. Suicide victims typically have experienced an increase in stressful life events in the months prior to the suicide attempt. Among older adults, these events generally involve physical illness and loss (for example, loss of a loved one, retirement, threatened loss of autonomy through nursing home placement). Research suggests that most older suicide victims die as a result of their first episode of major depressive illness, a disorder that, if diagnosed, is very responsive to treatment.

Researchers are actively looking for biological markers of suicide, with a growing body of work suggesting a link between violent suicidal behavior and changes in the functioning of the neurotransmitter serotonin (Conwell, 1993). Should such a marker be found, it could aid in the detection of those at highest risk of suicide. In the meantime, efforts to increase the awareness of the symptoms of depression, to encourage older adults to seek help from mental health workers, and to educate primary care physicians about the nature and treatment of depression in late life should be undertaken (Pearson & Brown, 2000). Early recognition and treatment are likely to save lives.

Alzheimer's Disease

Dementia refers to a progressive deterioration in intellectual functions such as thinking, remembering, and reasoning, which is severe enough to interfere with the individual's ability to function in daily life. It is almost exclusively a problem of old age. Alzheimer's disease (pronounced *Altz-hi-merz*) is the leading cause of dementia (and is technically referred to as dementia of the Alzheimer's type), accounting for an estimated 60 to 90 percent of all cases and afflicting as many as 4.5 million Americans. (Other causes of dementia include stroke and Parkinson's disease.) Though it was first described by a physician named Alois Alzheimer in 1907, it is not a modern scourge. Sophocles may have been describing it in the fifth century B.C.: "All evils are engrained in long old age, with vanished, useless actions, empty thoughts." But for most of human history, few people lived long enough to develop the symptoms.

Defining Alzheimer's Disease: A Slow Death of the Mind

Alzheimer's disease (AD) is a progressive, degenerative neurological disease that attacks the brain and impairs memory, thinking, and behavior. As the disease progresses,

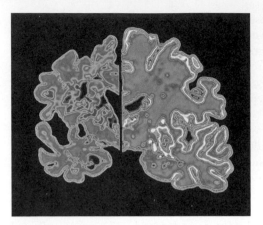

The neural destruction caused by Alzheimer's disease is evident in this computer graphic comparing a vertical slice through one of the hemispheres of the brain of an Alzheimer's victim (at left) with that of a normal brain (at right).

victims are robbed of their personalities, their ability to care for themselves, and the capacity to relate to others. AD results from the degeneration of neurons in the brain, particularly in the hippocampus and the frontal and temporal lobes of the cerebral cortex. These are the areas of the brain involved in memory, language, and higher-order thought. Primary motor and sensory areas are relatively unaffected. For unknown reasons, these neurons develop two characteristic abnormalities: **amyloid plaques,** which are spherical deposits consisting mostly of a protein fragment called beta-amyloid that builds up in the fluid surrounding the neurons, and neurofibrillary **tangles,** which are large accumulations of twisted nerve fibers called "tau" inside the neuron. Though plaques are found in all aged brains, they occur in much higher numbers in Alzheimer's patients. Because the affected neurons both produce and use acetylcholine, an important neurotransmitter involved in the storage of memory and other functions, the AD patient suffers from a depletion of acetylcholine supplies. Why these particular neurons are selectively attacked and destroyed is not known. The degree of cognitive impairment an individual exhibits is related to the extent of the pathological changes taking place in the brain.

Though it is more common among those over age 65, Alzheimer's disease can strike people in their 40s and 50s, as it did the famous actress Rita Hayworth. As many as 10 percent of those over 65 suffer from probable Alzheimer's disease, and the percentage increases with age, such that over 47 percent of those over age 85 are afflicted (Evans, 1989; Ritchie & Kildea, 1995). (See Figure 11.2.) The growth of the over-65 population means that by the year 2050, over 14 million older adults may have Alzheimer's disease (Hebert, Scherr, Bienias, Bennett, & Evans, 2003). Cognitive impairment is one of the major reasons for institutionalization of older adults. In fact, it has been estimated that when we eliminate Alzheimer's disease, we will empty half our country's nursing home beds (Butler, 1993). AD crosses all economic, racial, and ethnic lines. An estimated 100,000 deaths annually are attributed to this disease, making it a leading cause of death among adults.

Symptoms

AD is a progressive disease, meaning that the symptoms gradually worsen over time. The duration of the disease varies from three to 20 or more years from the onset of symptoms to the death of the victim, with the average at eight. Brain activity gradually diminishes until the person lapses into a coma and dies. One of the extraordinary things about AD is that although it is a brain disorder, the primary symptoms are behavioral (Cohen, 1988). Unlike other causes of dementia, such as stroke, somatic symptoms are usually absent in AD. Physical functioning may remain essentially normal throughout most of the course of the disease—there are no motor, sensory, or coordination deficits in the early stages (McKhann et al., 1984). Instead, the changes occurring in the brain profoundly affect the way the individual feels, thinks, and behaves,

FIGURE 11.2 *Percentage of People 65+ with Probable Alzheimer's Disease, by Age Group (excludes those in nursing homes and other institutions)*

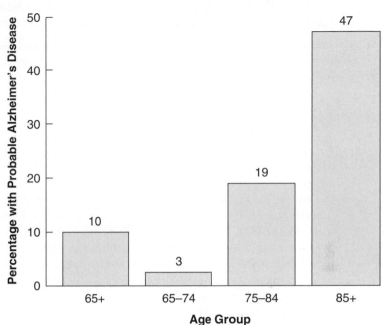

Source: U.S. Senate Special Committee on Aging et al., 1991, p. 116.

and disrupt interpersonal and psychosocial functioning. The rate of change as well as the particular constellation of symptoms vary from person to person. Symptoms include the following:

- Memory loss (initially short-term—the most obvious symptom in the early stages— but eventually long-term memory involvement)
- Confusion (disorientation as to time and place)
- Impaired judgment
- Loss of language and communication skills, such as difficulty in naming
- Personality and behavior changes—for example, agitation, irritability, wandering
- Difficulty performing routine tasks, such as dressing or bathing (Cohen, 1988; Lee, 1991; Teri et al., 1992)

Warning signs include getting lost in familiar places, forgetting simple words like *bread*, inability to operate simple appliances, inability to deal with numbers, or forgetting the uses or meaning of common things (e.g., that socks go on your feet).

Particularly in the early stages of the disease, the AD patient may continue to "act" normally by relying on highly routinized, well-socialized patterns of behavior. The appearance of normalcy can be deceiving. For example, Fontana and Smith (1989, p. 40) describe the behavior of a patient named Joe, who was sitting in a chair by the nurses' station when the telephone rang. He automatically reached over and answered it, "Hello." "He then held the phone out in front of himself, looked at it quizzically, and said confusedly, 'What on earth is this?' and handed the strange object to the nurse."

Similarly, Morella and Epstein (1983, p. 248) describe an encounter between Rita Hayworth and some old friends after the onset of the disease.

> Rita continued to be seen in public. She continued to look *great.* . . . She looked like her old self again. . . . Although she seemed to be functioning, she wasn't. People who had known her from the old days were shocked when they went up to say hello to her in public. It was obvious she didn't remember them.

Diagnosis

A diagnosis of Alzheimer's disease can only be confirmed at autopsy by the presence of plaques and tangles. There is at present no single clinical test that specifically identifies AD in a living patient. The behavioral quality of the primary symptoms of AD add to the confusion in diagnosis, as many other conditions, including other forms of dementia, mimic these symptoms. Among these are Parkinson's disease, stroke, depression, alcoholism, brain tumors, nutritional deficiencies, infections, head injuries, overmedication and adverse drug reactions, vitamin B12 deficiency, and thyroid problems. Since many of these conditions are treatable, it is imperative that all other possible diagnoses be ruled out before settling on a diagnosis of probable Alzheimer's disease. The elimination of all competing possibilities is known as a **diagnosis of exclusion.** This requires a thorough examination by a physician knowledgeable about dementia and the use of a number of neuropsychological tests and is best done at specialized centers, where diagnosis can reach 90 percent accuracy.

Some short tests have been developed to help physicians spot problems and refer the patient for a more complete evaluation. Sample items include questions such as What (year, day, month) is it? and Where are we (state, town, hospital)? or tasks such as counting backward from 100 by 7s (stop after five), following a three-stage command (take the pencil, put it on the table, put your hand over it), naming a common object, or copying a design. (See Figure 11.3.)

Investigators continue to search for a reliable and valid biological or chemical marker in the patient's blood, skin, or spinal fluid that would aid in the early diagnosis of this disease. The availability of brain imaging technologies such as MRI (magnetic resonance imaging) and PET (positron emission tomography)—which allow scientists to gather information about what is going on inside the brain without surgery—have assisted in the diagnosis of AD and other dementias and may eventually allow physicians to detect the earliest signs of the disease. Early diagnosis is critically important, as potential treatments to slow the progress of the disease will be most effective in the early stages before too much brain damage occurs (Epstein & Connor, 1999).

There seems to be special difficulty in distinguishing between depression and dementia. In fact, the symptoms of depression are frequently mistaken for signs of dementia (Kaszniak, 1990). These conditions can occur together, and when they do, cognitive deterioration is exaggerated. Studies indicate that treatment of the depressive symptoms can lead to improved cognitive functioning. Gatz (1988) points out that the rule of thumb used to be that if a patient complained of memory problems it was due to depression, and if a family member complained, it was due to dementia. However, it now appears that in the early stages of dementia, and especially in intelligent individuals, the patient may be the first one to recognize a cognitive deficit.

FIGURE 11.3 *Folstein Mini Mental Status Examination*

The Mini Mental Status Exam is a quick way to evaluate cognitive function and is often used to screen for dementia or monitor its progression.

TASK	INSTRUCTIONS	SCORING	
Date Orientation	"Tell me the date?" Ask for omitted items.	One point each for year, season, date, day of week, and month	5
Place Orientation	"Where are you?" Ask for omitted items.	One point each for state, county, town, building, and floor or room	5
Register 3 Objects	Name three object slowly and clearly. Ask the patient to repeat them.	One point for each item correctly repeated	3
Serial Sevens	Ask the patient to count backward from 100 by 7. Stop after five answers. (Or ask them to spell "world" backwards.)	One point for each correct answer (or letter)	5
Recall 3 Objects	Ask the patient to recall the objects mentioned above.	One point for each item correctly remembered	3
Naming	Point to your watch and ask the patient, "What is this?" Repeat with a pencil.	One point for each correct answer	2
Repeating a Phrase	Ask the patient to say, "No ifs, ands, or buts."	One point if successful on first try	1
Verbal Commands	Give the patient a plain piece of paper and say, "Take this paper in your right hand, fold it in half, and put it on the floor."	One point for each correct action	3
Written Commands	Show the patient a piece of paper with "CLOSE YOUR EYES" printed on it.	One point if the patient's eyes close	1
Writing	Ask the patient to write a sentence.	One point if sentence has a subject, a verb, and makes sense	1
Drawing	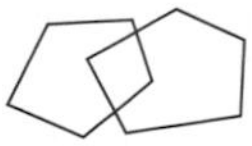 Ask the patient to copy a pair of intersecting pentagons onto a piece of paper.	One point if the figure has ten corners and two intersecting lines	1
Scoring	A score of 24 or above is considered normal.		**30**

Source: Adapted from Folstein, Folstein, and McHugh, 1975.

The presence of AD may result in missed diagnosis of other medical illnesses, both because patients may not be able to tell anyone if they don't feel well, and because the symptoms may be wrongly attributed to AD. In addition, medications prescribed for other conditions may aggravate the symptoms of AD if they block acetylcholine, which is already in short supply.

Possible Causes

The exact cause of the neural destruction at the heart of AD is not yet known, though researchers are pursuing a number of hypotheses. It seems likely that there is more than one form of the disease, with different patterns of causation. In addition, AD may result from a combination of causal factors interacting together, rather than from a single factor working alone. For example, a genetic predisposition could be set off by, say, a brain tumor followed by a metabolic disorder, and so on—a cascade of events leading to the full-blown disease. Some of the leading suspects are discussed briefly below.

Genetic Factors. A number of gene defects have been implicated in the development of Alzheimer's disease. In order to sort out the findings, it is necessary to distinguish between early- and late-onset forms of AD. Roughly 5 percent of cases are **early-onset Alzheimer's disease;** that is, they develop before age 60. This form of the disease clearly runs in families (known as **familial Alzheimer's disease** or FAD), and appears to follow an autosomal-dominant pattern of inheritance (meaning that only one defective gene is necessary for the disease to develop) (Tanzi & Blacker, 2000). A parent with this form of Alzheimer's will transmit the responsible gene to 50 percent of offspring. The search for the causative gene began with the finding that all Down syndrome individuals who survive to age 40 show signs of AD's hallmark plaques and tangles, leading investigators to suspect the involvement of chromosome 21. (Down syndrome is caused by an extra number 21 chromosome.) That suspicion was confirmed. In addition to a defective gene on chromosome 21 (the amyloid precursor protein or APP gene), defects on chromosomes 1 and 14 have also been identified as causes of early-onset Alzheimer's (Ross, Petrovitch, & White, 1997).

Those who suffer from **late-onset Alzheimer's disease** (which develops after age 60) may inherit various other genetic defects that, rather than actually causing the disease, instead function to increase the risk or predispose an individual to developing the

The lack of 100 percent concordance among identical twins suggests that factors other than genetics must play a causal role in Alzheimer's disease. One twin may develop the disease while the other does not, perhaps because of exposure to an as-yet-unidentified environmental trigger that activates a genetic predisposition to the disease.

disease if exposed to as-yet-unidentified environmental triggers. The greatest risk (estimated to be involved in 80 percent of cases) involves a gene on chromosome 19 that codes for a blood protein called apolipoprotein E (ApoE) (Beardsley, 1993). Everyone carries two copies of the ApoE gene, inheriting one copy from each parent. And there are three major versions (alleles) of this gene: ApoE2, ApoE3, and ApoE4. ApoE4 is associated with increased risk of AD. Those who inherit one ApoE4 gene (about 15 percent of the population) have a three times greater risk of developing the disease (Epstein & Connor, 1999). The 2 to 3 percent who carry two of the genes have a more than 80 percent risk of developing the disease between ages 60 and 85.

Exactly how the ApoE4 protein affects the brain is unclear. Brain-imaging studies have found that the hippocampus is smaller and more prone to atrophy in those carrying this allele. Perhaps E4 carriers have fewer neuroanatomical reserves or less efficient protection and repair mechanisms, making them more susceptible to injury and less able to recover from trauma (Smith, 2002). Thus, they would be more vulnerable to cognitive deficits later in life, when exposed to an additional factor that negatively affects brain structure and function. This idea, referred to as the *vulnerability hypothesis,* suggests a complex gene-environment interaction, with genotype modulating the brain's response to all sorts of insults. What kinds of factors might these be? One is a deficiency in vitamin B12 and folic acid (Bunce, Kivipelto, & Wahlin, 2004). That is, those who carry the E4 allele and are also deficient in vitamin B have a greater risk of cognitive impairment. Hendrie (2001) reports cross-cultural data suggesting the importance of diet in mediating the link between the E4 genotype and AD, with those eating a low-fat low-calorie diet at lower risk. ApoE4 may also interact with other factors, such as head injury, a number of medical conditions, and gender (with women being at greater risk).

Remember that the ApoE4 allele does not guarantee that an individual will develop Alzheimer's, but rather increases vulnerability: some who have the gene won't develop the disease, just as some who don't will. Cases of **sporadic Alzheimer's disease,** in which there is no family history of the disease, as well as the lack of 100 percent concordance among identical twins also suggest that other factors are involved. (For many reasons, the use of genetic testing in assessing risk, as well as in the diagnosis and treatment of Alzheimer's, is complex and controversial. The accuracy and utility of current methods of genetic screening for AD is reviewed in Tanzi and Blacker, 2000.)

Environmental Toxins. Toxins or poisons in the environment—for example, lead and mercury, pesticides, industrial chemicals, and so on—have also been investigated as possible causes of AD. These substances, if present in the body in sufficient quantities, could lead to nerve cell death. Aluminum is the most thoroughly examined of these toxins, as several studies have found elevated levels of aluminum in the brain tissue of AD victims. Aluminum is the third most common element in the earth's atmosphere, and we are regularly exposed to it in airborne dust. Therefore, the question is not where the aluminum comes from but why it is present in unusually large deposits in the brains of those suffering from AD. The consensus of opinion currently is that the aluminum concentrations are a consequence—not a cause—of the pathological changes occurring in the brain.

Biochemical Factors. In addition to changes in the levels of acetylcholine, there has been a lot of interest in the presence of a protein known as **beta-amyloid,** a major component of the plaques described earlier. Amyloid is apparently a minor by-product of the metabolism of a larger protein known as amyloid precursor protein (APP), the normal function of which is not known. This substance has been found throughout the

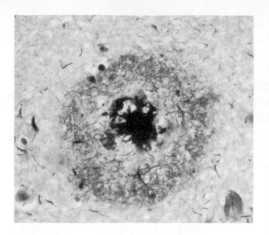

A neural plaque of beta-amyloid protein in the brain of a patient with Alzheimer's disease. This dark globular mass is surrounded by abnormal axons and dendrites and degenerating neural cell bodies that appear darker than the normal neurons.

From *Scientific American* (265, 1991, p. 71), "Amyloid Protein and Alzheimer's Disease," by J. D. Selko, used with permission.

bodies of healthy subjects, suggesting that perhaps AD patients metabolize it in some unusual way, resulting in the toxic buildup seen in plaques (Selkoe, 1993). It is not clear whether the accumulation of amyloid itself kills cells or whether its presence is mainly an indicator of other destructive processes at work in the cell. Whatever its exact role, most experts believe its presence is not incidental, but rather an essential component of the progress of the disease (Banner, 1992). Many neuroscientists support the amyloid cascade hypothesis—namely, that an accumulation of plaques triggers the progression of the disease process, which leads to the tangles. Whether these deposits result from the action of genetic mutations present in some family lines (Beardley, 1993) or some yet-unidentified environmental trigger is not known, but investigators believe that if the process by which beta-amyloid is produced can be blocked early in the disease course, it may be possible to stop or reverse the progression of the disease or prevent it altogether (Oddo, Billings, Kesslak, Cribbs, & LaFerla, 2004).

Other researchers are investigating the role of estrogen. Studies suggest that estrogen acts directly on brain cells throughout life, boosting the production of enzymes such as choline acetyltransferase (needed to build acetylcholine) and encouraging cells to maintain dense dendritic and axonic fibers (Angier, 1994). A reduction of estrogen may make neural cells more vulnerable to other risk factors by cutting the supply of critical enzymes or simplifying the neural architecture. Women experience a dramatic reduction of estrogen at menopause (see Chapter 9). This may partially explain women's higher risk of developing Alzheimer's disease, a finding previously attributed to their greater longevity. Research is under way to determine what role estrogen may play in the prevention of AD (Foy, Henderson, Berger, & Thompson, 2000). Hormone replacement therapy is not currently recommended for the prevention of cognitive decline or dementia.

Free Radicals.   Several lines of research suggest that an accumulation of free radicals (see Chapter 9) in the brain may contribute to the development of Alzheimer's disease (Connor, 1997). This view is supported by evidence that antioxidants such as vitamin E that neutralize free radicals can slow the disease process or play a role in prevention. Diets rich in antioxidants may thus be beneficial (Hendrie, 2001). What causes the buildup of free radicals? Some suspect they are a result of a failure in the brain's normal repair process or an inflammatory response to the presence of plaques. Nonsteroidal anti-inflammatory drugs are being studied to determine if they may prevent the disease in those who are at risk. In a review of the experimental evaluations of a number of nonprescription compounds thought to affect memory function, including antioxidants such as vitamin E, McDaniel, Maier, and Einstein (2002) conclude that the scientific evidence is inconclusive but is suggestive enough of potential benefit to justify more research.

Risk Factors.   Given the fact that no cause and no cure are in sight, what do we know about risk factors for the development of Alzheimer's disease? Clearly age is the biggest risk factor; most victims of AD are over 65, and the number of those affected doubles every five years beyond age 65. Family history seems to be another risk factor, particularly if the affected individual is a first-degree relative (that is, a parent or sibling). Other possibilities, such as a serious blow to the head and reduced neuronal reserve capacity (see Chapter 5) (Alexander et al., 1997; Snowdon et al., 1996), are being examined. Being knocked out may cause an acute buildup of amyloid and speed up the progress of the disease in those most vulnerable (e.g., those with a family history or who carry the ApoE4 allele). Lack of stimulation may also be devastating for the brain, leaving it more vulnerable in later years. This may explain the finding that those who are poor as well as those with less education, lower measured intelligence early in life, and less challenging occupational and leisure-time activities in adulthood have a significantly higher risk of developing Alzheimer's (Whalley et al., 2000; Wilson et al., 2002). These factors may interact with diet and other lifestyle variables to produce their effects. Finally, risk factors for heart disease, such as smoking, obesity, high blood pressure, and high cholesterol also increase the risk of developing AD, as does diabetes (associated with excess weight). A heart-healthy diet and lifestyle thus may have multiple benefits.

Treatment

Experts now view the development of Alzheimer's disease as a decades-long process. It may be possible to intervene at various points along the way. And once the different etiologies (causes) of AD are understood, effective treatments may be developed for various forms of the disease. Each of the lines of research described above could potentially lead to a treatment or cure for Alzheimer's disease. Dozens of clinical trials are currently under way to test treatments that may delay disease onset or slow its progression. (To review the National Institutes of Health data base of clinical trials, go to www.clinicaltrials.gov.) These include antioxidants such as vitamin E to protect against free radical damage, anti-inflammatory drugs, estrogen, and a class of cholesterol-lowering drugs called statins.

Enzyme-blocking therapy is a recent avenue of research. Identification of one of several enzymes (beta-secretase) believed to be involved in the formation of plaques has led to hope that medications might be developed to block the effects of these enzymes, thereby slowing the formation of plaques and the progression of the disease. Another approach is the use of a vaccine to prevent the formation of plaques or to tag existing plaques, which could then be removed by scavenger cells (Oddo et al., 2004). Others are experimenting with genetic engineering to introduce nerve growth factors into the brain that both prevent cell death and promote cell growth. Whether any of these options proves to be safe, effective, and practical in human subjects will require many more years of research. For now, the best advice is to reduce risk by building and sustaining a healthy brain through stimulation, diet, and exercise and by protecting it from injury (whether external—e.g., head trauma, or internal—e.g., high blood pressure).

Those patients and families already dealing with the disease must settle for techniques that assist in managing it and modifying some of its manifestations. Some of the symptoms of AD seem to be especially problematic for caregivers—these include aggression, agitation, an inability to bathe and dress oneself, incontinence, language disturbances, and sleeplessness (Finkel, 1994; Hutton et al., 1985; Heyman et al., 1987). Effective modification of these behaviors would not only improve the individual's quality of life (and that of the caregiver) but also reduce the need for institutionalization.

In addition, improved behavior within an institutional setting is correlated with enhanced staff morale and therefore better care (Finkel, 1994).

Medication may reduce the severity of some of the symptoms. The drugs currently available, Cognex, Exelon, and Aricept, increase supplies of acetylcholine by blocking the enzyme cholinesterase. However, they have serious side effects, don't work for everyone, and have a limited useful life of about six to nine months. Their effectiveness is probably limited by the fact that by the time the disease is diagnosed, too much damage has already occurred. Again, researchers stress the importance of early detection. Namenda represents a new class of drugs to treat moderate to severe AD. Like the others, however, it may slow but not stop the disease progress.

Physical activity, social involvement, good nutrition and health care, and a calm and well-structured environment may be helpful in managing the disease. Caregivers may help support the memory of those with AD by maintaining a routine schedule for the day, keeping often-used items in the same place, writing down notes, using a calendar and a bulletin board to post activities and reminders, and using a large, prominent clock. Should the family not be able to provide care at home, many new residential treatment facilities are being designed to address the needs of Alzheimer's patients. Approaches include providing abundant light to help combat depression and creating a smaller, homier scale to encourage meaningful interaction. A good-quality residential facility can cost $4,000 per month or more.

Effect on the Family System: Taking Care of the Caregiver

Because the family is a system of interdependent relationships (see Chapter 6), any change in one member has ramifications—ripple effects—for the others. About 70 percent of the care given to victims of AD is provided by family members, especially female relatives. Adjustment to this caregiving role has psychological, social, financial, and physical health consequences (Dillehay & Sandys, 1990). The financial strain can be enormous, both in terms of the direct costs of providing care as well as in time lost from work, and so on. Insurance coverage for AD is presently not available, though recent legislation for the first time allows out-of-pocket expenses for long-term care for a chronically ill individual (including personal care) to be deducted as medical expenses.

Much attention has been focused on the degree of burden experienced by the caregiver—the psychological state resulting from the combination of the physical work, emotional pressure, social limitations, and financial demands involved in this caregiving experience. (See Chapter 7 for a discussion of the caregiver role.) The Alzheimer's Association released results of a survey of more than 1,000 adults indicating that they were as afraid of caring for a loved one with AD as they were of getting the disease themselves (Alzheimer's Association, 2004). Indeed, family members have been described as the hidden victims of Alzheimer's disease (for example, Zarit, Orr, & Zarit, 1985). The caregiver's degree of burden is related to the likelihood that the patient will be institutionalized (Zarit, Todd, & Zarit, 1986). In addition to the stress of caregiving, family members are also adjusting to the gradual loss of someone they love. And the patient's lucid, insightful moments often give false hope to family caregivers. The family's material and psychosocial resources may also be diverted from other family members in order to care for the Alzheimer's patient.

Intervention to assist these families has a dual benefit: reducing the caregiver's stress and the family ripple effects while also reducing the likelihood of institutionalization of the patient. Mittelman and her colleagues found that AD patients lived at home almost a year longer when spouse-caregivers were given counseling and joined support groups (Mittelman, Ferris, Shulman, Steinberg, & Levin, 1996). Effective interventions include the following: the provision of knowledge about the disorder, its course, and prognosis; assistance in dealing with the behavioral symptoms of the disease; and social support. Caregivers should be encouraged to share their concerns with others, avoid isolation, get enough rest, and take time away from their caregiving responsibilities. In regard to the latter, the availability of respite care is considered vitally important. Adult day centers, which offer supervised, structured programs for AD patients, are becoming more widely available and help to meet needs of both caregivers and patients. Considered the "bible" for families with loved ones suffering from dementia, *The Thirty-Six Hour Day* (Mace & Rabins, 1999) has been available since 1981 and is now in its third edition. Help can also be found by contacting the Alzheimer's Association in Chicago (www.alz.org).

CRITICAL THINKING QUESTION
Should patients be told they have Alzheimer's disease? How many reasons can you think of for and against?

Concept Review 11.4

- Major depression is diagnosed on the basis of a number of persistent symptoms. Risk factors have been identified.

- For a variety of reasons, depression is twice as common among women as men.

- Though effective treatment is available, most people suffering from depression are not receiving help.

- Uncertainty persists about the relationship between age and depression, though it appears that there is substantial misdiagnosis and undertreatment of depression among the elderly.

- Alzheimer's disease (AD), the leading cause of senile dementia, is a progressive, degenerative neurological disorder that impairs thinking, memory, and behavior.

- Because the presence of AD can only be confirmed at autopsy, a diagnosis of probable AD is based on a combination of neuropsychological tests and exclusion of other explanations of the symptoms.

- Though the cause of AD is not yet known, it is likely that various forms of the disease exist, caused by different factors or combinations of factors.

- Risk factors may increase vulnerability to the disease in the presence of triggering events.

- Divergent perspectives on what initiates the neural destruction at the heart of AD have generated different theories on how best to intervene to prevent, delay, halt, or reverse disease progress. Dozens of clinical drug trials are currently under way.

(continued)

- The best way to reduce risk is to build and maintain a healthy brain.
- There is no cure for AD. Treatment focuses on efforts to modify the symptoms. Attempts to lesson the significant burden of family caregivers are also important.

REVIEW QUESTIONS

Happiness

1. Discuss the key dimensions of happiness, according to Ryff, Myers and Diener, and DeNeve.

Stress, Coping, and Locus of Control

1. What determines whether an individual experiences a situation as stressful?
2. What are the consequences of stress for the individual?
3. How can positive emotions be helpful in coping with stress?
4. Distinguish between an internal and an external locus of control.
5. How do control beliefs influence the experience of stress and an individual's responses to it?
6. Discuss the revisions in the locus-of-control model since it was first introduced.
7. Summarize the findings on age-related changes in individuals' personal control beliefs.
8. How do individuals maintain a sense of control even in low-control situations?

An Overview of the Mental Health Status of Adults

1. What does recent ECA data tell us about age-related trends in mental disorders among adults?
2. Discuss the special concerns related to the diagnosis and treatment of mental disorders among older adults.
3. How could age differences in risk for nonorganic psychiatric disorders be due to cohort effects? State what the age difference is, then discuss the possible causes of the cohort effect in this case.
4. Describe gender differences in rates of mental disorders.

5. Who is most likely to seek help with psychological problems?
6. Identify the most significant risk and protective factors.

A Look at Two Mental Disorders in Adulthood

1. On what basis is major depression diagnosed?
2. What forms of treatment are available?
3. What explanations are offered for the gender difference in rates of depression?
4. Define ruminative coping and explain how it might intensify and prolong depression.
5. Explain the paradoxical relationship between depression and age: the existence of large numbers of risk factors but low rates of major depression among older adults.
6. Who is most at risk for suicide?
7. What do we know about the state of mind of most suicide victims in the weeks before their death?
8. Why is Alzheimer's disease referred to as the slow death of the mind? Describe the symptoms and developmental course of the disease.
9. Explain how Alzheimer's disease is diagnosed. What are the difficulties, and why is accurate diagnosis so critical?
10. What are the two characteristic abnormalities found in the brains of Alzheimer's disease victims?
11. Discuss the major hypotheses about the causes of Alzheimer's disease.
12. What steps might one take to reduce the risk of developing Alzheimer's disease?
13. Who are the hidden victims of Alzheimer's disease, and what needs to be done to assist them?

KEY TERMS

12 Death, Dying, and Bereavement

DEATH WAS NOT A REAL PART of my experience until I was in my mid-30s, when the only grandparent I had ever known died. She was 89. Up to that point, I had only experienced death in a remote way, through the death of distant relatives or relatives of friends. Thus, I had no firsthand experience of the dying process, the death itself, or the grief and bereavement that follow. I discussed the topics in my classes, listened to the experiences of others, and read a lot on the subject. But I was insulated from the experience itself. This year, death became the dominant motif of my family's life, through the death of both my father and my mother-in-law. These experiences have changed me in a profound way, and, I am sure, in ways I have yet to comprehend. I am no longer insulated, and in a strangely reassuring way, I am also no longer isolated from this part of life.

This is a chapter about the end of life. It comes at the end of this book and probably at the end of your course and academic term. There is always some debate about this—should a book end with a "downer," should the course end on a sad note? In part, I think this is a reflection of the difficulty our society has in dealing with this subject. It seems natural to me that in a course about development in adulthood, the final topic would address the final stage in life. When else would we discuss it? At the beginning of the course? Somewhere in the middle? At any rate, either through logic or default, here it is at the end of the book. But I am hopeful that the treatment of the subject in this chapter will not depress or sadden you as much as it will enlighten you, confirm your experience, reassure you, prepare you, and perhaps challenge you to think about the issues of the end of life with the same intellectual curiosity you bring to the beginning and the middle of life.

So . . . this chapter has a number of objectives. We will begin by examining patterns in mortality in the late 20th and early 21st centuries—when, how, where, and among whom death typically occurs. Next, we will review attitudes toward death and what is known about the experience of dying from the perspective of the dying individual. We will address the growing emphasis on the concepts of "dying well" and patient autonomy, the right-to-die movement, and the controversial issues of euthanasia and assisted suicide. Our focus will then shift to the survivors and the grief experience. The final section examines societal rituals such as funerals, and their function in the bereavement process.

The Changed Nature of Death

I and most of you are members of what Robert Fulton has called the first "death-insulated" generation—that is, the first generation to be removed from death as a natural part of the life process. Chances are good that those of us born after World War II did not—or will not—experience death in our families prior to the age of 21. This is another of the consequences of extended life. The experience of death and the circumstances under which it occurs have changed dramatically. Let's consider some of these changes.

First, at the turn of the 20th century, children had a monopoly on death. Childbirth itself, along with infectious illnesses such as influenza and whooping cough, took many young lives. Death from occupational injuries killed many older individuals, and even deaths from cancer and heart disease were signaled only shortly before they occurred, since early diagnosis was unlikely and treatment ineffective. Thus, for people of all ages, death came quickly, usually only a few hours or days after they learned that death was imminent (Lynn, 1991). And until the mid-20th century, death occurred at home, with family and friends in attendance. Caring for the dying was an integral part of life, learned early in childhood. Women routinely attended to medical needs, dressing wounds and dispensing what medication was available (Abel, 1991). The body was prepared at home, a wake was held at home, and the funeral procession left from the home, with burial either on the family's property or in a local burying place—probably the churchyard, where the grave would be seen and visited regularly. Death was a natural part of life. In a mostly agrarian society, people were more intimately connected with the natural cycle of beginnings and endings, plantings and harvestings, births and deaths.

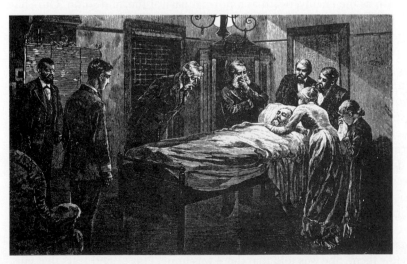

Until the mid-20th century, death was a more natural part of the life experience and was likely to take place at home with friends and family present. Today, 80 percent of all deaths occur in hospitals or nursing homes.

In contrast, today death is most common among the elderly, who are most likely to die of chronic, degenerative diseases. A lengthy period often exists in which the person knows that death is coming: thus, the dying phase of life has been extended. Few of us have witnessed the death of a loved one—a common experience a century ago. Eighty percent of all deaths now occur in hospitals or nursing homes, which have taken over the management of the dying process, an outgrowth of medical advances about 50 years ago that made it possible to delay or even prevent death by medical services provided in the hospital. Preparation of the body occurs in the institution and the funeral home, which also serves as the location for the wake or visitation and frequently for the funeral. Alternatively, the funeral or memorial service may occur in a church. Burial is at a remote site. Cremation is also common.

Thus, the home and family are no longer the centerpiece of the formal activities that mark a death. These functions have been delegated to professionals who have, quite literally, undertaken the business of dying. With some exceptions, most of what most of us know about death comes from its unrealistic portrayal on television, rather than as a product of our own experience. Our societal view of death has been transformed from what was once an accepted part of life experience to an unfamiliar and greatly feared event (Meier & Morrison, 1999).

CRITICAL THINKING QUESTION

What are the ramifications of the changes in the way death is experienced today, as compared to 100 years ago, both for the dying person and the family?

Attitudes toward Death

The Death-Denying Society

There are many historical and contemporary ways of thinking about death—for example, death as a prelude to eternal life, death as a punishment for sins, death as an end of everything, death as the enemy, death as a normal part of life, and so on. Ours has been called a **death-denying society.** Someone once said that Americans now deal with death the way the Victorians dealt with sex. We simply do not like to acknowledge that it goes on. We find it difficult, for example, to even use words like *dead, died,* or *death.* When extending our sympathy to others who have experienced the death of someone close, we find ourselves saying things like, "I'm so sorry to have heard the news," or "I'm so sorry about your mother." *Euphemisms*—substitutes considered to be less offensive—are often used. Examples include *passing, lost, slipped away,* and so on. You can probably think of others.

The American health care system is characterized by limitless optimism and shaped by our societal denial of death (Aries, 1981; Lynn, 1991). Medical advances have made it possible to prevent many of the traditional causes of death and to extend the lives of those who are sick. The goal is to overcome death. The classic example of the extent to which the medical establishment denies death is the experience of Elisabeth Kübler-Ross (1969), one of the pioneers in research on dying patients. She approached doctors at a large hospital in Chicago and asked for the names of terminally ill patients so that she could interview them. She was told that there was none. Fins (1999) fears that current advances in molecular medicine, such as work being done to manipulate the molecular basis of aging and thus to stave off death, will make it even more difficult to forgo treatment in the future and to accept death.

One of the consequences of death denial is that barriers are erected between the dying individual and family, friends, and medical personnel. Fear of confronting the issue causes people to begin avoiding the person, who becomes increasingly isolated. What has been referred to as a **conspiracy of silence** develops, in which no one addresses the issue on everyone's mind. The emphasis is on maintaining a charade and on prolonging life at all costs, rather than on attending to the needs of the dying individual and the family and making death as comfortable and dignified as possible. We will return to these issues later in the chapter.

According to Sankar (1993), the trend toward hospital death has been reversing in recent years, as home death has begun to reemerge. This is the result of the convergence of a number of factors: increasing emphasis on patient autonomy and the right to make health care decisions, the hospice movement, growing recognition of the limits of medical care and the undesirability of unnatural prolongation of life, improvements in pharmacology and the technology available in home health care, and changes in insurance reimbursements for hospital stays.

Sankar warns about the danger of romanticizing home death and of minimizing how difficult and strenuous this experience can be, especially in a society no longer equipped to support it. The dying person today is sicker (the primary disease is more advanced because death earlier in the course of the illness is generally prevented) and older—thus more debilitated and frail. This adds to the level of care—routine, medical, and psychological—required of the caregiver. Caregivers have also changed. Most work outside the home, may be single, and lack a network of friends and relatives available to assist.

On the other hand, home death allows family and friends to help manage the process of dying as the patient wants it and to experience the time remaining with them. Sankar (1993, p. 62) says that "many caregivers who have gone through a home death experience feel it was the finest moment in their lives; they also characterize it as the most difficult and challenging thing they have accomplished."

Psychology's Approach to Death

How do psychologists think about or conceptualize death? Reflecting attitudes prevalent in the society as a whole, the field of psychology has been slow to study death, the process of dying, and grief and bereavement. There is a field of study—**thanatology**—devoted to death and its related issues. Because this field studies the process of dying and the experience of the dying person, Kastenbaum (1992, p. 233) describes thanatology as "the study of death with life left in." He assesses the field as not far advanced, using clumsy methods and making shaky inferences. Yet he expresses the hope that thanatology might offer us some useful guidance based on the experience of others, leading to a perspective on life with death left in.

Individual views of death are a reflection of one's beliefs and values, upbringing, and cultural background. A psychologist's conception is also influenced by professional education and training, and the adoption of a particular theoretical perspective (psychoanalytic, learning theory, humanism, and so on). At the risk of overgeneralizing, life-span developmental psychologists tend to view death as a developmental task of late life. According to this view, accepting the inevitability of one's death and preparing for it constitute life's final developmental tasks. Thus, late adulthood is viewed as dominated by the psychosocial "work" of ending our lives.

This point of view is summarized by Munnichs (1980, p. 4) as follows: "When we ask ourselves what are the most characteristic features of old age, one difference . . . stands out most prominently, namely the fact that there is no other period following old age. . . . The experience of death . . . to realize and to know that life comes to an end, and adjustment to this fact, might possibly be considered as the focal point of the mentality of the aged."

Kastenbaum (1992) cautions us not to accept this developmental task view of death too enthusiastically. Though it has been dominant in psychology for about three decades, he asserts that it is not based on systematic research. Rather, it represents a way of thinking about human development. Developmental task theory reflects an idealized image of how human beings *should* cope with—and the goals that *should* be accomplished in—various stages of their lives. "Taking care of business," both practical and psychological, is a normative part of life. Thus, this approach assumes that thinking about and preparing for death in old age is "normal" and to be expected—death is viewed as a normal part of life. Research is needed to verify this assumption.

CRITICAL THINKING QUESTION

One might legitimately ask why older people "should" choose death as their number-one task. Why is this important or valuable? Are there other developmental tasks that might be considered primary at the end of life?

Finally, the developmental task approach links old age and death—making death into a "specialty of the aged" (Kastenbaum, 1992, p. 77). While it is true that this is when most people die these days, we must address deaths that occur at other times as well. Is there a difference, for example, when death occurs off-time?

Death Anxiety

How do people think and feel about death in their normal, everyday lives? Much of the research has focused on the degree of anxiety individuals experience about death. This is generally assessed on the basis of self-report surveys, the most common of which is the Death Anxiety Scale (Templer, 1970), containing 15 true-false items. Concerns have been raised about the validity of the death anxiety concept: for example, whether it is a unitary phenomenon or has subparts, whether there is a difference between concern about death and anxiety about death, and so on. The rather exclusive focus on death anxiety may overlook other important feelings and attitudes toward death, such as anger, sorrow, or more positive orientations. As we have discussed many times in earlier chapters, the use of self-report measures is problematic as well. Further, there is the question of how to interpret death anxiety scores. That is, what is the "correct" amount of death anxiety to have? What is too little? Too much? Finally, there are concerns over the heavy reliance on the cross-sectional design and the use of primarily White samples. With these concerns and limitations in mind, what do studies of death anxiety show?

First, although significant individual differences exist, most people seem to have a low to moderate level of concern about death in their daily lives (Kastenbaum,

1992). They do not seem to fear death much. This finding can be interpreted in a number of ways. For example, it could be taken at face value, or as an indication of denial. Any surge in death anxiety might, then, be seen as a warning signal—for example, perhaps the individual is having a lot of difficulty dealing with the death of a loved one.

Gender Differences

Women generally score higher on measures of death anxiety than men (Lonetto & Templer, 1986). Again, this is difficult to interpret. Are women "too anxious" or men "not anxious enough"? Perhaps women's higher scores reflect their greater involvement in caregiving and greater sensitivity to the needs of others, or a greater willingness to discuss these issues.

Age Differences

The evidence indicates that thoughts of death increase with age. This is understandable, given that older people are more likely to experience the death of friends and loved ones and to be closer to death themselves. Death is a common theme in published journals of late life (Berman, 1991). Vining (1978, p. 91) states: "I don't think about it every day. . . . It floats into my mind from time to time, awakened by a reference in a book, the death or serious illness of a friend, or just suddenly appearing out of nothing." She likens death to a shadow: "We may, of course, meet him unexpectedly in the earlier years, but after seventy we are certain to encounter him soon, and his shadow often walks beside us in this new landscape" (p. 5).

So, while death may be present in a new and more persistent way with increasing age, and individuals may think and talk about it more, this is not equivalent to an increased dread of death. Does level of death anxiety change with age? Does it increase, decrease, or remain the same? Though most of the research is cross-sectional and may therefore reflect cohort differences rather than the effect of age, existing studies clearly indicate that age per se does not tell us much about a person's attitudes toward death. Some studies have found that death anxiety remains about the same across adulthood, while others have found a reduction of death anxiety with age. It seems safe to conclude that death anxiety does not increase with age.

If age does not seem to predict level of death anxiety, does that mean that one's age is irrelevant in this regard? Kastenbaum (1992) suggests that while adults of different ages may have the same level of death anxiety, they may have different concerns about death. For example, Stricherz and Cunningham (1981–1982) surveyed three age groups about their death-related concerns: high school students, employed adults with a mean age of 42, and retirees. The students' primary concerns had to do with the fear of losing a loved one, the finality of death, and death as a punishment. The middle-aged adults were concerned about pain and the risk of premature death. There is some research suggesting that dread of death may be greatest among middle-aged adults, who may for the first time be grappling with the midlife issue of personal mortality (Kalish, 1976). The major concerns of older adults had to do with the *process* of dying rather than death itself. Specifically, individuals fear being helpless and dependent and kept alive in an undignified state. Consistent with this research, published diaries repeatedly emphasize that the writers do not fear death. Rather, they fear becoming disabled: "What

I fear is not death but illness—the paralysis following stroke, the agony of cancer, the long weariness of being cared for while deteriorating mentally and physically" (Vining, 1978, p. 146). May Sarton (1977, p. 53) fears "dying in some inappropriate or gruesome way, such as long illness requiring care." Scott-Maxwell (1979, p. 910) "had one fear. What if something went wrong and I became an invalid . . . a burden, ceased to be a person and became a problem, a patient, someone who could not die."

So individuals of different ages may have different ways of thinking about and different concerns about death. The best conclusion for now is that age itself does not seem to have a strong effect on death anxiety.

Cultural Differences

We must also remember that different cultures hold different attitudes about death. Kalish and Reynolds (1977) studied four samples in Los Angeles: African American, Japanese American, Mexican American, and Anglo-American. They found many differences in death-related attitudes, though the extent to which these were affected by socioeconomic status is not clear. One interesting finding was that Anglo-Americans viewed the Mexican Americans' reaction to death as highly emotional, while the Mexican Americans viewed the Anglo-American response as cold and cruel. In other words, the same level of death anxiety may be viewed differently depending on the frame of reference. Cultural norms, beliefs, and values affect death-related attitudes and behaviors.

In sum, then, most of us have a relatively low level of everyday anxiety about death, though there are gender, age, and cultural differences in level of anxiety, specific concerns about death, and death-related attitudes and behaviors.

Concept Review 12.1

- During the twentieth century, the nature of death and the experience of dying changed dramatically.

- The tendency in American culture to deny death has limited research in death and dying and affects the treatment of dying individuals.

- Most people experience a low to moderate degree of anxiety about death.

- Older adults express more concern about the process of dying than of death itself.

The Dying Person

Contributions of Kübler-Ross

Few researchers have contributed more to our understanding of the dying process or had greater impact on current attitudes toward the individual's experience of death than psychiatrist Elisabeth Kübler-Ross, who joined the faculty of the University of Chicago in 1965. Kübler-Ross spent literally thousands of hours interviewing over 200 middle-aged cancer patients. To gain access to these patients, she had to overcome entrenched societal barriers as well as the medical establishment's death denial. Her work culminated in the description of a series of five stages her subjects experienced as they coped with their own dying, detailed in her best-selling book *On Death and Dying* (1969). A brief overview of these stages follows.

The initial reaction to the news that one has a terminal illness is typically shock, disbelief, and denial, or a refusal to accept that one is dying. This is a defense that allows the individual to slowly adjust to the news that death is imminent. Once the diagnosis is acknowledged, anger develops. The individual asks, "Why me?" A sense of injustice may cause the patient to react with hostility toward others. The third stage, bargaining, reflects the individual's desire to have more time. In exchange, the individual may promise to be a better person, or to go to church regularly. The bargain is made with God and, if death does not come, is rarely kept. Depression represents the growing acceptance of reality in the face of deteriorating health and the resulting grieving for oneself. At this point, the individual may withdraw from others. If given enough time and support, many patients reach acceptance—a stage in which the earlier feelings have been worked through and death is approached with peace.

The stages themselves have been criticized for artificially standardizing the process of dying and ignoring the tremendous variability among individuals as they cope with death. In addition, Retsinas (1988) questions the applicability of these stages to the experience of dying among the elderly, who constitute the vast majority of people who die. She points out that Kübler-Ross's middle-aged cancer patients, who are described as frightened, confused, and angry, differ in a number of important ways from this group. For example, death is occurring at an unexpected time, when the individual is most likely still actively involved in family and work responsibilities and very concerned about the impact of the impending death on spouse, young children, and so on. Though her model has not been confirmed by subsequent research, Kübler-Ross's work has been significant in opening the subject for scientific inquiry and freeing terminally ill patients from the imposed isolation of the conspiracy of silence. The phases described by Kübler-Ross may be helpful in understanding some of the reactions of some individuals as they cope with significant losses, including the impending loss of their own lives.

Dying Well

We have seen that most deaths now occur late in life, and that most people will know that death is coming. We also know that medical and technological advances have made it possible to forestall death, to keep people alive longer after illness develops. Given this more prolonged period of dying, what becomes important to people at the end of their lives? What does it mean to "die well"? Lynn (1991, p. 70) provides an answer: "The most striking aspect of the period during which adults know they are dying is the variability of their priorities. More than any other criterion, what 'dying well' requires is that the life being lived as death comes near be one that is 'befitting' to the life that was being lived before serious terminal illness." This means that the uses to which individuals will want to put their remaining time, and the people, places, and activities that will be important to them, will vary. Some may want to get their financial affairs in order, or to make peace with loved ones; others may want to explore the spiritual meaning of their life and death; still others may want to share their feelings with others, to have one last fling, or to continue their lives as normally as possible for as long as possible, and so on.

It also means that people will vary in terms of how much control they want over events, including aspects of their health care. Many fear being kept alive artificially. For them, dying well means being allowed to die when the time comes. For example, a 1990

Gallup poll found that 84 percent of Americans would want treatment withheld if they were on life-support systems and had no hope of recovering (Ames, 1991). Regardless of age, the support of others, management of pain, maintenance of mental faculties, and control over the circumstances of death seem to be important (Tobin, 1990).

Advances in medical technology have raised a whole new set of issues that at their core have to do with the question, Whose life and death is it, anyway? More and more people are taking steps to ensure that their death appropriately represents their life and that they have a say in the most deeply personal decisions—those that bear on their life and death.

Patient Autonomy and Advance Directives

The notion of dying well includes the assumption that the needs, values, and priorities of the individual patient must be allowed to shape the course and extent of health care. Two legal tools—known as *advance directives*—have been developed to assist individuals in making their health care wishes known and ensuring that they will be honored in the event that they are no longer capable of speaking for themselves. All 50 states now have laws authorizing their use.

The first of these is the **living will,** which provides information relative to the patient's wishes regarding the use of life-prolonging technology. (See Figure 12.1 for an example.) The living will addresses some of the strongest fears people express about the experience of dying—that of indignity, dependency, and loss of control—and acknowledges the patient's right to die. That is, it states that if recovery is not possible, the individual prefers to be allowed to die, rather than be kept alive through artificial means. State statutes usually require that at least two people, preferably not family members, witness the signing of the document. Some also require that it be notarized. Some states require that their particular form be used. The living will should be given to the individual's physician to become a part of the medical record, as well as to the member of the clergy, lawyer, and anyone to be included in making health care decisions.

The second legal tool is the **durable power of attorney for health care,** which identifies one or more individuals who will have the authority to make health care decisions for the patient in the event that he or she can no longer do so. A durable power of attorney is more flexible than a living will and allows the individual to detail precise wishes regarding treatment. While the living will applies only in cases where death is imminent, the durable power of attorney is activated in any medical situation in which individuals are unable to make their own decisions. It also empowers someone to make decisions in situations that were not anticipated specifically in the instructions left by the patient. It is most effective if the surrogate decision maker fully understands the patient's values concerning medical care and quality of life issues—this assumes that the individuals involved have thoroughly discussed these subjects. Such understanding helps to guarantee that the power of attorney is not just a piece of paper, but a real extension of the patient's autonomy. (See Figure 12.2 for a sample document.)

The Patient Self-Determination Act of 1990, which went into effect in December 1991, requires hospitals and nursing homes participating in Medicare and Medicaid to ask all those adults admitted if they have executed advance directives and to provide information about them and help in executing them if they so desire. However, it does not require that any assessment be done of the patient's understanding of the information presented.

Figure 12.1 *The Living Will*

The living will is one of the two legal tools referred to as advance directives.

SAMPLE*

Declaration made this _____ day of _____ 20____

I, _____, being of sound mind, willfully and voluntarily make known my desires that my dying shall not be artificially prolonged under the circumstances set forth below, and do declare:

If at any time I should have an incurable injury, disease, or illness certified to be a terminal condition by two (2) physicians who have personally examined me, one of whom shall be my attending physician, and the physicians have determined that my death will occur whether or not life-sustaining procedures are utilized and where the application of life-sustaining procedures would serve only to artificially prolong the dying process, I direct that such procedures be withheld or withdrawn, and that I be permitted to die naturally with only the administration of medication or the performance of any medical procedure deemed necessary to provide me with comfort, care or to alleviate pain.

In the absence of my ability to give directions regarding the use of such life-sustaining procedures, it is my intention that this declaration shall be honored by my family and physician(s) as the final expression of my legal right to refuse medical or surgical treatment and accept the consequences from such refusal.

I understand the full import of this declaration and I am emotionally and mentally competent to make this declaration.

Signed _____

Address _____

I believe the declarant to be of sound mind. I did not sign the declarant's signature above for or at the direction of the declarant. I am at least 18 years of

Living Will

Declaration

age and am not related to the declarant by blood or marriage, entitled to any portion of the estate of the declarant according to the laws of interstate succession of the _____ or under any will of the declarant or codicil thereto, or directly financially responsible for declarant's medical care. I am not the declarant's attending physician, an employee of the attending physician, or an employee of the health facility in which the declarant is a patient.

Witness_____

Address _____

Witness_____

Address _____
ss.:

Before me, the undersigned authority, on this

_____ day of _____, 20____,

personally appeared _____

_____, and _____
known to me to be the Declarant and the witnesses, respectively, whose names are signed to the foregoing instrument, and who, in the presence of each other, did subscribe their names to the attached Declaration (Living Will) on this date, and that said Declarant at the time of execution of said Declaration was over the age of eighteen (18) years and of sound mind.

{Seal}
My commission expires:

_____

Notary Public

Check requirements of individual state statute.

Source: Sample form is from *A Matter of Choice,* prepared for the U.S. Senate Special Committee on Aging.

FIGURE 12.2 *The Durable Power of Attorney for Health Care*

Along with the living will, the durable power of attorney for health care helps ensure that an individual's wishes with regard to health care and the use of life-prolonging technology are honored.

SAMPLE*

DURABLE POWER OF ATTORNEY
FOR HEALTH CARE

I, _____

hereby appoint _____

name _____

home address _____

home telephone number _____

as my agent to make health care decisions for me if and when I am unable to make my own health care decisions. This gives my agent the power to consent to giving, withholding or stopping any health care, treatment, service, or diagnostic procedure. My agent also has the authority to talk with health care personnel, get information, and sign forms necessary to carry out those decisions.

If the person named as my agent is not available or is unable to act as my agent, then I appoint the following person(s) to serve in the order listed below:

1. name _____

   home address _____

   home telephone number _____

   work telephone number _____

2. name _____

   home address _____

   home telephone number _____

   work telephone number _____

By this document I intend to create a power of attorney for health care which shall take effect upon my incapacity to make my own health care decisions and shall continue during that incapacity.

My agent shall make health care decisions as I direct below or as I make known to him or her in some other way.

(a) Statement of desires concerning life-prolonging care, treatment, services, and procedures:

_____

_____

_____

_____

(b)   Special provisions and limitations:

_____

_____

_____

_____

_____

_____

_____

_____

(Continued)

BY SIGNING HERE I INDICATE THAT I UNDERSTAND THE PURPOSE AND EFFECT OF THIS DOCUMENT.

I sign my name to this form on _____
                                    (date)

My current home address:

_____

_____

_____
(You sign here)

WITNESSES

I declare that the person who signed or acknowledged this document is personally known to me, that he/she signed or acknowledged this durable power of attorney in my presence, and that he/she appears to be of sound mind and under no duress, fraud, or undue influence. I am not the person appointed as agent by this document, nor am I the patient's health care provider, or an employee of the patient's health care provider.

FIRST WITNESS

Signature: _____

Home Address: _____

Print Name: _____

Date: _____

SECOND WITNESS

Signature: _____

Home Address: _____

Print Name: _____

Date: _____

(At least one of the above witnesses must also sign the following declaration.)

I further declare that I am not related to the patient by blood, marriage, or adoption, and to the best of my knowledge, I am not entitled to any part of his/her estate under a will now existing or by operation of law.

Signature: _____

Signature: _____

I further declare that I am not related to the patient by blood, marriage, or adoption, and to the best of my knowledge, I am not entitled to any part of his/her estate under a will now existing or by operation of law.

Signature: _____

Signature: _____

Check requirements of individual state statute.

Source: Sample form is from *A Matter of Choice,* prepared for the U.S. Senate Special Committee on Aging.

High (1991) has expressed concern that the move toward the use of these legal tools may displace the traditional position of family members acting together as informal surrogates in making health care decisions. Life-and-death decisions are deeply personal and rest on moral, ethical, and spiritual grounds. Many people are uncomfortable with reducing them to the level of legal documents. Others argue that taken together, these legal tools provide critical information that can direct the actions of doctors and family members and spare them from making agonizing decisions at a time when what is most sought is an indication of what patients would decide for themselves if they were able to do so. Advance directives preserve self-determination and the right of the patient to refuse treatment, while also protecting physicians and surrogate decision makers from liability and the trauma and expense of going to court for permission to stop treatment when no hope of recovery exists.

These documents do not solve all the problems, however. For example, there is some question as to whether the use of these instruments is primarily a middle-class phenomenon. Might this mean that the self-determination of those who do not execute them (for example, those who are poor, uneducated, or distrustful of the legal system) could be undermined? Who would be empowered to make decisions for them? Holstein (1992) raises the issue of whether, if ever, the decision of a patient or a surrogate can be overturned. What if, for instance, the patient or surrogate demands that "everything" be done, including providing care that others judge to be futile? Could that mean that Medicare would have to continue to finance care no matter what the cost or the consensus of outside opinion on the benefit of the treatment? Finally, it must be pointed out that merely filling out the forms is no guarantee that they will be honored. Physicians may be unaware of the patient's wishes or may ignore them (SUPPORT Principal Investigators, 1995).

To sum up, the notion of individual autonomy has become an important issue in the area of health care. Dying well presumes that the values, priorities, and wishes of the dying individual will be understood, recognized, and implemented by family, friends, caregivers, and the health care system. The use of advance directives helps to ensure that this will occur.

Hospice

The hospice movement in the United States is another clear reflection of the growing attention being given to the needs of dying individuals and their families and caregivers. Based on the work of Cicely Saunders, medical director of St. Christopher's Hospice in London, **hospice** is an alternative concept of care for terminally ill patients and their families. It emphasizes maximizing the quality of life when the quantity of life cannot be extended. Although many variations exist, hospice care generally includes the following features:

- The dying patient and family—rather than the patient alone—are the focus of care.
- Care is ideally home based, but inpatient facilities are available to provide services that cannot be provided in the home.
- Services include physical, psychological, social, and spiritual care for both patients and family members. These services may continue after the patient dies.
- Services are medically supervised and are provided by an interdisciplinary team of professionals (which may include doctors, nurses, psychologists, clergy, social workers, homemakers, aides) and volunteers.

- Pain and symptom management and the comfort of the patient (referred to as *palliative care*) are the focus of medical care.
- Care is available seven days a week and 24 hours a day. This does not mean that the hospice team is present in the home constantly—the primary responsibility of care remains in the hands of the family or paid caregivers. But the services of the team are available on a prearranged or an on-call basis around the clock should they be needed.

Hospices do not turn patients away and they do not limit the length of service. Hospice volunteers typically receive extensive formal training and attend regular support groups. They must be dependable, nonjudgmental, and comfortable with death and the issues surrounding grief. Their role is to provide support for the patient and family. Hospice services are covered under Medicare and many private insurance plans.

The hospice care system is not without its problems. For example, though time of death is very difficult to predict, Medicare requires the physician to certify that the patient has six months or less to live. In addition to death denial discussed earlier, fear of being charged with fraud if the patient lives longer may cause some physicians to wait until death is imminent before recommending hospice care, far short of the three-month minimum most experts recommend. Thus, patients and their families may be denied access to these beneficial services.

Right-to-Die Movement: Suicide, Assisted Suicide, and Euthanasia

The philosophy behind the hospice movement and the development of the advance directives described above is that human beings, the only living things that can contemplate their deaths, have the right to die with dignity. Controversy has erupted over whether this right to die extends beyond letting nature take its course, rejecting treatment, and managing the experience of dying, to actually causing death. Clearly, public opinion on this subject has been changing. In 1975, 41 percent of those responding to a Gallup poll said that they believed someone in great pain, and with no hope of recovery, had the moral right to commit suicide; by 1990, the figure was 66 percent (Ames, 1991).

The book *Final Exit: The Practicalities of Self-Deliverance and Assisted Suicide for the Dying* hit bookstores in July 1991 and became an immediate best-seller. Written by Derek Humphry, president of the Hemlock Society—a euthanasia organization founded in 1980—the book represents the extreme edge of the growing effort to regain some control over the nature of dying and death. It is addressed to terminally ill elderly individuals and doctors and nurses to advise them on how to commit suicide successfully or to assist their patients to do so (the latter is referred to as *assisted suicide*). Though highly controversial, the book speaks to the growing concerns among Americans about the possibility that death will not come when it should and to the growing sentiment that elderly terminally ill patients should have the right to control the time, place, and manner of their death.

Adherents argue that it is common for people to be kept alive indefinitely, long after any quality of life or chance of improvement is possible and claim that this is unacceptable—that it robs the individual of dignity, prolongs suffering, and denies the right to choose in matters of life and death. Opponents view the right-to-die movement as an insult to the sanctity of life and fear embarking on a "slippery slope" leading to the devaluation of life in general and certain lives in particular, perhaps eventually leading from a right to die to an obligation to die.

Physician-assisted suicide has been legal in the state of Oregon since 1994. The law, known as the Death with Dignity Act, allows any mentally competent adult resident of the state who has been diagnosed as terminally ill by two physicians to obtain a lethal prescription for oral medication. The patient must make one written and two oral requests over a period of at least 15 days. Voters reaffirmed the law in 1997.

CRITICAL THINKING QUESTION
Is suicide ever justifiable? If not, why not? If so, under what circumstances?

Much of the debate centers on the practice of **euthanasia,** which means literally the good death. Euthanasia can take two forms: **passive euthanasia,** in which death is not actively prevented by any type of intervention, and **active euthanasia** (or mercy killing), in which definite steps are taken to cause death. While it is the latter that seems to arouse the most emotion, the difference between the two is not that clear-cut. For example, consider the case of an individual who cannot take food or water by mouth but is fed either by tube or intravenously. If the feedings are discontinued, is that passive euthanasia (letting nature take its course) or active euthanasia (actually causing death)?

Active euthanasia is legal in the Netherlands under certain conditions: the patient has repeatedly requested it; the doctor has consulted with the patient, the patient's family, and at least one other doctor; the patient's suffering cannot be alleviated; and the illness is terminal. Legalized active euthanasia means that a physician can end the life of a terminally ill patient and not be charged with murder.

Those who favor such legislation argue that this is the ultimate act of compassion, while opponents claim that it violates the Hippocratic oath to do no harm and changes the position of the doctor from that of trusted healer to potential executioner. They further argue that to devalue any life is to devalue all life, and that euthanasia would ultimately lead to the removal of barriers protecting the most vulnerable members of society. The debate over who should decide these issues and whether suicide, assisted suicide, and euthanasia are moral, compassionate, criminal, and/or dangerous will likely continue for many years. This debate is an outgrowth of the success of modern medicine in taking control over life and death out of the hands of nature and placing it in the hands of human beings, as well as its failure to deal adequately with the needs of dying patients, such as relief from pain and fear of abandonment.

Improving Care of the Dying

Part of the problem is poor communication between patients, doctors, and families. The experience of dying patients and their families can be improved through open communication from physicians about the patient's condition, prognosis, and treatment options. At the same time, patients and their families must directly communicate their values and wishes in regard to care. Such communication enhances individuals' sense of control as well as social support and contributes to effective and appropriate decision making. Critics also point out that there is little research on dying patients, and that medical school curricula and medical textbooks have largely ignored the care of the dying, known as *end-of-life care* (Sachs, 1994). The result is that physicians are inadequately trained to address the physical, not to mention the psychological and social, needs of dying patients. As many as 15 to 20 percent of terminally ill patients experience depression about their illness (Ballie, 2001). Anxiety is also prevalent, though neither is a "normal" aspect of terminal illness. These conditions can have far-reaching effects for the patient as well as the family, affecting quality of life, decision-making ability, communication, and physical condition. Few receive effective treatment, often the result of a missed diagnosis or the incorrect assumption that depression is normal under the circumstances and therefore does not require treatment. Larger societal issues regarding life and death—for example, whether a peaceful death is a legitimate goal—also play a role in physician behavior and attitudes. While relief of the symptoms of dying patients should be the focus of treatment, concerns have been expressed about significant undertreatment—for example, ineffective pain management, especially among aged patients (Meier & Morrison, 1999; Sachs, 1994). Though the hospice movement has made an important contribution, its impact has been limited by its peripheral position outside mainstream medicine in the United States (for example, some patients and their families may not even be informed about hospice) as well as the uneven quality and availability of hospice care.

In summary, the contributions of Kübler-Ross and others have focused attention on the needs of the dying patient. We have discovered that most terminally ill individuals benefit from the opportunity to share their feelings and to be a part of a social support system that acknowledges their experience. Growing belief in the right of the individual to die with dignity is reflected in the popularity of advance directives, the humane philosophy of the hospice movement, and ongoing debates about how far individual autonomy extends in matters of life and death.

Concept Review 12.2

- Kübler-Ross's landmark research on the experience of dying patients opened the door to research on death and dying.

- The meaning of "dying well" is determined by the beliefs, values, and needs of the individual.

- Increased emphasis on self-determination and patient autonomy has contributed to the use of advance directives.

- Hospice has made an important contribution to the care of dying individuals and their families.

- Debates about assisted suicide and euthanasia reflect the need for improvements in the care of dying patients.

Grief and Bereavement

Death involves not only the dying person but also those who must deal with the death and adjust to the loss of a loved one. The purpose of this last section is to explore the impact of death on emotionally involved survivors. **Bereavement** refers to the experience of the loss of a loved one by death. It comes from a root word meaning "shorn off or torn up," suggesting that one is stripped or dispossessed of something important, especially by death. Survivors are often referred to as *the bereaved*. **Grief** is the emotional suffering caused by such a loss—the normal, natural response to *any* significant loss, really—an experience of deep distress. It is as natural a response to loss as eating is to hunger. "Grief is nature's way of healing a broken heart" (Kleyman, 1996). And each of us grieves in our own way. Yet, though we all experience many losses over the course of our lives, "grieving is the most misunderstood and neglected growth process a person can go through. . . . Ironically, despite the inevitability and universality of the experience of loss, we know very little about recovery from it. . . . Incomplete recovery can have a lifelong effect on a person's capacity for happiness" (James & Cherry, 1988, pp. 3–5). What then is the nature of grief? What are its normal manifestations? How long does it last? How do people deal with it? These are the questions we will address in the remainder of this chapter.

Cultural and Historical Context of Grief

As Stroebe, Gergen, Gergen, and Stroebe (1992) remind us, the experience of grief and our understanding of it are influenced by both the cultural and historical context. Today, Western cultures view grief as a period of intense emotionality and a departure from normal functioning—something to be "worked through" and "gotten over" so that the individual can return to the normal business and routine of life. In this view, "reducing attention to the loss is critical, and good adjustment is often viewed as a breaking of ties between the bereaved and the dead" (p. 1206).

This way of thinking about grief is traceable to Freud, who is often credited with being one of the first theorists to offer a psychological explanation of the grief experience. In essence, Freud stated that grief is resolved through the "work of mourning"

Views of death reflect the historical and cultural context. The romantic view of death and mourning that predominated in the 19th century considered marriage to be an eternal communion of souls. The survivor was not expected to "get over" a death, but to maintain a bond with the deceased and to experience lasting sorrow.

(often referred to as *grief work*)—a process by which individuals gradually break the ties that bind them to the love object and withdraw the energy associated with those ties, energy that can then be reinvested in other relationships. The central idea is that to recover from the devastation of the death of a loved one, the individual must gain a new identity and develop an autonomous and independent life separate from the deceased.

The cultural and historical embeddedness of these views is more apparent when they are placed in contrast. For example, the romantic view of death and mourning that predominated in the 19th century considered marriage to be an eternal communion of souls (Stroebe et al., 1992). Grief signaled the significance of that bond and the depth of one's commitment. Breaking the ties to the deceased and "getting over" the grief would have trivialized the importance of the relationship and reflected badly on the spiritual depth of the survivor. Instead, the bonds were to be maintained, even in death. These ideas are clearly represented in the Romantic poetry of the period, which speaks of lasting sorrow and broken hearts, the clinging to memories and the hope of a reunion with the departed in the afterlife.

Contrary to the Western view described above, beliefs that stress the maintenance of ties with the dead persist in some non-Western cultures. In Japan, for instance, almost all homes contain an altar dedicated to deceased ancestors, and associated rituals encourage continued contact with and the maintenance of ties to these family members. Whereas placing food at the altar of a dead relative would be seen as normal in Japan, in our culture such behavior would be viewed as an indication that the individual was not facing reality, not getting past the death. Among the Hopi of Arizona, grief in response to the death of a loved one is discouraged, owing to fear of death and of the dead person. The Hopi believe that contact with death is polluting and therefore wish to break ties with the dead and get on with life as quickly as possible (Mandelbaum, 1959).

The point is that our views of death, our experience of grief, and our understanding of what is normal and pathological in response to the death of a loved one are relative to our historical and cultural context and the worldview that derives from it and provides us with a sense of the meaning of life events. As we have seen consistently throughout this book, diverse groups of people think and react in diverse ways. This diversity has implications for our research and theory on death and dying as well as on therapeutic approaches that address the difficulties experienced by the grieving individual. Sensitivity to these issues will be increasingly important as our society becomes more culturally diverse. See the Box for a brief overview of Lakota Sioux beliefs about life and death.

Though the Freudian grief work view of mourning has dominated the bereavement literature over most of the last 100 years, there is surprisingly little empirical evidence to support it (Bonanno & Kaltman, 1999). In fact, recent research often directly contradicts it. As a result, the notion that full recovery from a death requires that one confront and work through grief and sever attachment to the deceased is giving way to other views of grief and bereavement (see Bonanno & Kaltman, 1999, for an in-depth review). It is clear that the effect of the circumstances of the death as well as the age, gender, culture, personal history of loss, and other characteristics of the survivor also need to be better understood (Bonanno, 1999). The evidence does seem to suggest that for most people, making sense of or fully understanding the loss is difficult or impossible, but comfort may come from a sense of benefit in terms of personal growth. We'll return to this point at the end of the chapter.

UNDERSTANDING THE DEVELOPMENTAL CONTEXT

Death and Grief among the Lakota Sioux

There is a temptation to think of all Native Americans—including 350 distinct tribes in the United States and 596 different bands in Canada—as sharing a common belief system. But as Brokenleg and Middleton (1993) point out, values and beliefs vary widely. Because the focus of identity is on the tribe, not merely native heritage, it is important to understand and appreciate the diversity that makes, for example, the Cherokees and the Crows as culturally different as the English and the Chinese. The Lakota Sioux are the largest nation of Native Americans in the upper Midwest, and the second largest in the country. Their views of life and death represent a blend of the tribal elements that form the basic foundation of their belief system and Christian influence. A brief sketch offers an example of how culture colors and defines a universal human experience. Because the idea of a balanced universe is basic to Lakota thought, death and birth are viewed as natural counterparts and equally sacred. Life and death are part of a continuous process and not to be questioned. And though both people and animals are believed to go to the Spirit Land auto-matically after death, the emphasis is on living in the here and now in a complete and good way. The Lakota have great reverence for the body, both in life and after death, because it is the repository of a person's essence. Thus, it is to be respected and cared for. Lakota culture emphasizes cohesion among the extended family, which comes together in times of need. Because death is a sacred event to be shared, relatives (sometimes numbering over 1,000) go to great lengths to gather to support the family. Grief following death takes on a different quality among the Lakota, among whom it is inappropriate to ask "why?" and who therefore do not experience strong feelings of denial and anger. Mourning is viewed as natural, and unrestrained expression of grief is considered appropriate. Family members observe a year of mourning, during which individuals strive to avoid conflict, anger, jealousy, and so on, in an attempt to live an exemplary life. An individual's true character is thought to emerge in times of grief. The Lakota belief system also shapes attitudes about wakes, funerals, burials, and other rituals that honor the spirit of the deceased.

Resilience in the Face of Loss

Recent research confirms that people respond to loss in different ways. An estimated 10 to 15 percent experience the kind of severe and potentially chronic distress described in the traditional literature. Others experience less intense symptoms for a much shorter period of time. Still others, as many as 50 percent, exhibit what Bonanno (2004, p. 20) describes as **resilience** in the face of loss: "the ability of adults in otherwise normal circumstances who are exposed to an isolated and potentially highly disruptive event, such as the death of a close relation . . . , to maintain relatively stable, healthy levels of psychological and physical functioning." While they may experience transient disruptions, such as several weeks of preoccupation with thoughts of the loss or difficulty sleeping, they retain the ability to function at work and in close relationships and the capacity to experience positive emotions. (You may be familiar with the term *resilience* from studies of children who overcome adverse circumstances and continue to thrive.) He points out that most of the psychological literature on grief and bereavement was based on studies of those who experienced significant psychological problems or sought treatment following the death of a loved one. These responses were mistaken for the norm and served as the foundation on which theories of normal grief and recovery were based. Resilience was viewed as either rare (seen only in the exceptionally healthy) or pathological (a reflection of denial, a diminished capacity for feeling, or lack of attachment to the deceased). Contrary to traditional views, Bonanno asserts that resilience is one of several different trajectories in response to loss and is more common than previously believed. A number of factors contribute to resilience. One of these is the personality trait of hardiness, which consists of the following dimensions: being committed to finding meaningful purpose in life, the belief that one can control one's circumstances and the outcome of events (i.e., personal control), and the view that personal growth can come from both positive and negative experiences. Another factor is the capacity to use laughter and positive emotion (see Chapter 11). Resilient individuals are highly unlikely to need or benefit from grief counseling. It is important to enhance our understanding of the developmental origins of resilience, the protective factors that contribute to it as well as the risk factors that undermine it, and determine whether individuals can learn to be more resilient to aversive events. Bonanno and his colleagues (Bonanno, Wortman, & Nesse, 2004) conclude that we must move beyond simplistic views of grief and bereavement, maintain a healthy skepticism toward traditional perspectives, and acknowledge that we still have much to learn about the diverse ways in which people respond to loss.

Grief Process

Our traditional thinking about the nature of grief was shaped by Freudian theory, as mentioned above, and also by a classic study conducted by the psychiatrist Eric Lindemann in the 1940s. His goal was to sensitize physicians to the symptoms of grief and to suggest appropriate therapeutic interventions. The essence of his descriptive summary of the normal grief response was initially supported, and his ideas expanded, by subsequent research (for example, Parkes, 1972; Glick, Weiss, & Parkes, 1974). It was widely accepted that the grief process consisted of an orderly sequence of stages, that the characteristics of normal and abnormal grief could be clearly identified, and that people eventually recovered from their loss. However, more recent research using better methods and more representative samples has cast doubt on this traditional depiction of grief (Lund, 1993). Rather than conceptualizing grief as a linear process made up of stages with clearly defined boundaries, it is more accurate to think of a series of overlapping and fluid phases that vary from person to person. The phases described below are general guidelines and should not be used to prescribe appropriate behavior or timing in the process of dealing with grief (Stroebe, Stroebe, & Hansson, 1993).

Initial Response

The first phase begins with the death and continues for about three weeks, during which time the funeral and other leave-taking rituals take place. The initial reaction includes shock and disbelief. Individuals may feel numb, dazed, empty, and disoriented. These feelings, which have served as a barrier to the pain of loss, give way in a few days to deep sorrow, expressed through extended periods of weeping and crying, along with fear and free-floating or generalized anxiety. The intensity of these feelings may cause individuals to think that they cannot make it and to fear losing their minds or breaking down. There is a danger of overdependence on tranquilizers or alcohol during this period.

Physical symptoms include an empty feeling in the abdomen, shortness of breath, tightness in the throat, and loss of muscular power. Loss of appetite and inability to sleep are also common. After about three weeks, these symptoms begin to subside in frequency and intensity.

Intermediate Phase

The second phase of the grief process begins about three weeks after the death and lasts for about a year. As this phase begins, the business aspects of the death—the transferring of car titles, dealing with insurance companies, processing wills, and so on—are winding down, the busyness and chores are subsiding, and the reality of the death is sinking in. This is the time of "roller-coaster" emotions. Anger (at the loved one, God, the situation, or others who seem to be happy), guilt, longing, and loneliness are common. It may be best to defer important decisions.

Three behaviors typify this phase: an obsessional review of how the death occurred and might have been prevented (the "what ifs" and "if onlys"), a search for meaning in the death (the "whys"), and searching for the deceased. The bereaved may feel the presence of the deceased strongly and have hallucinations in which the person is seen and heard. This is especially likely if the death was sudden and unexpected.

All of these behaviors decrease over time. During this process, the individual may suddenly notice that for a short time, the suffering has subsided a bit. These experiences will become more frequent and longer-lasting and may offer a sense of hope. Most people are functioning fairly well within a few months after the death and enter the recovery phase within a year.

Recovery Phase

The final phase of bereavement usually starts around the beginning of the second year. Sleep and appetite have returned to normal, and the person is looking ahead and may even begin to form new relationships. This does not mean, however, that the mourning process is over. We now realize that mourning the death of a loved one may go on for a lifetime, although with decreased frequency and intensity. It may be reactivated in surprising ways and at surprising times, especially by anniversaries (of the death as well as wedding anniversaries, birthdays, and so on) and holidays. Thus, feelings of grief may never cease completely.

Despite this overview of the process of grief, it is important to stress that individuals grieve in their own unique way; there is no set pattern to grief.

Lund (1996) offers the following general conclusions based on research on the grief process.

- While bereavement may be very stressful, many individuals exhibit considerable resiliency in dealing with their loss. Two of the most important predictors of adjustment, regardless of age or gender, are self-esteem and coping skills that allow the individual to meet the changing demands of daily life.
- There is diversity in the thoughts, feelings, and behaviors people experience as they progress through the grief process. This diversity is also seen within individuals, who may experience simultaneously both negative feelings (such as anger and loneliness) as well as positive feelings (such as personal strength).

- Because of the considerable diversity in the way grief is experienced and manifested, it is better to use terms such as *common* and *uncommon,* rather than *normal* and *abnormal,* to describe feelings and behaviors during bereavement.
- Rather than describing the grief process as a succession of clearly defined stages leading to full resolution and recovery, it is more accurate to use the metaphor of a rollercoaster ride with ups and downs. These fluctuations have to do with rapidly changing feelings, dealing with personal weaknesses and limitations, coping with fatigue and loneliness, and meeting the challenges of learning new skills and behavior patterns and forming new relationships. While there are no clear time markers, the ride gradually becomes more manageable, though it may never end completely.

Unanticipated and Anticipated Death

Lindemann's description of grief was based on postdeath reactions to a death that was both sudden and unexpected. Subsequent research has confirmed that the experience of grief is greatly affected by the circumstances surrounding the death. As a result, a number of researchers have stressed the importance of whether a death is **unanticipated,** such as due to an accident, or **anticipated** or expected, as in the case of a long terminal illness.

High-Grief versus Low-Grief Death

Fulton (1970) makes a distinction between a **high-grief death,** in which death is accidental, sudden, or involves a young person, and a **low-grief death,** in which death comes after a prolonged illness or involves an old person. High-grief deaths cause the profound psychological, behavioral, and physiological reactions described above, which are con-

The extraordinary outpouring of grief following the death of Diana, Princess of Wales, was in part a result of its sudden and unexpected nature.

sidered to constitute the normal grief response. In contrast, Fulton has argued that a low-grief death causes a less intense response because the bereaved begins to anticipate the death and to grieve prior to its actual occurrence. This is the concept of anticipatory grief (Lindemann, 1944; Fulton, 1987).

Anticipatory Grief

Anticipatory grief has been observed in adult sons and daughters who have been anticipating the death of an elderly parent for 5 to 10 years or more. According to Zilberfein (1999), anticipatory grief may be just as intense as that occurring after a death, though this is often overlooked. Fulton believes the survivors discharge a lot of their feelings prior to the death and therefore do not display the normal pattern of grief in response to the death itself. Goldberg (1973) noted that if the death was long and painful, relief may be the primary experience of the bereaved once death occurs.

An anticipated death provides the survivors the opportunity to absorb the reality gradually, be of assistance to the dying person, tie up the loose ends of their relationship, complete unfinished business, prepare for the death, and adjust to its consequences. The death is also perceived to be less mysterious and frightening. When death occurs suddenly and unexpectedly, survivors may never be able to understand it and may fear that it can happen again at any time, either to them or someone they love. This increased sense of vulnerability may interfere with motivation to form new relationships or to remarry (Glick et al., 1974).

The idea is, then, that an anticipated death is experienced as more predictable and offers more opportunities to have at least some control over aspects of the death. Years of research on stress have shown that stress is reduced to the extent that it is predictable and controllable. Regardless of the circumstances of death, however, most people are never fully prepared.

The notion of anticipatory grief has been controversial. Parkes and Weiss (1983) do not believe that actual grieving can begin prior to the death, though they do acknowledge that an anticipated death allows some preparation to occur and that reactions to an unanticipated death are more severe. In reviewing the literature on this subject, Huber and Gibson (1990) conclude that there is evidence that some people do begin to grieve prior to the actual death of a loved one, and that this may alter their postdeath reaction and speed the recovery process. Thus, they believe that anticipatory grief can serve as a mediating force that affects the bereavement experience and its outcome.

Death of a Child

The death of a child is especially devastating for the survivors and is often cited as a classic example of a high-grief death. Because this type of death is now so rare and unexpected, it is experienced as especially incomprehensible and unjust. Knapp (1987) interviewed more than 155 families who had lost a child between the ages of 1 and 28 through terminal illness, sudden death, suicide, or murder. He found six similarities in the way the parents responded: an intense need to remember and a desire never to forget the child; a need to talk about their experience and about the child; contemplation of their own deaths; the need to find a cause or reason for their loss; a significant change in values, including a greater sensitivity to and understanding of the suffering of others; and the experience of **shadow grief,** or grief that is never totally resolved.

Studies document that parents who suffer the loss of a child through miscarriage or stillbirth go through the same grief process, although the fact that family members and friends often discount this type of loss as less significant may mean that the support system is not activated (Cole, 1987). In addition, reactions to miscarriage and stillbirth may be complicated by a tendency to blame oneself, a feeling of isolation caused by the fact that few people may have even known about the pregnancy, and the fact that the parents are mourning a fantasy, a child that they did not know and may never have seen.

Health and Mortality Risks of Bereavement

The danger of grief in terms of negative effects on health and increased risk of mortality has been recognized for centuries. For example, grief is cited as a specific cause of death in a report published in London in 1657 (Parkes, 1972). Intense emotions and an inability to concentrate in the early stages of grief increase the risk of accidental injury, while depression increases the risk of suicide. In addition, the immunosuppressive effects of the body's response to stress increase the risk of infectious illness, while other aspects of the stress response increase the likelihood of other stress-related illnesses.

Rees and Lutkins (1967) found that the death rate among those in the first year of bereavement was almost seven times higher than that of the general population. Similarly, Rowland (1977) found that the mortality rate among the bereaved in the years after the death of a spouse was much greater than among those matched in age and health status who had not experienced this loss. The death rate was highest in the first 6 to 12 months, after which it gradually returned to normal. As we have seen in regard to other life stresses, the individual's coping skills and degree of social support have a great effect on the risk of ill health and mortality during bereavement.

The Funeral and Other Leave-Taking Rituals

Functions

I used to believe that wakes and funerals were disgusting and barbaric, and the family gatherings ("parties") that often followed them, hypocritical. But having now experienced the deaths of several loved ones, I have a great appreciation for the important role of these formal activities in the grief process. First, the preparations necessary for these events help to focus the bereaved in the early hours and days after a death. At a time when people have trouble knowing what to do, the need to make decisions and plans imposes a structure (though not a pleasant one) on them. These rituals also serve as a way of activating the survivors' support system, which can help the bereaved cope with the stress of the loss.

The process of going through the preparations and the actual events helps the reality of the death to sink in, and allows the family, friends, and the community to acknowledge the death, to emphasize the importance of the loss of the individual, and to pay their respects. Like other rites of passage—graduations, weddings, baptisms—the funeral (or memorial service or whatever) is a public acknowledgment that something significant has happened, that some transition has occurred, and brings a sense of closure to the death. Funerals are a way of honoring the dead, but their most important function is to assist the living.

Funerals activate the survivors' support system, provide a focus for activities in the period immediately following a death, and help survivors acknowledge the reality of their loss.

Funeral Transaction

In her classic and highly critical study of the funeral industry, *The American Way of Death* (1963), Jessica Mitford described a number of ways in which the planning of a funeral differed from other types of business transactions. These included disorientation caused by grief (and the desire to "do right" by the deceased), the lack of standards by which to judge the products being offered to the consumer (how do you know what makes a good casket, for example), the need to make an on-the-spot decision (no chance or desire to comparison shop—this is impulse buying), general ignorance of the law in regard to death and burial and the likelihood of being misled (for example, being told that the body must be embalmed), and the ready availability of insurance money to finance the transaction (in other words, funeral directors know that their bills will be paid first, and thus do not worry much about what the buyer can afford).

One of the outgrowths of the hue and cry that went up after Mitford's exposé of funeral practices was the passage of legislation in 1984 to regulate the funeral industry, which until that time had been rather freewheeling in the way it did business. For example, the Federal Trade Commission now mandates that the funeral home must provide the consumer with an itemized list of all expenses so that the buyer knows exactly what is being purchased and how much it will cost. However, critics charge that the law is loosely enforced and inadequate (for example, the rules apply only to funeral homes, not cemeteries, monument sellers, casket sellers, or crematories). Moreover, state regulations vary widely, which is confusing to consumers. In recent years, aggressive marketing has encouraged prepayment (generally not a good idea); in fact, nearly 25 percent of funerals are now prepaid (Baker, 1999). And the consumers' reluctance to shop around allows funeral homes to maintain inflated prices. According to one survey, 53 percent of respondents chose a funeral home because it had been used by the family in the past, while 33 percent chose the one closest to home (Baker, 1999). Finally, the funeral industry is increasingly dominated by large corporate chains, which now own 15 percent of all homes and conduct 25 percent of the business. Though the average funeral costs about $5,000, chains charge up to $10,000, not including the costs of the cemetery and monument. (See Figure 12.3 for an example of a general price list provided by a funeral home. You may be surprised at some of the items included and some of the decisions that must be made. You may be even more surprised at the costs involved.)

My experience is that there are huge numbers of decisions that must be made quickly on the basis of limited information. I distinctly remember all of us (my mother, sister, and brother) sitting in the funeral director's office after Dad died, looking at each other quizzically after each question was posed, sometimes expressing a strong opinion (casket open or closed, for example), but most times saying things like, "Well, I don't know, what do you think (or want or prefer)?" I felt fortunate that we were able to share this experience and the responsibility of making these decisions.

Individuals can relieve family members from the burden of making all of these arrangements by prearranging (but *not* prepaying for) their funeral. Yes, I know, it does not sound like the kind of thing you would like to do on a Sunday afternoon, but it does help guarantee that your wishes will be carried out and that your survivors will be spared some difficult decisions. My grandmother prearranged much of her service (chose the funeral home, selected the music, decided on cremation, and so on), and my mother-in-law also prearranged her funeral (down to having the headstone in place and engraved, except for the death date!). I thought it was grotesque when she did it but quickly ate my words after her death, at which time I much appreciated her thoughtfulness. There was still plenty to do.

So, in sum, the funeral and other leave-taking rituals perform an important function in helping the bereaved to acknowledge the reality of a death and to begin the work of grieving for their loss. While specific practices vary tremendously among families and cultures and have changed historically, their contribution to the experience of bereavement endures.

Condolence Behavior

The irony is that the most difficult part of the grief process occurs after the initial "business" prompted by the death is taken care of, after the cards and gifts and visits taper off, after relatives and friends have returned to their homes and normal routines, when the bereaved are left to face the day-to-day-reality and the changes in their lives alone. I have tried very hard to remember this as I work to improve my own "condolence" behavior. Phone calls, social invitations, notes, and other remembrances can be important sources of support in the weeks and months following the funeral.

Our fear of not knowing what to say or saying the wrong thing often causes us to avoid family and friends who have experienced a death. In doing so, we further isolate them from our support. I remember hearing a sermon on this subject a few years ago, the title of which was "The Quiet Ministries." Our minister, Dr. Butler, spoke in particular about the ministry of silence and the ministry of acceptance. He pointed out that whatever we say is less important than our presence, and that sometimes the most helpful thing is simply to be with someone, to be there if needed, and to be silent. The best gift you can give is yourself.

Acceptance of the feelings, thoughts, and behaviors of the bereaved is also healing. Remember that acceptance is one of the qualities of a supportive relationship, since it conveys the sense that one is heard, understood, and cared for. Rigdon (1986) interviewed 570 bereaved individuals age 55 and over and found that the help that was most appreciated was keeping in touch through calls and visits and giving them an opportunity to

FIGURE 12.3 *An Example of a General Price List for Funeral Arrangements, Showing Itemization of Goods and Services*

The Federal Trade Commission has mandated this GENERAL PRICE LIST as a means of consumer protection and requires the enclosed information along with their mandatory disclosures shown in quotes. These prices are effective October 1, 2004 and are subject to change without notice.

Information and/or pre-arrangement charge when applicable $75

TRADITIONAL CEREMONY

Professional services of the staff to respond to initial request for service, consultation with responsible person, preparation of documents, and allocated portion of the overhead expenses. Use of facilities, equipment, materials and personnel for embalming, dressing, casketing and cosmetology. Use of vehicles within DuPage Co. for; transporting the remains to the funeral home, the funeral coach, and the service utility vehicles for all errands. Use of facilities and personnel to setup/cleanup visitation area, display floral arrangements, oversee private family time prior to and public hours of 3 P.M. to 9 P.M. Use of facilities and personnel to arrange, setup/cleanup, and direct the funeral ceremony. Personnel to supervise the committal at the cemetery.

Traditional Ceremony $5330

Merchandise and cash advances are separate and in addition to the above.

"The goods and services shown below are those we can provide to our customers. You may choose only the items you desire. However, any funeral arrangements you select will include a charge for our basic services and overhead. If legal or other requirements mean you must buy any items you did not specifically ask for, we will explain the reason in writing on the statement we provide describing the funeral goods and services you selected."

Professional Services of Funeral Director and Staff $2,410

This charge includes, but is not limited to, twenty-four hour availability of funeral director and staff to respond to the initial request for service, consultation with responsible person to determine the type of services and the disposition desired, and the preparation of all necessary authorizations and permits.

Incorporated within the above figure is a fee of $990 for an allocated portion of the overhead expenses such as, professional licensing, legal and accounting fees, record keeping, insurance, taxes, maintenance, equipment and furnishings.

"This fee for our services and overhead will be added to the total cost of the funeral arrangements you selected. (This fee is already included in our charges for direct cremations, immediate burials, and forwarding or receiving remains.)"

USE OF FUNERAL HOME FACILITIES

Visitation:

Facilities and personnel to setup/cleanup, display floral arrangements, oversee visitation, and family private time either inside or outside our facility.

One Full day of visitation (3 PM to 9 PM) $995

One Evening of visitation (6 PM to 9 PM) $645

Obsequies:

Facilities, equipment and personnel for setup/cleanup, coordination and directing the ceremony or service.

Held within the facility

Funeral Ceremony $515
Memorial Service $515
Visitation per hour prior to Obsequies $150

Held outside the facility

Funeral Ceremony $515
Memorial Service $190
Graveside Service $190

Shelter:

A per day charge for sheltering the remains beyond the normal 4 days $40

Miscellaneous:

Extra lounge cleanup (if necessary) $50

Embalming..$495

"Except in certain special cases, embalming is not required by law. Embalming may be necessary, however, if you select certain funeral arrangements, such as a funeral with viewing. If you do not want embalming, you usually have the right to choose an arrangement that does not require you to pay for it, such as direct cremation or immediate burial."

(continued)

FIGURE 12.3 *Continued*

OTHER PREPARATIONS

Dressing, Casketing, Cosmetology $165
Hairstyling (rinse or dye additional $20) $40
Special Care of autopsy or harvested remains.........$150
Care of unembalmed remains "disinfecting
& dressing" $50

AUTOMOTIVE EQUIPMENT

Transfer of Remains $250
Funeral Coach $350
Service Utility Vehicles.....................................$150
Limousine...$390
(waiting time $60 with a 2 hr minimum)

Additional $50 per service in counties neighboring
DuPage

MERCHANDISE

Caskets ....$1075 to $5820
   "A complete price list will be provided at the
   funeral home."

Other Burial Containers...............................$575 to $3585
   "A complete price list will be provided at the
   funeral home."

Cremation Urns...$190 to $1990
Burial Clothing ....$20 to $200
Register Book $30
Memorial Folders with printing.......................$45 to $82
Prayer Cards with printing.............................$40 to $212
Crucifix (inside or outside) ....$25 to $40
Acknowledgment Cards (per box)...............................$12

CASH ADVANCES

Certified Death Certificates

Coroner's Cremation Permits

Cremation Charge

Long Distance phone calls or Fax

Newspaper notices

Organist

Soloist

Stipend-Religious

Tent

Vault Installation Charge

The above cash advances will vary in charges. We also exercise our right to cash discounts for prompt payment.

Immediate Burial...$2970

Our charge for immediate burial only includes: local removal of remains, shelter of the remains, transportation to any local place of disposition, and necessary services of the staff. Casket provided by purchaser.

If a casket is selected from the funeral home, it will be added to the above charge for an immediate burial. Caskets range from $1075 to $5820.

Direct Cremation $2190

Our charge for direct cremation only includes: necessary service of the staff, proportionate amount of the overhead costs, local removal of the remains, shelter of the remains, transportation to local crematory, and obtaining necessary authorizations and/or permits. Cremation charge and cremation container are not included.

"If you want to arrange a direct cremation, you can use an alternative container. Alternative containers encase the body and can be made of materials like fiberboard or composition materials (with or without an outside covering). The containers we provide are:"

   Beech—light stained hardwood with
   light interior..$760

   Faith—cloth covered unit with interior...............$620

   Flattop—cloth covered...$445

   Cardboard—cardboard with wood
   bottom $190

FORWARDING AND RECEIVING

Forwarding...$1850

This charge includes: local removal of remains, embalming, temporary shelter of the remains, transportation to airport, shipping container, services of staff, and any necessary authorizations.

Receiving...$1995

This charge includes: temporary shelter of remains, necessary transportation from airport, professional services of the funeral director and staff. It does not include any charge for visitation or services.

talk about their loss. These individuals expressed resentment toward those who told them they understood or that it would get easier.

Bereavement as a Transition

As Huber and Gibson (1990) point out, bereavement has been viewed at various times as an illness, a crisis, a series of stages or developmental tasks, and, more recently and broadly, a complex psychosocial transition that takes a considerable amount of time to complete. Seen in this light, bereavement represents a major life change that will have long-lasting effects. It includes changes in lifestyle as well as changes in the way one thinks of life, self, and others, and corresponding changes in roles and schemas (Horowitz, 1990). According to Murphy (1987), the outcome of this transition will depend on three sets of variables: the circumstances of the death, such as the relationship to the deceased and whether the death was anticipated or sudden; the individual's personal attributes, such as gender, income, and health; and mediating processes, such as social support and anticipatory grief.

In a survey of 134 bereaved individuals, Huber and Gibson (1990) found evidence suggesting that hospice care facilitated the respondents' ability to come to terms with the reality of the impending death, provided them with tools useful in coping with grief, and encouraged them to engage in some anticipatory grief. Hospice care had "a strong and positive impact on survivors' subsequent bereavement" (p. 63). Thus, the provision of hospice services may be a useful mediator affecting bereavement outcome.

A number of observers, such as Schlossberg (1984), have noted that individuals' own self-assessments are the best indicators of where they are in the bereavement process. Huber and Gibson (1990) have offered a simple instrument called the *10-Mile Mourning Bridge,* which allows a bereaved individual to assess progress in working through grief. Individuals are asked to visualize a hypothetical 10-mile bridge, which represents the grief process. The bridge begins with their first knowledge of an impending death and ends when they are able to reinvest their emotional energies and get on with their lives, identified by Worden (1982) as the final stage of recovery. Individuals are then asked various questions that require them to plot themselves, based on their own individual criteria, at some point on the bridge. For example, subjects might be asked, "Where are you now?" Six miles, eight miles, and so on. Though this instrument requires further validation, it may be useful both to the individual and to researchers, allowing them to plot individual progress and to compare the progress of various individuals on the basis of such criteria as relationship to the loved one, use of hospice services, and so on.

Surviving Survival: Positive Outcomes of the Grief Process

Those who have found a way to cope with their grief often feel a sense of pride in having survived the unsurvivable, the terrible pain caused by the loss of someone close. They feel more confident of their ability to face the challenges of life, armed with the tools they acquired in their struggle through the grief process: "Like a phoenix rising out of the ashes, a widow or widower often comes out of the bereavement experience a more capable and stronger person" (Schulz, 1978, p. 148). A greater sensitivity to and compassion for others may also result from these experiences, along with a sense of being touched by and connected with one of the most difficult of life's events. An increased sense of competence and mastery may encourage the survivor to take on new challenges and pursue activities that were previously viewed as too difficult. Schulz (1978, p. 149) has the last word: "If there is anything positive about surviving the death of someone close to us it is the possibility of increased growth and self-confidence, although this self-improvement comes at a very high price."

> As is the generation of leaves, so too of men:
> At one time the wind shakes the leaves to the ground
>   but then the flourishing woods
> Gives birth, and the season of spring comes
>   into existence;
> So it is with the generations of men, which
>   alternately come forth and pass away.
>
> —Homer, *Iliad,* Sixth Book

Concept Review 12.3

- The traditional view of grief and bereavement is currently being challenged and revised.

- The experience of grief is shaped by cultural beliefs and historical period, relationship to the deceased, personal qualities, and the circumstances of the death.

- Though each person grieves differently, research has suggested some common phases in the grief process in Western culture.

- Funerals and other rituals surrounding death play an important role in helping individuals cope with grief.

- Those who are bereaved benefit from expressions of social support that extend beyond the immediate aftermath of the death.

- The experience of grief and learning to cope with it may contribute in important ways to personal development.

REVIEW QUESTIONS

The Changed Nature of Death

1. Discuss the ways death has changed in the modern era.

Attitudes toward Death

1. What is meant by the statement that ours is a death-denying society? What are the consequences of death denial?
2. Explain the developmental task view of death.

3. Evaluate the main findings of death anxiety research.

The Dying Person

1. Assess Kübler-Ross's contributions to our understanding of death.
2. What does it mean to "die well"?
3. Identify factors that have led to the increased use of advance directives.
4. Explain the function of a living will and a durable power of attorney for health care.

5. Discuss the philosophy and essential features of hospice care.
6. What is the right-to-die movement?
7. Identify and assess the arguments for and against euthanasia.
8. How might care of the dying be improved?

Grief and Bereavement

1. Contrast current Western views of death and grief with those predominant in other periods and cultures.
2. Describe the traditional "grief work" view of mourning developed by Freud. How do contemporary approaches to grief and bereavement differ from it?
3. Discuss the meaning and prevalence of resilience in response to loss and factors that contribute to it.

4. Outline the three phases of the grief process.
5. Compare the impact of an anticipated versus an unanticipated death on the bereaved.
6. Why is the death of a child considered to be especially devastating?
7. Identify the health and mortality risks of grief.
8. Defend the statement that funerals are for the living. What are the functions of such leave-taking rituals?
9. What makes the business transaction of planning a funeral unique, according to Jessica Mitford?
10. What are some of the most helpful ways to be supportive toward those who are bereaved?
11. Identify potential positive outcomes for the individual once grief has been successfully resolved.

KEY TERMS

active euthanasia, 473
anticipated death, 480
anticipatory grief, 481
bereavement, 474
conspiracy of silence, 463
death-denying society, 462
durable power of attorney for health care, 468

euthanasia, 473
grief, 475
high-grief death, 480
hospice, 471
living will, 468
low-grief death, 480
passive euthanasia, 473
resilience, 477

shadow grief, 481
thanatology, 463
unanticipated death, 480

Glossary

accommodation   Piaget's term for modifying an existing cognitive schema or creating a new one; a strategy of successful cognitive aging whereby an older individual disengages from activities that stress cognitive limits and diverts energy to areas of expertise

active elements of mate selection   aspects of mate selection that result from personal preferences and choices and that weed out potential mates

active euthanasia   active steps are taken to cause death; mercy killing

active life expectancy   refers to the average number of years individuals of a given cohort can expect to live free from disability and dependency

activities of daily living (ADLs)   basic functions necessary to live independently, such as bathing, toileting, and eating

activity theory   a theory of social aging that holds that life satisfaction is a function of remaining actively involved in a variety of behaviors and relationships

adult development   subfield of developmental psychology concerned with development in the period of life after adolescence

adulthood   not tied to a particular chronological age, but characterized by relative independence from parents and acceptance of responsibility for one's actions

affectional bond   a long-lasting emotional tie to another person who is viewed as unique and not interchangeable with any other

age-complexity effect   the finding that the magnitude of age differences in cognitive performance increases with the complexity of the task

age-irrelevant society   Neugarten's term referring to the fact that, because of changes in biological and social aging, chronological age has become an inadequate indicator of psychological development; thus, its significance has lessened, along with the power of age norms to govern behavior

age norm   socially defined standards or expectations of behavior based on age

ageism   prejudice and discrimination against an individual based on age

ageless self   Kaufman's term referring to the finding that elderly people tend to maintain a consistent concept of themselves that is generally unaffected by age

agentic generativity   Kotre's term for acts of generativity that are primarily monuments to the self, as opposed to communal generativity

aging   see *primary aging, secondary aging*

agreeableness   one of McCrae and Costa's five personality traits; represents the degree to which a person is compassionate, good-natured, cooperative, and motivated to avoid conflict

Alzheimer's disease (AD)   the leading cause of senile dementia; a progressive degenerative disease that attacks the brain and impairs memory, thinking, and behavior

anticipated death   a death that is expected, such as that due to a long illness

anticipatory grief   in the case of an expected death, grief experienced before the actual death of a loved one

anxious/ambivalent attachment   the result of inconsistent and/or inappropriate caregiving, infants are drawn to the caregiver but are unable to trust him or her

applied cognitive aging   the research field that attempts to solve real-life problems of older adults by utilizing what is known about their cognitive abilities

arteriosclerosis   a pathological condition in which plaque begins to accumulate on the inside of arteries, reducing blood flow

assimilation   Piaget's term for adding information to an existing schema

attachment   an emotional bond between two people

attachment behavioral system   a group of actions and feelings that enhance the likelihood of survival by promoting proximity between infant and caregiver

attachment theory   explains the development of an emotional bond between infant and caregiver in the first year of life

attention   an important resource in the information-processing system, determining which information is processed; it is thought to be limited in quantity and under the direction of some executive control mechanism

automatic processing   information processing that can be carried out with few or no demands on attention

average life expectancy   refers to the average number of years an individual can expect to live, given the circumstances present during her or his lifetime

avoidant attachment   a form of attachment in which infants derive no comfort from the caregiver, and which results from unresponsive or even rejecting caregiving

axon   the long neural fiber extending away from the cell body of the neuron, responsible for transmitting a nerve impulse

baby boom   the large cohort born between 1946 and 1964

baby bust   the smaller cohort born after the baby boom, beginning in 1965

behavioral pathogen   behavior (attitudes, habits, and so on) that contributes to disease, disability, and death

behavioral system   a genetically determined, biologically based constellation of behaviors and feelings that exists in all members of the species, has survival value, and has evolved through natural selection

behaviorism a school of psychology founded by John Watson in 1913; stresses observable behavior as the only proper subject matter for the field and emphasizes the use of rigorous scientific methods, especially the laboratory experiment

bereavement the experience of losing a loved one through death

beta-amyloid a protein found in characteristic plaques in the brains of Alzheimer's victims; its role in the disease is not clear

biographical interviewing the method used by Levinson in his study of adult men; involves extensive interviews with the subject, the subject's spouse, and others, in an attempt to document the story of a man's life

biological generativity Kotre's term for the conception, delivery, and nursing of offspring

blood-brain barrier a characteristic of the vascular system of the brain that prevents many potentially harmful blood-borne substances from entering the brain

bridge job a transitional job following retirement from a career job, usually either self-employment or part-time work in a new field

calling an old term referring to a calling from God to do a particular type of work that makes a positive contribution to society; experienced as an inner desire or urge

care manager the individual who arranges for and coordinates caregiving services provided by others

care provider the individual who actually performs the caregiving tasks

career a relatively new term that describes work in which upward mobility requiring increased mastery and offering increased compensation is available

career primary track a level of career development reserved for women whose careers take precedence over family roles; these women are often unmarried and/or childless

career self-efficacy belief in one's ability to choose, prepare for, and be successful in a given occupation

caregiving career for many women, caregiving (for children, elderly parents and other relatives, and husbands) is a long-term role, extending into late middle and early old age—it is not a single, time-limited episode in their lives

Cartesian dualism the belief espoused by René Descartes that mind and body are separate entities

case-study method an in-depth investigation of one individual

cataract clouding of the lens of the eye, common among older adults

central executive a component of working memory that oversees information processing, assisted by the articulatory loop and the visuospatial scratch pad

cerebral cortex the one-fourth-inch covering over the cerebrum, where higher-order mental activity takes place

chronological age chronological age in years

cognition a broad term referring to the collection of mental processes and activities used in perceiving, remembering, and thinking, and the act of using them

cognitive closure a need for definite knowledge on an issue and a desire to avoid confusion and uncertainty

cognitive permanence the desire to maintain cognitive closure

cognitive psychology subfield of psychology that studies mental activities and processes

cognitive urgency the inclination to reach cognitive closure as quickly as possible

cohort a group of people born at about the same time and therefore subject to the same sociohistorical events

cohort effect the effect of one's year of birth and subsequent sociohistorical experience on development

collagen a fibrous, elastic protein that constitutes the basic structural component of connective tissue, found throughout the body; a loss of elasticity with age has adverse effects on skin, muscle, bone, and so on

collectivist culture a culture in which individuals define themselves as members of a group(s), subordinate personal to group goals, and feel strong attachment to and concern for the well-being of the group

commitment according to Sternberg, a component of companionate love that refers to intent to maintain the relationship; according to Erikson, refers to making choices from among alternatives and pursuing relevant goals—a key developmental task in identity formation as well as career development

communal generativity Kotre's term for generative acts that focus primarily on the well-being of the generative object—as opposed to agentic generativity

communal orientation an attitude toward close relationships that emphasizes the needs and well-being of the other person

companionate love warm, trusting affection

compensation in reference to strategies of successful cognitive aging, the maintenance of level of performance by changing the way a task is performed

competence in comparison to performance, what one is capable of achieving under optimal conditions

compression-of-morbidity hypothesis the idea that disease and disability will be delayed against a fixed life span; thus, poor health will develop later in life and last for a shorter period of time before death

confounding the variables a situation in a poorly controlled experiment when the outcome could be due to a mixture of variables—in other words, the cause of the behavior is not clear

conscientiousness McCrae and Costa's trait representing self-discipline, organization, ambition, and achievement

conspiracy of silence a mutual pretense in which no one speaks of or acknowledges an impending death, even though everyone knows that it will occur

construct validity refers to the quality and appropriateness of the tool used for measuring behavior

contextual model of development   views behavior as the result of a complex, reciprocal interaction between the individual's biogenetic characteristics and the sociohistorical environment; acknowledges the influence of both nature and nurture

continued-potential view   the idea that cognitive development continues throughout life, in opposition to the decrementalist view

continuity theory of retirement adaptation   a model of retirement adaptation that holds that retirement produces few long-term effects

contrasexual transition   Gutmann's term for the transformation that occurs in men and women as the active parenting role subsides; each integrates qualities of the opposite sex into their sense of self

control group   in an experiment, the group used for comparison, not exposed to the independent variable

convergent thought   a kind of thinking in which the one true answer is sought

convoy model   the idea that individuals move through life with a set of significant others from whom they derive benefits such as social support

corporate eldercare   a service provided by a company to assist employees with responsibilities for caring for elderly family members

correlation coefficient   a numerical value between 0 and 1.0 that indicates the strength of relationship between two or more variables

correlational study   seeks to determine if a relationship exists between two or more naturally occurring variables

creativity   a cognitive process that is dependent on divergent thought and that leads to an extraordinary product or achievement that is novel, original, unique, and relevant

crisis theory of retirement adaptation   a model of retirement adaptation that holds that the loss of the work role is so significant that it is hazardous to the retiree's physical and mental health

cross-era transition   Levinson's term for a fundamental turning point in the life cycle, lasting about five years, during which one is terminating a major era and entering a succeeding one

cross-linkage theory of aging   maintains that many characteristics of aging are due to a gummy substance produced when glucose attaches itself to body proteins, thereby impairing tissue function

cross-sectional study   groups of subjects of different age cohorts are compared at one point in time to determine if age-related differences in behavior exist

crystallized intelligence   accumulated knowledge

cultural generativity   Kotre's term for generative acts that pass on the value system and meanings of a culture to the next generation

death-denying society   refers to the difficulty American society has in dealing with the reality of death and a preference to avoid the subject as well as dying individuals

decrementalist view   in opposition to the continued potential view, the idea that adult cognitive development is characterized by inevitable and universal decline

demand characteristics   subjects' interpretation of what is expected of them as research participants

dementia   progressive deterioration in intellectual functions such as thinking, reasoning, and remembering, which is severe enough to interfere with daily activities

demographic trends   changes in the characteristics of populations

dendrite   short, branching neural fiber that extends from the cell body of the neuron and that receives information from elsewhere in the nervous system

dependency ratio   the number of workers paying into the system compared with the number receiving benefits

dependent variable   the behavior measured at the conclusion of an experiment; the subjects' responses

depletion syndrome   a form of depression hypothesized to be more common among older individuals, characterized by pervasive feelings of worthlessness and a loss of interest in things

development   systematic changes in behavior over time that result from interaction between the individual and the internal and external environment

developmental era   a series of four 25-year segments of the life cycle in Levinson's model of development; each era has its own psychosocial qualities, though it contributes to and is integrated with the whole (the eras partly overlap)

developmental health psychology   the study of the interaction among age, behavior, and health

developmental period   substage of the major developmental era in Levinson's model, usually lasting about five years; stable (structure-building) periods alternate with transitional (structure-changing) periods

developmental psychology   the subfield of psychology concerned with the nature and direction of change associated with age

developmental reciprocities   the effects that developmental events in one individual's life have on others in the social network

developmental research   interested in whether and how people change over time; studies relationships between age and another variable

developmental task   an ability, skill, or responsibility that, if accomplished at the appropriate stage in life, contributes to future growth and happiness

diagnosis of exclusion   because there are no clinical tests that can confirm a diagnosis of Alzheimer's disease in a living patient, all other possible causes of the symptoms must be ruled out before a diagnosis of probable AD is reached

dialectical paradigm   synonym for *contextual model*

diathesis   a predisposition to developing a mental disorder

discontinuous work history   a characteristic of women's career development, in which work is interrupted by family responsibilities such as caring for children

discrimination   unfair treatment of an individual

disease   refers to the objective diagnosis of a particular disorder with a specific cause and characteristic symptoms

disengagement theory   a theory of social aging that maintains that successful aging consists of a process of mutual withdrawal between the aging individual and society in anticipation of death

disuse hypothesis   the idea that the poorer performance of older adults on some measures of cognitive ability is due to lack of use of the relevant skills—the "use it or lose it" idea

divergent thought   a kind of thinking in which alternative solutions or answers are sought

DNA-damage theories of aging   view aging as the result of damage to the DNA of somatic cells, which negatively affects protein manufacture

domestic violence   a pattern of physical, sexual, and/or psychological maltreatment used by one person in an intimate relationship to unfairly gain or maintain the misuse of power, control, and authority over another

dopamine   a neurotransmitter that affects frontal cortex functions—such as attention, processing speed, and working memory—also affects motor function

double-blind study   an experiment in which neither the subjects nor those interacting with the subjects know who has been assigned to the experimental and control groups

Dream   Levinson's term for a vision of the kind of life one wants to lead as an adult; the Dream facilitates separation from the family of origin and entrance into the adult world, providing purpose and direction

dual-earner/dual-career family   the predominant family form, in which both husband and wife work outside the home

durable power of attorney for health care   a legal document that details the individual's wishes in regard to health care decisions and identifies the person who will be delegated responsibility for these decisions

dyad   a relationship between two people who pay attention to or participate in each other's activities

early-onset Alzheimer's disease   a form of the disease that develops before age 60

early retirement   retirement prior to age 65

ecological experiments   also called experiments of nature; the natural environment is changed in order to investigate its effect on development

ecological transitions   Bronfenbrenner's term for changes in roles and the resultant changes in the settings in which one participates

ecological validity   refers to the relevance of laboratory-based research findings to explaining real-life behavior

ecology   the scientific study of organism-environment relationships

ecology of human development   Bronfenbrenner's term for the scientific study of the progressive, mutual accommodation between an active, growing human being and the changing properties of the immediate settings in which the developing person lives, as this process is affected by relations between these settings and by the larger contexts in which the settings are embedded

effortful operations   information-processing operations that require attention

egalitarian marriage   a relationship in which power and authority are shared equally by husband and wife; division of labor tends to be more equal as well

ego identity versus role confusion   in stage 5 in Erikson's theory of psychosocial development, the individual is challenged to develop an integrated sense of self, making commitments in regard to occupation, ideology, and sexual orientation and role

emerging adulthood   Arnett's conception of a transitional stage between adolescence and young adulthood in industrialized societies

emphysema   an obstructive disease in which air flow to the lungs is restricted, resulting in "oxygen hunger"

empty nest   refers to the home once children have grown and left

encoding   perceiving and comprehending information during information processing; transforming sensory information into a code that the information-processing system can handle

endocrine system   composed of the cells and tissues that produce hormones

epidemiology   the study of the incidence, distribution, and control of disease

epigenetic principle   basic to Erikson's theory of development; the personality develops as a composite of its parts, each of which emerges at a particular time in development, so that the parts give rise to the whole

episodic memory   memory for events experienced by the individual, stored with contextual information such as time and place

equilibration   Piaget's term for a state of cognitive harmony or balance

equity theory   a theory of social interaction that asserts that individuals strive to maintain relationships that are equitable or fair—that is, each person receives benefits from the relationship in proportion to contributions made to it

estrogen   the female sex hormone produced in the ovaries that influences as many as 300 body functions

ethnic subculture   groups that differ from the majority in race, national background, and/or shared cultural history and values

euthanasia   a term that literally means the good death

evolutionary hypothesis   the idea that males and females have developed different criteria for mate selection based on their reproductive capacity—females place more weight on characteristics associated with resource acquisition, while males place more weight on physical attractiveness

excess-disabilities syndrome   a condition in which individuals function at a level lower than that of which they are capable; often caused by overmedication

exchange orientation   an attitude toward close relationships that emphasizes comparability of benefits derived by each partner

exosystem   Bronfenbrenner's term for a part of the ecological environment made up of settings in which individuals do not participate but that influence the microsystems in which they do participate

experimental group   in an experiment, the group exposed to the independent variable

experimental study   a study in which the investigator creates an artificial situation to which subjects are exposed; their responses are recorded and attempts are made to determine causal relationships

expertise   the development of advanced skills and knowledge in a particularly well practiced activity

explicit memory   conscious recollection of previous experience

exploration   the seeking of information about the self and the external world and the active consideration of alternatives; a key developmental task in identity formation as well as career development

expressive role   the female gender role, emphasizing relationships with others

extended family   composed of the nuclear family and all others directly related to them: grandparents, aunts, uncles, and cousins; these people are known as kin

external locus of control   the belief that control over the events of one's life resides outside oneself

external validity   the extent to which research results can be generalized to groups, settings, and times other than those studied

extraneous variable   a factor other than the independent variable that could affect the outcome of an experiment; investigators try to control as many of these as possible

extraversion   according to McCrae and Costa, one of the five basic personality traits; refers to preferences for social interaction and social activity

familial Alzheimer's disease   runs in families and is believed to reflect a genetic predisposition

family development perspective   an approach to the study of the family that examines changes in the family unit from its formation to its dissolution

family developmental task   a responsibility that must be accomplished at a certain stage in the family life cycle in order for the family to successfully meet its obligations and promote future success of its members and itself

family life cycle model   maintains that families pass through predictable, universal stages in their development

family myth   family members' shared perception of the family's identity, the nature of the world, and the family's place in it

family of origin   the family of one's birth

family ripple effects   the ramifications of developmental change in one family member for other family members

felt capacity for generativity   a sense that one is able to carry out generative behavior

felt identity   identity as the person feels or experiences it

feminization of poverty   refers to the fact that poverty has become increasingly concentrated among women (and children)

fertility rate   the number of births per female

field   a real-life setting in which research is conducted

filial   refers to being a son or daughter, as in the term *filial role*

fluid intelligence   inherited ability to think and reason; basic information-processing capabilities

fluid life cycle   Neugarten's term for the fact that the traditional periods in the life cycle are beginning to break down, as rates of biological development and social definitions of age change and age norms weaken, resulting in a blurring of age divisions and the creation of new life periods

formal operations   the final stage in Piaget's model of cognitive development, characterized by abstract thought and a hypothetico-deductive approach to problem solving

free radical   a highly reactive molecule produced during oxygen metabolism

free radical theory of aging   argues that most aging changes are the result of damage from free radicals produced during oxygen metabolism

friendship   a voluntary association between equals who are high in similarity and whose primary orientation in the relationship is toward enjoyment and personal satisfaction

frontal lobe   the front portion of each cerebral hemisphere, involved in executive functions such as planning and decision making

functional age   actual competence and performance

functional magnetic resonance imaging (fMRI)   an advancement in magnetic resonance imaging that provides information about brain function

functional-specificity-of-relationships model   asserts that different social relationships in an individual's life tend to meet particular kinds of needs and serve different purposes

gender   the sociocultural aspects of being a female or male, as distinct from the biological aspects

gender identity   one's concept of self as either male or female

gender role   society's description of appropriately masculine or feminine characteristics and behaviors; the expressive and instrumental roles

gender splitting   Levinson's term to refer to the rigid division between male and female, feminine and masculine, that pervades all aspects of human life

generalized other   Mead's concept that we begin to take the perspective of other people in judging ourselves, incorporating their standards into our sense of who we are

generalized slowing hypothesis   the idea that all information-processing activities slow with age, affecting both quality and quantity of cognitive abilities

generational acceleration   a shortening of the age distance between generations

generative accomplishment   a sense of having achieved a generative goal

generative desires   the wish to be productive and to make a contribution to society

generativity   Erikson's term for a concern for future generations and the kind of legacy one will leave behind; stage 7 in his theory of psychosocial development

gerontology   scientific study of aging

glass ceiling   structural, though invisible, barriers that keep women out of top management positions

global self-esteem   an overall sense of self-worth, based on the synthesis of separate self-esteems in specific areas of our lives (such as academic self-esteem, social self-esteem, and so on)

glucocorticoids   chemicals secreted by the adrenal cortex during stress that suppress immune function

grief   the emotional suffering caused by a significant loss, as in the death of a loved one

health   the absence of disease; more broadly, a state of complete physical, mental, and social well-being

hierarchy of importance   George's idea that some aspects of the self-concept are more central and critical to the sense of self than others; these are core qualities

hierarchy of pervasiveness   George's notion that some self-conceptions are so central to our sense of who we are that they affect every aspect of our lives; others are less influential

high-grief death   a death that is accidental, sudden, or involves a younger person and causes a more severe grief response than usual

hippocampus   a finger-shaped structure in the limbic system that is involved in memory

homogamy   similarity; one of the criteria in mate selection

homunculus   a preformed being

hormone replacement therapy (HRT)   a treatment for the symptoms of menopause that involves supplementing estrogen and progesterone

hospice   an alternative concept of care for terminally ill patients and their families

human factors   the research field that makes use of what is known about cognitive, perceptual, and motor behaviors to design safer and more efficient tools and environments

human wealth span   a concept from financial gerontology, based on the idea that events earlier in life affect how we live in later years; composed of the accumulation and expenditure/retirement phases

hypokinesia   degeneration and functional loss of muscle and bone tissue due to disease

hypothesis   a tentative explanation of behavior

identity   Erikson's term for a sense of who one is, what one believes in, and where one is headed in life

identity achievement   the most mature of Marcia's identity statuses; refers to an individual who has made self-chosen commitments in the areas critical to identity formation

identity diffusion   an individual who is not in a state of identity crisis and has made no identity-related commitments; the least mature of Marcia's statuses

identity foreclosure   Marcia's term for an individual who has made commitments chosen by others

identity moratorium   Marcia's term for an individual currently in a state of identity crisis and unable to make the necessary commitments

identity status   Marcia's model of a style of coping with the crisis of identity formation

illness   the existence of disease, along with the individual's subjective perception of and response to the disease

immune system   composed of the thymus, bone marrow, spleen, and lymph nodes, the immune system protects us from infection by identifying and destroying foreign organisms

immune theory of aging   cites programmed changes in the immune system as a cause of reduced resistance to infection and increased incidence of autoimmune disorders with age

immunosuppression   refers to conditions that inhibit activity in the immune system, thereby increasing susceptibility to illness (for example, the secretion of glucocorticoids during stress)

implicit memory   unintentional, nonconscious recollection

independent variable   in an experiment, the variable that the experimenter manipulates to determine its effect

individualist culture   a culture in which individuals define themselves as separate from the group, place personal goals above group goals, and feel less attachment to and concern for the group than in collectivist cultures

individuation   Jung's term for a process of self-discovery and self-development, marked by increasing introspection and the integration of polarities within the self, which begins about age 40

information-loss model   the idea of Myerson and associates that cognitive processes slow with age as a result of cumulative and accelerating loss of information at each processing step

information-processing theory   a collection of concepts that attempts to explain what the mind does with information

instrumental activities of daily living (IADLs)   in addition to fundamental activities of daily living (ADLs), these are tasks that have to do with carrying out the business of daily life—shopping, housework, getting around in the community, and so forth

instrumental role   the male gender role, emphasizing independent achievement

intelligence   the mental activity involved in successful adaptation to the changing demands of the environment

intergenerational relationships   relationships between individuals in different generations, as between parent and child or grandparent and grandchild

intergenerational transmission of violence   the idea that a cycle of family violence is learned and passed down from one generation to another

internal locus of control   the belief that control over the events of one's life resides within the self

internal validity   in an experiment, the extent to which the results are likely to be due to the independent variable

interobserver reliability   refers to the consistency in the ratings of two or more observers

intimacy   a component of companionate love, according to Sternberg, referring to sharing, warmth, and closeness

I-self   James's term for the part of the self that actually knows and experiences things: the knower; also called the phenomenal self, it constructs the Me-self

job   connotes work limited in upward mobility and in which movement is primarily horizontal

kinkeeper   the role of maintaining ties with family members, normally adopted by females

labor-force participation rate   the percentage of those of working age who are actually working or actively looking for work

late-onset Alzheimer's disease   a form of the disease that develops after age 60

leaving home   a psychological transition in which one finishes the developmental tasks of adolescence, establishes an identity, and begins to make the choices and commitments expected of adults

leisure   time to do things one is not obligated to do and that are done for pleasure

levels-of-processing model   Craik and Lockhart's hypothesis that memory is affected by the quality and extent of processing the individual engages in during encoding; semantic processing (processing at the level of meaning) is considered to be a deeper and more powerful level

life expectancy   see *average life expectancy*

life review   Butler's term for a normal and universal period of purposeful reminiscence prompted by impending death; the life review may enable the person to integrate life experiences into a meaningful whole, leading to resolution of conflict and acceptance

life span   a theoretical construct that refers to the genetically based upper limit to life

life-span development   the scientific study of age-related changes in behavior

life-span developmental perspective   views development as an ongoing process from conception to death; concerned with change over time and the influence of genetic, biological, historical, and environmental factors

life structure   Levinson's term for the overall pattern or design of a person's life, usually composed of two major areas of choice and commitment

living will   a legal document that states an individual's wishes in regard to the use of life-prolonging technology

locus of control   refers to expectations about the ability to control the events and circumstances of one's life

longevity revolution   Butler's term for the 25-year gain in average life expectancy during the 20th century

longitudinal study   data are collected on one group of same-age subjects over a long period of time to detect age-related changes

long-term memory   the unlimited-capacity, permanent-storage component of the human memory system

looking glass self   Cooley's idea that our sense of self is largely derived from our evaluation of feedback received from others, as if they served as a social mirror

low-grief death   a death that comes after a long illness or involves an elderly person and that causes a less severe grief response than usual

macrosystem   Bronfenbrenner's term for a part of the ecological environment composed of the beliefs and values that govern how social groups are organized

macular degeneration   an age-related blinding disease that affects the small center of the retina called the macula

major depression   a depressed mood or the loss of interest in all or almost all activities of life, along with associated symptoms that occur together and persist for at least two weeks; in general, the individual feels helpless, hopeless, worthless, and exhausted and experiences changes in sleeping and eating patterns and the ability to carry out normal activities

matching hypothesis   the idea that people are more likely to develop relationships with those whose physical attractiveness is similar to their own

means test   income criteria that would determine eligibility to receive retirement benefits; Social Security is not means tested but is a system of earned income based on contributions, regardless of need

mechanics of intelligence   according to Baltes and associates, the cognitive processes and structures that form the basic architecture of information processing and problem solving

mechanistic model of development   views the individual as a tabula rasa, passively reacting to environmental influences; takes the nurture side of the nature-nurture debate

melatonin   a hormone produced by the pineal gland; a decline or change in production with age may contribute to sleep disorders among older adults

menopause   the permanent cessation of menstruation and resulting loss of fertility

mental flexibility   the capacity to use a variety of approaches and perspectives, resulting in alternative solutions to cognitive problems

mentor   an individual who is usually older and more experienced in one's field of work and who facilitates one's career progress

Me-self   synonymous with the self-concept, James's term for what is known about the self

mesosystem   Bronfenbrenner's term for a level of the ecological environment composed of relationships among settings in which the individual participates

metabolic theories of aging   focus on the relationship between metabolic rate and longevity; overly simplistic in original form, newer versions focus on damage to mitochondria

microsystem   Bronfenbrenner's term for the innermost level of the nested structures that make up the ecological environment—the immediate setting containing the developing person and the objects and people with whom the individual interacts

midcourse   an emerging life stage from 50 to 75 characterized by expanding options for productive activity

middle-generation squeeze   the competing demands of filial and parental roles experienced by middle-age family members

midlife transition   a major period of reassessment postulated by Levinson and others to occur around age 40 and precipitated by an increased awareness of mortality; one of the most controversial aspects of his model

miniature adult   the view of the child as smaller in physical size but in no other way different from an adult

minor depression   significant symptoms of depression that fail to meet the diagnostic criteria for major depression

mitochondria   components of the cell that produce energy needed for cell function

mommy track   a level of restricted career development reserved for women who choose to combine work and family roles, and for whom their career is not primary

naturalistic observation (field method)   describes the behavior of real-life subjects in a natural setting without intervention by the researcher

need for affiliation   an innate desire to seek interpersonal relationships; varies in strength among individuals

negative correlation   indicates that two factors are inversely related

neo-Freudian   literally, new Freudians; followers of Sigmund Freud who have expanded his theory of psychoanalysis

nerve growth factor   a chemical substance produced in the brain that may regulate the sprouting of nerve fibers

neuroendocrine theories of aging   focus on degeneration of the endocrine system and the hypothalamus as a cause of aging

neuron   a nerve cell

neuronal reserve capacity   the hypothesis that education early in life may increase the number and strength of synapses in the brain, thus providing a reserve supply that may help to offset neuronal loss with aging

neuroticism   one of the five traits in McCrae and Costa's model of personality development, it has to do with how likely an individual is to experience unpleasant, disturbing emotions and their corresponding thoughts and actions

neurotrophins   a family of proteins, including nerve growth factor, that may facilitate the growth and regeneration of neural tissue

niche picking   a model of gene-environment interaction in which people seek out and prefer environments, activities, and relationships compatible with their genetic predispositions

nonadherence   failure to take medication as prescribed

nondevelopmental research   looks for relationships among non-age-related variables

nonnormative influence   experiences unique to the individual, not the norm, not predictable

normative age-graded influence   predictable experiences that happen universally and are closely tied to age

normative history-graded influence   experiences shared by people because they are alive during a particular period

novice phase   in Levinson's theory of male adult development, a period between about ages 17 and 33, during which the individual enters the adult world

nuclear family   a family unit consisting of parents and young children

occupation   a general term referring to all types of paid employment

occupational segregation   the concentration of women in occupations traditionally defined as feminine, in which few males are found, and that offer lower pay and other economic benefits

off-time event   a life event that happens either earlier or later than normally expected; more stressful than on-time events

old-old   Neugarten's term referring to those older individuals who are frail and dependent

omission error   failure to respond to a test item

on-time event   a life event that happens at about the expected time in the life cycle; less stressful than off-time events

openness   one of McCrae and Costa's personality traits; refers to an individual's receptiveness to new ideas and experiences

organismic model of development   a view that stresses the natural unfolding of behavior according to a genetic blueprint; stresses the nature side of the nature-nurture debate

osteoarthritis   degenerative joint disease, the most common form of arthritis

osteoporosis   an age-related, pathological decrease in bone mass and strength, more common in women, especially after menopause

parental generativity   Kotre's term for generative acts involving the raising and guiding of children

passionate love   characterized by intense emotion, sexual feeling, and complete absorption in the other

passive elements of mate selection   aspects of mate selection resulting from educational, social, and geographic propinquity; these elements operate to weed out potential mates without the individual's active participation

passive euthanasia   a situation in which death is not actively prevented

performance   in comparison to competence, what one actually does in a given assessment situation

phenomenal self   equivalent to the I-self, the part of the self that actually experiences things subjectively

phenomenology   the view that one must understand reality as it is subjectively perceived by the individual

phonological loop   a term proposed by Baddeley and Hitch to refer to the component of working memory that temporarily stores speech-based information

placebo   a pharmaceutically inactive substance

plaques   deposits of waste material from the degenerating neuron around a core of beta-amyloid protein; characteristic of Alzheimer's disease

plasticity within-person modifiability—the idea that an individual's development is modifiable, within limits, based on one's life conditions and experiences; in regard to the brain, its capacity to modify its structure and function in response to damage

polypharmacy the use of multiple medications

portable pension benefits pension benefits that follow employees when they change jobs—most pension benefits are not portable

positive cohort trend the finding that later-born individuals perform at a higher level than did earlier-born individuals at the same age

positive correlation indicates that the variables are directly related; as one increases (or decreases), the other increases (or decreases)

positive psychology an approach that emphasizes the scientific study of positive subjective experience, positive individual traits, and positive social institutions

postformal thought a stage of thought hypothesized to develop after formal operations and that represents a qualitative change in adult cognition

pragmatics of intelligence according to Baltes and associates, the ability to apply knowledge of facts and procedures appropriately in a variety of contexts

predictive validity refers to how well test performance predicts actual performance in real life

prejudice prejudgment of or bias toward an individual or group

presbycusis decreased sensitivity to high-frequency sounds, characteristic of older hearing, especially among men

presbyopia difficulty in focusing on objects at close visual range; farsightedness

primary aging the normal age-related changes that are intrinsic, inevitable, progressive, deleterious, irreversible, and universal

primary prevention focuses on preventing or delaying the development of a disease or condition

principle of encoding specificity the idea that the nature of the task determines the best encoding strategy

procedural memory the effect of past experience on present performance; skill memory

programmed theories of aging argue that aging is the result of a built-in genetic program

propinquity physical proximity or closeness

prospective memory remembering to perform an action in the future

protective factors variables that increase an individual's resistance to risk factors and therefore disorders

PsychLit a computerized database listing psychological books and articles

psychoanalysis a theory of psychology developed by Sigmund Freud, emphasizing stages of psychosexual development and the importance of early experience; also refers to a type of therapy based on the theory

psychological stress a negative state in which an individual feels that the demands of the environment exceed the ability to cope

psychological trait according to McCrae and Costa, a dimension of individual differences in tendencies to show consistent patterns of thoughts, feelings, and actions

psychology the scientific study of behavior and mental processes

psychometric approach an approach to the study of cognitive development that utilizes standardized tests to describe cognitive performance

psychometrics the field that attempts to develop valid and reliable measures of psychological traits

psychoneuroimmunology refers to the interactions between the mind, the nervous system, the endocrine system, and the immune system

psychosocial crisis in Erikson's theory, a turning point in development, when there is heightened vulnerability but also opportunity for growth (Erikson described eight crises in the life cycle)

qualitative change change in the form or structure of an attribute

quantitative change variations in the amount of an attribute

quasi- or natural experiments studies of groups to whom events of interest have occurred naturally and could not be ethically induced

racial mortality crossover effect refers to the fact that at about age 80, Black life expectancy exceeds that of Whites

redundancy refers to functional duplication in the brain, with many sets of neurons responsible for similar tasks

relationship orientation the general attitude a person holds toward the exchange of resources in close relationships, either communal or exchange

relative risk describes the rate of a particular disease among those who have the risk factor(s) versus those who do not

reliability the extent to which consistent results are obtained

remarried family a family in which the husband, wife, or both are in a second or subsequent marriage

remediation in reference to strategies of successful cognitive aging, intervention to restore abilities to a previous level

repeated-exposure effect the idea that we develop increasingly positive feelings toward any neutral or mildly positive stimulus after multiple contacts

repulsion hypothesis the idea that dissimilarity leads to avoidance of social interaction

research design the way a research project is set up and organized

resilience the capacity to maintain healthy levels of psychological and physical functioning despite experiencing adverse events

retirement incentive program (RIP) a package of economic benefits offered to employees if they retire early and within a specified period

retrieval finding and activating a stored memory

risk factor a biological or behavioral characteristic that increases the likelihood that an individual will develop a particular disease

role context perspective   a complex view of multiple roles that stresses the effect of the quality of an individual's roles, their reciprocal interaction, and the individual's subjective assessment of them for a sense of well-being

role enhancement/role expansion perspective   a view of multiple roles that emphasizes the advantages of occupying various positions concurrently

role strain perspective   a view of multiple roles that holds that occupying a variety of roles may lead to difficulty in meeting role demands, resulting in stress or overload

rumination   a style of coping with depression characterized by thoughts and feelings that focus one's attention on the symptoms of distress and their meanings and consequences

schema   Piaget's term for a cognitive concept, a unit of knowledge

secondary aging   age-related declines due to extrinsic factors, such as disease

secondary prevention   aimed at early diagnosis and early treatment to cure or prevent the progression of a disease or condition

secure attachment   infants who are securely attached have experienced sensitive and responsive caregiving and are generally happy, secure, exploratory, and comforted by the caregiver; the norm in our society

selective optimization with compensation   Baltes and associates' view that successful cognitive aging involves maximizing cognitive strengths while developing compensatory skills to shore up weaknesses

self   consists of all the knowledge, feelings, and attitudes we have about our own being as unique, functioning individuals

self-concept   our knowledge about ourselves; synonymous with Me-self

self-efficacy   our beliefs and expectations about whether we have the ability to successfully complete a particular task

self-esteem   refers to feelings we have toward ourselves—an evaluation of self-worth; those with high self-esteem have assessed the self and find it to have value

self-reference effect   information seen as pertinent to the self is processed and retained more efficiently

self-report method   research that relies on the subjects' responses to questions about beliefs, experiences, and behaviors

self-schema   a theory or concept of the self; a concept based on information-processing theory

semantic memory   general knowledge of facts and vocabulary

senile miosis   a reduction in the size of the pupil with age

sequential design   newer and complex designs that attempt to combine the strengths and minimize the weaknesses of traditional developmental research approaches

sex   refers to the biological, as opposed to the sociocultural, aspects of being female or male

shadow grief   grief that is never totally resolved—for example, the grief over the death of a child

short-term memory   a component of the memory system characterized by limited duration, capacity, and resulting rapid turnover; a holding system for information as it is processed for long-term memory

siblings   individuals who share common biological parents

sociable system   an innate behavioral system that motivates us to seek and maintain relationships with peers because of the survival value in doing so

social age clock   Neugarten's term for an internalized social calendar, which tells us when in our lives we should be doing what

social cognition   refers to knowledge we hold about other people, how they function, how to interact with them, and so on

social desirability bias   bias introduced into self-report data because of subjects' tendency to want to portray themselves in the best possible light

social network   the web of relationships one has with others

social role   a set of activities and relations expected of an individual who occupies a particular social position, and of others in relation to the individual

Social Security   a federal system of earned income that provides retirement and other benefits based on years of employment

social support   the quality of social relationships, which includes comfort, assistance, and emotional closeness and warmth, and which contributes to a positive self-concept, higher self-esteem, and greater self-efficacy

socioemotional selectivity theory   the idea that social networks become increasingly selective over time as we attempt to maximize social and emotional gains and minimize social and emotional risks

somatic mutation theories of aging   view aging as the result of mutations in the DNA of somatic cells, which negatively affect protein manufacture

special woman   according to Levinson, a unique and important relationship in which a woman supports a young man's Dream and assists his pursuit of it

sporadic Alzheimer's disease   cases in which the patient has no family history of the disease

sprouting   the growth of new dendritic or axonic fibers of neurons

stage theory   the notion that all of us, at about the same time in our lives, experience the same events, problems, or challenges; emphasizes universal sequences of change

stepfamily   a remarried family that includes children under age 18 in the home who were born before the remarriage occurred

stereotyping   thinking of all members of a group as if they were alike

stochastic theories of aging   argue that aging is the result of the accumulated damage wrought by random events of living

storage   maintaining information over time

structural lag   the tendency for social change to occur more rapidly than social norms and structures can adjust to it, resulting in a poor fit between the reality of individuals' lives and the institutions of society

subjective age   the age that one feels psychologically

successful aging   in the biological sense, refers to individuals with minimal physiological losses across a range of functions as compared to younger individuals

successive-hurdles principle   the idea that potential mates are progressively filtered out by successive criteria (also called filters or screens)

superoxide dismutase   an enzyme produced by the body that neutralizes free radicals

swan-song phenomenon   Simonton's term for the change in the nature of musical creations produced late in life by classical composers; also known as last-works effect

synapse   the small, fluid-filled space between two neurons or between a neuron and a muscle or gland

synergistic effects   the interactive effect achieved when drugs are combined as opposed to taken singly

tabula rasa   literally, blank slate or blank tablet; the view of the human mind as empty at birth, to be written on by experience (an extreme environmental position in the nature-versus-nurture debate)

tangles   the twisting of nerve fibers in a degenerating neuron; one of the hallmarks of Alzheimer's disease

technical generativity   Kotre's term for acts of generativity that involve the teaching of skills to younger individuals

terminal drop   the rapid decline in performance on measures of cognitive ability in the period before death

tertiary prevention   services provided after a diagnosis of a serious disease or condition, aimed at restoring function and limiting further disability

test-retest reliability   the extent to which a subject receives comparable scores when retested

thanatology   the study of death and related issues

thymosin   a hormone secreted by the thymus gland, important to the functioning of the immune system

thymus   an endocrine gland, one of the principal components of the immune system; secretes thymosin

time-lag study   same-age groups are observed at different historical times

time-of-measurement effect   an influence at work in the environment between and during the times behavior is measured and that can change it

traditional family structure   a hierarchical family structure in which more power and status are assigned to males and older family members. These families include an extensive kinship system and place high value on respect, obligation, and intergenerational ties; common among Asians, Hispanics, and some European Catholic immigrant families.

traditional marriage   a relationship in which the husband holds greater status, power, and authority; the wife defers to him in important decisions; division of labor tends to follow stereotyped gender roles

traditional marriage enterprise   Levinson's term for a marriage structure characterized by a clear division between the roles of female homemaker and male provisioner

traditional population pyramid   a population structure characterized by larger numbers of younger than older people

trait   see *psychological trait*

transforming experiment   an experiment that changes the macrosystem and therefore has the potential for changing the behavior of those within the social group in significant ways

transgenerational design   the concept that products and environments should be designed to accommodate the widest possible range of needs and abilities of users, regardless of age

traumatic bonding   the strong ties of affection and dependency forged by a victim toward his or her abuser

unanticipated death   death that is unexpected, such as that due to an accident

validity   the extent to which a study examined what the investigator meant to examine; the quality of the study

vested   entitled to draw retirement benefits from a pension plan; usually requires that an employee be in the job for 10 years

visual acuity   the ability to see detail clearly

visuospatial sketchpad   the term used by Baddeley and Hitch to refer to a component of working memory that temporarily stores visual and spatial information

vital capacity   the total amount of air that can be forced into or out of the lungs

vocation   a general term referring to all forms of paid employment

wage gap   the difference between male and female earnings

widow   a woman whose husband has died

widower   a man whose wife has died

widowhood   loss of a spouse through death

wisdom   expertise in the conduct and meaning of life

working memory   a place in the human memory system where current mental activity occurs—characterized by limited resources and consisting of the central executive, the phenological loop, and the visuospatial sketchpad

working model   inner mental representations of self, other, and the nature of relationships that develop as a result of attachment experience

young-old   Neugarten's term for older adults who remain healthy and active, more in line with the stereotypical behavior of late middle age; the majority of older adults currently fit this definition, in contrast to the old-old

References

Abel, E. (1991). *Who cares for the elderly: Public policy and experiences of adult daughters.* Philadelphia: Temple University Press.

Aber, J. L., & Cicchetti, D. (1984). The socio-emotional development of maltreated children: An empirical and theoretical analysis. In H. Fitzgerald, B. Lester, & M. Yogman (Eds.), *Theory and research in behavioral pediatrics* (Vol. 2, pp. 147–199). New York: Plenum.

Abramson, T. A., Trejo, L., & Lai, D. W. (2002). Culture and mental health: Providing appropriate services for a diverse older population. *Generations, 26,* 21–27.

Achenbaum, W. A., & Levin, J. S. (1989). What does gerontology mean? *Gerontologist, 29,* 393–399.

Adamchak, D. J. (1993). Demographic aging in the industrialized world: A rising burden? *Generations, 17*(4), 6–9.

Adams, B. (1967). Interaction theory and the social network. *Sociometry, 30,* 64–78.

Adams, J. S. (1965). Inequity in social exchange. In L. Berkowitz (Ed.), *Advances in experimental social psychology* (Vol. 2, pp. 267–299). New York: Academic Press.

Addis, M. E., & Mahalik, J. R. (2003). Men, masculinity, and the contexts of help seeking. *American Psychologist, 58*(1), 5–14.

Adelman, C. (1991). *Women at thirtysomething: Paradoxes of attainment.* Washington, DC: U.S. Government Printing Office.

Adelson, B. (1984). When novices surpass experts: The difficulty of a task may increase with expertise. *Journal of Experimental Psychology: Learning, Memory, and Cognition, 10,* 483–495.

Adler, J., Springen, K., Glick, D., & Gordon, J. (1991, June 24). What do men really want? *Newsweek,* pp. 46–51.

Adler, N. E., Boyce, T., Chesney, M. A., Cohen, S., Folkman, S., Kahn, R. L., & Syme, S. L. (1994). Socioeconomic status and health: The challenge of the gradient. *American Psychologist, 49,* 15–24.

Adler, N., & Matthews, K. (1994). Health psychology: Why do some people get sick and some stay well? *Annual Review of Psychology, 45,* 229–259.

Adler, T. (1991, July). Memory researcher wins Troland Award. *APA Monitor,* p. 12.

Ahmed, I., & Takeshita, J. (1997). Late-life depression. *Generations, 20*(4), 17–21.

Ainsworth, M. D. S. (1989). Attachments beyond infancy. *American Psychologist, 44,* 709–716.

Ainsworth, M. D. S., Blehar, M. C., Waters, E., & Wall, S. (1978). *Patterns of attachment: A psychological study of the strange situation.* Hillsdale, NJ: Erlbaum.

Aizenberg, R., & Treas, J. (1985). The family in later life: Psychosocial and demographic considerations. In J. E. Birren & K. W. Schaie (Eds.), *Handbook of the psychology of aging* (2nd ed., pp. 169–189). New York: Van Nostrand Reinhold.

Albert, M. S. (1989). Assessment of cognitive dysfunction. In M. S. Albert & M. B. Moss (Eds.), *Geriatric neuropsychology* (pp. 57–81). New York: Guilford Press.

Albert, M S., Jones, K., Savage, C. R., Berkman, L., Seeman, T., Blazer, D., & Rowe, J. W. (1995). Predictors of cognitive change in older persons: MacArthur studies of successful aging. *Psychology and Aging, 10*(4), 578–589.

Albrecht, T. L., & Adelman, M. B. (1987). *Communicating social support.* Newbury Park, CA: Sage.

Aldous, J. (1978). *Family careers.* New York: Wiley.

Aldous, J. (1990). Family development and the life course: Two perspectives on family change. *Journal of Marriage and the Family, 52,* 571–583.

Aldwin, C. M. (1995). The role of stress in aging and adult development. *Adult Development and Aging News, 23*(2), 3, 7, 16. (Newsletter of Division 20, American Psychological Association, available from Roger W. Morrell, Newsletter Editor, University of Michigan, Ann Arbor, MI 48109-2007.)

Alecxih, L. (2001). The impact of sociodemographic change on the future of long-term care. *Generations, 25*(1), 7–11.

Alexander, G. E., Furey, M. L., Grady, C. L., Pietrini, P., Brady, D. R., Mentis, M. J., & Schapiro, M. B. (1997). Association of premorbid intellectual function with cerebral metabolism in Alzheimer's disease: Implications for the cognitive reserve hypothesis. *American Journal of Psychiatry, 154*(2), 165–172.

Allport, G. (1955). *Becoming.* New Haven, CT: Yale University Press.

Alzheimer's Association. (2004, October 5). Americans as afraid of caring for a loved one with Alzheimer's as they are of getting Alzheimer's: New report reveals tremendous burden on Alzheimer caregivers. Retrieved October 12, 2004, from www.alz.org/Media/newsreleases/2004/100404_caregiver.asp.

Amabile, T. M. (1996). *Creativity in context.* Boulder, CO: Westview Press.

Amato, P., & Booth, A. (1997). *A generation at risk: Growing up in an era of family upheaval.* Cambridge, MA: Harvard University Press.

American Association of University Women. (1991). *Shortchanging girls, shortchanging America.* Washington, DC: Greenberg-Lake Analysis Group.

American Cancer Society. (2004). *Cancer facts and figures, 2003.* Retrieved from www.cancer.org/downloads/STT/CAFF2003pwsecured.pdf.

American Heart Association. (2004). 2004 heart disease and stroke statistics. Retrieved from www.americanheart.org.

American Heart Association. (1997a). *Heart and stroke facts.* (Available from the American Heart Association National Center, 7272 Greenville Avenue, Dallas, TX 75231-4596.)

American Heart Association. (1997b). *1997 heart and stroke statistical update.* (Available from the American Heart Association National Center, 7272 Greenville Avenue, Dallas, TX 75231-4596.)

American Psychiatric Association. (1987). *Diagnostic and statistical manual of mental disorders* (3rd ed., rev.). Washington, DC: Author.

American Psychiatric Association. (1994). *Diagnostic and statistical manual of mental disorders* (4th ed.). Washington, DC: Author.

American Psychological Association. (1994). *Publication manual of the American Psychological Association* (4th ed.). Washington, DC: Author.

American Psychological Association. (1996). *APA presidential task force on violence and the family report.* Washington, DC: Author.

American Psychological Association. (2004a). Guidelines for psychological practice with older adults. *American Psychologist, 59*(4), 236–260.

American Psychological Association. (2004b, May). APA poll: Most Americans have sought mental health treatment but cost, insurance still barriers. Retrieved from www.apa.org/releases/practicepoll_o4.html.

Ames, K. (1991, August 26). Last rights. *Newsweek,* pp. 40–41.

Amster, L E., & Krass, H. H. (1974). The relationships between life crises and mental deterioration in old age. *International Journal of Aging and Human Development, 5,* 51–55.

Andersen, B. L., Kiecolt-Glaser, J. K., & Glaser, R. (1994). A biobehavioral model of cancer stress and disease course. *American Psychologist, 49*(5), 389–404.

Andersen, M. L. (1988). *Thinking about women* (2nd ed.). New York: Macmillan.

Anderson, D., & Palmore, E. (1974). Longitudinal evaluation of ocular function. In E. Palmore (Ed.), *Normal aging: II. Reports from the Duke Longitudinal Studies, 1970–1973* (pp. 166–230). London: Butterworth.

Anderson, H., Borger, G., Hager, M., & Fineman, H. (1983, January 24). The Social Security crisis. *Newsweek,* pp. 18–28.

Anderson, J. R. (1993). Problem solving and learning. *American Psychologist, 48,* 35–44.

Anderson, T. B. (1984). Widowhood as a life transition: Its impact on kinship ties. *Journal of Marriage and the Family, 46,* 105–114.

Andres, R., & Hallfrisch, J. (1989). Nutrition intake recommendations needed for the older American. *Journal of the American Dietetic Association, 89,* 1739–1741.

Angier, N. (1994, March 8). How estrogen may work to protect against Alzheimer's. *New York Times,* pp. B6(N), C3(L).

Anthony, J. C., & Aboraya, A. (1992). The epidemiology of selected mental disorders in later life. In J. E. Birren, R. B. Sloane, & G. D. Cohen (Eds.), *Handbook of mental health and aging* (2nd ed.). San Diego, CA: Academic Press.

Antonovsky, A. (1987). *Unraveling the mystery of health: How people manage stress and stay well.* San Francisco: Jossey-Bass.

Antonucci, T. C. (1986). Hierarchical mapping techniques. *Generations, 10*(4), 10–12.

Antonucci, T. C. (1989). Understanding adult social relationships. In K. Kreppner & R. M. Lerner (Eds.), *Family systems and life-span development* (pp. 303–317). Hillsdale, NJ: Erlbaum.

Antonucci, T. C., & Akiyama, H. (1991, Winter). Social relationships and aging well. *Generations, 15,* 39–44.

Antonucci, T. C., & Akiyama, H. (1995). Convoys of social relations: Family and friendships within a life span context. In R. Blieszner & V. H. Bedford (Eds.), *Handbook of aging and the family* (pp. 355–371). Westport, CT: Greenwood Press.

Antonucci, T. C., & Jackson, J. (1983). Physical health and self-esteem. *Family and Community Health, 6,* 1–9.

Antonucci, T. C., & Jackson, J. (1987). Social support, interpersonal efficacy, and health: A life course perspective. In L. L. Carstensen & B. A. Edelstein (Eds.), *Handbook of clinical gerontology* (pp. 291–311). Elmsford, NY: Pergamon Press.

Antonucci, T. C., & Jackson, J. S. (1990). The role of reciprocity in social support. In I. G. Sarason, B. R. Sarason, & G. R. Pierce (Eds.), *Social support: An interactional view* (pp. 173–189). New York: Wiley.

Aquilino, W. S. (1990). The likelihood of parent-adult child coresidence: Effects of family structure and parental characteristics. *Journal of Marriage and the Family, 52,* 405–419.

Aquilino, W. S. (1991). Parent-child relations and parents' satisfaction with living arrangements when adult children live at home. *Journal of Marriage and the Family, 53,* 13–27.

Arbuckle, T. Y., Maag, U., Pushkar, D., & Chaikelson, J. S. (1998). Individual differences in trajectory of intellectual development over 45 years of adulthood. *Psychology and Aging, 13*(4), 663–675.

Arbuckle, T., Gold, D., Andres, D., Schwartzman, A., & Chaikelson, J. (1992). The role of psychosocial context, age, and intelligence in memory performance of older men. *Psychology and Aging, 7,* 25–36.

Archbold, P. G. (1983). Impact of parent-caring on women. *Family Relations, 32,* 39–45.

Archer, J. (1996). Sex differences in social behavior: Are the social role and evolutionary explanations compatible? *American Psychologist, 51*(9), 909–917.

Aries, E., & Moorehead, K. (1989). The importance of ethnicity in the development of identity of black adolescents. *Psychological Reports, 65,* 75–82.

Aries, P. (1981). *The hour of our death.* New York: Knopf.

Arking, R. (1991). *Biology of aging: Observations and principles.* Englewood Cliffs, NJ: Prentice Hall.

Arlin, P. K. (1984). Adolescent and adult thought: A structural interpretation. In M. Commons, F. Richards, & C. Armom (Eds.), *Beyond formal operations: Late adolescent and adult cognitive development* (pp. 258–271). New York: Praeger.

Arluke, A., & Levin, J. (1984, August–September). Another stereotype: Old age as a second childhood. *Aging, 7*–11.

Arnett, J. J. (2000). Emerging adulthood: A theory of development from the late teens through the twenties. *American Psychologist, 55* (5), 469–480.

Arnetz, B. B., Theorell, T., Levi, L., Kallner, A., & Eneroth, P. (1983). An experimental study of social isolation of elderly people: Psychoendocrine and metabolic effects. *Psychosomatic Medicine, 45,* 395–406.

Aron, A., & Aron, E. N. (1986). *Love and the expansion of self: Understanding attraction and satisfaction.* New York: Hemisphere/Harper & Row.

Aron, A., Dutton, D. G., Aron, E. N., & Iverson, A. (1989). Experiences of falling in love. *Journal of Social and Personal Relationships, 6,* 243–257.

Arond, M. (1991). *First year of marriage: What to expect, what to accept, and what you can change.* New York: Warner Books.

Ashcraft, M. (1989). *Human memory and cognition.* Glenview, IL: Scott, Foresman.

Atchley, R. (1976). *The sociology of retirement.* New York: Schenkman.

Atchley, R. (1980). *The social forces in later life* (3rd ed.). Belmont, CA: Wadsworth.

Atchley, R. (1982). The aging self. *Psychotherapy: Theory, Research, and Practice, 19,* 388–396.

Atchley, R. (1988). *Social forces and aging: An introduction to social gerontology.* Belmont, CA: Wadsworth.

Atchley, R., Pignatiello, L., & Shaw, E. (1975). *The effect of marital status on social interaction patterns of older women.* Oxford, OH: Scripps Foundation.

Atkinson, R. (1987). The development of purpose in adolescence: Insights from the narrative approach. *Adolescent Psychiatry, 14,* 149–161.

Atkinson, R., & Shiffrin, R. (1968). Human memory: A proposed system and its control processes. In K. W. Spence & J. T. Spence (Eds.), *The psychology of learning and motivation* (Vol. 2, pp. 89–195). New York: Academic Press.

Attneave, C. (1982). American Indians and Alaska Native families: Emigrants in their own homeland. In M. McGoldrick, J. Pearce, & J. Giordano (Eds.), *Ethnicity and family therapy* (pp. 55–83). New York: Guilford Press.

Avolio, B., & Waldman, D. (1990). An examination of age and cognitive test performance across job complexity and occupational types. *Journal of Applied Psychology, 75,* 43–50.

Azar, B. (2000, July/August). A new stress paradigm for women. *Monitor on Psychology,* 42–43.

Azar, B. (2001, December). Blueberries + exercise = healthy minds? *Monitor on Psychology,* (pp. 26–28). Washington, DC: American Psychological Association.

Backman, L., Small, B. J., Wahlin, A., & Larsson, M. (2000). Cognitive functioning in very old age. In F. I. M. Craik & T. A. Salthouse (Eds.), *The handbook of aging and cognition* (2nd ed., pp. 499–558). Mahwah, NJ: Erlbaum.

Baddeley, A. D. (1986). *Working memory.* Oxford, England: Clarendon Press.

Baddeley, A. D. (2000). The episodic buffer: A new component of working memory? *Trends in Cognitive Sciences, 4,* 417–423.

Baddeley, A. D. (2001). Is working memory still working? *American Psychologist, 56*(11), 851–864.

Baddeley, A. D., & Hitch, G. J. (1974). Working memory. In G. Bower (Ed.), *Advances in learning and motivation* (Vol. 8, pp. 47–90). New York: Academic Press.

Baker, B. (1999, November). Fighting for funeral rights. *AARP Bulletin,* pp. 18–20.

Baker, R. (1991, September 7). Cultural gaps separate generations. *Arizona Republic,* p. A19.

Ballie, R. (2001, October). Congressional briefing puts psychology at forefront of end-of-life issues. *Monitor on Psychology,* p. 15.

Ballweg, J. A. (1969). Extensions of meaning and use for kinship terms. *American Anthropologist, 71,* 84–87.

Baltes, M. M., & Baltes, P. B. (1986). *The psychology of control and aging.* Hillsdale, NJ: Erlbaum.

Baltes, P. B. (1979). Life-span development psychology: Some converging observations on history and theory. In P. B. Baltes & O. G. Brim, Jr. (Eds.), *Life-span development and behavior* (Vol. 2, pp. 255–279). New York: Academic Press.

Baltes, P. B. (1987). Theoretical propositions of life-span developmental psychology: On the dynamics between growth and decline. *Developmental Psychology, 23,* 611–626.

Baltes, P. B. (1997). On the incomplete architecture of human ontogeny: Selection, optimization, and compensation as foundation of developmental theory. *American Psychologist, 52*(4), 366–380.

Baltes, P. B., & Baltes, M. M. (1990). Psychological perspectives on successful aging: A model of selective optimization with compensation. In P. B. Baltes & M. M. Baltes (Eds.), *Successful aging: Perspectives from the behavioral sciences* (pp. 1–34). Cambridge, England: Cambridge University Press.

Baltes, P. B., & Labouvie, G. V. (1973). Adult development of intellectual performance: Description, explanation, and modification. In C. Eisdorfer & M. P. Lawton (Eds.), *The psychology of adult development and aging.* Washington, DC: American Psychological Association.

Baltes, P. B., & Lindenberger, U. (1997). Emergence of a powerful connection between sensory and cognitive functions across the life span: A new window to the study of cognitive aging? *Psychology and Aging, 12*(1), 12–21.

Baltes, P. B., & Nesselroade, J. R. (1979). History and rationale of longitudinal research. In J. R. Nesselroade & P. B. Baltes (Eds.), *Longitudinal research in the study of behavior and development* (pp. 1–40). New York: Academic Press.

Baltes, P. B., & Staudinger, U. M. (2000). Wisdom: A meta-heuristic (pragmatic) to orchestrate mind and virtue toward excellence. *American Psychologist, 55*(1), 122–136.

Baltes, P. B., Dittmann-Kohli, F., & Dixon, R. A. (1984). New perspectives on the development of intelligence in adulthood: Toward a dual-process conception and a model of selective optimization with compensation. In P. B. Baltes & O. G. Brim, Jr. (Eds.), *Life-span development and behavior* (Vol. 6, pp. 33–76). San Diego, CA: Academic Press.

Baltes, P. B., Dittmann-Kohli, F., & Kliegl, R. (1986). Reserve capacity of the elderly in aging-sensitive tests of fluid intelligence: Replication and extension. *Psychology and Aging, 1,* 172–177.

Baltes, P. B., Staudinger, U. M., & Lindenberger, U. (1999). Lifespan psychology: Theory and application to intellectual functioning. *Annual Review Psychology, 50,* 471–507.

Baltes, P. B., Staudinger, U. M., Maercker, A., & Smith, J. (1995). People nominated as wise: A comparative study of wisdom-related knowledge. *Psychology and Aging, 10*(2), 155–166.

Bandura, A. (1977a). Self-efficacy: Toward a unifying theory of behavioral change. *Psychological Review, 84,* 191–215.

Bandura, A. (1977b). *Social learning theory.* Englewood Cliffs, NJ: Prentice Hall.

Bandura, A. (1991, May 2). *Explorations in self-efficacy.* Paper presented at the meeting of the Midwestern Psychological Association, Chicago.

Bandura, A., Cioffi, D., Taylor, C. B., & Brouillard, M. E. (1988). Perceived self-efficacy in coping with cognitive stressors and opioid activation. *Journal of Personality and Social Psychology, 55,* 479–488.

Bane, S. (1991). Rural minority populations. *Generations, 15*(4), 63–65.

Bankoff, E. A. (1983a). Aged parents and their widowed daughters: A support relationship. *Journal of Gerontology, 38,* 226–230.

Bankoff, E. A. (1983b). Social support and adaption to widowhood. *Journal of Marriage and the Family, 45,* 827–839.

Banner, C. (1992). Recent insights into the biology of Alzheimer's disease. *Generations, 16*(4), 31–34.

Bardwick, J. (1990). Where we are and what we want: A psychological model. In R. A. Nemiroff & C. A. Colarusso (Eds.), *New dimensions in adult development* (pp. 186–213). New York: Basic Books.

Barefoot, J. C., Dodge, K. A., Peterson, B. L., Dahlstrom, W. G., & Williams, R. B., Jr. (1989). The Cook-Medley Hostility Scale: Item content and ability to predict survival. *Psychosomatic Medicine, 51,* 46–57.

Barinag, M. (1991). How long is the human life-span? *Science, 254,* 936–938.

Barker, R. (1968). *Ecological psychology: Concepts and methods for studying the environments of human behavior.* Stanford, CA: Stanford University Press.

Barnes-Farrell, J., & Piotrowski, M. (1989). Workers' perceptions of discrepancies between chronological age and personal age: You're only as old as you feel. *Psychology and Aging, 4,* 376–377.

Barnett, R. C., & Baruch, G. K. (1987). Determinants of fathers' participation in family work. *Journal of Marriage and the Family, 49,* 29–40.

Barnett, R. C., & Hyde, J. S. (2001). Women, men, work, and family. *American Psychologist, 56*(10), 781–796.

Barnett, R. C., Marshall, N. L., & Singer, J. D. (1992). Job experiences over time, multiple roles, and women's mental health: A longitudinal study. *Journal of Personality and Social Psychology, 62,* 634–644.

Baron, A., & Cerella, J. (1993). In J. Cerella, J. Rybash, W. Hoyer, & M. L. Commons (Eds.), *Adult information processing: Limits on loss* (pp. 176–206). San Diego, CA: Academic Press.

Baron, R. A., & Byrne, D. (1991). *Social psychology: Understanding human interaction* (6th ed.). Boston: Allyn & Bacon.

Barresi, C. M. (1990). Ethnogerontology: Social aging in national, racial, and cultural groups. In K. F. Ferraro (Ed.), *Gerontology: Perspectives and issues* (pp. 247–265). New York: Springer.

Barton, W. E. (1976). *Abraham Lincoln and his books: With selections from the writings of Lincoln and a bibliography of books in print relating to Abraham Lincoln.* Folcroft, PA: Folcroft Library Editions.

Baruch, G., Barnett, R., & Rivers, C. (1983). *Lifeprints: New patterns of love and work for today's women.* New York: McGraw-Hill.

Barusch, A. S., & Steen, P. (1996). Keepers of community in a changing world. *Generations, 20*(1), 49–52.

Bashore, T. R., & Goddard, P. H. (1993). Preservative and restorative effects of aerobic fitness. In J. Cerella, J. Rybash, W. Hoyer, & M. L. Commons (Eds.), *Adult information processing: Limits on loss* (pp. 207–230). San Diego, CA: Academic Press.

Basic Behavioral Science Task Force, National Advisory Mental Health Council. (1996). Basic behavioral science research for mental health: Family processes and social networks. *American Psychologist, 51*(6), 622–630.

Basow, S. (1992). *Gender: Stereotypes and roles* (3rd ed.). Pacific Grove, CA: Brooks/Cole.

Basseches, M. A. (1984). Dialectal thinking as a metasystematic form of cognitive organization. In M. Commons, F. Richards, & C. Armon (Eds.), *Beyond formal operations: Late adolescent and adult cognitive development* (pp. 216–238). New York: Praeger.

Bates, D. W., Spell, N., Cullen, D. J., Burdick, E., Laird, N., Petersen, L. A., Small, S. D., Sweitzer, B. J., & Leape, L. L. (1997). The costs of adverse drug events in hospitalized patients. *Journal of the American Medical Association, 277*(4), 307–311.

Baum, A., & Posluszny, D. M. (1999). Health psychology: Mapping biobehavioral contributions to health and illness. *Annual Review of Psychology, 50,* 137–163.

Baumeister, R. F., & Leary, M. R. (1995). The need to belong: Desire for interpersonal attachments as a fundamental human motivation. *Psychological Bulletin, 117,* 497–529.

Baumrind, D. (1995). Commentary on sexual orientation: Research and social policy implications. *Developmental Psychology, 31*(1), 130–136.

Beard, G. M. (1874). *Legal responsibility in old age.* New York: Russell.

Beardsley, T. (1993). Unraveling Alzheimer's: A major cause of the disease yields to researchers. *Scientific American, 269,* 28–30.

Becker, G. S. (1957). *The economics of discrimination.* Chicago: University of Chicago Press.

Beckman, L. J. (1981). Effects of social interaction and children's relative inputs on older women's psychological well-being. *Journal of Personality and Social Psychology, 41,* 1075–1086.

Bedard, J., & Chi, M. T. H. (1992). Expertise. *Current Directions in Psychological Science, 1,* 135–139.

Bedford, V. H. (1989). A comparison of thematic apperceptions of sibling affiliation, conflict, and separation at two periods of adulthood. *International Journal of Aging and Human Development, 28,* 53–66.

Beers, M. H. (2001). Age-related changes as a risk factor for medication-related problems. *Generations, 24*(4), 22–27.

Belsky, J. (1985a). Child maltreatment: An ecological integration. *American Psychologist, 35,* 320–335.

Belsky, J. (1985b). Exploring individual differences in marital change across the transition to parenthood: The role of violated expectations. *Journal of Marriage and the Family, 47,* 1037–1044.

Bengtson, V. L., & Robertson, J. F. (Eds.). (1985). *Grandparenthood.* Beverly Hills, CA: Sage.

Bengtson, V. L., & Schaie, K. W. (Eds.). (1989). *The course of later life: Research and reflections.* New York: Springer.

Bengtson, V. L., Burgess, E. O., & Parrott, T. M. (1997). Theory, explanation, and a third generation of theoretical development in social gerontology. *Journal of Gerontology: Social Sciences, 52b*(2), S72–S88.

Bengtson, V. L., Reedy, M. N., & Gordon, C. (1985). Aging and self-conceptions: Personality processes and social contexts. In J. E. Birren & K. W. Schaie (Eds.), *Handbook of the psychology of aging* (2nd ed., pp. 544–594). New York: Van Nostrand Reinhold.

Bengtson, V. L., Rosenthal, C. J., & Burton, L. M. (1995). Paradoxes of families and aging. In R. H. Binstock and L. K. George (Eds.), *Handbook of aging and the social sciences* (4th ed.). San Diego, CA: Academic Press.

Bengtson, V. L., Rosenthal, C., & Burton, L. (1990). Families and aging: Diversity and heterogeneity. In R. H. Binstock & L. K. George (Eds.), *Handbook of aging and the social sciences* (pp. 263–287). San Diego, CA: Academic Press.

Bennett, S. (1994). The American Indian: A psychological overview. In W. Lonner & R. Malpass (Eds.), *Psychology and culture* (pp. 35–39). Boston: Allyn & Bacon.

Bentler, P. M., & Newcomb, M. (1978). Longitudinal studies of marital success and failure. *Journal of Consulting and Clinical Psychology, 40,* 1053–1070.

Berardo, D., Shehan, C., & Leslie, G. (1987). A residue of tradition: Jobs, careers, and spouses' time in housework. *Journal of Marriage and the Family, 49,* 381–390.

Berardo, F. (1970). Survivorship and social isolation: The case of the aged widower. *Family Coordinator, 19,* 11–25.

Berg, C. A., Klaczynski, P. A., Calderone, K. S., & Strough, J. (1994). In J. D. Sinnott (Ed.), *Interdisciplinary handbook of adult lifespan learning* (pp. 371–388). Westport, CT: Greenwood Press.

Berg, C., & Sternberg, R. (1992). Adults' conceptions of intelligence across the adult life span. *Psychology and Aging, 7,* 221–231.

Berger, C., & Gold, D. (1979). Do sex differences in problem-solving still exist? *Personality and Social Psychology Bulletin, 5,* 109–113.

Bergman, M. (1966). Hearing in the Mabaans. *Archives of Otalaryngology, 84,* 411–415.

Berk, L. (1991). *Child development* (2nd ed.). Boston: Allyn & Bacon.

Berkman, L. F., Berkman, C. S., Kasl, S., Freeman, D. H., Jr., Leo, L., Ostfeld, A. M., Cornoni-Huntley, J., & Brody, J. A. (1986). Depressive symptoms in relation to physical health and functioning in the elderly. *American Journal of Epidemiology, 124,* 372–388.

Berman, J. (1991). From the pages of my life. *Generations, 15*(2), 33–40.

Bernal, M. E., & Castro, F. G. (1994). Are clinical psychologists prepared for service and research with ethnic minorities? Report of a decade of progress. *American Psychologist, 49*(9), 797–805.

Bernstein, W. M., Stephenson, B. O., Snyder, M. L., & Wicklund, R. A. (1983). Causal ambiguity and heterosexual affiliation. *Journal of Experimental Social Psychology, 19,* 78–92.

Berry, J. M., & West, R. L. (1993). Cognitive self-efficacy in relation to personal mastery and goal setting across the life span. *International Journal of Behavioral Development, 16*(2), 351–379.

Berscheid, E. (1988). Some comments on love's anatomy. In R. J. Sternberg & M. L. Barnes (Eds.), *The psychology of love.* New Haven, CT: Yale University Press.

Berscheid, E., & Reis, H. T. (1998). Attraction and close relationships. In D. T. Gilbert, S. T. Fiske, & G. Lindzey (Eds.), *The handbook of social psychology* (4th ed., Vol. 2, pp. 193–281). New York: McGraw-Hill.

Berscheid, E., & Walster, E. (1974). A little bit about love. In T. L. Huston (Ed.), *Foundations of interpersonal attraction* (pp. 355–381). New York: Springer-Verlag.

Berscheid, E., Walster, E., & Bohrnstedt, G. (1973). The body image report. *Psychology Today, 7,* 119–131.

Berzonsky, M. (1988). Self-theorists, identity status, and social cognition. In D. K. Lapsley & F. C. Power (Eds.), *Self, ego, and identity: Integrative approaches* (pp. 243–262). New York: Springer-Verlag.

Berzonsky, M. (1989a). Identity style: Conceptionalization and measurement. *Journal of Adolescent Research, 4,* 268–282.

Berzonsky, M. (1989b). The self as a theorist: Individual differences in identity formation. *International Journal of Personal Construct Psychology, 2*(4), 363–376.

Betancourt, H., & Lopez, S. R. (1993). The study of culture, ethnicity, and race in American psychology. *American Psychologist, 48,* 629–637.

Betz, N. E., & Fitzgerald, L. F. (1987). *The career psychology of women.* New York: Academic Press.

Betz, N. E., & Hackett, G. (1981). The relationship of career-related self-efficacy expectations to perceived career options in college women and men. *Journal of Counseling Psychology, 28,* 399–410.

Betz, N. E., & Hackett, G. (1986). Applications of self-efficacy theory to understanding career choice behavior. *Journal of Social and Clinical Psychology, 4,* 279–289.

Biederman, I. (1995). Visual object recognition. In S. F. Kosslyn & D. N. Osherson (Eds.), *An invitation to cognitive science: Vol. 2. Visual cognition* (2nd ed., pp. 121–165). Cambridge, MA: MIT Press.

Binion, V. (1990). Psychological androgyny: A black female perspective. *Sex Roles, 22,* 487–507.

Binney, E. A., & Swan, J. H. (1991). The political economy of mental health care for the elderly. In M. Minkler & C. L. Estes (Eds.), *Critical perspectives on aging: The political and moral economy of growing old* (pp. 165–188). Amityville, NY: Baywood.

Birren, J. E. (1964). *The psychology of aging.* Englewood Cliffs, NJ: Prentice Hall.

Birren, J. E. (1969). The concept of functional age: Theoretical background. *Human Development, 12,* 214–215.

Birren, J. E. (1985). Age, competence, creativity, and wisdom. In R. N. Butler & H. P. Gleason (Eds.), *Productive aging: Enhancing vitality in later life* (pp. 29–36). New York: Springer.

Birren, J. E. (1988a). Behavior as a cause and a consequence of health and aging. In J. J. F. Schroots, J. E. Birren, & A. Svanborg (Eds.), *Health and aging* (pp. 25–41). New York: Springer.

Birren, J. E. (1988b). A contribution to the theory of the psychology of aging: As a counterpart of development. In J. E. Birren & V. L. Bengtson (Eds.), *Emergent theories of aging* (pp. 153–176). New York: Springer.

Birren, J. E. (1989). My perspective on research on aging. In V. L. Bengtson & K. W. Schaie (Eds.), *The course of later life: Research and reflections* (pp. 135–149). New York: Springer.

Birren, J. E., & Birren, B. A. (1990). The concepts, models, and history of the psychology of aging. In J. E. Birren & K. W. Schaie (Eds.), *Handbook of the psychology of aging* (3rd ed., pp. 3–20). San Diego, CA: Academic Press.

Birren, J. E., & Renner, V. J. (1983). Health, behavior, and aging. In J. E. Birren, J. M. A. Munnichs, H. Thomae, & M. Maurois (Eds.), *Aging: A challenge to science and society* (Vol. 3, pp. 9–35). Oxford, England: Oxford University Press.

Birren, J. E., & Zarit, J. M. (1985). Concepts of health, behavior, and aging. In J. E. Birren & J. Livingston (Eds.), *Cognition, stress, and aging* (pp. 1–20). Englewood Cliffs, NJ: Prentice Hall.

Birren, J. E., Riegel, K. F., & Morrison, D. F. (1962). Age differences in response speed as a function of controlled variations of stimulus conditions: Evidence of a general speed factor. *Gerontologia, 6,* 1–18.

Bjorksten, J. (1968). The cross linkage theory of aging. *Journal of the American Geriatric Society, 16,* 408–427.

Black, J. E., Greenough, W. T., Anderson, B. J., & Isaacs, K. R. (1987). Environment and the aging brain. *Canadian Journal of Psychology, 41*(2), 111–130.

Blake, A. J., Morgan, K., Bendall, M. J., Dallasso, H., Ebrahim, S. B. J., Arie, T. H. D., Fentem, P. H., & Bassey, E. J. (1988). Falls by elderly people at home: Prevalence and associate factors. *Age and Aging, 17,* 365–372.

Blanchette, P. L., & Flynn, B. (2001). Geriatric medicine: An approaching crisis. *Generations, 25*(1), 80–84.

Blau, Z. S. (1973). *Old age in a changing society.* New York: New View Points.

Blazer, D. G. (1982). Social support and morality in an elderly population. *American Journal of Epidemiology, 115,* 684–694.

Blazer, D. G. (1985). Psychiatric disorders: A rural/urban comparison. *Archives of General Psychiatry, 42,* 651–656.

Blazer, D. G., Hughes, D., & George, L. (1987). The epidemiology of depression in an elderly community population. *Gerontologist, 27,* 281–287.

Blieszner, R., & Bedford, V. H. (1995). The family context of aging: Trends and challenges. In R. Blieszner & V. H. Bedford (Eds.), *Handbook of aging and the family* (pp. 3–12). Westport, CT: Greenwood Press.

Bloom, B. S. (1964). *Stability and change in human characteristics.* New York: Wiley.

Blum, R. W., Harmon, B., Harris, L., Bergeisen, L., & Resnick, M. D. (1992). American Indian-Alaska native youth health. *Journal of the American Medical Association, 267,* 1637–1644.

Bodnar, J. C., & Kiecolt-Glaser, J. K. (1994). Caregiver depression after bereavement: Chronic stress isn't over when it's over. *Psychology and Aging, 9*(3), 372–380.

Bolger, N., DeLongis, A., Kessler, R. C., & Wethington, E. (1990). The microstructure of daily role-related stress in married couples. In J. Eckenrode & S. Gore (Eds.), *Stress between work and family.* New York: Plenum Press.

Bonanno, G. A. (1999). Factors associated with the effective accommodation to loss. In C. Figley (Ed.), *The traumatology of grieving* (pp. 37–52). Tallahassee, FL: Taylor & Francis.

Bonanno, G. A. (2004). Loss, trauma, and human resilience: Have we underestimated the human capacity to thrive after extremely aversive events? *American Psychologist, 59*(1), 20–28.

Bonanno, G. A., & Kaltman, S. (1999). Towards an integrative perspective on bereavement. *Psychological Bulletin, 125*(6), 760–776.

Bonanno, G. A., Wortman, C. B., & Nesse, R. M. (2004). Prospective patterns of resilience and maladjustment during widowhood. *Psychology and Aging, 19*(2), 260–271.

Bond, J., Briggs, R., & Coleman, P. (1990). The study of aging. In J. Bond & P. Coleman (Eds.), *Aging in society: An introduction to social gerontology* (pp. 17–47). London: Sage.

Bonnie, R. J., & Wallace, R. B. (Eds.). (2003). *Elder mistreatment: Abuse, neglect, and exploitation in an aging America.* Washington, D.C.: National Academy of Sciences.

Bookwala, J., & Schulz, R. (2000). A comparison of primary stressors, secondary stressors, and depressive symptoms between elderly caregiving husbands and wives: The Caregiver Health Effects Study. *Psychology and Aging, 15*(4), 607–616.

Bookwala, J., Yee, J. L., & Schulz, R. (2000). Caregiving and detrimental mental and physical health outcomes. In G. M. Williamson, P. A. Parmalee, & D. R. Shaffer (Eds.), *Physical illness and depression in older adults: A handbook of theory, research, and practice* (pp. 93–131). New York: Plenum.

Bordage, G., & Zacks, R. (1984). The structure of medical knowledge in the memories of medical students and general practitioners: Categories and prototypes. *Medical Education, 18*, 406–416.

Bossard, J. H. S. (1945, January). The law of family interaction. *American Journal of Sociology, 50*(4), 292–294.

Botwinick, J. (1984). *Aging and behavior: A comprehensive integration of research findings.* New York: Springer.

Bourne, E. (1978). The state of research on ego identity: A review and appraisal: Pt. II. *Journal of Youth and Adolescence, 7*, 371–392.

Bourne, L. (1992). Cognitive psychology: A brief overview. *Psychological Science Agenda, 5*(5), 5, 20. Washington, DC: American Psychological Association.

Bowen, G., & Orthner, D. (1983). Sex-role congruency and marital quality. *Journal of Marriage and the Family, 45*, 223–230.

Bowlby, J. (1969). *Attachment and loss: Vol. 1. Attachment.* New York: Basic Books.

Bowlby, J. (1973). *Attachment and loss: Vol. 2. Separation: Anxiety and anger.* New York: Basic Books.

Bowlby, J. (1979). *The making and breaking of affectional bonds.* London: Tavistock.

Bowlby, J. (1980). *Attachment and loss: Vol. 3. Loss.* New York: Basic Books.

Bowlby, J. (1982). *Attachment and loss: Vol. 1. Attachment* (2nd ed.). New York: Basic Books.

Bowlby, J. (1988). Attachment, communication, and the therapeutic process. In J. Bowlby, *A secure base: Clinical applications of attachment theory* (pp. 137–157). London: Routledge.

Boyd, S. T. (1985). Study of the father: Research methods. *American Behavioral Scientist, 29*, 112–128.

Bramlett, M. D., & Mosher, W. D. (2002). Cohabitation, marriage, divorce, and remarriage in the United States. *Vital Health Statistics, 23*, 22. Hyattsville, MD: National Center for Health Statistics.

Branch, L. G., Horowitz, A., & Carr, C. (1989). The implications for everyday life of incident reported visual decline among people over age 65 living in the community. *Gerontologist, 29*, 359–365.

Brandt, N. (2001). On the horizon: New medicines for older adults. *Generations, 24*(4), 37–42.

Brandtstadter, J., & Greve, W. (1994). The aging self: Stabilizing and protective processes. *Developmental Review, 14*, 52–80.

Brandtstadter, J., & Rothermund, K. (1994). Self-percepts of control in middle and later adulthood: Buffering losses by rescaling goals. *Psychology and Aging, 9*(2), 265–273.

Brandtstadter, J., Wentura, D., & Greve, W. (1993). Adaptive resources of the aging self: Outlines of an emergent perspective. *International Journal of Behavioral Development, 16*, 323–349.

Braverman, L. B. (1989). Beyond the myth of motherhood. In M. McGoldrick, C. M. Anderson, & F. Walsh (Eds.), *Women and families* (pp. 227–243). New York: Free Press.

Brennan, M. (2002). When vision *and* hearing fail: Dual sensory impairment among older adults. *Aging and Vision, 14*(2), 6–7.

Bretherton, I. (1992). The origins of attachment theory: John Bowlby and Mary Ainsworth. *Developmental Psychology, 28*, 759–775.

Brewer, M. B., & Caporael, L. R. (1990). Selfish genes vs. selfish people: Sociobiology as origin myth. *Motivation and Emotion, 14*, 237–243.

Breytspraak, L. M. (1984). *The development of self in later life.* Boston: Little, Brown.

Brody, E. M. (1981). "Women in the middle" and family help to older people. *Gerontologist, 21*, 471–480.

Brody, E. M. (1985). Parent care as a normative family stress. *Gerontologist, 25*, 19–29.

Brody, E. M. (1989). The family at risk. In E. Light & B. D. Lebowitz (Eds.), *Alzheimer's disease treatment and family stress: Directions for research* (pp. 2–49) (DHHS Publication No. ADM 89–1569). Washington, DC: U.S. Government Printing Office.

Brody, J. A. (1988). Changing health needs of the aging population. In D. Evered & J. Whelan (Eds.), *Research in the aging population* (pp. 208–215). New York: Wiley.

Brody, J. A., Brock, D. B., & Williams, T. F. (1989). Trends in health of the elderly population. In L. Breslow, J. E. Fielding, & L. B. Love (Eds.), *Annual Review of Public Health, 8*, 211–234.

Brokenleg, M., & Middleton, D. (1993). Native Americans: Adapting, yet retaining. In D. P. Irish, K. F. Lundquist, & V. J. Nelsen (Eds.), *Ethnic variations in dying, death, and grief: Diversity in universality* (pp. 101–112). Washington, DC: Taylor & Francis.

Bronfenbrenner, U. (1979). *The ecology of human development: Experiments by nature and design.* Cambridge, MA: Harvard University Press.

Bronfenbrenner, U. (1989). Ecological systems theory. In R. Vasta (Ed.), *Annals of child development: Vol. 6. Six theories of child development: Revised formulations and current issues* (pp. 187–249). Greenwich, CT: JAI Press.

Bronfenbrenner, U., Kessel, F., Kessen, W., & White, S. (1986). Towards a critical social history of developmental psychology: A propaedeutic discussion. *American Psychologist, 41*, 1218–1230.

Broughton, J. M. (1984). Not beyond formal operations but beyond Piaget. In M. Commons, F. Richards, & C. Armon (Eds.), *Beyond formal operations: Late adolescent and adult cognitive development* (pp. 395–411). New York: Praeger.

Brown, J. D. (1977). *Essay on Social Security.* Princeton, NJ: Princeton University Press.

Browne, A. (1993). Violence against women by male partners: Prevalence, outcomes, and policy implications. *American Psychologist, 48*, 1077–1087.

Browne, A., & Williams, K. R. (1989). Exploring the effect of resource availability and the likelihood of female-perpetrated homicides. *Law and Society Review, 23*, 75–94.

Brubaker, T. (1985). *Later life families.* Beverly Hills, CA: Sage.

Bruckner, R. (1967). Longitudinal research on the eye. *Gerontologia Clinica, 9*, 87–95.

Buckner, R. L., & Logan, J. M. (2001). Functional neuroimaging methods: PET and fMRI. In R. Cabeza & A. Kingstone (Eds.), *Handbook of functional neuroimaging of cognition* (pp. 27–48). Cambridge, MA: MIT Press.

Bulhan, H. (1985). Black Americans and psychopathology: An overview of research and therapy. *Psychotherapy, 22*, 370–378.

Bunce, D., Kivipelto, M., & Wahlin, A. (2004). Utilization of cognitive support in episodic free recall as a function of apolipoprotein E and vitamin B12 or folate among adults aged 75 years and older. *Neuropsychology, 18*(2), 362–370.

Burns, B. J., & Kamerow, D. B. (1988). Psychotropic drug prescriptions in nursing home residents. *Journal of Family Practice, 26*(2), 155–160.

Bursik, K. (1991). Correlates of women's adjustment during the separation and divorce process. *Journal of Divorce and Remarriage, 14*(3–4), 137–162.

Burton, L. M. (1992). Black grandparents rearing children of drug-addicted parents: Stressors, outcomes, and social service needs. *Gerontologist, 32*, 744–751.

Burton, L., & Bengtson, V. (1985). Black grandmothers: Issues of timing and continuity of roles. In V. Bengtson & J. F. Robertson (Eds.), *Grandparenthood* (pp. 61–77). Beverly Hills, CA: Sage.

Burton, L., Dilworth-Anderson, P., & Bengtson, V. (1991). Creating culturally relevant ways of thinking about diversity and aging. *Generations, 15*(4), 67–72.

Buss, D. M. (1989). Sex differences in human mate preferences: Evolutionary hypotheses tested in 37 cultures. *Behavioral and Brain Sciences, 12*, 1–49.

Buss, D. M. (1995). Psychological sex differences: Origins through sexual selection. *American Psychologist, 50*(3), 164–168.

Buss, D. M. (2000). The evolution of happiness. *American Psychologist, 55*(1), 15–23.

Buss, D. M., & Schmitt, D. P. (1993). Sexual strategies theory: An evolutionary perspective on human mating. *Psychological Review, 100*, 204–232.

Busse, E. W. (1969). Theories of aging. In E. W. Busse & E. Pfeiffer (Eds.), *Behavior and adaptation in later life* (pp. 11–32). Boston: Little, Brown.

Butler, R. N. (1963). The life review: An interpretation of reminiscence in the aged. *Psychiatry, 26*, 65–76.

Butler, R. N. (1968). The life review: An interpretation of reminiscence in the aged. In B. Neugarten (Ed.), *Middle age and aging* (pp. 486–496). Chicago: University of Chicago Press.

Butler, R. N. (1969). Age-ism: Another form of bigotry. *Gerontologist, 9*, 243–246.

Butler, R. N. (1988). Health and aging: The new gerontology. In J. J. F. Schroots, J. E. Birren, & A. Svanborg (Eds.), *Health and aging: Perspectives and prospects* (pp. 143–153). New York: Springer.

Butler, R. N. (1993). Dispelling ageism: The cross-cutting intervention. *Generation, 17*(2), 75–78.

Butler, R. N. (2000). Butler reviews life review. *Aging Today, 21*(4), 1, 12.

Butler, R. N., Lewis, M., & Sunderland, T. (1991). *Aging and mental health: Positive psychosocial and biomedical approaches* (4th ed.). New York: Merrill.

Butt, D., & Beiser, M. (1987). Successful aging: A theme for international psychology. *Psychology and Aging, 2*, 87–94.

Cacioppo, J. T., & Berntson, G. G. (1992). Social psychological contributions to the decade of the brain. *American Psychologist, 47*, 1019–1028.

Caldwell, M. A., & Peplau, L. A. (1982). Sex differences in same-sex friendship. *Sex Roles, 8*, 721–732.

Cameron, K. A., & Richardson, A. W. (2001). A guide to medications and aging. *Generations, 24*(4), 8–21.

Campbell, A. J., Borrie, M. J., & Spears, G. F. (1989). Risk factors for falls in a community-based prospective study of people 70 years and older. *Journal of Gerontology, 44*, M112–M117.

Campos, J. J., Barrett, K. C., Lamb, M. E., Goldsmith, H. H., & Stenberg, C. (1983). Socioemotional development. In M. M. Haith & J. J. Campos (Eds.), *Handbook of child psychology: Vol. 2. Infancy and psychobiology* (pp. 783–915). New York: Wiley.

Candy, S., Troll, L., & Levy, S. (1981). A developmental exploration of friendship functions of women. *Psychology of Women Quarterly, 5*, 456–472.

Cantor, M. (1980). The informal support system: Its relevance in the lives of the elderly. In E. Borgotta & N. McCluskey (Eds.), *Aging and society.* Beverly Hills, CA: Sage.

Cantor, M. (1983). Strain among caregivers: A study of experience in the United States. *Gerontologist, 23*, 597–604.

Cappell, C., & Heiner, R. B. (1990). The intergenerational transmission of family aggression. *Journal of Family Violence, 5*, 135–152.

Caranasos, G. J., Stewart, G. B., & Cluff, L. E. (1974). Drug-induced illness leading to hospitalization. *Journal of the American Medical Association, 228,* 713–717.

Carstensen, L. L. (1991). Socioemotional selectivity theory: Social activity in life-span context. In K. W. Schaie & M. P. Lawton (Eds.), *Annual Review of Gerontology and Geriatrics* (Vol. 11, pp. 195–217). New York: Springer.

Carstensen, L. L. (1992). Social and emotion patterns in adulthood: Support for socioemotional selectivity theory. *Psychology and Aging, 7,* 331–338.

Carstensen, L. L. (1995). Evidence for a life-span theory of socioemotional selectivity. *Current Directions in Psychological Science, 4*(5), 151–156.

Carstensen, L. L., & Charles, S. T. (1998). Emotion in the second half of life. *Current Directions, 7*(5), 144–149.

Carstensen, L. L., Gottman, J. M., & Levenson, R. W. (1995). Emotional behavior in long-term marriage. *Psychology and Aging, 10*(1), 140–149.

Carstensen, L. L., Isaacowitz, D. M., & Charles, S. T. (1999). Taking time seriously: A theory of socioemotional selectivity. *American Psychologist, 54*(3), 165–181.

Carter, B., & McGoldrick, M. (1988). *The changing family life cycle: A framework for family therapy* (2nd ed.). New York: Gardner Press.

Case, R. B., Moss, A. J., Case, N., McDermott, M., & Eberly, S. (1992). Living alone after myocardial infarction: Impact on prognosis. *Journal of the American Medical Association, 267,* 515–519.

Caspi, A., & Herbener, E. (1990). Continuity and change: Assortative marriage and the consistency of personality in adulthood. *Journal of Personality and Social Psychology, 58,* 250–258.

Cassel, C. (1992). Ethics and the future of aging research. *Generations, 16*(4), 61–65.

Cattell, R. (1963). Theory of fluid and crystallized intelligence: A critical experiment. *Journal of Educational Psychology, 54,* 1–22.

Cazenave, N. A., & Straus, M. A. (1990). Race, class, network embeddedness, and family violence: A search for potent support systems. In M. A. Straus & R. J. Gelles (Eds.), *Physical violence in American families* (pp. 321–339). New Brunswick, NJ: Transaction.

Ceci, S. J. (1993). Contextual trends in intellectual development. *Developmental Review, 13,* 403–435.

Centers for Disease Control. (1999). Suicide deaths and rates per 100,000. Retrieved from www.cdc.gov/ncipc/data/us9794/suic.htm.

Centers for Disease Control. (2004a). *Health consequences of smoking: A report of the Surgeon General.* Retrieved from www.cdc.gov/tobacco/sgr/sgr_2004/index.htm.

Centers for Disease Control. (2004b). *Overweight and obesity.* Retrieved September 14, 2004, from www.cdc.gov/nccdphp/dnpa/obesity/.

Centers for Disease Control. (2004c). *The state of aging and health in America 2004.* Retrieved from www.cdc.gov/aging/pdf/State_of_Aging_and_Health_in_America_2004.pdf.

Centers for Disease Control. (2004d). *Young people at risk: HIV/AIDS among America's youth.* Retrieved from www.cdc.gov/hiv/pubs/facts/youth.htm.

Centers for Disease Control and Prevention. (1994). *HIV/AIDS surveillance report: Year-end edition.*

Centers for Disease Control, Division of Chronic Disease Control. (1989). Years of life lost due to cancer—United States, 1968–1985. *Journal of the American Medical Association, 261,* 209–216.

Cerami, A. (1985). Glucose as a mediator of aging. *Journal of the American Geriatric Society, 33,* 626–634.

Cerami, A., Vlassara, H., & Brownlee, M. (1987). Glucose and aging. *Scientific American, 256*(5), 90–97.

Cerella, J. (1990). Aging and information-processing rate. In J. E. Birren & K. W. Schaie (Eds.), *Handbook of the psychology of aging* (3rd ed., pp. 201–221). San Diego, CA: Academic Press.

Cerella, J., Poon, L., & Williams, D. (1980). Age and the complexity hypothesis. In L. W. Poon (Ed.), *Aging in the 1980's* (pp. 332–340). Washington, DC: American Psychological Association.

Cerella, J., Rybash, J., Hoyer, W., & Commons, M. L. (Eds.). (1993). *Adult information processing: Limits on loss.* San Diego, CA: Academic Press.

Chalk, R., & King, P. A. (Eds.). (1998). *Violence in families: Assessing prevention and treatment programs.* Washington, DC: National Research Council.

Charness, N. (1992). Human factors and age. In F. I. M. Craik & T. A. Salthouse (Eds.), *The handbook of aging and cognition* (pp. 495–552). Hillsdale, NJ: Erlbaum.

Charness, N., & Bosman, E. (1992). Human factors and age. In F. I. M. Craik & T. A. Salthouse (Eds.), *The handbook of aging and cognition* (pp. 495–552). Hillsdale, NJ: Erlbaum.

Chase, W. G., & Simon, H. A. (1973). The mind's eye in chess. In W. G. Chase (Ed.), *Visual information processing* (pp. 215–281). San Diego, CA: Academic Press.

Chawla, S. (1993). Demographic aging and development. *Generations, 17*(4), 20–23.

Cherlin, A., & Furstenberg, F. F. (1985). Styles and strategies of grandparenting. In V. L. Bengtson & J. F. Robertson (Eds.), *Grandparenthood* (pp. 97–116). Beverly Hills, CA: Sage.

Chi, M. T., Glaser, R., & Rees, E. (1982). Expertise in problem solving. In R. J. Steinberg (Ed.), *Advances in the psychology of human intelligence* (Vol. 1, pp. 7–75). Hillsdale, NJ: Erlbaum.

Chitwood, D., & Bigner, J. (1980). Young children's perceptions of old people. *Home Economics Research Journal, 8,* 369–374.

Choi, N. G. (1989, March). Differential life expectancy, socioeconomic status, and Social Security benefits. *Social Work, 34,* 147–150.

Christensen, H., MacKinnon, A. J., Korten, A. E., Jorm, A. F., Henderson, A. S., Jacomb, P., & Rodgers, B. (1999). An analysis of diversity in the cognitive performance of elderly community dwellers: Individual differences in change scores as a function of age. *Psychology and Aging, 14,* 365–379.

Christensen, K., Moye, J., Armson, R., & Kern, T. (1992). Health screening and random recruitment for cognitive aging research. *Psychology and Aging, 7,* 204–208.

Cicirelli, V. G. (1981). *Helping elderly parents: Role of adult children.* Boston: Auburn.

Cicirelli, V. G. (1983). Adult children and their elderly parents. In T. Brubaker (Ed.), *Family relationships in later life.* Beverly Hills, CA: Sage.

Cicirelli, V. G. (1985). Sibling relationships throughout the life cycle. In L. L'Abate (Ed.), *Handbook of family psychology* (pp. 225–251). Homewood, IL: Dorsey.

Cicirelli, V. G. (1991). Sibling relationships in adulthood. *Marriage and Family Review, 16*(3–4), 291–310.

Cicirelli, V. G. (1993). Attachment and obligation as daughters' motives for caregiving behavior and subsequent effect on subjective burden. *Psychology and Aging, 8,* 144–155.

Clark, A. L., & Wallin, P. (1965). Women's sexual responsiveness and the quality of their marriage. *American Journal of Sociology, 71,* 187–196.

Clark, D.C. (1991, January 28). *Final report to the AARP Andrus Foundation: Suicide among the elderly.* Washington, DC: AARP.

Clark, M. C., Czaja, S. J., & Weber, R. A. (1990). Older adults and daily living task profiles. *Human Factors, 32*(5), 537–549.

Clark, M. S., Mills, J., & Powell, M. C. (1986). Keeping track of needs in communal and exchange relationships. *Journal of Personality and Social Psychology, 51,* 333–338.

Clark, R. D., & Hatfield, E. (1989). Gender differences in receptivity to sexual offers. *Journal of Psychology and Human Sexuality, 2,* 39–55.

Clark, R., Anderson, N. B., Clark, V. R., & Williams, D. R. (1999). Racism as a stressor for African Americans. *American Psychologist, 54*(10), 805–816.

Clarkson, P. M., & Dedrick, M. E. (1988). Exercise-induced muscle damage, repair, and adaption in old and young subjects. *Journal of Gerontology, 43,* M91–M96.

Classen, D.C., Pestotnik, S. L., Evans, R. S., Lloyd, J. F., & Burke, J. P. (1997). Adverse drug events in hospitalized patients: Excess length of stay, extra costs, and attributable mortality. *Journal of the American Medical Association, 277*(4), 301–307.

Clayton, V. P., & Birren, J. E. (1980). The development of wisdom across the lifespan: A reexamination of an ancient topic. *Life-Span Development and Behavior, 3,* 103–135.

Clemens, A. W., & Axelson, L. J. (1985). The not-so-empty nest: The return of the fledgling adult. *Family Relations, 34,* 259–264.

Coberly, S. (1991). Older workers and the Older Americans Act. *Generations, 15*(3), 27–30.

Cohen, A. G., & Gutek, B. A. (1991). Sex differences in the career experiences of members of two APA divisions. *American Psychologist, 46,* 1292–1298.

Cohen, G. (1993). Comprehensive assessment: Capturing strengths, not just weaknesses. *Generations, 17*(1), 47–50.

Cohen, G. D. (1988). Disease models of aging: Brain and behavior considerations. In J. E. Birren & V. L. Bengtson (Eds.), *Emergent theories of aging* (pp. 83–89). New York: Springer.

Cohen, G. D. (1990). Psychopathology and mental health in the mature and elderly adult. In J. E. Birren & K. W. Schaie (Eds.), *Handbook of the psychology of aging* (3rd ed., pp. 359–371). San Diego, CA: Academic Press.

Cohen, J. (2002, February). I/Os in the know offer insights on Generation X workers. *Monitor on Psychology,* pp. 66–67.

Cohen, S. (1996). Psychological stress, immunity, and upper respiratory infections. *Current Directions in Psychological Science, 5*(3), 86–90.

Cohen, S., & Herbert, T. B. (1996). Health psychology: Psychological factors and physical disease from the perspective of human psychoneuroimmunology. *Annual Review of Psychology, 47,* 113–142.

Cohen, S., Doyle, W. J., Skoner, D. P., Rabin, B. S., & Gwaltney, J. M. (1997). Social ties and susceptibility to the common cold. *Journal of the American Medical Association, 277,* 1940–1944.

Cohen, S., Tyrrell, D. A. J., & Smith, A. P. (1993). Negative life events, perceived stress, negative affect, and susceptibility to the common cold. *Journal of Personality and Social Psychology, 64,* 131–140.

Coie, J. D., Watt, N. F., West, S. G., Hawkins, J. D., Asarnow, J. R., Markman, H. J., Ramey, S. L., Shure, M. B., & Long, B. (1993). The science of prevention: A conceptual framework and some directions for a national research program. *American Psychologist, 48,* 1013–1022.

Colcombe, S. J., Erickson, K. I., Raz, N., Webb, A. G., Cohen, N. J., McAuley, E., & Kramer, A. F. (2003). Aerobic fitness reduces brain tissue loss in aging humans. *The Journals of Gerontology, Series A, 58*(2), 176–180.

Colcombe, S. J., Kramer, A. F., Erickson, K. I., Scalf, P., McAuley, E., Cohen, N. J., Webb, A., Jerome, G. J., Marquez, D. X., & Elavsky, S. (2004). Cardiovascular fitness, cortical plasticity, and aging. *Proceedings of the National Academy of Sciences, 101*(9), 3316–3321.

Cole, D. (1987, July). It might have been: Mourning the unborn. *Psychology Today,* pp. 64–65.

Cole, M. (1990). Cognitive development and formal schooling: The evidence from cross-cultural research. In L. C. Moll (Ed.), *Vygotsky and education: Instructional implications and applications of socio-historical psychology* (pp. 89–110). Cambridge, England: Cambridge University Press.

Cole, T. (1992, July-August). Ageism and the journey of life in America. *Aging Today,* p. 17.

Coleman, P., & Bond, J. (1990). Aging in the twentieth century. In J. Bond & P. Coleman (Eds.), *Aging in society* (pp. 1–16). London: Sage.

Coleman, P., & Flood, D. (1986). Dendritic proliferation in the aging brain as a compensatory repair mechanism. *Progress in Brain Research, 70,* 227–236.

Coley, R. L. (2001). (In)visible men: Emerging research on low-income, unmarried, and minority fathers. *American Psychologist, 56*(9), 743–753.

Colten, H. R. (1999). The coin has two sides. *Newsletter of the Center on Aging, Northwestern University Medical Center, 15*(1), 1.

Combs, A. W., & Snygg, D. (1959). *Individual behavior* (rev. ed.). New York: Harper & Row.

Commons, M. L., & Richards, F. A. (1984). A general model of stage theory. In M. L. Commons, F. A. Richards, & C. Armon (Eds.), *Beyond formal operations: Late adolescent and adult cognitive development* (pp. 120–140). New York: Praeger.

Commons, M. L., Richards, F. A., & Armon, C. (Eds.). (1984). *Beyond formal operations: Late adolescent and adult cognitive development.* New York: Praeger.

Conger, R. D., Cui, M., Bryant, C. M., & Elder, G. H. (2001). Competence in early adult romantic relationships: A developmental perspective on family influences. *Prevention and Treatment, 4* (article 11), 1–24.

Connidis, I. (1989). The subjective experience of aging: Correlates of divergent views. *Canadian Journal of Aging, 8*(1), 7–18.

Connidis, I., & Davies, L. (1990). Confidants and companions in later life: The place of family and friends. *Journal of Gerontology: Social Sciences, 45*(4), S141–S149.

Connor, J. R. (1997). *Metals and oxidative damage in neurological disorders.* New York: Plenum Press.

Conwell, Y. (1993). Suicide in the elderly. In L. S. Schneider, C. F. Reynolds, B. D. Lebowitz, & A. J. Friedhoff (Eds.), *Diagnosis and treatment of depression in late life.* Washington, DC: American Psychiatric Press.

Conwell, Y. (1996). Outcomes of depression. *Journal of the American Geriatrics Society, 4* (suppl. 1), S34–S44.

Cooley, C. (1902). *Human nature and the social order.* New York: Scribner's.

Coons, S. J., Hendricks, J., & Sheahan, S. L. (1988). Self medication with nonprescription drugs. *Generations, 12*(4), 22–27.

Coopersmith, S. (1967). *The antecedents of self-esteem.* San Francisco: Freeman.

Coopersmith, S. (1975). Studies in self-esteem. In *Readings from Scientific American: Psychology in progress* (pp. 218–224). San Francisco: Freeman.

Cornelius, S., & Caspi, A. (1986). Self-perceptions of intellectual control and aging. *Educational Gerontology, 12,* 345–357.

Corso, J. F. (1981). *Aging sensory systems and perception.* New York: Praeger.

Costa, P. T., & McCrae, R. R. (1982). An approach to the attribution of aging, period, and cohort effects. *Psychological Bulletin, 92,* 238–250.

Costa, P. T., & McCrae, R. R. (1984). Personality as a lifelong determinant of wellbeing. In C. Z. Malatesta & C. E. Izard (Eds.), *Emotion in adult development* (pp. 141–155). Beverly Hills, CA: Sage.

Costa, P. T., & McCrae, R. R. (1999). Personality across cultures: Studies focus on age factor. *Aging Today, 20*(2), 5.

Costa, P. T., Jr., & McCrae, R. R. (1992). *Revised NEO Personality Inventory (NEO-PI-R) and NEO Five-Factor Inventory (NEO-FFI) professional manual.* Odessa, FL: Psychological Assessment Resources.

Cotman, C. (1990). The brain: New plasticity/new possibility. In R. N. Butler, M. R. Oberlink, & M. Schechter (Eds.), *The promise of productive aging: From biology to social policy* (pp. 70–84). New York: Springer.

Coultas, V. (1989). Black girls and self-esteem. *Gender and Education, 1,* 283–294.

Cowan, C. P., & Cowan, P. A. (1992). *When partners become parents: The big life change for couples.* New York: Basic Books.

Cowan, C., Cowan, P., Coie, L., & Coie, J. (1978). Becoming a family: The impact of a first child's birth on the couple's relationship. In L. Newman & W. Miller (Eds.), *The first child and family formation* (pp. 296–326). Chapel Hill, NC: Carolina Population Center.

Cowan, P. A., & Cowan, C. P. (1988). Changes in marriage during the transition to parenthood: Must we blame the baby? In G. Y. Michaels & W. A. Goldberg (Eds.), *The transition to parenthood: Current theory and research.* Cambridge, England: Cambridge University Press.

Cowley, G., & Church, V. (1992, May 18). Live longer with vitamin C. *Newsweek,* p. 60.

Craik, F. I. M. (1986). A functional account of age differences in memory. In F. Klix & H. Hagendorf (Eds.), *Human learning and cognitive capabilities, mechanisms and performance* (pp. 407–422). Amsterdam: North-Holland/Elsevier.

Craik, F. I. M. (1994). Memory changes in normal aging. *Current Directions in Psychological Science, 3*(5), 155–158.

Craik, F. I. M., & Jennings, J. M. (1992). Human memory. In F. I. M. Craik & T. A. Salthouse (Eds.), *The handbook of aging and cognition* (pp. 51–110). Hillsdale, NJ: Erlbaum.

Craik, F. I. M., & Lockhart, R. S. (1972). Levels of processing: A framework for memory research. *Journal of Verbal Learning and Verbal Behavior, 11,* 671–684.

Craik, F. I. M., & Salthouse, T. (Eds.). (1992). *The handbook of aging and cognition.* Hillsdale, NJ: Erlbaum.

Craik, F. I. M., & Salthouse, T. A. (Eds.). (2000). *The handbook of aging and cognition* (2nd ed.). Mahwah, NJ: Erlbaum.

Craik, F. I. M., & Simon E. (1980). Age differences in memory: The roles of attention and depth of processing. In L. W. Poon, J. L. Fogard, L. S. Cermak, D. Arenberg, & L. W. Thompson (Eds.), *New directions in memory and aging.* Hillsdale, NJ: Erlbaum.

Craik, F. I. M., Morris, R. G., & Gick, M. L. (1989). Adult age differences in working memory. In G. Vallar & T. Shallice (Eds.), *Neuropsychological impairments of short-term memory.* New York: Cambridge University Press.

Cramer, D. (1990a). Disclosure of personal problems, self-esteem, and the facilitativeness of friends and lovers. *British Journal of Guidance and Counseling, 18,* 186–197.

Cramer, D. (1990b). Helpful actions of close friends to personal problems and distress. *British Journal of Guidance and Counseling, 18*, 281–293.

Crandell, L. E. (1992, May). *Continuities and discontinuities in attachment relationships across the life span: A qualitative study.* Paper presented at the meeting of the Midwestern Psychological Association, Chicago.

Crawford, M., & Marecek, J. (1989). Psychology reconstructs the female. *Psychology of Women Quarterly, 13,* 147–165.

Creighton, L. (1991, December 16). Grandparents: Silent saviors. *U.S. News and World Report,* pp. 80–89.

Cristofalo, V. J. (1988). An overview of the theories of biological aging. In J. E. Birren & V. L. Bengtson (Eds.), *Emergent theories of aging* (pp. 118–127). New York: Springer.

Crocker, J., & Major, B. (1989). Social stigma and self-esteem: The self-protective properties of stigma. *Psychological Review, 96,* 608–630.

Crosby, F. J. (Ed.). (1987). *Spouse, parent, worker: On gender and multiple roles.* New Haven, CT: Yale University Press.

Crossley, M., & Hiscock, M. (1992). Age-related differences in concurrent-task performance of normal adults: Evidence for a decline in processing resources. *Psychology and Aging, 7,* 499–506.

Crossman, L., London, C., & Barry, C. (1981). Older women caring for disabled spouses: A model for supportive services. *Gerontologist, 21,* 464–470.

Crouter, A. C., & Bumpus, M. F. (2001). Linking parents' work stress to children's and adolescents' psychological adjustment. *Current Directions in Psychological Science, 10*(5), 156–159.

Crowder, R. G. (1982). The demise of short-term memory. *Acta Psychologica, 50,* 291–323.

Crowell, J. A., Treboux, D., & Waters, E. (2002). Stability of attachment representations: The transition to marriage. *Developmental Psychology, 38*(4), 467–479.

Crystal, S. (1988). Work and retirement in the twenty-first century. *Generations, 12*(2), 60–64.

Culbertson, F. M. (1997). Depression and gender: An international review. *American Psychologist, 52*(1), 25–31.

Cumming, E., & Henry, W. H. (1961). *Growing old: The process of disengagement.* New York: Basic Books.

Cunningham, W. (1989). Intellectual abilities, speed of response, and aging. In V. L. Bengtson & K. W. Schaie (Eds.), *The course of later life: Research and reflections.* New York: Springer.

Curtis, L. H., Ostbye, T., Sendersky, V., Hutchison, S., Dans, P. E., Wright, A., Woosley, R. L., & Schulman, K. A. (2004). Inappropriate prescribing for elderly Americans in a large outpatient population. *Archives of Internal Medicine, 164,* 1621–1625.

Cushman, P. (1990). Why the self is empty: Toward a historically situated psychology. *American Psychologist, 45,* 599–611.

Cutler, N. (1991). Targeting and means testing, aging and need. *Generations, 15*(3), 17–18.

Darden, E., & Zimmerman, T. S. (1992). Blended families: A decade review, 1979 to 1990. *Family Therapy, 19,* 25–31.

Dasen, P. R. (1984). The cross-cultural study of intelligence: Piaget and the Baoule. *International Journal of Psychology, 19*(4–5), 407–434.

Davis, K., Grant, P., & Rowland, D. (1990). Alone and poor: The plight of elderly women. *Generations, 14*(2), 43–47.

Davis, M. S. (1973). *Intimate relations.* New York: Free Press.

DeAngelis, T. (2004, January). What's to blame for the surge in super-size Americans? *Monitor on Psychology,* pp. 46–49.

Deary, I., Whiteman, M C., Pattie, A., Starr, J., Hayward, C., Wright, A. F., Visscher, P. M., Tynan, M. C., & Whalley, L. J. (2004). Apolipoprotein E gene variability and cognitive functions at age 79: A follow-up of the Scottish Mental Survey of 1932. *Psychology and Aging, 19*(2), 367–371.

DeNavas, C., Proctor, B. D., & Mills, R. J. (2004). Income, poverty, and health insurance coverage in the United States: 2003. U.S. Bureau of the Census, *Current Population Reports (P60-226).* Washington, DC: U.S. Government Printing Office.

DeNeve, K. M. (1999). Happy as an extraverted clam? The role of personality for subjective well-being. *Current Directions, 8*(5), 141–144.

Denmark, F. L. (1994). Engendering psychology. *American Psychologist, 49*(4), 329–334.

Denmark, F., Russo, N. F., Frieze, I. H., & Sechzer, J. A. (1988). Guidelines for avoiding sexism in research: A report of the Ad Hoc Committee on Nonsexist Research. *American Psychologist, 43,* 582–585.

Dennis, W. (1966). Creative productivity between the ages of 20 and 80 years. *Journal of Gerontology, 21,* 1–8.

Deutsch, F. M. (2001). Equally shared parenting. *Current Directions in Psychological Science, 10*(1), 25–28.

Devins, G. M., Binik, Y. M., Gorman, P., Dattel, M., McCloskey, B., Oscar, G., & Briggs, J. (1982). Perceived self-efficacy, outcome expectancies, and negative mood states in end-stage renal disease. *Journal of Abnormal Psychology, 91,* 241–244.

deWaal, F. (1989). *Peacemaking among primates.* Cambridge, MA: Harvard University Press.

Diamond, M. C. (1993). An optimistic view of the aging brain. *Generations, 17*(1), 31–33.

Diener, E. (2000). Subjective well-being: The science of happiness and a proposal for a national index. *American Psychologist, 55*(1), 34–42.

Diener, E., & Diener, C. (1996). Most people are happy. *Psychological Science, 7*(3), 181–185.

Dillehay, R. C., & Sandys, M. R. (1990). Caregivers for Alzheimer's patients: What we are learning from research. *International Journal of Aging and Human Development, 30,* 263–285.

Dion, K. K. (1985). Socialization in adulthood. In G. Lindzey & E. Aronson (Eds.), *Handbook of social psychology* (Vol. 2, pp. 123–148). New York: Random House.

Dittmann, M. (2003, May). Fighting ageism. *Monitor on Psychology,* pp. 50–52.

Dosser, D. A., Balswick, J. O., & Halverson, C. F. (1986). Male inexpressiveness and relationships. *Journal of Social and Personal Relationships, 3,* 241–258.

Doty, R. L., Shaman, P., Applebaum, M. S. L., Gilberson, R., Siksorski, L., & Rosenberg, L. (1984). Smell identification ability: Changes with age. *Science, 226,* 1441–1443.

Doucette, D., & Roueche, J. E. (1991, October). Arguments with which to combat elitism and ignorance about community colleges. *Leadership Abstracts, 4*(13), 1–2.

Douvan, E., & Adelson, J. (1966). *The adolescent experience.* New York: Wiley.

Downs, B. (2003). Fertility of American women: June 2002. U.S. Census Bureau, *Current Population Reports* (P20-548). Washington, DC: U.S. Government Printing Office.

Drinkwater, B. (1988). Exercise and aging: The female master athlete. In J. L. Puhland & R. O. Voy (Eds.), *Sport science perspectives for women.* Champaign, IL: Human Kinetics.

Dutton, D. B., & Levine, S. (1989). Overview, methodological critique, and reformulation. In J. P. Bunker, D. S. Gomby, & B. H. Kehrer (Eds.), *Pathways to health* (pp. 29–69). Menlo Park, CA: Henry J. Kaiser Family Foundation.

Dutton, D. G., & Painter, S. L. (1981). Traumatic bonding: The development of emotional attachments in battered women and other relationships of intermittent abuse. *Victimology, 6*(1), 139–155.

Duvall, E. M. (1977). *Marriage and family development* (5th ed.). New York: Harper & Row.

Dychtwald, K., & Flower, J. (1989). *Age wave: The challenges and opportunities of an aging America.* Los Angeles: Tarcher.

Dykstra, P. (1995). Loneliness among the never and formerly married: The importance of supportive friendships and a desire for independence. *Journals of Gerontology: Psychological Sciences and Social Sciences, 50B,* S321–S329.

Easterlin, R. A., Macdonald, C., & Macunovich, D. J. (1990). Retirement prospects of the baby boom generation: A different perspective. *Gerontologist, 30,* 776–783.

Ehrlich, E. (1989, March 20). The mommy track. *Business Week,* pp. 126–134.

Eiden, R. D., Teti, D. M., & Corns, K. M. (1995). Maternal working models of attachment, marital adjustment, and parent-child relationship. *Child Development, 66,* 1504–1518.

Einstein, G. O., McDaniel, M. A., Manzi, M., Cochran, B., & Baker, M. (2000). Prospective memory and aging: Forgetting intentions over short delays. *Psychology and Aging, 15*(4), 671–683.

Einstein, G. O., McDaniel, M. A., Smith, R. E., & Shaw, P. (1998). Habitual prospective memory and aging: Remembering intentions and forgetting action. *Psychological Science, 9*(4), 284–288.

Eisenhandler, S. (1990). The asphalt identikit: Old age and the driver's license. *International Journal of Aging and Human Development, 30*(1), 1–14.

Ekerdt, D. J. (1989). Introduction: Retirement comes of age. *Generations, 13*(2), 5–6.

Elder, G. H. (1984). Families, kin, and the life course: A sociological perspective. In R. D. Parke (Ed.), *Review of child development research* (Vol. 7, pp. 80–135). Chicago: University of Chicago Press.

Elder, G. H., Jr. (1986). Military times and turning points in men's lives. *Developmental Psychology, 22,* 233–245.

Elias, M. F., Elias, J. W., & Elias, P. K. (1990). Biological and health influences on behavior. In J. E. Birren & K. W. Schaie (Eds.), *Handbook of the psychology of aging* (3rd ed., pp. 79– 102). San Diego, CA: Academic Press.

Elkind, D. (1996). Inhelder and Piaget on adolescence and adulthood: A postmodern appraisal. *Psychological Science, 7*(4), 216–220.

Ellis, A. (1991). How to fix the empty self. *American Psychologist, 46,* 539–540.

Ellor, J. R., & Kurz, D. J. (1982). Misuse and abuse of prescription and nonprescription drugs by the elderly. *Nursing Clinics of North America, 17,* 319–329.

Emery, R. E. (1989). Family violence. *American Psychologist, 44,* 321–328.

Emery, R. E., & Laumann-Billings, L. (1998). An overview of the nature, causes, and consequences of abusive family relationships: Toward differentiating maltreatment and violence. *American Psychologist, 53*(2), 121–135.

Enns, C. Z. (1994). On teaching about the cultural relativism of psychological constructs. *Teaching of Psychology, 21*(4), 205–211.

Epstein, C. F. (1987). Multiple demands and multiple roles: The conditions of successful management. In F. J. Crosby (Ed.), *Spouse, parent, worker: On gender and multiple roles* (pp. 23–35). New Haven, CT: Yale University Press.

Epstein, D. K., & Connor, J. R. (1999). Dementia in the elderly: An overview. *Generations, 23*(3), 9–16.

Epstein, E., & Guttman, R. (1984). Mate selection in man: Evidence, theory, and outcome. *Social Biology, 31,* 243–278.

Erber, J., & Rothberg, S. (1991). Here's looking at you: The relative effect of age and attractiveness on judgments about memory failure. *Journal of Gerontology: Psychological Sciences, 46,* P116–P123.

Erber, J., Etheart, M., & Szuchman, L. (1992). Age and forgetfulness: Perceiver's impressions of targets' capability. *Psychology and Aging, 7,* 479–483.

Erber, J., Szuchman, L., & Rothberg, S. (1990). Age, gender, and individual differences in memory failure appraisal. *Psychology and Aging, 5,* 236–241.

Erdner, R. A., & Guy, R. F. (1990). Career identification and women's attitudes toward retirement. *International Journal of Aging and Human Development, 30*(2), 129–139.

Ericsson, K. A., & Charness, N. (1994). Expert performance: Its structure and acquisition. *American Psychologist, 49*(8), 725–747.

Ericsson, K. A., Krampe, R. T., & Tesch-Romer, C. (1993). The role of deliberate practice in the acquisition of expert performance. *Psychological Review, 100,* 363–406.

Erikson, E. (1950). *Childhood and society.* New York: Norton.

Erikson, E. (1959). Identity and the life cycle. *Psychological Issues, 1*(1).

Erikson, E. (1963). *Childhood and society* (2nd ed.). New York: Norton.

Erikson, E. (1964). *Insight and responsibility.* New York: Norton.

Erikson, E. (1968). *Identity: Youth and crisis.* New York: Norton.

Erikson, E., Erikson, J., & Kivnick, H. (1986). *Vital involvement in old age.* New York: Norton.

Ershler, W. B. (1992). Cancer biology and aging. *Generations, 16*(4), 27–30.

Estes, C. L., & Binney, E. A. (1991). The biomedicalization of aging: Dangers and dilemmas. In M. Minkler & C. L. Estes (Eds.), *Critical perspectives on aging: The political and moral economy of growing old* (pp. 117–134). Amityville, NY: Baywood.

Evans, D. A., et al. (1989). Prevalence of Alzheimer's disease in a community population of older persons. *Journal of the American Medical Association, 262*(18), 2251–2256.

Evans, R. (1981). *Dialogue with Erik Erikson.* New York: Praeger.

Exeter, T. (1991). Demographic forecasts: Birthrate debate. *American Demographics, 13*(9), 55.

Falicov, C. (1984). Commentary: Focus on stages. *Family Process, 23,* 329–334.

Fay, R. E., Turner, C. F., Klassen, A. D., & Gagnon, J. H. (1989). Prevalence and patterns of same-gender contact among men. *Science, 243,* 338–348.

Featherman, D., & Petersen, T. (1986). Markers of aging: Modeling the clocks that time us. *Research on Aging, 8,* 339–365.

Federal Interagency Forum on Aging-Related Statistics. (2004). *Older Americans 2004: Key indicators of well-being.* Retrieved December 22, 2004, from www.agingstats.gov/chartbook2004/population.html.

Feeney, J. A., & Noller, P. (1990). Attachment style as a predictor of adult romantic relationships. *Journal of Personality and Social Psychology, 58,* 281–291.

Feinberg, J. L. (2001). Introduction: Ensuring appropriate, effective, and safe medication use for older people. *Generations, 24*(4), 5–7.

Feingold, A. (1988). Matching for attractiveness in romantic partners and same-sex friends: A meta-analysis and theoretical critique. *Psychological Bulletin, 104,* 226–235.

Feingold, A. (1992). Gender differences in mate selection preferences: A test of the parental investment model. *Psychological Bulletin, 112,* 125–139.

Ferraro, K. (1990). The gerontological imagination. In K. Ferraro (Ed.), *Gerontology: Perspectives and issues* (pp. 3–18). New York: Springer.

Fiatarone, M. A., Marks, E. C., Ryan, N. D., Meredith, C. N., Lipsitz, L. A., & Evans, W. J. (1990). High intensity strength training in nonagenarians. *Journal of the American Medical Association, 263,* 3029–3034.

Field, D. (1981). Retrospective reports by healthy intelligent elderly people of personal events of their adult lives. *International Journal of Behavioral Development, 4,* 77–97.

Field, D., & Minkler, M. (1988). Continuity and change in social support between young-old, old-old, and very-old adults. *Journal of Gerontology, 43,* P100–P106.

Field, D., & Weishaus, S. (1992). Marriage over half a century: A longitudinal study. In M. Bloom (Ed.), *Changing lives* (pp. 269–273). Columbia: University of South Carolina Press.

Fields, J. (2003a). America's Families and Living Arrangements: 2003. U.S. Census Bureau, *Current Population Reports,* (p20-553). Washington, DC: U.S. Government Printing Office.

Fields, J. (2003b). Children's living arrangements and characteristics: March 2002. U.S. Census Bureau, *Current Population Reports* (P20-547). Washington, DC: U.S. Government Printing Office.

Fields, J., & Casper, L. (2001). America's families and living arrangements: March 2000. U.S. Bureau of the Census, *Current Population Reports* (P20-537). Washington, DC: U.S. Government Printing Office.

Finch, C. E. (1988). Aging in the female reproduction system: A model system for analysis of complex interactions during aging. In J. E. Birren & V. L. Bengtson (Eds.), *Emergent theories of aging.* New York: Springer.

Finch, C. E., & Landfield, P. W. (1985). Neuroendocrine and automatic functions in aging mammals. In C. E. Finch & E. L. Schneider (Eds.), *Handbook of the biology of aging* (pp. 567–594). New York: Van Nostrand Reinhold.

Finch, C. E., & Tanzi, R. (1997). The genetics of aging. *Science, 278,* 407–411.

Finch, J., & Mason, J. (1990). Gender, employment, and responsibilities to kin. *Work, Employment, and Society, 4,* 349–367.

Fingerman, K. L. (2001). A distant closeness: Intimacy between parents and their children in later life. *Generations, 25*(3), 26–33.

Finkel, J. S., & Hansen, F. J. (1992). Correlates of retrospective material satisfaction in long-lived marriages: A social constructivist perspective. *Family Therapy, 19,* 1–16.

Finkel, S. I. (1994, January-February). Treating the symptoms of dementia. *Aging Today,* p. 3.

Finley, N. (1989). Theories of family labor as applied to gender differences in caregiving for elderly parents. *Journal of Marriage and the Family, 51,* 79–86.

Finn, S. (1986). Stability of personality self-ratings over 30 years: Evidence for an age/cohort interaction. *Journal of Personality and Social Psychology, 50,* 813–818.

Fins, J. J. (1999). Death and dying in the 1990s: Intimations of reality and immortality. *Generations, 23*(1), 81–86.

Fisher, C. B., Reid, J. D., & Melendez, M. (1989). Conflict in families and friendships of later life. *Family Relations, 38,* 83–89.

Fisher, H. E. (1992). *Anatomy of love: The natural history of monogamy, adultery, and divorce.* New York: Norton.

Fisk, A. D., & Rogers, W. A. (2002). Psychology and aging: Enhancing the lives of an aging population. *Current Directions in Psychological Science, 11*(3), 107–110.

Flavell, J. (1992). Cognitive development: Past, present, and future. *Developmental Psychology, 28,* 998–1005.

Flavell, J. H. (1996). Piaget's legacy. *Psychological Science, 7* (4), 200–203.

Fleming, A. S., Ruble, D. N., Flett, G. L., & Shaul, D.C. (1988). Postpartum adjustment in first-time mothers: Relations between mood, maternal attitudes, and mother-infant interactions. *Developmental Psychology, 24,* 71–81.

Fleming, A. S., Ruble, D. N., Flett, G. L., & Van Wagner, V. (1990). Adjustment in first-time mothers: Changes in mood and mood content during the early postpartum months. *Developmental Psychology, 26,* 137–143.

Floyd, F. J., Haynes, S. N., Doll, E. R., Winemiller, D., Lemsky, C., Burgy, T. M., Werle, M., & Heilman, N. (1992). Assessing retirement satisfaction and perceptions of retirement experiences. *Psychology and Aging, 7,* 609–621.

Folkman, S., & Moskowitz, J. T. (2000). Stress, positive emotion, and coping. *Current Directions, 9*(4), 115–118.

Follingstad, D. R., Neckerman, A. P., & Vormbrock, J. (1988). Reactions to victimization and coping strategies of battered women: The ties that bind. *Clinical Psychology Review, 8,* 373–390.

Folstein, M. F., Folstein, S., & McHugh, P. R. (1975). "Mini-Mental State." A practical method for grading the cognitive state of patients for the clinician. *Journal of Psychiatric Research, 12*(3), 189–198.

Fonagy, P., Steele, H., & Steele, M. (1991). Maternal representations of attachment during pregnancy predict the organization of infant-mother attachment at one year of age. *Child Development, 62,* 891–905.

Fontana, A., & Smith, R. (1989). Alzheimer's disease victims: The "unbecoming" of self and the normalization of competence. *Sociological Perspectives, 32,* 35–46.

Ford, M., & Widiger, T. A. (1989). Sex bias in the diagnosis of histrionic and antisocial personality disorder. *Journal of Consulting and Clinical Psychology, 57,* 301–305.

Foucault, M. (1981). *The history of sexuality: Vol. 1. An introduction.* Harmondsworth, England: Viking.

Fowler, R. D. (2002). Running commentary: APA's directory tells us who we are. *Monitor on Psychology, 33*(2), 3.

Fowlkes, M. R. (1987). Role combinations and role conflict: Introductory perspective. In F. J. Crosby (Ed.), *Spouse, parent, worker: On gender and multiple roles* (pp. 3–10). New Haven, CT: Yale University Press.

Foy, M. R., Henderson, V. W., Berger, T. W., & Thompson, R. F. (2000). Estrogen and neural plasticity. *Current Directions in Psychological Science, 9*(5), 148–152.

Fozard, J. (1990). Vision and hearing in aging. In J. E. Birren & K. W. Schaie (Eds.), *Handbook of the psychology of aging* (3rd ed., pp. 150–170). San Diego, CA: Academic Press.

Fraiberg, S., Adelson, E., & Shapiro, V. (1975). Ghosts in the nursery: A psychoanalytic approach to the problems of impaired infant-mother relationships. *Journal of the American Academy of Child Psychiatry, 14,* 387–422.

Fredrickson, B. L. (2000). Cultivating positive emotions to optimize health and well-being. *Prevention and Treatment, 3.* Available at http://journals.apa.org. prevention.

Fredrickson. B. L. (2001). The role of positive emotions in positive psychology. *American Psychologist, 56*(3), 218–226.

Freeman, S. M., Whartenby, K. A., & Abraham, G. N. (1992). Gene therapy: Applications to diseases associated with aging. *Generations, 16*(4), 45–48.

Freudenberger, H. J. (1987, December). Today's troubled men. *Psychology Today,* pp. 46–47.

Freund, A. M., & Baltes, P. B. (1998). Selection, optimization, and compensation as strategies of life management: Correlations with subjective indicators of successful aging. *Psychology and Aging, 13*(4), 531–543.

Friedmann, E. A., & Orbach, H. L. (1974). Adjustment to retirement. In S. Arieti (Ed.), *American handbook of psychiatry: Vol. 1. Foundations of psychiatry* (2nd ed.). New York: Basic Books.

Friends of the San Francisco Commission on the Status of Women (1980, December). *Womannews,* pp. 1ff.

Fries, J. F. (1980). Aging, natural death, and the compression of morbidity. *New England Journal of Medicine, 303,* 130–136.

Fries, J. F. (1990). The sunny side of aging. *Journal of the American Medical Association, 263,* 2354–2355.

Frieze, I., & Sechzer, J. (1988). Guidelines for avoiding sexism in psychological research: A report of the Ad Hoc Committee on Nonsexist Research. *American Psychologist, 43,* 582–585.

Fry, A. F., & Hale, S. (1996). Processing speed, working memory, and fluid intelligence: Evidence for a developmental cascade. *Psychological Science, 7*(4), 237–241.

Fuller-Thomson, E., Minkler, M., & Driver, D. (1997). A profile of grandparents raising grandchildren in the United States. *Gerontologist, 37*(3), 406–411.

Fullerton, H. N., Jr. (1999, November). The labor force: Steady growth, changing composition. *Monthly Labor Review,* pp. 19–32.

Fullerton, H. N., Jr., & Toossi, M. (2001, November). Employment outlook: 2000–2010. Labor force projections to 2010: Steady growth and changing composition. *Monthly Labor Review, 124*(11).

Fulton, R. (1970). Death, grief, and social recuperation. *Omega: Journal of Death and Dying, 1,* 23–28.

Fulton, R. (1987). The many faces of grief. *Death Studies, 11,* 243–256.

Funder, D. C., & Colvin, C. (1991). Explorations in behavioral consistency: Effects of persons, situations, and behaviors. *Journal of Personality and Social Psychology, 60,* 773–794.

Furstenberg, F. F., Brooks-Gunn, J., & Chase Lansdale, L. (1989). Teenaged pregnancy and childbearing (Special issue: Children and their development: Knowledge base, research agenda, and social policy application). *American Psychologist, 44,* 313–320.

Furumoto, L., & Scarborough, E. (1986). Placing women in the history of psychology. *American Psychologist, 41,* 35–42.

Fyock, C. D. (1995, November-December). Golden workers in gray America. *Aging Today,* p. 11.

Gabrieli, J. D. E., Desmond, J. E., Demb, J. B., Wagner, A. D., Stone, M. V., Vaidya, C. J., & Glover, G. H. (1996). Functional magnetic resonance imaging of semantic memory processes in the frontal lobes. *Psychological Science, 7*(5), 278–283.

Gallant, M. P., & Connell, C. M. (2003). Neuroticism and depressive symptoms among spouse caregivers: Do health behaviors mediate this relationship? *Psychology and Aging, 18*(3), 587–592.

Gallo, J. J., Ryan, S. D., & Ford, D. E. (1999). Attitudes, knowledge, and behavior of family physicians regarding depression in late life. *Archives of Family Medicine, 8*(3), 249–256.

Gannon, L. (1985). *Menstrual disorders and menopause.* New York: Praeger.

Gannon, L., Luchetta, T., Rhodes, K., Pardie, L., & Segrist, D. (1992). Sex bias in psychological research: Progress or complacency? *American Psychologist, 47,* 389–396.

Gardner, H. (1983). *Frames of mind: The theory of multiple intelligences.* New York: Basic Books.

Gardner, H. E. (1998). Extraordinary cognitive achievements (ECA): A symbol systems approach. In W. Damon & R. M. Lerner (Eds.), *Handbook of child psychology: Vol. I. Theoretical models of human development* (5th ed., pp. 415–466). New York: Wiley.

Gardner, H. E. (1999). Are there additional intelligences? The case for naturalist, spiritual, and existential intelligences. In J. Kane (Ed.), *Education, information, and transformation.* Englewood Cliffs, NJ: Prentice Hall.

Garland, H., Weinberg, R., Bruya, L., & Jackson, A. (1988). Self-efficacy and endurance performance: A longitudinal field test of cognitive mediation theory. *Applied Psychology: An International Review, 37,* 381–394.

Gatz, M. (1989). Clinical psychology and aging. In M. Storandt & G. R. VandenBos (Eds.), *The adult years: Continuity and change* (pp. 83–114). Washington, DC: American Psychological Association.

Gatz, M., & Hurwicz, M. (1990). Are old people more depressed? Cross-sectional data on Center for Epidemiological Studies depression scale factors. *Psychology and Aging, 5,* 284–290.

Gatz, M., & Pearson, C. G. (1988). Ageism revised and the provision of psychological services. *American Psychologist, 43,* 184–188.

Gatz, M., & Smyer, M. A. (1992). The mental health system and older adults in the 1990s. *American Psychologist, 47,* 741–751.

Gatz, M., & Smyer, M. A. (2001). Mental health and aging at the outset of the twenty-first century. In J. E. Birren & K. W. Schaie (Eds.), *Handbook of the psychology of aging* (5th ed., pp. 523–544). San Diego, CA: Academic Press.

Gatz, M., Bengtson, V. L., & Blum, M. J. (1990). Caregiving families. In J. E. Birren & K. W. Schaie (Eds.), *Handbook of the psychology of aging* (3rd ed., pp. 404–426). San Diego, CA: Academic Press.

Gazmarian, J., Petersen, P., Spitz, A., Goodwin, M., Saltzman, L., & Marks, J. (2000). Violence and reproductive health: Current knowledge and future directions. *Maternal and Child Health Journal, 4,* 79–84.

Geffner, R., & Rosenbaum, A. (1990). Characteristics and treatment of batterers. *Behavioral Sciences and the Law, 8,* 131–140.

Geiger, B. (1996). *Fathers as primary caregivers.* Westport, CT: Greenwood Press.

Gelles, R. J., & Straus, M. A. (1988). *Intimate violence.* New York: Simon & Schuster.

Gelles, R. J., & Straus, M. A. (1990). The medical and psychological costs of family violence. In M. A. Straus & R. J. Gelles (Eds.), *Physical violence in American families* (pp. 425–430). New Brunswick, NJ: Transaction.

Gelman, D., & Kandell, P. (1993, January 18). Isn't it romantic? *Newsweek,* pp. 60–61.

George, L. K. (1980). *Role transitions in later life.* Monterey, CA: Brooks/Cole.

George, L. K. (1990a). Caregiver stress studies: There really is more to learn. *Gerontologist, 30,* 580–581.

George, L. K. (1990b). Gender, age, and psychiatric disorders. *Generations, 14*(3), 22–27.

George, L. K. (1990c). Social structure, social processes, and social-psychological states. In R. H. Binstock & L. K. George (Eds.), *Handbook of aging and the social sciences* (3rd ed., pp. 186–204). San Diego, CA: Academic Press.

George, L. K. (1993). Depressive disorders and symptoms in later life. *Generations, 17*(1), 35–38.

George, L. K., & Clipp, E. (1991). Subjective components of aging well. *Generations, 15*(1), 57–60.

George, L. K., Blazer, D. G., Winfield-Laird, I., Leaf, P. J., & Fishbach, R. L. (1988). Psychiatric disorders and mental health service use in later life: Evidence from the Epidemiologic Catchment Area program. In J. Brody & G. Maddox (Eds.), *Epidemiology and aging* (pp. 189–219). New York: Springer.

Gerhard, G. S., & Cristofalo, V. J. (1992). The limits of biogerontology. *Generations, 16*(4), 55–59.

German, P. S. (1994). The meaning of prevention for older people: Changing common perceptions. *Generations, 18*(1), 28–32.

Gesell, A., & Ilg, F. (1949). *Child development: An introduction to the study of human growth.* New York: Harper & Row.

Ghisletta, P., & Lindenburger, U. (2003). Age-based structural dynamics between perceptual speed and knowledge in the Berlin Aging Study: Direct evidence for ability dedifferentiation in old age. *Psychology and Aging, 18* (4), 696–713.

Giarrusso, R., Silverstein, M., & Bengtson, V. L. (1996). Family complexity and the grandparent role. *Generations, 20*(1), 17–23.

Gibbons, A. (1990). Gerontology research comes of age. *Science, 250,* 622–625.

Gibson, R. C., & Burns, C. J. (1991, Fall-Winter). The health, labor force, and retirement experiences of aging minorities. *Generations, 15,* 31–35.

Gignac, M. A. M., & Gottlieb, B. H. (1996). Caregivers' appraisals of efficacy in coping with dementia. *Psychology and Aging, 11*(2), 214–225.

Gilbert, L. A. (1994). Current perspectives on dual-career families. *Current Directions in Psychological Science, 3*(4), 101–106.

Gilford, R. (1986). Marriages in later life. *Generations, 10*(4), 16–20.

Gilford, R., & Bengtson, V. (1979). Measuring marital satisfaction in three generations: Positive and negative dimensions. *Journal of Marriage and the Family, 41*(2), 15–50.

Gilligan, C. (1982). *In a different voice: Psychological theory and women's development.* Cambridge, MA: Harvard University Press.

Glaser, R. (1984). Education and thinking: The role of knowledge. *American Psychologist, 39*, 93–104.

Glick, I. O., Weiss, R. S., & Parkes, C. M. (1974). *The first year of bereavement.* New York: Wiley.

Glick, P. (1977). Updating the life cycle of the family. *Journal of Marriage and the Family, 39*, 5–13.

Glick, P. (1979). Future marital status and living arrangements of the elderly. *Gerontologist, 19*, 301–310.

Glick, P. (1984). Marriage, divorce, and living arrangements: Prospective changes. *Journal of Family Issues, 5*, 7–26.

Glick, P. (1988). Fifty years of family demography: A record of social change. *Journal of Marriage and the Family, 50*, 861–873.

Gobet, F., & Simon, H. A. (1996). The roles of recognition processes and look-ahead search in time-constrained expert problem-solving: Evidence from grand-master-level chess. *Psychological Science, 7*(1), 52–55.

Goetting, A. (1986). The developmental tasks of siblingship over the life cycle. *Journal of Marriage and the Family, 48*, 703–714.

Goff, K., & Torrance, P. (1991). The Georgia studies of creative behavior: Venturing into studies of creativity in elders. *Generations, 15*(2), 53–54.

Gold, D. T. (1987). Siblings in old age: Something special. *Canadian Journal on Aging, 6*(3), 199–215.

Gold, D. T. (1989). Sibling relationships in old age: A typology. *International Journal of Aging and Human Development, 28*, 37–50.

Gold, D. T., Woodbury, M. A., & George, L. K. (1990). Relationship classification using grade of membership analysis: A typology of sibling relationships in later life. *Journal of Gerontology: Social Sciences, 45*, S43–S51.

Gold, P. E., Cahill, L., & Wenk, G. L. (2002). *Ginkgo biloba:* A cognitive enhancer? *Psychological Science in the Public Interest, 3*(1), 2–11.

Goldberg, S. (1973). Family tasks and reactions in the crisis of death. *Social Casework, 54*, 398–405.

Goleman, D. (1980a, August). Leaving home: Is there a right time to go? *Psychology Today,* pp. 54–61.

Goleman, D. (1980b, February). 1,528 little geniuses and how they grew. *Psychology Today,* pp. 28ff.

Gonyea, J. G. (1998). Midlife and menopause: Uncharted territories for baby boomer women. *Generations, 22*(1), 87–89.

Goodman, L. A., Koss, M. P., Fitzgerald, L. F., Russo, N. F., & Keita, G. P. (1993). Male violence against women. *American Psychologist, 48*, 1054–1058.

Goodnow, J. J. (1976). The nature of intelligent behavior: Questions raised by cross-cultural studies. In L. B. Resnick (Ed.), *The nature of intelligence.* Hillsdale, NJ: Erlbaum.

Gordon, C., & Gergen, K. J. (Eds.). (1968). *The self in social interaction: Classic and contemporary perspectives.* New York: Wiley.

Gorman, C. (1991, September 30). How old is too old? *Time,* p. 62.

Gornick, M. E., Eggers, P. W., Reilly, T. W., Mentnech, R. M., Fitterman, L. K., Kucken, L. E., & Vladeck, B. C. (1996). Effects of race and income on mortality and use of services among Medicare beneficiaries. *New England Journal of Medicine, 335*(11), 791–799.

Gorrell, J. (1990). Some contributions of self-efficacy research to self-concept theory. *Journal of Research and Development in Education, 23*(2), 73–81.

Gould, E., Reeves, A. J., Graziano, M. S. A., & Gross, C. G. (1999). Neurogenesis in the neocortex of adult primates. *Science, 286*, 548–551.

Gould, E., Tanapat, P., McEwen, B. S., Fluge, G., & Fuchs, E. (1998). *Proceedings of the National Academy of Sciences, USA, 95*, 3168.

Gould, R. (1978). *Transformations.* New York: Simon & Schuster.

Goulding, M. (2004). Elderly patients prescribed inappropriate medications at 8 percent of doctor visits. *Archives of Internal Medicine, 164*(3), 305–312.

Gove, W. (1972). Sex, marital status, and mortality. *American Journal of Sociology, 79*, 45–67.

Gove, W. R., Ortega, S. T., & Style, C. B. (1989). The maturational and role perspectives on aging and self through the adult years: An empirical evaluation. *American Journal of Sociology, 94*, 1117–1145.

Goyal, A., & Fine, S. L. (1993). Update on medical and surgical techniques. *Aging and Vision News, 5*, 3. (Published by the Lighthouse National Center for Vision and Aging.)

Grady, C. L. (2002). Introduction to the special section on aging, cognition, and neuroimaging. *Psychology and Aging, 17*(1), 3–6.

Graf, P., & Schacter, D. (1985). Implicit and explicit memory for new associations in normal and amnesic subjects. *Journal of Experimental Psychology: Learning, Memory, and Cognition, 11*, 501–518.

Graham, S. (1992). "Most of the subjects were white and middle class": Trends in published research on African Americans in selected APA journals, 1970–1989. *American Psychologist, 47*, 629–639.

Grambs, J. D. (1989). *Women over forty: Visions and realities* (rev. ed.). New York: Springer.

Greenberg, J., & Cohen, R. L. (Eds.). (1982). *Equity and justice in social behavior.* New York: Academic Press.

Greenberg, J., Solomon, S., Pyszczynski, T., Rosenblatt, A., Burling, J., Lyon, D., Simon, L., & Pinel, E. (1992). Why do people need self-esteem? Converging evidence that self-esteem serves an anxiety-buffering function. *Journal of Personality and Social Psychology, 63,* 913–922.

Greenberg, M. T., & Marvin, R. S. (1982). Reactions of preschool children to an adult stranger: A behavioral system analysis. *Child Development, 53,* 481–490.

Greenough, W. T. (1984). Structural correlates of information storage in the mammalian brain: A review and hypothesis. *Trends in Neurosciences, 7*(7), 229–233.

Greenough, W. T. (1988). The anatomy of a memory: Convergence of results across a diversity of tests (Special issue: Learning and memory). *Trends in Neurosciences, 11*(4), 142–147.

Greenough, W. T., Larson, J. R., & Withers, G. S. (1985). Effect of unilateral and bilateral training in a reaching task on dendritic branching of neurons in the rat motor-sensory forelimb cortex. *Behavioral Neural Biology, 44,* 301–314.

Greenwald, A. (1988). A social-cognitive account of the self's development. In D. K. Lapsley & F. C. Power (Eds.), *Self, ego, and identity: Integrative approaches* (pp. 30–42). New York: Springer-Verlag.

Greenwald, A. (1992). New look: 3. Unconscious cognition reclaimed. *American Psychologist, 47,* 766–779.

Greenwald, A., Carnot, C. G., Beach, R., & Young, B. (1987). Increasing voting behavior by asking people if they expect to vote. *Journal of Applied Psychology, 71,* 314–318.

Greer, M. (2004, July/August). Strengthen your brain by resting it. *Monitor on Psychology,* pp. 60–62.

Gribbin, K., Schaie, K. W., & Parham, I. A. (1980). Complexity of life style and maintenance of intellectual abilities. *Journal of Social Issues, 36,* 47–61.

Griffin, E., & Sparks, G. G. (1990). Friends forever: A longitudinal exploration of intimacy in same-sex friends and platonic pairs. *Journal of Social and Personal Relationships, 7,* 29–46.

Griffin, J., Thomas, K., & Curry, G. (1991a, November 24). Odds against growing up black and male. *Chicago Tribune,* pp. 1, 20–21.

Griffin, J., Thomas, K., & Curry, G. (1991b, November 25). Lost fortunes, lost futures: Black men confront job, drug, and health problems. *Chicago Tribune,* pp. 1, 16.

Griffin, J., Thomas, K., & Curry, G. (1991c, November 26). Discrimination following black men into middle class. *Chicago Tribune,* pp. 1, 8.

Griffiths, T. D., & Meechan, P. J. (1990). Biology of aging. In K. F. Ferraro (Ed.), *Gerontology: Perspectives and issues* (pp. 45–57). New York: Springer.

Gruber, A. L., & Schaie, K. W. (1986, November). *Longitudinal-sequential studies of marital assortativity.* Paper presented at the annual meeting of the Gerontological Society of America, Chicago.

Gur, R. C., Mozley, P., Resnick, S., Gottlieb, G., Kohn, M., Zimmerman, R., Herman, G., Atlas, S., Grossman, R., Beretta, D., Erwin, R., & Gur, R. E. (1991). Gender differ-

ences in age effect on brain atrophy measured by magnetic resonance imaging. *Proceedings of the National Academy of Sciences of the United States of America, 88,* 2845–2849.

Gurucharri, C., & Selman, R. L. (1982). The development of interpersonal understanding during childhood, preadolescence, and adolescence: A longitudinal follow-up study. *Child Development, 53,* 924–927.

Gurung, R. A. R., Taylor, S. E., & Seeman, T. E. (2003). Accounting for changes in social support among married older adults: Insights from the MacArthur Studies of Successful Aging. *Psychology and Aging, 18*(3), 487–496.

Gutmann, D. (1988). The two faces of gerontology. *Newsletter of the Buehler Center on Aging* (McGaw Medical Center, Northwestern University), *4*(1), 1–2.

Gutmann, D. (1990). Psychological development and pathology in later adulthood. In R. A. Nemiroff & C. A. Colarusso (Eds.), *New dimensions in adult development* (pp. 170ff.). New York: Basic Books.

Haan, N., Millsap, R., & Hartka, E. (1986). As time goes by: Change and stability in personality over fifty years. *Psychology and Aging, 1,* 220–232.

Haas, A. P., & Hendin, H. (1983). Suicide among older people: Projections for the future. *Suicide and Life-Threatening Behavior, 13,* 147–154.

Haber, C. (1993). "And the fear of the poorhouse": Perceptions of old age impoverishment in early twentieth-century America. *Generations, 17*(2), 46–50.

Hackel, L. S., & Ruble, D. N. (1992). Changes in the marital relationship after the first baby is born: Predicting the impact of expectancy disconfirmation. *Journal of Personality and Social Psychology, 62,* 944–957.

Hackett, G. (1985). Role of mathematics self-efficacy in the choice of math-related majors of college women and men: A path analysis. *Journal of Counseling Psychology, 32,* 47–56.

Hackett, G., & Betz, N. E. (1981). A self-efficacy approach to the career development of women. *Journal of Vocational Behavior, 18,* 326–339.

Hacking, I. (Ed.). (1975). *The emergence of probability: A philosophical study of early ideas about probability, induction, and statistical inference.* London: Cambridge University Press.

Hackler, C. (2002). Troubling implications of doubling the human lifespan. *Generations, 24*(4), 15–19.

Hagestad, G. O. (1981). Problems and promises in the social psychology of intergenerational relations. In R. Fogel, E. Hatfield, S. Kiesler, & J. March (Eds.), *Aging: Stability and change in the family.* New York: Academic Press.

Hagestad, G. O. (1982). Divorce: The family ripple effect. *Generations, 7*(2), 24–25.

Hagestad, G. O. (1985). Continuity and connectedness. In V. L. Bengtson & J. F. Robertson (Eds.), *Grandparenthood* (pp. 31–48). Beverly Hills, CA: Sage.

Hagestad, G. O. (1987). Parent-child relations in later life: Trends and gaps in past research. In J. B. Lancaster, J. Altman, A. S. Rossi, & L. R. Sherrod (Eds.), *Parenting across the life span: Biosocial dimensions.* New York: Aldine de Gruyter.

Hagestad, G., & Neugarten, B. (1985). Age and the life course. In R. Binstock & E. Shanas (Eds.), *Handbook of aging and the social sciences* (pp. 35–61). New York: Van Nostrand Reinhold.

Haight, B. K. (1991). Reminiscing: The state of the art as a basis for practice. *International Journal of Aging and Human Development, 33,* 1–32.

Haimov, I., & Lavie, P. (1996). Melatonin—a soporific hormone. *Current Directions in Psychological Science, 5*(4), 106–111.

Haley, J. (1980). *Leaving home.* New York: McGraw-Hill.

Haley, W. E., West, C. A. C., Wadley, V. G., Ford, G. R., White, F. A., Barrett, J. J., Harrell, L. E., & Roth, D. L. (1995). Psychological, social, and health impact of caregiving: A comparison of black and white dementia family caregivers and noncaregivers. *Psychology and Aging, 10*(4), 540–552.

Hall, J. L., Gonder-Fredericks, L., Vogt, J., & Gold, P. E. (1986). Glucose enhancement of memory in aged humans. *Society for Neuroscience Abstracts, 12,* 1312.

Hamachek, D. (1990). Evaluating self-concept and ego status in Erikson's last three psychosocial stages. *Journal of Counseling and Development, 68,* 677–683.

Hamburg, D. A., & Takanishi, R. (1989). Preparing for life: The critical transition of adolescence. *American Psychologist, 44,* 825–827.

Harman, D. (1956). Aging: A theory based on free radical and radiation chemistry. *Journal of Gerontology, 11,* 298–300.

Harris, L. (1981). *Aging in the eighties.* Washington, DC: National Council on Aging.

Harter, S. (1988). The construction and conversation of the self: James and Cooley revisited. In D. K. Lapsley & F. C. Power (Eds.), *Self, ego, and identity: Integrative approaches* (pp. 43–70). New York: Springer-Verlag.

Harter, S. (1990). Issues in the assessment of the self-concept of children and adolescents. In A. La Greca (Ed.), *Through the eyes of a child* (pp. 292–325). Boston: Allyn & Bacon.

Hartfield, B. W. (1996). Legal recognition of the value of intergenerational nurturance: Grandparent visitation statutes in the nineties. *Generations, 20*(1), 53–56.

Hartin, W. H. (1990). Re-marriage: Some issues for clients and therapists. *Australian and New Zealand Journal of Family Therapy, 11,* 36–42.

Hartlage, S., Alloy, L. B., Vazquez, C., & Dykman, B. (1993). Automatic and effortful processing in depression. *Psychological Bulletin, 113,* 247–278.

Hartup, W. W., & Stevens, N. (1999). Friendships and adaptation across the life span. *Current Directions in Psychological Science, 8*(3), 76–79.

Hasher, L., & Zacks, R. (1979). Automatic and effortful processes in memory. *Journal of Experimental Psychology: General, 108,* 356–388.

Hasher, L., & Zacks, R. T. (1988). Working memory, comprehension, and aging: A review and a new view. In G. H. Bower (Ed.), *The psychology of learning and motivation* (Vol. 22, pp. 193–225). New York: Academic Press.

Hashimoto, A. (1993). Family relations in later life: A cross-cultural perspective. *Generations, 17*(4), 24–26.

Hatch, L. R. (1990). Gender and work: At midlife and beyond. *Generations, 14*(2), 48–51.

Hatfield, E. (1988). Passionate and compassionate love. In R. J. Sternberg & M. L. Barnes (Eds.), *The psychology of love.* New Haven, CT: Yale University Press.

Havighurst, R. (1953). *Human development and education.* New York: Longmans, Green.

Hawkins, H. L., Kramer, A. F., & Capaldi, D. (1992). Aging, exercise, and attention. *Psychology and Aging, 7,* 643–653.

Hayes, J. R. (1985). Three problems in teaching general skills. In S. Chipman, J. Segal, & R. Glaser (Eds.), *Thinking and learning skills* (pp. 391–406). Hillsdale, NJ: Erlbaum.

Hayflick, L. (1965). The limited in vitro lifetime of human diploid cell strains. *Experimental Cell Research, 37,* 614–636.

Hayflick, L. (1994). *How and why we age.* New York: Ballantine Books.

Hayflick, L. (2002). Anti-aging medicine: Hype, hope, and reality. *Generations, 24*(4), 20–26.

Hayflick, L. (2003). The one billion dollar misunderstanding. *Contemporary Gerontology, 10*(2), 65–69.

Hayflick, L., & Moorhead, P. S. (1961). The serial cultivation of human diploid cell strains. *Experimental Cell Research, 25,* 585–621.

Hays, R. B. (1985). A longitudinal study of friendship development. *Journal of Personality and Social Psychology, 48,* 909–924

Hays, R. B. (1989). The day-to-day functioning of close versus casual friendships. *Journal of Social and Personal Relationships, 6,* 21–37.

Hayslip, B., & Patrick, J. H. (Eds.). (2002). *Working with custodial grandparents.* New York: Springer.

Hazan, C., & Shaver, P. R. (1987). Romantic love conceptualized as an attachment process. *Journal of Personality and Social Psychology, 52,* 511–524.

Hebert, L. E., Scherr, P. A., Bienias, J. L., Bennett, D. A., & Evans, D. A. (2003, August). Alzheimer's disease in the U.S. population: Prevalence estimates using the 2000 census. *Archives of Neurology, 60*(8), 1119–1122.

Heckhausen, J., & Schulz, R. (1995). A life-span theory of control. *Psychological Review, 102*(2), 284–304.

Heckler, M. (1985). *Report of the secretary's task force on black and minority health.* Bethesda, MD: U.S. Department of Health and Human Services.

Heidrich, S. M., & Ryff, C. D. (1993). Physical and mental health in later life: The self-system as mediator. *Psychology and Aging, 8,* 327–338.

Heilman, K. M., Watson, R. T., Valenstein, E., & Goldberg, M. E. (1987). Attention: Behavioral and neural mechanisms. In V. B. Mountcastle (Ed.), *Handbook of physiology: Section 1. The nervous system* (pp. 461–481). Bethesda, MD: American Physiological Society.

Heilman, M. E., Wallen, A. S., Fuchs, D., & Tamkins, M. M. (2004). Penalties for success: Reactions to women who succeed at male gender-typed tasks. *Journal of Applied Psychology, 89*(3), 416–427.

Heine, S. H., Lehman, D. R., Markus, H. R., & Kitayama, S. (1999). Is there a universal need for positive self-regard? *Psychological Review, 106*(4), 766–794.

Heise, D. (1987). Sociocultural determination of mental aging. In C. Schooler & K. W. Schaie (Eds.), *Cognitive functioning and social structure over the life course* (pp. 247–261). Norwood, NJ: Ablex.

Hellman, L. (1974). *Pentimento.* New York: Signet.

Helms, J. (1992). Why is there no study of cultural equivalence in standardized cognitive ability testing? *American Psychologist, 47*, 1083–1101.

Helson, R., & Moane, G. (1987). Personality change in women from college to mid-life. *Journal of Personality and Social Psychology, 53*, 176–186.

Helson, R., & Wink, P. (1992). Personality change in women from the early 40s to the early 50s. *Psychology and Aging, 7*, 46–55.

Henderson, B. E., Ross, R. K., & Pike, M. C. (1991). Toward the primary prevention of cancer. *Science, 254,* 1131–1138.

Henderson, V. W., Paganini-Hill, A., Emanuel, C. K., Dunn, M. E., & Buckwalter, J. G. (1994). Estrogen replacement therapy in older women. Comparisons between Alzheimer's disease cases and nondemented control subjects. *Archives of Neurology, 51*, 896–900.

Hendrick, C., Hendrick, S., Foote, F. H., & Slapion-Foote, M. J. (1984). Do men and women love differently? *Journal of Social and Personal Relationships, 1,* 177–195.

Hendricks, J., & Hendricks, C. D. (1986). *Aging in mass society: Myth and realities.* Boston: Little, Brown.

Hendrie, H. C. (2001). Exploration of environmental and genetic risk factors for Alzheimer's disease: The value of cross-cultural studies. *Current Directions in Psychological Science, 10*(3), 98–101.

Henry, J. D., MacLeod, M. S., Phillips, L. H., & Crawford, J. R. (2004). A meta-analytic review of prospective memory and aging. *Psychology and Aging, 19*(1), 27–39.

Hering, E. (1920). Memory as a universal function of organized matter. In S. Butler (Ed.), *Unconscious memory.* London: Jonathan Cape.

Hermans, H., Kempen, H., & van Loon, R. (1992). The dialogical self: Beyond individualism and rationalism. *American Psychologist, 47*, 23–33.

Hertzog, C., & Hultsch, D. F. (2000). Metacognition in adulthood and old age. In F. I. M Craik & T. A. Salthouse (Eds.), *The handbook of aging and cognition* (2nd ed., pp. 417–466). Mahwah, NJ: Erlbaum.

Hertzog, C., & Schaie, K. W. (1988). Stability and change in adult intelligence: 2. Simultaneous analysis of longitudinal means and covariance structures. *Psychology and Aging, 3*, 122–130.

Herzog, A. R. (1989). Physical and mental health in older women. In A. R. Herzog, K. C. Holden, & M. M. Seltzer (Eds.), *Health and economic status of older women* (pp. 35–91). Amityville, NY: Baywood.

Hess, B. (1990). Gender and aging: The demographic parameters. *Generations, 14*(3), 12–15.

Hess, B., & Soldo, B. (1985). Husband and wife networks. In W. J. Sauer & R. T. Coward (Eds.), *Social support networks and the care of the elderly: Theory, research, and practice* (pp. 67–92). New York: Springer.

Hewlett, S. A. (1986). *A lesser life: The myth of women's liberation in America.* New York: Morrow.

Heyman, A., Wilkinson, W. E., Hurwitz, B. J., et al. (1987). Early-onset Alzheimer's disease: Clinical predictors of institutionalization and death. *Neurology, 37*, 980–984.

Higginbottom, S. F., Barling, J., & Kelloway, E. K. (1993). Linking retirement experiences and marital satisfaction: A mediational model. *Psychology and Aging, 8*, 508–516.

Higgins, E. T., & Bargh, J. A. (1987). Social cognition and social perception. *Annual Review of Psychology, 38*, 369–425.

High, D. M. (1991). A new myth about families of older people? *Gerontologist, 31*, 611–618.

Hightower, E. (1990). Adolescent interpersonal and familial precursors of positive mental health at midlife. *Journal of Youth and Adolescence, 19*, 257–275.

Hill, C. A. (1987). Affiliation motivation: People who need people but in different ways. *Journal of Personality and Social Psychology, 52*, 1008–1018.

Hill, C. A., & Christensen, A. J. (1989). Affiliative need, different types of social support, and physical symptoms. *Journal of Applied Social Psychology, 19*, 1351–1370.

Hill, R. (1986). Life cycle stages for types of single parent families: Of family development theory. *Family Relations, 35,* 19–29.

Hill, R., & Mattessich, P. (1979). Family development theory and life-span development. In P. Baltes & O. Brim (Eds.), *Life-span development and behavior* (Vol. 3, pp. 161–204). New York: Academic Press.

Hinde, R. A. (1984). Why do the sexes behave differently in close relationships? *Journal of Social and Personal Relationships, 1,* 471–501.

Hirschfeld, R. M. A., et al. (1997). The National Depressive and Manic-Depressive Association statement on the undertreatment of depression. *Journal of the American Medical Association, 277*(4), 333–340.

Hobfoll, S. (1989). Conservation of resources: A new attempt at conceptualizing stress. *American Psychologist, 44*, 513–524.

Hobman, D. (1981). *The impact of aging: Strategies for care.* New York: St. Martin's Press.

Hochschild, A. R. (1973). *The unexpected community.* Berkeley: University of California Press.

Hochschild, A. R. (1989). *The second shift: Working parents and the revolution at home.* New York: Viking.

Hoffman, E. (2000, November 20). Nursing homes don't have to break you. *Businessweek Online.* Available at www.businessweek.com:/2000/00 47/b3708183.htm.

Hoffman, L., & Manis, J. (1979). The value of children in the United States: A new approach to the study of fertility. *Journal of Marriage and the Family, 41,* 583–596.

Hogg, J. R., & Heller, K. (1990). A measure of relational competence for community-dwelling elderly. *Psychology and Aging, 5,* 580–588.

Holahan, C. K. (1984). Marital attitudes over 40 years: A longitudinal cohort analysis. *Journal of Gerontology, 39,* 49–57.

Holland, J. L. (1973). *Making vocational choices: A theory of careers.* Englewood Cliffs, NJ: Prentice Hall.

Holland, J. L. (1977). *Manual for the Vocational Preference Inventory.* Palo Alto, CA: Consulting Psychologists Press.

Holland, J. L. (1985). *Making vocational choices: A theory of vocational personalities and work environments.* Englewood Cliffs, NJ: Prentice Hall.

Holland, J. L. (1996). Exploring careers with a typology: What we have learned and some new directions. *American Psychologist, 51*(4), 397–406.

Hollon, S. D., Thase, M. E., & Markowitz, J. C. (2002). Treatment and prevention of depression. *Psychological Science in the Public Interest, 3*(2), 39–77.

Holmes, T. H., & Rahe, R. H. (1967). The social readjustment rating scale. *Journal of Psychosomatic Research, 11,* 213–218.

Holstein, M. (1992, February-March). Beyond the PSDA: The wisdom and heart of choice in dying. *Aging Today,* p. 3.

Holtzworth-Munroe, A., & Stuart, G. L. (1994). Typologies of male batterers: Three subtypes and the differences among them. *Psychological Bulletin, 116,* 476–497.

Honel, R. (1988). *Journey with grandpa: Our family's struggle with Alzheimer's disease.* Baltimore, MD: Johns Hopkins University Press.

Honig, M. (1996). Retirement expectations: Differences by race, ethnicity, and gender. *Gerontologist, 36*(3), 373–382.

Hooker, K., Monahan, D., Shifren, K., & Hutchison, C. (1992). Mental and physical health of spouse caregivers: The role of personality. *Psychology and Aging, 7,* 367–375.

Horn, J. L. (1982). The theory of fluid and crystallized intelligence in relation to concepts of cognitive psychology and aging in adulthood. In F. I. M. Craik & E. E. Trehub (Eds.), *Aging and cognitive processes* (pp. 237–278). New York: Plenum Press.

Horn, J. L. (1986). Intellectual ability concepts. In R. J. Sternberg (Ed.), *Advances in the psychology of human intelligence* (pp. 35–75). Hillsdale, NJ: Erlbaum.

Horner, K. L., Rushton, J. P., & Vernon, P. A. (1986). Relation between aging and research productivity. *Psychology and Aging, 1,* 319–324.

Horner, M. (1970). Femininity and successful achievement: A basic inconsistency. In J. Bardwick, E. Douvan, M. Horner, & D. Gutmann (Eds.), *Feminine personality and conflict.* Belmont, CA: Brooks/Cole.

Horowitz, M. J. (1990). A model of mourning: Changes in schemas of self and others. *Journal of the American Psychoananalytic Association, 38,* 297–324.

House, J. S., Landis, K. R., & Umberson, D. (1988). Social relations and health. *Science, 241,* 540–545.

Howard, G. (1991). Culture tales: A narrative approach to thinking, cross-cultural psychology, and psychotherapy. *American Psychologist, 46,* 187–197.

Howard, J. H., Marshall, J., Rechnitzer, P. A., Cunningham, D. A., & Donner, A. (1982). Adapting to retirement. *Journal of the American Geriatrics Society, 30,* 488–500.

Hoyer, W. (1987). Acquisition of knowledge and the decentralization of g in adult intellectual development. In C. Schooler & K. W. Schaie (Eds.), *Cognitive functioning and social structure over the life course* (pp. 120–141). Norwood, NJ: Ablex.

Hoyer, W., & Rybash, J. M. (1994). Characterizing adult cognitive development. *Journal of Adult Development, 1*(1), 7–12.

Huber, R., & Gibson, J. W. (1990). New evidence for anticipatory grief. *Hospice Journal, 6*(1), 49–67.

Hudson, R. B. (1993). The "graying" of the federal budget revisited. *Generations, 17*(2), 79–82.

Hudson, R. B., & Kingson, E. R. (1991). Inclusive and fair: The case for universality in social programs. *Generations, 15*(3), 51–56.

Hughes, M., & Demo, D. (1989). Self-perceptions of black Americans: Self-esteem and personal efficacy. *American Journal of Sociology, 95,* 132–159.

Hull, R. (1980). Thirteen commandments for talking to the hearing-impaired older person. *Asha, 22,* 427.

Hultsch, D. F., Hertzog, C., Small, B. J., & Dixon, R. A. (1999). Use it or lose it: Engaged lifestyle as a buffer of cognitive decline in aging? *Psychology and Aging, 14*(2), 245–263.

Hultsch, D., & Dixon, R. (1990). Learning and memory in aging. In J. E. Birren & K. W. Schaie (Eds.), *Handbook of the psychology of aging* (3rd ed., pp. 258–274). San Diego, CA: Academic Press.

Human Capital Initiative. (1993). *Vitality for life: Psychological research for productive aging.* Washington, DC: American Psychological Association.

Humphry, D. (1991). *Final exit: The practicalities of self-deliverance and assisted suicide for the dying.* Eugene, OR: Hemlock Society.

Hunt, E. (1993). What do we need to know about aging? In J. Cerella, J. Rybash, W. Hoyer, & M. L. Commons (Eds.), *Adult information processing: Limits on loss* (pp. 587–598). San Diego, CA: Academic Press.

Hutton, T. J., Dippel, R. L., Loewenson, R. B., et al. (1985). Predictors of nursing home placements in patients with Alzheimer's disease. *Hospital Community Psychiatry, 37,* 1199–1201.

Huyck, M. (1990). Gender differences in aging. In J. E. Birren & K. W. Schaie (Eds.), *Handbook of the psychology of aging* (3rd ed., pp. 124–132). San Diego, CA: Academic Press.

Huyck, M. H. (1995). Marriage and close relationships of the marital kind. In R. Blieszner & V. H. Bedford (Eds.), *Handbook of aging and the family* (pp. 181–200). Westport, CT: Greenwood Press.

Inglehart, R. (1990). *Culture shift in advanced industrial society.* Princeton, NJ: Princeton University Press.

Ivy, G., MacLeod, C., Petit, T., & Markus, E. (1992). A physiological framework for perceptual and cognitive changes in aging. In F. I. M. Craik & T. A. Salthouse (Eds.), *The handbook of aging and cognition* (pp. 273–314). Hillsdale, NJ: Erlbaum.

Jackson, J. J. (1985). Race, national origin, ethnicity, and aging. In R. B. Binstock & E. Shanas (Eds.), *Handbook of aging and the social sciences.* New York: Van Nostrand Reinhold.

Jackson, J. S., Antonucci, T., & Gibson, R. (1990). Cultural, racial, and ethnic minority influences on aging. In J. E. Birren & K. W. Schaie (Eds.), *Handbook of the psychology of aging* (3rd ed., pp. 103–123). San Diego, CA: Academic Press.

Jakubiak, C. H., Jr., & Callahan, J. J., Jr. (1996). Treatment of mental disorders among nursing home residents: Will the market provide? *Generations, 19*(4), 39–42.

James, J. W., & Cherry, F. (1988). *The grief recovery handbook.* New York: Harper & Row.

James, J. W., & Haley, W. E. (1995). Age and health bias in practicing clinical psychologists. *Psychology and Aging, 10*(4), 610–616.

James, W. (1890). *Principles of psychology.* New York: Henry Holt.

James, W. (1892). *Psychology.* New York: Henry Holt. (Adapted in Gordon & Gergen, *Self in Social Action,* 1968, chap. 3.)

James, W. (1952). The principles of psychology. In R. M. Hutchinson (Ed.), *Great books of the western world.* Chicago: Encyclopaedia Britannica. (Original work published 1890.)

Janoff-Bulman, R., & Frieze, I. H. (1983). A theoretical perspective for understanding reactions to victimization. *Journal of Social Issues, 39,* 1–17.

Jarvis, P. S. (1990). A nation at risk: The economic consequences of neglecting career development. *Journal of Career Development, 16*(3), 157–171.

Jenkins, S. R. (1989). Longitudinal prediction of women's careers: Psychological, behavioral, and socio-structural influences. *Journal of Vocational Behavior, 34,* 204–235.

Jensen-Campbell, L. A., Graziano, W. G., & West, S. G. (1995). Dominance, prosocial orientation, and female preferences: Do nice guys really finish last? *Journal of Personality and Social Psychology, 68*(3), 427–440.

Jeste, D. V., Alexopoulos, G. S., Bartels, S. J., Cummings, J. L., Gallo, J. J., Gottlieb, G. L., Halpain, M. C., Palmer, B. W., Patterson, T. L., Reynolds, C. F., & Lobowitz, B. D. (1999). Consensus statement on the upcoming crisis in geriatric mental health. *Archives of General Psychiatry, 56*(9), 848–853.

Johnson, C. L. (1985a). Grandparenting options in divorcing families: An anthropological perspective. In V. L. Bengtson & J. F. Robertson (Eds.), *Grandparenthood* (pp. 81–96). Beverly Hills, CA: Sage.

Johnson, C. L. (1985b). The impact of illness on late life marriages. *Journal of Marriage and Family, 47,* 165–172.

Johnson, C. L. (1995). Cultural diversity in the late-life family. In R. Blieszner & V. H. Bedford (Eds.), *Handbook of aging and the family* (pp. 307–331). Westport, CT: Greenwood Press.

Johnson, C. L., & Catalano, D. J. (1981). Childless elderly and their family supports. *Gerontologist, 21,* 610–618.

Johnson, W., McGue, M., Krueger, R. F., & Bouchard, Jr., T. J. (2004). Marriage and personality: A genetic analysis. *Journal of Personality and Social Psychology, 86*(2).

Johnston, W. B. (1991, March-April). Global work force 2000: The new world labor market. *Harvard Business Review,* pp. 115–127.

Johnston, W. B., & Packer, A. H. (1987). *Workforce 2000: Work and workers for the twenty-first century.* Indianapolis, IN: Hudson Institute.

Jones, C. J., & Meredith, W. (2000). Developmental paths of psychological health from early adolescence to later adulthood. *Psychology and Aging, 15*(2), 351–360.

Jones, D.C., & Vaughan, K. (1990). Close friendships among senior adults. *Psychology and Aging, 5,* 451–457.

Jones, D.C., Bloys, N., & Wood, M. (1990). Sex roles and friendship patterns. *Sex Roles, 23,* 133–145.

Jones, W. H., Hobbs, S. A., & Hockenbury, D. (1982). Loneliness and social skill deficits. *Journal of Personality and Social Psychology, 42,* 682–689.

Jung, C. (1933). *Modern man in search of a soul* (W. S. Dell & C. F. Baynes, Trans.). New York: Harcourt.

Kahana, E., & Kahana, B. (1970). Grandparenthood from the perspective of the developing grandchild. *Development Psychology, 3,* 98–105.

Kahn, R. L. (1979). Aging and social support. In M. W. Riley (Ed.), *Aging from birth to death.* Boulder, CO: Westview Press.

Kahn, R. L., & Antonucci, T. C. (1980). Convoys over the life-course: Attachment, roles, and social support. In P. B. Baltes & O. G. Brim (Eds.), *Life-span development and behavior* (pp. 253–286). San Diego, CA: Academic Press.

Kahn, R. L., Wethington, E., & Ingersoll-Dayton, B. (1987). Social support and social networks. In R. P. Abeles (Ed.), *Life-span perspectives and social psychology* (pp. 139–165). Hillsdale, NJ: Erlbaum.

Kalick, S. M., & Hamilton, T. E. (1986). The matching hypothesis reexamined. *Journal of Personality and Social Psychology, 4,* 673–682.

Kalish, R. A. (1975). *Late adulthood: Perspectives on human development.* Monterey, CA: Brooks/Cole.

Kalish, R. A. (1976). Death and dying in a social context. In R. H. Binstock & E. Shanas (Eds.), *Handbook of aging and the social sciences.* New York: Van Nostrand.

Kalish, R. A., & Reynolds, D. (1977). *Death and ethnicity: A psychocultural study.* Los Angeles: University of Southern Califoria Press.

Kantor, G. K., & Straus, M. A. (1990). The "drunken bum" theory of wife beating. In M. A. Straus & R. J. Gelles (Eds.), *Physical violence in American families* (pp. 203–224). New Brunswick, NJ: Transaction.

Kantrowitz, B., Rosenberg, D., Springen, K., & King, P. (1992, November 16). Giving women the business. *Newsweek,* p. 98.

Kaplan, M. (1983). A woman's view of DSM-III. *American Psychologist, 38,* 786–792.

Kaplan, S. (1987, March-April). The new generation gap: The politics of generational justice. *Common Cause Magazine,* pp. 13–15.

Karlin, W. A., Brondolo, E., & Schwartz, J. (2003). Workplace social support and ambulatory cardiovascular activity in New York City traffic agents. *Psychosomatic Medicine, 65*(2), 167–176.

Karney, B. R., & Bradbury, T. N. (1995). The longitudinal course of marital quality and stability: A review of theory, method, and research. *Psychological Bulletin, 118*(1), 3–34.

Karp, D. (1988). A decade of reminders: Changing age consciousness between fifty and sixty years old. *Gerontologist, 28,* 727–738.

Kastenbaum, R. (1992). *The psychology of death* (2nd ed.). New York: Springer.

Kastenbaum, R. (1995). To which self be true? *Contemporary Gerontology, 2*(2), 34–37.

Kaszniak, A. W. (1990). Psychological assessment of the aging individual. In J. E. Birren & K. W. Schaie (Eds.), *Handbook of the psychology of aging* (3rd ed., pp. 427–445). San Diego, CA: Academic Press.

Katakis, C. D. (1976). An exploratory multilevel attempt to investigate interpersonal and intrapersonal patterns of 20 Athenian familes. *Mental Health and Society, 3,* 1–9.

Katakis, C. D. (1978). On the transaction of social change processes and the perception of self in relation to others. *Mental Health and Society, 5,* 275–283.

Katakis, C. D. (1984). *Oi tris tautotites tis Ellinikis oikogenoias [The three identities of the Greek family].* Athens, Greece: Kedros.

Kaufman, S. R. (1986). *The ageless self: Sources of meaning in later life.* Madison: University of Wisconsin Press.

Kaufman, S. R. (1988). Illness, biography, and the interpretation of self following a stroke. *Journal of Aging Studies, 2,* 217–227.

Kaufman, S. R. (1993). Reflections on "the ageless self." *Generations, 17*(2), 13–16.

Kausler, D. H. (1994). *Learning and memory in normal aging.* San Diego, CA: Academic Press.

Kausler, D. H., Wiley, J. G., & Lieberwitz, K. J. (1992). Adult age differences in short-term memory and subsequent long-term memory for actions. *Psychology and Aging, 7,* 309–316.

Keinan, G., & Hobfoll, S. E. (1989). Stress, dependency, and social support: Who benefits from husband's presence in delivery? *Journal of Social and Clinical Psychology, 8,* 32–44.

Keith, P. M. (1986). The social context and resources of the unmarried in old age. *International Journal of Aging and Human Development, 23,* 81–96.

Keith, P. M., & Schafer, R. B. (1991). *Relationships and well-being over the life stages.* New York: Praeger.

Keller, M., Leventhal, E., & Larson, B. (1989). Aging: The lived experience. *International Journal of Aging and Human Development, 29*(1), 67–82.

Kelley, H. H. (1979). *Personal relationships.* Hillsdale, NJ: Erlbaum.

Kelley, H. H., Berscheid, E., Christensen, A., Harvey, J. H., Huston, T. L., Levenger, G., McClintock, E., Peplau, L. A., & Peterson, D. R. (1983). *Close relationships.* New York: Freeman.

Kelly, E. L., & Conley, J. J. (1987). Personality and compatibility: A prospective analysis of marital stability and marital satisfaction. *Journal of Personality and Social Psychology, 52,* 27–40.

Kelly, J. R. (1988). *Peoria winter.* Lexington, MA: Heath.

Kempe, C. H., Silverman, F., Steele, B., Droegemueller, W., & Silver, H. (1962). The battered child syndrome. *Journal of the American Medical Association, 181,* 17–24.

Kemper, S., Greiner, L. H., Marquis, J. G., Prenovost, K., & Mitzner, T. L. (2001). Language decline across the life span: Findings from the Nun Study. *Psychology and Aging, 16*(2), 227–239.

Keniston, K. (1971). *Youth and dissent: The rise of a new opposition.* New York: Harcourt Brace Jovanovich.

Kenrick, D. T., & Keefe, R. C. (1992). Age preferences in mates reflect sex differences in human reproductive strategies. *Behavioral and Brain Sciences, 15*(1), 75–133.

Kessler, R. C., Brown, R. L., & Borman, C. L. (1981). Sex differences in psychiatric help-seeking: Evidence from four large-scale surveys. *Journal of Health and Social Behavior, 22,* 49–64.

Kessler, R. C., McGonagle, K. A., Zhao, S., Nelson, C. B., Hughes, M., Eshelman, S., Wittchen, H., & Kendler, K. S. (1994). Lifetime and 12-month prevalence of DSM-III-R psychiatric disorders in the United States: Results from the National Comorbidity Survey. *Archives of General Psychiatry, 51,* 8–19.

Kiecolt-Glaser, J. K., & Glaser, R. (1988). Psychological influences on immunity: Implications for AIDS. *American Psychologist, 43,* 892–898.

Kiecolt-Glaser, J. K., & Glaser, R. (2001). Stress and immunity: Age enhances the risks. *Current Directions in Psychological Science, 10*(1), 18–21.

Kiecolt-Glaser, J. K., McGuire, L., Robles, T. F., & Glaser, R. (2002). Emotions, morbidity, and mortality: New perspectives from psychoneuroimmunology. *Annual Review of Psychology, 53,* 83–107.

Kiecolt-Glaser, J. K., Page, G. G., Marucha, P. T., MacCallum, R. C., & Glaser, R. (1998). Psychological influences on surgical recovery: Perspectives from psychoneuroimmunology. *American Psychologist, 53*(11), 1209–1218.

Killoran, M. M. (1984). The management of tension: A case study of *Chatelaine Magazine,* 1939–1980. *Journal of Comparative Family Studies, 15,* 407–426.

Kim, J. E., & Moen, P. (2001). Is retirement good or bad for subjective well-being? *Current Directions in Psychological Science, 10*(3), 83–86.

Kim, J. E., Nesselroade, J. R., & Featherman, D. L. (1996). The state component in self-reported worldviews and religious beliefs of older adults: The MacArthur successful aging studies. *Psychology and Aging, 11*(3), 396–407.

Kimmel, D., & Moody, H. (1990). Ethical issues in gerontological research and services. In J. E. Birren & K. W. Schaie (Eds.), *Handbook of the psychology of aging* (3rd ed., pp. 489–501). San Diego, CA: Academic Press.

Kingson, E. R. (1989). Don't panic; it's working: What baby boomers need to know about Social Security. *Generations, 13*(2), 15–20.

Kinsey, A., Pomeroy, W., & Martin, C. (1948). *Sexual behavior in the human male.* Philadelphia: Saunders.

Kinsey, A., Pomeroy, W., & Martin, C. (1953). *Sexual behavior in the human female.* Philadelphia: Saunders.

Kirkwood, T. B. L. (2000). Evolution of aging: How genetic factors affect the end of life. *Generations, 24*(2), 12–18.

Kite, M., & Johnson, B. (1988). Attitudes toward older and younger adults: A meta-analysis. *Psychology and Aging, 3,* 233–244.

Kivnick, H. (1982a). Grandparenthood: An overview of meaning and mental health. *Gerontologist, 22,* 59–66.

Kivnick, H. Q. (1982b). *The meaning of grandparenthood.* Ann Arbor, MI: UMI Research Press.

Kivnick, H. (1993). Everyday mental health: A guide to assessing life's strengths. *Generations, 17*(1), 13–20.

Klaus, M. H., & Kennell, J. H. (1982). *Maternal-infant bonding* (2nd ed.). St. Louis: Mosby.

Klein, D. M., Jorgenson, S. R., & Miller, B. (1979). Research methods and developmental reciprocity in families. In R. M. Lerner & G. B. Spanier (Eds.), *Child influences on marital and family interactions: A life-span perspective* (pp. 107–136). New York: Academic Press.

Kleyman, P. (1996, January–February). Living with loss, healing with hope. *Aging Today,* pp. 7–8.

Kling, K. C., Hyde, J. S., Showers, C. J., & Buswell, B. (1999). Gender differences in self-esteem: A meta-analysis. *Psychological Bulletin, 125*(4), 470–500.

Klohnen, E. C., & Luo, S. (2003). Interpersonal attraction and personality: What is attractive—self similarity, ideal similarity, complementarity, or attachment security? *Journal of Personality and Social Psychology, 85*(4).

Knapp, R. (1987, July). When a child dies. *Psychology Today,* pp. 60–67.

Kobak, R. R., & Sceery, A. (1988). Attachment in late adolescence: Working models, affect regulation, and representation of self and others. *Child Development, 59,* 135–146.

Kogan, N. (1990). Personality and aging. In J. E. Birren & K. W. Schaie (Eds.), *Handbook of the psychology of aging* (3rd ed., pp. 330–346). New York: Academic Press.

Kogan, N., & Mills, M. (1992). Gender influences on age cognitions and preferences: Sociocultural or sociobiological? *Psychology and Aging, 7,* 98–106.

Kohen, J. A. (1983). Old but not alone: Informal social supports among the elderly by marital status and sex. *Gerontologist, 23,* 57–63.

Kohlberg, L. (1969). Stage and sequence: The cognitive-developmental approach to socialization. In D. A. Goslin (Ed.), *Handbook of socialization and research* (pp. 347–480). Chicago: Rand McNally.

Kohn, M. L. (1969). *Class and conformity.* Homewood, IL: Dorsey.

Kohn, M. L. (1987). Cross-national research as an analytic strategy. *American Sociological Review, 52,* 713–731.

Kohn, M. L., & Schooler, C. (1983). In collaboration with J. Miller, K. A. Miller, C. Schoenbach, & R. J. Schoenberg, *Work and personality: An inquiry into the impact of social stratification.* Norwood, NJ: Ablex.

Kohn, R. R. (1978). *Principles of mammalian aging.* Englewood Cliffs, NJ: Prentice Hall.

Kohn, R. R. (1985). Aging and age-related diseases: Normal processes. In H. A. Johnson (Ed.), *Relations between normal aging and disease* (pp. 1–43). New York: Raven Press.

Kolata, G. (2000, April 5). Estrogen use tied to slight increase in risks to heart. *New York Times,* p. 1.

Kotre, J. (1984). *Outliving the self: Generativity and the interpretation of lives.* Baltimore: Johns Hopkins University Press.

Kotre, J. (1992, May 1). *Emerging perspectives in adult personality development: Research concerning generativity. Generative outcome.* Symposium presented at the meeting of the Midwestern Psychological Association, Chicago.

Kotulak, R. (1993, April 11). Unraveling hidden mysteries of the brain. *Chicago Tribune,* pp. 1, 10.

Kozma, A., & Stones, M. J. (1978). Some research issues and findings in the study of psychological well-being in the aged. *Canadian Psychological Review, 19,* 241–249.

Kramer, A. F., & Willis, S. L. (2002). Enhancing the cognitive vitality of older adults. *Current Directions in Psychological Science, 11*(5), 173–177.

Kramer, A. F., Hahn, S., Cohen, N. J., Banich, M. T., McAuley, E., Harrison, C. R., Chason, J., Vakil, E., Bardell, L., Boileau, R. A., & Colcombe, A. (1999). Ageing, fitness and neurocognitive function. *Nature, 400*(6743), 418–420.

Krantz, D. S., & McCeney, M. K. (2002). Effects of psychological and social factors on organic disease: A critical assessment of research on coronary heart disease. *Annual Review of Psychology, 53*(1), 341–369.

Krantz, D. S., Sheps, D. S., Carney, R. M., & Natelson, B. H. (2000). Effects of mental stress in patients with coronary artery disease. *Journal of the American Medical Association, 283*(14), 1800–1802.

Krause, N. (2003). Stress, social support, and health in late life: Key issues for future research. *Contemporary Gerontology, 10*(1), 3–6.

Krause, N., & Baker, E. (1992). Financial strain, economic values, and somatic symptoms in later life. *Psychology and Aging, 7,* 4–14.

Krause, N., & Shaw, B. A. (2000). Role-specific feelings of control and mortality. *Psychology and Aging, 15*(4), 617–626.

Krause, N., & Wray, L. A. (1991). Psychosocial correlates of health and illness among minority elders. *Generations, 15*(4), 25–30.

Kraut, R. E. (1973). Effects of social labeling on giving to charity. *Journal of Experimental Social Psychology, 9,* 551–562.

Kremer, J. (1988). Effects of negative information about aging on attitudes. *Educational Gerontology, 14,* 69–80.

Kroger, J. (1990). Ego structuralization in late adolescence as seen through early memories and ego identity status. *Journal of Adolescence, 13,* 65–77.

Kruglanski, A. W., & Webster, D. M. (1996). Motivated closing of the mind: "Seizing" and "freezing." *Psychological Review, 103*(2), 263–283.

Kübler-Ross, E. (1969). *On death and dying.* New York: Macmillan.

Kuhn, M. H., & McPartland, T. S. (1954). An empirical investigation of self-attitudes. *American Sociological Review, 19,* 68–76.

Kulik, J. A., Mahler, H. I. M., & Moore, P. J. (1996). Social comparison and affiliation under threat: Effects on recovery from major surgery. *Journal of Personality and Social Psychology, 71*(5), 967–979.

Kunkel, S. (1989). An extra eight hours a day. *Generations, 13*(2), 57–60.

Kupfer, C. (1995). Measuring quality of life in low vision patients. *Aging and Vision News, 7*(2), 5.

Kutza, E. A. (1998). A look at national policy and the baby boom generation. *Generations, 22*(1), 16–21.

La Rue, A., Dessonville, C., & Jarvik, L. F. (1985). Aging and mental disorders. In J. E. Birren & K. W. Schaie (Eds.), *Handbook of the psychology of aging* (2nd ed., pp. 664–702). New York: Van Nostrand Reinhold.

Labouvie-Vief, G. (1984). Logic and self-regulation from youth to maturity: A model. In M. Commons, F. Richards, & C. Armon (Eds.), *Beyond formal operations: Late adolescent and adult cognitive development* (pp. 158–180). New York: Praeger.

Labouvie-Vief, G. (1985). Intelligence and cognition. In J. E. Birren & K. W. Schaie (Eds.), *Handbook of the psychology of aging* (2nd ed.). New York: Van Nostrand Reinhold.

Labouvie-Vief, G., Chiodo, L. M., Goguen, L. A., Diehl, M., & Orwoll, L. (1995). Representations of self across the life span. *Psychology and Aging, 10*(3), 404–415.

Lachman, M. E. (1985). Personal efficacy in middle and old age: Differential and normative patterns of change. In G. H. Elder (Ed.), *Life-course dynamics: Trajectories and transitions, 1968–1980.* Ithaca, NY: Cornell University Press.

Lachman, M. E., & Weaver, S. L. (1998). Sociodemographic variations in the sense of control by domain: Findings from the MacArthur studies of midlife. *Psychology and Aging, 13*(4), 553–562.

Lamb, M. E. (1978). Influence of the child on marital quality and family interaction during the prenatal, perinatal, and infancy periods. In R. Lerner & G. Spanier (Eds.), *Child influences on marital and family interaction: A life-span perspective.* New York: Academic Press.

Lamb, M. E. (1986). The changing roles of fathers. In M. E. Lamb (Ed.), *The father's role: Applied perspectives* (pp. 3–27). New York: Wiley.

Landis, S. H., Murray, T., & Bolden, S. (2000). Cancer statistics, 2000. *CA: A Cancer Journal for Clinicians, 50*(1), 2398–2424.

Lang, F. R., & Carstensen, L. L. (1994). Close emotional relationships in late life: Further support for proactive aging in the social domain. *Psychology and Aging, 9*(2), 315–324.

Lang, F. R., & Carstensen, L. L. (2002). Time counts: Future time perspective, goals, and social relationships. *Psychology and Aging, 17*(1), 125–139.

Langer, E. J., & Rodin, J. (1976). The effects of choice and enhanced personal responsibility for the aged: A field experiment in an institutional setting. *Journal of Personality and Social Psychology, 34,* 191–198.

Langer, E. J., Janis, I. L., & Wolfer, J. A. (1975). Reduction of psychological stress in surgical patients. *Journal of Experimental Social Psychology, 11,* 155–165.

Langer, P. A. (1986). *Preventing domestic violence against women.* Washington, DC: U.S. Department of Justice.

Lansford, J. E., Sherman, A. M., & Antonucci, T. C. (1998). Satisfaction with social networks: An examination of socioemotional selectivity theory across cohorts. *Psychology and Aging, 13*(4), 544–552.

Lapsley, D. K., & Power, F. C. (Eds.). (1988). *Self, ego, and identity: Integrative approaches.* New York: Springer-Verlag.

Larson, E. B. (1991). Geriatric medicine. *Journal of the American Medical Association, 265,* 3125–3126.

Larson, R. (1978). Thirty years of research on the subjective well-being of older Americans. *Journal of Gerontology, 33,* 109–125.

Larson, R., Mannell, R., & Zuzanek, J. (1986). Daily well-being of older adults with friends and family. *Psychology and Aging, 1,* 117–126.

Laursen, B., Pulkkinen, L., & Adams, R. (2002). The antecedents and correlates of agreeableness in adulthood. *Developmental Psychology, 38*(4), 591–603.

Lavee, Y., McCubbin, H., & Olson, D. (1987). The effect of stressful life events and transitions on family functioning and well-being. *Journal of Marriage and the Family, 49,* 857–875.

Lawrence, B. S. (1984). Age grading: The implicit organizational time-table. *Journal of Occupational Behaviour, 5,* 23–35.

Lawson, C. (1990, April 12). Tracking the life of the new father. *New York Times,* sec. C, p. 1.

Lazarus, R. S., & Folkman, S. (1984). *Stress, appraisal, and coping.* New York: Springer.

Lee, R. A. (1995). *Ageism in advertising: A study of advertising agency attitudes towards mature and maturing consumers.* Roseville, MN: High-Yield Marketing.

Lee, V. K. (1991). Language changes and Alzheimer's disease: A literature review. *Journal of Gerontological Nursing, 17,* 16–20.

Lehman, H. C. (1953). *Age and achievement.* Princeton, NJ: Princeton University Press.

Leigh, G. K. (1982). Kinship interaction over the family life-span. *Journal of Marriage and the Family, 44,* 197–208.

Lent, R. W., & Hackett, G. (1987). Career self-efficacy: Empirical status and future directions. *Journal of Vocational Behavior, 30,* 347–382.

Lerner, R. M. (1984). *On the nature of human plasticity.* New York: Cambridge University Press.

Lesar, T. S., Briceland, L., & Stein, D. S. (1997). Factors related to errors in medication prescribing. *Journal of the American Medical Association, 277*(4), 312–318.

Levenson, R. W., Carstensen, L. L., & Gottman, J. M. (1993). Long-term marriage: Age, gender, and satisfaction. *Psychology and Aging, 8,* 301–313.

Levine, R. L., & Stadtman, E. R. (1992). Oxidation of proteins during aging. *Generations, 16*(4), 39–42.

Levinson, D. J. (1978). *The seasons of a man's life.* New York: Ballantine Books.

Levinson, D. J. (1986). A conception of adult development. *American Psychologist, 41,* 3–13.

Levinson, D. J. (1996). *The seasons of a woman's life.* New York: Knopf.

Levitan, S. J., & Kornfeld, D. S. (1981). Clinical and cost benefits of liaison psychiatry. *American Journal of Psychiatry, 138*(6), 790–793.

Levitt, M. J., Weber, R. A., & Guacci, N. (1993). Convoys of social support: An intergenerational analysis. *Psychology and Aging, 8,* 323–326.

Levy, B. R., Slade, M. D., Kunkel, S. R., & Kasl, S. V. (2002). Longevity increased by positive self-perceptions of aging. *Journal of Personality and Social Psychology, 83*(2), 261–270.

Lewin, K. (1935). *A dynamic theory of personality.* New York: McGraw-Hill.

Lewis, R. (1999a). Older workers vow to stay on the job. *AARP Bulletin, 40*(9), 4.

Lewis, R. (1999b). Suddenly, older workers find they're in demand. *AARP Bulletin, 40*(10), 22.

Lewis, R. A. (1978). Emotional intimacy among men. *Journal of Social Issues, 34,* 108–121.

Li, J., & Caldwell, R. (1987). Magnitude and directional effects of marital sex-role incongruence on marital adjustment. *Journal of Family Issues, 8,* 97–110.

Li, S. (2002). Connecting the many levels and facets of cognitive aging. *Current Directions in Psychological Science, 11*(1), 38–43.

Liang, J., Shaw, B. A., Krause, N. M., Bennett, J. M., Blaum, C., Kobayashi, E., Fukaya, T., Sugihara, Y., & Sugisawa, H. (2003). Changes in functional status among older adults in Japan: Successful and usual again. *Psychology and Aging, 18*(4), 684–695.

Libman, E., Creti, L., Amsel, R., Brender, W., & Fichten, C. S. (1997). What do older good and poor sleepers do during periods of nocturnal wakefulness? The sleep-behaviors scale: 60+. *Psychology and Aging, 12*(1), 170–182.

Licata, A. A. (1987). Osteoporosis in older women. *Generations, 11*(4), 12–15.

Light, L. (1988). Preserved implicit memory in old age. In M. M. Gruneberg, P. E. Morris, & R. N. Sykes (Eds.), *Practical aspects of memory: Current research and issues* (Vol. 2, pp. 90–95). New York: Wiley.

Light, L. (1991). Memory and aging: Four hypotheses in search of data. *Annual Review of Psychology, 42,* 333–376.

Lindemann, E. (1991). The symptomatology and management of acute grief. *American Journal of Psychiatry, 144,* 141–148.

Lindenberger, U., & Baltes, P. B. (1994). Sensory functioning and intelligence in old age: A strong connection. *Psychology and Aging, 9*(3), 339–355.

Linn, M. C., & Hyde, J. S. (1989). Gender, mathematics, and science. *Educational Researcher, 18*(8), 17–19, 22–27.

Linville, P. W. (1982). Affective consequences of complexity regarding the self and other. In M. S. Clark & S. T. Fiske (Eds.), *Affect and cognition* (pp. 79–110). Hillsdale, NJ: Erlbaum.

Linville, P. W. (1987). Self-complexity as a cognitive buffer against stress-related illness and depression. *Journal of Personality and Social Psychology, 52,* 663–676.

Lipsey, M. W., & Wilson, D. B. (1993). The efficacy of psychological, educational, and behavioral treatment: Confirmation from meta-analysis. *American Psychologist, 48*(12), 1181–1209.

Litt, M. D. (1988). Self-efficacy and perceived control: Cognitive mediators of pain tolerance. *Journal of Personality and Social Psychology, 54,* 149–160.

Lonetto, R., & Templer, D. (1986). *Death anxiety.* New York: Hemisphere.

Longino, C. F., Jr., & Earle, J. R. (1996). Who are the grandparents at century's end? *Generations, 20*(1), 13–16.

Longino, C. F., Jr., & Lipman, A. (1981). Married and spouseless men and women in planned retirement communities. *Journal of Marriage and the Family, 43,* 169–177.

Longworth, R. C. (1992, April 24). UN data offers disturbing view of U.S. *Chicago Tribune,* pp. 1, 16.

Lopata, H. Z. (1973). *Widowhood in an American city.* Cambridge, MA: Schenkman.

Lopata, H. Z. (1979). *Women as widows.* New York: Elsevier.

Lopata, H. Z., & Norr, K. R. (1980). Changing commitments of American women to work and family roles. *Social Security Bulletin, 43*(6), 3–14.

Lore, R. K., & Schultz, L. A. (1993). Control of human aggression: A comparative perspective. *American Psychologist, 48,* 16–25.

Lorge, I. (1936). The influence of the test upon the nature of mental decline as a function of age. *Journal of Educational Psychology, 27,* 100–110.

Lund, D. A. (1993). Widowhood: The coping response. In R. Kastenbaum (Ed.), *Encyclopedia of adult development* (pp. 537–541). Phoenix, AZ: Oryx Press.

Lund, D. A. (1996). Bereavement and loss. *Encyclopedia of gerontology* (Vol. 1, pp. 173–183). San Diego, CA: Academic Press.

Lund, D. A., Caserta, M. S., & Dimond, M. F. (1993). The course of spousal bereavement in later life. In M. S. Stroebe, W. Stroebe, & L. O. Hansson (Eds.), *Handbook of bereavement* (pp. 240–254). Cambridge, England: Cambridge University Press.

Luria, A. R. (1976). *Cognitive development: Its cultural and social foundations.* Cambridge, MA: Harvard University Press.

Lurie, N., Slater, J., McGovern, P., Ekstrum, J., Quam, L., & Margolis, K. (1993). Preventive care for women: Does the sex of the physician matter? *New England Journal of Medicine, 329*(7), 478–482.

Lykken, D., & Tellegen, A. (1996). Happiness is a stochastic phenomenon. *Psychological Science, 7*(3), 186–189.

Lynn, J. (1991). Dying well. *Generations, 15*(1), 69–72.

Lyubomirsky, S. (2001). Why are some people happier than others? The role of cognitive and motivational processes in well-being. *American Psychologist, 56*(3), 239–249.

Mac Rae, H. (1990). Older women and identity maintenance in later life. *Canadian Journal on Aging, 9*(3), 248–267.

Maccoby, E. E., & Jacklin, C. N. (1974). *The psychology of sex differences.* Stanford, CA: Stanford University Press.

Mace, N. L., & Rabins, P. V. (1999). *The 36-hour day: A family caregiving guide for persons with Alzheimer's disease, related dementing illnesses, and memory loss in later life.* Baltimore, MD: Johns Hopkins University Press.

Maddox, G. L. (1965). Fact and artifact: Evidence bearing on disengagement theory from the Duke Geriatric Project. *Human Development, 8,* 117–130.

Maddox, G. L. (1991). Aging with a difference. *Generations, 15*(1), 7–10.

Maier, H. W. (1969). *Three theories of child development.* New York: Harper.

Main, M., & Goldwyn, R. (1984). Predicting rejection of her infant from mother's abuse representation of her own experience: Implications for the abuse-abusing intergenerational cycle. *Child Development, 8,* 203–217.

Main, M., Kaplan, N., & Cassidy, J. (1985). Security in infancy, childhood and adulthood: A move to the level of representation. *Monographs of the Society for Research in Child Development, 50* (1–2, Serial No. 209).

Mair, M. (1988). Psychology as storytelling. *International Journal of Personal Construct Psychology, 1,* 125–138.

Majerovitz, S. D. (1995). Role of family adaptability in the psychological adjustment of spouse caregivers to patients with dementia. *Psychology and Aging, 10*(3), 447–457.

Malonebeach, E. E., & Zarit, S. H. (1991). Current research issues in caregiving to the elderly. *International Journal of Aging and Human Development, 32*(2), 103–114.

Mandelbaum, D. G. (1959). Social uses of funeral rites. In H. Feifel (Ed.), *The meaning of death.* New York: McGraw-Hill.

Mansfield, P. K., Jorgensen, C. M., & Yu, L. (1989). The menopausal transition: Guidelines for researchers. *Health Education, 20*(6), 44–49, 59.

Manson, J. E., Hu, F. B., Rich-Edwards, J. W., Colditz, G. A., Stampfer, M. J., Willett, W. C., Speizer, F. E., & Hennekens, C. H. (1999). A prospective study of walking as compared with vigorous exercise in the prevention of coronary heart disease in women. *New England Journal of Medicine, 341*(9), 650–659.

Manton, K. G. (1989). Epidemiological, demographic, and social correlates of disability among the elderly. *Milbank Quarterly, 67* (Suppl. 1, Disability policy: Restoring socioeconomic independence), 13–58.

Manton, K. G., Corder, L., & Stallard, E. (1993). Estimates of change in chronic disability and institutional incidence and prevalence rates in the U.S. elderly population from the 1982, 1984, and 1989 National Long Term Care Survey. *Journal of Gerontology, 48*(4), S153–S166.

Marcia, J. (1966). Development and validation of ego-identity status. *Journal of Personality and Social Psychology, 3,* 551–558.

Marcia, J. (1976). *Studies in ego identity.* Burnaby, British Columbia: Simon Fraser University.

Marcia, J. (1980). Identity in adolescence. In J. Adelson (Ed.), *Handbook of adolescent psychology.* New York: Wiley.

Marcia, J. (1988). Ego identity, cognitive/moral development, and individuation. In D. K. Lapsley & F. C. Power (Eds.), *Self, ego, and identity: Integrative approaches* (pp. 211–225). New York: Springer-Verlag.

Marecek, J. (1995). Gender, politics, and psychology's ways of knowing. *American Psychologist, 50*(3), 162–163.

Maret, E., & Finlay, B. (1984). Distribution of household labor among women in dual-career families. *Journal of Marriage and the Family, 46,* 357–364.

Mariani, P. (1982). *William Carlos Williams.* New York: McGraw-Hill.

Marin, G. V., Marin, G., Otero-Sabogal, R., Sabogal, F., & Perez-Stable, E. (1987). *Cultural differences in attitudes toward smoking: Developing messages using the theory of reasoned action* (Tech. Rep.). San Francisco: Division of Adolescent Medicine, University of California.

Marin, G., & Marin, B. (1991). *Research with Hispanic populations.* Newbury Park, CA: Sage.

Markides, K. S., & Mindel, C. H. (1987). *Aging and ethnicity.* Newbury Park, CA: Sage.

Markides, K. S., Levin, J. S., & Ray, L. A. (1987). Religion, aging, and life satisfaction: An eight-year, three-wave longitudinal study. *Gerontologist, 27,* 660–665.

Marks, S. R. (1977). Multiple roles and role strain: Some notes on human energy, time, and commitment. *American Sociological Review, 42,* 921–936.

Markson, E. W. (1992). On behalf of older women: An apologia and review. *AGHE Exchange, 15*(3), 1–3.

Markus, H. (1977). Self-schemata and processing information about the self. *Journal of Personality and Social Psychology, 35,* 63–78.

Markus, H., & Herzog, A. G. (1991). The role of the self-concept in aging. In K. W. Schaie & M. P. Lawton (Eds.), *Annual review of gerontology and geriatrics* (Vol. 11, pp. 110–143). New York: Springer.

Markus, H. R., & Kitayama, S. (1991). Culture and the self: Implications for cognition, emotion, and motivation. *Psychological Review, 98,* 224–253.

Markus, H., & Nurius, P. (1986). Possible selves. *American Psychologist, 41,* 954–969.

Markus, H., & Zajonc, R. B. (1985). The cognitive perspective in social psychology. In G. Lindsey & E. Aronson (Eds.), *The handbook of social psychology* (3rd ed., Vol. 1, pp. 137–230). New York: Random House.

Marsh, H. W., & Shavelson, R. (1985). Self-concept: Its multi-faceted hierarchical structure. *Educational Psychologist, 20,* 107–123.

Martin, J. A., Hamilton, B. E., Sutton, P. D., Ventura, S. J., Menacker, P. A., & Munson, M. S. (2003, December 17). Births: Final data for 2002. *National Vital Statistics Reports, 52*(10). Retrieved from www.cdc.gov/nchs/data/nvsr/nvsr52/nvsr52_10.pdf.

Martire, L. M., Stephens, M. A. P., & Townsend, A. L. (2000). Centrality of women's roles: Beneficial and detrimental consequences for psychological well-being. *Psychology and Aging, 15*(1), 148–156.

Martocchio, J. J. (1989). Age-related differences in employee absenteeism: A meta-analysis. *Psychology and Aging, 4*(4), 409–414.

Marvin, R. S. (1977). An ethological-cognitive model for the attenuation of mother-child attachment behavior. In T. Alloway, P. Pliner, & L. Krames (Eds.), *Advances in the study of communication and affect* (Vol. 3, pp. 25–68). New York: Plenum.

Marvin, R. S., & Greenberg, M. T. (1982). Preschoolers' changing conceptions of their mothers: A social-cognitive study of mother-child attachment. In D. Forbes & M. T. Greenberg (Eds.), *Developing plans for behavior* (New Directions in Child Development, No. 14, pp. 47–60). San Francisco: Jossey-Bass.

Mascie-Taylor, C. G. N., & Vandenberg, S. G. (1988). Assortative mating for IQ and personality due to propinquity and personal preference. *Behavior Genetics, 18,* 339–345.

Masnick, G., & Bane, M. J. (1980). *The nation's families: 1960–1990.* Cambridge, MA: Joint Center for Urban Studies of M.I.T. and Harvard Universities.

Masters, W., & Johnson, V. (1966). *Human sexual response.* Boston: Little, Brown.

Masunaga, H., & Horn, J. (2001). Expertise and age-related changes in components of intelligence. *Psychology and Aging, 16*(2), 293–311.

Matarazzo, J. D. (1984). Behavioral health: A 1990 challenge for the health sciences professions. In J. D. Matarazzo, A. Herd, N. E. Miller, & S. M. Weiss (Eds.), *Behavioral health: A handbook of health enhancement and disease prevention* (pp. 3–39). New York: Wiley.

Mattessich, P., & Hill, R. (1987). Life cycle and family development. In M. Sussman & S. Steinmetz (Eds.), *Handbook of marriage and the family* (pp. 437–469). New York: Plenum.

Matthews, A. M., & Brown, K. (1988). Retirement as a critical life event: The differential experiences of women and men. *Research on Aging, 9*(4), 548–571.

Matthews, K. A., & Rodin, J. (1989). Women's changing work roles: Impact on health, family, and public policy. *American Psychologist, 44,* 1389–1393.

Matthews, K. A., Shumaker, S. A., Bowen, D. J., Langer, R. D., Hunt, J. R., Kaplan, R. M., Klesges, R. C., & Ritenbaugh, C. (1997). Women's Health Initiative: Why now? What is it? What's new? *American Psychologist, 52*(2), 101–116.

Matthews, S. H., & Rossner, T. T. (1988). Shared filial responsibility: The family as the primary caregiver. *Journal of Marriage and the Family, 50,* 185–195.

Matthews, S. H., & Sprey, J. (1984). The impact of divorce on grandparenthood: An exploratory study. *Gerontologist, 24,* 41–47.

Matthews, S. H., & Sprey, J. (1985). Adolescents' relationships with grandparents: An empirical contribution to conceptual clarification. *Journal of Gerontology, 40,* 621–626.

Maxwell, N. (1985). The retirement experience: Psychological and financial linkages to the labor market. *Social Science Quarterly, 66,* 22–23.

Mayer, K. U., Baltes, P. B., Baltes, M. M., Borchelt, M., Delius, J., Helmchen, H., Linden, M., Smith, J., Staudinger, U. M., Steinhagen-Thiessen, E., & Wagner, M. (1999). What do we know about old age and aging? Conclusions from the Berlin Aging Study. In P. B. Baltes & K. U. Mayer (Eds.), *The Berlin Aging Study: Aging from 70 to 100.* Cambridge, England: Cambridge University Press.

Maylor, E., & Valentine, T. (1992). Linear and nonlinear effects of aging on categorizing and naming faces. *Psychology and Aging, 7,* 317–323.

Mays, B., & Nicholoson, J. (1971). The genius of the negro church. In H. M. Nelsen, R. L. Yokley, & A. K. Nelsen (Eds.), *The black church in America* (pp. 287–291). New York: Basic Books.

Mays, V. M., Rubin, J., Sabourin, M., & Walker, L. (1996). Moving toward a global psychology: Changing theories and practice to meet the needs of a changing world. *American Psychologist, 51*(5), 485–487.

McAdams, D. P., & de St. Aubin, E. (1992). A theory of generativity and its assessment through self-report, behavioral acts, and narrative themes in autobiography. *Journal of Personality and Social Psychology, 62,* 1003–1015.

McAdams, D. P., de St. Aubin, E., & Logan, R. L. (1993). Generativity among young, midlife, and older adults. *Psychology and Aging, 8,* 221–230.

McAuliffe, K. (1988, May 23). Prescription for a healthy old age. *U.S. News & World Report,* p. 72.

McCandless, N.J., Lueptow, L. B., & McClendon, M. (1989). Family socioeconomic status and adolescent sex-typing. *Journal of Marriage and the Family, 51,* 627–635.

McCarter, R. (1978). Effects of age on contraction of mammalian skeletal muscle. In G. Kaldor & W. J. DiBattista (Eds.), *Aging in muscle* (pp. 1–21). New York: Raven Press.

McCarthy, S. (1983). Geropsychology: Meaning in life for adults over seventy. *Psychological Reports, 53,* 497–498.

McClelland, D. (1975). *Power: The inner experience.* New York: Irvington.

McClelland, D., Atkinson, J., Clark, R., & Lowell, E. (1953). *The achievement motive.* New York: Irvington.

McConnell, S., & Beitler, D. (1991). The Older Americans Act after 25 years: An overview. *Generations, 15*(3), 5–10.

McCormick, A. (1992). Tools for aging research. *Generations, 16*(4), 15–20.

McCrae, R. R., & Costa, P. T., Jr. (1984). *Emerging lives, enduring dispositions: Personality in adulthood.* Boston: Little, Brown.

McCrae, R. R., & Costa, P. T., Jr. (1990). *Personality in adulthood.* New York: Guilford Press.

McCrae, R. R., & Costa, P. T., Jr. (1994). The stability of personality: Observations and evaluations. *Current Directions in Psychological Science, 3*(6), 173–175.

McCrae, R. R., & Costa, P. T., Jr. (1997). Personality trait structure as a human universal. *American Psychologist, 52*(5), 509–516.

McCrae, R. R., Arenberg, D., & Costa, P. T., Jr. (1987). Declines in divergent thinking with age: Cross-sectional, longitudinal, and cross-sequential analyses. *Psychology and Aging, 2,* 130–137.

McCrae, R. R., Costa, P. T., Jr., deLima, M. P., Simoes, A., Ostendorf, F., Angleitner, A., Marusic, I., Bratko, D., Caprara, G. V., Barbaranelli, C., Chae, J., & Piedmont, R. L. (1999). Age differences in personality across the life-span: Parallels in five cultures. *Developmental Psychology, 35*(2), 466–477.

McDaniel, M. A., Maier, S. F., & Einstein, G. O. (2002). "Brain-specific" nutrients: A memory cure? *Psychological Science in the Public Interest, 3*(1), 12–38.

McDermott, D., & Snyder, C. R. (1999). *Making hope happen: A workbook for turning possibilities into reality.* Oakland, CA: New Harbinger Publications.

McDowd, J., & Birren, J. (1990). Aging and attentional processes. In J. E. Birren & K. W. Schaie (Eds.), *Handbook of the psychology of aging* (3rd ed., pp. 222–233). San Diego, CA: Academic Press.

McDowd, J., & Filion, D. (1992). Aging, selective attention, and inhibitory processes: A psychophysiological approach. *Psychology and Aging, 7,* 65–71.

McDowd, J. M., & Shaw, R. J. (2000). Attention and aging: A functional perspective. In F. I. M. Craik & T. A. Salthouse (Eds.), *The handbook of aging and cognition* (2nd ed., pp. 221–292). Mahwah, NJ: Erlbaum.

McGinnis, J. M., & Foege, W. H. (1993). Actual causes of death in the United States. *Journal of the American Medical Association, 270,* 2207–2212.

McHale, S. M., & Huston, T. L. (1985). The effect of the transition to parenthood on the marriage relationship. *Journal of Family Issues, 6,* 409–433.

McHugh, M., Koeske, R., & Frieze, I. (1986). Issues to consider in conducting nonsexist psychological research: A guide for researchers. *American Psychologist, 41,* 879–890.

McKhann, G., Drachman, D., Folstein, M., Katzman, R., Price, D., & Stadlan, E. M. (1984). Clinical diagnosis of Alzheimer's disease: Report of the NINCDS-ADRDA Work Group under the auspices of Department of Health and Human Services Task Forces on Alzheimer's Disease. *Neurology, 34,* 939–944.

McKinlay, J. B. (1981). A case for refocusing upstream: The political economy of illness. In P. Conrad & R. Kern (Eds.), *The sociology of health and illness: Critical perspectives.* New York: St. Martin's Press.

McLanahan, S., & Adams, J. (1987). Parenthood and psychological well-being. *Annual Review of Sociology, 13,* 237–257.

McLaughlin, S. D., & Micklin, M. (1983). The timing of first birth and changes in personal efficacy. *Journal of Marriage and the Family, 45,* 47–53.

McLeroy, K. R., & Crump, C. E. (1994). Health promotion and disease prevention: A historical perspective. *Generations, 18*(1), 9–17.

Mead, G. H. (1934). *Mind, self, and society.* Chicago: University of Chicago Press.

Meehan, P. J., Saltzman, L. E., & Sattin, R. W. (1991). Suicides among older United States residents: Epidemiological characteristics and trends. *American Journal of Public Health, 81,* 1198–1200.

Meeks, S., Murrell, S. A., & Mehl, R. C. (2000). Longitudinal relationships between depressive symptoms and health in normal older and middle-aged adults. *Psychology and Aging, 15*(1), 100–109.

Meier, D. E., & Morrison, R. S. (1999). Old age and care near the end of life. *Generations, 23*(1), 6–11.

Mellins, C. A., Blum, M. J., Boyd-Davis, S. L., & Gatz, M. (1993). Family network perspectives on caregiving. *Generations, 17*(1), 21–24.

Mercer, R. T., Nichols, E. G., & Doyle, G. C. (1989). *Transitions in a woman's life: Major life events in developmental context.* New York: Springer.

Merriam, S. B. (1994). Learning and life experience: The connection in adulthood. In J. D. Sinnott (Ed.), *Interdisciplinary handbook of adult lifespan learning* (pp. 74–89). Westport, CT: Greenwood Press.

Meyer, B. J. F., & Rice, G. E. (1989). Prose processing in adulthood: The text, the learner, and the task. In L. W. Poon, D.C. Rubin, & B. A. Wilson (Eds.), *Everyday cognition in adulthood and old age.* New York: Cambridge University Press.

Meyerhoff, B. (1978). *Number our days.* New York: Dutton.

Meyerson, D. E., & Fletcher, J. K. (2000). A modest manifesto for shattering the glass ceiling. *Harvard Business Review, 78*(1), 127.

Michael, R. T., Gagnon, J. H., Laumann, E. O., & Kolata, G. (1994). *Sex in America: A definitive survey.* New York: Warner Books.

Miletti, M. A. (1984). *Voices of experience: 1500 retired people talk about retirement.* New York: TIAA/CREF.

Miller, G. A. (1956). The magical number seven, plus or minus two: Some limits on our capacity for processing information. *Psychological Review, 63,* 81–97.

Miller, J. B. (1986). *Toward a new psychology of women* (2nd ed.). Boston: Beacon Press.

Miller, N. (1992). Introducing and teaching much-needed understanding of the scientific process. *American Psychologist, 47,* 848–850.

Miller, R. (1995, August 9). It's not prime time on networks for over-50 viewers. *Chicago Tribune,* sec. 1, p. 16.

Miller, W. R., & Thoresen, C. E. (2003). Spirituality, religion, and health: An emerging research field. *American Psychologist, 58*(10), 24–35.

Minckler, T. M., & Boyd, E. (1968). Physical growth. In J. Minckler (Ed.), *Pathology of the nervous system* (Vol. 1, pp. 98–122). New York: McGraw-Hill.

Minkler, M., & Roe, K. M. (1996). Grandparents as surrogate parents. *Generations, 20*(1), 34–38.

Minkler, M., & Stone, R. (1985). The feminization of poverty and older women. *Gerontologist, 25*, 351–357.

Mitchell, J., & Register, J. C. (1984). An exploration of family interaction with the elderly by race, socioeconomic status, and residence. *Gerontologist, 24*, 48–54.

Mitford, J. (1963). *The American way of death.* New York: Simon & Schuster.

Mittelman, M. S., Ferris, S. H., Shulman, E., Steinberg, G., & Levin, B. (1996). A family intervention to delay nursing home placement of patients with Alzheimer's disease. *Journal of the American Medical Association, 276*(21), 1725–1731.

Mittenberg, W., Seidenberg, M., O'Leary, D. S., & DiGiulio, D. V. (1989). Changes in cerebral functioning associated with normal aging. *Journal of Clinical and Experimental Neuropsychology, 11*, 918–932.

Moen, P. (1998a). Recasting careers: Changing reference groups, risks, and realities. *Generations, 22*(1), 40–45.

Moen, P. (1998b). Reconstructing retirement: Careers, couples, and social capital. *Contemporary Gerontology, 4*(4), 123–125.

Moen, P. (2003). Midcourse: Reconfiguring careers and community service for a new life stage. *Contemporary Gerontology, 9*(3), 87–94.

Moen, P., Dempster-McClain, D., & Williams, R. M. (1989). Social integration and longevity: An event history analysis of women's roles and resilience. *American Sociological Review, 54*, 635–647.

Moen, P., Kim, J. E., & Hofmeister, H. (2001). Couples' work/ retirement transitions, gender, and marital quality. *Social Psychology Quarterly, 64*, 55–71.

Moghaddam, F. M. (1987). Psychology in three worlds: As reflected by the crisis in social psychology and the move toward indigenous third-world psychology. *American Psychologist, 42*, 912–920.

Mokdad, A. H., Marks, J. S., Stroup, D. F., & Gerberding, J. L. (2004). Actual causes of death in the United States, 2000. *Journal of the American Medical Association, 291*(10), 1238–1245.

Monane, M., Gurwitz, J. H., & Avorn, J. (1993). Pharmacotherapy with psychoactive medications in the long-term-care setting: Challenges, management, and future directions. *Generations, 17*(1), 57–60.

Montepare, J., & Lachman, M. (1989). "You're only as old as you feel": Self-perceptions of age, fears of aging, and life satisfaction from essence to old age. *Psychology and Aging, 4*, 73–78.

Montgomery, R. J. V., & Datwyler, M. M. (1990). Women and men in the caregiving role. *Generations, 14*(2), 34–38.

Montgomery, R. J. V., & Kamo, Y. (1989). Parent care by sons and daughters. In J. A. Mancini (Ed.), *Aging parents and adult children.* Lexington, MA: Heath.

Moody, H. R. (1988). The contradictions of an aging society: From zero sum to productive society. In R. Morris & S. A. Bass (Eds.), *Retirement reconsidered: Economic and social roles for older people* (pp. 15–34). New York: Springer.

Morella, J., & Epstein, E. A. (1983). *Rita: The life of Rita Hayworth.* New York: Dell.

Morgan, D. L. (1986). Personal relationships as an interface between social networks and social cognitions. *Journal of Social and Personal Relationships, 3*, 403–422.

Morgan, P. I., Patton, J., & Baker, H. K. (1985, January). The organization's role in managing midlife crisis. *Training and Development Journal,* pp. 56–59.

Morin, C. M. (1993). *Insomnia: Psychological assessment and management.* New York: Guilford Press.

Moritz, D., Kasl, S., & Berkman, L. (1989). The health impact of living with a cognitively impaired spouse: Depressive symptoms and social functioning. *Journal of Gerontology, 44*(1), S17–S27.

Morley, J. (1997). Update on men's health. *Generations, 20*(4), 13–16.

Morrell, R. W. (2002). Older adults are getting online in the "internet century." *Aging and Vision, 14*(2), 4–5.

Morris, R., & Bass, S. A. (1988). Toward a new paradigm about work and age. In R. Morris & B. A. Bass (Eds.), *Retirement reconsidered: Economic and social roles for older people* (pp. 3–14). New York: Springer.

Morris, R., & Caro, F. G. (1995). The young-old, productive aging, and public policy. *Generations, 19*(3), 32–37.

Morrison, N. A., Ql, J. C., Tokita, A., Kelly, P. J., Crofts, L., Nguyen, T. V., Sambrook, P. N., & Eisman, J. A. (1994). Prediction of bone density from vitamin D receptor alleles. *Nature, 367*, 284–287.

Morrow, D., Leirer, V., Altieri, P., & Fitzsimmons, C. (1994). When expertise reduces age differences in performance. *Psychology and Aging, 9*(1), 134–148.

Mortimer, J. A., & Hutton, J. T. (1985). Epidemiology and etiology of Alzheimer's disease. In J. T. Hutton & A. D. Kenny (Eds.), *Senile dementia of the Alzheimer's type* (pp. 177–196). New York: Liss.

Moses-Zirkes, S. (1993, August). APA asks Congress to fund more training for minorities. *APA Monitor,* p. 57.

Mosocitch, M., & Winocur, G. (1992). The neuropsychology of memory and aging. In F. Craik & T. Salthouse (Eds.), *The handbook of aging and cognition* (pp. 315–372). Hillsdale, NJ: Erlbaum.

Mrazek, P. J., & Haggerty, R. J. (Eds.). (1994). *Reducing risks for mental disorders: Frontiers for preventive intervention research.* Washington, DC: National Academy Press.

Mueller, P., & Major, B. (1989). Self-blame, self-efficacy, and adjustment to abortion. *Journal of Personality and Social Psychology, 57*, 1059–1068.

Munnichs, J. M. (1980). *Old age and finitude: A contribution to psychogerontology.* New York: Arno Press.

Murphy, C. M., & O'Farrell, T. J. (1996). Marital violence among alcoholics. *Current Directions in Psychological Science, 5*(6), 183–186.

Murphy, E. M. (2003). Being born female is dangerous for your health. *American Psychologist, 58*(3), 205–210.

Murphy, S. (1987). Self-efficacy and social support: Mediators of stress on mental health following a natural disaster. *Western Journal of Nursing Research, 9*(1), 58–86.

Mutran, E. (1985). Integrational family support among blacks and whites: Response to culture or to socioeconomic differences. *Journal of Gerontology, 40,* 382–389.

Mutran, E., & Reitzes, D. (1990). Integrational exchange relationships in the aging family. In K. F. Ferraro (Ed.), *Gerontology: Perspectives and issues* (pp. 149–162). New York: Springer.

Myers, D. G. (2000). The funds, friends, and faith of happy people. *American Psychologist, 55*(1), 56–67.

Myers, D. G., & Diener, E. (1995). Who is happy? *Psychological Science, 6*(1), 10–19.

Myers, J. K., et al. (1984). Six-month prevalence of psychiatric disorders in three communities, 1980 to 1982. *Archives of General Psychiatry, 41,* 959–967.

Myers, R. J. (1998). Does Social Security need fixing? Can it be fixed? *Contemporary Gerontology, 4*(3), 79–83.

Myerson, J., Ferraro, F. R., Hale, S., & Lima, S. (1992). General slowing in semantic priming and word recognition. *Psychology and Aging, 7,* 257–270.

Myerson, J., Hale, S., Poon, L., Wagstaff, D., & Smith, G. (1990). The information-loss model: A mathematical theory of age-related cognitive slowing. *Psychological Review, 97,* 475–487.

Myles, J. (1991, March–April). A short history of retirement. *Aging Today,* p. 8.

Nathanson, C. A. (1977). Sex roles as variables in preventive health behavior. *Journal of Community Health, 3,* 142–155.

National Center for Education Statistics. (2000). Postsecondary education. In *Digest of Education Statistics, 1999* (NCES Publication No. 2000031, chapter 3). Washington, DC: Author.

National Center for Health Statistics. (1989, March). *Health. United States, 1988* (DHHS Publication No. PHS 89-1232). Washington, DC: Department of Health and Human Services.

National Center for Health Statistics. (1990a, March). *Health, United States, 1988* (Series 90, No. 1232). Washington, DC: U.S. Government Printing Office.

National Center for Health Statistics. (1990b, October). Current estimates from the National Health Interview Survey, 1989. In *Vital and Health Statistics* (Series 10, No. 176). Washington, DC: Department of Health and Human Services.

National Center for Health Statistics. (1990c). *Health, United States, 1990.* Washington, DC: Department of Health and Human Services.

National Center for Health Statistics. (1991). Advance report of final marriage statistics, 1988. *Monthly Vital Statistics Report,* Vol. 40, No. 4, Supplement (DHHS Publication No. 91–1120). Hyattsville, MD: Public Health Service.

National Center for Health Statistics. (1999, December 13). *National vital statistics report, 47*(28), table 12. Washington, DC: Department of Health and Human Services.

National Center for Health Statistics. (2000). www.cdc.gov/nchs/fastats/lifexpec.htm and www.cdc.gov/nchs/fastats/pdf/10200t57.pdf.

National Center for Health Statistics. (2003). Health, United States, 2003. In *National Vital Statistics Reports, 52*(3). Hyattsville, MD: Author.

National Center for Health Statistics. (2004a). Retrieved from www.cdc.gov/nchs/fastats/lifexpec.htm.

National Center for Health Statistics. (2004b). Health, United States, 2004. Retrieved from www.cdc.gov/nchs/data/hus/hus04trend.pdf#031.

National Council on Aging. (1981). *The myth and reality of aging in American.* Washington, DC: Author.

National Council on Aging. (2000). *Myths and realities of aging 2000.* Washington, DC: Author.

National Institute on Aging. (1986). *Established populations for epidemiological studies of the elderly.* Washington, DC: National Institutes of Health.

National Osteoporosis Foundation. (1991). *Boning up on osteoporosis.* Washington, DC: Author.

Neisser, U. (1976). *Cognition and reality.* San Francisco: Freeman.

Neisser, U., Boodoo, G., Bouchard, T. J., Jr., Boykin, A. W., Brody, N., Ceci, S. J., Halpern, D. F., Loehlin, J. C., Perloff, R., Sternberg, R. J., & Urbina, S. (1996). Intelligence: Knowns and unknowns. *American Psychologist, 51*(2), 77–101.

Nemiroff, R., & Colarusso, C. (1990). Frontiers of adult development in theory and practice. In R. A. Nemiroff & C. A. Colarusso (Eds.), *New dimensions in adult development* (pp. 97–124). New York: Basic Books.

Nemschoff, H. L. (1992). A view from the middle: Fear for many retirees. *Aging Today, 15*(5), 7, 9.

Neugarten, B. (1968). Adult personality: Toward a psychology of the life cycle. In B. Neugarten (Ed.), *Middle age and aging* (pp. 137–147). Chicago: University of Chicago Press.

Neugarten, B. (1974). Age groups in American society and the rise of the young-old. In F. R. Eisele (Ed.), *Political consequences of aging* (pp. 187–198). Philadelphia: American Academy of Political and Social Sciences.

Neugarten, B. (1977). Personality and aging. In J. E. Birren & K. W. Schaie (Eds.), *Handbook of the psychology of aging* (pp. 626–649). New York: Van Nostrand Reinhold.

Neugarten, B. (1993). Obituary: Robert J. Havighurst (1900–1991). *American Psychologist, 48,* 1290–1291.

Neugarten, B. (1995–96, Winter). The costs of survivorship. *Newsletter of the Buehler Center on Aging* (McGaw Medical Center, Northwestern University), *11*(4), 1.

Neugarten, B., & Hagestad, G. (1976). Age and life course. In R. Binstock & E. Shanas (Eds.), *Handbook of aging and the social sciences* (pp. 35–55). New York: Van Nostrand Reinhold.

Neugarten, B., & Neugarten, D. (1987, May). The changing meanings of age. *Psychology Today,* pp. 29–33.

Neugarten, B., & Weinstein, K. (1964). The changing American grandparent. *Journal of Marriage and the Family, 26,* 199–204.

Newcomb, M. (1990). Social support by many other names: Toward a unified conceptualization. *Journal of Social and Personal Relationships, 7,* 479–494.

Newcomb, M. D. (1986). Cohabitation, marriage, and divorce among adolescents and young adults. *Journal of Social and Personal Relationships, 3,* 473–494.

Newman, J. P., Engel, R. J., & Jensen, J. E. (1991). Age differences in depressive symptom experiences. *Journal of Gerontology, 46,* 224–235.

Newman, J. P., Klein, M. H., Jensen, J. E., & Essex, M. J. (1996). Depressive symptom experiences among older women: A comparison of alternative measurement approaches. *Psychology and Aging, 11*(1), 112–126.

Newsom, J. T. (1999). Another side to caregiving: Negative reactions to being helped. *Current Directions in Psychological Science, 8* (6), 183–187.

Newsom, J. T., & Schulz, R. (1996). Social support as a mediator in the relation between functional status and quality of life in older adults. *Psychology and Aging, 11*(1), 34–44.

Newsom, J. T., Nishishiba, M., Morgan, D. L., & Rook, K, S. (2003). The relative importance of three domains of positive and negative social exchanges: A longitudinal model with comparable measures. *Psychology and Aging, 18*(4), 746–754.

NIMH Prevention Research Steering Committee. (1994). *The prevention of mental disorders: A national research agenda.* Washington, DC: Author.

Noam, G. (1988). The self, adult development, and the theory of biography and transformation. In D. K.-Lapsley & F. C. Power (Eds.), *Self, ego, and identity: Integrative approaches* (pp. 3–29). New York: Springer-Verlag.

Noble, J., Cover, J., & Yanagishita, M. (1996). *The world's youth.* Washington, DC: Population Reference Bureau.

Noell, E. (1996). Design in nursing homes: Environment as a silent partner in caregiving. *Generations, 19*(4), 14–19.

Nolen-Hoeksema, S. (1987). Sex differences in unipolar depression: Evidence and theory. *Psychological Bulletin, 101,* 259–282.

Nolen-Hoeksema, S. (1990). *Sex differences in depression.* Stanford, CA: Stanford University Press.

Nolen-Hoeksema, S. (1991). Responses to depression and their effects on the duration of depressive episodes. *Journal of Abnormal Psychology, 100,* 569–582.

Nolen-Hoeksema, S. (2001). Gender differences in depression. *Current Directions in Psychological Science, 10*(5), 173–176.

Nolen-Hoeksema, S., Larson, J., & Grayson, C. (1999). Explaining the gender difference in depression. *Journal of Personality and Social Psychology, 77,* 1061–1072.

Nolen-Hoeksema, S., Morrow, J., & Fredrickson, B. L. (1993). Response styles and the duration of episodes of depressed mood. *Journal of Abnormal Psychology, 102*(1), 20–28.

Nolen-Hoeksema, S., Parker, L. E., & Larson, J. (1994). Ruminative coping with depressed mood following loss. *Journal of Personality and Social Psychology, 67*(1), 92–104.

Norenzayan, A., & Nisbett, R. E. (2000). Culture and causal cognition. *Current Directions in Psychological Science, 9*(4), 132–135.

Norton, A. J. (1983). Family life cycle: 1980. *Journal of Marriage and the Family, 45,* 267–277.

O'Brien, S. J., & Vertinsky, P. A. (1991). Unfit survivors: Exercise as a resource for aging women. *Gerontologist, 31,* 347–357.

O'Bryant, S. L., & Hansson, R. O. (1995). Widowhood. In R. Blieszner & V. H. Bedford (Eds.), *Handbook of aging and the family* (pp. 355–371). Westport, CT: Greenwood Press.

O'Connell, A. (1976). The relationship between life style and identity synthesis and resynthesis in traditional, neotraditional, and non-traditional women. *Journal of Personality, 44,* 675–688.

O'Connor, B. P., & Vallerand, R. J. (1994). Motivation, self-determination, and person-environment fit as predictors of psychological adjustment among nursing home residents. *Psychology and Aging, 9*(2), 189–194.

O'Connor, D. J., & Wolfe, D. M. (1987). On managing midlife transitions in career and family. *Human Relations, 40,* 799–816.

O'Grady-LeShane, R. (1993). Changes in the lives of women and their families: Have old age pensions kept pace? *Generations, 17*(4), 27–31.

Ochberg, F. M. (1980). Victims of terrorism. *Journal of Clinical Psychiatry, 41,* 73–74.

Oddo, S., Billings, L., Kesslak, J. P., Cribbs, D. H., & LaFerla, F. M. (2004). A-beta immunotherapy leads to clearance of early, but not late, hyperphosphorylated tau aggregates via the proteasome. *Neuron, 43,* 321–332.

Oliver, M B., & Hyde, J. S. (1993). Gender differences in sexuality: A meta-analysis. *Psychological Bulletin, 114,* 29–51.

Olshansky, S. J., Carnes, B. A., & Cassel, C. (1990). In search of Methuselah: Estimating the upper limits to human longevity. *Science, 250,* 634–640.

Ornstein, S., & Isabella, L. (1990). Age vs. stage models of career attitudes of women: A partial replication and extension. *Journal of Vocational Behavior, 36,* 1–19.

Ornstein, S., Cron, W. L., & Slocum, J. W., Jr. (1989). Life stage versus career stage: A comparative test of the theories of Levinson and Super. *Journal of Organizational Behavior, 10,* 117–133.

Orwoll, L., & Achenbaum, W. A. (1993). Gender and the development of wisdom. *Human Development, 36,* 274–296.

Overholser, J. C., & Moll, S. H. (1990). Who's to blame: Attributions regarding causality in spouse abuse. *Behavioral Sciences and the Law, 8,* 107–120.

Owens, W. A. (1956). Research on age and mental abilities. In J. E. Anderson (Ed.), *Psychological aspects of aging* (pp. 155–157). Washington, DC: American Psychological Association.

Oyserman, D., Coon, H. M., & Kemmelmeier, M. (2002). Rethinking individualism and collectivism: Evaluation of theoretical assumptions and meta-analyses. *Psychological Bulletin, 128*(1), 3–72.

Pagelow, M. (1984). *Family violence.* New York: Praeger.

Palmore, E. B. (1982). Predictors of the longevity difference: A 25 year followup. *Gerontologist, 22,* 513–518.

Palmore, E. B., Burchett, B. M., Fillenbaum, G. G., George, L. K., & Wallman, L. M. (1985). *Retirement: Causes and consequences.* New York: Springer.

Park, D.C. (1992). Applied cognitive aging research. In F. I. M. Craik & T. A. Salthouse (Eds.), *The handbook of aging and cognition* (pp. 449–493). Hillsdale, NJ: Erlbaum.

Park, D.C., & Cherry, K. (1989). Human subjects and cognitive aging research: A unique solution to a perennial problem. *Educational Gerontologist, 15,* 563–571.

Park, D.C., & Kidder, D. P. (1996). Prospective memory and medication adherence. In M. Brandimonte, G. O. Einstein, & M. A. McDaniels (Eds.), *Prospective memory: Theory and applications* (pp. 369–390). Mahwah, NJ: Erlbaum.

Park, D.C., Smith, A. D., Lautenschlager, G., Earles, J. L., Frieske, D., Zwahr, M., & Gaines, C. L. (1996). Mediators of long-term memory performance across the life span. *Psychology and Aging, 11*(4), 621–637.

Parkes, C. M. (1972). *Bereavement: Studies of grief in adult life.* New York: International Universities Press.

Parkes, C. M., & Weiss, R. S. (1983). *Recovery from bereavement.* New York: Basic Books.

Parkin, A. J., & Walter, B. M. (1992). Recollective experience, normal aging, and frontal dysfunction. *Psychology and Aging, 7,* 290–298.

Parry-Billings, M., & Walter, B. M. (1992). Recollective experience, normal storage, and release of metabolites by muscle. In J. G. Evans & T. F. Williams (Eds.), *Oxford textbook of geriatric medicine.* London: Oxford University Press.

Parry-Billings, M., Newsholme, E. A., & Young, A. (1992). The uptake, storage, and release of metabolites by muscle. In J. G. Evans & T. F. Williams (Eds.), *Oxford textbook of geriatric medicine.* London: Oxford University Press.

Parsons, T. (1949). The social structure of the family. In R. Anshem (Ed.), *The family: Its function and destiny.* New York: Harper.

Patterson, C. J. (1995). Sexual orientation and human development: An overview. *Developmental Psychology, 31*(1), 3–11.

Pearce, D. (1978). The feminization of poverty: Women, work, and welfare. *Urban and Social Change Review, 11,* 28–36.

Pearlin, L. I. (1983). Role strains and personal stress. In H. B. Kaplan (Ed.), *Psychosocial stress: Trends in theory and research.* New York: Academic Press.

Pearlin, L. I., & Turner, H. A. (1987). The family as a context of the stress process. In S. Kasl & C. L. Cooper (Eds.), *Stress and health issues in research methodology* (pp. 143–165). Chichester, England: Wiley.

Pearlin, L. I., Mullan, J. T., Semple, S. J., & Skaff, M. M. (1990). Caregiving and the stress process: An overview of concepts and their measures. *Gerontologist, 30,* 583–594.

Pearson, J. L., & Brown, G. K. (2000). Suicide prevention in late life: Directions for science and practice. *Clinical Psychology Review, 20,* 685–705.

Peck, R. (1968). Psychological developments in the second half of life. In B. Neugarten (Ed.), *Middle age and aging* (pp. 88–92). Chicago: University of Chicago Press.

Perlmutter, M. (1988). Cognitive potential throughout life. In J. E. Birren & V. L. Bengtson (Eds.), *Emergent theories of aging* (pp. 247–267). New York: Springer.

Peterson, B. E., & Klohnen, E. C. (1995). Realization of generativity in two samples of women at midlife. *Psychology and Aging, 10*(1), 20–29.

Peterson, B. E., & Stewart, A. J. (1996). Antecedents and contexts of generativity motivation at midlife. *Psychology and Aging, 11*(1), 21–33.

Peterson, C. (2000). The future of optimism. *American Psychologist, 55*(1), 44–55.

Peterson, R. R. (1996). A re-evaluation of the economic consequences of divorce. *American Sociological Review, 61,* 528–536.

Petrovitch, H., Masaki, K., & Rodriguez, B. (1997). Update on women's health: Pros and cons of postmenopausal hormone replacement therapy. *Generations, 20*(4), 7–12.

Pfaff, L. A. (1999). Five year study shows gender differences in leadership skills. Study summary available from Lawrence A. Pfaff and Associates, Suite 3, 5950 Portage Road, Portage, MI 49002.

Pfost, K. S., & Fiore, M. (1990). Pursuit of nontraditional occupations: Fear of success or fear of not being chosen? *Sex Roles, 23,* 15–24.

Phares, V. (1992). Where's poppa? The relative lack of attention to the role of fathers in child and adolescent psychopathology. *American Psychologist, 47,* 656–664.

Phinney, J. S. (1996). When we talk about American ethnic groups, what do we mean? *American Psychologist, 51*(9), 918–927.

Piaget, J. (1972). Intellectual evolution from adolescence to adulthood. *Human Development, 15,* 1–12.

Piaget, J., & Inhelder, B. (1969). *The psychology of the child.* New York: Basic Books.

Pillemer, K., & Suitor, J. J. (1998). Baby boom families: Relations with aging parents. *Generations, 22*(1), 65–70.

Pinel, J. P. J., Assanand, S., & Lehman, D. R. (2000). Hunger, eating, and ill health. *American Psychologist, 55* (10), 1105–1116.

Pineo, P. E. (1961). Disenchantment in the later years of marriage. *Marriage and Family Living, 23,* 3–11.

Pinquart, M., & Sorensen, S. (2000). Influences of socioeconomic status, social network, and competence on subjective well-being in later life: A meta-analysis. *Psychology and Aging, 15*(2), 187–224.

Pion, G. M., Mednick, M. T., Astin, H. S., Hall, C. C. I., Kenkel, M. B., Keita, G. P., Kohout, J. L., & Kelleher, J. C.

(1996). The shifting gender composition of psychology: Trends and implications for the discipline. *American Psychologist, 51*(5), 509–528.

Piotrkowski, C., Rapoport, R., & Rapoport, R. (1987). Families and work. In M. Sussman & S. Steinmetz (Eds.), *Handbook of marriage and the family.* New York: Plenum.

Pirkl, J. J. (1995). Transgenerational design: Prolonging the American dream. *Generations, 19*(1), 32–36.

Poon, L. W., Krauss, I. K., & Bowles, N. L. (1984). On subject selection in cognitive aging research. *Experimental Aging Research, 10,* 43–49.

Porter, J., & Washington, R. (1979). Black identity and self-esteem: A review of studies of black self-concept, 1968–1978. *Annual Review of Sociology, 5,* 53–74.

Powell, L. H., Shahabi, L., & Thoresen, C. E. (2003). Religion and spirituality: Linkages to physical health. *American Psychologist, 58*(1), 36–52.

Preston, S. (1984). Children and the elderly: Divergent paths for America's dependents. *Demography, 21,* 435–457.

Preston, S. H., & Taubman, P. (1994). Socioeconomic differences in adult mortality and health status. In L. G. Martin & S. H. Preston (Eds.), *Demography of aging* (pp. 279–318). Washington, DC: National Academy Press.

Problems with prescription drugs highest among the elderly. (1983). *American Family Physician, 28*(6), 236.

Pruchno, R. A., Blow, F. C., & Smyer, M. A. (1984). Life events and interdependent lives. *Human Development, 27,* 31–41.

Quadagno, J., & McClellan, S. (1989). The other functions of retirement. *Generations, 13*(2), 7–10.

Quindlen, A. (1988). *Living out loud.* New York: Random House.

Quinn, J. B. (2000, July 3). A challenge, not a crisis. *Newsweek,* p. 26.

Quinn, J. F., & Kozy, M. (1996). The role of bridge jobs in the retirement transition: Gender, race, and ethnicity. *Gerontologist, 36*(3), 363–372.

Rabbitt, P. M. A. (1993). Does it all go together when it goes? The nineteenth Bartlett memorial lecture. *Quarterly Journal of Experimental Psychology, 46A,* 385–434.

Rabbitt, P., Donlan, C., Watson, P., McInnes, L., & Bent, N. (1995). Unique and interactive effects of depression, age, socioeconomic advantage, and gender on cognitive performance of normal healthy older people. *Psychology and Aging, 10*(3), 307–313.

Raichle, M. E. (2001). Functional neuroimaging: A historical and physiological perspective. In R. Cabeza & A. Kingstone (Eds.), *Handbook of functional neuroimaging of cognition* (pp. 3–26). Cambridge, MA: MIT Press.

Rank, M. R., & Hirschl, T. A. (1999). Estimating the proportion of Americans ever experiencing poverty during their elderly years. *Journals of Gerontology: Social Sciences, 54B*(4), S184–S193.

Ratner, H. (1987, October). Memory: Age or practice? *Psychology Today,* p. 24.

Ratner, H., Schell, D., Crimmins, A., Mittelman, D., & Baldinelli, L. (1987). Changes in adults' prose recall: Aging or cognitive demands? *Developmental Psychology, 23,* 521–525.

Ray, O. (2004). How the mind hurts and heals the body. *American Psychologist, 59*(1), 29–40.

Reardon, P. T. (1993, January 15). How poverty's weight cracks families. *Chicago Tribune,* pp. 1, 16.

Rees, W. D., & Lutkins, S. G. (1967). The mortality of bereavement. *British Medical Journal, 4,* 13–16.

Regier, D. A., Myers, J. K., Kramer, M., Robins, L. N., Blazer, D. G., Hough, R. L., Eaton, W. W., & Locke, B. Z. (1984). The NIMH Epidemiological Catchment Area program: Historical context, major objectives, and study population characteristics. *Archives of General Psychiatry, 41,* 934–941.

Reis, H. T., Collins, W. A., & Berscheid, E. (2000). The relationship context of human behavior and development. *Psychological Bulletin, 126*(6), 844–872.

Rennison, M., & Welchans, W. (2000). *Intimate partner violence.* U.S. Department of Justice (NCJ178247). Washington, DC: U.S. Government Printing Office.

Renwick, P. A., & Lawler, E. E. (1978). What do you really want from your job? *Psychology Today, 11*(12), 53–65.

Repetti, R. L., Matthews, K. A., & Waldron, I. (1989). Employment and women's health: Effects of paid employment on women's mental and physical health. *American Psychologist, 44,* 1394–1401.

Retsinas, J. (1988). A theoretical reassessment of the applicability of Kübler-Ross's stages of dying. *Death Studies, 12,* 207–216.

Richards, F., Armon, C., & Commons, M. (1984). Perspectives on the development of thought in late adolescence and adulthood: An introduction. In M. Commons, F. Richards, & C. Armon (Eds.), *Beyond formal operations: Late adolescent and adult cognitive development* (pp. xiii–xxviii). New York: Praeger.

Riegel, K. (1973). Dialectical operations: The final period of cognitive development. *Human Development, 16,* 346–370.

Ries, L. A. G., Kosary, C. L., & Hankey, B. F. (1999). *SEER cancer status review, 1973–1996.* Bethesda, MD: National Cancer Institute.

Rigdon, I. S. (1986). Help and hope for the elderly bereaved. *Gerontologist, 26,* 128.

Riger, S. (1992). Epistemological debates, feminist voices: Science, social values, and the study of women. *American Psychologist, 47,* 730–740.

Riley, M. W., Kahn, R. L., & Foner, A. (Eds.). (1994). *Age and structural lag.* New York: Wiley.

Ritchie, K., & Kildea, D. (1995). Is senile dementia "age-related" or "ageing-related"?—evidence from meta-analysis of dementia prevalence in the oldest old. *Lancet, 346,* 931–934.

Rix, S. E. (1990). *Older workers.* Santa Barbara, CA: ABC-CLIO.

Roberto, K. A., & Kimboko, P. J. (1989). Friendships in later life: Definitions and maintenance patterns. *International Journal of Aging and Human Development, 28,* 9–19.

Roberts, B. W., & Donahue, E. M. (1994). One personality, multiple selves: Integrating personality and social roles. *Journal of Personality, 62*(2), 199–218.

Roberts, P., & Newton, P. (1987). Levinsonian studies of women's adult development. *Psychology and Aging, 2,* 154–163.

Robertson, J. F. (1977). Grandmotherhood: A study of role conceptions. *Journal of Marriage and the Family, 39,* 165–174.

Robins, L. N., Helzer, J. E., Weissman, M. M., Orvaschel, H., Gruenberg, E., Burke, J. D., & Regier, D. A. (1984). Lifetime prevalence of specific psychiatric disorders in three sites. *Archives of General Psychiatry, 41,* 949–958.

Robins, R. W., Trzesniewski, K. H., Tracy, J. L., Gosling, S. D., & Potter, J. (2002). Global self-esteem across the life span. *Psychology and Aging, 17*(3), 423–434.

Rodin, J. (1986). Aging and health: Effects of the sense of control. *Science, 233,* 1271–1276.

Rodin, J. (1987). Personal control through the life course. In R. P. Abeles (Ed.), *Life-span perspectives and social psychology* (pp. 103–119). Hillsdale, NJ: Erlbaum.

Rodin, J., & Langer, E. J. (1977). Long-term effects of a control-relevant intervention with the institutional aged. *Journal of Personality and Social Psychology, 35,* 897–902.

Roe, K. M., & Minkler, M. (1998–1999). Grandparents raising grandchildren: Challenges and responses. *Generations, 22*(4), 25–32.

Rogers, C. (1951). *Client-centered therapy.* Boston: Houghton Mifflin.

Rogers, W. A. (2000). Attention and aging. In D. C. Park & N. Schwarz (Eds.), *Cognitive aging: A primer* (pp. 57–73). Philadelphia: Psychology Press.

Rogers, W. A., & Fisk, A. D. (2004). Psychological science and intelligent home technology: Supporting functional independence of older adults. *Psychological Science Agenda, 18*(2). Retrieved from www.apa.org/science/psa/sb-rogersprt.html.

Rogoff, B., & Chavajay, P. (1995). What's become of research on the cultural basis of cognitive development? *American Psychologist, 50*(10), 859–877.

Roizen, M. F. (1999). *RealAge: Are you as young as you can be?* New York: Cliff Street Books.

Roland, A. (1984). The self in India and America: Toward a psychoanalysis of social and cultural contexts. In V. Kovolis (Ed.), *Designs of selfhood* (pp. 123–130). Cranbury, NJ: Associated University Presses.

Rolf, J., Masten, A. S., Cicchetti, D., Neuchterlein, K. H., & Weintraub, S. (Eds.). (1990). *Risk and protective factors in the development of psychopathology.* New York: Cambridge University Press.

Rollins, B. C. (1989). In S. Hunter and M. Sundel (Eds.), *Midlife myths* (pp. 184–194). Beverly Hills, CA: Sage.

Rollins, B. C., & Feldman, H. (1970). Marital satisfaction over the family life cycle. *Journal of Marriage and the Family, 32*(1), 20–28.

Rook, K. S. (1987). Social support versus companionship: Effects on life stress, loneliness, and evaluations of others. *Journal of Personality and Social Psychology, 52,* 1132–1147.

Roscoe, B., & Benaske, N. (1985). Courtship violence experienced by abused wives: Similarities in patterns of abuse. *Family Relations, 34,* 419–424.

Rosenbaum, M. E. (1986). The repulsion hypothesis: On the nondevelopment of relationships. *Journal of Personality and Social Psychology, 51,* 1156–1166.

Rosenberg, M. (1979). *Conceiving the self.* New York: Basic Books.

Rosenberg, M. (1989). Self-concept research: A historical overview. *Social Forces, 68*(1), 34–44.

Rosenblatt, R. A. (1996, July–August). Boomer fever rises at AARP and in DC. *Aging Today,* p. 1.

Rosenthal, C. J. (1985). Kinkeeping in the familial division of labor. *Journal of Marriage and the Family, 47,* 965–974.

Rosow, I. (1973). The social context of the aging self. *Gerontologist, 13,* 82–87.

Ross, G. W., Petrovitch, H., & White, L. R. (1997). Update on dementia. *Generations, 20*(4), 22–27.

Rothbaum, F., Weisz, J., Pott, M., Miyake, K., & Morelli, G. (2000). Attachment and culture: Security in the United States and Japan. *American Psychologist, 55*(10), 1093–1104.

Rothermund, K., & Brandtstadter, J. (2003a). Depression in later life: Cross-sequential patterns and possible determinants. *Psychology and Aging, 18*(1), 80–90.

Rothermund, K., & Brandtstadter, J. (2003b). Coping with deficits and losses in later life: From compensatory action to accommodation. *Psychology and Aging, 18*(4), 896–905.

Rotter, J. B. (1966). Generalized expectancies for internal versus external control of reinforcement. *Psychological Monographs, 80*(1, entire No. 609).

Rovner, B. W., German, P. S., Brant, L. J., Clark, R., Burton, L., & Folstein, M. F. (1991). Depression and mortality in nursing homes. *Journal of the American Medical Association, 265,* 993–996.

Rovner, B. W., German, P. S., Broadhead, J., et al. (1990). The prevalence and management of dementia and other psychiatric disorders in nursing homes. *International Psychogeriatrics, 147,* 299–302.

Rowe, D.C., Vazsonyi, A. T., & Flannery, D. J. (1994). No more than skin deep: Ethnic and racial similarity in developmental process. *Psychological Review, 101*(3), 396–413.

Rowe, J. W., & Kahn, R. L. (1987). Human aging: Usual and successful. *Science, 237,* 143–149.

Rowe, J. W., & Kahn, R. L. (1998). *Successful aging.* Westminster, MD: Pantheon.

Rowland, K. F. (1977). Environmental events predicting death for the elderly. *Psychological Bulletin, 84,* 349–372.

Rozanski, A., Blumenthal, J. A., & Kaplan, J. (1999). Impact of psychological factors on the pathogenesis of cardiovascular disease and implications for therapy. *Circulation, 99*(16), 2192–2217.

Rubenstein, L. Z. (1997). Update on preventive medicine for older people. *Generations, 20*(4), 47–53.

Rubin, Z. (1981, May). Does personality really change after 20? *Psychology Today,* pp. 18–27.

Ruble, D., Fleming, A. S., Hackel, L., & Stangor, C. (1988). Changes in the marital relationship during the transition to first-time motherhood: Effects of violated expectations and concerning division of household labor. *Journal of Personality and Social Psychology, 55,* 78–87.

Rudinger, G. (1976). Correlates of changes in cognitive functioning. In H. Thomas (Ed.), *Patterns of aging* (pp. 20–35). London: Karger.

Rudman, D., Feller, A. G., & Nagra, H. S. (1990). Effects of human growth hormone in men over 60 years old. *New England Journal of Medicine, 323,* 1–6.

Ruhm, C. J. (1995). Secular changes in the work and retirement patterns of older men. *Journal of Human Resources, 30,* 362–385.

Ryan, V. C. (1989). Relationship of socioeconomic status and living arrangements to nutritional intake of the older person. *Journal of the American Dietetic Association, 89,* 1805–1807.

Ryan, W. (1971). *Blaming the victim.* New York: Vintage Books.

Rybash, J. M., Hoyer, W., & Roodin, P. (1986). *Adult cognition and aging.* New York: Pergamon Press.

Ryff, C. (1985). The subjective experience of life-span transitions. In A. Rossi (Ed.), *Gender and the life course.* New York: Aldine.

Ryff, C. D. (1995). Psychological well-being in adult life. *Current Directions in Psychological Science, 4*(4), 99–104.

Ryff, C. D., Lee, Y. H., Essex, M. J., & Schmutte, P. S. (1994). My children and me: Midlife evaluations of grown children and of self. *Psychology and Aging, 9*(2), 195–205.

Sabatelli, R. M., & Cecil-Pigo, E. F. (1985). Relational interdependence and commitment in marriage. *Journal of Marriage and the Family, 47,* 931–937.

Sachs, G. A. (1994). Improving care of the dying. *Generations, 18*(4), 19–22.

Sakuye, K. (1992). The elderly Asian patient. *Journal of Geriatric Psychiatry, 25,* 69–84.

Salovey, P., Rothman, A. J., Detweiler, J. B., & Steward, W. T. (2000). Emotional states and physical health. *American Psychologist, 55*(1), 110–121.

Salthouse, T. A. (1984). Effects of age and skill in typing. *Journal of Experimental Psychology: General, 113,* 345–371.

Salthouse, T. A. (1985). Speed of behavior and its implications for cognition. In J. E. Birren & K. W. Schaie (Eds.), *Handbook of the psychology of aging* (2nd ed., pp. 400–426). New York: Van Nostrand Reinhold.

Salthouse, T. A. (1987). Age, experience, and compensation. In C. Schooler & K. W. Schaie (Eds.), *Cognitive functioning and social structure over the life course* (pp. 142–150). New York: Ablex.

Salthouse, T. A. (1988). The role of processing resources in cognitive aging. In M. L. Howe & C. J. Brainerd (Eds.),

Cognitive development in adulthood: Progress in cognitive development research (pp. 185–239). New York: Springer-Verlag.

Salthouse, T. A. (1991a). Cognitive facets of aging well. *Generations, 15*(1), 35–38.

Salthouse, T. A. (1991b). *Theoretical perspectives on cognitive aging.* Hillsdale, NJ: Erlbaum.

Salthouse, T. A. (1994). The nature of the influence of speed on adult age differences in cognition. *Developmental Psychology, 30*(2), 240–259.

Salthouse, T. A. (1996). The processing-speed theory of adult age differences in cognition. *Psychological Review, 103*(3), 403–428.

Salthouse, T. A., Atkinson, T. M., & Berish, D. E. (2003). Executive functioning as a potential mediator of age-related cognitive decline in normal adults. *Journal of Experimental Psychology: General, 132*(4), 566–594.

Salthouse, T. A., Berish, D. E., & Miles, J. D. (2002). The role of cognitive stimulation on the relations between age and cognitive functioning. *Psychology and Aging, 17*(4), 548–557.

Salts, C. J. (1985). Divorce stage theory and therapy: Therapeutic implications throughout the divorcing process. *Journal of Psychotherapy and the Family, 1*(3), 13–23.

Sampson, E. E. (1993). Identity politics: Challenges to psychology's understanding. *American Psychologist, 48,* 1219–1230.

Sankar, A. (1993). Images of home death and the elderly patient: Romantic versus real. *Generations, 17*(2), 59–63.

Sano, M., et al. (1997). A controlled trial of selegiline, alpha-tocopherol, or both as treatment for Alzheimer's disease. *New England Journal of Medicine, 336*(17), 1216–1222.

Sapadin, L. A. (1988). Friendship and gender: Perspectives of professional men and women. *Journal of Social and Personal Relationships, 5,* 387–403.

Sapolsky, R. M. (1992). Stress and neurendocrine changes during aging. *Generations, 16*(4), 35–38.

Sarason, B. R., Sarason, I. G., & Pierce, G. R. (Eds.). (1990). *Social support: An interactional view.* New York: Wiley.

Sarason, S. (1977). *Work, aging, and social change.* New York: Free Press.

Sarton, M. (1977). *The house by the sea: A journal.* New York: Norton.

Sarton, M. (1988). *After the stroke.* New York: Norton.

Savishinsky, J. (2000). *Breaking the watch: The meanings of retirement in America.* Ithaca, NY: Cornell University Press.

Savishinsky, J. (2001). Images of retirement: Finding the purpose and the passion. *Generations, 25*(3), 52–56.

Scanzoni, J. (1978). *Sex roles, women's work, and marital conflict.* Lexington, MA: Heath.

Scanzoni, J. (1980). Contemporary marriage types. *Journal of Family Issues, 1,* 125–140.

Scarr, S. (1988). Race and gender as psychological variables: Social and ethical issues. *American Psychologist, 43,* 56–59.

Scarr, S., & Gracek, S. (1982). Similarities and differences among siblings. In M. E. Lamb & B. Sutton-Smith (Eds.),

Sibling relationships: Their nature and significance across the lifespan (pp. 357–381). Hillsdale, NJ: Erlbaum.

Scarr, S., & McCartney, K. (1983). How people make their own environments: A theory of genotype environment effects. *Child Development, 54,* 424–435.

Schachter, S. (1959). *The psychology of affiliation.* Stanford, CA: Stanford University Press.

Schacter, D. (1989). Memory. In M. I. Posner (Ed.), *Foundations of cognitive science* (pp. 683–725). Cambridge, MA: MIT Press.

Schacter, D. (1992). Understanding implicit memory: A cognitive neuroscience approach. *American Psychologist, 47,* 559–569.

Schacter, D., Cooper, L., & Valdisseri, M. (1992). Implicit and explicit memory for novel visual objects in older and younger adults. *Psychology and Aging, 7,* 299–308.

Schaie, K. W. (1965). A general model for the study of developmental problems. *Psychological Bulletin, 64,* 92–107.

Schaie, K. W. (1977). Quasi-experimental research designs in the psychology of aging. In J. E. Birren & K. W. Schaie (Eds.), *Handbook of the psychology of aging* (pp. 39–58). New York: Van Nostrand Reinhold.

Schaie, K. W. (1978). External validity in the assessment of intellectual development in adulthood. *Journal of Gerontology, 33,* 696–701.

Schaie, K. W. (1983). The Seattle longitudinal study: A twenty-one-year exploration of psychometric intelligence in adulthood. In K. W. Schaie (Ed.), *Longitudinal studies of adult psychological development* (pp. 64–135). New York: Guilford Press.

Schaie, K. W. (1988). Ageism in psychological research. *American Psychologist, 43,* 179–183.

Schaie, K. W. (1989). Individual differences in rate of cognitive change in adulthood. In V. L. Bengtson & K. W. Schaie (Eds.), *The course of later life: Research and reflections* (pp. 65–85). New York: Springer.

Schaie, K. W. (1990). Intellectual development in adulthood. In J. E. Birren & K. W. Schaie (Eds.), *Handbook of the psychology of aging* (3rd ed., pp. 291–309). San Diego, CA: Academic Press.

Schaie, K. W. (1994). The course of adult intellectual development. *American Psychologist, 49*(4), 304–313.

Schaie, K. W. (1996). *Intellectual development in adulthood: The Seattle Longitudinal Study.* Cambridge, England: Cambridge University Press.

Schaie, K. W., & Geiwitz, J. (1982). *Adult development and aging.* Boston: Little, Brown.

Schaie, K. W., & Willis, S. L. (1993). Age difference patterns of psychometric intelligence in adulthood: Generalizability within and across ability domains. *Psychology and Aging, 8,* 44–55.

Schell, T. L., Klein, S. B., & Babey, S. H. (1996). Testing a hierarchical model of self-knowledge. *Psychological Science, 7*(3), 170–173.

Schlenker, E. D. (1984). *Nutrition in aging.* St. Louis, MO: Times Mirror/Mosby.

Schlossberg, N. (1984). *Counseling adults in transition: Linking practice with theory.* New York: Springer.

Schmich, M. T. (1991, October 18). Employee benefit of the 90's. *Chicago Tribune,* pp. 1, 6.

Schmotkin, D. (1999). Affective bonds of adult children with living versus deceased parents. *Psychology and Aging, 14*(3), 473–482.

Schneider, B. A., Daneman, M., Murphy, D. R., & See, S. K. (2000). Listening to discourse in distracting settings: The effects of aging. *Psychology and Aging, 15*(1), 110–125.

Schneider, E. L. (1992). Biological theories of aging. *Generations, 16*(4), 7–10.

Schoenborn, C. A., & Horm, J. (1993). *Negative moods as correlates of smoking and heavier drinking: Implications for health promotion.* Hyattsville, MD: National Center for Health Statistics.

Schooler, C. (1990). Psychosocial factors and effective cognitive functioning in adulthood. In J. E. Birren & K. W. Schaie (Eds.), *Handbook of the psychology of aging* (3rd ed., pp. 347–358). San Diego, CA: Academic Press.

Schooler, C., & Mulatu, M. S. (2001). The reciprocal effects of leisure time activities and intellectual functioning in older people: A longitudinal analysis. *Psychology and Aging, 16*(3), 466–482.

Schooler, C., Mulatu, M. S., & Oates, G. (1999). The continuing effects of substantively complex work on the intellectual functioning of older workers. *Psychology and Aging, 14*(3), 483–506.

Schroots, J. J. F. (1988). Current perspectives on aging health, and behavior. In J. J. F. Schroots, J. E. Birren, & A. Svanborg (Eds.), *Health and aging: Perspectives and prospects* (pp. 3– 24). New York: Springer.

Schroots, J., & Birren, J. (1990). Concept of time and aging in science. In J. E. Birren & K. W. Schaie (Eds.), *Handbook of the psychology of aging* (3rd ed., pp. 45–64). San Diego, CA: Academic Press.

Schulz, J. H. (1992). The early retirement time-bomb. *Aging Today, 15*(5), 9.

Schulz, R. (1978). *The psychology of death, dying, and bereavement.* Reading, MA: Addison-Wesley.

Schulz, R. (1994). Introduction: Debate on generalized theories of slowing. *Journal of Gerontology: Psychological Sciences, 49*(2), P59.

Schulz, R., & Beach, S. R. (1999). Caregiving as a risk factor for mortality: The Caregiver Health Effect Study. *JAMA, 282*(23), 2215–2219.

Schulz, R., & Heckhausen, J. (1996). A life-span model of successful aging. *American Psychologist, 51*(7), 702–714.

Schulz, R., Martire, L. M., Beach, S. R., & Scheier, M. F. (2000). Depression and mortality in the elderly. *Current Directions in Psychological Science, 9*(6), 204–208.

Schulz, R., Musa, D., Staszewski, J., & Siegler, R. S. (1994). The relationship between age and major league baseball performance: Implications for development. *Psychology and Aging, 9*(2), 274–286.

Schulz, R., Visintainer, P., & Williamson, G. M. (1990). Psychiatric and physical morbidity effects of caregiving. *Journal of Gerontology, 45,* 181–191.

Schwartz, F. (1989). Management women and the new facts of life. *Harvard Business Review, 67,* 65–76.

Schwartz, J. B. (1997, Spring). Medications in the elderly: The good news and the bad news. *Newsletter of Buehler Center on Aging* (McGaw Medical Center, Northwestern University), *13*(1), 1–2.

Schwartz, J., & Barrett, T. (1991, November 25). Retire or bust. *Newsweek,* pp. 50, 52.

Scott, K. (2001). The anatomy of a geriatric education. *Aging Today, 22*(4), 10, 12.

Scott-Maxwell, F. (1979). *The measure of my days.* New York: Penguin Books.

Sedlak, A. J. (1988). Prevention of wife abuse. In V. B. Van Hasselt, R. L. Morrison, A. S. Bellack, & M. Hersen (Eds.), *Handbook of family violence* (pp. 457–481). New York: Plenum.

Seelbach, W. C., & Hansen, C. J. (1980). Satisfaction with family relations among the elderly. *Family Relations, 29,* 91–96.

Seeman, T. E., Dubin, F., & Seeman, M. (2003). Religiosity/spirituality and health: A critical review of the evidence for biological pathways. *American Psychologist, 58*(1), 53–63.

Seeman, T., McAvay, G., Merrill, S., Albert, M., & Rodin, J. (1996). Self-efficacy beliefs and change in cognitive performance: MacArthur studies of successful aging. *Psychology and Aging, 11*(3), 538–551.

Sekuler, R., & Blake, R. (1987, December). Sensory underload. *Psychology Today,* pp. 48–51.

Seligman, J., Rosenberg, D., Wingert, P., Hannah, D., & Annin, P. (1992, December 14). It's not like Mr. Mom. *Newsweek,* pp. 70–73.

Seligman, M. E. P., & Csikszentmihalyi, M. (2000). Positive psychology: An introduction. *American Psychologist, 55*(1), 5–14.

Selkoe, D. J. (1991). Amyloid protein and Alzheimer's disease. *Scientific American, 265*(5), 68–78.

Selkoe, D. J. (1993). Physiological production of the beta-amyloid protein and the mechanism of Alzheimer's disease. *Trends in Neurosciences, 16*(10), 403–409.

Sells, L. W. (1973). *High school math as the critical filter in the job market.* Alexandria, VA: Eric Document Reproduction Service (ED 080 351).

Selman, R. L. (1980). *The growth of interpersonal understanding.* New York: Academic Press.

Selman, R. L., & Byrne, D. F. (1974). A structural-developmental analysis of levels of role taking in middle childhood. *Child Development, 45,* 803–806.

Seltzer, M. (1976). Suggestions for the examination of time-disordered relationships. In J. F. Gubrium (Ed.), *Time, roles, and self in old age* (pp. 111–125). New York: Human Sciences Press.

Seltzer, M. M., & Ryff, C. D. (1994). Parenting across the life span: The normative and nonnormative cases. In D. L.

Featherman, R. M. Lerner, & M. Perlmutter (Eds.), *Life-span development and behavior* (Vol. 12, pp. 1–40). Hillsdale, NJ: Erlbaum.

Serow, W. J., & Sly, D. F. (1988). The demography of current and future aging cohorts. In Committee on an Aging Society (Ed.), *America's aging: The social and built environment in an older society* (pp. 42–102). Washington, DC: National Academy Press.

Serrano, J. P., Latorre, J. M., Gatz, M., & Montanes, J. (2004). Life review therapy using autobiographical retrieval practice for older adults with depressive symptomatology. *Psychology and Aging, 19*(2), 272–277.

Seybold, K. S., & Hill, P. C. (2001). The role of religion and spirituality in mental and physical health. *Current Directions in Psychological Science, 10*(1), 21–24.

Shanas, E. (1979a). The family as a social support system in old age. *Gerontologist, 19,* 169–174.

Shanas, E. (1979b). Social myth as hypothesis: The case of the family relations of older people. *Gerontologist, 19,* 3–19.

Shapiro, D. H., Jr., Schwartz, C. E., & Astin, J. A. (1996). Controlling ourselves, controlling our world: Psychology's role in understanding positive and negative consequences of seeking and gaining control. *American Psychologist, 51*(12), 1213–1230.

Shapiro, J. L. (1987, January). The expectant father. *Psychology Today,* pp. 36–42.

Shavelson, R. J., Hubner, J. J., & Staton, G. C. (1976). Self-concept: Validation and construct interpretations. *Review of Educational Research, 46,* 407–441.

Shaver, P. R., & Hazan, C. (1988). A biased overview of the study of love. *Journal of Social and Personal Relationships, 5,* 473–501.

Shaw, B. A., Krause, N., Chatters, L. M., Connell, C. M., & Ingersoll-Dayton, B. (2004). Emotional support from parents early in life, aging, and health. *Psychology and Aging, 19*(1), 4–12.

Shaw, L. B. (1984). Retirement plans of middle-aged married women. *Gerontologist, 24*(2), 154–159.

Sheehy, G. (1976). *Passages: Predictable crises in adult life.* New York: Dutton.

Sherman, E. (1993). Mental health and successful adaptation in later life. *Generations, 17*(1), 43–46.

Sherman, L. W., & Berk, R. A. (1984). The specific deterrent effects of arrest for domestic assault. *American Sociological Review, 49,* 261–272.

Shimamura, A. P. (1996). Unraveling the mystery of the frontal lobes: Explorations in cognitive neuroscience. *Psychological Science Agenda, 9*(5), 8–9.

Shimp, L. A., & Ascione, F. J. (1988). Causes of medication misuse and error. *Generations, 12*(4), 17–21.

Shneidman, E. (1989). The indian summer of life: A preliminary study of septuagenarians. *American Psychologist, 44,* 684–694.

Sieber, S. D. (1974). Toward a theory of role accumulation. *American Sociological Review, 39,* 567–578.

Siegler, I. (1975). The terminal drop hypothesis: Fact or artifact? *Experimental Aging Research, 1*(1), 169–185.

Siegler, I. (1989). Developmental health psychology. In M. Storandt & G. R. VandenBos (Eds.), *The adult years: Continuity and change* (pp. 119–142). Washington, DC: American Psychological Association.

Silverstein, L. B. (1991). Transforming the debates about child care and maternal employment. *American Psychologist, 46,* 1025–1032.

Silvestri, G. (1997, November). Occupational employment projections to 2006. *Monthly Labor Review,* p. 59.

Simonton, D. K. (1975). Age and literary creativity: A cross-cultural and transhistorical survey. *Journal of Cross-Cultural Psychology, 6,* 259–277.

Simonton, D. K. (1988). Age and outstanding achievement: What do we know after a century of research? *Psychological Bulletin, 104,* 251–267.

Simonton, D. K. (1989). The swan-song phenomenon: Last-works effects for 172 classical composers. *Psychology and Aging, 4,* 42–47.

Simonton, D. K. (1990). Creativity and wisdom in aging. In J. E. Birren & K. W. Schaie (Eds.), *Handbook of the psychology of aging* (3rd ed., pp. 320–329). San Diego, CA: Academic Press.

Simonton, D. K. (1991). Creative productivity through the adult years. *Generations, 15*(2), 13–16.

Simonton, D. K. (2000). Creativity: Cognitive, personal, developmental, and social aspects. *American Psychologist, 55*(1), 151–158.

Singer, T., Verhaeghen, P., Ghisletta, P., Lindenburger, U., & Baltes, P. B. (2003). The fate of cognition in very old age: Six-year longitudinal findings in the Berlin Aging Study (BASE). *Psychology and Aging, 18*(2), 318–331.

Sinnott, J. (1993). Commentary. *Human Development, 36,* 297–299.

Sinnott, J. D. (1994a). The future of adult lifespan learning: Learning institutions face change. In J. D. Sinnott (Ed.), *Interdisciplinary handbook of adult lifespan learning* (pp. 449–466). Westport, CT: Greenwood Press.

Sinnott, J. D. (1998). *The development of logic in adulthood: Postformal thought and its applications.* New York: Plenum Press.

Sinnott, J. D. (Ed.). (1994b). *Interdisciplinary handbook of adult lifespan learning.* Westport, CT: Greenwood Press.

Skolnick, A. (1981). Married lives: Longitudinal perspectives on marriage. In D. Eichorn, J. Clausen, N. Haan, M. Honzig, & P. Mussen (Eds.), *Present and past in middle age* (pp. 270–300). New York: Academic Press.

Sliwinski, M. J., Hofer, S. M., Hall, C., Buschke, H., & Lipton, R. B. (2003). Modeling memory decline in older adults: The importance of preclinical dementia, attrition, and chronological age. *Psychology and Aging, 18*(4), 658–671.

Sliwinski, M. J., Lipton, R. B., Buschke, H., & Stewart, W. F. (1996). The effect of preclinical dementia on estimates of normal cognitive function in aging. *Journal of Gerontology: Psychological Sciences, 51B,* P217–225.

Small, B. J., Fratiglioni, L., von Strauss, E., & Backman, L. (2003). Terminal decline and cognitive performance in

very old age: Does cause of death matter? *Psychology and Aging, 18*(2), 193–202.

Smallegan, M. (1989). Level of depressive symptoms and life stresses for culturally diverse older adults. *Gerontologist, 29,* 45–50.

Smith, D. E., Roberts, J., Gage, F. H., & Tuszynski, M. H. (1999). Age-associated neuronal atrophy occurs in the primate brain and is reversible by growth factor gene therapy. *Proceedings of the National Academy of Sciences USA, 96,* 10893–10898.

Smith, E. E. (2000). Neuronal bases of human working memory. *Current Directions in Psychological Science, 9*(2), 45–49.

Smith, J. D. (2002). Apolipoproteins and aging: Emerging mechanisms. *Aging Research Reviews, 1,* 345–365.

Smith, J., & Baltes, M. M. (1998). The role of gender in very old age: Profiles of functioning and everyday life patterns. *Psychology and Aging, 13*(4), 676–695.

Smith, Z. N. (1996, March 8). Golden ceilings and glass floors. *Chicago Sun-Times,* p. 30.

Snowdon, D. A., Kemper, S. J., Mortimer, J. A., Greiner, L. H., Wekstein, D. R., & Markesbery, W. R. (1996). Linguistic ability in early life and cognitive function and Alzheimer's disease in late life: Findings from the Nun Study. *Journal of the American Medical Association, 275*(7), 528–532.

Snyder, C. R. (1994). *The psychology of hope: You can get there from here.* New York: Free Press.

Snyder, C. R. (Ed.). (2000). *Handbook of hope: Theory, measures, and applications.* Orlando, FL: Academic Press.

Snyder, C. R., Harris, C., Anderson, J. R., Holleran, S. A., Irving, L. M., Sigmon, S. T., Yoshinobu, L., Gibb, J., Langelle, C., & Harney, P. (1991). The will and the ways: Development and validation of an indvidual differences measure of hope. *Journal of Personality and Social Psychology, 60,* 570–585.

Snygg, D. (1941). The need for a phenomenological system of psychology. *Psychological Review, 48,* 404–424.

Snygg, D., & Combs, A. W. (1949). *Individual behavior: A new frame of reference for psychology.* New York: Harper.

Social Security Administration. (2004). Women and Social Security. Retrieved December 23, 2004, from www.ssa.gov/pressoffice/factsheets/women.htm.

Solomon, J., & Fuchsberg, G. (1990, January 26). Great number of older Americans seen ready to work. *Wall Street Journal,* p. B1.

Somerfield, M. R., & McCrae, R. R. (2000). Stress and coping research: Methodological challenges, theoretical advances, and clinical applications. *American Psychologist, 55*(6), 620–625.

Sontag, S. (1979). The double standard of aging. In J. Williams (Ed.), *Psychology of women* (pp. 462–478). San Diego, CA: Academic Press.

Speigel, D., Bloom, J. R., Kraemer, H. C., & Gottheil, E. (1989). Effect of psychosocial treatment on survival of patients with metastatic breast cancer. *Lancet, 334,* 888–891.

Sperling, M. B., & Berman, W. H. (Eds.). (1994). *Attachment in adults: Clinical and developmental perspectives*. New York: Guilford Press.

Spitze, G. (1988). Women's employment and family relations: A review. *Journal of Marriage and the Family, 50,* 595–618.

Spokane, A. R. (1985). A review of research on person-environment congruence in Holland's theory of careers. *Journal of Vocational Behavior, 26,* 306–343.

Srivastava, S., John, O. P., Gosling, S. D., & Potter, J. (2003). Development of personality in early and middle adulthood: Set like plaster or persistent change? *Journal of Personality and Social Psychology, 84*(5), 1041–1053.

Sroufe, L. A. (1978). Attachment and the roots of competence. *Human Nature, 1,* 50–51.

Sroufe, L. A., & Fleeson, J. (1986). Attachment and the construction of relationships. In W. Hartup & Z. Rubin (Eds.), *Relationships and development* (pp. 51–72). Hillsdale, NJ: Erlbaum.

Stacey-Konnert, C. (1993). Preventative interventions for older adults. *Generations, 17*(1), 77–78.

Stamler, J. (2001). Is it ever too late to make lifestyle changes? *Center on Aging* (Buehler Center on Aging, Northwestern University), *17*(1), 1–3.

Stanford, E. P., & Schmidt, M. G. (1996). The changing face of nursing home residents: Meeting their diverse needs. *Generations, 19*(4), 20–23.

Stanford, E. P., & Yee, D. (1991). Gerontology and the relevance of diversity. *Generations, 15*(4), 11–14.

Stangor, C., & Ruble, D. N. (1989). Strength of expectancies and memory for social information: What we remember depends on how much we know. *Journal of Experimental Social Psychology, 25,* 18–35.

Stark, E., & Flitcraft, A. (1988). Violence among intimates: An epidemiological review. In V. B. Van Hasselt, R. L. Morrison, A. S. Bellack, & M. Hersen (Eds.), *Handbook of family violence* (pp. 293–317). New York: Plenum.

Staudinger, U. M., Smith, J., & Baltes, P. B. (1992). Wisdom-related knowledge in a life review task: Age difference and the role of professional specialization. *Psychology and Aging, 7,* 271–281.

Steinberg, L., Dornbusch, S. M., & Brown, B. B. (1992). Ethnic differences in adolescent achievement: An ecological perspective. *American Psychologist, 47,* 723–729.

Steinhauser, S. (1999). Beyond age bias: Successfully managing an older workforce. *Aging Today, 20*(5), 9, 12.

Stephen, T. (1986). Communication and interdependence in geographically separated relationships. *Human Communication Research, 13,* 191–210.

Stephens, M. A. P., & Townsend, A. L. (1997). Stress of parent care: Positive and negative effects of women's other roles. *Psychology and Aging, 12*(2), 376–386.

Stephens, M. A. P., Franks, M. M., & Atienza, A. A. (1997). Where two roles intersect: Spillover between parent care and employment. *Psychology and Aging, 12*(1), 30–37.

Stephens, M. A. P., Franks, M. M., & Townsend, A. L. (1994). Stress and rewards in women's multiple roles: The case of women in the middle. *Psychology and Aging, 9*(1), 45–52.

Sternberg, R. J. (1985a). *Beyond IQ: A triarchic theory of human intelligence.* Cambridge, England: Cambridge University Press.

Sternberg, R. J. (1985b). Implicit theories of intelligence, creativity, and wisdom. *Journal of Personality and Social Psychology, 49,* 607–677.

Sternberg, R. J. (1988). Triangulating love. In R. J. Sternberg & M. L. Barnes (Eds.), *The psychology of love.* New Haven, CT: Yale University Press.

Sternberg, R. J. (2001). What is the common thread of creativity? Its dialectical relation to intelligence and wisdom. *American Psychologist, 56*(4), 360–362.

Sternberg, R. J. (2004). Culture and intelligence. *American Psychologist, 59*(5), 325–338.

Sternberg, R. J. (Ed.). (1997). Intelligence and lifelong learning (Special issue). *American Psychologist, 52*(10).

Sternberg, R. J., & Lubart, T. I. (1996). Investing in creativity. *American Psychologist, 51*(7), 677–688.

Sterns, H. L., Matheson, N. K., & Schwartz, L. S. (1990). Work and retirement. In K. F. Ferraro (Ed.), *Gerontology: Perspectives and issues* (pp. 163–178). New York: Springer.

Stets, J. E., & Straus, M. A. (1990). Gender differences in reporting marital violence and its medical and psychological consequences. In M. A. Straus & R. J. Gelles (Eds.), *Physical violence in American families* (pp. 151–165). New Brunswick, NJ: Transaction.

Stevens-Long, J. (1979). *Adult life: Developmental processes.* Palo Alto, CA: Mayfield.

Stevens-Long, J. (1990). Adult development: Theories past and future. In R. Nemiroff & C. Colarusso (Eds.), *New dimensions in adult development* (pp. 125–169). New York: Basic Books.

Stewart, A. J., & Ostrove, J. M. (1998). Women's personality in middle age: Gender, history, and midcourse corrections. *American Psychologist, 53,* 1185–1194.

Stewart, A. J., & Vandewater, E. A. (1998). The course of generativity. In D. P. McAdams & E. de St. Aubin (Eds.), *Generativity and adult development: Psychosocial perspectives on caring for and contributing to the next generation* (pp. 75–100). Washington, DC: American Psychological Association Press.

Stokols, D. (1992). Establishing and maintaining healthy environments: Toward a social ecology of health promotion. *American Psychologist, 47,* 6–22.

Stoller, E. P., & Earl, L. L. (1983). Help with activities of everyday life: Sources of support for the nonistitutionalized elderly. *Gerontologist, 23,* 64–70.

Stone, R., Cafferata, G. L., & Sangl, J. (1987). Caregivers of the frail elderly: A national profile. *Gerontologist, 27,* 616–626.

Stoppard, J. M. (1989). An evaluation of the adequacy of cognitive/behavioral theories for understanding depression in women. *Canadian Psychologist, 47,* 1205–1212.

Straus, M. A. (1990a). The National Family Violence Surveys. In M. A. Straus & R. J. Gelles (Eds.), *Physical violence in American families* (pp. 3–16). New Brunswick, NJ: Transaction.

Straus, M. A. (1990b). Ordinary violence, child abuse, and wife beating: What do they have in common? In M. A. Straus & R. J. Gelles (Eds.), *Physical violence in American families* (pp. 403–424). New Brunswick, NJ: Transaction.

Straus, M. A. (1990c). Social stress and marital violence in a national sample of American families. In M. A. Straus & R. J. Gelles (Eds.), *Physical violence in American families* (pp. 181–201). New Brunswick, NJ: Transaction.

Straus, M. A., & Gelles, R. J. (1986). Societal change and change in family violence from 1975 to 1985 as revealed by two national surveys. *Journal of Marriage and the Family, 48,* 465–479.

Straus, M. A., & Gelles, R. J. (1990). How violent are American families? Estimates from the National Family Violence Resurvey and other studies. In M. A. Straus & R. J. Gelles (Eds.), *Physical violence in American families* (pp. 94–112). New Brunswick, NJ: Transaction.

Strehler, B. (1982). *Time, cells, and aging.* New York: Academic Press.

Stricherz, M., & Cunningham, L. (1981–1982). Death concerns of students, employed persons, and retired persons. *Omega: Journal of Death and Dying, 12,* 373–380.

Strickland, B. R. (1989). Internal-external control expectancies: From contingency to creativity. *American Psychologist, 44,* 1–12.

Strickland, B. R. (1992). Women and depression. *Current Directions in Psychological Science, 1,* 132–135.

Stroebe, M., Gergen, M. M., Gergen, K. J., & Stroebe, W. (1992). Broken hearts or broken bonds: Love and death in historical perspective. *American Psychologist, 47,* 1205–1212.

Stroebe, M. S., Stroebe, W., & Hansson, R. O. (1993). *Handbook of bereavement.* New York: Cambridge University Press.

Stroebe, W., & Stroebe, M. S. (1987). *Bereavement and health: The psychological and physical consequences of partner loss.* London: Cambridge University Press.

Stuen, C. (2002). Accessibility benefits all. *Aging and Vision, 14*(2), 1.

Sue, S. (1999). Science, ethnicity, and bias: Where have we gone wrong? *American Psychologist, 54,* 1070–1077.

Suitor, J. J., Pillemer, K., & Straus, M. A. (1990). Marital violence in a life course perspective. In M. A. Straus & R. J. Gelles (Eds.), *Physical violence in American families* (pp. 305–317). New Brunswick, NJ: Transaction.

Super, D. E. (1957). *The psychology of careers.* New York: Harper & Row.

Super, D. E. (1984). Career and life development. In D. Brown & L. Brooks (Eds.), *Career choice and development.* San Francisco: Jossey-Bass.

Super, D. E. (1985). Coming of age in Middletown: Careers in the making. *American Psychologist, 40,* 405–414.

SUPPORT Principal Investigators. (1995). A controlled trial to improve care for seriously ill hospitalized patients: The Study to Understand Prognoses and Preferences for Outcomes and Risks of Treatments (SUPPORT). *Journal of the American Medical Association, 274*(20), 1591–1598.

Suter, L. E., & Miller, H. P. (1973). Income differences between men and career women. *American Journal of Sociology, 59,* 962–974.

Sweetser, D. A. (1963). Asymmetry in intergenerational family relationships. *Social Forces, 41,* 346–352.

Swenson, C., Esker, R., & Kohlhepp, K. (1984). Five factors in long-term marriages. *Lifestyles, 7,* 94–106.

Swindle, R., Jr., Heller, K., Pescosolido, B., & Kikuzawa, S. (2000). Responses to nervous breakdowns in America over a 40-year period: Mental health policy implications. *American Psychologist, 55,* 740–749.

Symons, D. (1979). *The evolution of human sexuality.* New York: Oxford University Press.

Szinovacz, M. (1987). Preferred retirement timing and retirement satisfaction in women. *International Journal of Aging and Human Development, 24*(4), 301–317.

Tanzi, R. E., & Blacker, D. (2000). Genetic screening in Alzheimer's disease. *Generations, 24*(1), 58–63.

Taylor, S. E. (2002). *The tending instinct: How nurturing is essential to who we are and how we live.* New York: Holt.

Taylor, S. E., Kemeny, M. E., Reed, G. M., Bower, J. E., & Gruenewald, T. L. (2000). Psychological resources, positive illusions, and health. *American Psychologist, 55*(1), 99–109.

Templer, D. I. (1970). The construction and validation of a Death Anxiety Scale. *Journal of General Psychology, 8,* 165–177.

Teri, L., Truax, P., Logsdon, R., Uomoto, J., Zarit, S., & Vitaliano, P. P. (1992). Assessment of behavioral problems in dementia: The Revised Memory and Behavior Problems Checklist. *Psychology and Aging, 7,* 622–631.

Tesch, S. A. (1983). Review of friendship development across the life span. *Human Development, 26,* 266–276.

Thoits, P. A. (1986). Multiple identities: Examining gender and marital status differences in distress. *American Sociological Review, 51,* 259–272.

Thomas, W., & Thomas, D. (1928). *The child in America.* New York: Knopf.

Thompson, A. (1997, March-April). U.S. healthcare system fails to detect elders' malnutrition. *Aging Today,* pp. 1, 6.

Thompson, M. G., & Heller, K. (1990). Facets of support related to well-being: Quantitative social isolation and perceived family support in a sample of elderly women. *Psychology and Aging, 5,* 535–544.

Thompson, S. C., Sobolew-Shubin, A., Galbraith, M. E., Schwankovsky, L., & Cruzen, D. (1993). Maintaining perceptions of control: Finding perceived control in low-control circumstances. *Journal of Personality and Social Psychology, 64,* 293–304.

Thurstone, L. L., & Thurstone, T. G. (1949). *Examiner manual for the SRA Primary Mental Abilities Test.* Chicago: Science Research Associates.

Tiger, L. (1969). *Men in groups.* New York: Random House.

Tiger, L. (1979). *Optimism: The biology of hope.* New York: Simon & Schuster.

Tobin, S. S. (1990). *Acceptance of death at the end of life.* Chicago: Center for Applied Gerontology.

Tolman, R. M., & Bennett, L. W. (1990). A review of quantitative research on men who batter. *Journal of Interpersonal Violence, 5,* 87–118.

Tonti, M. (1988). Relationships among adult siblings who care for their aged parents. In M. D. Kahn & K. D. Lewis (Eds.), *Siblings in therapy* (pp. 417–434). New York: Norton.

Tornstam, L. (1992). The quo vadis of gerontology: On the scientific paradigm of gerontology. *Gerontologist, 32*(3), 318–326.

Townsend, A. L., & Franks, M. M. (1995). Binding ties: Closeness and conflict in adult children's caregiving relationships. *Psycholgy and Aging, 10*(3), 343–351.

Townsend, J. M. (1989). Mate selection criteria: A pilot study. *Ethology and Sociobiology, 10,* 241–253.

Travis, S. S. (1987). Older adults' sexuality and remarriage. *Journal of Gerontological Nursing, 13*(6), 9–14.

Treas, J., & Bengtson, V. L. (1987). The family in later years. In M. B. Sussman & S. K. Steinmetz (Eds.), *Handbook of marriage and the family* (pp. 625–648). New York: Plenum.

Triandis, H. C. (1989). The self and social behavior in differing cultural contexts. *Psychological Review, 96,* 506–520.

Triandis, H. C. (1995). *Individualism and collectivism.* Boulder, CO: Westview Press.

Triandis, H. C. (1996). The psychological measurement of cultural syndromes. *American Psychologist, 51*(4), 407–415.

Triandis, H. C., & Suh, E. M. (2002). Cultural influences on personality. *Annual Review of Psychology, 53,* 133–160.

Triandis, H. C., Bontempo, R., Villareal, M. J., Asai, M., & Lucca, N. (1988). Individualism and collectivism: Cross-cultural perspectives on self-ingroup relationships. *Journal of Personality and Social Psychology, 54,* 323–338.

Trivers, R. (1972). Parental investment and sexual selection. In B. Campbell (Ed.), *Sexual selection and the descent of man* (pp. 136–179). Chicago: Aldine.

Trivers, R. (1985). *Social evolution.* Menlo Park, CA: Benjamin/Cummings.

Troll, L. E. (1982). *Continuations: Adult development and aging.* Monterey, CA: Brooks/Cole.

Troll, L. E. (1983). Grandparents: The family watchdogs. In T. Brubaker (Ed.), *Family relationships in later life* (pp. 63–74). Beverly Hills, CA: Sage.

Troll, L. E. (1986). *Family issues in current gerontology.* New York: Springer.

Troll, L. E., & Skaff, M. M. (1997). Perceived continuity of self in very old age. *Psychology and Aging, 12*(1), 162–169.

Troll, L. E., & Stapely, J. (1986). Elders and the extended family system: Health, family salience, and affect. In J. M. A. Munnich (Ed.), *Life span and change in a gerontological perspective.* New York: Academic Press.

Troll, L. E., Miller, S. J., & Atchley, R. C. (1979). *Families in later life.* Belmont, CA: Wadsworth.

Tschann, J. M. (1988). Self-disclosure in adult friendship: Gender and marital status differences. *Journal of Social and Personal Relationships, 5,* 65–81.

Tulving, E. (1972). Episodic and semantic memory. In E. Tulving (Ed.), *Organization of memory.* New York: Academic Press.

Tulving, E. (1983). *Elements of episodic memory.* New York: Oxford University Press.

Tulving, E., & Schacter, D. (1990). Priming and human memory systems. *Science, 247,* 301–306.

Turkington, C. (1993, January). More funding urged to study biology of mental disorders. *APA Monitor,* p. 40.

Turner, A. M., & Greenough, W. T. (1985). Differential rearing effects on rat visual cortex synapses: 1. Synaptic and neuronal density and synapses per neuron. *Brain Research, 329,* 195–203.

Twenge, J. M., & Crocker, J. (2002). Race and self-esteem: Meta-analyses comparing Whites, Blacks, Asians, and American Indians and comment on Gray-Little and Hafdahl. (2000). *Psychological Bulletin, 128*(3), 371–408.

U.S. Bureau of the Census. (1965, July). Estimates of the population of the United States, by single years of age, color, and sex: 1900 to 1959. *Current Population Reports,* Series P-25, No. 311. Washington, DC: U.S. Government Printing Office.

U.S. Bureau of the Census. (1983, September). America in transition: An aging society, by Cynthia M. Taeuber. *Current Population Reports,* Series P-23, No. 128. Washington, DC: U.S. Government Printing Office.

U.S. Bureau of the Census. (1984, December). *Statistical abstract of the United States: 1985.* Washington, DC: U.S. Government Printing Office.

U.S. Bureau of the Census. (1989, January). Projections of the population of the United States, by age, color, and sex: 1988 to 2080, by Gregory Spencer. *Current Population Reports,* Series P-25, No. 1018. Washington, DC: U.S. Government Printing Office.

U.S. Bureau of the Census. (1990a). Child support and alimony: 1987. *Current Population Reports,* Series P-23, No. 167. (Publication No. S/N 803-005-10020-1.) Washington, DC: U.S. Government Printing Office.

U.S. Bureau of the Census. (1990b). Household and family characteristics: March 1990 and 1989. *Current Population Reports,* Series P-20, No. 447. Washington, DC: U.S. Government Printing Office.

U.S. Bureau of the Census. (1990c). Need for personal assistance with everyday activities. *Current Population Reports,* Series P-70, No. 19. (Publication No. S/N 803-044-00007-4.) Washington, DC: U.S. Government Printing Office.

U.S. Bureau of the Census. (1990d, March). U.S. population estimates, by age, sex, race, and Hispanic origin: 1989, by Frederick W. Hollman. *Current Population Reports,* Series P-25, No. 1057. Washington, DC: U.S. Government Printing Office.

U.S. Bureau of the Census. (1991a, May). Marital status and living arrangements: March 1990. *Current Population Reports,* Series P-20, No. 450. Washington, DC: U.S. Government Printing Office.

U.S. Bureau of the Census. (1991b, September). Child support and alimony: 1989. *Current Population Reports,* Series P-60, No. 173. Washington, DC: U.S. Government Printing Office.

U.S. Bureau of the Census. (1991c). Pensions: Worker coverage and retirement benefits (Publication No. S/N 803-

044-00013-9). Washington, DC: U.S. Government Printing Office.

U.S. Bureau of the Census. (1991d). What's it worth? Educational background and economic status: Spring 1987. *Current Population Reports,* Series P-25. Washington, DC: U.S. Government Printing Office.

U.S. Bureau of the Census. (1992a). Households, families, and children: A 30-year perspective. *Current Population Reports,* Series P-23, No. 181. Washington, DC: U.S. Government Printing Office.

U.S. Bureau of the Census. (1992b). Marriage, divorce, and remarriage in the 1990's. *Current Population Reports,* Series P-23, No. 180. Washington, DC: U.S. Government Printing Office.

U.S. Bureau of the Census. (1992c). Population projections of the United States, by age, sex, race, and Hispanic origin. *Current Population Reports,* Series P-25, No. 1092. Washington, DC: U.S. Government Printing Office.

U.S. Bureau of the Census. (1992d). 65+ in America. *Current Population Reports,* Series P-23, No. 178. Washington, DC: U.S. Government Printing Office.

U.S. Bureau of the Census. (1992e). *Statistical abstract of the United States: 1992* (112th ed.). Washington, DC: U.S. Government Printing Office.

U.S. Bureau of the Census. (1993a). How we're changing: Demographic state of the nation, 1993. *Current Population Reports,* Series P-23, No. 184. Washington, DC: U.S. Government Printing Office.

U.S. Bureau of the Census. (1993b). Marital status and living arrangements: March 1993. *Current Population Reports,* Series P-20, No. 478. Washington, DC: U.S. Government Printing Office.

U.S. Bureau of the Census. (1995). Population profile of the United States: 1995. *Current Population Reports,* Series P-23-189. Washington, DC: U.S. Government Printing Office.

U.S. Bureau of the Census. (1998a). *Statistical abstract of the United States: 1998* (118th ed.). Washington, DC: U.S. Government Printing Office.

U.S. Bureau of the Census. (1998b, June). Fertility of American women: June 1998. *Current Population Reports,* Series P20-526. Washington, DC: U.S. Government Printing Office.

U.S. Bureau of the Census. (1998c, March). Marital status and living arrangements: March 1998 (update). *Current Population Reports,* Series P20-514. Washington, DC: U.S. Government Printing Office.

U.S. Bureau of the Census. (1999). *Statistical abstract of the United States: 1999* (119th ed.). Washington, DC: U.S. Government Printing Office.

U.S. Bureau of the Census. (2001, September). Gender: 2000. *Census 2000 Brief* (C2KB/01-9). Washington DC: U.S. Government Printing Office.

U.S. Bureau of the Census. (2003a). Marital status by sex for the population 15 years and over (P031). Retrieved December 22, 2004, from http://factfinder.census.gov.

U.S. Bureau of the Census. (2003b, August). Employment status: 2000. *Census 2000 Brief* (C2KBR-18). Washington, DC: U.S. Government Printing Office.

U.S. Bureau of the Census. (2003c, March). Disability status: 2000. *Census 2000 Brief* (C2KBR-17). Washington, DC: U.S. Government Printing Office.

U.S. Bureau of the Census. (2003d, October). Custodial mothers and fathers and their child support: 2001. *Current Population Reports* (P60-225). Washington, DC: U.S. Government Printing Office.

U.S. Congress, Office of Technology Assessment. (1986). *Hearing impairment and elderly people: A background paper* (Publication No. OTA-BP-BA-30). Washington, DC: U.S. Government Printing Office.

U.S. Department of Health and Human Services. (1990). *Healthy people 2000: National health promotion and disease prevention objectives* (PHS Publication No. 91-50213). Washington, DC: U.S. Government Printing Office.

U.S. Department of Health and Human Services. (1991). *Family violence: An overview.* Washington, DC: U.S. Government Printing Office.

U.S. Department of Health and Human Services. (1999). *Mental health: A report of the Surgeon General.* Rockville, MD: Author.

U.S. Department of Health and Human Services. (2000). *Healthy people 2010.* Washington, DC: U.S. Government Printing Office.

U.S. Department of Justice, Federal Bureau of Investigation. (1984). *Uniform crime reports for 1983.* Washington, DC: U.S. Government Printing Office.

U.S. Department of Labor. (1985, September). *Employment and earnings.* Washington, DC: U.S. Government Printing Office.

U.S. Department of Labor. (1991, June). *What work requires of schools: A SCANS report for America 2000* (a report of the Labor Secretary's Committee on Achieving Necessary Skills). Washington, DC: U.S. Government Printing Office.

U.S. Department of Labor. (2000). *Futurework: Trends and challenges for work in the 21st century.* Washington, DC: U.S. Government Printing Office.

U.S. Department of Labor, Bureau of Labor Statistics. (1991). *Employment and earnings, February 1991.* Washington, DC: U.S. Government Printing Office.

U.S. Department of Labor, Bureau of Labor Statistics. (2002, February). Contingent and alternative employment arrangements, February 2001. Retrieved December 23, 2004, from www.bls.gov/news.release.conemp.nr0.htm.

U.S. Department of Labor, Bureau of Labor Statistics. (2002, March). Work at home in 2001. Special supplement to the May 2001 *Current Population Survey.* Retrieved December 23, 2004, from www.bls.gov/news.release/homey.nr.htm.

U.S. Department of Labor, Bureau of Labor Statistics. (2004a, February). *Women in the labor force: A databook (report 973).* Washington, DC: U.S. Government Printing Office.

U.S. Department of Labor, Bureau of Labor Statistics. (2004b, September). Highlights of women's earning in 2003 (Report 978). Retrieved December 23, 2004, from www.bls.gov/cps/cpswom2003.pdf.

U.S. Department of Labor, Bureau of Labor Statistics. (2004–2005). *Occupational outlook handbook.* Washington, DC: U.S. Government Printing Office.

U.S. Food and Drug Administration, Center for Drug Evaluation and Research. (2004). Preventable adverse drug reactions: A focus on drug interactions. Available at www.fda.gov/cder/drug/drugReactiosn/default.htm.

U.S. General Accounting Office. (2003, April). *Retirement income—intergenerational comparisons of wealth and future income.* Washington, DC: U.S. Government Printing Office.

U.S. House of Representatives, Committee on Ways and Means. (1991). *Background material and data on programs within the jurisdiction of the Committee on Ways and Means: 1991 Green Book.* Washington, DC: U.S. Government Printing Office.

U.S. House of Representatives, Committee on Ways and Means. (1992). *Overview of entitlement programs: 1992 Green Book.* Washington, DC: U.S. Government Printing Office.

U.S. Senate Judiciary Committee. (1992, October). *Violence against women: A week in the life of America,* prepared by the majority staff of the Senate Judiciary Committee. (Available from Hart Office Building, Room B04, Washington, DC 20510.)

U.S. Senate Special Committee on Aging, American Association of Retired Persons, Federal Council on Aging, and U.S. Administration on Aging. (1991). *Aging America: Trends and projections* (DHHS Publication No. FCoA 91-28001). Washington, DC: U.S. Department of Health and Human Services.

U.S. Surgeon General. (1989). *Reducing the health consequences of smoking: 25 years of progress. Report of the Surgeon General* (DHHS Publication No. CDCV 89-8411). Washington, DC: U.S. Government Printing Office.

U.S. Surgeon General. (1990). *The health benefits of smoking cessation: A report of the Surgeon General* (DHHS Publication No. CDC 90–8416). Washington, DC: U.S. Government Printing Office.

Uba, L. (1994). *Asian Americans: Personality patterns, identity, and mental health.* New York: Guilford Press.

Uchino, B. N., Cacioppo, J. T., & Kiecolt-Glaser, J. K. (1996). The relationship between social support and physiological processes: A review with emphasis on underlying mechanisms and implications for health. *Psychological Bulletin, 119*(3), 488–531.

Uchino, B. N., Uno, D., & Holt-Lunstad, J. (1999). Social support, physiological processes, and health. *Current Directions in Psychological Science, 8*(5), 145–148.

Uhlenberg, P. (1980). Death and the family. *Journal of Family History, 5,* 313–320.

Umberson, D., & Gove, W. R. (1989). Parenthood and psychological well-being: Theory, measurement, and stage in the family life course. *Journal of Family Issues, 10,* 440–462.

United Nations. (1991). *The world's women 1970–1990: Trends and statistics.* New York: United Nations.

Utne, M. K., Hatfield, E., Traupman, J., & Greenberger, D. (1984). Equity, marital satisfaction, and stability. *Journal of Social and Personal Relationships, 1,* 323–332.

Vaillant, G. (1977). *Adaptation to life.* Boston: Little, Brown.

Van IJzendoorn, M. H. (1995). Adult attachment representations, parental responsiveness, and infant attachment: A meta-analysis on the predictive validity of the Adult Attachment Interview. *Psychological Bulletin, 117,* 387–403.

Van Lehn, K. (1989). Problem-solving and cognitive skill acquisition. In M. Posner (Ed.), *The foundations of cognitive science* (pp. 527–580). Cambridge, MA: MIT Press.

Vandenberg, S. G. (1972). Assortive mating, or who marries whom? *Behavior Genetics, 2,* 127–157.

Verbrugge, L. M. (1979). Marital status and health. *Journal of Marriage and the Family, 41,* 267–285.

Verbrugge, L. M. (1983). Multiple roles and physical health of women and men. *Journal of Health and Social Behavior, 24,* 16–30.

Verbrugge, L. M. (1987). From sneezes to adieux: Stages of health for American men and women. In R. A. Ward & S. S. Tobin (Eds.), *Health in aging: Sociological issues and policy directions* (pp. 17–57). New York: Springer.

Verbrugge, L. M. (1989). Pathways of health and death. In R. D. Apple (Ed.), *The history of women, health, and medicine in America.* New York: Garland.

Verhaeghen, P., Marcoen, A., & Goossens, L. (1992). Improving memory performance in the aged through mnemonic training: A meta-analytic study. *Psychology and Aging, 7,* 242–251.

Verhaeghen, P., Steitz, D. W., Sliwinski, M. J., & Cerella, J. (2003). Aging and dual-task performance: A meta-analysis. *Psychology and Aging, 18*(3), 443–460.

Vestal, R. E., & Dawson, G. W. (1985). Pharmacology and aging. In C. E. Finch & E. L. Schneider (Eds.), *Handbook of the biology of aging* (2nd ed.). New York: Van Nostrand Reinhold.

Vinick, B. H. (1978). Remarriage in old age. *Family Coordinator, 27,* 359–363.

Vinick, B. H., & Ekerdt, D. J. (1989). Retirement and the family. *Generations, 13*(2), 53–56.

Vining, E. (1978). *Being seventy: The measure of a year.* New York: Viking.

Visher, G. B., & Visher, J. S. (1990). Dynamics of successful stepfamilies. *Journal of Divorce and Remarriage, 14,* 1–12.

Vollmer, F. (1986). Why do men have higher expectancy than women? *Sex Roles, 14,* 351–362.

Vormbrock, J. K. (1993). Attachment theory as applied to wartime and job-related marital separation. *Psychological Bulletin, 114,* 122–144.

Vygotsky, L. S. (1978). *Mind in society.* Cambridge, MA: Harvard University Press.

Wachtel, P. L. (1977). *Psychoanalysis and behavior therapy: Toward an integration.* New York: Basic Books.

Waldman, S. (1992, May 4). Deadbeat dads. *Newsweek,* pp. 46–52.

Walford, R. (1969). *The immunological theory of aging.* Copenhagen: Munksgaard.

Walker, K. (1970, June). Time spent by husbands in household work. *Family Economics Review,* pp. 8–11.

Walker, L. E. (1979). *The battered woman.* New York: Harper & Row.

Walker, L. E. (1984). *The battered woman syndrome.* New York: Springer.

Walker, L. E. (1989). Psychology and violence against women. *American Psychologist, 44,* 695–702.

Walker, L. E. (1999). Psychology and domestic violence around the world. *American Psychologist, 54*(1), 21–29.

Walsh, M. W. (2004, June 13). Healthier and wiser? Sure, but not wealthier. *Wall Street Journal.*

Walsh, W. B., & Betz, N. E. (1985). *Tests and assessment.* Englewood Cliffs, NJ: Prentice Hall.

Walster, E., Walster, G. W., & Berscheid, E. (1978). *Equity: Theory and research.* Boston: Allyn & Bacon.

Wamboldt, F. S., & Wolin, S. J. (1989). Reality and myth in family life: Changes across generations. *Journal of Divorce and Remarriage, 12,* 141–165.

Ward, R., & Spitze, G. (1996). Will the children ever leave? Parent-child coresidence history and plans. *Journal of Family Issues, 17*(4), 514–539.

Warr, P. (1992). Age and occupational well-being. *Psychology and Aging, 7,* 37–45.

Waterman, A. (1982). Identity development from adolescence to adulthood: An extension of theory and a review of research. *Developmental Psychology, 18*(3), 341–358.

Watkins, S. C., Menken, J. A., & Bongaarts, J. (1987). Demographic foundations of family change. *American Sociological Review, 52,* 346–358.

Watson, J. B. (1913). Psychology as the behaviorist views it. *Psychological Review, 20,* 158–177.

Weeks, J. (1984). *Aging: Concepts and social issues.* Belmont, CA: Wadsworth.

Weibel-Orlando, J. (1990). Grandparenting styles: Native American perspectives. In J. Sokolovsky (Ed.), *The cultural context of aging.* New York: Bergin & Garvey.

Weiland, S. (1993). Erik Erikson: Ages, stages, and stories. *Generations, 17*(2), 17–22.

Weinmann, L., & Newcombe, N. (1990). Relational aspects of identity: Late adolescents' perceptions of their relationships with parents. *Journal of Experimental Child Psychology, 50,* 357–369.

Weiss, L., & Lowenthal, M. F. (1975). Life-course perspectives on friendship. In M. F. Lowenthal, M. Thurnher, & D. Chiriboga (Eds.), *Four stages of life* (pp. 48–61). San Francisco: Jossey-Bass.

Weiss, R. S. (1974). *Loneliness: The experience of emotional and social isolation.* Cambridge, MA: MIT Press.

Wellesley College Center for Research on Women and the American Association of University Women. (1992). *How schools shortchange girls: The AAUW report: A study of major findings on girls and education.* Washington, DC: AAUW Educational Foundation/National Education Association.

Welsh, W. M., & Stewart, A. J. (1995). Relationships between women and their parents: Implications for midlife well-being. *Psychology and Aging, 10*(2), 181–190.

West, R., Crook, T., & Barron, K. (1992). Everyday memory performance across the life span: Effects of age and noncognitive individual differences. *Psychology and Aging, 7,* 72–82.

Westkott, M. (1989). Female relationality and the idealized self. *American Journal of Psychoanalysis, 49*(3), 239–250.

Whalley, L. J., Starr, J. M., Athawes, R., Hunter, D., Pattie, A., & Deary, I. (2000). Childhood mental ability and dementia. *Neurology, 55,* 1455–1459.

Wheeler, L., Reis, H. T., & Nezlek, J. (1983). Loneliness, social interaction, and sex roles. *Journal of Personality and Social Psychology, 45,* 943–953.

Whitbourne, S. K. (1985). *The aging body: Physiological changes and psychological consequences.* New York: Springer-Verlag.

Whitbourne, S. K. (1987). Personality development in adulthood and old age: Relationships among identity style, health, and well-being. In K. W. Schaie & C. Eisdorfer (Eds.), *Annual review of gerontology and geriatrics* (Vol. 7, pp. 189–216). New York: Springer.

Whitbourne, S. K., & Hulicka, I. (1990). Ageism in undergraduate psychology texts. *American Psychologist, 45,* 1127–1136.

Whitbourne, S. K., Zuschlag, M. K., Elliot, L. B., & Waterman, A. S. (1992). Psychosocial development in adulthood: A 22-year sequential study. *Journal of Personality and Social Psychology, 63,* 260–271.

White, L. K., Booth, A., & Edwards, J. N. (1986). Children and marital happiness: Why the negative correlation? *Journal of Family Issues, 7,* 131–149.

Whittington, F. J. (1988). Making it better: Drinking and drugging in old age. *Generations, 12*(4), 5–7.

Wicklund, R. A., & Gollwitzer, P. M. (1982). *Symbolic self-completion.* Hillsdale, NJ: Erlbaum.

Widom, C. S. (1989). Does violence beget violence? A critical examination of the literature. *Psychological Bulletin, 106*(1), 3–28.

Wiley, E. (1990). Cool posing: Misinterpreted expressions often lead to educational deprivation. *Black Issues in Higher Education, 7*(19), 5–7.

Willcox, S. M., Himmelstein, D. U., & Woolhandler, S. (1994). Inappropriate drug prescribing for the community-dwelling elderly. *Journal of the American Medical Association, 272*(4), 292–296.

Williams, F. T. (1992). Aging versus disease. *Generations, 16*(4), 21–25.

Williams, J. (1987). *Psychology of women: Behavior in a biosocial context* (3rd ed.). New York: Norton.

Williams, T. F. (1995). Educating professionals about low vision. *Aging and Vision News, 7*(2), 6.

Williamson, G. M., & Schulz, R. (1992). Physical illness and symptoms of depression among elderly outpatients. *Psychology and Aging, 7,* 343-351.

Wilson, R. S., Beckett, L. A., Barnes, L. L., Schneider, J. A., Bach, J., Evans, D. A., & Bennett, D. A. (2002). Individual differences in rates of change in cognitive abilities of older persons. *Psychology and Aging, 17*(2), 179–193.

Wilson, R. S., Mendes de Leon, C. F., Barnes, L. L., Schneider, J. A., Bienias, J. L., Evans, D. A., & Bennett, D. A. (2002). Participation in cognitively stimulating activities and risk of incident Alzheimer disease. *Journal of the American Medical Association, 287,* 742–748.

Wingfield, A., Stine, E. A. L., Lahar, C. J., & Aberdeen, J. S. (1988). Does the capacity of working memory change with age? *Experimental Aging Research, 14,* 103–107.

Wink, P., & Dillon, M. (2003). Religiousness, spirituality, and psychosocial functioning in late adulthood: Findings from a longitudinal study. *Psychology and Aging, 18*(4), 916–924.

Winocur, G., & Moscovitch, M. (1990). A comparison of cognitive function in institutionalized and community-dwelling old people of normal intelligence. *Canadian Journal of Psychology, 44,* 435–444.

Winters, R. (1999, November 22). Half-retired: The first generation of two-income couples is starting to retire. Now she works, and he doesn't. *Time,* pp. 110ff.

Wise, P. M. (1986). Changes in the central nervous system and neuroendocrine control of reproduction in males and females. In L. Mastroianni, Jr., & C. A. Paulsen (Eds.), *Aging, reproduction, and the climacteric* (pp. 81–96). New York: Plenum.

Wiseman, J. P. (1986). Friendship: Bonds and binds in a voluntary relationship. *Journal of Social and Personal Relationships, 3,* 191–211.

Wisniewski, H. M., & Terry, R. D. (1976). Neuropathology of the aging brain. In R. D. Terry & S. Gershod (Eds.), *Neurobiology of aging* (pp. 65–78). New York: Raven.

Wisocki, P. A., & Keuthen, N. K. (1988). Later life. In E. A. Blechman & K. D. Brownell (Eds.), *Handbook of behavioral medicine for women* (pp. 48–58). New York: Pergamon Press.

Wodarski, J. S. (1987). An examination of spouse abuse: Practice issues for the profession. *Clinical Social Work Journal, 15,* 172–187.

Wolfe, D., O'Connor, D., & Crary, M. (1990). Transformation of life structure and personal paradigm during the midlife transition. *Human Relations, 43,* 957–973.

Wolinsky, F. D., & Johnson, R. J. (1992). Widowhood, health status, and the use of health services by older adults: A cross-sectional and prospective approach. *Journal of Gerontology: Social Sciences, 47,* S8–S16.

Wollenberg, C. (2000). Nursing home costs vary by state. *Medical Economics, 77*(18), 22.

Wood, V., & Robertson, J. F. (1978). Friendship and kinship interaction: Differential effects in the morale of the elderly. *Journal of Marriage and the Family, 40,* 367–375.

Woodruff-Pak, D. S. (1993). Neural plasticity and aging. In J. Cerella, J. Rybash, W. Hoyer, & M. L. Commons (Eds.), *Adult information processing: Limits on loss* (pp. 13–36). San Diego, CA: Academic Press.

Worchel, S., & Shebilske, W. (1992). *Psychology: Principles and applications* (4th ed.). Englewood Cliffs, NJ: Prentice Hall.

Worden, W. (1982). *Grief counseling and grief therapy: A handbook for the mental health practitioner.* New York: Springer.

Wright, L. (1988). The Type A behavior pattern and coronary heart disease. *American Psychologist, 43,* 2–14.

Wright, P. H. (1982). Men's friendships, women's friendships, and the alleged inferiority of the latter. *Sex Roles, 8,* 1–20.

Wright, P. H. (1984). Self-referent motivation and the intrinsic quality of friendship. *Journal of Social and Personal Relationships, 1,* 115–130.

Wyckle, M. L., & Musil, C. M. (1993). Mental health of older persons: Social and cultural factors. *Generations, 17*(1), 7–12.

Yee, B. W. K., & Weaver, G. D. (1994). Ethnic minorities and health promotion: Developing a "culturally competent" agenda. *Generations, 18*(1), 39–44.

Yee, J. L., & Schulz, R. (2000). Gender differences in caregiving: A critical review. *Gerontologist, 40,* 147–164.

Yoder, J. D., & Kahn, A. S. (1993). Working toward an inclusive psychology of women. *American Psychologist, 48,* 846–850.

Youngstrom, N. (1992a, February). Adapt to diversity or risk irrelevance, field warned. *APA Monitor,* p. 44.

Youngstrom, N. (1992b, April). Poverty can exacerbate risk of developmental ills. *APA Monitor,* p. 30.

Youngstrom, N. (1992c, June). Grim news from national study of rape. *APA Monitor,* p. 38.

Youngstrom, N. (1992d, June). Psychology's memory lane packed with myth, anecdote. *APA Monitor,* p. 12.

Zajonc, R. B. (1968). Attitudinal effects of mere exposure. *Journal of Personality and Social Psychology, Monographs Supplement, 9,* 1–27.

Zarit, S. H., Birkel, R. C., & Malonebeach, E. (1989). Spouses as caregivers: Stresses and interventions. In M. Z. Goldstein (Ed.), *Family involvement in the treatment of the frail elderly.* Washington, DC: American Psychiatric Association.

Zarit, S. H., Orr, N. K., & Zarit, J. M. (1985). *The hidden victims of Alzheimer's disease: Families under stress.* New York: New York University Press.

Zarit, S. H., Pearlin, L. I., & Schaie, K. W. (Eds.). (2003). *Personal control in social and life course contexts.* New York: Springer.

Zarit, S. H., Todd, P. A., & Zarit, J. M. (1986). Subjective burden of husbands and wives as caregivers: A longitudinal study. *Gerontologist, 26,* 260–266.

Zeiss, A. M., & Kasl-Godley, J. (2001). Sexuality in older adults' relationships. *Generations, 24*(3), 18–25.

Zilberfein, F. (1999). Coping with death: Anticipatory grief and bereavement. *Generations, 23*(1), 69–74.

Zucker, A. N., Ostrove, J. M., & Stewart, A. J. (2002). College-educated women's personality development in adulthood: Perceptions and age differences. *Psychology and Aging, 17*(2), 236–244.

Zweig, R. A., & Hinrichsen, G. A. (1993). Factors associated with suicide attempts by depressed older adults: A prospective study. *American Journal of Psychiatry, 150,* 1687–1692.

Name Index

548

Subject Index

psychological approach to, 463–464
and right to die, 471–472
of spouse (*See* Widowhood)
stages of coping with, 467
unanticipated, 480
Demand characteristics, 16
Dementia. *See also* Alzheimer's disease
definition of, 447
as effect of disease, 355–356
Demographic trends
definition of, 2
in life expectancy, 2–4
Dendrites, 191. *See also* Nerves
sprouting of, 192–193
Dependency ratio, 342
Dependent variable, 18
Depletion syndrome, 445
Depression
age differences in, 444–446
among family caregivers, 287
causes of, 441–442
and cognition, 167–168
diagnosis of, 441
and domestic violence, 294–295
gender differences in, 443
major, 440–447
minor, 445
misdiagnosed as Alzheimer's disease, 450
and relationships, 205–206
ruminative coping in, 443–444
and suicide, 440
treatment of, 442–443
in women *vs.* men, 436
Depression, The Great. *See* Great Depression
Dermis, 360
Desires, generative, 54. *See also* Generativity
Development
vs. aging, 356–357
complexity of, 9–10
contexts and, 10–12
contextual model of, 39
definition of, 2
Eriksonian theory of, 46–48
five factor model of, 66–68
Freudian theory of, 46
gains and losses in, 9
goals of study in, 12
Jungian theory of, 46
Levinsonian theory of, 54–60
mechanistic model of, 38–39
multidisciplinary nature of, 12
organismic model of, 38
perspectives on, 8–12
physical, 359–381
plasticity of, 10
psychosocial, 37–73
Development-in-context, 40
Developmental psychology, definition of, 2
DHEA (dehydroepiandros-terone), 379
Diagnosis of exclusion, 450
Diagnostic and Statistical Manual. *See* DSM

Dialectic thought, 147
Diathesis, 441
Diet
and aging, 354
and bone health, 361
and brain, 194
and heart disease, 390–391
as preventive measure, 407–408
Disability
fear of, 465–466
trends in, 394–396
Disconnection hypothesis, 176
Discrimination. *See also* Ageism; Ethnicity; Gender
and self concept, 82
and wages, 306
against working women, 325
Disease. *See also* Health; Illness
definition of, 387
effects of, *vs.* effects of aging, 355–356
vs. illness, 387
Disengagement theory, 209. *See also* Relationships
Disuse hypothesis, 164
Divergent thought, 154
Divorce, 259–262. *See also* Marriage
adjustment to, 260
and adults living alone, 248
changes in rate of, 259–260
economic consequences of, 261
and ethnicity, 260
and grandparenthood, 277–278
remarriage after, 262
DNA, and aging, 380
Domestic violence, 290–297
and age, 291
causal factors of, 293
changing views of, 290
and community violence, 291
consequences of, 294–295
in crime surveys, 292
cycle of, 295
definition of, 290
and developmental patterns, 295
and ecological systems theory, 293
and gender of abusers, 291
incidence of, 291–293
intervention for, 296–297
vs. maltreatment, 292
profiles of victims and perpetrators of, 294
statistics on, 292–293
through generations, 291
Dopamine, 192
Double blind, 19. *See also* Experimental studies
Down syndrome, 452
Dream (developmental task), 319
in women, 319–320
Driving, and old age identity, 116
Drugs. *See* Medication
DSM (Diagnostic and Statistical Manual of Mental Disorders), 433
ethnic and cultural issues in, 436
gender bias in, 436
Dual-career family, 322

Dual-earner, 322
Dualism, Cartesian, 403–406
Dyad, 41, 201–202, 223
Dying well, 467–471. *See also* Death

Ecological systems theory, 39–45. *See also* Ecology
development of, 39–40
and domestic violence, 293
environment in, 40–44
phenomenology in, 40
Ecological transitions, 42
Ecological validity, 162–163
Ecology. *See also* Ecological systems theory
definition of, 39
of human development, 40
and human difference, 44
Education
African American experience in, 108
ageism in, 27, 30
and cognition, 168
and ethnicity, 43
and gender, 106, 326–327
gender discrimination in, 329
postsecondary, and labor market, 303–304, 307–308
Effortful operations *vs.* automatic, 173
Egalitarian marriage, 254–255
Ego, 78
Eldercare, corporate, 289
Elderly. *See also* Age
diagnosis of mental health of, 434
suicide among, 446–447
Emerging adulthood, 231
Emotional states
and cognition, 167–168
and stress, 423
Emphysema, 365
Empty-nest syndrome, 272–273
Encoding, 172
Encoding specificity, 181
Endocrine system
and aging, 366–367
overview of, 366
and sleep disturbances, 366–367
Environment, physical and aging, 354, 355
Environment, psychological complex, and cognition, 165–166
levels of, in ecological systems theory, 40–44
and relationships, 202–203
Epidemiological Catchment Area Survey (ECA), 431
Epidemiology, 431
Epidermis, 360
Epigenetic principle, 47
Episodic memory, 182
Equilibrium, of schemas, 80
Equity theory, 213–214
Era, developmental, 56–57
Erectile dysfunction, 367
Erikson, Erik
theory of development, 46–49
theory of identity, 91–92

Estrogen, 367–368
Ethics, in research, 26
Ethnic group, definition of, 104
Ethnicity. *See also* Racism; *specific ethnic groups*
bias in research, 31–32
and breast cancer, 393
and caregiver stress, 287
categories of, 34
and cognitive differences, 170–171
definition of, 104
and divorce, 260
and education, 43
and fertility rate, 265
and health, 398–400
and help seeking for mental illness, 436–437
and ideas of self, 104–109
and intelligence testing, 132
and long-term care, 416
and parenting styles, 43
and relationships, 214–215
and research relevance, 32–35
and socioeconomic status, 108–109
and surrogate parenthood by grandparents, 280
and wages, 306
of working women, 321
Euthanasia, 471–472
Evolutionary hypothesis, of mate selection, 234
Excess-disabilities syndrome, 414. *See also* Medication
Exchange orientation, 214
Exercise
benefits of, 408–410
and bone health, 361, 362
and brain, 193, 409
and cognition, 409
Exosystem, 42–43
Experimental group
definition of, 19
diversity of, and validity, 18–19
Experimental studies, 18–20
advantages of, 19
definition of, 18
disadvantages of, 19–20, 39–40
diversity of subjects in, 18–19
vs. naturalistic observation, 39–40
variables in, 18
Experiments, natural, 20
Expertise, 148–151. *See also* Cognition; Intelligence; Wisdom
and aging, 150–151
in chess, 148–149
cognitive advantages of, 149
cognitive disadvantages of, 149, 150
definition of, 148
and memory, 150
Explicit memory, 183
Expressive role, 100
External validity, 14
and bias, 32–33
in experimental studies, 18–19, 20

562